PRAISE FOR *Lincoln President-Elect*

"Holzer . . . is the Muhammad Ali of Lincoln biographers. His command of Lincoln—the man, the politician, the orator—is unmatched."

—Jessica Reaves, *Chicago Tribune*

"Lincoln Prize–winner Holzer has written a brilliantly crafted book. . . . *Lincoln President-Elect* is an extraordinary piece of historical reporting."

—Larry Cox, *Tucson Citizen*

"A devourable history [that] does the impossible—reveals a Lincoln nobody knows."

—*Men's Vogue*

"A fascinating, new look at Lincoln's tricky time as president-elect. . . . Holzer blends excellent research with skillful writing to make the period come alive. . . . Adds a new dimension to a little-examined period."

—Lee Davidson, *Deseret Morning News*

"A new book by a remarkable historian. . . . It is pure, well-researched and well-written revisionist history."

—Richard Reeves, syndicated columnist

"Holzer vividly re-creates the intrigue and danger that surrounded the president-elect as he waited to assume office. . . . Holzer's invaluable contribution is to show that Lincoln, while reluctant to discuss his intentions while James Buchanan remained president, was not disconnected from events and was not silent."

—James R. Carroll, *The Courier-Journal* (Louisville, Kentucky)

"Holzer's well-written biography meticulously documents the phenomenal challenges and frustrations Lincoln confronted in the four-month interregnum between his November election and inauguration the following March. . . . History buffs and dilettantes alike will savor this compelling human portrait of 'The Great Liberator.'"

—Sheila Anne Feeney, *The Star-Ledger* (Newark, New Jersey)

"Holzer renders Lincoln's last weeks in Springfield, his eventful journey by rail to Washington, and his first days in the capital in lavish and loving detail."

—Mark Dunkelman, *Providence Journal-Bulletin*

"Highly recommended to those interested in Lincoln, history of the presidency, transitional periods of the presidency, and the Civil War."

—Benet Exton, *The Oklahoman*

"Holzer writes with grace about an important period in Lincoln's career."

—John M. Taylor, *The Washington Times*

"An engrossing narrative. . . . Holzer shows Lincoln shrewdly and methodically manipulating friend and foe alike, while also taking the first cautious steps toward preparing both himself and his country for a grim trial by fire."

—*Publishers Weekly*

"Award-winning Lincoln scholar Holzer meticulously examines the ominous period between the 16th president's election and his swearing in. . . . A learned chronicle of a massively significant few months. Effectively brings this tense interlude to vivid life."

—*Kirkus Reviews*

"Drawing on Lincoln's many letters and carefully crafted speeches, as well as his strategic public silences, Holzer reveals an engaged President-elect, rapidly learning, with few missteps, to control the confusing swirl of competing political interests and personal expectations surrounding him. The public—including our next President-elect—will profit from this book. Highly recommended for university and large public libraries."

—*Library Journal* (starred review)

"One of our greatest Lincoln scholars. . . . Holzer deals effectively with a lingering controversy in a work that will be an excellent addition to Lincoln collections."

—Jay Freeman, *Booklist*

"A nearly 600-page tour de force. . . . Holzer's writing is superb and a pleasure to read. . . . The definitive work on Lincoln as President-Elect has been written, and Holzer's book will replace previous studies as being definitive."

—Michael Burkhimer, *Lincoln Herald*

"This is a stunningly original work that casts completely new light on the most turbulent and critical presidential transition in American history. Holzer's superb narrative skill, along with his abundant use of colorful details, creates an atmosphere of such immediacy that the reader feels transported back to 'the Great Secession Winter' as an eyewitness to Lincoln's gifted leadership during this dramatic period. This groundbreaking book will take its place with the most valuable and indispensable works in the Lincoln canon."

—Doris Kearns Goodwin, author of
Team of Rivals: The Political Genius of Abraham Lincoln

"No one has a finer intuitive understanding of Abraham Lincoln than Harold Holzer. In this fascinating book, he throws a searchlight on a crucial and surprisingly underexamined episode of Lincoln's life to show us the essential elements of Lincoln's political and moral greatness."

—Michael Beschloss, author of *Presidential Courage:
Brave Leaders and How They Changed America, 1789–1989*

"Harold Holzer's *Lincoln President-Elect* is the most complete account of the interregnum between Lincoln's election and his first inaugural. Examining every source for this critical time, the author puts to rest the perception that the President-elect could have, but failed to, prevent secession and civil war."

—Frank J. Williams, Founding Chair, The Lincoln Forum

Other Books by Harold Holzer

Lincoln and Freedom: Slavery, Emancipation,
and the Thirteenth Amendment
(coedited with Sara Vaughn Gabbard)

Lincoln's White House Secretary:
The Adventurous Life of William O. Stoddard

Lincoln Revisited: New Insights from the Lincoln Forum
(coedited with John Y. Simon and Dawn Vogel)

Abraham Lincoln Portrayed in the Collections
of the Indiana Historical Society

The Emancipation Proclamation: Three Views—Social, Political,
Iconographic (with Edna Greene Medford and Frank J. Williams)

The Battle of Hampton Roads: New Perspectives on the USS Monitor
and CSS Virginia (coedited with Tim Mulligan)

Lincoln in the Times: The Life of Abraham Lincoln as
Originally Reported in the New York Times
(coedited with David Herbert Donald)

Lincoln at Cooper Union:
The Speech That Made Abraham Lincoln President

The President Is Shot! The Assassination of Abraham Lincoln

State of the Union: New York and the Civil War (editor)

The Lincoln Forum: Rediscovering Abraham Lincoln
(coedited with John Y. Simon)

Abraham Lincoln the Writer: A Treasury of His Greatest Speeches
and Letters (editor)

Lincoln Seen and Heard

Prang's Civil War Pictures: The Complete Battle Chromos of Louis Prang

The Union Image: Popular Prints of the Civil War North
(with Mark E. Neely, Jr.)

*Lincoln as I Knew Him: Gossip, Tributes, and Revelations from His Best
Friends and Worst Enemies* (editor)

The Lincoln Forum: Abraham Lincoln, Gettysburg and the Civil War
(coedited with John Y. Simon and William D. Pederson)

*The Union Preserved: A Guide to the Civil War Records in
the New York State Archives* (editor)

The Lincoln Mailbag: America Writes to the President, 1860–1865
(editor)

Witness to War: The Civil War

The Civil War Era

Dear Mr. Lincoln: Letters to the President (editor)

Washington and Lincoln Portrayed: National Icons in Popular Prints

*The Lincoln-Douglas Debates:
The First Complete, Unexpurgated Text* (editor)

Mine Eyes Have Seen the Glory: The Civil War in Art
(with Mark E. Neely, Jr.)

Lincoln on Democracy (coedited with Mario Cuomo)

The Lincoln Family Album (with Mark E. Neely, Jr.)

The Confederate Image: Prints of the Lost Cause
(with Gabor S. Boritt and Mark E. Neely, Jr.)

The Lincoln Image: Abraham Lincoln and the Popular Print
(with Gabor S. Boritt and Mark E. Neely, Jr.)

LINCOLN

Abraham Lincoln and
the Great Secession Winter
1860–1861

Simon & Schuster Paperbacks

PRESIDENT-ELECT

HAROLD HOLZER

New York London Toronto Sydney

To the memory of Charles Holzer
And the future of his namesake
Charles Ezra Kirsch

Simon & Schuster Paperbacks
A Division of Simon & Schuster
1230 Avenue of the Americas
New York, NY 10020

First Simon & Schuster trade paperback edition October 2009

SIMON & SCHUSTER PAPERBACKS and colophon are registered
trademarks of Simon & Schuster, Inc.

For information about special discounts for bulk purchases,
please contact Simon & Schuster Special Sales at
1-866-506-1949 or business@simonandschuster.com.

The Simon & Schuster Speakers Bureau can bring authors
to your live event. For more information or to book an event,
contact the Simon & Schuster Speakers Bureau at
866-248-3049 or visit our website at www.simonspeakers.com.

Designed by Paul Dippolito

Manufactured in the United States of America

1 3 5 7 9 10 8 6 4 2

The Library of Congress has cataloged the hardcover edition as follows:

Holzer, Harold.
Lincoln president–elect : Abraham Lincoln and the great secession
winter 1860–1861 / Harold Holzer.
p.   cm.
Includes bibliographical references and index.
1. Lincoln, Abraham, 1809–1865.   2. Lincoln, Abraham, 1809–1865—Political career
before 1861.   3. United States—Politics and government—1857–1861.
4. United States—History—Civil War, 1861–1865—Causes.   I. Title.
E457.4.H69   2008
973.7092—dc22   2008021520
ISBN 978-0-7432-8947-4
ISBN 978- 0-7432-8948-1 (pbk)
ISBN 978-1-4165-9440-6 (ebook)

The Lincoln's Inaugural Rail Journey Map, which originally appeared in *Abraham Lincoln:
Great American Historians on Our Sixteenth President* (PublicAffairs, 2008), appears here with
the permission of PublicAffairs.

⊰ CONTENTS ⊱

Introduction　*1*

PART ONE · THE PROMISE OF SOMETHING BETTER

Chapter One　The Government Is About to Fall
into Our Hands　*11*

Chapter Two　My Troubles Have Just Commenced　*46*

Chapter Three　We Won't Jump That Ditch　*79*

Chapter Four　A Masterly Inactivity　*114*

Chapter Five　The Tug Has to Come　*148*

Chapter Six　Very Much Like the Critter　*184*

PART TWO · THE MOMENTOUS ISSUE OF CIVIL WAR

Chapter Seven　If We Surrender, It Is the End of Us　*221*

Chapter Eight　Will You Hazard So Desperate a Step?　*254*

Chapter Nine   With a Task Before Me   *288*

Chapter Ten   No Occasion for Any Excitement   *325*

Chapter Eleven   I Would Rather Be Assassinated   *361*

Chapter Twelve   Plain as a Turnpike Road   *397*

Chapter Thirteen   The Ultimate Justice of the People   *430*

Epilogue   Mystic Chords of Memory   *459*

What Became of . . . ?   *477*

Acknowledgments   *485*

Notes   *493*

Index   *597*

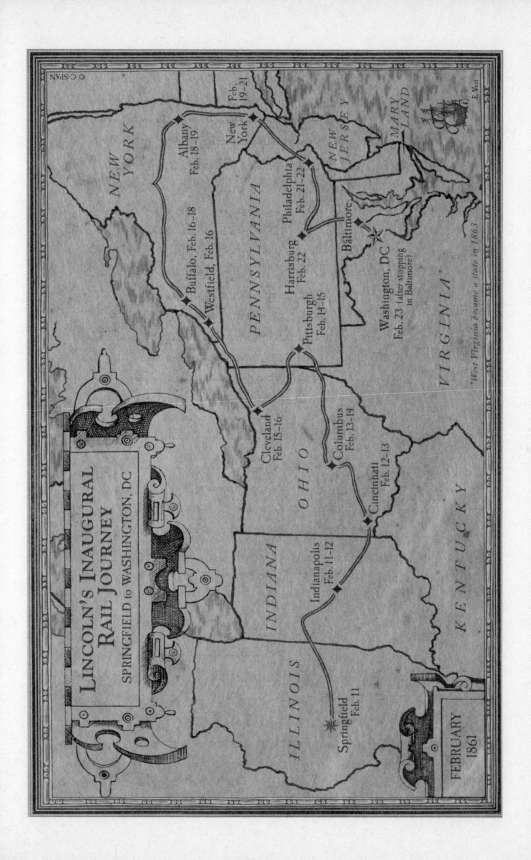

LINCOLN'S INAUGURAL
RAIL JOURNEY
SPRINGFIELD to WASHINGTON, DC

FEBRUARY
1861

© C-SPAN

E. West

NEW
YORK

Albany
Feb. 18–19

New
York
Feb.
19–21

Buffalo, Feb. 16–18

Westfield, Feb. 16

PENNSYLVANIA

Harrisburg
Feb. 22

Philadelphia
Feb. 21–22

NEW
JERSEY

MARY
LAND

Baltimore

Pittsburgh
Feb. 14–15

Washington, DC
Feb. 23 (after stopping
in Baltimore)

VIRGINIA*

*West Virginia became a state in 1863

Cleveland
Feb. 15–16

OHIO

Columbus
Feb. 13–14

Cincinnati
Feb. 12–13

INDIANA

Indianapolis
Feb. 11–12

ILLINOIS

Springfield
Feb. 11

KENTUCKY

⊰ INTRODUCTION ⊱

THE "GREAT SECESSION Winter of 1860–1861," to use the memorable phrase Henry Adams coined, has often been regarded among professional scholars and ordinary Americans alike as Abraham Lincoln's historical Achilles' heel—the vulnerable soft spot in an otherwise sterling reputation.

Although he has long and almost universally been regarded as America's greatest president, the story persists that in the months leading up to his inauguration, Lincoln not only failed to do all that was required to prevent secession and war, but made his mighty challenge all the more difficult by souring the public he had just been elected to lead.

According to this interpretation, Lincoln remained silent for far too long after his victory, emboldening traitors and dismaying supporters, dithered on the vital issues of slavery and states' rights, all but ignored blatant treachery in the South, and then made his way to Washington offering a series of bumbling, inconsistent speeches that veered toward compromise on the sectional crisis one moment, and toward defiant coercion the next. He chose too few cabinet appointees in a timely fashion, showered too many favors on unqualified job-seekers, told too many unsavory jokes to his cronies, and lavished improbable attention on his own physical appearance and the artists and photographers who recorded it, all the while failing to grasp the peril of the crisis awaiting his attention.

It was almost as if the memory of Lincoln the transformative leader required the legend of the unprepared leader-in-waiting to add to the luster of his later accomplishments. As his first vice president, Hannibal Hamlin, agreed, Lincoln's "extreme eulogists made the mistake of constructing a Lincoln who was as great the day he left Springfield as when he made his earthly exit four years later."[1] In Hamlin's view, Lincoln made countless mistakes during this period. Was he right? Or was Lincoln simply ingenious at diverting attention from dangers over which he still had no control, leaving his record as president-elect understandably overshadowed by his record as president.

The founders did not foresee a lengthy or closely observed interregnum when they established March 4 as inauguration day. Washington, Adams, and Jefferson were each elected just a few weeks prior to his swearing in, limiting the potential for fractiousness and mischief between administrations. Of course, those men had not anticipated the subsequent rise of political parties, much less the introduction of popular voting; they expected that new presidents would be forever chosen by electoral colleges every fourth winter and sworn in shortly thereafter. Later custom shifted elections back to November, but left the inauguration in March, assuming it would take weeks for electors, not to mention future presidents, to travel from their homes to Washington from remote parts of the growing nation. The outdated tradition remained fixed until Franklin D. Roosevelt's second term began on January 20, 1937.

What the framers failed to anticipate was the resulting, and potentially dangerous, void that long transitions might encourage. *Webster's* defines "interregnum" as "the time during which a throne is vacant between two successive reigns or regimes." So, in a sense, the word does not literally apply to American presidential transition. Yet, in a way, from late 1860 until early 1861, America endured an interregnum of its own, and during this time the country could more accurately be said to have had no president than to have had two. The incumbent was paralyzed, and his successor powerless. Almost from the moment votes are counted, lame-duck chief executives invariably recede into superfluity, but Lincoln's hapless predecessor, James Buchanan, made procrastination into an art form. He could not have excused himself from responsibility at a more portentous moment, or left his successor with graver problems to address once he was constitutionally entitled to do so.

In the void, the public and press invariably turned expectantly to the next leader for reassuring hints of policy and personality, even though the law empowered him to wield absolutely no authority, and political tradition encouraged him to attempt no influence. The scrutiny was no less intense during this age of politically operated broadsheet newspapers than it is in today's world of all-day broadcast news and Internet blogs. However limited his authority between November and March, Lincoln was intensely analyzed. In the eyes of many, he failed the test.

Whatever his subsequent achievements, the reputation of Lincoln as president-elect remained a matter of dispute for generations, even if he seemed wanting only in comparison with his accomplishments once in office. As William O. Stoddard, a White House clerk who later became his biographer, noted as early as 1884, the "majority of those who have written" about this period "have strangely taken it for granted that he was in a manner ignorant of the course of events. They have regarded him as being as much taken by surprise by each development as might be any private citizen who puzzled over the news brought to him, correctly or incorrectly, by his favorite newspaper." To this reigning view, Stoddard would only add: "The difficulties of Mr. Lincoln's position at that time have been but little understood."[2] Time did not improve that understanding. At the very least, as journalist Noah Brooks maintained ten years later, there were those Americans in late 1860 who "hoped . . . that he would be sent back to Illinois dead or alive, and that 'President [Jefferson] Davis' would come and take his place."[3]

To be sure, Lincoln had his share of defenders, especially in the afterglow of his assassination and martyrdom. The early biographer Phoebe Hanaford, for one, took pains to depict him as the "prepared man," and in her section entitled "Called to the Presidential Chair" called "Abe Lincoln" the "best contribution which America has made to history."[4] Her contemporary L. P. Brockett judged Lincoln's protracted pre-inaugural silence to be "wise,"[5] and citing the "enormity" of his challenges, described Lincoln as an oasis of calm in a storm of "feverish apprehension."[6] Isaac N. Arnold, the Illinois congressman-turned-biographer, lauded his old friend for demonstrating "clear and positive convictions of his duty" during the transition.[7]

Subsequent writers took a different view. Historian David M. Potter pointed out in 1942 that as president-elect, Lincoln was no more than "simply a lawyer from Springfield, Illinois—a man of great undeveloped capacities and narrowly limited background. He was more fit to *become* President than to *be* President."[8] Eight years later, Allan Nevins argued similarly that while Lincoln "possessed more qualifications than men dreamed . . . great public prestige he sadly lacked." As president-elect, Nevins maintained, Lincoln's "clumsy attempts at wit were inappropriate to the tension of the hour" and "jarred on anxious citizens."[9] Even when the influential James G. Randall insisted that "few leaders have met such a situation with greater grace," he conceded that the fact that Lincoln managed to hold his party together between his election and inauguration "seems now something of a miracle."[10]

James M. McPherson spoke for a later generation of scholars when he asserted in 1988 that Lincoln's entire, public inaugural journey might have been a "mistake," because in his effort to avoid "a careless remark or slip of the tongue" that might "inflame the crisis further," the president-elect "indulged in platitudes and trivia," producing "an unfavorable impression on those who were already disposed to regard the ungainly president-elect as a commonplace prairie lawyer."[11] Mark E. Neely, Jr., has similarly noted that Lincoln's remarks en route to Washington were "widely quoted in the press to show that Lincoln was insensitive and unequipped to cope with the secession crisis."[12] And Richard Carwardine spoke of "Lincoln's larger misreading of the southern surge toward secession," arguing: "Lincoln may also have misjudged things in not doing more to reassure anxious southerners that he would not use his patronage powers to place hard-line Republicans in federal appointments in the slave states."[13]

On the other hand, Phillip Shaw Paludan has credited Lincoln with using this period of his career "to bring to life the political philosophy his party espoused"—it being a new political organization "that needed unity as desperately as the Union did."[14] And Doris Kearns Goodwin has pointed out that President-elect Lincoln, "not oblivious to the abyss that could easily open beneath his feet," demonstrated admirable "strength of will."[15] The professional historical debate continues, as it should.

Significantly, not a single scholar among all those cited above ever minimized the desperate challenges Lincoln faced, or questioned that his was the most dangerous transition period in history. While attending to the customary tasks of assembling a cabinet, rewarding political loyalists with federal appointments, and drafting an inaugural address alone—he employed no speechwriters—Lincoln was uniquely forced to confront the collapse of the country itself, with no power to prevent its disintegration. Bound to loyalty to the Republican party platform on which he had run and won, he could yield little to the majority that had in fact voted against him.

During the four months—a full third of a year—between his election and inauguration, seven Southern states seceded from the Union, set up their own independent government, chose their own president, seized federal property, and dared Lincoln to resist their defiant independence. Within thirty days of the November 1860 popular vote—in which, notably, he failed to amass even 40 percent of the total cast, and earned none at all in much of the South—the minority president-elect could not even be certain that he would have a nation to lead. At a minimum, he faced the very real possibility that the Electoral College obligated to certify his victory might not be able to assemble safely, and that the formal inaugural pageant might be difficult to stage without both interference and considerable personal risk. Certainly no president ever faced such audacious impediments to taking lawful office.

Some critics then and now still indict Lincoln for remaining uncharacteristically aloof as the country began breaking apart, either unable or unwilling out of deference to both political tradition and his own rigid party platform to take a stand as the crisis widened. Torn by conflicting advice, they maintain, he showed too much hesitancy in assembling his ministerial family, unable to make final decisions—in one case, making one choice, retracting it, and then making it again. He not only fumbled badly in his attempts at impromptu oratory en route to the capital, but worst of all, ended his journey in the dead of night, embarrassingly fearful for his safety, after encouraging unseemly partisan demonstrations in friendly Northern cities. He was too conspicuous. He was too sequestered. He was too careless. He was too calculating. He was too conciliatory. He was too coercive. He was too sloppy. He was too preening. Either way, he ultimately, tragically, bungled his last, best hope of preventing a war that cost America 600,000 of her sons. In the anti-Lincoln tradition—most recently renewed improbably by gadfly 2008 Republican presidential candidate Ron Paul—Lincoln could easily have achieved freedom for the slaves without resorting to military force.[16]

This book is an attempt to reexamine and thoroughly illuminate this complex record by exploring Lincoln's—and America's own—experience at the time. It will show how seriously Lincoln regarded the transition, not resting whiggishly in preparation for his presidency, but working tirelessly to unite his party, assemble a cabinet, fill hundreds of patronage jobs, assess the constitutional and military threats to the Union, open communications with Southerners, keep an eye on America's role in the world—and, most of all, draw a line in the sand to prevent the spread of human slavery. Lincoln later told Congress that it—and he—could not "escape history." But every monument needs a pedestal. And Lincoln's monumental place in American history could not have been secured without the pedestal he built as president-elect.[17] Making full use of period recollections by the people around him, along with newspaper and magazine accounts and rarely analyzed material culture, it offers a week-by-week exploration of Lincoln's own evolving thoughts, declarations, and actions as he prepared to introduce himself to the American people (having never campaigned for the presidency, he needed to do so after his election). It will examine what he said, what he wrote, and what he declined to say and do; how he dextrously, often covertly, manipulated individuals and factions, resisted flattery, faced down disloyalty, and endured criticism and hatred along with almost unimaginable personal discomfort along the road to his inauguration; how he relaxed, what he read, and, when possible, what he thought; how contemporaries reacted to him, and how he responded in turn, maintaining public silence while somehow gathering the intelligence and momentum needed to arm himself for the brutal challenge awaiting him.

In so doing, the book aims to paint the most accurate and detailed picture yet offered of America's gravest crisis through the eyes of this altogether original leader—"inexperienced in wielding great power"[18] yet astonishingly intuitive and gifted with remarkable instincts for communication—whom Americans chose to confront that crisis, then by tradition compelled to wait so long before doing so.

One fact remains inarguable. Abraham Lincoln faced obstacles, challenges, citizen apprehension, disloyalty, even threats greater than that which confronted any president-elect before or since. He said so himself rather immodestly at the time, and history has generated no convincing rebuttal since. He would somehow survive all of them and go on to preserve the country and substantially remake it by validating majority rule and eradicating the stain of human slavery. But first came the extraordinary transition that might easily have tainted or even doomed all that followed.

This book aims to show how ingeniously Abraham Lincoln worked within the constraints of reigning political tradition to make certain that he had that opportunity, and how close he came to losing it.

Rye, New York
February 12, 2008

The first photograph of President-Elect Abraham Lincoln with his new beard, taken by Samuel G. Alschuler, Chicago, Illinois, Sunday, November 25, 1860. (LIBRARY OF CONGRESS)

PART ONE

THE PROMISE OF
SOMETHING BETTER

Chapter One

The Government Is About to Fall into Our Hands

THE CANNON SALVO that thundered over Springfield, Illinois, to greet the sunrise on November 6, 1860, signaled not the start of a battle, but the end of one. The bitter, raucous, and exhilarating six-month-long campaign for president of the United States was over at last. Election Day was finally dawning.[1]

Ignited to rouse the Republican faithful to the polls that morning, the explosions were soon augmented by other "manifestations of popular feeling" designed to "enliven" the city. Crowds of boisterous partisans took up positions outside the city's one and only polling place and began a long day devoted to outshouting each other. Providing clamorous accompaniment were bands of musicians parading through the streets aboard horse-drawn wagons, giving ear-shattering performances while waving banners like the one that proclaimed, "A Home President for Springfield."[2] There was little danger that Abraham Lincoln's hometown would slumber through this decisive day of days.

As for Lincoln himself, the Republican presidential nominee probably awoke, like his neighbors, at the first cannon blast—that is, if he had been able to sleep at all. Victory—probable but not quite certain—might, he knew, prove Pyrrhic. Just a few days earlier, warning that "the existence of slavery is at stake," South Carolina's leading newspaper, the

Charleston Mercury, had defiantly called for a prompt secession convention in "each and all of the Southern states" should the "Abolitionist white man" Lincoln capture the White House.[3] That same day, a prominent New York Democrat prophesied that if the Republican were elected, "at least Mississippi, Alabama, Georgia, Florida, and South Carolina would secede."[4] Yet the danger that winning could prove more cataclysmic than losing did little to deflate the celebratory mood among Republicans in Lincoln's hometown. By the time the polls opened at 8 A.M., a journalist reported, "tranquility forsook Springfield" altogether, and "the out-door tumult" awoke "whatever sluggish spirits there might be among the populace."[5]

Lincoln himself had seemed uncharacteristically skittish. Less than three weeks earlier, he had confided to a caller, not for the first time, that he would have preferred contending for a full six-year term in the Senate, "where there was more chance to make reputation and less chance of losing it—than four years in the presidency."[6] It was a startling admission. But having lost not one but two senatorial races over the past five years, most recently to Stephen A. Douglas—one of the Democrats now standing in the way of his election to the White House—Lincoln's conflicted thoughts were understandable. Surely his mood did not improve when he read an Election Eve letter demanding he withdraw from the race unilaterally, simply because, as its author put it, "we do not want you for President of the United States. . . . The Spirit says so."[7] Jitters and divination notwithstanding, there was, of course, no turning back now from the nation's judgment day.

Looking at his prospects coolly—and Lincoln was an expert vote-counter—he had reason enough to expect he would prevail. In a pivotal state election two months earlier, widely seen as a harbinger of the presidential contest, Maine had elected a Republican governor with a healthy majority. In bellwether contests that soon followed, Republicans had earned similarly impressive majorities in Pennsylvania, Ohio, and Indiana. Ward Hill Lamon, Lincoln's old friend from their circuit-riding days, wrote the candidate to joke that on hearing the news, his campaign manager, three-hundred-pound Judge David Davis, had "turned a double somersault and adjourned court until after the presidential election—and in his delirium he actually talks of Lincoln's Election as being a fixed fact."[8] Lincoln finally allowed himself to believe that the "splendid victories . . . seem to fore-shadow the certain success of the Republican cause in November."[9]

To Senator William H. Seward of New York, the onetime front-runner he had defeated for the Republican presidential nomination six months earlier, Lincoln went even further, admitting the recent successes "surpassed all expectation, even the most extravagant." In a rare burst of optimism, he told Seward: "It now really looks as if the Government is about to fall into our hands."[10] But it was always part of Lincoln's complex nature to greet impending success with some foreboding.[11] Besides, the recent local victories in the North, however encouraging, hardly guaranteed victory in the national election. The black leader Frederick Douglass, for one, acknowledged that the "efforts and appliances resorted to by the enemies of the Republican party . . . could not fail to cause doubt and anxiety in the minds of the most sanguine."[12]

Complicating matters was the fact that four candidates were competing for the presidency. Earlier in the year, the sectionally riven Democratic party had split into Northern and Southern factions, promising a dilution of its usual strength—1,838,169 votes in the last national election, or 45.3 percent of the total in that three-way race. Perceptions of extremism from both parties had inspired the formation of a new Constitutional Union party, which nominated Tennessee politician John Bell as its own candidate for president. The rupture in the nation's oldest political organization left Lincoln convinced, by the end of September, that no "ticket can be elected by the People, unless it be ours."[13] Still, no one could be absolutely certain that any candidate would amass enough *electoral* votes to win the presidency outright. If none secured an absolute majority of electors on November 6, the Constitution punted the contest to the House of Representatives, where only the top three vote-getters would be eligible. And if the House—where Republicans had yet to amass an outright majority—got to choose the next president, slaveholding Southern states, overwhelmingly Democratic, would exercise more power than they could in the Electoral College. Each state would cast a single presidential vote. Anything might yet happen.[14]

Stephen A. Douglas, now the presidential standard-bearer of Northern Democrats, took care to deny he harbored hopes for such an outcome, but privately dreamed of an outcome in which he might yet end up battling in the "Ho[use] of Reps."[15] So serious were concerns that the South would exercise disproportionate influence under such a scenario, that in hotly contested New York, anxious business leaders rallied on Election Eve to warn voters that transferring "the present contest for the Presidency to the Halls of Congress" could "subject our Government to more fearful peril than any it has hitherto encountered."[16] Another speaker, James S. Thayer, raised ominous doubts "that Lincoln would ever be President of this nation,"[17] whatever the verdict of the people.

Thayer was referring to last-minute efforts among Northern and Southern Democrats to forgo their differences on slavery and unite around "fusion" tickets to stop Lincoln. Outgoing President James Buchanan's endorsed choice, Vice President John C. Breckinridge of Kentucky, candidate of the Southern Democrats, had improbably emerged as the favorite of Democrats in the president's home state of Pennsylvania, where "Old Buck" still enjoyed popularity and influence. In New York, opposition to Lincoln coalesced around Douglas. Horace Greeley, editor of the pro-Lincoln *New York Tribune*, warned on November 1 that a fusion "triumph" was "not an impossibility." Nervously, he exhorted the Republican faithful to allow no "call of business or pleasure, any visitation of calamity, bereavement, or moderate illness, to keep you from the polls."[18]

DESPITE THE UNPRECEDENTED tension and lingering uncertainty—intensified by the growing sense that the election held historic significance—Lincoln, over the last six months, had done next to nothing publicly, and precious little privately, either in person or in print, to advance his own cause. Prevailing political tradition called for silence from presidential candidates. In earlier elections, nominees who had defied custom appeared desperate, and invariably lost.[19] Besides, the choice seemed clear enough from the outset of the 1860 campaign, especially when it came to the smoldering issue of slavery. Douglas championed the idea that settlers in new Western territories were entitled to vote slavery up or down for themselves, while Breckinridge argued that slave-owners could take their human property anywhere in the country they chose. Against both stood Lincoln. As Frederick Douglass acknowledged, only the Republican believed it "the power and duty of the National Government to prevent the spread and perpetuation of slavery."[20]

Such profound disagreement might have provided fodder for serious debate—at least in modern campaigns. But no such opportunities existed within the reigning political culture of mid-nineteenth-century America, not even when the canvass involved proven debaters like Lincoln and Douglas, who had famously battled each other face-to-face in seven senatorial debates two years earlier. Worried that Lincoln might be tempted to resume politicking, William Cullen Bryant, editor of the pro-Republican *New York Evening Post*, bluntly reminded him that "the vast majority of your friends . . . want you to make no speeches, write no letters as a candidate, enter into no pledges, make no promises, nor even give any of those kind words which men are apt to interpret into promises."[21]

Obligingly, the acclaimed prairie orator silenced himself from the day of his nomination onward. The gifted campaigner retreated to the proverbial back porch—resisting even a tempting offer to campaign in "the place of my nativity," overwhelmingly Democratic Kentucky, by jokingly worrying: "Would not the people Lynch me?"[22] To his dismay, a newspaper unearthed the playful correspondence and gravely reported that Lincoln feared "the invitation was a trap led by some designing person to inveigle him into a slave State for the purpose of doing violence to his person."[23] Charges of cowardice could be fatal to politicians—a harsh reality with which Lincoln would soon have to contend as president-elect. He promptly drafted a reply.

For the most part, however, the skillful writer wisely let his correspondence ebb to a trickle, taking pains to mark his few interesting letters "private" or "confidential" to discourage their release to the public. Though Americans continued to revel in politics, thronging rallies, loyally affiliating with one party or the other, and voting in overwhelming numbers—a record-breaking 82 percent would turn out this Election Day nationwide[24]—Lincoln surprised no one when he assured an Ohio ally that "in my present position . . . by the lessons of the past, and the united voice of all discreet friends, I am neither [to] say or write a word for the public."[25]

When the crush of campaign correspondence became burdensome anyway, a "sensible and discreet"[26] young man named John George Nicolay left his clerkship in the Illinois secretary of state's office to join Lincoln's staff—to *become* his staff, more accurately—as private secretary for $75 a month.[27] The slightly built, dark-haired, German-born "George," as intimates knew him, could barely keep up with the ensuing flood of letters.[28]

As the 1860 campaign reached its climax, Lincoln received and rejected anxious last-minute appeals, from supporters and opponents alike, that he simply assure the South that, if elected, he had no intention of interfering with slavery. Less astute politicians might have regarded such reassurances as pabulum: easy to concoct, easier to swallow. Lincoln not only kept quiet; he spoke out to explain his silence, contending that any such policy reiterations would not only be superfluous, but a sign of indecisiveness that could cripple him as president-elect—and as president.

He was already on record as viewing slavery as "a moral, political and social wrong" that "ought to be treated as a wrong . . . with the fixed idea that it must and will come to an end."[29] These sentiments alone had proven enough to alarm Southerners. But Lincoln had never embraced immediate abolition, knowing, if nothing else, that such a position would have isolated him from mainstream white American voters and rendered him unelectable. Unalterably opposed to the extension of slavery, Lincoln remained willing to "tolerate" its survival where it already existed, believing that containment would place it "in the course of ultimate extinction."[30] That much about him voters already knew.

When a worried visitor from New England nonetheless urged him, the very day before the election, to "reassure the men honestly alarmed" over the prospect of his victory, Lincoln flew into a rare fury, and with a "warmth of retort he seldom reached," Nicolay observed, branded such men "liars and knaves." As Lincoln hotly explained: "This is the same old trick by which the South breaks down every Northern victory. Even if I were personally willing to barter away the moral principle involved in this contest, for the commercial gain of a new submission to the South, I would go to Washington without the countenance of the men who supported me and were my friends before the election; I would be as powerless as a block of buckeye wood."[31]

As for "[t]hose who will not read, or heed, what I have already publicly said," he insisted, they "would not read, or heed, a repetition of it."[32] Somewhat ponderously quoting Scripture, he added: " 'If they hear not Moses and the prophets, neither will they be persuaded though one rose from the dead.' " As he insisted: "What is it I could say which would quiet the alarm? Is it that no interference by the government, with slaves or slavery within the states, is intended? I have said this so often already, that a repetition of it is but mockery, bearing an appearance of weakness, and cowardice. . . ."[33]

In the very last letter of his noncampaign for the White House, composed a week before Election Day, one can almost hear the presumptive president-elect refusing to be drawn into further debate:

For the good men of the South—and I regard the majority of them as such—I have no objection to repeat seventy and seven times. But I have *bad* men also to deal with, both North and South—men who are eager for something new upon which to base new misrepresentations—men who would like to frighten me, or, at least, to fix upon me the character of timidity and cowardice. They would seize upon almost any letter I could write, as being an "*awful coming down*." I intend keeping my eye upon these gentlemen, and to not unnecessarily put any weapons in their hands.[34]

There would be no "awful coming down." Lincoln's "campaign" for president ended how and where it began: in adamant silence, and in the same Illinois city to which he had so tenaciously clung since the national convention. Like the solar eclipse that had obscured the Illinois sun in July, Lincoln remained in Springfield, hidden in full view.[35]

INSIDE WHAT ONE visiting reporter described as the "plain, neat looking, two story" corner house[36] where he had lived with his family for sixteen years, Abraham Lincoln awoke on Election Day 1860 and prepared to face the verdict of the people.

Inside his small, second-floor bedroom, Lincoln dressed in his usual formal black suit, pulling his long arms into a frock coat worn over a stiff white shirt and collar, a black waistcoat in between. As always, he wound a black tie carelessly round his sinewy neck and pulled tight-fitting boots—how could they be otherwise?—over his gargantuan feet. He likely greeted Mary and their two younger sons, nine-year-old Willie and seven-year-old Tad, at the dining table. (The eldest, Robert, had recently begun his freshman year at Harvard.)

Lincoln probably took his usual spare breakfast with the family, an egg and toast washed down with coffee.[37] Neither husband nor wife ever confided their routine or mood at home that morning. Nor did they welcome visitors who might have left such recollections. All we know is that eventually Lincoln donned the signature stovepipe hat he kept pegged on a wooden rack in the front hall. Then, as always—unaccompanied by retinues of security men or political aides—he stepped outside and turned toward the Illinois State Capitol some five blocks northwest of his home. As ever looking tough as "a whip-cord," he strode atop the "dead drift of leaves" that littered the sidewalks this brisk autumn morning, and marched on toward his headquarters.[38]

The bracing air that greeted Lincoln may have surprised—even worried—him. It was unseasonably chilly. How might the weather affect Election Day turnout? The sun shone from an encouragingly cloudless sky, but "Frost & ice" caked the ground throughout central Illinois, as Lincoln ally Orville Hickman Browning recorded in his diary from Quincy, a hundred miles away.[39] As the morning warmed, however, reports of sun-drenched, cloudless skies from one end of the state to the other stirred Republican hearts, clement weather being crucial to the task of enticing widely scattered rural voters, predominantly Republican in loyalty, to their distant polling places. "[C]ontray to all precedent," reported an excited editor from Chicago, "it was a glorious fall day . . . , a marvel." In pro-Lincoln Bloomington, the weather grew so obliging that one enfeebled citizen who had not been able to leave his house in months allowed himself to be hauled painlessly to the polls "in a carriage with a bed in it."[40]

Springfield, for nearly a quarter of a century Illinois's capital city, seemed, in visiting journalist Noah Brooks's harsh view, "a commonplace, sprawling sort of town."[41] Once notorious for its muddy streets and freely roaming herd of pigs, at least it now boasted outdoor, gas-fed lighting, a large and growing population of lawyers, doctors, and merchants, and clusters of two- and three-story brick structures surmounting wood-plank sidewalks. To a New York journalist, the town now presented "a handsome appearance," with streets "well planned and wide," and "a noble expanse" for a public square, around which huddled a ring of retail shops and professional offices, marked by an awning of vividly painted signs.[42] For the last few weeks, another New York reporter noticed, it was also alive "with the florid emblazonry of banner, and flared with unnumbered torches." A veritable "torrent of hurrahs" echoed repeatedly through its "usually tranquil streets."[43] Springfield was in a happy uproar.

Looming with stunning, almost incongruous grandeur over the city was the imposing State House, its red-painted copper cupola rising twice as tall as any other structure in town. Here, ever since his nomination in May, Lincoln had maintained his official headquarters—and his official silence—in a second-floor corner suite customarily reserved for the state's reigning governor. For six months, attended by Nicolay, Lincoln had here welcomed visitors, told "amusing stories,"[44] posed for painters, accumulated souvenirs, worked on selected correspondence, and scoured newspapers. Now he headed back to pass his final hours there as a candidate for president.

Lincoln entered the limestone State House from the south through its oversized pine doors. He ambled past its Supreme Court chamber, where he had argued many cases during his twenty-four-year-long legal career, and past the adjacent libraries where he had researched the sensational address delivered at Cooper Union nine months earlier.[45] Then he climbed the interior staircase, at the top of which stood the ornate Assembly chamber where, back in 1858, he had accepted the Republican Senate nomination with his rousing "House Divided" address.

The building brimmed with many such indelible memories, but what Lincoln felt as he encountered these touchstones on Election Day remains unknown. Lincoln "never had a confidant," law partner William H. Herndon explained, and "never unbosomed himself to others."[46] Keeping his thoughts to himself as usual, Lincoln headed to the so-called gubernatorial "residences"—a fifteen-foot-by-twenty-five-foot carpeted reception room and smaller adjacent office, simply furnished with both upholstered and plain wooden chairs, a desk, and a table—ceded to him these many months by the new governor, John Wood[47]

Here, since May, he had received and displayed an avalanche of gifts: "pieces of old rails that he had split, fragments of the log cabin in which he had lived, dilapidated specimens of the furniture he had made and used, stray bits of the surveyor's instruments he had once owned, mementoes of the Black Hawk War, in which he took part, books, pictures and engravings." The official who occupied the adjoining suite— Newton Bateman, the diminutive superintendent of public education whom Lincoln called "my little friend, the big schoolmaster of Illinois"— observed "articles of all sorts and sizes" in the room, "some very quaint and curious, some cheap and homemade, others elegant and costly."[48] One miraculous novelty dominated an entire wall: a twelve-foot-long wood-link chain a disabled Iowan had carved out of a single piece of timber "to symbolize the indissoluble union of the states."[49]

Here the journalists who arrived on the scene to cover Lincoln's movements this Election Day first encountered the candidate, "surrounded by an abattis [sic] of disheveled newspapers and in comfortable occupancy of two chairs, one supporting his body, the other his heels."[50] Under the watchful eye of friends and reporters, Lincoln, perhaps nervously, shifted from seat to seat, at one point all but disappearing into an "arm chair of liberal proportions . . . which he hardly seemed to fill to anything like repletion." Soon he was seen with his "long legs . . . elevated to the top of a stove, as he sat in a chair tipped backward." His "great height" multiplied the comic effect.[51]

Entering the crowded room to a hearty "come in, sir," a New York newspaperman was struck by the candidate's "easy, old fashioned, offhanded manner," and surprised to find "none of that hard, crusty, chilly look about him" that "dominated most campaign portraits." Doing his best to display his "winning manner" and "affability,"[52] Lincoln spent the early part of the day "receiving and entertaining such visitors as called upon him" with extravagant formality, respectfully rising each time a new delegation arrived. "These were both numerous and various—representing, perhaps as many tempers and as many nationalities as could easily be brought together at the West."[53]

When, for example, "some rough-jacketed constituents" burst in who, "having voted for him . . . expressed a wish to look at their man," Lincoln received them "kindly" until they "went away, thoroughly satisfied in every manner." To a delegation of New Yorkers, Lincoln feigned displeasure at seeing them so far from home, chiding them that he would have felt better had they stayed home to vote. He said much the same thing when a New York reporter arrived to shadow him, raising an eyebrow and scolding, "a vote is a vote; every vote counts."[54]

But when one visitor daringly asked the candidate a substantive question about the nation's future—whether he was worried Southern states would secede if he won—Lincoln turned serious, confidently replying, "they might make a little stir about it before, but if they waited until after the inauguration and for some overt act, *they would wait all their lives.*"[55] Unappreciated in the excitement of the hour was this hint at a policy of nonaggression. Few took notice—least of all in the South.

A visiting correspondent, this one from St. Louis, seemed surprised to detect no evidence of Lincoln's supposedly tasteless humor. Samuel R. Weed took special care to report that the candidate "did not jest or crack jokes (as his enemies charged was his daily habit)." Yet he did regale his guests with a full platter of funny stories. On the subject of "personal beauty," for example, Lincoln merrily confided he felt fortunate that " 'the women couldn't vote,' otherwise the monstrous portraits of him which had been circulated during the canvas by friends as well as by foes would surely defeat him."[56]

On this tense day, Lincoln offered the hopeful view that "elections in this country were like 'big boils'—they caused a great deal of pain before they came to a head, but after the trouble was over the body was in better health than before." He trusted that "the bitterness of the canvass would pass away 'as easily as the core of a boil.' " Eager as he was for the campaign to "come to a head," however, Lincoln delayed casting his own vote. As the clock ticked away, he remained secluded in the Governor's suite, occasionally glancing out the window to the crowded polling place across Capitol Square. Inside, he remained secluded, "surrounded by friends . . . apparently as unconcerned as the most obscure man in the nation."[57]

AS LINCOLN OCCUPIED himself greeting allies and supporters while waiting to learn his political fate, the rest of America—the first trickle among the more than four million white males who would go to the polls nationwide this day—began registering their choices for the presidency.

In must-win New York, Lincoln's supporters loudly made sure the metropolis was awake—"wide awake," joked the *New York Times*. This was a humorous reference to the indefatigable paramilitary Wide-Awake

Clubs whose members had for months marched the streets for Lincoln, carrying blazing torches atop wooden poles to illuminate nighttime rallies, dressed in oilskin hats and slickers to shield themselves from dripping oil and sparks. Now the Wide-Awakes worked one final day to pull the vote, determined to seize a "once in a lifetime" opportunity.[58] For the most part, as the pro-Democratic *New York World* reported, "the quiet of the city . . . reached even the point of dullness."[59]

Patrician New York lawyer George Templeton Strong, an ardent Lincoln supporter, sensed history in the making. "A memorable day," he confided in his diary. "We do not know yet for what. Perhaps for the disintegration of the country, perhaps for another proof that the North is timid and mercenary, perhaps for demonstration that Southern bluster is worthless. We cannot tell yet what historical lesson the event of November 6, 1860, will teach, but the lesson cannot fail to be weighty."

Strong attempted to cast his own ballot first thing in the morning, but "found people in a queue extending a whole block from the polls." Retreating, he rode to his Wall Street office, and attended a meeting at which bankers predicted there would be no financial panic no matter who won the election. Though another New Yorker sneered that most of the "Bulls, Bears, and Snakes of Wall Street assumed the air of deeply injured men" as the day unfolded,[60] Strong reported little gloom within the investment community. Optimistically, he returned to his polling place at 2 P.M., where he finally "got in my vote after only an hour's detention. I voted for Lincoln."[61]

Not so the colorful old Virginia extremist Edmund Ruffin, much as he wanted Lincoln to win—though for a different reason. Like many fellow secessionist ultras, Ruffin hoped a Lincoln victory would nerve the South to quit the Union. Earlier that year, the agricultural theorist and political agitator had nudged his section toward the inevitable by publishing a visionary piece of speculative fiction entitled *Anticipations of the Future*. The book flatly predicted that "the obscure and coarse Lincoln" would be "elected by the sectional Abolition Party of the North," which in turn would justify Southern resistance to "oppression and impending subjugation"—namely, a fight for "independence."[62] The uncanny, long-since-forgotten tome erred in only one detail: forecasting that these events would unfold four years later—in 1864.

On the eve of Election Day 1860, Ruffin reiterated in his diary: "I most earnestly & anxiously desire Lincoln to be elected. . . . I wish the question tested & settled now." He cast his personal ballot, however, for John C. Breckinridge, though he claimed that the Kentuckian did "not come up to my standard of what a southern candidate should be." Then, fully anticipating a Lincoln victory that would "serve to show whether these southern states are to remain free, or to be politically enslaved," Ruffin boarded a train bound for South Carolina, his baggage stuffed with political pamphlets advocating secession. Once in Charleston, he expected to begin agitating for disunion as soon as a Lincoln victory was confirmed.[63]

Nearly a thousand miles north, Election Day morning brought a sudden downpour and a single dramatic thunderclap to the abolitionist hotbed of Quincy, Massachusetts, "a thing which I never remember to have happened here so late in the year." So marveled Charles Francis Adams—Republican congressional candidate, son of one American president, grandson of another, and proud heir to a long family tradition of ant-slavery. Finding "quite a crowd" at the polling place at Town Hall despite the weather, Adams proudly "voted the entire ticket of the Republicans," exulting: "It is a remarkable idea to reflect that all over this broad land at this moment the process of changing the ruler is peacefully going on and what a change in all probability. . . . The prospect is great for a victory."[64] Even so, for Adams it would be at best bittersweet. Contending for that victory was not the Republican he had hoped would win the presidency—William Seward—but a Westerner whose success had upended so many Easterners' dreams.

Back across the continent, much closer to Lincoln's Springfield— and perhaps more reflective of the divided spirit of America—a newly relocated Galena, Illinois, Mexican War veteran evinced conflicted emotions about the choices his neighbors faced this Election Day. "By no means a 'Lincoln man,' "[65] he nonetheless seemed resigned to the

Republican's success. "The fact is I think the Democratic party want a little purifying and nothing will do it so effectually as a defeat," admitted the retired soldier, now starting life anew in the family's leather-tanning business. "The only thing is, I don't like to see a Republican beat the party."[66] The veteran's name was Ulysses S. Grant, and he would not remain a tanner for long. Grant had not lived in the river town "long enough to gain citizenship and could not, therefore, vote." But he was "really glad of this at the time," he later claimed, "for my pledges would have compelled me to vote for Stephen A. Douglas, who had no possible chance of election."[67]

In Stephen A. Douglas's hometown of Chicago, meanwhile, voters braved crowds as large as those flocking to the polls in New York. Four-block-long lines and two-hour waits prevailed. But Douglas was not in residence to cast a vote of his own. En route home after a multicity tour through the South, he found himself stranded in the unlikely town of Mobile. There, the Democrat perhaps found solace in the fact that Lincoln's name did not even appear on Alabama's ballots—or on those of nine additional states in the Deep South.

Yet the man who had beaten Lincoln for the Senate only two years earlier now stood a good chance of losing his home state—and with it, the biggest prize in American politics—to the very same man. Even Douglas's running mate seemed convinced of Lincoln's imminent success—and equally fearful that, in anticipation, "the fires of sectionalism in the South are waxing hot."[68]

As of Election Day, Lincoln had successfully avoided not only his three opponents, but also his own running mate, Hannibal Hamlin. Republicans had nominated the Maine senator for vice president without Lincoln's knowledge, much less his consent—true to another prevailing political custom that left such choices exclusively to the delegates—in an attempt to balance the Chicago convention's choice of a Westerner for the presidency. For a time, the man at the top of the ticket seemed to extend his vow of campaign silence to Hamlin, too. After asking a mutual acquaintance to convey his "respects" a week after the convention, Lincoln waited a full two months before initiating direct communication. Even then, pointing out that both of them had served in the 30th Congress from 1847 to 1849—Lincoln as a congressman and Hamlin as a senator—Lincoln admitted, "I have no recollection that we were introduced." Almost grudgingly did he now concede, "It appears to me that you and I ought to be acquainted."[69]

There the correspondence temporarily ceased, until September, when Lincoln got wind of Hamlin's fear that Republicans in Maine might soon lose House seats and barely survive the gubernatorial election. Making clear he expected "a splendid victory for us," Lincoln complained that such loose talk would "put us on the down-hill track, lose us the state elections in Pennsylvania and Indiana, and probably ruin us on the main turn in November."[70] The senator attempted a feeble response, denying he had leaked the story, then admitting the identical concerns. Their correspondence would not be resumed even when Maine voters in the state elections put the lie to Hamlin's concerns. Now, on this national Election Day the Republican party's running mates would be voting much as they had "run"—separately and silently.

Lincoln and Hamlin agreed on one thing: their party would no longer tolerate compromise that would make possible the further spread of slavery. So the party platform declared—in an era when party platforms still very much mattered—attesting incontrovertibly: "We deny the authority of Congress, of a Territorial Legislature, or of any individuals, to give legal existence to slavery in any territory of the United States."[71]

One anti-slavery champion who remained skeptical was the passionate African American civil rights pioneer, Frederick Douglass. A former slave, he was, much like the Republican presidential candidate, self-educated, a brilliant writer, and a captivating orator. And while both men rejected the idea that the Constitution gave Americans the right to own slaves, Lincoln differed with Douglass by reluctantly conceding that the Constitution protected slavery in the states where it had existed since the founding of the republic (and long before), while state laws sanctioned it in southern states that had joined the Union since. Certainly no other 1860 presidential candidate gave Douglass any better hope that slavery might end under his rule—and one, Stephen A. Douglas, had for years cruelly used "Fred," as he derisively called him,[72] as a rhetorical punching bag. But still the editor of the abolitionist newspaper *Douglass' Monthly* did not see in Lincoln the ideal answer to the black man's prayers for freedom and equality.[73]

Much as Douglass decried the "mobs gotten up to put down the Republican [state] Conventions at Baltimore, Alexandria, and Wheeling, the threats of violence" against Republicans in Kentucky, "and the threats of dissolution of the Union in case of the election of Lincoln," he could not bring himself to praise Lincoln directly.[74] Whether Lincoln himself ever read Douglass's increasingly critical editorials or speeches remains a matter of historical conjecture. Their own warm personal acquaintance would not begin for several more years.

On Election Day, Douglass tirelessly worked the polls in his home city of Rochester, encouraging neighbors not only to support the Republican party, but also to back a statewide universal suffrage referendum especially dear to his heart. In New York, free blacks still had to prove that they owned at least $250 in property and assets in order to vote, though the ballot initiative proposed at last to give all free blacks that right.[75] If Douglass himself voted that day remains a mystery. With or without his ballot, indicative of the intractable racism gripping even the Northern states in 1860, the suffrage referendum went down to a resounding defeat.[76]

FROM MORNING UNTIL dusk, an immense crowd of both Douglas Democrats and Lincoln Republicans milled noisily outside the polling place at the oblong-shaped, two-story Sangamon County Court House at Sixth and Washington Streets.[77] Here partisans gave voice to their beliefs by cheering at each approach by the inexhaustible roving musicians, and shouting their respective approval whenever a partisan hoisted a banner or shouted a slogan. The din could be heard for blocks.

Squabbles broke out repeatedly among so-called ticket-peddlers—

party agents who tried pushing prepared ballots on voters as they arrived.[78] Each time one agent or another tried pressing ballots into
prospective voters' hands, rivals on the scene cried out their disapproval
and offered substitute ballots instead.

The actual polling place, set up in a courtroom two flights upstairs,
consisted of two partially enclosed "voting windows close beside each
other," one for Democrats, one for Republicans. It was "a peculiar arrangement" in the view of the correspondent from St. Louis, but one
that had been "practiced in Springfield for several years." A voter had
only to pick up the preprinted ballot of his choice outside, and then as-
cend the stairs to announce his own name to an election clerk and deposit his ticket in a clear glass bowl. This was a secret ballot in name
only: voters openly clutching their distinctly tinted, ornately designed
forms while waiting on line unavoidably signaled to those of their neighbors gathered about the polls precisely how they intended to vote. The
system all but guaranteed bickering and ill feelings, which most of the
protagonists savored. Some voters, nearly as frantic over local legislative
races as they were over the big contest for the presidency, took out their
frustrations by accusing ticket agents of printing fraudulent ballots that
intentionally omitted the name of one minor candidate or another.

In this roiling atmosphere, it was hardly surprising that, the evening
before, quizzed by a neighbor at the post office on how he himself
planned to vote, Lincoln had replied almost defensively, "for Yates"—
Richard Yates, the Republican candidate for governor of Illinois. But
"*How vote*" on "the presidential question?" persisted the bystander. To
which Lincoln, his arms comically burdened with a pile of mail, drolly
replied: "Well . . . by ballot," leaving his neighbors "all laughing."[79]
Until Election Day afternoon, Lincoln's law partner Herndon was convinced that Lincoln would not cast a ballot at all, bowing to the "feeling
that the candidate for a Presidential office ought not to vote for his own
electors."[80]

But this was one tradition Lincoln thought of breaking. At around
3:30 P.M., after examining a "fragment of good news" about voter turnout, he peered out the window toward the crowd surrounding the Court

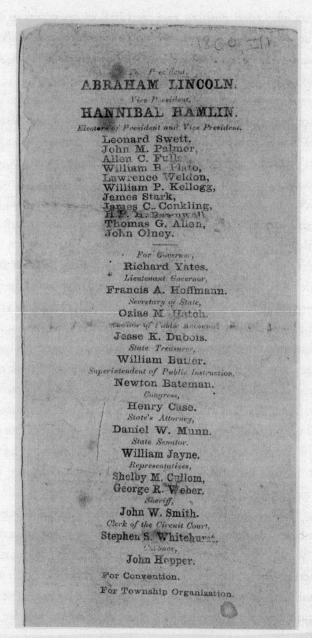

A typical Republican ballot for Springfield, Illinois. Lincoln modestly cut his own name—and those of his pledged electors'—from his ticket, voting only for his party's candidates for state and local office. (ABRAHAM LINCOLN PRESIDENTIAL LIBRARY)

House. Determining that the "multitude" had thinned a bit, he slipped out of the Governor's Room, headed downstairs, and then "walked leisurely over to deposit his vote,"[81] accompanied by a small group of friends and protectors to "see him safely through the mass of men at the voting place."[82] Burly fellow lawyer Ward Hill Lamon hovered close to Lincoln on one side. Positioned on the other was the spruce young drillmaster and onetime Lincoln law student, Ephraim Elmer Ellsworth, "an admirable specimen of an American soldier-citizen" in the words of one of his many admirers.[83] John Nicolay, along with Illinois secretary of state Ozias M. Hatch and William Herndon, trailed close behind.[84] But if Lincoln thought that this imposing retinue would guarantee his right to exercise his franchise quietly he was mistaken.

As he reached the Court House to cheers and shouts from surprised Republicans—many of whom had also convinced themselves Lincoln would not vote—"friends almost lifted him off the ground and would have carried him to the polls by [sic] for interference."[85] The "dense crowd," Lincoln's future assistant secretary John M. Hay recalled, "began to shout with . . . wild abandon" even as they "respectfully opened a passage for him from the street to the polls."[86] People shouted out "Old Abe!" "Uncle Abe!" "Honest Abe!" and "The Giant Killer!" Meanwhile, the "Giant's" usually combative Democratic supporters, Herndon marveled, "acted politely—civilly & respectfully, raising their hats to him as he passed on through them to vote." Lincoln took note of the welcome, Herndon recalled, "& was glad of it."[87]

As a *New York Tribune* reporter on the scene confirmed, "All party feelings seemed to be forgotten, and even the distributors of opposition tickets joined in the overwhelming demonstrations of greeting."[88] Every Republican agent in the street of course fought for "the privilege of handing Lincoln his ballot."[89] A throng followed Lincoln inside, Nicolay reported, pursuing him "in dense numbers along the hall and up the stairs into the court room which was also crowded." The cheering that greeted him there was even more deafening than in the street, and once again came from both sides of the political spectrum. As Nicolay testified: "from the time he entered the room until he cast his vote and again left it, there was wild huzzahing, waving of hats, and all sorts of demonstrations of applause rendering all other noises insignificant and futile."

The "object of all this irrepressible delight took it as calmly as he could," the *New York Tribune* reporter observed. The "crowd gathered about him with such excess of zeal that it was with some difficulty that he made his way through" as fellow voters expressed "the heartiest and most undivided delight at his appearance."[90] After he "urged his way" to the voting table, Lincoln followed ritual by formally identifying himself in a subdued tone: "Abraham Lincoln."[91] Then he "deposited the straight Republican ticket" after first cutting his own name, and those of the electors pledged to him, from the top of his preprinted ballot so he could vote for other Republicans without immodestly voting for himself. Snipped from Lincoln's ticket were the names of the eleven allies pledged to vote for him in the electoral college, among them his friends Leonard Swett, William Pitt Kellogg, John M. Palmer, and James Cook Conkling.[92]

Making his way back to the door, the candidate found himself again surrounded by well-wishers. He smiled broadly at them and, doffing the black top hat that made him appear, in the words of a popular campaign song, "in h[e]ight somewhat less than a steeple,"[93] bowed with as much grace as he could summon. Though the "crush was too great for comfortable conversation,"[94] a number of excited neighbors grabbed Lincoln by the hand or tried offering a word or two as he inched forward.

Somehow, the man of the hour eventually made his way through this gauntlet and back downstairs, where he encountered yet another throng of frenzied well-wishers. Now they shed all remaining inhibitions, "seizing his hands, and throwing their arms around his neck, body or legs and grasping his coat or anything they could lay hands on, and yelling and acting like madmen."[95] Somehow, Lincoln made his way back to the Capitol. By 4 P.M. he was safely back inside "his more quiet quarters," where he again "turned to the entertainment of his visitors as unconcernedly as if he had not just received a demonstration which anybody might well take a little time to think of and be proud over."[96]

Even with the people's decision only hours away, Lincoln still managed to look relaxed and to exchange stories with his intimates, perhaps keeping busy in order to remain calm himself. Samuel R. Weed thought it remarkable that "Mr. Lincoln had a lively interest in the election, but . . . scarcely ever alluded to himself." To hear his comments, noted Weed, "one would have concluded that the District Attorneyship of a county in Illinois was of far more importance than the Presidency itself." Lincoln's "good nature never deserted him and yet underneath I saw an air of seriousness, which in reality dominated the man."[97]

After four o'clock, telegrams bearing scattered early returns at last began trickling into the State House, uniformly predicting Republican successes across the North. When one cantankerous dispatch arrived from a pro-secession ex-congressman in South Carolina, expressing the Ruffin-like hope that the Republican would triumph so his state "would soon be free," Lincoln at first scoffed, recalling that he had received several such threatening letters in recent weeks, some signed, others anonymous. Then his expression darkened and he handed the telegram to Ozias Hatch with the remark that its author "would bear watching."[98] Indirect as it was, this was the very first expression from the candidate that he indeed expected soon to be president-elect, with responsibilities that included isolating potential traitors. Shortly thereafter, around 5 P.M. Lincoln finally broke away and returned to his home a few blocks away, presumably to take dinner. There he remained in private seclusion with his family for more than two hours.[99]

THE REAL "FUN began" around seven, when Lincoln returned to the State House and resumed reading dispatches in the Governor's suite, still displaying "a most marvelous equanimity."[100] Down the corridor, inside cavernous, gas-lit Representative Hall, nearly five hundred Republican faithful massed for a "lively time" of their own. The chamber "was filled nearly all night," Nicolay recalled, by a crowd "shouting, yelling, singing dancing, and indulging in all sorts [of] demonstrations of happiness as the news came in."[101]

Weed distinctly remembered the candidate's silent but evocative reaction when the first real returns finally arrived at the Governor's suite. "Mr. Lincoln was calm and collected as ever in his life, but there was a nervous twitch on his countenance when the messenger from the telegraph office entered, that indicated an anxiety within that no coolness from without could repress." It turned out to be a wire from Decatur "announcing a handsome Republican gain" over the presidential vote four years earlier. The room erupted with shouts at the news, and supporters bore the telegram into the hallway toward Representative Hall "as a trophy of victory to be read to the crowd."[102]

Further numbers proved agonizingly slow in coming. Not until eight o'clock did Hatch receive a wire reporting a Republican gain in nearby Jacksonville. "The news seemed to gratify Mr. Lincoln exceedingly." The " 'boys' kept bringing various reports of the progress of counting, but none of them were satisfactory."[103] When the delirium from nearby Representative Hall grew irresistible, Lincoln decided to make an appearance there. Supporters greeted his visit with a loud "outburst of enthusiasm"[104] and ushered him to the speaker's chair. Enthroned awkwardly in the place of honor, he listened to a few tribute orations, declined to say much himself, then retreated back to the relative privacy of the Governor's rooms to await more results.[105]

The day before, the town's principal telegraph operator had invited Lincoln to await the returns at the nearby Illinois & Mississippi Telegraph Company headquarters on the north side of Capitol Square, in whose second-floor office, he promised, "you can receive the good news without delay," and without "a noisy crowd inside."[106] Lincoln fully appreciated telegraphy. As he had predicted a year earlier, "the lightening [sic] stands ready harnessed to take and bring his tidings in a trifle less than no time."[107] The local station now linked to "all the other lines in the United States and Canada," using Western Union to connect to both the Mid-Atlantic and New England states.[108] The office would certainly get the election news fast. By nine o'clock, Lincoln could resist the opportunity no longer. Accompanied by Hatch, Nicolay, and Jesse K. Dubois, Lincoln strode across the square, ascended the stairs of the telegraph building, and installed himself on a sofa "comfortably near the instruments." Here he remained, sitting or lying down "snugly," waiting for "lightening" to strike.[109]

At some point onetime Illinois congressman Edward Dickinson Baker, now a rising star in Oregon politics, arrived on the scene, as did Springfield's mayor, Goyn Sutton. For a time, the growing knot of on-lookers notwithstanding, the small room remained eerily quiet, the only sounds coming from "the rapid clicking of the rival instruments, and the restless movements of the few most anxious among the party of men who hovered" around the clattering machines.[110] All eyes focused on the wood-and-brass contraptions whose worn ivory keys pulsated magi-cally, untouched by human hands, each time a new message set the relay magnet clacking away audibly.[111]

At first the "throbbing messages from near and far" arrived in "frag-mentary driblets," Nicolay remembered, then in a "rising and swelling stream of cheering news."[112] Each time a telegraph operator transcribed the latest coded messages onto a mustard-colored paper form, the three-by-five-inch sheet was quickly "lifted from the table . . . clutched by some of the most ardent news-seekers, and sometimes, in the hurry and scramble, would be read by almost every person present before it reached him for whom it was intended."[113]

For a while, the telegraph company's resident superintendent, John J. S. Wilson, grandly announced every result aloud.[114] But eventually the telegraph operators began handing Lincoln each successive message, which, with slow-motion care, "he laid on his knee while he adjusted his spectacles, and then read and re-read several times with deliberation."[115] Despite the uproar provoked by each, the candidate received every piece of news "with an almost immovable tranquility." It was not that he at-tempted to conceal "the keen interest he felt in every new develop-ment," an onlooker believed, only that his "intelligence moved him to less energetic display of gratification" than his supporters.[116] "It would have been impossible," another witness agreed, "for a bystander to tell that that tall, lean, wiry, good-natured, easy-going gentleman, so anx-iously inquiring about the success of the local candidates, was the choice of the people to fill the most important office in the nation."[117]

Heartening bulletins soon began arriving in rapid succession from across Illinois, with a particular "thrill of delight" ignited by the news that Democratic Joliet had given Douglas a majority of only 432, when a win by five hundred had been expected. Then the tiny downstate town of Du Quoin reported, giving Lincoln twice as many votes as its entire county had awarded Republican candidate John C. Frémont four years earlier. From neighboring Alton came the news that Republicans there had successfully "checkmated" a Democratic "scheme of fraud."[118] At this report, Lincoln "laughed heartily and exclaimed that that was a tribute from Egypt [the period nickname for Southern Illinois] to the success of the public school fund.' "[119] Better education, he was saying, had produced more Republicans. An even "more joyful thrill" greeted the report that Lincoln had won Chicago by 2,500 votes, and all of Cook County by four thousand. Handing over the crucial dispatch, Lincoln ordered, "Send it to the boys," and supporters whisked it across the square to the State House. Moments later, the cheering from the Capitol could be heard all the way to the telegraph office. The ovation lasted a full thirty seconds.[120]

These fragmentary returns were "Greek to me," journalist Weed confessed, "but Mr. Lincoln seemed to understand their bearing on the general result in the State and commented upon every return by way of comparison with previous elections. He understood at a glance whether it was a loss or gain to his party."[121]

This was an understatement. In Nicolay and Hay's words: "He was completely at home among election figures. All his political life he had scanned tables of returns with as much care and accuracy as he analyzed and scrutinized maxims of government and platforms of parties. Now, as formerly, he was familiar with all the turning-points in contested counties and 'close' districts, and knew by heart the value of each and every local loss or gain, and its relation to the grand result."[122] But the candidate relied on more than instinct. Lincoln brought with him for easy comparative reference a handwritten, county-by-county chart of Illinois returns from the 1856 Buchanan–Frémont–Millard Fillmore race.[123]

Tonight the gains overwhelmingly predominated. Indiana reported a majority of "over twenty thousand for honest old Abe,"[124] followed by similarly good news from Wisconsin and Iowa. Pittsburgh declared: "Returns already recd indicate a maj for Lincoln in the city by Ten Thousand[.] All the counties heard from give Lincoln large increase."[125] From the City of Brotherly Love came the news that "Philadelphia will give you maj about 5 & plurality of 15" thousand.[126] Connecticut reported a "10,000 Rep. Maj."[127]

Notwithstanding this growing arsenal of good news, by 10 P.M. the group remained nervously impatient for news from the swing state of New York, whose mother lode of thirty-five electoral votes might determine whether the election ended up decided this very night, or later in the uncertain House of Representatives. Breaking the tension, Senator Lyman Trumbull arrived at the telegraph office door, fresh from a long

One of the many telegrams Lincoln read on election night at the Springfield telegraph office, this one brought good news from Pennsylvania's leading Republican, Simon Cameron. (LINCOLN PAPERS, LIBRARY OF CONGRESS)

train journey from his Alton residence just north of St. Louis.[128] Five years earlier, Trumbull had bested Lincoln in a fractious legislative battle for the U.S. Senate seat he now held. But the two had resumed a cautious friendship—based largely on a shared antipathy for Stephen A. Douglas—and Trumbull had become a valuable ally in the presidential campaign. Now the senator studied the returns for himself, looked up, and exclaimed, "We've got 'em, we've got 'em." In Weed's words, "if there was joy upon the countenance of Mr. Lincoln before, it was then a positive blaze of light."[129]

Even the trickle of negative news that arrived from Southern states like Virginia, Delaware, and Maryland left the nominee "very much pleased" because the numbers from these solidly Democratic strongholds might have been far worse. Soon after Lincoln pronounced the latest returns from Pittsburgh to be likewise "better than . . . expected—far better," Pennsylvania senator Simon Cameron so confirmed by wiring the candidate to predict a seventy-thousand-vote majority statewide, adding in an exhilarating postscript: "New York safe Glory enough."[130] Then came a momentous report from the Empire State. Its Republican chairman, Simeon Draper, was thought by many to be "impulsive," but no one in Springfield's telegraph office doubted him when he wired: "The city of New York will more than meet your expectations."[131] Between the lines, the report signaled that the overwhelmingly Democratic metropolis had failed to produce the majorities Douglas needed to offset the Republican tide upstate.

Amid the euphoria that greeted this news, Lincoln remained the "coolest man in that company."[132] When the report of a probable fifty-thousand-vote victory quickly followed from Massachusetts, Lincoln merely commented in mock triumph that it was "a clear case . . . of the Dutch taking Holland."[133] Meanwhile, with only a few intimates able to fit inside the modest telegraph office, crowds built in the square outside, where rumors "of the most gigantic and imposing dimensions" soon began wildly circulating, the New York Tribune reported. Even Lincoln's most trusted associates seemed powerless to contain or refute them.

The southerners in Washington had set fire to the capital. Jeff Davis had proclaimed rebellion in Mississippi, and Douglas had been seized as a hostage in Alabama. Blood was running in the streets of New York and could not be stopped. The negroes of Virginia had risen in insurrection. Buchanan had resigned the presidency. Any person emerging from the telegraph station and denying these and kindred rumors was set down as having his own reasons for concealing the dreadful truth. As for Mr. Lincoln, it was, of course, preposterous to look to him for a square statement or any statement of the facts. The privileged half dozen who went freely in and out, being unable to confirm the catalogue of horrors, became extremely unpopular, and were compelled to listen to unflattering remarks concerning their character, vocation, manners and appearance.[134]

Shortly after midnight, with the definitive tally from New York still lagging, Lincoln and his party decided to take a break, walking to the nearby "ice cream saloon" operated by William W. Watson & Son on the opposite side of Capitol Square.[135] Here a contingent of Republican ladies had set up "a table spread with coffee, sandwiches, cake, oysters and other refreshments for their husbands and friends."[136] At Watson's, the *Missouri Democrat* reported, "he came as near to being killed by kindness as a man can conveniently be without serious results."[137]

Lincoln's entrance unleashed the usual "commotion" and greetings of "How do you do, Mr. President?" from a chorus of friendly female voices. As the women formed a circle "in Indian style"[138] around their buffet table to take turns clutching his hand, a glee club of "Lincoln boys" loudly let out with the popular campaign song: "Ain't you glad you joined the Republicans . . . Down in Illinois?"[139] Several female admirers grew bolder and "saluted him with hearty kisses on the cheek," to which he offered "good-natured resistance" at first, then yielded, joking that the display of affection was "a form of coercion not prohibited by the Constitution or Congress." Correspondent Weed recalled that he "surrendered meekly enough and took the proffered kisses as one of the duties of the high office" he was about to win.[140]

If he was worried that definitive returns might now be arriving unread at the telegraph office he had abandoned, Lincoln showed no outward sign of anxiety, calmly indulging "in pleasant chat and his propensity for story-telling."[141] He probably resisted the "lakes of fluid and islands of confection" that in other guests invited "submission to absolute gluttony."[142] Food and drink had never much interested the abstemious Lincoln, though for many others, they provided the fuel that nourished politics.

Mary Lincoln attended the collation, too, as "an honored guest," by one account helping to set out the repast along with the other wives. For a time, she sat near her husband in what was described as "a snug Republican seat in the corner," surrounded by friends and "enjoying her share of the triumph."[143] A fervent, repressed political partisan in her own right who had viewed the October state results in both Indiana and Pennsylvania as extremely hopeful signs, Mary had become more anxious than her husband in the final days of the campaign. "I scarcely know, how I would bear up, under defeat," she had confided.[144] As thrilled as she must have been that night at the likely prospect of victory, it is hard to imagine that the preternaturally jealous Mary was able to enjoy a reception for her husband that featured what one journalist suggestively described as the "wildest climax of feminine ecstasy."[145]

"Instead of toasts and sentiment," remembered Newton Bateman, another eyewitness, "we had the reading of telegrams from every quarter of the country." Each time the designated reader mounted a chair to announce the latest results, the numbers—depending on which candidate it favored—elicited either "anxious glances" or "shouts that made the very building shake." According to Bateman, the candidate himself read one newly arrived telegram from Philadelphia. "All eyes were fixed upon his tall form and slightly trembling lips, as he read in a clear and distinct voice: 'The city and state for Lincoln by a decisive majority,' and immediately added in slow, emphatic terms, and with a significant gesture of the forefinger: 'I think that settles it.'"[146]

If the matter remained in doubt, the long-anticipated dispatch soon arrived from New York. The tally all but confirmed that Lincoln would indeed win the biggest electoral prize of the evening—and with it, the presidency. The celebrants instantly crowded around him, "overwhelming him with congratulations." Describing the reaction—in which "men fell into each other's arms shouting and crying, yelling like mad, jumping up and down"—one of the celebrants compared the experience to "bedlam let loose."[147] Hats flew into the air, "men danced who had never danced before," and "huzzahs rolled out upon the night."[148]

In the State House, upon hearing the news, "Men pushed each other—threw up their hats—hurrahed—cheered for Lincoln—cheered for Trumbull—cheered for New York—cheered for everybody—and some actually laid down on the carpeted floor and rolled over and over."[149] One eyewitness reported a "perfectly *wild*" scene, with Republicans "*singing, yelling! Shouting!! The boys (not children) dancing. Old men, young, middle aged, clergymen, and all . . . wild with excitement and glory.*"[150]

"I thought I had seen all the excitement which could possibly be produced on such an occasion," a reporter for a New Hampshire newspaper wired to his paper, "but I must confess that I never witnessed real, genuine enthusiasm until then. I saw men who at other times would have thought it beneath their dignity to have joined in giving three moderate cheers, who were now throwing up their hands and shouting for Uncle Abe."[151]

The vast roar from the canyon of streets surrounding Capitol Square "seemed to startle men and women from their beds and many a window in Springfield was lifted" by residents shouting down for "the cause of the shouting." As church bells began pealing,[152] Lincoln eased past the dense throng of well-wishers at Watson's, having spent in total only half an hour at this "first testimonial delight over his success."[153] A fellow celebrant there observed that "Mr. Lincoln slipped out quietly looking grave and anxious,"[154] and headed back toward the telegraph office to receive the final reports.

First, he appeared to steel himself for these life-altering moments.

One observer saw him pacing up and down the sidewalk alone before reentering the Illinois & Mississippi building. Another glimpsed his silhouette, his head bowed to stare at the latest dispatch while "standing under the gas jets" that lit the streets.[155] Once back inside, wires from Buffalo sealed the state—and the White House—for the Republicans. The final telegram from New York ended with the words: "We tender you our congratulations upon this magnificent victory."[156]

Though the crowd inside the telegraph office greeted this climactic news with lusty cheering, Lincoln merely stood up to read the pivotal telegram "with evident marks of pleasure," then sank back into his seat, silently. Lyman Trumbull tried to break the tension by embracing his old friend and shouting: "Uncle Abe, you're the next President, and I know it." All Lincoln allowed himself to say was: "Well, the agony is most over and you will soon be able to go to bed."[157]

The revelers in the State House, however, had no intention of retiring for the night. Instead they emptied into the streets and massed outside the telegraph office, shouting "New York 50,000 majority for Lincoln—whoop, whoop hurrah!" The entire city "went off like one immense cannon report, with shouting from houses, shouting from stores, shouting from house tops, and shouting everywhere."[158]

Others reacted more solemnly. One of the final telegrams Lincoln received that night came from an anonymous admirer who signed himself only as "one of those who am glad today." It read: "God has honored you this day, in the sight of all the people. Will you honor Him in the White House?"[159]

ABRAHAM LINCOLN WON election as the sixteenth president of the United States by carrying every Northern state save New Jersey. No candidate had ever before taken the presidency with such an exclusively regional vote. (Even the Jefferson-Adams contests of 1796 and 1800 had featured exceptions to lopsided regional voting, with Pennsylvania going to Jefferson in their first contest, and New York in their second.) In the end, Lincoln would amass 180 electoral votes in all—comfortably more than the 152 required for an absolute majority.[160] In the raw count, Lincoln could take comfort from the fact that the rapidly growing nation awarded him more popular votes than any man who had ever run for president—1,866,452 in all, 28,000 more votes than Democrat James Buchanan had earned in winning the presidency four years earlier. But Lincoln's votes amounted to only a shade under 40 percent of the total cast, the smallest share ever collected by an outright victor. And the national tally alone did not tell the full story.

Testifying alarmingly to the deep rift cleaving North from South, and presaging the challenges soon to face his administration, was the anemic support Lincoln garnered in the few Southern states where his name was allowed to appear on the ballot. In Virginia, the Lincoln ticket received just 1,929 votes out of 167,223 statewide—barely one percent. The result was even worse in his native Kentucky, where only 1,364 out of 146,216 voters cast their ballots for the Republicans, in this case amounting to less than one percent. Lincoln could find some solace in the fact that both of these Upper South states, along with Missouri, at least went for the moderate John Bell, rather than the Southern choice, John C. Breckinridge. When news of the Virginia result reached him, Lincoln greeted it with the hope that it "represented a sentiment of love for the Union which would destroy the hopes of the ultra secessionists."[161]

Yet as the ominously divided vote confirmed, just as Southern foes had warned, Lincoln's victory proved entirely sectional—an outcome all but guaranteed when most Southern states refused to list Lincoln's name on ballots. Analyzed geographically, the total result gave Lincoln a decisive 54 percent in the North and West, but only 2 percent in the South—the most lopsided vote in American history. Moreover, most of the 26,000 votes Lincoln earned in all five slaveholding states where he was allowed to compete came from a single state—Missouri, whose biggest city, St. Louis, included many German-born Republicans.[162]

Would Lincoln have prevailed had the House of Representatives been compelled to choose the nation's sixteenth president? Possibly not. Although he won seventeen states in all, to sixteen for all three of his opponents combined, the House would have voted by congressional delegation. Each would have caucused to choose a designee, with none harnessed by the obligation to respect its Election Day outcome. Deals and compromises would have remained a possibility—especially if Congress concluded that denying Lincoln the White House might preserve the Union. In the end, the Republicans did not fare well enough in the 1860 congressional elections to ensure victory for its presidential candidate that year even had the decision been left to the newly elected House.

Forced to "the lamentable conclusion that Abraham Lincoln has been elected President of the United States," the pro-Democratic, pro-Southern *Washington Constitution* forecast "gloom and storm and much to chill the heart of every patriot in the land" only hours after the votes were tabulated. "We can understand the effect that will be produced in every Southern mind when he reads the news this morning—that he is now called on to decide for himself, his children, and his children's children whether he will submit tamely to the rule of one elected on account of his hostility to him and his, or whether he will make a struggle to defend his rights, his inheritance, and his honor."[163]

CONTEMPORARY REPORTS DIFFER as to how long the victory celebrations continued in the hometown of the nation's brand-new president-elect. Lincoln's neighbor and freshly elected Republican presidential elector, James Conkling, for one, happily admitted that he stayed out till 2 A.M. after spending the earlier part of the evening celebrating at the State Capitol.[164]

According to a visiting journalist, the tireless city remained "alive and animated throughout the night." Rallies continued until dawn, growing so "uncontrollable" by 4 A.M. that revelers toted back the cannon with which they had inaugurated Election Day and now made it again "thunder rejoicings for the crowd."[165] John Nicolay tried going to bed at 4:30 but "couldn't sleep for the shouting and firing guns."[166] By most accounts, the celebrations ended only with daybreak.

No one is entirely sure when Lincoln himself finally retired. According to one eyewitness account, he left the telegraph office for his house at 1:30 A.M., according to another, shortly after two.[167] Not until 4:45 A.M. did the *New York Tribune* receive a final bulletin from its Springfield correspondent confirming: "Mr. Lincoln has just bid good-night to the telegraph office and gone home."[168]

Moments before his departure, whenever it came, Lincoln at last received the final returns from his hometown base—a matter about which he admitted he "did not feel quite easy," national victory notwithstanding. But Lincoln could take heart. Though he lost Sangamon County to Douglas by a whisker, 3,556 to 3,598, he won the hotly contested city of Springfield—by all of twenty-two votes.[169] At this latest news, "for the first and only time" that night, Lincoln "departed from his composure, and manifested his pleasure by a sudden exuberant utterance—neither a cheer nor a crow, but something partaking of the nature of each"—after which he "contentedly" laughed out loud.[170]

Not everyone laughed with him. The anti-Republican *Washington Constitution* could "almost hear the veritable cockadoodledoo with which, according to friendly scribes, the village politician celebrated his exit from the crowd on the gloomy morning of the seventh November." With displeasure, it frowned: "It is plain that on that occasion Mr. Lincoln had not the faintest conception of the true import of what had happened to him and to the country. He was elated, buoyant, and disposed to crow; rather after the fashion of a rail-splitter whose game rooster comes out conqueror from a hard-fought main than of a statesman solemnly alive to the responsibilities of his position."[171]

But no opposition grumbling could spoil the moment for the new president-elect. He donned his overcoat, thanked the telegraph operators for their hard work and hospitality, and stuffed the final dispatch from New York into his pocket as a souvenir. It was about time, he announced to one and all, that he "went home and told the news to a tired woman who was sitting up for him."[172]

Yet to several observers, Lincoln suddenly seemed graver—his thoughts focused far away. Though the celebratory frenzy intensified through Capitol Square, Nicolay could see the "pleasure and pride at

the completeness of his success" melt into melancholy. The "momen-
tary glow" of triumph yielded to "the appalling shadow of his mighty
task and responsibility. It seemed as if he suddenly bore the whole world
upon his shoulders, and could not shake it off." Even as the outer man
continued absentmindedly studying final election returns, the "inner
man took up the crushing burden of his country's troubles, and traced
out the laborious path of future duties."[173] Only later did Lincoln tell
Gideon Welles of Connecticut that from the moment he allowed himself to believe he had won the election, he indeed felt "oppressed with
the overwhelming responsibility that was upon him."[174]

From "boyhood up," as Lincoln once confided to his old friend Ward
Hill Lamon, "my ambition was to be President."[175] Now a leavening
dose of reality worked like a toxin to poison the fulfillment of that lifelong dream. Amid "10,000 crazy people" outside, "shouting, throwing
up their hats, slapping and kicking one another," the president-elect of
the United States—"still perfectly cool, the coolest man" in that feverish town—slowly descended the stairs of the Illinois & Mississippi telegraph office and disappeared down the street, "without a sign of anything
unusual."[176]

A contemporary later heard that Lincoln arrived home to find his
wife not "sitting up for him," after all, but fast asleep. He "gently touched
her shoulder" and whispered her name, "to which she made no answer."
Then, as Lincoln recounted: "I spoke again, a little louder, saying 'Mary,
Mary! *we are elected!*' "[177]

Minutes before, the final words his friends heard him utter that night,
were: "God help me, God help me."[178]

Chapter Two

My Troubles Have Just Commenced

EVEN AS ILLINOIS Republicans continued boisterously celebrating the victory of their favorite son—the demonstrations would, in fact, persist on and off for days to come—a sizable portion of the rest of America greeted the November 6 election results with emotions ranging from trepidation to outrage.

True, residents of the village of Bladensburg, Illinois, in happy conspiracy with visiting Republicans from out of town, burned up so many fireworks in those first seventy-two hours that they had to send to Chicago for fresh supplies. To one Lincoln man, the result signaled that "the reign of the slaveholders is at an end, and we are more free and independent." An eyewitness reported everyone from street "urchins" to "wide awakes" hoarse from shouting "Hurrah for Lincoln!" a full three days after the election.[1] But in distant Virginia, a stronghold of support for the failed compromise candidacy of John Bell, one furious newspaper editor branded Lincoln's triumph "a calamity," likening the victorious Republicans to "John Brown's Kansas brand of fanatics, cut-throats, and horse-stealers."[2] The disappointed editor of the *Richmond Enquirer* lamented that "Lincoln owed his election to the worst enemies of the South" and warned he would now "naturally and necessarily select his counsellors from among them."[3]

Some embittered Southerners quickly began talking openly of resistance. Deep in Breckinridge country, the *Fayetteville North Carolinian* warned its readers that "if we submit now to Lincoln's election . . . your home will be visited by one of the most fearful and horrible butcheries that has cursed the face of the globe."[4] The *Charleston Mercury* was equally emphatic, harking back to the colonies' century-old grievances against the throne of England to proclaim, just two days after the election: "The tea has been thrown overboard; the revolution of 1860 has been initiated."[5]

As if in response, precisely as the old firebrand Edmund Ruffin had hoped, the South Carolina legislature promptly convened to begin planning "the mode and measure of redress." Three years earlier, Ruffin had urged "preparation for war."[6] Now, Charleston provocatively called for ten thousand volunteers between the ages of eighteen and forty-five to join the ranks of its state militia.[7] In the same defiant spirit, the governor of Mississippi greeted Lincoln's triumph by calling a special legislative session of his own with an identical agenda: consideration of a secession convention. The state's most prominent U.S. senator, Jefferson Davis, remembered the moment proudly.[8] "A paper parchment is all that holds us together," echoed an Alabama disunionist, "and the sooner that bond is severed the better it will be for both parties."[9] Left unmentioned by such declarations was the fact that the new president-elect had long maintained he would do nothing to threaten slavery where it was long entrenched and constitutionally protected.

Similarly ignoring Lincoln's long-held moderate positions, Southern-born members of President Buchanan's administration, now relegated to lame-duck status, began exchanging private correspondence with their home state governors about the growing prospects for disunion. As Louisiana senator John Slidell admitted to Buchanan: "I see no probability of preserving the Union, nor indeed do I consider it desirable to do so if we could."[10] Rumors abounded that Southern senators were about to resign their seats en masse in anticipation of secession. Was Buchanan's successor, far from Washington, alert to these danger signs? Lincoln's own secretary came to believe that at least three members of

Buchanan's Democratic "cabinet cabal" were guilty of nothing less than a "flagrant conspiracy in the early stages of rebellion." Surely Lincoln had confided these impressions to Nicolay at the time. But the president-elect did and said nothing outside his headquarters to damp down these initial post-election brushfires.[11]

Nor did he react publicly to smaller, but equally troubling, anti-Union outbursts throughout the South. At a celebration in Savannah ostensibly organized to mark completion of a new railroad line, the mayor roused the crowd by pledging fifty thousand militiamen from Georgia "to rush to the assistance of South Carolina if coerced." A few days later, at a banquet at the other end of the line—Charleston—the city's swank Mills House hotel resounded to fiery disunion threats from well-fed ultras. Somehow forgotten in the din of separatist rhetoric was the ironic fact that the Savannah–Charleston tracks had been built by black slave labor to carry trains that would transport only white passengers.[12] A local poet stoked the growing ultra spirit by warning that a Northern invasion was likely, and must be resisted:

> *Ready for "Lincoln's cattle"*
> *In all their boasted might.*
> *Ready till death to battle*
> *In defence of Southern right.*
>
> *Gallant sons of Carolina,*
> *O'er your head the Lone Star waves—*
> *Fight ye now beneath that banner,*
> *Or fore'er we will be slaves!*[13]

Around this same time, a gang of "white boys" in the South Carolina outpost of Mount Pleasant—supposedly "aided by negroes," although, of course, slaves could be ordered to do anything their masters desired—burned " 'Old Abe' in effigy." When one local resident objected, he suffered forty lashes for his interference, and was thrown in jail.[14] In several Alabama counties, Minutemen, pledged to fight to the death for Southern independence, began sporting ribbons proclaiming: "Resistance to Lincoln is obedience to God."[15]

In state after state, one portentous incident after another, breathlessly reported in newspapers throughout the country in the days following the election, alarmed even confident Republicans who had insisted that a Lincoln victory could never loosen the bonds that held the Union together. As early as November 9, pro-secession placards appeared on the streets of New Orleans, calling for the formation of a defense corps of Minutemen. Dissidents unfurled palmetto flags in Charleston, where artillery saluted their appearance by opening fire with a defiant fifteen-gun cannonade.[16] A U.S. District Court judge there dramatically tore off his official robes "in rage and disgust at Lincoln's election."[17] In Lynchburg, Virginia, a federally appointed postmaster resigned his seat and offered the job "to any Lincolnite who wanted it."[18] There were no known takers.

Anti-Union talk was not restricted to the Deep South. Even out west in the Golden State, secessionist whispers intensified following the bitterly contested canvass. This was nothing new for California. The huge state, which sprawled from Oregon all the way down to Mexico, mirrored the national North–South divide. Just a year earlier, a pro-Southern Supreme Court justice there had killed a pro-Northern U.S. senator in a politically inspired duel. Now two of its congressmen publicly suggested that the time was ripe for California to become an independent republic.[19] With the Democrats split, Lincoln had won the state, but by a hair—only 657 votes—amassing less than 33 percent of the total ballots cast. Reportedly "elated" when he first got this good news two full weeks after Election Day[20]—it still took a fortnight to move messages across the mountains from the West Coast to Illinois—Lincoln now faced the unhappy prospect that his victory there might actually trigger a California secession movement. Days after the Eastern results reached the state, the *San Francisco Daily Herald* still prayed for "the defeat somehow of the Black Republicans" and their "perversion of the Divine Law."[21]

Of course, not all the response to the Republican triumph was negative. In the North, reaction to Lincoln's election predictably split along immutable party lines. In New Jersey, for example, the only Northern state Lincoln failed to carry, Newark's local Republican paper blamed the defeat on the local Democrats' "mean and slavish obsequiousness to the South." With a smirk, the Douglas paper replied: "Both branches of Congress will have a majority against Lincoln, and for the next two years he may amuse himself by splitting rails and appointing Northern postmasters."[22]

The day after the election, the pro-Lincoln *Chicago Tribune* exulted, "The battle has been fought and the victory won. Hail! All Hail!!" But within the week, Springfield's pro-Douglas organ, the *Register*, cast a shadow over the celebration by charging that a wholesale system of bribery and corruption had elevated "negro lovers and abolitionists" to high office.[23] Throughout the North, Republican enthusiasts congratulated Lincoln and each other, while Northern Democrats lamented the result—and in one instance painfully close to home, questioned it. At Mount Holyoke, a band of female Wide-Awakes described as "running hither and thither . . . laughing and shouting, and drinking lemonade," marched in a celebratory torchlight procession, unfurling a banner that read: "PRESIDENT—ABRAHAM LINCOLN. Behind a homely exterior, we recognize inward beauty."[24] But the *Boston Advertiser* warned, it is a matter of doubt whether the Union is *busted* or not. We suppose it is."[25]

Few such concerns were expressed in New England—although former President Franklin Pierce, a Democrat from New Hampshire who had quietly supported Breckinridge, sadly concluded that any attempt to stave off disunion would now be "vain." "How can I urge the men of the South to take a view I should not take if I were there?" he asked.[26] Purists on the other end of the political spectrum seemed equally dissatisfied, but for different reasons. Like radical Southerners, they wanted revolution, not continued compromise that forestalled a crisis they believed unavoidable. Abolitionist Wendell Phillips, for one, worried that Lincoln was nothing more than "a pawn on the political chessboard . . . hardly an anti-Slavery man." Oddly, the entire crisis might have been averted had Southern extremists harbored the same reservations as this Northern one. At that same Boston meeting, however, Massachusetts governor John A. Andrew countered by predicting that the new administration would prove "successful, patriotic, brilliant, faithful and true."[27] In nearby Cambridge, "a large body" of Harvard students rallied on campus to offer formal, but "cordial," congratulations to their fellow student, Robert T. Lincoln, son of the president-elect and newly dubbed—in honor of the Prince of Wales's recent triumphant American tour—the "Prince of Rails."[28]

Next door in Concord, the anti-slavery martyr, Senator Charles Sumner, marked the Republican triumph by marching to the home of another abolitionist icon, Ralph Waldo Emerson, in the company of an exhilarated Wide-Awake corps. Called on to speak at this symbolic spot, Sumner hailed Lincoln's victory as a historic "landmark" for the anti-slavery movement. "A poet has said that the shot fired here was heard round the world," Sumner declared, thereby making another, quite different reference to America's Revolutionary War heritage, "and I doubt not that this victory which we have achieved in our country will cause a reverberation that will be heard throughout the globe."

Still, like many other Northerners, abolitionists included, the senator strongly urged "moderation" and "wisdom" in the face of Southern hostility. He left little doubt that he thought the president-elect possessed these virtues—and yet another quality he valued even more. Explained the man who had once been beaten nearly to death by a Southern congressman on the floor of the U.S. Senate: "I believe that bravery is necessary in directing the affairs of government, as much as prudence. I believe he is the man especially called to see to it that we are not in any way checked or set back by the menaces of disunion which sometimes come to us from the South."[29]

Such menaces came occasionally from the North as well. Just before Election Day, Philadelphian James A. Bayard had declared himself "unable to see how disunion can be avoided if the Blacks elect Lincoln," using the shorthand du jour for "Black Republicans." Bayard worried that the "business men of Phila" were not as "awake" as their New York counterparts to the dangers certain to "follow the election of Lincoln."[30] But a week after the vote, a local newspaper sternly insisted that if disunion resulted, "the South will be its sole author, and the South will be its worst sufferer."[31] Such warnings often found their way into Southern journals, where they were bitterly denounced, just as fire-eating secession editorials earned frequent republication—and rebuke—in the North. The posturing was thus not localized; frequently adapted in the opposing section of the nation, journals that typically preached only to converted locals now succeeded in inflaming readers in all parts of the country, expanding the uproar exponentially. Southern newspapers hungry for fodder to roil the secession debate fed their subscribers the most inciteful material they could unearth in the Northern press. Northern journals scoured Southern papers for similarly provocative reports designed to confirm hotheaded Southern disloyalty.

Sensational incidents, however isolated, thus assumed disproportionate consequence by earning major coverage in the press. Many Northerners heard the news that in the communications hub of New York, a Northern city where the president-elect had won scant support, 150 Southern-born medical students called an emergency post–Election Day meeting to decide how to respond. To shouts of "let's all go home," they agreed to return South when—not *if*—"each state secedes." Nervous teachers agreed to forward their diplomas later.[32]

The mood in America's commercial capital had been bleak for days, particularly in its jittery financial community. Investors talked of an imminent panic "out of fears aroused by the ferment in the Southern States."[33] But by November 9, George Templeton Strong insisted, "things are not so bad as I expected they would be three days after Lincoln's election." Despite all the "gasconading from the sunny South," Strong seemed sure at first that "the storm will blow over and die away without uprooting anything."[34]

To make certain, New York newspapers went into overdrive urging caution. Even the contrarian *New York World*, while conceding that "we may have a flurry," insisted: "there can be no disunion." Unrealistically, the paper also suggested that the only way to prevent revolution and maintain the nation's "prosperity, freedom and greatness" was by banishing the issue of slavery from the public discourse—hardly likely. Decades earlier, such a gag rule had choked off congressional debate year after frustrating year. The chance that Congress might reimpose such a veil was nil. Besides, as the *World* admitted, echoing Sumner, Lincoln's victory constituted not just a realignment, but a "revolution."[35] The very next day, the paper urged Lincoln to publish a conciliatory message to the South. Yet it conceded that if the brand-new president-elect thought it more dignified to remain silent, his previously published speeches should prove sufficient to demonstrate his "moderation and conservatism"—a defense of silence that Lincoln himself would soon appropriate for himself.[36]

Suspecting that its readers still hardly knew the president-elect, and might be dismayed by reports of his roughness and lack of breeding, the *World* took pains to reassure "that many-headed monster, the general public," that "judicious observers" would "hesitate before pronouncing him ugly," adding: "His face is quick and mobile in expression; his eyes, dark and lustrous, set deeply in his head, like [Daniel] Webster's." The paper went on to praise Lincoln's rise in life from flatboat pilot and railsplitter, and even added the prediction that Mrs. Lincoln was destined to "adorn and grace" her new position as well.[37] The pro-Republican *New York Times* ran a "private letter" from an unnamed "professional gentleman in Springfield" extolling Lincoln's "goodness of soul, generous nature . . . simplicity of character . . . [and] honesty of heart," adding as if in answer to decades-old whispers about his lack of religious orthodoxy: "He respects religion, believes in its doctrines, feels them important, though he has not made religion a personal matter."[38]

Some New Yorkers required no such reassurances. Striking a defiant tone, the Young Men's Republican Union—the organization that had hosted Lincoln's Cooper Union speech back in February—filled Stuyvesant Institute to hear victory orations from pro-Republican editors Horace Greeley and William Cullen Bryant. After the Rocky Mountain Glee Club performed the comic song "Where! Oh where, is Jimmy Buchanan?" Bryant declared Lincoln's election "one of the most important moral and political victories that had ever been achieved." The "enemy," the old poet-editor declared, "was conquered." Greeley, at least, expressed the hope that "the moderate men of the South" would "cheerfully" acquiesce to Republican rule.[39]

At first, pro-Union journals in the Upper South did urge caution. The *Baltimore Exchange*, for example, pledged to support "all lawful efforts to check any further agitation" on the slavery issue, insisting it "would trust to the guidance of worse than Mr. Lincoln, rather than sanction at this juncture any step that would imperil the bonds of the Union or shake the stability of the Republic."[40] A major Memphis daily concurred, insisting four days after the election that Lincoln could surely be trusted to mete out "equal justice to the South." But soon enough, separatist rhetoric began drowning out the moderates. Some withered into lonely voices striving vainly to hold off the secessionist tide. Others gave up and joined the tidal wave for disunion—like the very same Memphis paper, which soon acknowledged "an irrepressible conflict . . . between the two sections, which it is impossible ever to reconcile."[41]

Similarly, the influential *Richmond Dispatch*, while branding Lincoln's election "a calamity," and his party "fanatical," at first urged Virginians to "take time to consider" any irrevocable response, acknowledging that "hot-headed young gentlemen" agitating for armed resistance might "distort the problem" and make matters worse. Then the paper promptly contradicted itself by warning Virginians not to nap until overtly provoked by the president-elect. "We do not 'wait for a sign,'" it editorialized. "The outrage perpetuated is great, and cannot be wiped out by the failure of Lincoln to commit an 'overt act.'"[42] Tennessee's *Murfreesboro Citizen* concurred: "It will be difficult to induce the Southern people, loyal to their institutions as they are to transfer to the incoming Administration the traditional respect and reverence which American citizens accord to the National Government."[43]

Vague comments about "respect and reverence" skirted the volatile issue underlying much Southern post-election panic: the subject of race. Lincoln's record on the subject was complicated. Three years earlier, he had coldly conceded "a natural disgust in the minds of nearly all white people, to the idea of an indiscriminate amalgamation of the white and black races." But he also maintained that in "the natural right to eat the bread" they earn "with their own hands," African Americans were "my equal, and the equal of all others."[44] Such comments, retrograde as they seemed to abolitionists, were more than sufficient to inflame slave-owners in regions like the Carolinas, where blacks nearly outnumbered whites, keeping the minority in a state of constant fear of slave revolt. Enslaved persons there were regarded as unthreatening to their masters only as long as the natural rights of which Lincoln spoke were denied.

No newspaper produced a franker acknowledgment of the region's unofficial policy of perpetual race subjugation than the *Charlotte Daily Bulletin*, which ignored Lincoln's history of moderation to claim: "The head and front of the Abolitionists actually claims for the negro social and political equality with you and me." Added the writer, in what the famous South Carolina diarist Mary Boykin Chesnut liked to call "the hot, fervid, after-supper Southern style":[45] "I would prefer to live under the government of a wise and enlightened King than that of a Black Republican fanatic like old ABE LINCOLN whose whole political life is *deadly hostility* to us and our institutions."[46]

Reflecting this view—and worse—a small-town Georgia newspaper warned: "Can we suppose, for a moment, that the South will submit to a Black Ruler of our Government?" Vowing never to recognize a so-called "negro President," the journal labeled Lincoln "a notorious *nigger thief*" and posted a $10,000 reward for "Hannibal's and ABE's heads without their bodies," hinting that Vice President–elect Hannibal Hamlin was himself of African descent. Lincoln kept the vile clipping in his files.[47]

Powerful as was the intensity of racial hatred, racism alone did not adequately explain Southern panic over Lincoln's election. Economics and politics played crucial roles, too, at least as they related to the preservation of slavery. The region had long guaranteed the survival of its slave-based system by maintaining political control of all branches of the federal government—"slaveholders have ruled the American government for the last fifty years," is how Frederick Douglass disgustedly put it a few months earlier.[48] The slaveholders' grip encompassed a durable, if aging, majority on the Supreme Court, a decisive voice in Congress, and, since 1853, a succession of sympathetic Northerners in the White House. Though the Constitution assumed the perpetuation of slavery, the prospect of an authentic anti-slavery man in the presidency was enough to drive many Southern radicals to raging talk of disunion.[49]

Even the region's moderates saw their future as hopeless under a Lincoln presidency. President Buchanan's treasury secretary, Howell Cobb of Georgia, for one, conceded: "It is true that without a majority in Congress, Lincoln will not be able to carry out *at present* all the aggressive measures of his party. But let me ask if that feeble and constantly decreasing majority in Congress against him can arrest that tide of popular sentiment in the North against slavery which, sweeping down all barriers of truth, justice, and Constitutional duty, has borne Mr. Lincoln into the Presidential chair." Not even a safe congressional majority, Cobb predicted, could protect the South from "the power and patronage of President Lincoln."[50] This was key. The prospect of ceding Southern-based federal jobs to anti-slavery Republicans was just too much for Cobb—and many others.

Still wandering through the South en route home to Illinois in defeat, Lincoln's longtime rival, Senator Stephen A. Douglas, wasted little time in speaking out, too. Anxious New Orleans merchants had asked his advice in the wake of the Republican victory, and his response, however grudging in some respects, constituted one of the unreconstructed partisan's finer hours. "No man in America regrets the election of Mr. Lincoln more than I do," he began a frank open letter, "none made more strenuous exertions to defeat him; none differ with him more radically and irreconcilably upon all the great issues involved in the contest." Perhaps gilding the lily a bit, the senator added: "No man living is [more] prepared to resist, by all the legitimate means, sanctioned by the Constitution and laws of our country, the aggressive policy which he and his party are understood to represent."[51]

But then Douglas trumpeted a warning note: "I am bound, as a good citizen and law-abiding man, to declare my conscientious conviction that the mere election of any man to the Presidency by the American people, in accordance with the Constitution and the laws, does not itself furnish any just cause or reasonable ground for dissolving the Federal Union." Besides, he argued, checks and balances would surely curtail excesses by one branch of government or another—Lincoln included. A "reliable majority" in the Congress, Douglas pointed out, would negate executive hostility. A president who sought to act without its consent would find himself "before the High Court of Impeachment." Any "outrage" on Lincoln's part was bound to "arouse and consolidate all the conservative elements of the North in firm and determined resistance."[52]

"Four years will soon pass away," Douglas concluded soothingly, at which time "the ballot-box will furnish a peaceful, legal and constitutional remedy for all the grievances with which the country may be afflicted." Until then, he ended his impassioned appeal, "the election of Mr. Lincoln, in my humble opinion, presents no just cause, no reasonable excuse for disunion"—and no "pretext" for those "who look upon disunion and a Southern Confederacy as a thing desirable in itself."[53]

However welcome the Democratic lion's remarks—they were promptly published in the crucial Upper South state of Missouri—Lincoln may well have given them greater importance than they deserved. His only public response was a "smile," a signal that some supporters misunderstood, one paper blasting the tome as a "graceless exhibition of morbid jealousy."[54] If Lincoln truly regarded Douglas's sentiments, viewed together with the cautionary editorials that appeared early on in some Southern newspapers, as vindication of his recent policy of silence and invisibility, it proved a miscalculation. As he should have realized, such appeals had previously failed to win the Little Giant much support in precisely the region he was now trying to mollify: the South.

THE PRESIDENT-ELECT'S UNWAVERING, months-long public posture—that of confident silence—was belied by the private worries that plagued, and now began haunting, him. Determined to maintain an aura of strength for the public, he confided these anxieties, signs, and omens to only a handful of intimates.

On Election Night, for example, when one journalist observed that overconfident foes had "turned tail as soon as they got the news" of Lincoln's election, the victor cautioned: "There are plenty left. A little while ago I saw a couple of shooting stars fall down hissing and sputtering. Plenty left for many a bright night."[55]

Soon thereafter, Lincoln glimpsed another "mysterious" and, he feared, "ominous" vision in his own bedroom mirror. While reclining on a lounge, he glanced up to notice a "double-image of himself in the looking-glass," one clear, the other pallid. For a moment, it was vivid; then it vanished—at first, two Lincolns side by side, then none at all. As he recounted the eerie vision to his friend Ward Hill Lamon: "There was Abraham Lincoln's face reflecting the full glow of health and hopeful life; and in the same mirror, at the same moment of time, was the face of Abraham Lincoln showing a ghostly paleness." Then it "melted away, and in the excitement of the hour [I] forgot all about it," Lincoln told another friend, "—nearly, but not quite, for the thing would once in a while come up, and give me a little pang as if something uncomfortable had happened."[56]

In Lincoln's mind, at least as Lamon interpreted the story, "the illusion was a sign." Both the president-elect and his wife believed it meant he would not only survive his term in office, but four years later win reelection to a second one, only to die before it ended. "With that firm conviction, which no philosophy could shake," Lamon believed, "Mr. Lincoln moved on through a maze of mighty events, calmly awaiting the inevitable hour of his fall by a murderous hand."[57]

Lamon's version of Lincoln's premonition, like many of his stories, was probably exaggerated. It seems highly unlikely that a freshly elected president would have spoken about a second term only days after first winning the White House, especially since no chief executive had sought and won reelection since Andrew Jackson. And yet, other contemporaneous evidence suggests that Lincoln did indeed harbor faith in dreams and signs—and would do so for the rest of his life.[58] A more reliable source—a politician who hungered to join the cabinet, Connecticut editor Gideon Welles—held that, at the very least, Lincoln lay awake, sleepless, in the aftermath of his election, his mind crowded with thoughts of George Washington and Andrew Jackson, recalling "what all his predecessors had done" when faced with crises of their own.[59] Welles insisted, however, that Lincoln confided he used his insomnia not to interpret optical illusions but to plan the future. In his own way, Welles created an equally exaggerated countermyth of the post-election Lincoln; not the troubled spirit Lamon depicted, but a leader of absolute certainty and unshakable conviction.

Lincoln told Welles he did not "get much sleep" on Election Night, "for I then felt, as I never had before, the responsibility that was upon me. I began at once to feel that I needed support,—others to share with me the burden." Over and over, his restless mind grappled with the names of "men on whom he could depend, and who would be his support in the trials that were before him." By the time "the sun went down" the next night, so Lincoln told Welles, "I had made up my Cabinet. It was almost the same that I finally appointed." Indeed, sometime after Election Day, a sleepless Lincoln supposedly even jotted down the names of prospective cabinet appointees on a note card. He never made the list public. As it happened, most—but not all—the politicians would eventually join the administration, though the path to their appointments would prove rocky. Furthermore, close examination of the original suggests someone else pencilled the wish list, not Lincoln, though it surely reflected his hopes for a balanced government, both geographically (westerners and easterners) and politically (ex-Whigs and ex-Democrats).[60]

Lincoln	Judd
Seward	Chase
Bates	M. Blair
Dayton	Welles

Private secretaries John Nicolay and John Hay later confirmed Welles's startling claim and went one night better, testifying: "The work of framing the new Cabinet was mainly performed on the evening of the Presidential election." As Lincoln told the secretaries a few years later: "When I finally bade my friends good-night . . . I had substantially created the framework of my Cabinet as it now exists."[61] Yet another White House secretary, William O. Stoddard, further hyperbolized that Lincoln was "busy" with the "duty" of cabinet formation "even before election-day."[62] In truth, the path between framework and formal appointments would be littered with formidable roadblocks and detours.

Lincoln would ultimately select for his administration what historian Doris Kearns Goodwin ingeniously called "a team of rivals."[63] As Nicolay and Hay put it, he sought "a council of distinctive and diverse, yet able, influential, and representative, men, who should be a harmonious group of constitutional advisers and executive lieutenants—not a board of regents holding the great seal in commission and intriguing for the succession."[64] But assembling the team was neither an overnight, nor straightforward, task. With so many approaches to weigh—political obligations, personal loyalties, press opinion, and regional balance (including the question of whether to offer one of the coveted cabinet spots to a loyal Southerner)—Lincoln was hardly prepared to choose his ministers the day after the vote, much as Honest Abe liked to claim in retrospect. In fact, his cabinet-making would be marked in the weeks to come by false starts, wild speculation, political intrigue, and a battle royal over representation for Pennsylvania.

THIS MUCH WE know for certain. Around ten o'clock the morning after the election, Lincoln left his home and headed back to the State Capitol "as usual." So observed one visiting journalist, startled to see the newly elevated leader following his customary routine "as though nothing of importance had happened."[65] For years, Springfielders had seen their neighbor tread the very same path, more often than not "absorbed . . . gazing upward and noticing no one." But today was different, at least in one respect: "He was hailed with cheers as he passed some knot of Republicans who still lingered in the city to hear the final result."[66]

Lincoln returned to the Governor's suite at the State House surprised to find it overflowing with friends, strangers, reporters, and an entirely new class of visitor destined to plague the next president to the end of his days: office-seekers. The room was still anchored by one table groaning under the weight of a huge pile of books, and another "littered" with "heaps and hills of . . . newspapers, enough to supply a country journalist with items for a year."[67] A capacious tank of water stood near the reception room window, offering visitors their only refreshment.[68] But now, according to one observer, it seemed as if the "entire community" had lodged itself inside to greet the new president-elect.[69] Overnight, while the tired candidate had tossed and turned in bed, these visitors, ostensibly eager to congratulate Lincoln, had flooded into town on horseback or aboard farm wagons and carriages. By dawn, they were joined by additional "loads of people" who dashed to Springfield aboard the earliest trains, jostling with each other for scarce hotel rooms and then making a beeline for the president-elect's headquarters in quest of attention, favors, and employment.[70]

Campaign manager David Davis lumbered into town, too, all three hundred pounds of him, disgusted to find all of Springfield "as drunk as Bacchus." But neither Mr. nor Mrs. Lincoln seemed particularly "elated" by the victory, he observed with surprise, perhaps insensitive to their likely exhaustion. "There is no use anticipating the future," Davis wrote home.[71] James C. Conkling's wife, Mercy, found her old friend Mary Lincoln in quite a different mood a few days later—"in fine spirits as you may imagine."[72]

If the president-elect himself showed no visible elation, the same could not be said of his neighbors. At the State House, Lincoln found a "host of friends" on hand to slap his back and call him "Mr. President." Notwithstanding his new status, he struck one journalist on the scene as still "emphatically the man of the people," as he "greeted the meanest dressed with equal cordiality as the best."[73]

Watching this scene unfold, newspaperman Samuel Weed, like several other eyewitnesses, thought he could discern, lurking behind the president-elect's "sincere pleasure and good nature," a "sort of sadness in his face which was remarked [upon] by more than one of those present. But Lincoln left his anxieties unexpressed, amid the warm congratulations which poured in upon him, and conversed with all who got near enough to him for the purpose with his old-time freedom."[74]

Flopping into the copious armchair he had occupied the day before, casually hoisting his boots to the top of the castiron stove, Lincoln greeted his friends and neighbors by "throwing out hearty western welcomes" to all visitors. At least half a dozen times, he was heard to drawl: "Well, boys, your troubles are over now, but mine have just commenced." Every so often, Lincoln would excuse himself, and retreat to a corner table with John Nicolay, to dictate correspondence—"maybe a leaf of history," one observer speculated giddily.[75]

Before long, the crush in the modest suite grew so thick that Lincoln felt compelled to turn the unscheduled down-home reception into "a regular levee." Unwinding his long legs and rising slowly from his seat, he commenced formally shaking hands with every visitor who pushed his way in—yet in a manner Weed described as "so natural, sincere and hearty that no one could question the admiration with which Mr. Lincoln was regarded by his neighbors." Weed believed Lincoln would never seem more "manly or self-possessed in any emergency" that might follow.[76]

Another reporter was startled to see, among the "constant stream, coming and going, from every part of the lands," two big, sandy-haired boys who loudly claimed to be as tall as the new president-elect. Lincoln immediately offered to stand back-to-back, after which the young men took their leave, enormously pleased that they had measured up. An "elderly and very good looking lady" came to apologize to Lincoln for offering him a meager dinner on the prairie a quarter century before. "Madam," he had consoled her, "it was good enough for a President." Her story stood in stark contrast to the warning of a country boy whose father had sent him to alert Lincoln that he might be poisoned. The young man left only after advising him: "dad says you must look out and eat nothing only what your old woman cooks; and mother says so too."[77]

Before this outpouring of affection and respect could go to his head, a "grizzled" old farmer arrived at the door, elbowed his way into the

Governor's suite and through the throng, grasped Lincoln's hand, and happily exclaimed: "Uncle Abe, I didn't vote for yer, but I am mighty glad yer elected just the same." To which Lincoln jovially shot back: "Well, my old friend, when a man has been tried and pronounced not guilty he hasn't any right to find fault with the jury."[78] In a way, the analogy was inapt. Few Americans doubted that—victory or not—with a crisis looming, and less than two-fifths of the electorate on his side, the jury on Abraham Lincoln was still very much deadlocked.

With the crush of happy visitors on hand, it was easy—too easy—to forget that even Lincoln's Springfield had been almost evenly divided on Election Day. No doubt speaking for many disappointed Democrats, local teenager Anna Ridgely ruefully admitted in her diary on November 11: "We were disappointed, for we had hoped that such a man as he without the least knowledge of state affairs, without any polish or manner would not be chosen to represent this great nation, but so it is.—I tremble for our country."[79]

Lincoln received one more painful reminder that he was still a target for criticism. Walking between his home and office, he noticed a group of young boys teasing an agitated stray goat. When the animal hungrily spied the taller target, it turned from the children and tried butting Lincoln instead, until he was forced to seize it by the horns in self-defense. As the youngsters watched in delight, the president-elect of the United States gave his first post-election speech—to an angry goat. He might as well have been speaking to the South when he shouted: "I didn't bother you. It was the boys. Why don't you go and butt the boys. I wouldn't trouble you."[80]

LINCOLN HAD ANOTHER way to take the measure of public opinion, which he valued highly.[81] Before the introduction of political polling, and while party newspapers remained unwaveringly one-sided and therefore unreliable in reflecting the national mood, the people's voice could be heard in but one way: direct contact—either in person, or through the mails.

Among the many letters and telegrams that poured into his office in the days following his election, Lincoln could take comfort from a wide range of congratulations from both celebrities and ordinary citizens, friends and strangers, military men and civilians, senior citizens and children, politicians and poets.[82] Private secretary Nicolay opened some fifty such letters in just three days—a minuscule outpouring by modern measurements, but a virtual avalanche to a mid-nineteenth-century staff of one. The crush of correspondence became "appalling," one newspaperman sympathized, and mostly "impertinent."[83] By November 18, the load had grown to about seventy letters daily—most of them falling into three categories: congratulations, demands for patronage (neither of which the secretary answered), and endless requests for Lincoln's autograph, which he fulfilled.[84] With "other things claiming my attention," the punctilious Nicolay admitted, he invariably found himself "somewhat behind" at the end of each hectic day.[85]

Some letters, of course, seemed to call out for instant attention. "You are President elect," wrote Senator Salmon P. Chase of Ohio, one of the elite Republicans who had sought the nomination Lincoln won instead. "I congratulate you and thank God. . . . The space is now clear for the establishment of the policy of Freedom on safe & firm grounds. The lead is yours. The responsibility is vast. May God strengthen you for your great duties."[86] Lincoln made no immediate reply—perhaps preferring to wait until he could thank Chase properly—with the offer of a cabinet post. Nor did he answer the influential German-American leader Carl Schurz, who rather ponderously reminded Lincoln that he now faced "the greatest mission that ever fell to the lot of mortal man: the restoration of original principle in the model republic of the world."[87] No known answer went to Republican national committeeman George G. Fogg, either, even though Fogg had kept a protective eye on Lincoln's son Robert during his time at prep school in New Hampshire, and though he wrote only to join "in the general rejoicing with which the great victory is being hailed all over the land."[88] Such politicians had more than congratulations on their minds, Lincoln knew. They also sought influence, power, and patronage, and he was not yet ready to deal with them.

Among his many less famous correspondents, Vincennes, Indiana, lawyer Cyrus M. Allen wrote to salute Lincoln's victory "because it enables us to turn out the Goths & Vandals who have so long had possession of the government." Helen Haskell, a self-described "little girl" from Hillsboro, Illinois, expressed her rather grown-up hope that "the South will soon learn, that they can trust a northern man to be President, and that the states and people will be happy under your government." Equally heartening news came from Lincoln's cousin-in-law James Shoaff, who reported from the family homestead in Decatur that his wife, Nancy Hanks Shoaff—named for Lincoln's late mother—"had our cottage beautifully illuminated last night in honor of *your* election to the Presidency."[89] And a group of students from Indiana Asbury University wrote "to congratulate you in your happy success," adding, "now for a little advice we want you to split the Democratic platform into Shivers all." They signed their letter: "Abes boys."[90]

The newest of "Abes boys" was born in Germantown, Pennsylvania, while the votes were still being counted. His father, insurance man William F. Smith, promptly informed the president-elect that on "Wednesday Mor, about 2 A M when the whole United States were looking for the returns wether [sic] Old Abe (Excuse the familiarity) was elected President, just at that particular period 'Young Abe' made his appearance[.] I desire to have you record the fact that we are the first to Honor your Election, by naming the New Candidate . . . after the New President of the same date and Trust that he may have as you have now, the Confidence of his fellow man." Smith was something of a confidence man himself. He shamelessly enclosed a brochure entitled, *Some among the many reasons why you should Insure your Life*, along with a less-than-subtle list of premium rates, should Lincoln feel "honored" enough to purchase a policy from him.[91]

Eager to take some credit (and perhaps reward) for the Republican triumph in the Empire State, New York's Young Men's Republican Union mailed Lincoln a brochure enumerating its many contributions to the campaign. Not only had the group marched in local parades and demonstrations, it reported, it had also circulated tens of thousands of copies of Lincoln's Cooper Union address and Lincoln-Douglas debates. This was precisely the degree of mass distribution the president-elect believed should be adequate to assuage Southern concerns about his intentions, however doubtful it was that copies had ever circulated where Lincoln hoped they would extinguish fires: in the South itself.

Ohio boasted its share of celebrants, too, and a letter scrawled by one enthusiast must have brought Lincoln particular delight. One H. Jeffords wrote to say he believed the Republican triumph owed at least something to its candidate's superior height. "I raised the tallest Lincoln Pole in Ohio," Jeffords boasted, "I helped to elect the tallest President in the United States. I married a wife of 5 ft 11 inches high. I produced the largest turnips in the State of Ohio and a pumkin [sic] 182 lbs in weight. honest *Abe* aint I some pumpkins[?]"[92]

But even the most cheerful news from the Buckeye State could carry a chill of foreboding. Writing from the Lake County town of Mentor to exult that "This last battle pays for 1858"—the year Lincoln had painfully lost the Senate race to Douglas—an old legal associate, Clifton H. Moore, unknowingly echoed the very sentiments Lincoln was expressing at the time to his visitors in Springfield: "Your problems have just commenced[;] that of your friends who are not politicians measurably ended."[93]

In nonresponse to this outpouring, the president-elect wrote precious few letters of his own—still uncertain whether his private correspondence could remain private, determined that it should be. Two days after Election Day, he did pen a note to invite the newly chosen vice president, Hannibal Hamlin, if he could do so "without much inconvenience," to meet him soon in Chicago. He thanked only a handful of correspondents for gifts and congratulations.[94] Certainly no reply went to the Virginian who importuned Lincoln "to allay the excitement in the Southern States" by quickly announcing that he "would not interfere with the right of the South in their slaves, but administer the government according to the Constitution as interpreted by the illustrious Henry Clay—if such are your intentions."[95] Not even an irresistible eleven-year-old Ohio girl who wrote to "honest old abe the rail splitter" asking for a "presant" because "I hirarr for you" got a reply from the usually softhearted president-elect.[96]

But he did respond pointedly when Thomas Haycraft, a Kentucky acquaintance of his late father's, wrote movingly to "pray God that you may be enabled manfully to bear up under the weight and skillfully to pilot the vessel through the breakers of the threatened storm." Lincoln's birth state of Kentucky had given him but a fraction of the votes it cast on November 6. And Haycraft acknowledged that in the wake of the result, "Those Hotspurs of the South will no doubt try a while to kick up a dust." But the old man remained hopeful that "sober second thoughts may calm them down into a decent acquiescence of the choice of the Nation." Acknowledging that the boy he once knew was likely being "annoyed to death with letters & all sorts of petitions and communications," Haycraft still could not help asking that one of Lincoln's brave supporters from his old family home in Elizabethtown could be "remembered while favours are being dispersed."[97] The job-seeking was well under way.

Though Lincoln made clear that he would not "as yet, make any committal as to offices," he did give Haycraft the kind of policy commitment he seemed reluctant to offer the rest of the South. "Rest fully assured," Lincoln replied a week after Election Day, "that the good people of the South who will put themselves in the same temper and mood towards me which you do, will find no cause to complain of me."[98] As usual, Lincoln marked the letter "Private, and confidential," but likely would not have objected had Haycraft shared the spirit of his conciliatory message with other citizens of that vital border state. Its loyalty to the Union Lincoln knew he must keep.

Yet another Kentuckian, the president-elect's old friend and roommate, Joshua Fry Speed, offered Lincoln a similar opportunity after penning perhaps the most appreciated of all these post-election congratulations. From Farmington, his elegant mansion near Louisville, Speed, who had evidently cast his own ballot against Lincoln on Election Day, wrote to "tender you my sincere congratulations upon your election to the highest position in the world—by the suffrage of a free people." Though now estranged from Lincoln politically, Speed took pains to point out: "As a friend, I am rejoiced at your success—as a political opponent I am not disappointed." Lincoln must have studied this text with particular care, for his former roommate had been the closest friend—perhaps the only truly close friend—he had ever had. Speed's letter went on to say:

> That you will bring an honest purpose to bear upon all subjects upon which you are called to act I do not doubt. Knowing you as I do and feeling for you as I have ever done—I can not but tremble for you. But all men and all questions sink into utter insignificance when compared with the good of our whole country and the preservation of our glorious Union. You are I know as proud of its past glories as any man in the nation.
>
> Its continuance and its future will depend very much upon how you deal with the inflammable material by which you are, and will be surrounded.
>
> The *eyes* of the *whole* nation will be upon you, while unfortunately the *ears* of one *half* of it will be closed to any thing you might say. How to deal with the combustible material lying around you without setting fire to the edifice of which we are all so proud and of which you will be the chief custodian is a difficult task.[99]

Evidently deeply moved, Lincoln asked Speed to meet him on the trip he was planning, urging him to bring his wife to keep Mary company, and cautioning him to keep the plan secret, "as I prefer a very great crowd should not gather at Chicago."[100] For the benefit of the public, Lincoln hoped to damp down the secessionist firestorm Speed described. But he would not—or could not—admit it was as "combustible" as his friend warned, especially if the "eyes" and "ears" of the nation were indeed as focused on the president-elect as Speed suggested. To acknowledge so publicly, he believed, would only make the tense situation worse. Perhaps a man who had won 39 percent of the popular vote might feel compelled to speak out to reassure the majority who had opposed him. But the man who had also won 52 percent of the electoral vote could afford to keep silent.

Besides, lacking anything but symbolic power, and with four long months remaining before his inauguration, Lincoln convinced himself he could do nothing tangible, certainly nothing official, to avert the crisis as long as the lame-duck Buchanan administration remained in office. A keen student of American history, Lincoln likely knew that the most anxiety-producing previous change of administrations—the tense 1801 transition between John Adams and Thomas Jefferson—had mercifully lasted only three weeks.[101] His own agony was not scheduled to end for four months. Until then, talk was cheap—and might prove fatally dangerous as well, especially before state electors cast their votes in December, and then the Electoral College votes were counted in Washington in February and made the November 6 results official.

For better or for worse, the new president-elect concluded as well that whatever he might say would unavoidably alarm at least part of the country that he would not be able to govern for more than a hundred days. Soothing words of reassurance on the rights of slaveholders might inflame freedom-loving Republicans who had just voted for him. Defiant pronouncements on the sanctity of Union would probably arouse Southern Democrats who had not, and for whom anything less than conciliation amounted to coercion. Saying nothing was preferable to saying too much. Well versed in the Bible, Lincoln may also have remembered the lines from Isaiah: "You silence the uproar of foreigners; as heat is reduced by the shadow of a cloud, so the song of the ruthless is stilled."[102]

Lincoln likely believed, too, that expending political capital too early might render him less effective when he took over the government in March. Historians who have suggested that he misjudged the growing crisis have both overestimated his legal and political ability to allay the growing panic, and underestimated Lincoln's conviction that he could confront disunion only after his inauguration.[103] But the suggestion that he was unaware of the severity of the problem is both unfair and inaccurate.

Besides, many of his supporters believed silence remained the best policy. "Mr. Lincoln does admirably well in refusing to be catechized, or give new pledges, or declare his policy, under the threats now made," observed Mason Brayman, a Democrat whose daughter was married to the editor of Springfield's Republican newspaper. "Let Mr. Buchanan face that music. While Mr. L preserves himself and holds to the dignity belonging to his position, his friends can do much by conciliatory language to disarm the blusterers."[104]

The painful truth about the national unease could be gleaned from the president-elect's own mailbag. Lincoln's initial post-election correspondence was hardly all congratulatory. Though it is likely that some of the most disobliging letters, certainly the more threatening among them, were kept from Lincoln and discarded by the prudent Nicolay—making an accurate analysis of incoming mail impossible—the secretary did file away some of these angry missives, and they still survive. Reading them in the days that followed his election, the president-elect surely came quickly to understand that, victory notwithstanding, the country remained a house divided. Did he regard these warnings as the work of extremists, false prophets, and crackpots? It remains impossible to know for sure. But the fact that he kept some of their ravings in his files suggests he took them seriously, even if he had yet to find the appropriate way to respond.

Even before the election, correspondents began warning Lincoln to guard his life against assassination.[105] One army veteran had even offered to come to Springfield to serve as his personal bodyguard.[106] Now, a "Maine country girl" who had "received the glad tidings" of Lincoln's victory "with great joy" ominously reminded the president-elect that the sudden deaths of Whig presidents William Henry Harrison and Zachary Taylor back in the 1840s should now sound an alarm for Lincoln. "Remembering my childish tears and disappointments over the doom of my favorite hero's" [sic]—which she and a surprising number of other letter-writers attributed to "subtle poisons"—the writer urged Lincoln to take his own physician to Washington, and there employ kitchen servants whom he was sure he could trust.[107] In the same spirit, a writer signing himself only "A. W. H." insisted that both Harrison and Taylor (though the latter owned slaves of his own) had been "sacrifices to Slavery," and urged Lincoln: "Be continually on your guard. 'A word to the wise is sufficient—' "

In a similar vein, R. C. Carter of Cincinnati begged Lincoln to "be careful that your enemies do not administer Poison to you, they feel desperate & I fear they will resort to desperate measures[.]" And one Joseph I. Irwin wrote from Indiana to warn that Lincoln would be "until the end of your Presidential term in personal danger from *Border Ruffians* at all times," adding: "I have heard some of them say that you should be killed. . . . We must not—we cannot lose you."[108]

Some letter-writers thought otherwise, convinced the country would be better off without Lincoln. "I think, Sir," suggested yet another anonymous correspondent, "that nothing short of your resignation & Mr Hamlin's, accompanied with a warm, patriotic & fraternal appeal to the whole country to cease from strife and henceformost be brothers will suffice to save our beloved country at this time[.]" Otherwise, he would be forever "stigmatized as ambitious, fanatical, and the destroyer of this glorious confederacy."[109]

Were such threats and warnings to be taken seriously? "Brave" as Charles Sumner thought him, Lincoln had every reason to believe so. Just two days after his election, he received an anonymous report from "A Citizen" of Pensacola, Florida, that surely chilled him—and punctuated all the bad news he had been reading in the press: "You were last night hung in effigy in this city."[110]

IN LINCOLN'S OWN city, Republicans began planning a quite different public demonstration. By Thursday, November 8, as the ever-expanding crowd of well-wishers swelled to include Democrats and John Bell–Edward Everett Unionists, town fathers committed themselves to mark Lincoln's victory with an official celebration.[111] But another week would pass before they formally scheduled it, nearly a fortnight before it came off. Local Republicans first wanted every vote counted in the local contests still in dispute.

While Lincoln waited, he attended to household matters and personal chores he had put off for months, picking up two pairs of wool socks at his brother-in-law's dry goods store, and purchasing a bottle of hair balsam at the local druggist's. Not unlike modern fathers who support sons away at college, he sent a fifty-dollar check to Robert at Harvard.[112] Lincoln actually had good cause to worry about money: he had all but abandoned his lucrative law practice after his nomination, at most working with Herndon only to clear away a backlog of outstanding cases, and perhaps review a few pending appeals. He had been substantially without income for six months, and had no prospect of earning money again until his $25,000 annual presidential salary began flowing in March.[113]

In the meantime, visiting reporters had little else to do but speculate endlessly on what, if anything, the president-elect might now say to reassure his new national constituency. The answer should have surprised none of those who had waited in vain through the entire campaign for a new sign from Lincoln that he posed neither a threat to slavery in the South, nor to anti-slavery sentiment in the North: he would say nothing at all. Nonetheless, pressure grew, even from friendly newspapers, for some kind of formal reassurance.[114] Inevitably, apprehension and wild proposals filled the void left by Lincoln's profound silence. One New Yorker actually suggested that Lincoln "repair at once in person to Charleston S C and other southern cities and by direct intercourse with the people through the medium of public addresses make known to them your determination to administer the Government, not only according to the letter, but in the Spirit of the Constitution."[115] Not surprisingly, Lincoln held his ground—literally.

Determined to guard his tongue, he had no intention of going anywhere but Chicago, and there, he hoped, only to meet Hamlin and Speed. Despite what the press called "the greatest eagerness" from all quarters "to ascertain in some manner the new President's intentions, as regards his own course and the character of his appointments," Lincoln remained, in the words of the *New York Tribune*, "the last man to gratify this curiosity until the proper time shall arrive. Not the slightest indication of his future movements is yielded to anybody."[116]

With some exceptions. On November 8, a worried veteran diplomat named Henry S. Sanford arrived unexpectedly in Springfield bearing a letter "of great delicacy & importance" from Lincoln's onetime Whig colleague in Congress years before, ex-Senator Truman Smith of Connecticut. Still conducting an open house for all callers, Lincoln received Sanford at the State Capitol and opened and read the letter in his presence. "Many of our friends speak lightly of the threatened disorders of the South," Smith confided in his earnest note, "but I shall not be surprised should we meet with very serious difficulties from that Quarter. Possibly these may be encountered even before your advent to office." The time had come, suggested the old politician, for Lincoln to offer "the public some exposé of views to counteract falsehood and allay excitement, particularly at the South."[117] Protracted silence, he feared, might also imperil the nation's economy, perhaps encouraging mischief-makers to sabotage the cotton crop. It was up to Lincoln to "allay causeless anxiety" and "induce all good citizens" to "judge the tree by its fruit."

Lincoln remained unconvinced. But Senator Smith at least enjoyed the benefit of a "Private & confidential" explanation, not to be released to the public. As Sanford waited in the Governor's Room, Lincoln painstakingly wrote out his answer. "It is with the most profound appreciation of your motive, and highest respect for your judgment too," Lincoln began his carefully worded reply, "that I feel constrained, for the present, at least, to make no declaration for the public." Convinced that such a "declaration" might undo the perilous balance under which he had been voted into office, he would not modify the policy of eloquent silence that had won him the election in the first place. Still fearful that he might embolden his foes by appearing weak or worried, and doubtless recognizing that the all-important Electoral College would not cast its votes for president for another three months, and must not be impeded or threatened, Lincoln further justified his position to Smith this way:

First, I could say nothing which I have not already said, and
which is in print, and open for the inspection of all. To press a
repetition of this upon those who *have* listened, is useless; to press
it upon those who have *refused* to listen, and still refuse, would be
wanting in self-respect, and would have an appearance of syco-
phancy and timidity, which would excite the contempt of good
men, and encourage bad ones to clamor the more loudly.

To answer new charges would require him to acknowledge that his election was justifiable cause for concern, and this he was not willing to do.
As he wrote Smith: "nothing is to be gained by fawning around the '*respectable scoundrels*' who got it up."[118] But Lincoln did not want the financial markets roiled by his silence, either.

So for good measure, he also wrote out one of those anodyne third-
person statements he occasionally composed for publication or dissemi-
nation anonymously—though many readers invariably recognized his
distinctive style and regarded such statements as authoritative. Now he
penned just such a narrative for Ambassador Sanford to carry home.
The statement was designed to assure skeptics that, however reluctant
to speak out, the president-elect fully recognized the serious challenges
ahead: "I find Mr. Lincoln is not insensible to any uneasiness in the
minds of candid men, nor to any commercial, or financial, depression, or
disturbance, in the country if there be such," announced the extraordinary message; "still he does not, so far as at present advised, deem it
necessary, or proper for him to make, or authorize, any public declaration. He thinks candid men need only to examine his views already
before the public."[119]

Before handing the statement to Sanford, Lincoln evidently showed
it first to the resident correspondent for the pro-Republican *New York
Tribune*, who was undoubtedly eager for news. It was no coincidence
that soon thereafter, the newspaper obligingly parroted, without comment or criticism, that while "not unmindful of the uneasiness which
may exist in many parts of the country, nor of the unfortunate commercial troubles that may have been threatened," the president-elect still

did not "discover any cause for . . . offering any public expression of his views."[120]

Lincoln held his ground on the "reassurance" issue even when Nathaniel P. Paschall, the editor of an anti-Republican newspaper ironically still called—from Jefferson's day—the *Missouri Republican*, disputed Lincoln's familiar argument that his speeches were long in print and required no further elaboration. The Democratic editor warned that the publication of mere "extracts from your speeches . . . sent forth from newspapers known to be the bitterest enemies of the South," would "fail to have any effect whatever in the States now on the point of seceding from the Union." Paschall proposed an alternative. He challenged Lincoln simply to "collate" and distribute his most recent speeches himself. A new authorized edition, Paschall suggested, would convince Southerners that as president, Lincoln would enforce the Fugitive Slave Laws that compelled the return of escapees, and oppose Personal Liberty bills and other local legislation aimed at whittling away these slave-owners' rights.[121] This seemed in some respects a reasonable compromise. Though "wary of appeasement," even William H. Seward's political guru, Thurlow Weed, similarly believed Lincoln should now at least reissue excerpts from the Lincoln-Douglas debates.[122]

But even as "the reign of the winter king" commenced earlier than usual in Springfield, leaving its streets depressingly "dressed in very sloppish outer garments,"[123] and as grain and cotton shipments simultaneously began shrinking in the West and South, Lincoln steadfastly—some said stubbornly—refused to show his hand and issue "some public declaration with a view to favorably affect the business of the country."[124] But Lincoln's policy of selective silence only went so far. He would soon begin dropping enough scattered hints to assuage Southern slave-owners without outraging Northern slavery foes, enough at a minimum to head off a new financial panic that could further weaken an economy still struggling to emerge from a four-year-long depression.

For the time, Lincoln's response to Paschall would be his final word. "I could say nothing which I have not already said, and which is in print and accessible to the public," Lincoln insisted to the Democratic editor he probably categorized as one of those "respectable scoundrels" about whom he had warned Senator Smith. This was especially true with regard to "papers like yours," he added in a rare display of irritation that must have come as an enormous relief to the writer, "which heretofore have persistently garbled, and misrepresented what I have said." All Paschall need do now, Lincoln insisted, was accurately publish the "copious abstracts from my many public speeches, which would at once reach the whole public if your class of papers would also publish them.

"I am not at liberty to shift my ground—that is out of the question," Lincoln concluded. "If I thought a *repetition* of it would do any good I would make it. But my judgment is it would do positive harm. The secessionists, *per se* believing they had alarmed me, would clamor all the louder."[125] An enthusiastic reader of English poetry, Lincoln forgot or ignored Dryden's warning from "Astraea Redux": "An horrid stillness first invades the ear,/ And in that silence we the tempest fear."

Lincoln refused to be publicly alarmed, refused to envision a tempest. But if he truly believed that his previously issued speeches might stave off political and financial crises, he soon learned otherwise. On November 13, New York stocks plunged, and George Templeton Strong confided in his diary: "I think they will fall much lower before the game is played out." Secession talk was having its effect on the investment community. "Southern securities are waste paper in Wall Street," Strong lamented. "Not a dollar can be raised on them. Who wants to buy paper that must be collected by suit in the courts of South Carolina and Georgia?"[126]

The markets fluctuated alarmingly for the rest of the month, falling one day, recovering the next, then plummeting another, leaving speculators alternating between relief and hysteria. By the end of November, with many nervous New Yorkers clamoring for reassurances, Strong confided he was as fearful about Northern capitulation as he was about Southern belligerence. "Our national mottoes must be changed to '*e pluribus duo*' (at least) and 'United we stand, divided we stand easier.'" He had heard nothing from Springfield to ease his fears that "a great civil war" was "inevitable," and that democracy might "disappear forever."[127] But despite the jitters on Wall Street, Lincoln would have little to say on economic policy during the interregnum, save for his politically inspired determination to satisfy both free trade and high tariff men with cabinet representation. His economic priority, as historian Gabor Boritt has described it, was "stopping slavery extension in the name of the American Dream."[128] For a time, however, the reiteration of this commitment did little to stabilize the volatile markets.

The news from Washington was marginally more heartening. Just before Election Day, Lincoln was able to take solace from a long memorandum from the capital entitled "Views suggested by imminent danger." Now it seemed to hold crucial meaning. The memo was the careful work of "Old Fuss and Feathers," the white-haired, orotund, seventy-four-year-old general-in-chief of the army, Winfield Scott. Virginia born, a veteran of the War of 1812 and a hero of the Mexican War, Scott had been in service to the American armed forces since before Lincoln was born.[129] Eight years ago, he had himself been a candidate for president on the Whig ticket—unsuccessfully. Now, he was writing to President Buchanan—with copies earmarked for Lincoln and others—to express his view that to "break this glorious Union by whatever line or lines that political madness may contrive" would mean no hope of reunification without "the laceration and despotism of the sword." Though he admitted that he had privately hoped for John Bell's success on Election Day, General Scott refused to believe "any unconstitutional violence, or breach of law," would greet a Lincoln victory.

But danger did exist, Scott conceded, "of an early act of rashness, preliminary to secession," specifically the seizure of a number of federal forts on the Mississippi River and on the Eastern coast—including the vulnerable installations at Charleston harbor.[130] To head off the threat, Scott recommended that "all those works should be immediately so garrisoned as to make any attempt to take any one of them by surprise or coup de main ridiculous." President Buchanan, at least, possessed the power to act that Lincoln still lacked. Adding the kind of unctuous advice to which Lincoln would soon become accustomed from Scott, the venerable military giant offered his hope that a "federal executive" committed to both "firmness and moderation" could avert a secession crisis "without conflict of arms, one execution or one arrest for treason."

In Washington, Buchanan dismissed his general's warning as "calculated to do much injury in misleading the South." The president went so far as to complain, "it would be difficult to estimate whether they did most harm in encouraging or in provoking secession." It would remain his chief mission, he reassured himself, to "refrain from any act which might provoke or encourage the cotton States into secession."[131]

The president-elect's reaction was quite different. Desperate for good news, a grateful Lincoln, buoyed by the communiqué, profusely thanked Scott three days after the election, adapting the general's officious third-person style, "for this renewed manifestation of his patriotic purposes as a citizen, connected, as it is, with his high official position, and most distinguished character, as a military captain."[132] Lincoln's respectful tone paid enormous dividends, undoubtedly pleasing the old soldier, already disposed to loyalty, and further cementing Scott's fealty to both the old Union and the new president. For his part, Lincoln undoubtedly took solace from Scott's confidence—not only in the chief-executive-in-waiting, but also in the moderation and loyalty the general expected from his fellow Southerners, including high-ranking Southern-born military officers like himself. As it turned out, that confidence would prove misplaced. But for a time, it steeled Lincoln to silent resistance.

It came as no surprise that another visitor to Springfield found Lincoln on November 14 "reading up anew" on the history of Andrew Jackson's response to the 1832 Nullification Crisis. While he made no effort to conceal "the uneasiness which the contemplated treason gives him," Lincoln assured his guest that, like Jackson, he would not "yield an inch."[133]

Chapter Three

We Won't Jump That Ditch

ABRAHAM LINCOLN'S HOMETOWN Republicans scheduled their victory celebration for November 20. In "honor of the triumphant election of our honored fellow citizen, Abraham Lincoln, to the highest office in the world," organizers blanketed the town with handbills breathlessly declaring that the "Grand Meeting of Rejoicing" would feature "A Grand Torch Light Procession! General Illumination! Pyrotechnic Display, Bonfires," and speeches.[1]

But two weeks had elapsed since Election Day, and Lincoln's private secretary feared that the air had already gone out of the balloon. "People look and act as if they were almost too tired to feel at all interested in getting up a grand hurrah over the victory," he admitted nine days before the jubilee, "and I believe they would not do it at all were it not that it is a formality which in this case cannot well be omitted."[2]

Still, when he learned that the " 'Jollification' is at last set for next Tuesday night," the overworked Nicolay summoned the enthusiasm to invite his fiancée to attend. Anticipating a crush of out-of-towners, he urged her to decide quickly so he could secure her a room before Springfield's hotels were fully booked.[3] The "hunters for office" had not yet assembled there "in great force,"[4] the New York Tribune reported, but Lincoln and his friends were girding for the expected onslaught of celebrants and job-seekers alike. Hunting season began in earnest within days.

To accommodate the growing crush of visitors, the president-elect established a surprisingly generous and highly visible routine. Arriving at the Governor's Room each morning at eight, he spent some two hours working alone with Nicolay on correspondence. Then, he invited the public to pour in twice daily for informal receptions—later, in the White House, Lincoln would call these open office hours his "public-opinion baths"[5]—from 10 A.M. to noon, and again from 3:30 to 5:30 P.M. The State Journal carried a notice alerting the public that "To-day, and till further notice, Mr. Lincoln will see visitors at the Executive Chamber in the State House" at these specified hours only.[6] Between these ordeals, Lincoln would take a 1 P.M. dinner break and try to get some desperately needed rest. By mid-November, hewing to this taxing schedule, he was greeting up to 160 visitors per day. Each morning they assembled hungrily outside the Governor's Room, lining up from the upstairs hallway down the State House staircase, sometimes spilling out the front door of the building. As they waited their turn for an interview, "the clear voice and often ringing laughter of the President" sounded in the corridor to "guide them to the right door."[7]

Once inside—fortunately for history—they were closely observed by a Bavarian-born journalist named Henry Villard (he had shortened it from the aristocratic-sounding original, Ferdinand Heinrich Gustav Hilgard Villard). The young reporter came to town on assignment from the Democratic-leaning New York Herald. Over the next three months, Villard would colorfully report Lincoln's activities, filing well-observed firsthand accounts of the president-elect's daily routine.

One can only speculate that the correspondent's access to the Governor's Room was eased by Nicolay, who hailed from the Rhine valley hamlet of Essingen, located just a few miles west of Villard's birthplace of Speyer. Once Lincoln introduced them, the two young German-Americans, both in their mid-twenties, must have bonded instantly.[8] Whatever the secret to his limitless opportunities to observe Lincoln,

Villard went on to produce a vivid portrait of an increasingly weary president-elect, trying his best to maintain his good humor and boundless patience amid throngs of strangers in a crowded suite "altogether inadequate for the accommodation" of his visitors—most of whom wanted something.

Villard arrived in Springfield very much doubting the newly elected chief executive. A disappointed Seward supporter, he could not understand why this "uncouth, common Illinois politician" had defeated "the foremost figure . . . in the country."[9] Recognizing at once that the journalist was far more sympathetic to the anti-slavery cause than to his racist publishers, Lincoln wisely treated him as a potential friend, not an adversary, entertaining him with stories and exposing him to public receptions at which he demonstrated his uncanny ability to impress and appease visitors with bluff frontier directness. The president-elect seldom confided policy matters to Villard, but the reporter came to appreciate—and report sympathetically on—the exhausting burdens that sycophants and office-seekers alike placed on his valuable time. The *Herald* in turn printed Villard's dispatches undistorted, and they ultimately provided the only sustained firsthand portrait produced at the time of this uniquely tested leader-in-training.

Complaining, for example, that "the Jacksonian 'doctrine' that to the 'victors belong the spoils' " remained "universally the creed of all politicians," Villard nonetheless marveled at Lincoln's willingness to "submit to this tribulation."[10] The army of "importunate office seekers . . . greatly annoyed" him, his hometown newspaper agreed.[11] Those who failed to squeeze into the Governor's Room to stake their often dubious claims wrote presumptuous letters, or made overtures to Lincoln's friends. One particularly audacious—and unqualified—job-seeker begged state Secretary of State Ozias Hatch to "consider me in" among the applicants to "Old Abe." Describing his so-called credentials, the office-seeker made it clear he no longer expected to work very hard: "Poverty is no disgrace, but as the fellow said, I find it d——d inconvenient, and I should like to get something that would keep my nose and the grindstone apart for a while."[12] Lincoln's old law associate Ward Hill Lamon reported Springfield's hotels "filled with gentlemen who came with light baggage and heavy schemes."[13]

Their greed notwithstanding, most such visitors earned a hearty welcome. "On opening the door," Villard reported of the arrival of one delegation, "the tall, lean form of 'Old Abe' directly confronts the leader of the party. Seizing the latter's hand with a hearty shake, Lincoln leads him in, and bids the rest to follow suit with an encouraging, 'Get in, all of you.' The whole party being in, he will ask for their names, and then immediately start a running conversation."[14]

To another eyewitness, these "daily receptions" became more than "merely occasions for the interchange of social and personal courtesies, but for the study of the general situation, and of those intricate and delicate questions which would inevitably confront his administration, at its very opening. That room was a school to him, and to the uttermost did he improve its advantages."[15]

As a host, Lincoln was "never at a loss as to the subjects that please the different classes of visitors and there is a certain quaintness and originality about all he has to say, so that one cannot help feeling interested. His 'talk' is not brilliant," Villard observed. "His phrases are not ceremoniously set, but pervaded with a humorousness and, at times, with a grotesque joviality, that will always please. I think it would be hard to find one who tells better jokes, enjoys them better and laughs oftener than Abraham Lincoln."[16]

The reporter quickly came to understand how much these jokes meant—both to the president-elect and to the invading army of favorseekers, so few of whose requests he could accommodate. "His neverfailing stories helped many times to heal wounded feelings and mitigate disappointments," testified Villard. But he added that "None of his hearers enjoyed the wit—and wit was an unfailing ingredient—of his stories half as much as he did himself." To the journalist, it was "a joy indeed to see the effect upon him. A high-pitched laughter lighted up his otherwise melancholy countenance with thorough merriment. His body shook all over with gleeful emotion, and when he felt particularly good over his performance, he followed his habit of drawing his knees, with his arms around them, up to his very face."[17] The most deeply disappointed job-seeker left the Governor's Room convinced he had enjoyed a precious glimpse into Lincoln's soul.

Not every observer approved. In a profile derisively entitled "The Old Storyteller," the *New York Daily News* condemned the president-elect's "mania for telling stories," adding: "We have no doubt if Mrs. Lincoln could be put in evidence, she would relate stories that he tells in his night cap. It is even possible the inveterate old anecdote monger babbles of stories in his peaceful slumber." The paper wondered: "Is the precious time of Cabinet Councils to be wasted with stories? Shall we have stories in his annual messages? Will he go down to South Carolina and assuage her wrath with incidents of his first flat boat experience?"[18]

Closer to home, journalists better understood Lincoln's style. "He converses fluently on all subjects," the local Republican newspaper marveled, and "illustrates everything by a merry anecdote, of which article he has a boundless supply." Political questions he adroitly deflected by protesting: "Ah! You have not read my speeches. Let me make you a present of my speeches." Lincoln also learned new strategies to repel boors. When one "hard-looking customer" plopped down into a comfortable chair he had temporarily vacated, Lincoln extended his massive paw from the other side of the room, forcing the interloper to abandon the seat in exchange for a handshake. Once the president-elect pumped his visitor's hand, he deftly reclaimed his chair.[19]

As a neighboring newspaper reported: "Mr. Lincoln receives his visitors with his accustomed cordiality, illustrates his conversation with apt anecdotes, and laughs very heartily when others laugh."[20] A bit sheepish about the resulting commotion, Lincoln told his office neighbor Newton Bateman, "If you can stand the noise, I can."[21] But even Lincoln's boundless supply of humor, "patience and shrewdness" sometimes proved insufficient to bear up to the sheer magnitude of the public crush. His commitment to openness, however admirable, made it increasingly difficult for him to focus on major issues like cabinet-building and the secession threat. Inevitably, the president-elect found less time for much needed reflection as he devoted more time to his visitors. Lincoln "gradually showed the wear and tear of these continuous visitations, and finally looked so careworn as to excite one's compassion."[22]

Villard professed horror at the "motley" crowd that pushed its way into Lincoln's headquarters day after day. As he put it, "Muddy boots and hickory shirts are just as frequent as broadcloth, fine linen, etc. The ladies, however, are usually dressed up in their very best, although they cannot hope to make an impression on old married Lincoln." Entertaining higher hopes was the "stampede" of office-seekers, many lusting after post office jobs and other obscure federal appointments.[23]

So great was the quest for patronage that Lincoln came to hope that Southerners would never leave the Union and abandon the plum government jobs they might retain if they remained loyal. As he joked rather cynically to the Ohio editor and politician Donn Piatt over a chicken dinner at the Lincoln home: "Were it believed that vacant places could be had at the North Pole, the road there would be lined with dead Virginians." Lincoln appeared unaware of—or yet unwilling to acknowledge—the growing Southern anxiety that he might replace home-state Democrats with Northern Republicans in local federal jobs like the post offices. Piatt thought that Lincoln for too long judged the secession threat as a "political game of bluff, gotten up by politicians, and meant solely to frighten the North."[24]

Not every job-questing politician behaved respectfully. "The President-elect had a hard time of it with the office-seekers," Villard acknowledged.[25] "Churlish fellows" burst in without removing their hats, cigars still lighted, and "their pantaloons tucked into their boots," he reported. "Dropping into chairs they sit puffing away and trying to gorgonize the President with their silent stares, until their boorish curiosity is fully satisfied." One eighty-three-year-old professing a close friendship with the president-elect came every day, spinning spurious Lincoln anecdotes so relentlessly that he excited "the scorn rather than the laughter of the hearers," and boring "Old Abe" in the bargain.[26] On yet another occasion, Villard saw "half a dozen rustics rush in, break their way through other visitors up to the object of their search and after calling out their names and touching the Presidential fingers, back out again."[27]

Not that Lincoln was a stickler for ceremony. Bringing one visitor home for a meal, where he looked to his guest like "a huge skeleton in clothes," he talked politics there without interruption while his two little boys clambered over his long legs, "patted his cheeks, pulled his nose, and poked their fingers in his eyes, without causing reprimand or even notice."[28] Another caller to his home declared, "Mr. L. has not altered one bit he amused us nearly all the evening telling funny stories and cracking jokes." Added the appreciative lady: "I could hardly realize that I was sitting in the august presence of a *real live President*."[29]

One day at the office, an especially tall visitor from Missouri exclaimed on first glimpsing the giant form of Lincoln, "I reckon one is about as big as the other." To which Lincoln delightedly shot back: "Let us measure." He then backed his guest against a wall, admonished him to stand flat on his heels and "be honest," and proceeded to calculate his height with a stick while other visitors doubtless stared in disbelief. Though amused, Villard neglected to report the result of the contest.[30] "Fifth Avenue snobs," he conceded, "if unaware who he was, would be horrified at walking across the street with him. And yet, there is something about the man that makes one at once forget these exterior shortcomings and feel attracted toward him."[31]

BUT LINCOLN APPARENTLY decided he was not attractive enough. And for once in his life, he did something about it. For the first time, he began cultivating a beard. The story goes that, one day, as his barber William Florville prepared to give him his customary shave, Lincoln stopped him. "Billy," he reportedly said, "let's give them a chance to grow!"[32]

The result transformed Lincoln. The strong-jawed rail-splitter disappeared and, at least on the surface, a wise-looking statesman emerged to replace him. "Old Abe . . . is commencing to raise a beautiful pair of whiskers, and looks younger than usual," noted an Illinois weekly, adding: "Still there is no disguising the fact that he is homely."[33] Taking note of "Old Abe's new whiskers," a Democratic journal teased: "The country does not want wisdom or courage in its Executive, but beauty; and Lincoln knows it, and he is up to the crisis! The oil that a less wise man would have thrown upon the troubled waters, he reserves for his nascent moustaches. What better evidence of fitness for empire, than to grow an imperial? Who knows but that the pillars of the Confederation may be held together by a Sampson that refuses to be shorn?"[34]

Henry Villard took sarcastic note of the sudden "adornment of whiskers" on November 19. "His old friends, who have been used to a great indifference as to the 'outer man,' on his part," the journalist punned, "say that 'Abe is putting on airs.' "[35]

Artist G.P.A. Healy might have been the first to hear directly from Lincoln that he had begun feeling uncomfortable in his own skin once he became president-elect. Commissioned to paint the president-elect's portrait for a proposed "National Gallery" of eminent Americans in Chicago,[36] Healy arrived in Springfield to present his credentials shortly after the election. He found Lincoln at the State House, studying a disobliging letter, which he proceeded to read aloud. It had come from a woman who objected to his appearance. "She complains of my ugliness," Lincoln helplessly reflected to Healy. "It is allowed to be ugly in this world, but not as ugly as I am. She wishes me to put on false whiskers, to hide my horrible lantern jaws." Perhaps only half in jest, he proposed a solution. "Will you paint me with false whiskers?" he asked the artist. "No? I thought not."[37] Instead, Healy went on to produce what turned out to be not only the first life portrait of Lincoln as president-elect, but also the last to show him before he began sporting his iconic beard.[38]

Lincoln left no other clues about why he decided to grow whiskers a few months shy of his fifty-second birthday, after rejecting or ignoring several earlier suggestions that he do so, and despite the recent publication of dozens of perfectly adequate, indeed flattering, portraits showing him clean-shaven. These would now require costly and time-consuming revision (though their sale undoubtedly profited the image-makers).

Just a month earlier, as the presidential campaign peaked, a group of anonymous correspondents signing themselves "True Republicans" had written the candidate to express their "candid determination" that Lincoln's appearance would be much improved "provided you would cultivate whiskers, and wear standing collars." It was their "earnest desire," they concluded, "that 'our candidate' should be the best looking as well as the best of the rival candidates." Then they warned in a postscript: "We really fear votes will be lost to 'the cause' unless our 'gentle hints' are attended to."[39] Lincoln neither replied nor obliged.

The following week, an eleven-year-old girl from upstate New York wrote a far more endearing version of the same entreaty. Grace Bedell of the tiny village of Westfield promised him: "I have got 4 brother's and part of them will vote for you any way and if you will let your whiskers grow I will try to get the rest of them to vote for you[.] you would look a great deal better for your face is so thin. All the ladies like whiskers and they would tease their husband's to vote for you and then you would be President."[40]

Testifying to the potent power of the popular images Lincoln would soon render obsolete, both of these letters had been inspired by unflattering portraits then in circulation. Perhaps the idea of forcing their alteration thus appealed to Lincoln. The "True Republicans" had recoiled at the daguerreotype likenesses that they wore "as tokens of our devotedness to you"; Grace Bedell was emboldened to express what she later called her "childish thoughts"[41] after studying a crude-looking campaign poster her father brought home from the county fair. Lincoln undoubtedly knew he had it within his power, by growing whiskers, to provide a more avuncular model for future presidential portraiture.

In his reply to little Grace, however, Lincoln had originally protested: "As to the whiskers, having never worn any, do you not think people would call it a silly piece of affect[at]ion if I were to begin it now?"[42] But as John Nicolay remembered, "Mr. Lincoln was, no doubt, touched by the unaffected sincere kindliness of this childish prattle."[43] By mid-November, his protests notwithstanding, whiskers began sprouting from his face. A few weeks later, his assistant private secretary, John Hay, approvingly punned:

Election news Abe's hirsute fancy warrant—
Apparent hair becomes heir apparent.[44]

Another itinerant artist, Philadelphian Jesse Atwood, had the bad luck to paint the president-elect on the cusp of this image transfiguration. Convinced that Lincoln was about to win the White House, he had arrived in Springfield at the end of October to make him the tenth presidential subject of his long career. Lincoln agreed to grant him sittings and within a week, Atwood produced a likeness that the local newspaper pronounced "perfect in feature and delineation." The canvas went on display to considerable acclaim in the Capitol's Senate Chamber, located just across the upstairs hallway from Lincoln's official headquarters.[45]

Two weeks later, with Lincoln safely elected, and after fulfilling lucrative additional commissions to paint portraits of other Springfielders, the artist left town a happy man. "If there is such a thing as a *hit* in the profession of portrait painting," the *Illinois State Journal* raved, "Mr. Atwood certainly has made it."[46] But the artist did not remain happy for long. Apparently chagrined when he learned that his subject had dramatically changed his appearance only days after sitting for him, he slapped a daub of whiskers onto his painting in an effort to bring it up to date. The altered result was no longer an authentic portrait from life, and worse, resembled neither the bearded nor the beardless Lincoln.[47] Oddly, it enjoyed little known subsequent success on exhibition, whereas Healy's portrait, which the artist declined to revise, went on view in Chicago.

Lincoln had only begun to vex the portrait-making trade. His tonsorial decision would soon roil the entire picture-publishing industry, forcing printmakers like Currier & Ives of New York, and Samuel Sartain of Philadelphia to superimpose haphazardly imagined beards onto their lithographic stones and steel engravers' plates in an effort to update their successful campaign images. These portraits they had surely hoped would enjoy sustained appeal with only a simple change in their captions to reflect Lincoln's new status as president-elect.[48] For some image-makers, the news came too late. The popular pictorial journal *Frank*

Leslie's Illustrated Newspaper published a "new" portrait of "President Elect Abraham Lincoln" on November 21.[49] But the clean-shaven image, based on a five-month-old photograph, was out of date before it was issued; by the time it went on sale, Lincoln had begun appearing in public bewhiskered. For months thereafter, Lincoln kept image-makers in distant cities guessing about his changing appearance. Did his new beard look Satanic or luxuriant? Would he trim it or allow it to flourish? Not until he sat for definitive new photographs and began his public journey east for the inauguration would the question finally be settled. One Southern critic was heard to observe, with chilling prescience, that Lincoln was "trying to disguise himself so as to get unrecognized through Maryland to Washington."[50]

More likely, for Lincoln, the decision to emphasize image over words offered a politically ingenious diversionary tactic. Coming after two weeks of irritating speculation about whether he should speak out publicly to assuage the South, the news that he was growing a beard changed the national conversation, at least temporarily.

Clearly, the decision impressed yet another young girl—the eighteen-year-old Stephen Douglas supporter from Springfield, Anna Ridgely. When she first glimpsed the newly bearded president-elect at his home, she admitted: "Mr L really looked handsome to me[. H]is whiskers are a great improvement and he had such a pleasant smile I could not but admire him."[51]

Henry Villard at first thought otherwise. "Always cadaverous," the reporter observed on November 19, "his aspect is now almost ghostly. His position is wearing him, terribly. Letters threatening his life are daily received from the South. . . . But these trouble him little compared with the apprehended difficulty of conciliating the South without destroying the integrity of his own party."

To Villard, the crisis imperiling the president-elect posed one of the greatest threats any newly elected chief executive was ever called upon to weather. And in these first weeks after his victory, the journalist did not believe Lincoln was up to it, writing: "I doubt Mr. Lincoln's capacity for the task of bringing light and peace out of the chaos that will surround him." Conceding that Lincoln was "a man of good heart and good intention," Villard concluded that "he is not firm," adding: "The times demand a Jackson."[52]

As of mid-November 1860, most of the country would have agreed. However much gravitas he had added to his public image by growing a beard, there were few who would yet disagree with Villard's conclusion that Abraham Lincoln was no Andrew Jackson.

Only Nicolay and a few other intimates believed otherwise. His secretary heard Lincoln authoritatively remind a caller on November 15 that "this government possesses both the authority and the power to maintain its own integrity." Here was Jacksonian firmness to spare. "That, however, is not the ugly point of this matter," Lincoln added grimly. "The ugly point is the necessity of keeping the government by force, as ours ought to be a government of fraternity."[53]

"JOLLIFICATION" DAY REQUIRED the president-elect to perform his most arduous work since winning the election. The especially large, impatient crowd poised to greet his morning arrival at the State House began massing at dawn, and rather than wait the two hours until his public hours officially began, surrounded him the minute he came into view, then "clung to his coat tail,"[54] and pursued him inside en masse, just as his admirers had done at the polls on Election Day.

Once inside the Governor's Room, his visitors trailing behind, Lincoln at first tried positioning himself at the doorway to facilitate quick handshakes and prompt goodbyes. But intruders pushed past him and made themselves comfortable on the chairs and sofas inside, some remaining immovably for hours. The most loquacious well-wishers and office-seekers cornered Lincoln against the far wall, haranguing him without mercy. Out-of-towners had packed local hotels, convinced that the three-dollar weekly investment for room and board would be more than repaid by a four-year appointment to a cushy federal job.[55] For the next ten hours, Lincoln was "tortured to death" by "the importunities of a steady tide of callers."[56]

Not until 6:30 in the evening was he able to free himself from this "tight jam"[57] and make his way back home. But there he found no rest either. Even at his private residence, Lincoln "was once more crowded upon in his parlor, and had to undergo another agony of presentations." Well-dressed and "ill-mannered" callers alike filled the downstairs parlors to overflowing all evening long, much to the delight of Lincoln's young sons Willie and Tad, who responded with "juvenile yells" through the open windows whenever the surging crowd in the street let out with a cheer. Mrs. Lincoln had less reason to applaud, watching helplessly as strangers trampled her carpets, and overhearing strangers rudely point her way and ask, "Is that the old woman?"[58]

Eventually, a regiment of noisy, uniformed Wide-Awakes under the direction of a "commandant" named Adam Johnston, a stonecutter who had helped build the State Capitol,[59] massed outside the house under the glare of blazing torchlights and called on Lincoln for a speech. Officially, tonight's victory rally was to feature an address by soon-to-be reelected Senator Lyman Trumbull (Senators were officially chosen by state legislatures, but Republicans had done well enough on November 6 to guarantee Trumbull's success)—presidents-elect were deemed above such vulgar demonstrations.

But his admirers were determined to lavish their enthusiasm on Lincoln, and in turn elicit some kind of response. Sensing danger days earlier, the *Chicago Tribune*'s editor, Joseph Medill, had rushed word to Springfield to caution, "We want no speech from Lincoln on the 20th on political questions." The party platform and previously published speeches should continue to suffice. As Medill warned: "There are a class of d——d fools or knaves who want him to make a 'union saving speech'—in other words to Set *down* to conciliate the Disunionists and fire-eaters. He must keep his feet out of all such wolf traps."[60] Two weeks after his election, it seemed that Lincoln's most ardent supporters were becoming, with little justification, as dubious about his political mettle as his detractors.

Medill need not have worried much. When Lincoln could ignore the tumultuous demonstrations no longer, he stepped outside and from his front porch, begged: "Please excuse me, on this occasion, from making a speech." Then he proceeded to give a little oration after all—but with exquisite care. "I thank you for the kindness and compliment of this call. I thank you, in common with all others, who have thought fit, by their votes, to indorse the Republican cause. I rejoice with you in the success which has, so far, attended that cause."[61]

At last, he had a message of sorts for Southerners, too—brief as it was, and obliquely as he expressed it: "Yet in all our rejoicing, let us neither express, nor cherish, any harsh feeling towards any citizen who, by his vote, has differed with us." The suggestion elicited loud cheers. To "immense applause,"[62] he added: "Let us at all times remember that all American citizens are brothers of a common country, and should dwell together in the bonds of fraternal feeling." And then, with another plea to be excused from "further speaking at this time," he retreated inside.

Once again, Lincoln had broken his selective silence with a somewhat conciliatory message that he must have known would be widely reprinted—which it was. Surely this was no slip. Lincoln had held his tongue too tightly for too long to speak out casually. There was calculation here—a small but purposeful departure by a master politician risking a modest break from self-imposed silence and historic precedent at an extraordinarily delicate moment.

The press sensed its importance immediately. Noting that the "brief expression of his thanks" to "local friends" constituted "the first speech he has uttered since he accepted his nomination," the *New York Evening Post* praised its "kindly and conciliatory spirit," adding: "He speaks as one who has been chosen to the Chief Magistracy, not of a party or a section, but of a great and united country."[63] Would more skeptical journals find similar reassurance in so brief and informal a chat? In the end, no. Lincoln was fortunate that the opposition papers did not make embarrassing comparisons between the paramilitary Wide-Awake audience that had heard it, and the home guard regiments parading with similar enthusiasm down south. The only major difference was that the Wide-Awakes bore torches while Southern militiamen toted rifles.

The "Great Republican Jubilee" later that night lured an "immense turnout of the people," the *New York Times* gushed. The grand illumination proved "brilliant beyond anything ever seen in the West." Public buildings, storefronts, and private homes alike defied the darkness, "ablaze with fantastic devices." Even the Democratic boarders at the Franklin House got into the spirit, stringing Chinese lanterns from hotel windows. The most blinding light of all shone from four locomotive headlights strung from the State House cupola, beaming so brightly in the crisp prairie night they could be seen for miles.[64] What had been planned as a mere "country jubilee" had "assumed gigantic proportions."[65]

To some observers, however, the illumination proved something of a fizzle, just as Nicolay had feared. Henry Villard estimated that only two thousand out-of-towners journeyed to Springfield for the event, with just a quarter of them actually participating in the anticlimactic festivities. "The American people are known not to be able to foster a protracted excitement on one particular subject," Villard philosophized. "Having been treated *ad nauseam* to Wide Awake processions, meetings, speeches, fireworks, etc., during the campaign, they are now sick of all such empty demonstrations."[66] Young Anna Ridgely agreed. Though she conceded that "some of the fireworks were beautiful," she complained that most of them "were rockets and Roman candles that we have seen all summer long, while the torch light procession was the smallest I ever saw."[67] Ada Bailhache, wife of the town's pro-Lincoln newspaper editor, loyally hung "all our fine chinese lanterns and transparencies that we have been making," but found the weather "extremely unpropitious." The cold, hard wind made her regret the delay in scheduling the celebration. "It is a pity we did not have it last week, for we had such quiet beautiful nights."[68]

However dazzling or disappointing the parades and fireworks, all ears turned with universal interest to the official proceedings that night at a temporary building erected for the ceremonies. There, observers sensed, Senator Trumbull's keynote would be more expansive than the president-elect's porch-front remarks, and surely expressed "under Mr. Lincoln's direct supervision."[69] What the crowd did not yet know is that

Lincoln himself had drafted some of the words Trumbull began pronouncing that evening.

Lincoln had decided that, speaking through a surrogate, he could safely reassure the South that under his administration, as his handwritten draft put it, "all of the States will be left in as complete control of their own affairs respectively, and at as perfect liberty to choose, and employ, their own means of protecting property, and preserving peace and order within their respective limits, as they have ever been under any administration." Writing of himself in the third person—if General Scott could do so, why not the president-elect?—he added: "Those who have voted for Mr. Lincoln, have expected, and still expect this; and they would not have voted for him had they expected otherwise."

"Disunionists *per se*," Lincoln's draft conceded, "are now in hot haste to get out of the Union, precisely because they perceive they can not, much longer, maintain apprehension among the Southern people that their homes, and firesides, and lives, are to be endangered by the action of the Federal Government. With such '*Now, or never*' is the maxim."[70]

Rather than recite the words verbatim, Trumbull decided to paraphrase Lincoln's draft[71]—but between the lines, the message sounded identical: the incoming administration posed no threat to Southern slavery, and in any case separation agitation was both unjustified and unlawful. Trumbull said it perhaps better than Lincoln when he added: "Secession is an impracticability—or rather, an impossibility. The Constitution provides no way by which a State may withdraw from the Union—no way for the dissolution of the Government it creates."[72] Whichever man crafted that particular thought, it certainly reflected Lincoln's firm view, which he had doubtless shared with the senator a number of times since Election Day. "It is believed by all," the *New York Herald* reported, that Trumbull's speech "will go a great ways in clearing the Southern sky of the clouds of disunion."[73]

If such was the goal, Trumbull was probably wise to delete altogether the rather provocative and infelicitous afterthought Lincoln suggested at the conclusion of his draft. "I am rather glad of the military preparation in the South," Lincoln astonishingly asked Trumbull to declare. "It will enable the people the more easily to suppress any uprisings there, which their misrepresentations of [my] purposes may have encouraged."[74] Lincoln still wanted to believe that Southern moderates could be relied upon to cap the geyser of anti-Unionism. This particularly tortured argument even an ally like Trumbull could not bring himself to repeat. The two Republican leaders shared the belief that it was prudent to advance the message of national harmony and damp down extreme reaction to the election. But Lincoln believed longer—and more strongly—than most of his fellow Republicans that secession agitation was limited to a radical fringe, and that good sense and patriotism might ultimately win back the hearts and minds of wavering Southerners.

In the end, Trumbull's widely reported speech failed to appease anyone. Secessionists remained unconvinced of Lincoln's commitment to noninterference, while anti-slavery men within Lincoln's own victorious party assailed him for sanctioning Trumbull's conservative message. The balancing act was proving nearly impossible to maintain.

AT ELEVEN O'CLOCK the following morning, Wednesday, November 21, Lincoln and a small traveling party of five—including Mary, Senator Trumbull and his wife, Julia, Donn Piatt with his writer-wife, Louise,[75] and at least one reporter ("one of the most unscrupulous & notorious of all the gang," warned a loyalist,[76]—boarded a train in Springfield with scant fanfare, and headed north for the trip to Chicago.

This would be Lincoln's first official foray outside Springfield since his nomination to the presidency six months before. It was more than a vacation, of course. Lincoln planned to meet Vice President–elect Hannibal Hamlin for the first time, and confer with him about cabinet choices and the secession threat. But there was no question there was an element of escape to the journey, too—and not just because treasured old friends Joshua and Fanny Speed had promised to join them there. The Lincolns desperately needed a change of scenery.

After unostentatiously securing their own tickets, the group boarded "a crowded and inconvenient car like other democratic sovereigns," journalist Villard marveled, "neither the company nor conductor showing him any courtesy whatever." Indeed, the local sheriff, a disappointed Douglas supporter, went so far as to haul two shackled convicts on board the same railroad car, one of them a murderer, and rudely seated them between the Lincolns and Trumbulls.[77]

Actually, the arrangement may have suited Mary Lincoln perfectly. Once a close personal friend of Julia Jayne Trumbull's, she had never forgiven either the senator or his wife for prevailing at the 1855 legislative convention that awarded Trumbull a U.S. Senate seat she believed was Lincoln's by right. The president-elect, characteristically, had long ago made his peace with that disappointment. Five years later, however, even after her husband had soared past Trumbull to win the presidency, relations between Mary and Julia remained frigid, and Lincoln's wife was never shy when it came to turning up her nose publicly at perceived enemies. Just a year earlier, Mary had icily dismissed Julia as "looking as stately & *ungainly* as ever," adding for good measure: "'Tis unfortunate, to be so unpopular." Their husbands may have regarded the imposition of a convicted murderer between the two ladies as a blessing.[78] Nonetheless, when he later heard about these arrangements, the horrified superintendent of the St. Louis, Alton & Chicago railroad line profusely apologized to Lincoln for not offering "a more comfortable ride" or excluding from the car persons who "had no right or business to be there."[79]

As fate would have it, just as Lincoln's train lurched out of Springfield, a train bearing another delegation of office-seekers pulled in. When its disappointed passengers learned that Lincoln had just left town, they simply bought northbound tickets of their own and headed off to Chicago "in search of the departed idol." In Lincoln's absence, Springfield, at best "as dull as a New England village on Sunday" save for political action, fell into slumber, as the first chill of winter froze the suddenly quiet, mud-caked streets.[80]

Lincoln was not yet accustomed to speaking to well-wishers at railroad depots. Nor was he "a successful impromptu speaker," New York congressman Reuben E. Fenton remembered. "He required a little time for thought and arrangement of the thing to be said." He needed, Lincoln once told him, "a peg to hang on."[81] But along the way to the Windy City, audiences prevailed on him to speak extemporaneously three different times, whenever his train stopped to refuel. Though hardly oratorical triumphs, these opportunities proved good practice for the inaugural journey yet to come.

Thirty miles from Springfield in Lincoln, Illinois—the first town ever named in his honor (back in 1853, he had followed local tradition and personally christened the village by breaking a watermelon on a rock[82])— he faced his first such crowd. To his longtime friends and supporters here, the president-elect made it clear he was thrilled to be liberated from his hometown. "I have been shut up in Springfield for the last few months," he declared, "and therefore have been unable to greet you, as I was formerly in the habit of doing" as a lawyer and campaigner. Now he was "glad to see so many happy faces, and to listen to so many pleasant expressions." But if the locals expected a statement of substance, they were in for a disappointment. After blandly extending the compliments of the Thanksgiving season, Lincoln explained, "I am not in the habit of making speeches now, and I would therefore ask to be excused from entering upon any discussion of the political topics of the day."[83]

A few hours later, when the train paused again, this time at David Davis's hometown of Bloomington, Lincoln rather lamely ventured into politics after all, offering the first of many versions of a supposedly reassuring story he would massage and repeat in the months to come. It was meant, in all its permutations, to implore Americans for patience by reminding them that no president could possibly prove wicked enough to destroy the country in the four brief years allotted him by the Constitution—not even, it implied, a Republican elected by a minority of the popular vote.

"I think very much of the people," Lincoln awkwardly began his initial attempt to convey this message, "as an old friend said he thought of woman. He said when he lost his first wife, who had been a great help to him in his business, he thought he was ruined—that he could never find another to fill her place. At length, however, he married another, who he found did quite as well as the first, and that his opinion now was that any woman would do well who was well done by." The audience must have been somewhat bewildered as Lincoln tried to explain the tortured symbolism. "So I think of the whole people of this nation—they will ever do well if well done by. We will try to do well by them in all parts of the country, North and South, with entire confidence that all will be well with all of us."[84]

Perhaps befuddled, the crowd demanded a follow-up speech by Senator Trumbull, then shouted for an appearance by the future first lady. Ever the political wife, Mary Lincoln obliged by stepping outside, bowing, and shaking a few hands.[85] Lincoln's tortured words were quickly forgotten, though they would soon appear in Northern newspapers, reminding the president-elect that he could say nothing now that did not constitute national news. Later, there was one more banal speech in Lexington, Illinois, before the train mercifully ended its journey and spared additional crowds from Lincoln's unrehearsed meanderings.[86]

However clumsily it began, the Chicago trip proved a tonic. As soon as the Lincolns arrived in town, hotelier George W. Gage ushered them to a fine parlor suite at the elegant Tremont House.[87] Never before had Lincoln earned such splendid accommodations. Then local Wide-Awakes massed outside to serenade him. It was almost like a vacation set to campaign music.

Here Lincoln at last greeted Hannibal Hamlin face-to-face at a meeting the press described as "cordial in the highest degree."[88] The vice president–elect recalled Lincoln launching into the conversation by asking, abruptly but pleasantly: "Have we ever been introduced to each other, Mr. Hamlin?"

"No, sir; I think not."

"That is also my impression, but I remember distinctly, while I was in Congress, to have heard you make a speech in the Senate. I was very much struck with that speech, Senator—particularly struck with it—and for the reason that it was filled 'chock up' with the very best kind of anti-slavery doctrine."

"Well now," answered Hamlin, laughing at Lincoln's rustic style of expression, "that is very singular; for my one and first recollection of yourself is of having heard you make a speech in the House—a speech that was so full of good humor and sharp points that I, together with other of your auditors, was convulsed with laughter. And I see that you and I remain in accord on our anti-slavery principles."[89]

Before they could get past this "social conversation" and begin serious discussions, their local hosts urged Hamlin and the Lincolns into carriages and off to see the Chicago Wigwam, the cavernous temporary arena where both men had been nominated to head the Republican ticket back in May. Neither candidate had attended the convention or seen the structure, and now it was scheduled for imminent demolition. Lincoln left no record of his reaction to the visit, but he, and particularly Mary, must have felt immense pride at glimpsing the site of his great triumph over party luminaries who had begun the balloting heavily favored to win the nomination. Here the Lincolns saw the platform where the votes had been counted and announced, and the public galleries from which Lincoln boosters had triumphantly "showered" the delegates with engravings of their man after he clinched the nomination.[90] Leaving the Wigwam, local leaders proudly piled on tours of the city's new post office, the Custom House, and the federal courthouse, too, before at last depositing Lincoln and Hamlin back at their hotel.[91] For the rest of the afternoon, the two future leaders finally got their initial opportunity to discuss "business of a private nature."[92]

The next day, temperatures plummeted and a storm blanketed Chicago with autumn snow, in spite of which crowds thronged a two-and-a-half-hour public reception that Lincoln and Hamlin hosted in the center parlor of the Tremont House beginning at 10 A.M.[93] There, they cheerfully welcomed a "constant stream of visitors" who poured through the Lake Street entrance to view their new leaders. The levee was formally structured, something new for the unassuming president-elect. He stood at the head of the receiving line greeting every visitor first, and introducing each in turn to his vice president. Further down the line, the editor of the *Chicago Journal* presented guests to the future first lady.[94]

"The affair was an ovation throughout," exulted the pro-Republican *Chicago Tribune*, noting that Lincoln appeared hale despite the "labor and pressure" of recent weeks, while another journal exaggerated that Lincoln bore himself "with great dignity." Actually, he addressed many of his callers by their first names, firmly ushering them along whenever the line stalled. "It was amusing," recalled one attendee, "to observe Lincoln's unfeigned enjoyment and to hear his hearty greetings in answer to familiar friends who exclaimed, 'How are you Abe?' he responding in like manner with 'Hello, Bill!' Or 'Jack' or 'Tom,' alternately pulling or pushing them along with his powerful hand and arm, saying: 'There's no time to talk now, boys; we must not stop this big procession, so move on.' "[95] But he did hold the line when he spied attorney J. S. Moulton, a Chicago friend who had never warmed to Lincoln's presidential candidacy—not to remonstrate, but to declare: "You don't belong in that line, Moulton. You belong here with me." With that, the president-elect took the lawyer by the shoulder and ushered him out of the crowd. "From that hour on," remembered an eyewitness, "every faculty that Moulton possessed was at the service of the President. A little act of kindness, skillfully bestowed, had won him; and he stayed on to the end."[96]

Altogether, Lincoln greeted an estimated three thousand well-wishers that morning, accommodating the shortest of them by stooping down to grasp their hands in both of his, and sometimes shaking so vigorously he resembled a "man a-mowing."[97] Whenever a tall attendee appeared, Lincoln raised his arms "in well affected astonishment" and with a merry look exclaimed to the amusement of the crowd: "You are up *some*."[98] One onlooker said much the same thing about Lincoln himself. Emerging from the levee, he was asked precisely how big the president-elect was. The Chicagoan reported, "he carries himself ordinarily (referring to his habit of stooping) . . . but when he stretches himself up to his full heighth [sic], the 'Lord only knows how tall he grows.' "[99]

Stretching himself thus at one point, Lincoln peered over the receiving line and spied a man who for years had cut his hair whenever he visited Chicago. Calling out, "There is my little barber," he walked over to greet an astonished C. Gustave Reich.[100] The rigid rules governing public levees were lost on Lincoln, but his informality only endeared him to the crowd.

Lincoln reserved his most tender greeting, as usual, for a child, in this case, an unrestrained four-year-old boy so "boiling over with enthusiasm" that at one point he shrieked an ear-splitting "Hurray for Uncle Abe!" When Lincoln heard it, "the youthful Republican was treated to a 'tossing up' toward the ceiling, which tickled him and the visitors hugely, and will be remembered through life by the boy."[101] In the words of the *New York Herald*, "Nothing could better illustrate the democratic way of doing things in this country than the ovation paid today to the 'Rail Splitter' and 'Type Sticker' [the sobriquet for Hamlin, a onetime printing house compositor] . . . elevated by the people of the nation to the two highest offices in it."[102]

For midday dinner that day, Lincoln visited the Tom Andrews Head Quarters Restaurant, where he enjoyed a hearty meal of wild game with oysters.[103] Surely prompted by Mary, Lincoln found time as well to visit the Lake Street "merchant tailors" Titsworth & Brother, where the supposedly fashion-unconscious Lincoln ordered a "magnificent suit" for his inaugural. The all-black ensemble featured cashmere pants, a vest "of the finest grenadier silk," and a coat "of the best cloth that could be bought in the country, and made up with a taste and in a style that cannot be surpassed in any country." Woven on the inside of the coat collar was a stitched inscription that suggests the suit was a gift: "To Hon. Abraham Lincoln, from A. D. Titsworth, Chicago, Illinois."[104]

Now well fed and richly clothed, he finally got down to serious political business later that afternoon, meeting with both Illinois congressman William Kellogg and German-American leader Carl Schurz, and then conferring through supper with Hamlin, Trumbull, and Piatt.

The principal subject was the cabinet—its composition by no means settled on Election Night, notwithstanding Lincoln's later claim. No one kept a formal record of these discussions, but "authoritative circles" in Chicago whispered that the "old Jacksonian Democrat" Gideon Welles (the paper called the little-known New Englander "Wills") was among the "prominent names" rumored for a place in Lincoln's official family. So was that of former Ohio congressman Robert C. Schenck, a onetime U.S. ambassador to Brazil who arrived in town allegedly lusting for a spot—perhaps, some suggested, too blatantly. Also mentioned was Congressman Henry Winter Davis of Maryland, a former Whig who could boast a special advantage on his résumé: he was a cousin of Lincoln's influential campaign manager, David Davis. Amid these confusing and conflicting reports, speculation mounted that Senator Salmon P. Chase of Ohio hoped to be named to the coveted senior post of secretary of state.[105]

Not if William H. Seward's allies had anything to do with it. The once prohibitive favorite to win the Republican presidential nomination in this same city of Chicago, the New Yorker, still smarting over the rejection he had endured in favor of Lincoln at the convention, now cast himself as the star player in the opening act of the cabinet-making drama. At issue was whether Seward, overcoming his ruffled feathers, would accept the highest post in Lincoln's power to dispose: secretary of state. The notion was not without controversy. Just a few days earlier, the president-elect had listened "attentively" as one of his wife's Kentucky relatives fulminated that a Seward appointment would surely drive his state out of the Union. In reply, Lincoln wondered "in what speech Mr. Seward had ever spoken menacingly of the South?" He "knew not one single prominent public Republican" who had ever "made himself obnoxious to the South," which, meantime, had "persistently bespotted and bespattered" Northern Republicans. No, to rule out Seward would require Republicans to "again surrender the Government into the hands of the men they had just conquered."[106] Lincoln would have none of it, and his determination constituted good news for Seward.

Tradition in fact dictated that the most prominent remaining member of the victorious party should be offered the State Department—even if he had battled the winner for the nomination. After John Quincy Adams bested Whig rival Henry Clay for the presidency in 1824, for example, he had appointed his rival as secretary of state. An even closer analogy had played out four administrations later in 1840. Now a revered senior senator, Clay had entered the Whig convention—much as

Seward would do twenty years later at the Republican convention of 1860—the clear favorite, only to be beaten out by the original log-cabin-born dark horse, William Henry Harrison. Once elected, Harrison had beseeched Clay to return to the State Department. Clay refused, though an equally prominent Whig lion, Daniel Webster, subsequently stepped in and took the post.

Seward's closest political advisor, the cunning Albany editor Thurlow Weed, certainly knew about the Harrison-Clay precedent. What was more, he believed Lincoln similarly owed Seward the courtesy of the State Department appointment, even if he let it be known that Seward, in the fashion of Henry Clay, would almost certainly refuse it. Weed went one audacious step further. Recalling that Harrison had traveled to Lexington, Kentucky, in early 1841 to consult (and be rejected by) Clay at his home, Weed suggested that Lincoln make a similar pilgrimage to Seward's residence in Auburn, New York, to make the cabinet offer in person. Wisely, as Gideon Welles put it, "Mr. Lincoln declined to imitate Harrison."[107]

According to Welles, Weed then tried inveigling Lincoln to invite Seward to the meetings in Chicago, but the president-elect rejected this proposal, too. Lincoln had no intention of being overshadowed on his first post-election trip. Outfoxed, Weed had no choice but to "intercept" Hamlin en route to the Chicago summit, and instead ask him to carry a message: "the offer of the State Department was due to Mr. Seward, but S. would decline it. The courtesy, however, was, he claimed, due to Mr. S. and to New York." Weed so persuaded Hamlin, and if Welles is to be believed, Hamlin in turn convinced Lincoln. Welles, who was about to mount his own campaign for a cabinet post, claimed that in Chicago, Lincoln entrusted Hamlin with a letter to carry back east formally offering Seward the job of secretary of state.[108] Even if he did, Seward's response was still weeks away. For now, the nation's two leading Republicans continued jockeying for advantage. Seward remained ambivalent about the plum assignment. Lincoln, by some accounts, remained hopeful Seward would accept; according to other reports, prayed he would decline.

The president-elect likely kept in mind the recent tradition of naming other convention rivals to key cabinet posts. Francis Preston Blair, Jr. (brother of current cabinet aspirant Montgomery Blair) recalled that Franklin Pierce, for one, had "put in his cabinet his enemies—men who felt his nomination a blow to their ambitions."[109] Buchanan had named former Democratic presidential candidate Lewis Cass secretary of state, and Millard Fillmore's cabinet had included such luminaries as Daniel Webster, Thomas Corwin, and John J. Crittenden.

Cabinet-making was a vexingly complicated matter, and the Chicago discussions understandably proceeded slowly. Politicians so frequently "annoyed" Lincoln with diversionary "invitations to dinner and tea," or pressed minor patronage claims for themselves or their friends, that he found himself "unable to transact the private business for which he came." The party faithful—prominent leaders and "lesser lights" alike—had flocked into town, some thirsting after cabinet posts, others "looking to take any office that pays well . . . anything they can get."[110] The *New York Herald* took to announcing the comings and goings of office-seekers in a series of mock bulletins: "E. R. Couch, of New York, is here, willing to take any office that pays well. J. A. Bronson is here, but doesn't know exactly what he wants. Gov. Wood, of Illinois, is here after something."[111] Another newspaperman described Chicago as "congested with political bores" and "hungry and expectant camp followers." The writer was reminded of the story of the Western stump orator who had once sought a foreign embassy from President Jackson, and was "only appeased by the gift of an old pair of breeches." Lincoln must have read the item. He later appropriated the story for himself, adding the punch line: "But it is well to be humble."[112]

Around the dinner table on the evening of November 23, discussions inevitably turned to secession. Still minimizing the threat, Lincoln told Hamlin, Piatt, and Schenck that he continued to doubt that the South would leave the Union, much less initiate a war for independence. Piatt remembered—in retrospect—blurting out that conditions were in reality so dangerous he "doubted whether he would be inaugurated in Washington." To which Lincoln laughed that the decline of pork prices in Cincinnati must have affected the Ohioan's judgment.[113]

Irritably, Piatt replied that "in ninety days the land would be whitened by tents." But Lincoln would not take the bait. He merely replied: "Well, we won't jump that ditch until we come to it," pausing before he added: "I must run the machine as I find it." Piatt left dinner wondering why the "strange and strangely gifted" Lincoln remained "so blind."[114] The president-elect "could not be made to realize the existence of the gathering storm," Piatt concluded, failing to comprehend Lincoln's determination to appear as confident as possible about the future, even to friends. "He would not admit that the masses could be aroused to a bloody war against their brothers."[115]

To everyone's surprise, Lincoln decided to extend his Chicago trip by another day to continue his talks with Hamlin. One newspaper predicted he at least would finally "have some peace tomorrow, as many of the vultures left tonight, supposing Mr. Lincoln would leave in the morning train."[116] Lincoln and Hamlin used their unscheduled extra time to retreat to the Lake View home of longtime local supporter Ebenezer Peck. Here, according to Hamlin's official biographer (and son), Lincoln, like many presidents before and after, supposedly told his running mate that he would always welcome his vice president's counsel in Washington.[117] In a way, Lincoln made his first "appointments" that day: Senators Hamlin and Trumbull would return to the capital, there to function as the president-elect's eyes and ears for the crucial and uncertain three and a half months left before the inauguration. But the makeup of the Lincoln cabinet continued to be, in a word, "unsettled."[118]

So unsettled did the matter remain—or so astutely did Lincoln mask his real intentions—that the well-placed *New York Herald* managed twice that week in sweeping sets of predictions to get almost everything wrong. First it hinted that Judge John McLean of Ohio was the certain choice for secretary of state.[119] Then it speculated that the old Missouri statesman Edward Bates, another highly regarded pre-convention Republican favorite, would get the post instead. Illinois state senator Norman Judd would have a spot, too, if he could convince his longtime friend Lincoln that their home state deserved a place in an administration headed by a fellow Illinoisan. George Ashmun of Massachusetts would represent New England as secretary of war, former Ohio congressman Robert C. Schenck would be awarded the Interior Department, Chicago railroad executive William B. Ogden would be secretary of the treasury, and Indiana congressman Schuyler Colfax, postmaster general. Lincoln would, the report claimed, offer the attorney general's post to a Southerner: either Maryland's Henry Winter Davis or Lincoln's one-time congressional colleague, the diminutive Georgia Whig, Alexander H. Stephens. For good measure, former congressman John Minor Botts of Virginia would have the Navy Department.

In the end, not a single one of these predictions came true. The *Herald's* only accurate conclusion was that "a thousand conflicting rumors" abounded.[120] For the rest of his days, Donn Piatt, for one, believed that Ohio's Schenck was denied a place only by "certain low intrigues hatched at Chicago by the newly created politicians of that locality, who saw in the coming administration opportunities for plunder."[121]

From the outset, Lincoln tried to organize the cabinet discussions by region. More than one historian has speculated that Lincoln's lieutenants had already promised plum cabinet spots to specific states in exchange for delegate support at the convention. Whether or not individual deals were struck back in May, Lincoln instructed David Davis shortly after the convention that he would not be "committed to any man, clique or faction."[122] Still, Lincoln did believe he had political debts to repay to whole sections of the country whose delegates had favored him from the beginning, abandoned Seward after the first ballot to join his bandwagon, or voted for the Republican ticket overwhelmingly on Election Day.[123] By this reasoning, New England deserved a place, along with Pennsylvania, Ohio, and Indiana. And so might Illinois, whether or not it was the new president's own state. But did Lincoln really owe a place in the government to Southern states where, in some cases, he had not even been allowed to contend for votes in November?

Voted in by an amalgam of Free Soilers, high tariff men, anti-slavery ex-Democrats, ex-Whigs (including the "Conscience" Whigs of New England), and radical abolitionists, from both the East and the West—all of whom now called themselves Republicans—Lincoln understood he must not only harmonize these elements in his cabinet, but nourish future party loyalty through the appointments process. This he could accomplish only by parceling out hundreds of additional well-paying jobs, and increasing lucrative government advertising in party newspapers. And this he proved willing—in fact eager—to do.[124]

Leaving the State Department aside, and keeping his other conclusions secret if in fact he had reached them, Lincoln further muddied the waters in Chicago by suggesting the possibility of naming both Henry Winter Davis and Montgomery Blair of Maryland, the latter a West Point graduate, lawyer, and onetime Democrat who had argued for Dred Scott's freedom in the century's most famous Supreme Court case; floated two Massachusetts men, Governor Nathaniel P. Banks (Judge Davis's choice), and the son of a former president, Congressman Charles Francis Adams; mentioned a pair of Hoosiers, Colfax and former congressman Caleb Blood Smith (whom Davis preferred); and suggested two North Carolinians, Representative John A. Gilmer and former congressman Kenneth Rayner. Then there was the venerable Edward Bates of Missouri—but likely for attorney general, certainly not for State, and if another Upper South candidate was needed, Congressman Emerson Etheridge of Tennessee. Finally, there was the fourth member of the "big four" who, like Seward, Chase, and Bates, once seemed far more likely than Lincoln to win the Republican nomination: Pennsylvania's smart but smarmy senator, Simon Cameron.[125] By the time they wrapped up their meeting, Lincoln and his advisors had bandied about nearly every leading name in the Republican party—along with a number of Democrats as well.

Lincoln had one additional, intriguing Southern possibility in mind about whom he spoke to no one—not even Hamlin. That was a cabinet post for his dear friend Joshua Fry Speed. A few weeks earlier, Lincoln had asked Speed and his wife to meet him in Chicago, and the Speeds

had obliged. When he finally gained admittance to the president-elect's
suite—annoyed at being compelled to produce his handwritten invitation to those guarding his onetime roommate's door—the president-
elect proposed adjourning to the privacy of Speed's rooms where they
could confer without being overheard. There, leaving Mary and Fanny
to catch up in the sitting room, Lincoln flopped down on his friend's
bed, apparently unconcerned by the knowledge—so often regurgitated
and overanalyzed today—that as young men they had been forced to
share the same bed in the tiny room above Speed's store.[126] Looking
"worn down & fatigued," Lincoln summoned the energy to ask him a
frank question.

"Speed what are your pecuniary Conditions—are you rich or poor?"

Speed guessed what was coming next and nipped the offer in the bud
before it could be tendered. "Mr. Presdt.," he replied, "I think I know
what you wish. I'll speak Candidly to you—My pecuniary Conditions
are good—I do not think you have any office within your gift that I can
afford to take."[127]

Lincoln was disappointed—for if he decided to take his home state
of Illinois out of cabinet contention, he faced the lonely prospect of
having few trusted old friends among his new official family in Washington. But he remained intrigued with the idea of attracting a Southerner
to his cabinet, even if it could not be Joshua Speed. Next best was a
Southerner he could invite unofficially without fear of being publicly
rejected, a potentially disabling political embarrassment. So Lincoln
asked Speed at least to return home and quietly initiate discussions with
fellow Kentuckian James Guthrie, a railroad tycoon who had served as
treasury secretary under Democrat Franklin Pierce. This overture would
fail, too. Guthrie soon got word back to the president-elect that while
he remained fiercely loyal to the Union, he felt himself, at sixty-eight,
too old to consider serving. With the Speed and Guthrie options fore-
closed, Abraham Lincoln himself would be the only Kentucky-born
leader in the incoming Lincoln administration.[128]

From Speed's recollections, shared some six years later, it is clear that
Lincoln for a time did weigh the possibility of including another South-

erner in his cabinet. Certainly there were advantages to such an appointment. Lincoln had attracted no support in the Deep South, and precious little in the border states, but a Southern member of his cabinet might quell the region's fears that his administration would be completely hostile to its interests. On the other hand, Lincoln knew, the appointment of a pro-slavery Southerner might outrage Republicans in the North. Equally frightening was an alternative scenario truly without precedent: what if he appointed a Southern cabinet officer whose state actually seceded? And what, then, if that minister suddenly resigned and headed south, throwing a doubtlessly chaotic situation into further chaos still? For weeks, the president-elect would ponder these alternatives before making a final decision. Lincoln and Hamlin adjourned the meeting uncertain as to whether their administration—the first ever to be elected exclusively by Northerners—would also become the first to exclude Southerners from appointed office.

On his final day in Chicago, Sunday, November 25, Hamlin, Lincoln, and the president-elect's friend and political ally Isaac N. Arnold sought divine, rather than political, guidance. Together they attended religious services at the elite St. James Episcopal Church on Cass Street,[129] with the city's leading merchants and officials occupying the surrounding pews. Afterward, Lincoln joined Mary for Sabbath dinner at their hotel, only to be interrupted by businessman John V. Farwell, with whom Lincoln had promised to visit a Sunday school in the slums north of the river. Asking only that he be excused from giving a speech there, Lincoln and Farwell headed off by carriage to the North Market Mission Sabbath School where, predictably, evangelist Dwight L. Moody called on him to speak anyway. In response, the president-elect offered a "short address to the destitute children,"[130] assuring them that "with close attention to your teachers" and "hard work to put in practice what you learn from them, some of you may become President of the United States." He exited to resounding cheers.[131]

His long "day of rest" was not yet over. At the urging of his longtime legal associate Henry Clay Whitney, Lincoln also visited the studio of the German-Jewish photographer Samuel G. Alschuler, for whom he had posed once before at Urbana during the Lincoln-Douglas debate year of 1858.[132] The result this day was anything but satisfactory—at the very least, unsuited for public consumption. Horace White, the *Chicago Tribune* reporter, believed that whenever Lincoln sat for a photo and put on "his most serious look," the result made him look "as though he had just been sentenced to death."[133] Even so, it was a historic image (see page 8): the first to show the subject unshaven.

Looking neither fully bearded nor totally beardless, Alschuler's portrait showed Lincoln sporting over-trimmed, smile-shaped chin whiskers beneath a closely shaved cheek. With one brow arched and a vacant look in his eyes, the goateed president-elect managed to look crafty, yet distant. Undaunted, Alschuler sent the picture home to Lincoln a few days later as "a small token of my esteem,"[134] but there is no evidence that it surfaced publicly at the time. Lincoln apparently gave it to its perpetrator, Henry Clay Whitney, who preserved the original copy for the rest of his life.[135]

With political pressures intensifying, Lincoln seemed to shed the interest in his image he had manifested when he began growing his beard days earlier. Chicago art entrepreneur Thomas B. Bryan had invited him to cap his visit to town by paying a personal visit to Bryan Hall to examine his "Gallery of Presidential Portraits from Washington to Lincoln inclusive"—which now boasted G. P. A. Healy's freshly made oil painting from life, "the best that has been taken of our next President," according to the local press.[136] But Lincoln scrawled an absent-minded reply that suggested he barely recalled the recent project: "I now fear I can not find leisure to avail myself of this Mr. Bryan's kindness."[137] There was time for only one more event—dinner with Hamlin at the home of newly elected Republican state legislator Jonathan Young Scammon.[138]

Lincoln and his party returned to Springfield the following morning at nine, this time suitably installed aboard a private railroad car.[139] With a chill rain pounding villages south of Chicago, no onlookers materialized along the route to cheer him or demand speeches. It was just as well. Lincoln arrived home at 6:30 in the evening looking to Henry Villard "rather the worse for wear" despite his so-called break. Writing home from New England, Lincoln's eldest son, Robert, perhaps sensed his parents' growing exhaustion. "I see by the papers that you have been to Chicago," Bob reprimanded his parents. "Aren't you beginning to get a little tired of this constant uproar?"[140] No doubt they were, but there was no rest in prospect.

"If he expects relief here he will be disappointed," Villard agreed. "A number of expectants have been lying in wait for him during the last twenty-four hours, who will swoop upon him in the morning with an eagerness doubled by the delay."[141] Facing a huge pile of accumulated correspondence before which, Villard believed, "a less determined soul might well have quailed," Lincoln labored far into that first night home and, uninterrupted, throughout the following day, in an effort to catch up, wading through the latest batch of advice, requests, and reports—little of it heartening.

Nor did the accumulated out-of-town newspapers provide much solace. Lincoln was wise enough to seek information beyond the rosy, image-enhancing reports filed by admirers like Villard. Now he would learn from back issues of other journals that secessionist agitator Edmund Ruffin had been serenaded in Charleston, responding to the salute by asserting to much applause that "the Union is gone already virtually." In Alabama, the Baptist State Convention had officially voiced its hostility to "Northern fanatics," vowing never to "live under Black Republican rule." Mississippi's governor had delivered his annual message to a legislature "unanimous for secession." And while a public meeting in Bath County, Virginia, had urged that the state remain true to the Union, it adopted a resolution officially deploring Lincoln's election as "a national misfortune."[142] The president-elect did not have to subscribe to Southern journals to read these dismaying accounts. They were all reprinted in the *New York Herald* and the *New York Times*.

Worse, the *Times* reported that there was still no solid indication that the Buchanan administration would devote its final months in office to defusing the secession crisis. Lincoln reasonably expected that the White House incumbent, regardless of his loyalty to the Democrats, would speak out firmly against disunion and for holding federal property in the South, perhaps keeping the lid on the powder keg until Lincoln could take office in March. Instead, the paper hinted, Buchanan might actually recognize the right not of nullification but of secession—hairsplitting it condemned as "a distinction without a difference," explaining that the president "must be dreadfully frightened."[143] At most, the outgoing chief executive was expected to reserve judgment and, like his successor, remain silent—at least until his annual message to Congress early in December.

Back home, Lincoln again lifted his own veil of silence, this time to pound critics within his own Republican family—some of whom worried that he was tilting too far to the South to cool the fire-eaters. Writing confidentially to the *Times*'s pro-Republican editor, Henry J. Raymond, Lincoln upbraided newspapers that "endeavor to inflame the North" with the belief that the widely published Lyman Trumbull speech, which he had helped draft, signaled "an abandonment of Republican ground by the incoming administration." Nor could he accept the corollary charge by secession agitators that the very same speech constituted "an open declaration of war" against the South.

Lincoln threw up his hands in frustration. "This is just what I expected," he fumed, "and just what would happen with any declaration I could make. These political fiends are not half sick enough yet. 'Party malice' and not 'public good' possesses them entirely. 'They seek a sign, and no sign shall be given them.' "[144]

All Lincoln would add in response to the "rub-a-dubbing now coming up from the Southern States" was his insistence that "the law should be upheld." Convinced that further words would hurt him in the North and South alike, Lincoln determined to say no more. But he did confide to visitors that he could not believe "the Disunionists can work their people up to the point of consummating their threatened treason," could not imagine "a Confederacy in which slave-holding and the Slave Trade are the bonds of union."[145] Either Lincoln completely misread the heightened secession agitation, or, more likely, believed that admitting his concern would only embolden the agitators.

Instead, with "his usual grotesque *bon hommie*," he regaled his latest visitors with stories of his trip to Chicago, of the meetings he was compelled to attend, the receptions he was obliged to host. "It seems that instead of enjoying relief, as expected," Villard concluded, "he was even more molested" than in Springfield. "Mr. Lincoln's experience at Chicago will probably deter him from undertaking another journey previous to his final departure for Washington City." [146]

But isolation held its dangers, too. It comes as little surprise that Lincoln preserved an editorial from the *New York Evening Post* in which William Cullen Bryant, the man who had introduced him at Cooper Union and supported him for president, appeared to question "whether that election is sufficient to clothe Mr. Lincoln with the authority of a Chief Magistrate." Warned Bryant: "The greatest question at issue in this country at present is, whether a majority of the nation, if they choose to live in non-slaveholding states, are competent to elect and inaugurate a President in a constitutional way. That question is not yet settled." [147]

Chapter Four

A Masterly Inactivity

THE APPROACH OF Thanksgiving on November 29 sent Springfield into a panic—not over the nation-imperiling crisis plaguing its leading citizen, but the apparently more dismaying prospect of a local turkey shortage.[1] In a formal proclamation, Illinois governor John Wood had optimistically urged citizens to assemble "in their places of worship" on Thanksgiving to "acknowledge, as a people, our gratitude and our adoring love to the Infinite Giver of all good."[2] But a local newspaper fretted that even Springfield's most pious churchgoers would be unable to sit through holiday sermons "if the ceremony of basting that persecuted fowl was not going on at home." Fortunately, even sacred holidays commingled with politics that year. Having lost a wager that Stephen A. Douglas would be elected president, a Democrat from nearby Williamsville announced he would pay off his debt by roasting a Thanksgiving ox and issuing "a general invitation to all comers to . . . digest it."[3]

On Thanksgiving Day, as it turned out, more people seemed to flock into town than leave it. Lincoln himself found little rest on the holiday, pausing only to join Mary for an 11 A.M. divine service at the First Presbyterian Church—"having special cause to thank his Maker," remarked one journalist[4]—and to enjoy a traditional roast turkey dinner with his

114

family, apparently unaffected by the scarcity of fowl. Then it was back to work at the Governor's Rooms.

There, he plunged anew into his escalating correspondence, "the perusal of which," Henry Villard lamented, "made him no wiser." The latest batch of letters suffered from "[b]ad grammar and worse penmanship . . . [im]pertinence of expression, vain glorious assurance and impudent attempts at exaction" from "all grades of society." These included: "The grave effusions of statesmen; the disinterested advice of patriots . . . seditious pamphlets and manifestos . . . the well-calculated, wheedling praises of the expectant politician and the meaningless commonplaces of scribblers from mere curiosity." Among the worst offenders, apparently, were shocking examples of "Female forwardness and inquisitiveness." Sadly, examples have vanished.[5]

"Poets hasten to tax their muse in his glorification," Villard continued. "Authors and speculative book-sellers freely send their congratulations, accompanied by complimentary volumes. Inventors are exceedingly liberal with circulars and samples. More impulsive than well-mannered, Southerners indulge in occasional missives containing senseless fulminations and, in a few instances, disgraceful threats and indecent drawings."[6] An opposition sheet acknowledged that "a dozen letters a day . . . threaten him with flaying alive, assassination, mayhem, fire and brimstone, and getting his nose pulled."[7] With the mail also overflowing with gifts, state superintendent of education Newton Bateman—peeking in from his own office next door—testified that Lincoln's State House reception offices now "resembled a museum of curiosities."[8]

"A perfect shower of 'able editorials' is clipped out and enclosed," Villard further revealed. "Artists express their happiness in supplying him with wretched wood-cut representations of his surroundings." For his part, John Nicolay seemed proud that one such Henri Lovie drawing, published in woodcut in *Frank Leslie's Illustrated Newspaper*, not only depicted the Governor's Reception Room, dominated by the tall figure of Lincoln greeting visitors, but in the foreground, seen from behind, showed a scribbler bent over his desk. This portrayal was meant to be Nicolay. "Aside from the fact that it makes the room look entirely too large," the secretary drolly commented of the clipping he sent on to his fiancée, "you will also be struck with the marvellous truthfulness of the representation of Mr. Lincoln, and his elegant and accomplished secretary, who sits writing at the desk." Nicolay cautioned her, tongue in cheek, to spend no more than an exorbitant $75 on a frame.[9]

It is easy to understand why the artist showed Nicolay laboring over his work. He was all but overwhelmed by the incoming mail: now hundreds of letters daily reflecting the full " 'light and shadow' of Anglo-American political humanity," as Villard put it. Nicolay finally got some desperately needed help when John Hay, a nephew of Lincoln's onetime law student Milton Hay, suspended his own legal studies to join the staff.

Hay would remain Nicolay's second in command until the president's assassination. Just twenty-two years old but Brown-educated, a good listener, dazzling conversationalist, and fine writer, the handsome young Hay was reported to be "helping" Nicolay with "footing up some columns of election returns" as early as November 26. On Thanksgiving, firmly ensconced in his new job, Hay wrote home from Springfield, dismissing it as "a miserable sprawling village which imagines itself a city," to report on "the dull routine of everyday labor" for the president-elect.[10] From then on, he was seldom far from the senior secretary's—or Lincoln's—side as together they faced what Nicolay called "the prospect of continual excitement as the new Administration takes shape and proportion." Nicolay undoubtedly had Hay's welcome arrival in mind when he predicted that new developments "will lighten the labor somewhat."[11]

The senior secretary proved too optimistic. As letters piled up, so did guests. Lincoln's horde of late-November callers included high-ranking politicians, old friends, distant relations, and slick patronage hustlers, many armed with letters of introduction and recommendation from supporters as far away as Connecticut, Iowa, and Pennsylvania.[12] The fact that the future president retained their endorsements in his files suggests that he obligingly welcomed most of these strangers to the State House and gave them a fair hearing.

A cynical newspaperman described him there as "serenely smiling at the ominous tidings that rush over the wires from the cotton-growing States." Complaining that "Panic and impending revolution seem to him as nothing," the paper charged: "He laughs and jokes, gulps down the largest doses of adulation that a village crowd can manufacture, and altogether deports himself with the air of one who fails to comprehend the task which abolition fanaticism has thrust upon him." [13]

In truth, shackled to the grinding routine of receiving office-seekers and simultaneously keeping up with both his mail and the nation's newspapers (he was reported to be "faithfully" reading all the New York dailies as well as journals from the South and West [14]), Lincoln found he indeed had less and less time for serious planning. He had almost none for relaxation or exercise, which he enjoyed and needed. The weather had grown too cold for handball, one of his favorite activities. [15] An observer noticed that even when he got the chance these days to play chess, he seemed to be "continually thinking of something else," using the game as "a mechanical pastime to occupy his hands while his mind is busy with some other subject." His chess opponents were no doubt further put off by Lincoln's irritating habit of whistling while he considered his next move, or worse, singing an "Ethiopian" parody tune called "Dixie's Land," [16] a new song he reportedly first heard earlier that year at what a friend called a "high toned n——r show" in Chicago. [17]

When one sympathetic caller warned Lincoln that "the vexatious slavery matter" would be the first he must confront in Washington, the president-elect showed he was no stranger to the racist epithet, either. The visitor's commiseration reminded him of the Kentucky justice of the peace whose very first case involved criminal prosecution for slave abuse. Lacking precedents, he angrily exclaimed: "I will be damned if I don't feel almost sorry for being elected when the n——s is the first thing I have to attend to." [18]

Offensive or banal, ribald or folksy, Lincoln had a story or joke ready for every occasion—he loved "witty sayings . . . as much as any mortal," Villard testified. [19] Yet, as Newton Bateman marveled, oblivious to the painful "N" word, not one of his tales featured "malice or venom. . . . However broad the travesty, or side-shaking the burlesque, he was careful never to wound the feelings or trifle with the sensibilities of any man, present or absent."[20] Bateman's blindness—not to mention Lincoln's insensitivity, both common for the time—reflect the reality that in Springfield in 1860, blacks were seen but not heard. Although African Americans lived in Lincoln's neighborhood, worked at menial jobs or operated small businesses, and worshipped at their own churches, no one ever reported a black visitor to Lincoln's post-election headquarters that year. Even in a Northern city—an anti-slavery city—such an event was unimaginable.[21]

As winter approached, Lincoln welcomed several distinguished guests (all white, of course), some eager to offer advice, others lusting after appointments. One visitor was New York Republican leader Hugh White, with whom Lincoln had served in Congress years—it must have seemed a lifetime—earlier.[22] The Ohio abolitionist Joshua Giddings arrived in town to give a speech, paying the obligatory courtesy call on the president-elect, too, though he failed to convince Lincoln to speak out anew against slavery.[23] New Hampshire's George Fogg, secretary of the Republican National Committee, arrived in Springfield and cornered Lincoln for a "long private interview" of his own,[24] in quest of an appointment he ultimately received.[25] And the German-born Illinois state committeeman Gustave Koerner came to plead the case of Norman Judd, who still harbored cabinet ambitions. In the bargain he expressed "a wish to hold an office" himself, namely the United States mission in Berlin. Koerner was mortified when his rumored appointment got into the papers in Germany, eliciting premature congratulations from overseas,[26] and was further embarrassed when Judd was rejected for the cabinet—either because he was too radical or because he hailed from Lincoln's own state. (Lincoln eventually consoled Judd with the very assignment Koerner had coveted: he sent Judd to Berlin.)

The press faithfully reported each of these meetings, volunteering speculation in the absence of facts. By the time former Kansas governor Andrew Reeder had come and gone, one New York newspaper insisted that Lincoln had offered him a cabinet post, a Senate seat, a foreign mission, and a federal judgeship.[27] Another New Hampshire Republican,

Lincoln's onetime congressional colleague Amos Tuck, worried that "a rush to reap where they have not sown" had infected "every slippery politician in the party."[28] Tuck responded by planning a visit to Springfield to seek an appointment for a politician he deemed more worthy: himself.

Villard described Lincoln's rooms as "crowded all day during reception hours" with visitors and job-seekers offering "no end of introductions, salutations, congratulations, compliments, etc. etc."[29] Occasional comic relief arrived in the form of the "country people" who streamed into town to take their own measure of the president-elect. When a grizzled yeoman worker appeared one morning to complain that as a state legislator many years earlier, in hard times, young Lincoln had inexcusably voted to raise his government salary from two to all of four dollars a day," Lincoln listened to the reproach calmly. "Now, Abe, I want to know what in the world made you do it?" demanded the old Democrat. With deadpan seriousness, Lincoln explained: "I reckon the only reason was that we wanted the money."[30]

A delegation from Lincoln's native Kentucky, apparently expecting to find their fellow native son a taciturn lout, went home genuinely surprised by Lincoln's unexpected "conversational powers." A particularly "garrulous old lady," on the other hand, also hailing from the Bluegrass State, announced to anyone who would listen that she vividly remembered Abe as a child—and not at all favorably. "She expressed great astonishment at his elevation to the highest office in the land," Villard reported in the *Herald*.

" 'Why,' she said, 'he was the gawkiest, dullest looking boy you ever saw,' but she added: 'There was one thing remarkable about him. He could always remember things better than any other boy in the neighborhood.' "[31]

Nowadays he seemed principally compelled to remember the debts that patronage claimants earnestly believed he owed them. "The President elect has been greatly annoyed by importunate office-seekers," his hometown newspaper announced gravely late in the month, "who, notwithstanding his unvarying assertion that he will make no promises until after the 4th of March next . . . continue to persist in approaching him on the subject of appointments."[32] Writing from Boston a few days before heading to Washington to take his seat in the House of Representatives, Charles Francis Adams huffed: "The indications of policy that come from Springfield are dubious, and the swarm that surround Mr. Lincoln are by no means the best."[33] (Predictably, Adams would ultimately accept a diplomatic appointment himself.)

As for those who could not make pilgrimages to Springfield by railroad, wagon, or on foot, to lay their cases before Lincoln personally, they did the next best thing: they wrote truckling or peremptory letters. Complete strangers, many with only the most tenuous claims to the president-elect's gratitude, forwarded pleas, proposals, and requests—the nineteenth-century equivalents of curricula vitae. The most unqualified applicants seemed certain they could perform almost any job in the federal bureaucracy. The ex-Whigs, ex-Democrats, ex-Know-Nothings, abolitionists, Free Soilers, and high tariff men that comprised the new Republican coalition seemed totally united in one regard: their belief that they were all entitled to federal patronage.[34] As Ward Hill Lamon put it: "It was a party that had never been fed; and it was voraciously hungry."[35]

When one ravenous Republican loyalist called to demand a position because, as he put it, he had made him president, Lincoln stopped him.

"So you made me President, did you?" Lincoln asked with a twinkle in his eye.

"I think I did," said the office-seeker.

"Then a pretty mess you've got me into, that's all," Lincoln replied, ending the interview.[36]

Unlike modern presidents-elect, Lincoln employed no formal transition committee to help him sort through and evaluate these pleas for office.[37] Such groups were unheard of in the nineteenth century. Well-placed friends might provide occasional guidance on major appointments—men like David Davis, Leonard Swett, or Ozias M. Hatch,[38] for example, or Senator Lyman Trumbull, who continued to send advice on cabinet

selection after returning to Washington for the December session of
Congress. The press feverishly speculated that Kansas politician Mark
Delahay would screen all of his state's office-seekers, Francis Preston
Blair, Missouri's, while Trumbull and state party chairman Norman Judd
would control Illinois's.[39] In reality, the president-elect faced the flood of
patronage requests more or less in solitary despair, overwhelmed and
dispirited by the avalanche of demands. Or so the myth goes.

The long-accepted notion that Lincoln detested the burdensome
process of filling minor jobs and granting favors to lower-level Republican loyalists deserves serious reappraisal. Likely invented to bolster the
notion that he rose above petty politics during the interregnum, and
afterward in the White House, the durable legend suggests that Lincoln
loathed the patronage process and wished he could have avoided it entirely.

To say the least, this is an exaggeration. As surprised and oppressed
as he was by the volume of requests and the persistence of undeserving
applicants, Lincoln had no reason to want to avoid office-seekers or
abrogate the right of making federal appointments. Quite the contrary:
this was precisely the privilege he had hoped (and Republicans had
campaigned for him) to enjoy. Democrats had controlled the federal
bureaucracy without interruption for eight years—ever since Pierce's inauguration in 1853—and, for that matter, for much of the century. The
Republicans, a new political organization, had waged two national election contests before electing its first president, and now had every reason to expect their full share of loaves and fishes.

A consummate politician who believed in the concept of out with
the old and in with the new, Lincoln understood that he now had the
opportunity—indeed, the obligation—to reward supporters and thus
guarantee the loyalty of the federal bureaucracy during the difficult years
sure to come. In the bargain he was also expected to purge Democrats—
some of them not only political foes but perhaps treacherously sympathetic to secession—from the federal payroll. Lincoln demonstrated his
political and public relations genius by fulfilling this role diligently,

while making himself appear, to both neighbors and the press, over-whelmed to the point of exhaustion by the sordid exercise of power.

As he wrote to William H. Seward in mid-December—betraying an aversion to office-seekers tempered with an enthusiasm for office-seeking: "In regard to the patronage, sought with so much eagerness and jealousy, I have prescribed for myself the maxim, 'Justice to all'."[40] The message was clear: all the soldiers in Abraham Lincoln's army of sup-porters had an equal and convincing claim to spoils.

Of course he hoped that applicants would be worthy of his rewards. But as Illinois newspaper editor William O. Stoddard complained a few months later—in words that might easily have described the pre-inaugural job competition as well: "A curious idea appeared to have entered the minds of many men, that if a fellow had made good speeches and torn around actively in the presidential campaign," or perhaps had merely "done well with a flour mill or a country store, he was just the right man for a presidential appointment."[41]

Stoddard left unspoken the fact that he understood this absurdity from both sides of the patronage desk: the journalist became an appli-cant for a job himself. He was persistent, too. "I do not wish to inflict any more letters upon Mr. Lincoln," he wrote in desperation to Lin-coln's law partner Herndon when his quest stalled. Seeking a place on the new president's personal staff, he insisted: "While I have reason to fear that I shall really need some position—you know how lucrative a business editing a country weekly is—there is no office with twice the net profits which would so highly gratify me as the one in question."[42] Ten days later he offered to take the job " 'on trial,' as the Dutch-man took his wife."[43] When this plea, too, went unfulfilled, Stoddard sought help from Senator Trumbull, "almost ashamed to trouble" so busy a man, but emphasizing, "I do not propose to be a mere leech on the new administration—I wish to work, with it and for it."[44] Stod-dard's persistence paid off. Eventually he got the job as White House clerk.[45]

He was hardly alone in waging such campaigns based on his own, not the country's, needs. At least Stoddard could claim—though it proved an overstatement—to have written the first newspaper editorial to propose Lincoln for the presidency.[46] The very day after Lincoln's election, an obscure Springfield neighbor named Henry Fawcett dispatched a note begging the president-elect to let him "go with you to the White House as *your* Body Servant." Fawcett, who listed among his qualifications his experience ringing a local church bell when Lincoln won the nomination, offered "to carry your Messages and so forth . . . even Shaving you as well."[47] Lincoln made no known reply. A few days later, sixty-year-old Peoria lawyer Charles Balance also submitted "to the mortification of asking an office at your hands," justifying his request by explaining that he had "spent time and money, and sometimes a good deal of both, every year, in supporting the principles you and I have both professed." The post of marshal of the Northern District of Illinois, he frankly calculated, would help him "pay my debts, and support my family."[48] Incompetents wore their sense of entitlement proudly.

Total strangers were no less forward. An Indiana Republican summed up the situation well when he candidly admitted that anyone who "Hurras [sic] Strong for Old Abe" in turn "expects a teat at the crib."[49] One Henry F. Johns applied for the job of White House steward, attaching a petition signed by thirty-seven ladies from Union Springs, New York, attesting to the fact that his wife could conveniently "fill the situation of Stewardess."[50] John J. Hendee of Blackman, Michigan, argued that he was entitled to a job simply because he was "governed by the principles" outlined on an enclosed card. Labeled, "God's Commands," the manifesto called on its bearers to worship God, tell the truth, abstain from "intoxicating drinks," and avoid marrying "blood relation[s]." The list of commandments ended with the warning: "Waste not your strength in any unnatural manner"—in other words, do not masturbate.[51] The president-elect ignored the request but kept the card. Lincoln weighed these bizarre written applications at the same time he was dodging the personal entreaties from job-aspiring strangers who pushed their way into his reception room on a daily basis.

The spectacle was ripe for satire. One of Lincoln's favorite humorists, Charles Farrar Browne—who wrote under the pen name Artemus

Ward—obliged with a rollicking parody in dialect describing an imaginary quest for office in "ABRAHAM'S buzzum":

> "Good God!" cride Old ABE, "they cum upon me from the skize—down the chimneys, and from the bowels of the yearth!" He hadn't more'n got them words out of his delikit mouth before two fat offis-seekers from Wisconsin, in endeverin to crawl atween his legs for the purpuss of applyin for the tollgateship at Milwaky, upset the President eleck & he would hev gone sprawlin' into the fire-place if I hadn't caught him in these arms.[52]

Lincoln might have been similarly amused by an equally outrageous but genuine letter, penned the day after Thanksgiving, from an anonymous correspondent signing himself "Unterified." Even Artemus Ward could not have invented such a message. After congratulating the president-elect "on your good fortune, in being elevated to the high cockolorem [sic] chair of the nation," he warned him that he was "not out of the reach of your forty seven millions of friends wanting office." Then the demented writer expressed his own expectations:

> Permit me Honest Abe to say that I am not particular of having any office higher than Secretary of State under your administration. I am going to Washington on the 4th of March next and shall have on my person a dozen howitzers to repel any attack, which shall be made upon you, you will see me while you are taking the oath and in order that you will be able better to recognize me I shall paint the 32d hair of the left eyebrow a sky blue. Till then good bye and dont forget to make me Secretary of State.[53]

THERE WAS LITTLE danger Lincoln could forget, even for a moment, the pressures that continued mounting for an official pre-inaugural statement. "Every newspaper he opened was filled with clear indications of an impending national catastrophe," Henry Villard observed. "Every mail brought him written, and every hour verbal, entreaties to abandon his paralyzed silence, repress untimely feelings of delicacy, and pour the oil of conciliatory conservative assurances upon the turbulent waves of Southern excitement." [54]

But still Lincoln would not budge, would not speak, well aware that he yet enjoyed no power to govern, but possessed limitless potential for inflaming further discontent through anything he might say. Lincoln came to believe he had as much to fear from dissatisfaction among his Northern allies as from secession-minded Southern fire-eaters. As if to punctuate that danger, Frederick Douglass, speaking in Boston on December 3, declared with impolitic frankness: "I want the slaveholders to be made uncomfortable. . . . I rejoice in every uprising in the South."

What was more, in Douglass's opinion, Lincoln had already gone too far in reassuring Southerners. He regarded "the clamor now raised by the slaveholders about 'Northern aggression' [and] 'sectional warfare' " to be unwarranted. "If Mr. Lincoln were really an Abolition President, which he is not; if he were a friend to the Abolition movement, instead of being, as he is, its most powerful enemy, the dissolution of the Union might be the only effective mode of perpetuating Slavery in the Southern States." As far as Douglass was concerned, "the South has no such cause for disunion." [55] How could Lincoln reply to such comments, without offending abolitionists or frightening slave-owning Unionists from the Upper South? Placating words were likewise out of the question. A plea from Virginia suggesting Lincoln need do no more than assure Southerners they had the right to bring their property into all American territories reminded the dubious president-elect of an apt story. It concerned a little girl who begged her mother to let her play outside. The mother repeatedly said no, the child persisted, and the mother finally lost patience and gave her a whipping, "upon which," Lincoln chortled, "the girl exclaimed: 'Now, Ma. I can certainly run out.' " Lincoln would not offer either encouragement or condemnation to his Southern "children": once chastised, he suspected, they might feel it their right to "run out." [56]

Lincoln had other good reasons to hold off on further public comments. Anxious as he was about the potential for mischief-making among lame ducks in Washington, he was determined to let President Buchanan offer his final annual message to Congress—the nineteenth-century equivalent of today's State of the Union address. The message would open the new congressional session in the first week of December. Though Buchanan's term of office was winding down to its final months, rarely had any presidential message been so breathlessly anticipated. This would be the incumbent's last major opportunity to declare his authority to resist, or at least frown on, disunion. A strong anti-secessionist message, Lincoln believed, might still succeed in halting the escalating momentum for secession in the Deep South without his own intervention. The president-elect's attention "fixed on Congress" as he waited the annual message "with the greatest anxiety." [57]

Lincoln hoped he could wait, too, for his own formal election to the presidency. Technically, that would not happen until February—with good luck and adequate military security—when the votes of the 303 members of the 1860 Electoral College, from all parts of the country, were finally counted in Washington. (It was a complicated process: First the victorious electors would meet in the various states on December 5 formally to name their presidential choices; then designated messengers would transport the sealed results to the nation's capital for the required February vote-counting ceremony.) Only then would Lincoln's November victory at the polls truly be official. For generations, Americans had regarded these sessions as mere formalities, a kind of post-election coronation devoid of suspense, with each "delegate" firmly pledged in advance to support the ticket on which he had run. But little about this interregnum was going according to tradition or plan. Never before had a president-elect been subjected to so much pressure to pronounce himself on doctrinal issues before his inauguration. Never before had an entire section of the country threatened to abandon the United States altogether in response to an election.

Would the Electoral College bring a pro forma confirmation of the November 6 popular result, or a free-for-all clouded, and perhaps influenced, by these unprecedented threats of secession? Only time would tell. But the signs grew darker within the void left by Lincoln's silence.

On Thanksgiving Day, one New Orleans preacher "deeply moved" his audience with "an eloquent and thrilling discourse in favor of secession" for Louisiana. Two days later, a "large and enthusiastic" meeting at Mobile nominated delegates to a formal state convention called to consider secession for Alabama, too.[58] Most threatening of all, perhaps, was the news that Alexander Hamilton's son had urged New York's and Pennsylvania's electors to give their votes not to Lincoln but to William A. Graham of North Carolina in order "to throw the election into the House." As the *New York World* pointed out the day before the scheduled state-by-state count, the electors were "bound only by custom and their sense of honor," not by law. However unlikely such a move, the *World* argued, the "fact that it is seriously proposed by a gentleman of honor and character betokens his deep sense of the impending danger."[59]

BEHIND CLOSED DOORS at the White House, the outgoing Democratic president was hard at work preparing an annual message that, he hoped, would indeed question the right of secession and establish his determination to defend public property and collect revenues in the particularly defiant state of South Carolina. But this mild show of resolve James Buchanan intended to accompany with a torturous explanation of how the federal government in fact had no power to enforce either goal. Nor was Buchanan prepared to bow without protest to the imposition of Republican party policy barring the future expansion of slavery.

Nearing age seventy, Buchanan was a tired man. For four years he had dithered as the last of the fragile compromises binding North and South were undone by Congress and the courts on his watch. The old Pennsylvania "doughface"—the period moniker for Northerners who tilted to Southern interests—had no sooner entered office in 1857 than the Supreme Court ruled for slaveholders in the epochal case, *Dred Scott v. Sanford*. That infamous decision, authored by the still reigning Chief Justice Roger B. Taney, denied citizenship to blacks and forbade Congress or state legislatures from banning slavery in the territories. Just days earlier, in his inaugural address, Buchanan had urged citizens to abide by the long-awaited decision, "*whatever it might be*." That had given an Illinois Republican named Abraham Lincoln the inspiration to suggest by 1858 the existence of a grand, prearranged plot to nationalize slavery—among "Stephen [Douglas], Franklin [Pierce, then the outgoing president], Roger [Taney] and James [Buchanan]." Quoting Scripture to insist that "a house divided against itself cannot stand," Lincoln had charged that these co-conspirators "all understood one another from the beginning, and all worked upon a common *plan* or *draft* drawn up before the first lick was struck."[60] However unconvincing, Lincoln's accusation proved grand political theater, and further relegated Buchanan to the status of enemy within his own region. As it turned out, the hapless president's troubles were just beginning.

Even before *Dred Scott* decision roiled the country, Kansas Territory—"Bleeding Kansas," as it came to be known—had erupted in horrific violence, as resident pro- and anti-slavery advocates went to war over the question of its admission into the Union as a free or slave state. Buchanan, while occasionally claiming moral opposition to slavery, maintained that the institution was fully protected in the federal Constitution, and must be tolerated whenever a local jurisdiction favored it. Even when anti-slavery Kansans proceeded to boycott a rigged state constitutional convention that endorsed the territory's admission as a slave state, Buchanan enthusiastically supported the tainted outcome and urged Congress to do likewise. When fellow Democrat, Senator Stephen A. Douglas of Illinois, broke with him and urged a new Kansas convention, this time with full public participation—true to his faith in so-called popular sovereignty—Buchanan refused.[61] Even after Kansas's own citizens decisively rejected the pro-slavery Lecompton Constitution in a subsequent referendum, the president clung to his now discredited policy. (Kansas was ultimately admitted to the Union as a free state in 1861.)

Yet another blow struck the beleaguered administration that same summer, when an insurance company in Ohio collapsed spectacularly. The failure set off the Panic of 1857, a financial depression that crippled the North and the West. The Southern economy sailed on, however, with foreign demand for cotton undiminished by either the panic or the Crimean War in Europe. Rising labor costs meant little to a region benefiting from the "advantage" of black slavery. For most of the president's term, the free states struggled to reverse the economic downturn.

By 1860, Buchanan concluded that through no fault of his own, Lincoln's election "had established two geographical parties, inflamed with malignant hatred against each other, in despite [sic] of the warning voice of Washington"—namely his own. "Terror and alarm everywhere prevailed," he remembered, but through no fault of Democrats. Buchanan assigned blame not to Southern ultras, but to "the agitation in the North against slavery in the South," including the so-called "virulence" and "hostility" directed against his own administration by the Northern press ever since Lincoln's victory.[62]

Reaching out to a leading Southerner who shared this view, Buchanan summoned Mississippi senator Jefferson Davis to the White House. There he read him "the rough draft" of his annual message and invited his suggestions. As Davis, a Buchanan admirer, recalled the experience, the president "very kindly accepted all the modifications which I suggested." But Buchanan's outreach backfired. The senator left the mansion convinced the final document would prove unqualifiedly supportive of Southerners' constitutional right to leave the Union if they so chose. Later, Davis realized that it was "afterward somewhat changed," adding, "in my judgment, the last alterations were unfortunate." The hapless president succeeded only in ensuring that his message would please no one. Only later—when it was too late to prevent secession—did Davis concede that the message was a "model" that the next president ought to have followed.[63]

Buchanan later confessed he found Southern secession agitation entirely illogical. "The people of the slaveholding States must have known there could be no danger of an actual invasion of their constitutional rights over slave property from any hostile action of Mr. Lincoln's administration," he argued in his memoirs. In *Dred Scott v. Sanford*, the Supreme Court had ruled "in their favor" on slavery expansion, and the newly elected Congress would include enough Democrats "to prevent any legislation to their injury" despite Lincoln's presence in the White House. Within this comforting political bubble, Buchanan believed, "it would be madness for them to rush into secession." But the president offered these observations in hindsight—six years later. Nothing he wrote in his final message to Congress conveyed nearly as sensible an argument for Southern restraint.[64] Buchanan's extreme caution may actually have produced the opposite effect. In arguing that only "a deliberate, palpable, and dangerous exercise of powers not granted by the Constitution" could ever justify secession, Buchanan played into the disunionists' hands. The fire-eaters had convinced themselves that Lincoln posed precisely such a threat.

Astonishingly, Buchanan's message also called for new concessions to the South. "The Southern States, standing on the basis of the Constitution," Buchanan argued, have every right "to demand this act of justice from the States of the North. Should it be refused," he added sympathetically, "then the Constitution, to which all the States are parties, will have been willfully violated by one portion of them in a provision essential to the domestic security and happiness of the remainder. In that event, the injured States, after having first used all peaceful and constitutional means to obtain redress, would be justified in revolutionary resistance to the Government of the Union."[65] Insisting that his "supreme object" was to "preserve the Union" and head off "the shock of civil war," the message condemned the "long-continued and intemperate interference of the Northern people with the question of slavery in the Southern States." To provide a permanent answer, the president called for a constitutional amendment "recognizing the rights of the Southern States in regard to slavery in the Territories."[66]

Further clouding the issue, Buchanan concluded that the Constitution gave no power to either Congress or the executive "to coerce a State into submission which is attempting to withdraw, or has actually withdrawn."[67] In other words, the government could enforce the law against rebellious individuals, but not against states. Secession might be wrong, but it could not be prevented.

Many constitutional experts thought otherwise, recalling that the federal Militia Acts of 1794 and 1807 gave the president explicit authority to enforce the law in the various states. Indeed, in 1794, George Washington had not only authorized sending national troops into battle against Pennsylvanians resisting the whiskey tax, he had taken to the field to lead the forces himself. Later, Andrew Jackson had acted boldly to crush South Carolina's attempt to nullify the 1832 tariff. Yet another military hero, Winfield Scott, forcibly reminded Buchanan of the Jackson precedent at a White House meeting and a follow-up memorandum, but the president increasingly resented the old general's intrusions into policy-making.[68] Not that Buchanan made any new policy. He chose instead to do nothing.

On December 3, Buchanan sent his annual message to Capitol Hill, where tradition required that it be read aloud by a clerk in each chamber of Congress. In the House, members strained "to catch every word. . . . Never was any document listened to with such marked attention before."[69] Listening from his seat on the Republican side in the new Senate chamber of the Capitol,[70] John Parker Hale of New Hampshire could hardly believe his ears. As he interpreted the president's convoluted argument, "South Carolina has just cause for seceding from the Union . . . she has no right to secede . . . [and] we have no right to prevent her from seceding." As Hale put it, "the power of the country, if I understand the President, consists in what Dickens makes the English constitution to be—a power to do nothing at all."[71]

William H. Seward's lacerating reaction was much the same: "It shows conclusively that it is the duty of the President to execute the laws—unless somebody opposes him—and that no State has the right to go out of the Union—unless it wants to."[72] Agreed freshman Massachusetts congressman Charles Francis Adams: "It was in all respects like the author, timid and vacillating in the face of slaveholding rebellion, bold and insulting toward his countrymen whom he does not fear."[73]

As always, the chief executive's words made headlines. Most major newspapers reprinted the text in full. But if Buchanan thought it would calm the crisis, he soon learned otherwise. Instead it managed to outrage Northerners and Southerners alike—some of the latter within his own cabinet, for a start, and even before the message arrived on the Hill. After learning that the president planned mildly to denounce secession, even though he would neither offer a plan nor cite lawful means to prevent it, Secretary of the Treasury Howell Cobb, a Georgian, and Secretary of the Interior Jacob Thompson, a Mississippian, both informed Buchanan they would resign from his administration in its final days.[74]

With only three short but dangerous months left in his term, the president's last few remaining allies now deserted him—including the Southerners he had worked so long and so hard to court. Jefferson Davis and the fire-eaters in Washington abruptly ended "all friendly intercourse" with the president, "political or social."[75] Anti-slavery Northerners became no less hostile. Although the Democratic press applauded the annual message—one Boston paper declared that Buchanan had "found a more excellent way than the common for settling a great family quarrel"[76]—Republican newspapers denounced it, the New York Times judging the message "the most elaborate effort Mr. Buchanan has ever made to appear bold without taking any risks."

As the paper continued: "It is hard to believe that Mr. Buchanan is a conscious accomplice in the treason he is doing so much to aid;—but we can arrive at no other conclusion without impeaching his intelligence and his personal courage." Mocking the president for arguing that, to subdue secession, he needed Congress to give him more power, though he doubted Congress's authority to do so, the paper concluded: "It seems incredible that any man holding a high official position should put forth such an argument. . . . The truth is, the Message is only laughed at by all parties."[77] To abolitionists like Harriet Beecher Stowe, the result was more a tragedy. " 'The fool hath said in his heart there is no God,' " she wrote, quoting the Bible.[78]

Back in Springfield, Lincoln was not smiling either. Instead, he "freely gave vent to his surprise" when he read the initial telegraphed synopsis of the annual message. According to one observer, he seemed particularly rankled by Buchanan's "desire to rest the whole responsibility of the secession movement on the Free States." His own views, he believed, had been badly "misrepresented." And he was further irritated when he read Buchanan's assertion that "the election of any one of our fellow-citizens to the office of President does not of itself afford just cause for dissolving the Union," even if, as Buchanan had disdainfully put it, "the antecedents of the President elect have been sufficient to justify the fears of the South that he will attempt to invade their constitutional rights."[79]

Quickly rising to Lincoln's defense, Springfield's pro-Republican *Illinois State Journal* huffed, "will Mr. Buchanan please explain where he gets such information in regard to Mr. Lincoln's 'antecedents'? What authority has he for making such reckless assertions in a grave State paper, or for throwing such suspicions in advance upon Mr. Lincoln's position?"[80] Sure as Buchanan remained that the secession crisis would ebb with no further intervention, one correspondent lamented to Lincoln: "Do you not think that the wicked schemes of the Disunionists might have been frustrated if the president had . . . declared that it was a matter not admitting of discussion and that he would use the whole power of the government to crush the first overt act toward accomplishing it[?]"[81] Unwilling to respond, Lincoln likely felt as frustrated as the *New York Times*, which worried: "The country has to struggle through three months more of this disgraceful imbecility and disloyalty to the Constitution."[82]

So did the president-elect. After reading the entire message, Lincoln "somewhat modified" his initial hostility, at least according to the press. He reportedly viewed Buchanan's anti-secession stand as "much bolder" than the first reports suggested.[83] But Lincoln never confirmed his generous second thoughts. And if anything, the public and press furor reenforced Lincoln's own vow of silence. If the sitting president's pandering valedictory message could arouse such indignation North as well as South, what chance did a minority president-elect have to mollify both regions with anything he might venture to say before his inauguration?

"Much has been said about the propriety of your saying or writing something now that you are President elect, to satisfy and appease the South," wrote Pennsylvania congressman George Nicholas Eckert, "to prove to them . . . that you are not the black republican and abolitionist alledged [sic] & insisted upon by the democracy and pretended by the South." But as Eckert cautioned the president-elect: "In my judgment any thing that you could or would say . . . would be perverted, misconstrued and prove worse than useless. They have hardened their hearts not only against you, but against all people of the free states (except the miserable creatures who justify the Southern States in their own course) and would not believe tho' one 'rose from the dead.' "[84]

Another congressman, Elihu Washburne of Illinois, said much the same thing in his own letter to the president-elect: "What we most want is a 'masterly inactivity.' "[85] For the time being, Lincoln agreed.

ON DECEMBER 5, Illinois's eleven victorious presidential electors braved a two-day-long "heavy fall of snow"[86] to gather in Springfield to register the official ballots that voters had elected them to cast a month earlier. Most of the out-of-towners made it a holiday, bringing friends and family to the ceremony, filling hotels and bars, and reenlivening the city after a brief post-Thanksgiving lull.[87] Lincoln treated those who made it into Springfield the evening before the caucus to "segars and things spirituous" at his State House headquarters.[88]

Among these electors were friends and allies who had loyally supported Lincoln for years, each of them now poised to culminate his longtime devotion with a ballot representing thousands of Republican voters. Here among them was bespectacled Leonard Swett, co-manager of the Lincoln team at May's Republican convention, now rumored to be advocating Simon Cameron's appointment to the cabinet—a deal, some whispered, he had engineered to woo Pennsylvania's delegates over to Lincoln. Here was Lincoln's fellow lawyer-politician John M. Palmer, a onetime Democrat who had chaired the 1856 convention at which the Illinois Republican party was founded. Here, too, were Republican committeeman James Cook Conkling, whose wife, Mercy, was a friend of Mary Lincoln's; Bloomington lawyer and state legislator Lawrence Weldon (destined for appointment as district attorney for the state's Southern District); and the Canton, Illinois, congressman, William Pitt Kellogg, soon to earn a federal appointment of his own from the incoming president.[89] At high noon, all eleven assembled in the Senate Chamber of the State Capitol, just across the hall from the president-elect's reception rooms.

This was a ritual nearly as old as the Constitution itself. As Illinois's electors gathered to cast votes, electors throughout the nation did likewise. John Greenleaf Whittier would be voting for Lincoln this day in Massachusetts, William Cullen Bryant in New York. "I think I have . . . told you that the people of the United States do not vote directly for President and Vice President, but only indirectly," John G. Nicolay felt obliged to explain to his finacée. "Each state votes for a number of Electors equal to the number of Representatives and Senators which the State has in Congress."[90] It was a sound enough description, even if it failed to detail the occasion's pageantry.

In Springfield, as a hundred excited witnesses, among them Governor-elect Richard Yates, looked on—conspicuously absent, Lincoln remained in his suite—the Illinois electors officially convened, selected a chairman and a recording secretary, and named Leonard Swett to serve as the messenger to transport the result to Washington. Then, one by one, each elector pronounced his credentials, and proceeded down the aisle to deposit his vote in a hat resting on a small table.[91] Once the ballots were counted, the chairman officially declared that Lincoln had received all of Illinois's eleven electoral votes for president. The electors nearly adjourned before someone remembered that they were also required to cast separate ballots for vice president. So they hastily repeated the procedure and, as expected, gave their votes unanimously to Hannibal Hamlin.

By two o'clock they certified the results, composed and signed two copies of the tabulations on blue-lined foolscap paper—what we would today call legal-size pads—each attesting that "Abraham Lincoln of Illinois received eleven votes being the whole number of votes cast for President at said balloting." Then, together with an authorizing document signed by outgoing Governor Wood, the clerk folded the paperwork into blue-colored, four-inch-by-nine-and-a-half-inch envelopes, and closed them shut with eagle-encrusted red wax seals. On the back of each envelope, all eleven electors signed a statement attesting that the true results of the voting were "contained herein." Both envelopes—one sent by mail, the other entrusted to Swett to carry to Washington—were then addressed to the president of the Senate in Washington. By a trick of history, he happened to be John C. Breckinridge, the Kentucky Democrat who had lost the election he would now be required to certify.[92]

"*C'est tout*," a relieved John Nicolay exhaled. "These Electors met today in every State in the Union (or at least it was their duty to do so) and voted for the future Executive. The vote so cast, is sealed up and forwarded by special messenger to Washington City, where it will be opened and counted by the Senate and House of Representatives next February."[93] Lincoln was at last, in the *New York Herald*'s words, "the *bona fide* President of the United States."[94] No doubt relieved, he celebrated the milestone with Mary at a "very pleasant" dinner for twenty hosted by elector Conkling at his Monroe Street home. While his host worried privately that Lincoln would "have a very troublesome administration provided he shall be inaugurated at all," supporters outside hoisted a flag over the State House and fired an exuberant forty-four-gun salute: thirty-three for the states of the Union, and eleven for the electors who had made Lincoln's victory official.[95]

There would be no other celebration. The only further acknowledgment of Lincoln's new status went on display that day in the nearby window of Springfield's leading tailor, Woods & Henckle, from whom Lincoln had purchased the ill-fitting $100 suit he wore at Cooper Union.[96] But the president-elect's days as a paying customer were apparently over. The haberdashery now placed on exhibit an "elaborate . . . handsome and elegantly made dress coat," which it now intended to present to Lincoln as a gift.[97] The press treated the balloting as a relatively minor story. Was Lincoln himself old news now? *Frank Leslie's Illustrated Newspaper* marked the momentous week by publishing what it called a "splendid" full-page engraving not of the president-elect but of Mary with her two boys.[98] She loathed it.

In truth, many Americans were still learning about their newly elected—and now newly reconfirmed—president. Until May, Abraham Lincoln had been little known outside Illinois. As late as November 27, the *Chicago Tribune* thought it necessary to publish yet another "sketch of Lincoln's early days," portraying him as "toiling under the weight of poverty with a view of better days."[99] By now the outlines of his biography had grown familiar. But readers were surely surprised when the reigning bible of technology, *Scientific American*—otherwise devoting its latest issue to newly invented carriage wheels and gas meters—focused, too, on an eleven-year-old device for buoying vessels over river shoals.[100] Neither the blueprint, nor the four-foot wooden model he had first floated in a Springfield trough more than eleven years earlier,[101] had matured to the development phase, and in truth seemed unlikely to work. But the editors had learned it had been invented "by no less a personage than the President elect of the United States." Abraham Lincoln's 1849 patent (number 6469), though it had failed to attract investors, much less revolutionize river travel as once he had dreamed, now received the full *Scientific American* treatment, with the would-be inventor's handmade wooden model exhaustively described and faithfully reproduced in woodcut.[102]

The journal tactfully sidestepped the scientific merits of Lincoln's idea, gently conceding that "we hope the author of it will have better success in presiding as Chief Magistrate over the people of the entire Union than he has had as an inventor." But the magazine was clearly impressed, suggesting that Lincoln's little-known foray into science demonstrated "the variety of talents possessed by men"—one man in particular. In fact, no other president before or since has ever held a federal patent. As the magazine pointed out, "it is probable that among our readers there are thousands of mechanics who would devise a better apparatus for buoying steamboats over [sand]bars, but how many of them would be able to compete successfully in the race for the Presidency?"[103]

Not everyone would have agreed. William H. Prentice, a local Methodist minister who, like many of the twenty-four preachers in Springfield,[104] had supported Stephen A. Douglas for president and doubtless wished that the Little Giant, not Lincoln, was headed for the White House, heard directly from the senator himself around the same time. "I regret to say that our country is now in imminent danger," Douglas wrote gloomily. "I know not that the Union can be saved. . . . We must put our trust in God as our only hope."[105]

The situation tested Lincoln's faith, too. Years later, his office neighbor Newton Bateman alleged that Lincoln confided to him: "I know there is a God, and that He hates injustice and slavery. I see the storm coming, and I know that his hand is in it. If He has a place and work for me—and I think He has—I believe I am ready." Far easier to believe was Bateman's further recollection that of God's ministers in Springfield, most of whom were Democrats, Lincoln had added ruefully: "these men will find that they have not read their Bibles right."[106] Where the slavery issue was concerned, Lincoln hinted, God knew better than his messengers.

A few weeks earlier, a voice of almost equal influence had been heard from Georgia. On November 14, the spectrally frail but widely respected Senator Alexander H. Stephens addressed his state legislature, "not to stir up strife," he began his oration, "but to allay it; not to appeal to your passions, but to your reason." Asking himself—and his fellow Southerners—"shall the people of the South secede from the Union in consequence of the election of Mr. Lincoln to the Presidency of the United States," Stephens answered unequivocally in the negative. "My countrymen, *I tell you frankly, candidly, and earnestly, that I do not think that they ought*. In my judgment, the election of no man, constitutionally chosen to that high office, is sufficient cause for any State to separate from the Union."[107]

This was just the sort of news Lincoln hoped to hear. Desperate for signs of loyalty from the Deep South, but incurably cautious, Lincoln's first reaction was to write to Stephens, his onetime Whig congressional colleague back in the late 1840s, merely to ask whether the first newspaper reports of the oration were accurate.[108] As Lincoln surely understood, the senator had no way of knowing whether Northern papers had faithfully reprinted, or hopelessly mangled, his speech. Perhaps recognizing that Lincoln may have posed the unanswerable question in order to open a dialogue with a leading Southerner, Stephens courteously replied that he believed that the initial reports could be relied on.

It came as little surprise when Springfield's Republican paper went on to hail Stephens as "a patriotic, Union-loving man" with "the spirit of a hero in opposing the mad schemes of the Secessionists."[109] Indiana editor John Defrees reported hopefully to Lincoln that "a re-action has set in at the South, as shown by Stephen's [sic] speech," adding: "Prudence (or what is called a 'masterly inactivity,') on our part, at present, will bring all right in the end."[110] For the next few weeks, the president-elect pondered a conciliatory reply to his onetime fellow Whig. He seemed oblivious to the contrary message of Stephens's fiery Senate colleague, Robert Toombs, who on December 7 urged Georgians to "strike while it is yet to-day. Withdraw your sons from the army, the navy, and every department of the federal public service. Keep your own taxes in your own coffers; buy arms with them and throw the bloody spear into this den of incendiaries and assassins, and let God defend the right."[111]

Perhaps silence—or the phrase du jour, "masterly inactivity"—was still golden, but was Lincoln really in a conciliatory mood? A subtle indication that such was not the case came when a Springfield hardware dealer asked his famous neighbor to write out the most celebrated passage from the most radical speech he had ever given on slavery. The president-elect might easily have declined the request for the incendiary souvenir and as usual referred Edward D. Pease to existing published versions. Instead, perhaps just to vent his frustrations, Lincoln took a pencil in hand and meticulously copied, then signed, the very phrases that had convinced many Southerners that he now posed a serious danger. "A house divided against itself cannot stand," he scribbled afresh.

I believe this government cannot endure permanently half slave and half free. I do not expect the Union to be dissolved. I do not expect the house to fall; but I do expect it will cease to be divided. It will become all one thing or all the other. Either the opponents of slavery will arrest the further spread of it, and place it where the public mind shall rest in the belief that it is in the course of ultimate extinction; or its advocates will push it forward till it will become alike lawful in all the States old as well as new—North as well as South.[112]

What did Lincoln really think? Did he believe that Southern moderates like Alexander H. Stephens could successfully convince secessionists that a Lincoln administration would pose no threat to slavery where it existed? Or did he see some advantage to reiterating extracts from his most dire predictions of a do-or-die national upheaval over the same slavery issue? In John Nicolay's view, while "not unmindful of the troubles which are on hand, and while he sincerely wishes they were not existing," Lincoln was ". . . nevertheless not in the least intimidated or frightened by them."[113] The exasperated private secretary insisted: "If the caprices of one or half a dozen States is to be stronger than our Constitution, then in God's name the sooner we make the discovery the better."[114]

A MONTH AND MORE had passed since Election Day, and now Lincoln made one more crucial decision. He would postpone cabinet selection—at least the appointment of his leading cabinet minister—no longer. On December 8, he dispatched two separate personal notes to Senator William H. Seward, via Vice President–elect Hamlin, who was back in Washington to serve out his final weeks in the Senate.

Lincoln invited Hamlin to read the enclosures first, consult as needed with Senator Trumbull, and then, if he saw "no reason to the contrary, deliver the letter to Governor Seward at once." Though Hamlin raised no objections after studying the letters, he hesitated—first trying to enlist Seward's fellow New York senator, Preston King, to act as an intermediary. But King insisted that Hamlin go directly to Seward after all, and Hamlin, though still convinced Seward "will not desire a place in your Cabinet,"[115] dutifully handed him Lincoln's letters on December

14. The first handwritten note was the long-expected formal appointment to the highest office within Lincoln's powers to devolve: "With your permission, I shall, at the proper time, nominate you to the Senate, for confirmation as Secretary of State, for the United States."[116]

The second *"Private & Confidential"* letter made clear that the president-elect meant the appointment as more than a courtesy. "Rumors have got into the newspapers to the effect that the Department . . . would be tendered you, as a compliment, and with the expectation that you would decline it," Lincoln conceded, diplomatically ignoring the fact that the rumors had originated with Seward's own political patron, Thurlow Weed. "I beg you to be assured that I have said nothing to justify these rumors. On the contrary, it has been my purpose, from the day of the nomination at Chicago, to assign you, by your leave, this place in the administration." Lincoln here went one astonishing step further than he did later in recounting the selection process for the benefit of Gideon Welles. Not only had he settled on Seward as secretary of state on Election Day. He wanted Seward to believe he had done so on *nomination* day, six months earlier! In which case, the president-elect must explain his seeming hesitation:

> I have delayed so long to communicate that purpose, in deference to what appeared to me to be a proper caution in the case. Nothing has been developed to change my view in the premises; and I now offer you the place, in the hope that you will accept it, and with the belief that your position in the public eye, your integrity, ability, learning, and great experience, all combine to render it an appointment pre-eminently fit to be made.[117]

If Lincoln believed Seward would leap at the invitation, he was mistaken. Now it was the senator's turn to express "proper caution." Cagily arguing that he needed "a little time to consider whether I possess the qualifications and temper of a minister and whether it is in such a capacity that my friends would prefer that I should act if I am to continue at all in the public service," the wily Seward left his own "conclusions" unstated. Congressman Elihu Washburne admitted to Lincoln that he could not discern precisely "how Seward feels about Cabinet matters . . . for he guards himself with such vigilance in regard to such matters that his most intimate friends are not able to ascertain his views or wishes."[118] It would be more than two weeks before Seward deigned to share his decision with the president-elect.[119] Meantime, Springfield faced a premature winter, as temperatures plunged below zero and fierce winds whipped through the frozen streets.[120] As a man who believed in signs and omens, Lincoln must have hoped the change in the weather did not presage a chill in his relationship with the senator from the Empire State.

It did not help matters that Seward's New York enemies—many of whom had helped make Lincoln's nomination possible—now moved aggressively to block the appointment. Arguing that "Seward & Sewardism" were "the potent & original causes" of the secession crisis, Long Island nursery owner William P. Prince, for example, warned the president-elect that Seward's name "would be a blight & a curse to your Admina which he has striven *to blight in* advance by the malign influence of his fanatic harangues since your nomination."[121] Influential *Evening Post* editor William Cullen Bryant urged Lincoln to instead give the highest cabinet post to "one of the noblest and truest among the great leaders" of the party—namely the "wise, pure, fair-minded, practical" Salmon P. Chase.[122] Personally greeting Senator Trumbull as he passed through the city en route to the capital, Bryant advised Lincoln's Washington emissary that Seward's political operative, Thurlow Weed, was mired in a job corruption scheme involving New York's state legislature. The scandal, Bryant insisted, tarnished the senator beyond repair. A Seward appointment was bound to "bring with it a set of dishonest men."[123]

Lincoln would hear none of it; his mind was made up. "I regret exceedingly the anxiety of our friends in New-York," he instructed Trumbull. But now to snub the state's loyal Seward supporters—they had, after all, remained unified behind their senator throughout the balloting at the Republican convention—would constitute a grave political insult. "I will, myself, take care of the question of 'corrupt jobs[,]' " assured the president-elect, "and see that justice is done to all, our friends, of whom you write, as well as others." Even cabinet appointments seemed tethered to patronage issues.

While Seward kept Lincoln dangling, the president-elect turned his attention to his remaining cabinet options, leaving further evidence that, other than Seward for State, he had settled on no other choices by early December. With Hannibal Hamlin, for example, he shared "an intimation that Governor [Nathaniel] Banks [of Massachusetts] would yet accept a place in the Cabinet." If Lincoln thought this would settle the need for a New Englander, he quickly learned otherwise. Taking the opportunity to speak authoritatively for his region, Hamlin replied that he not only preferred Massachusetts governor-elect John A. Andrew, or Connecticut editor Gideon Welles, but regarded Banks as "wonderfully cold and selfish," adding: "I do not hear him talked of by our N. E. friends."[124] Much as Welles later preferred to believe—with Lincoln's encouragement—that he was the future president's first and only cabinet choice from New England, the correspondence with Hamlin suggests that as late as the first week of December, Lincoln remained undecided, and was looking elsewhere.

Lincoln's mailbag continued to bring him a conflicting raft of suggestions—some practical, some intriguing, others ridiculously farfetched, but all of them read and preserved in Lincoln's files. What was he to make of such advice, if anything? One correspondent who had served as sergeant-at-arms in the House of Representatives during Lincoln's sole term in Congress suggested Ohio senator Thomas Ewing for State, claiming he possessed "the most elephantine mental proportions of any man now living in the United States."[125] A former Republican congressman from Wisconsin thought the party's 1856 presidential candidate, John C. Frémont, "would be found equal to any emergency" as secretary of war.[126] A freshly reelected Michigan congressman believed his state's U.S. senator, Zachariah Chandler, ought to be postmaster general because he "knows how to do business as Homer knew *how* to write poetry."[127] From Washington came the plea that Lincoln appoint Stephen A. Douglas as secretary of the interior to "give him a chance to pursue his desire of many years, a rail road to the Pacific Ocean."[128] And one Pennsylvania Republican urged Lincoln to consider someone who had served as a cabinet official decades earlier under James Monroe— Supreme Court Justice John McLean—conceding the old man would probably not accept (in fact he died soon after Lincoln's inauguration).[129] On the other hand, an anonymous "friend" from Washington begged Lincoln to deny a rumored place for Indiana congressman Schuyler Colfax, "a plodding little fellow, who edits a six by nine Country paper, and would make a good Clerk at $1,000 a year."[130]

The clamor grew, too, for Southern representation in the cabinet. A Peekskill, New York, editor called on Lincoln to open a spot for the old Texas hero Sam Houston.[131] A bitter Illinois banker, ruined by the Panic of 1857, recommended Kentucky's Cassius M. Clay as secretary of war because "he understands the temper of the South better than any Northern-man, and [is] better *entitled* to it than any Southern-man."[132] The president of the Pennsylvania Railroad suggested Lincoln soothe "disaffection at the South" by naming former Democratic senator John Pendleton King of Georgia.[133] And Indiana's John Defrees expressed his belief that the inclusion of Winfield Scott of Virginia, Alexander Stephens of Georgia, and Edward Bates of Missouri "would do much to bring about a re-action among the people of all the Southern States except S. Carolina, which is insane beyond hope of cure."[134] (Stephens himself later branded as "totally groundless" the "rumor" that he had ever discussed a cabinet appointment with the president-elect.[135])

"You are a Kentuckian," chided an anonymous, self-described kinsman from Louisville. "Why not announce your Cabinet with some *Southern* conservatism in it? Or show yr kindly disposition to the South by *making the offer* to such men as [John] Crittenden, H[o]uston, Stevens, Bell, et. al. If they do not accept, you will have done your duty so far as yr feelings to the South is concerned.[136] Hoosier Defrees agreed that a Southern appointee, especially Stephens, would signal "that the Republicans do not intend making war upon the Constitutional rights of the South."[137] Even the quintessential Yankee, Maine's Hannibal Hamlin, concurred. "Should not *one* man of the South of Dem. Ante-

cedents be in your Cabinet?" he inquired on December 4, adding: "I think so—."[138]

Nearing mid-month, however, Lincoln seemed to be leaning to the view that he could not, should not, include a Deep South Democrat in the cabinet of the first Republican president. "The secessionists are still rampant," John Nicolay reported on December 9, no doubt reflecting Lincoln's own grim view, "and everybody in the extreme southern states is settled in the belief that the Union is to be dissolved."[139] The raw political reality was this: even if Lincoln were determined to find such a minister—Seward, for one, recommended John A. Gilmer of North Carolina—indications grew stronger by the day that no qualified Southerner would be willing to join his administration. A public rebuff would be humiliating.

On December 12, Lincoln decided to make his quandary public. That morning, Springfield's pro-Republican newspaper—"Lincoln's organ," his enemies suggestively called it—published an extraordinary editorial wondering "what terms" would be required in order to bring "two or three Southern gentlemen, from the parties opposed to him politically," into his cabinet. "Does he surrender to Mr. Lincoln, or Mr. Lincoln to him, on the political difference between them? Or do they enter upon the administration in open opposition to each other?"[140] Within days, the New York papers reprinted the editorial.[141] Its pugnacious literary style left little doubt as to its authorship. Lincoln wrote the words himself[142]—and with their publication made it clear he was close to ruling out the possibility of placing opposition Southerners in his official family. This view, too, would change again.

At the end of the month, Lincoln confided to Seward that he still harbored the hope that Gilmer would consider an appointment. "I wrote him, requesting him to visit me here; and my object was that if, on full understanding of my position, he would accept a place in the cabinet, to give it to him. He has neither come, nor answered me." Now Lincoln beseeched Seward to "ascertain his feelings, and write me." To Lincoln's disappointment or relief, the North Carolina congressman concluded that a face-to-face interview "would not be useful."[143]

No potential appointment, however, stirred as much controversy, anxiety, speculation, or sheer bulk of correspondence as Lincoln's supposed obligation to Simon Cameron of Pennsylvania. There could be no doubt that the mid-convention switch of Cameron's delegates to Illinois's favorite son had crushed Seward's chances and propelled Lincoln to the Republican nomination. The only question was whether Lincoln's managers had secured this momentum-altering support by promising Pennsylvania's favorite son a place in the future cabinet. The mystery has never been definitively solved—no hard evidence has ever been uncovered to prove that Lincoln men and Cameron men struck such a bargain. Still, Pennsylvania's voters had gone on to give Lincoln a decisive victory in November, bolstering the state's already formidable claims to a cabinet post in an era when regional representation—especially in the wake of sectional discord—remained important.

The only obstacle was Cameron himself. Though he had campaigned loyally and effectively for Lincoln, helping to repel President Buchanan's efforts to unite their state's Democrats around the candidacy of John C. Breckinridge, the senator and former governor had never quite shed the image of corrupt politician. Over the years, Cameron had assembled a vast personal fortune from a dizzying array of enterprises, nearly all of them at least in part facilitated, many believed, by political influence.

Many of Cameron's fellow senior Republicans distrusted him, and were inclined to oppose his inclusion in the cabinet, particularly for the job to which he aspired: secretary of the treasury. Lincoln's problem was that if he rewarded Pennsylvania at all, Cameron alone deserved to be recognized—there was no one else in the Keystone State with an equal claim to an appointment. As Philadelphia printer R. P. King put it: "Should you determine to have our goodly state represented in your Cabinet, pray give us a man . . . acceptable to the masses," namely Cameron, "who, by his own unaided industry, and indomitable energy, has risen, from being the poor Printer's boy, to the high & honorable position of United States Senator. He is emphatically one of *us*—one of the *People*."[144]

Once the press began speculating that Cameron might be in the running, Lincoln found himself inundated with correspondence—pro and con alike, much of the former well organized by Cameron's efficient political machine. On December 12, ten Pennsylvania congressmen signed a letter testifying to "the fitness of Hon. Simon Cameron for this distinguished, honorable and influential position." [145] On the other hand, an anonymous correspondent warned: "Do not be persuaded to give dishonest Ungodly Men eny [sic] office whatever." [146] Countered State Senator G. Rush Smith of Philadelphia: Cameron is the "representative man of our state, towering above all others in power and influence." [147] It was but the opening volley in a relentless torrent of both ardently supportive and bitterly hostile Cameron correspondence that poured into Springfield for weeks.

By this time, Lincoln might have wished he had paid more attention to John Defrees's pre-Thanksgiving recommendation: "The adoption of a rule, excluding members of Congress from Executive appointments, during the term for which they were elected, would be right in itself, and would remove many difficulties which now surround you." As Defrees saw it: "If the wisdom and statesmanship of the country was monopolized by Congress, it might be different; but fortunately it is not. The people did not go to Congress for a President; nor, is it necessary, or expedient, to go there for his appointees for office." [148] By then, it was too late. Lincoln had already "gone to Congress" for one prospective appointment. Now, as he pondered an offer to Cameron, he anxiously awaited Senator William H. Seward's reply.

Chapter Five

The Tug Has to Come

IT WAS MID-DECEMBER, an early winter had sapped the election season exuberance from Springfield, and to make matters worse, the president-elect still had no cabinet. William H. Seward was yet to accept Lincoln's invitation to take the State Department, while potential candidates and their supporters clamored for the remaining posts.

"It has been raining, snowing, sleeting, blowing, and freezing for eight days," Henry Villard complained on the 15th. Springfield had degenerated into "one grand mud hole." With every wet street reduced to "a miniature 'slough of despond,' " the local Republican newspaper reported, it was no wonder that even the president-elect seemed infected with "melancholy feelings."[1] Springfield's opposition *Daily State Register* did not disagree, though it mischievously saw a silver lining. Facing both miserable weather and "no encouragement," many office-seekers were now "saving their travelling expenses" and avoiding the "desperately muddy and dull" city. Lincoln's exhausting public receptions were "about played out."[2]

Even in the temporary absence of visitors, however, letters continued pouring into Springfield advising the president-elect to choose (or reject) Salmon P. Chase of Ohio, Simon Cameron of Pennsylvania, Norman Judd of Illinois, defeated presidential candidate John Bell of

Tennessee, and both Schuyler Colfax or Caleb B. Smith of Indiana. Weighing the cascading rumors, Chicago editor Joseph Medill counseled Lincoln to reject "discordant elements" that might "add fuel to the flames" and include only cabinet candidates who were "homogenous in sentiment."[3] Against all expectations, even as the secession crisis worsened, Lincoln again looked south.

Turning to another disappointed onetime aspirant for his party's 1860 presidential nomination, Lincoln reached out to the venerable Missouri politician Edward Bates, proposing that the two men meet in St. Louis to discuss the future. Virginia born, sixty-seven years old, and, most usefully, the conservative favorite son of an Upper South slave state, Bates had been the most conservative of the Republican aspirants for the nation's highest office. On the other side of the political ledger, Missouri's influential German-born Republicans disliked him intensely for his earlier flirtation with the anti-immigrant Know-Nothing party.

Lincoln apparently concluded, now that the election was won, that the struggle to hold the Union together outweighed any obligation to his loyal German-American supporters. Just a week earlier, coincidentally, he had quietly terminated a little known year-and-a-half-long stint as silent co-owner of Springfield's German language newspaper. Lincoln had invested $400 in the publication in 1859 to ensure its total loyalty to the Republican party. Mission accomplished, he now turned over full ownership of the *Illinois Staats-Anzeiger*, presses, type, and all, to his neighbor, editor Theodore Canisius. (Later, Lincoln further rewarded Canisius with a more valuable commodity: the consulate in Vienna.)[4]

Showing much grace, Bates told Lincoln he "saw an unfitness in *his coming to see me*," and instead proposed journeying "*to see him*" in Springfield.[5] While they exchanged messages, Lincoln welcomed to town another Missourian, Congressman Francis Preston Blair, Jr., whose powerful, Kentucky-born family yearned for cabinet recognition as well.[6] It was the Blair meeting that apparently inspired Lincoln to pen the little anonymous editorial questioning his obligation to appoint *any* Southerner. Yet here he was, conferring with one Missouri politician and arranging to meet another. Lincoln's behind-the-scenes maneuvering leaves little doubt he remained willing to explore all of his options when it came to cabinet-making. Finding a Deep South candidate still seemed unlikely. As Lincoln irritably pointed out—not for the first time—when Indiana party chairman John Defrees proposed cabinet appointments for Virginian Robert E. Scott and Georgian Alexander H. Stephens: "Would Scott or Stephens go into the cabinet? And if yea, on what terms?" Perhaps unconsciously echoing Bates's recently expressed concerns about travel protocol, he wondered: "Do they come to me? or I go to them? or are we to lead off in open hostility to each other?" [7]

Burdened with no such hostility to Lincoln, Bates arrived in Springfield on Friday night, December 14, and took a room at the Chenery House. The next morning, one of the hotel's residents, John Nicolay,[8] spotted him at the breakfast table. "He is not of impressive exterior," the secretary grimly observed. "His hair is gray, his beard quite white, and his face shows all the marks of age quite strongly." But he proved energetic. Bates called on Lincoln at the Capitol at 9 A.M., an hour before visiting hours officially commenced, offering "profuse civilities and apologies." Only after a three-hour break to allow Lincoln to fulfill his daily obligations to the public did he settle in for a "very cordial" private meeting.[9] Bates likely discovered Lincoln, as did a Philadelphia reporter who first glimpsed him around the same time, seated close to his office stove, his long body so oddly angled it looked like it could be "cut in two three times," his face "strongly-marked and by no means handsome."[10]

Lincoln tried mightily to charm his distinguished visitor. Taking the same tack he had employed in his week-old letter to Seward, he asked Bates to believe that he had hoped to interview him ever since the May nominating convention in order to offer a cabinet position. He had hesitated, he professed, only "to be enabled to act with caution," but now was prepared to bestow on Bates a place in his official family. Explaining that he had already offered Seward the post of secretary of state, but did not want to "burden" the elderly Missourian "with one of the drudgery offices," Lincoln asked him to take the attorney generalship, "for which he was certainly in every way qualified."[11]

As Bates interpreted the conversation, Lincoln already regretted his overture to Seward and his supporters. The New Yorker's appointment would invariably both offend anti-Seward Republicans and "exasperate the feelings of the South," making "conciliation impossible, because they consider Mr. S. the embodiment of all that they hold odious in the Republican party." Yet the president-elect confided it would "*rupture*" the party to deny him, even though his acceptance was bound to "weaken the administration."

Digesting all this, Bates inferred that he might yet get the top cabinet position if Seward declined. He left his meeting with Lincoln convinced that "I am the only man that he desired in the Cabinet, to whom he has yet spoken [or] . . . written a word, about their own appointments[.]" As "a matter of duty," Bates recalled, fully under Lincoln's spell, "I accepted his invitation."[12] It was Lincoln's singular talent for manipulating subordinates and peers alike that he could so easily convince two sophisticated men simultaneously that they were each his first and only choice for the same job. Unbeknown to the Missourian, at around the same time the president-elect began wooing Bates, David Davis—surely at Lincoln's urging—wrote Thurlow Weed to urge that he head to Springfield "at once," no doubt to shore up the Seward appointment to the very post Bates was being led to believe might yet be his.[13]

Ignorant of that summons, Bates returned home and conferred with his own advisors, then wrote Lincoln to declare himself "fully committed to the work," suggesting that "a good effect might be produced on the public mind—especially in the border Slave States—by letting the people know (substantially) the relations which now subsist between us."[14] Lincoln agreed—that is, as long as he could once again convey his intentions through one of his favorite means of communication: the anonymously planted newspaper notice.

"Let a little editorial appear in the Missouri Democrat, in about these words," he wrote: " 'We have the permission of both Mr. Lincoln and Mr. Bates to say that the latter will be offered, and will accept, a place in the new Cabinet, subject of course to the action of the Senate. It is not yet definitely settled which Department will be assigned to Mr. Bates.' "[15] Within days, the *Missouri Democrat*—a Republican paper—obligingly published the news under the headline: "A Cabinet Appointment—Missouri First on the List," hailing the development as a triumph for "conservatism and union."[16]

As Lincoln's communiqué made clear, a Southerner would be joining the Lincoln administration after all. The effect on the South of having in the cabinet another of the contenders for the 1860 Republican presidential nomination, however, was yet untested.[17] Back in Springfield, the Democratic *State Register* made light of the entire issue, joking: "The question is . . . did the 'southern gentleman' 'surrender' to Mr. Lincoln or did Mr. Lincoln 'surrender' to the 'southern gentleman.' Just now, the opinion here is, the surrender was mutual."[18]

With the Bates matter settled, Lincoln turned his attention to other problems—including, to his annoyance, the impertinent correspondents who wrote in increasing numbers to predict his death or propose revolution or resignation to keep him from taking office.

There was the anonymous Wide-Awake who alerted him that a "clairvoyant" had, in a trance, foretold his death by poison. The correspondent advised him to "drink hot milk in Large Quantities—in order to frustrate the diabolicol [sic] plot." The warning did not inhibit Lincoln from gratefully telling a local fishmonger trying to press a free sample on him as he walked along Capitol Square: "I hardly think that I can carry it along now; but if you will take it up to my house, I reckon we will keep it."[19] In a more serious vein, Chicago journalist Horace White reported that "$40,000 had been subscribed in the St Charles Hotel, New Orleans, to procure the assassination of yourself & Hamlin." White worried that "some fool or fanatic might attempt to claim the reward."[20]

A self-described "humble citizen of St Louis" begged Lincoln to decline the vote of the Electoral College and resign the presidency before taking office, arguing it was the only way "to save this Glorious Union from the horrors of dissolution." A similar suggestion came from an anonymous correspondent from Alabama, promising that by declining the presidency Lincoln would earn "the thanks of millions of your fellow beings." Besides, the writer assured him, "The Government will vote you your salrey [sic] and a thousand thanks for the sacrifice[.]"[21] On the other hand, General David Hunter, whose grandfather had signed the Declaration of Independence, wrote from Fort Leavenworth to warn Lincoln that Southerners were plotting to send troops to Washington to prevent his inauguration, and must be stopped. He recommended that "a hundred thousand Wide Awakes, wend their way quietly to Washington," where they would be armed to guarantee "a triumphant result."[22] Lincoln advised Hunter to remain calm but alert: "The most we can do now is to watch events, and be as well prepared as possible for any turn things may take."[23] Soon Lincoln would invite Hunter to "watch events" at his side.

With South Carolina hurtling toward secession, Lincoln found little solace in the letter he received a few days earlier from "Yours in 'Israel' " who implored Lincoln to consult "Isaiah 41 Chapter 8, 9, 10, 11, 12 & 13." If indeed he turned to those verses, they painfully reminded him of God's words: "gird yourselves, and ye shall be broken in pieces."[24] Not that Lincoln lost faith. Newton Bateman, whose office sat next door to Lincoln's suite at the State House, claimed he saw the president-elect at the time removing from his coat pocket a "pocket New Testament," which he had supposedly been consulting as the pressure of earthly matters increased.[25] With spirituality in mind, perhaps, he changed druggists shortly before Christmas and began patronizing a new shop owned by a fellow parishioner at Springfield's First Presbyterian Church, Dr. Samuel Melvin. To Melvin, Lincoln turned for something else that ailed him: blue pills for his chronic constipation.[26]

It was little wonder that journalist Henry Villard reported around this time that, beard or no beard, "The appearance of Mr. Lincoln has somewhat changed to the worse . . . he looks more pale and careworn than heretofore." It was a relief to the correspondent to note that "the vigor of his mind and the steadiness of his humorous disposition" remained "obviously unimpaired." But it was precisely "his good nature" that concerned Villard.

"To receive everybody with uniform kindness—to indulge the general curiosity with untiring patience—to reply to all questions with unvarying readiness—to grant willing compliance to all requests . . . may be a very good and pleasing rule in private life," the journalist lectured,

"... but its general observation by so high-stationed a personage as the President of the United States . . . is fraught with many hazards and that from the very abuse of those for whose benefit it is practiced." Villard urged the president-elect to spend less time with "the groveling time-wasters, fawners, sycophants and parasites" plaguing him for office.[27] "Reserve must take the place of indiscriminating affability. His ears and eyes must learn to be closed at certain times. His lips must be trained to less ready and unqualified responses. If not, the crowd will unbalance and overwhelm him."[28]

Villard need not have worried. Behind the scenes, Lincoln was acting with a steely firmness the journalist would scarcely have recognized. While the president-elect chose not to respond to most of the warnings piling up on his desk at the State Capitol, he replied indignantly when Henry J. Raymond, the pro-Republican editor of the *New York Times*, forwarded Lincoln a heated letter from a racist Mississippi legislator named William C. Smedes. Smedes had seen a false report charging that Lincoln once delivered a speech in Cincinnati at an event at which free blacks presented a pitcher of some sort to Ohio senator Salmon P. Chase. This was more than enough to give offense to the white supremacist Mississippian. Smedes fulminated that he would regard "death by a stroke of lightning to Mr Lincoln as but a just punishment from an offended deity" for the outrage.[29]

Lincoln was mystified—and every bit as furious as his attacker. "What a very mad-man your correspondent, Smedes is," he replied to editor Raymond. "As to the pitcher story, it is a forgery out and out. I never made but one speech in Cincinnati. . . . I have never yet seen Gov. Chase. I was never in a meeting of negroes in my life; and never saw a pitcher presented by anybody to anybody." Lincoln might have ended his letter there, but decided the implication that he supported racial equality was worth rebutting—even though he still hoped to lure the liberal Chase, too, into his official family. Proud as he was of his anti-slavery record, Lincoln knew disaster would follow if wavering Southern states regarded him as pro–equal rights.

"Mr. Lincoln is not pledged to the ultimate extinctinction [sic] of slavery," he closed, struggling over the spelling of the word "extinction" as if he could hardly bear to write it—no surprise, since he had been saying precisely the opposite for years. Writing of himself uncharacteristically in the third person, he added that Lincoln "does not hold the black man to be the equal of the white, unqualifiedly . . . and never did stigmatize white people as immoral & unchristian."[30] Judged by modern attitudes on race, of course, this was not his finest moment. But it was wholly true to his long-expressed beliefs. The 1860 Republican platform guaranteed that the party would not interfere with slavery where it existed. And there is no evidence that Lincoln himself yet favored equality between the races. Most important of all, the president-elect knew that the mere rumor of such radical views would lose him whatever loyal friends he had in the border states—and perhaps mean the quick end of the Union, before his "inaugeration" could take place.[31]

EQUALLY IMPORTANT TO Lincoln—and potentially far more troubling—was the intelligence from Washington that the legislative branch had filled the void left by Lincoln's silence and seized the initiative on compromise.

On December 4, Trumbull reported from Washington that the House of Representatives had created what he described as "a committee on the State of the Union."[32] This "Committee of Thirty-three"—one member for each state (Kansas had yet to join the Union)—would draft its own plan to avert disunion and try to enact it before the new president and new Congress took office. Anti-slavery men like William Kellogg of Illinois and Charles Francis Adams of Massachusetts joined the panel, but so did pro-slavery Southerners. The parallel Senate Committee of Thirteen, though its creation was delayed and debated, came into being soon thereafter. It soon boasted such prestigious senior members as William H. Seward, Jefferson Davis, abolitionist Benjamin Wade of Ohio, and ultra Robert Toombs of Georgia, along with respected veterans Stephen A. Douglas of Illinois and John J. Crittenden of Kentucky, who had backed Douglas over Lincoln for the Senate in 1858.[33]

The news that Congress might appropriate to itself a legislative compromise to avert secession unsettled Lincoln. Much as he yearned for a peaceful resolution of the crisis before Inauguration Day, he did not want a lame-duck Congress to enact policy that would bind the new administration. Not if a compromise wedged the government into a proslavery position. Not if it permitted slavery to expand westward in violation of the 1860 Republican platform. Not if it arrogated powers Lincoln believed he was elected to exercise. And not if it left future decisions on

Benjamin Day's 1861 political cartoon showed Seward (right) and other pro-conciliation politicians trying to force compromise down Lincoln's throat, as the president-elect clings to the antislavery tenets of the Republican platform. (LIBRARY OF CONGRESS)

slavery to local constituencies, in total disregard of his longtime opposition to Stephen A. Douglas's doctrine of popular sovereignty.

Even before the political details crystallized, Lincoln began worrying that his fellow Republicans serving on these committees might waver on the vital test of barring the extension of slavery. After a visit to Washington during the first week of December, one confidant sought to reassure him that Republicans were holding fast to "one language, and that was—no yielding, even though the heavens fall."[34]

But Lincoln's concern only grew. Keeping the Western territories open to limitless opportunity for paid labor—and free of slaves—had been his holy grail since 1854, the year Douglas had engineered passage of the Kansas-Nebraska Act, which made possible the reverse. In Lincoln's mind, the Free Soil issue had elected him in November, and bound him for the future. Now, to his dismay, before he began his presidency, he sensed congressional Republicans might entertain softening the party's opposition to slavery extension in return for guarantees against secession. Lincoln could either remain silent or speak out—or something in between. One way or another, even before his inauguration, he might be compelled to choose what was more important: freedom or Union.

Lincoln's alternatives were not only ugly but potentially dangerous. By speaking out, the man who had taken such pains to maintain official silence could conceivably enter office facing either a sundered Republican base, or a shattered nation. Although it is inconceivable to think that Lincoln yet envisioned the possibility that a long and bloody civil war might be required to settle the question, he realized he now faced a decision every bit as momentous as any in his life. No president since Washington, the *New York Herald* editorialized, had ever had "so glorious an occasion . . . to have his memory revered by future generations, as the deliverer of his country from disunion, anarchy and disgrace."[35] Lincoln certainly read these words for himself.

One choice before Lincoln was to acquiesce through silence to conciliation that might well keep the country intact: up to and including exhumation of the discarded Missouri Compromise, which Douglas's Kansas-Nebraska legislation had effectively overturned and whose revival now might again limit slavery to the South but now allow it to migrate west. Or he could draw his own line in the sand and oppose compromise entirely, hoping that, until his swearing in, President Buchanan would at least enforce the laws, holding federal forts and collecting government revenues in the South, even if confronted with secession and resistance.[36] While Buchanan dithered, Lincoln chose. Discarding his longtime Whiggish belief in congressional supremacy, Lincoln forcefully interjected himself into the congressional debate. No previous president-elect ever made such a show of power and influence before his swearing in. He delivered no public speeches and issued no state papers on the compromise issue—to do so, he still believed, would only exacerbate matters by angering both antislavery men and border state conservatives. Instead, he made his views clear in a series of remarkably tough letters to key allies on Capitol Hill, which he knew would be widely shared with other Republicans. Hoping still to embolden Southern Unionists, or at best steel the rest of the country for the possible use of force to protect federal property and collect revenues, he now made it clear he would reject fundamental concessions that might guarantee both, but at the expense of slavery expansion.[37]

Lincoln's reply to Trumbull left little doubt where he stood. "Let there be no compromise on the question of *extending* slavery," came the pointed instructions. "If there be, all our labor is lost, and, ere long, must be done again. The dangerous ground—that into which some of our friends have a hankering to run—is Pop[ular]. Sov[reignty]. Have none of it. Stand firm. The tug has to come, & better now, than any time hereafter."[38]

The very next day, Lincoln employed the same emphatic phrase in a similar message to Illinois congressman William Kellogg, who had joined the new House committee seeking "the remedy for the present difficulties."[39] Reiterated Lincoln: "the tug has to come & better now than later."[40]

From Washington, Congressman Elihu B. Washburne worriedly alerted Lincoln that the "secessionist feeling has assumed proportions of which I had but a faint conception when I saw you at Springfield. . . . I am certainly no alarmist, but it is folly to attempt to shut one's eyes as to what is transpiring around us." In the congressman's grim view, South Carolina, Florida, and Mississippi were now as good as gone from the Union.[41]

That somber assessment failed to weaken the president-elect's resolve. Lincoln told Washburne that he would still not bend on the crucial issue of slavery expansion. What was more, as the new head of the Republican party, he expected loyalty and obedience from others. His self-assurance and literary panache on full display, Lincoln reiterated his firm policy on December 13: "Prevent, as far as possible, any of our friends from demoralizing themselves, and our cause, by entertaining propositions for compromise of any sort, on '*slavery extention* [sic].' There is no possible compromise upon it, but which puts us under again, and leaves all our work to do over again." Efforts to revive popular sovereignty, under which the residents of new territories could approve slavery by referendum, must be resisted. Plans to exhume the Missouri Compromise, effectively permitting slavery to expand westward south of the 36°30' parallel, must be rejected.

"Let either be done," warned the president-elect, "& immediately filibustering and extending slavery recommences. On that point hold firm, as with a chain of steel."[42]

After reading and no doubt sharing the president-elect's instructions with his colleagues, Washburne reported "a firmer feeling among our Republicans here, though we are not out of danger of a compromise."[43]

Four days later, Lincoln instructed Senator Trumbull to hold firm, too. "If any of our friends do prove false, and fix up a compromise on the territorial question, I am for fighting again—that is all. (It is but repetition for me to say I am for an honest inforcement of the constitution—fugitive slave clause included)." Then, the very next day, he warned Indiana state chairman John Defrees: "I am sorry any republican inclines to dally with Pop. Sov. of any sort. It acknowledges that slavery has equal rights with liberty, and surrenders all we have contended for."[44] Lincoln would not "surrender."

With Seward—still wavering on Lincoln's cabinet offer—now entertaining compromise proposals with growing ardor as a member of the new Senate committee, the president-elect also confided his anti-conciliation position in yet another strong "Private & confidential" letter to the New Yorker's chief political operative, Thurlow Weed, obviously intending its sentiments to reach the senator.

Lincoln was willing to bend on only one controversial issue: he would condemn all opposition, "real and apparant," [sic] to the Fugitive Slave Laws that distastefully required Northerners to return escapees to their Southern masters. But he would remain "inflexible on the territorial question," maintaining that "either the Missouri line extended or . . . Pop. Sov. would lose us every thing we gained by the election" and create new slave states "in spite of us."

Conceding that there was nothing anxious Americans might find in his previous speeches to cover the overarching issue of the day—secession—Lincoln was now willing to let this much more be known: "My opinion is that no state can, in any way lawfully, get out of the Union, without the consent of the others; and that it is the duty of the President, and other government functionaries"—this presumably included Seward—"to run the machine as it is."[45]

IN THE MIDDLE of the month, that machine finally and fatally crashed. The long-feared South Carolina secession convention opened in rainy Charleston on December 17. Just a few days before the debate commenced, Lincoln was still endeavoring to remain publicly optimistic. "I think, from all I can learn, that things have reached their worst point in the South," he conceded to a Philadelphia journalist. But then he went on to insist, "they are likely to mend in the future." And "if the South Carolinians do not intend to resist the collection of the revenue, after they ordain secession," he reasoned, "there need be no collision with the federal government. The Union may still be maintained."[46]

Lincoln's strangely calm, and seemingly inaccurate, estimate of the situation—he went on to fuss about how the U.S. government might find judges, marshals, and court officers to keep South Carolina's federal legal system functioning after secession—made him seem, to some, oblivious to the revolutionary nature of the pending Charleston vote. After all, a newly independent South Carolina would hardly permit federal courts to function there in the foreseeable future. But Lincoln intended his reaction to reach beyond Charleston. Focusing on Virginia, Kentucky, Missouri, and other Upper South states, he coolly insisted, "there can be no advantage in taunting and bantering the South."[47] Too optimistically, he still believed coolness alone might yet confine the secession infection to one state only. To an old congressional colleague from upstate New York, Lincoln did admit, "the political horizon looks dark, and lowering." But even as North Carolina's John A. Gilmer warned him of a "stampede" for secession,[48] Lincoln persisted in the optimistic belief—at least publicly, in a last-ditch effort to prevent the "stampede"—that "the people, under Providence, will set all right."[49]

On December 20, in an atmosphere of defiant celebration, secession delegates in Charleston chose the opposite course, formally adopting an ordinance to take South Carolina out of the Union and "resume a separate, equal rank among nations."[50] Hearing cheers from the hall, the dean of the fire-eaters, Edmund Ruffin, his dream realized at last, gleefully joined in the "enthusiasm & joy."[51]

Rushing into print, the Charleston Mercury published its now famous broadside, declaring in oversize bold type: "THE UNION IS DISSOLVED." From the "Palmetto Boys of the Palmetto State" came an unwelcome original copy mailed to Lincoln. Trying to "give the deed of a most malignant enemy the guise of a friendly act," in the words of a houseguest, Lincoln calmly assured his worried eldest son, Robert, home from college for holiday vacation, that "it must have been intended for a Christmas gift."[52]

The president-elect folded the "gift" and stored it away, later taking it with him on to Washington. From that day forward, the ominous proclamation never left his files.[53] It would remind him for the rest of his life that the impossible nightmare had really begun. While President Buchanan reacted to the secession news with "childish despair," Henry

Villard reported, "instead of intimidating the President elect" it made him "firmer and more decided in his views on the reckless and unfortunate attempt to break up the Union."[54]

Yet over the next nineteen days, while Lincoln watched despairingly from Springfield and Congress debated compromises that no longer seemed to matter, six more Southern states held referenda and elected delegates to secession conventions of their own: Mississippi, Florida, Alabama, Georgia, Louisiana, and Texas. Historians have labored in vain to subject these ballot measures to analyses that might show whether voters fully understood their choices at this crucial moment— whether they truly supported the movement to dissolve the Union.[55] That issue has never been settled, but at the very least, the momentum unleashed in South Carolina became impossible to contain. Secession fever had grown incurable.[56] As Charleston's Christopher Memminger recalled years later, "Oh! It was a whirlwind, and all we could do was try to guide it."[57]

To David Hunter's warning that President Buchanan might soon order the abandonment of the three federal garrisons in South Carolina— Fort Moultrie, Fort Sumter, and Castle Pinckney—Lincoln hinted at a more defiant future policy: "If the forts fall, my judgment is that they are to be retaken."[58] He said much the same thing to Elihu Washburne, urging the congressman to make these views clear to General Winfield Scott: "I shall be obliged to him to be as well prepared as he can to either *hold*, or *retake*, the forts, as the case may require, at, and after the inaugeration [sic]."[59] With yet another of his effective "confidential" letters, the president-elect who refused to speak publicly thus once again pronounced his position on a crucial matter of national policy.

Lincoln grew increasingly exercised over the prospect of losing the forts before he took office. Once abandoned, he knew, they would have to be recaptured, an act that could set off a chain reaction of Southern secession—and, conceivably, armed revolt. As he continued to insist on December 22, "If Mr. B. surrenders the forts, I think they must be retaken." Two days later he was even willing to break his official public silence whatever the cost. "I will, if our friends at Washington concur, announce publicly at once that they are to be retaken after the inaugeration [sic]," he wrote Trumbull. "This will give the Union men a rallying cry."[60]

Privately, Lincoln was even angrier. He confided to John G. Nicolay that if Buchanan really intended to abandon the forts, "they ought to hang him."[61] To William H. Herndon, Lincoln proudly repeated the outburst, adding: "There can be no doubt that in *any* event that is good ground to live and die by."[62] Buchanan, for his part, did nothing. The day after Christmas, Colonel Robert Anderson quietly moved his small force across the harbor to Sumter. And on December 27, South Carolinians seized Forts Moultrie and Pinckney and hoisted the Palmetto flag over both. Two days later, Secretary of War John B. Floyd resigned rather than lead an effort to retake the property, and not long thereafter, Secretary of State Lewis Cass quit because the president refused to do so. Buchanan "whines and weeps and prays," Nicolay bitterly observed, "entirely unmanned and unnerved by a remote and worse than babyish fear of losing his own paltry life!"[63]

BACK IN WASHINGTON, Senator Crittenden took the lead in crafting a compromise plan to hold off the inevitable. Passionately committed to keeping the country together, the seventy-three-year-old Kentuckian stitched together a series of six constitutional amendments, none of which, he stipulated, could ever be modified in the future.[64] Just as Lincoln anticipated, Crittenden's plan called for reviving and extending the old Missouri Compromise line. On the one hand this meant that in any territory above latitude 36°30', slavery would be prohibited forever. Within all territory to the South, however—including land "now held, or hereafter acquired" all the way to the West Coast and potentially into the Caribbean as well—slavery would be all but permanently enshrined in law. This meant the likely creation of new, pro-Democratic slave states, reversing recent Republican gains in the House and Senate.

Crittenden's compromise package tilted heavily toward Southern interests. Additional amendments would: bar the federal government from prohibiting slavery in any federal property in the South (including military installations); prohibit Congress from interfering with the domestic, interstate slave trade; protect slavery in the District of Columbia unless residents consented (and only *after* slavery was first prohibited in Maryland and Virginia); and reaffirm the Fugitive Slave Laws by compensating Southern slave-owners unable to recapture their runaways in the North. Perhaps most important of all, the Crittenden Compromise proposed to bar any and all future federal legislation or constitutional amendment against slavery where it already existed. In effect, the package would protect the institution in perpetuity.

Some Eastern Republicans—Seward, for a time, included—concluded that resistance to compromise might trigger a financial downturn even more crippling than the Panic of 1857. Northern Democrats supported the plan with open enthusiasm. The anti-Lincoln *Chicago Times*, for one, praised defeated presidential candidate Stephen A. Douglas for backing the compromise, calling it "the effort of a great and patriotic mind to yield to the necessities of the time and to save his country." In the newspaper's rosy view, the amendments, "drawn with great thought and care, and with a patriotic desire to meet the emergency," would "forever exclude from Congress the exciting topic of slavery."[65]

Against this tide, Lincoln ever so slightly shifted his ground, attempting to demonstrate flexibility without really sacrificing principle. On December 20, the same day South Carolina seceded, he entered the compromise debate more overtly than ever. Drafting his own counterproposal, albeit a halfhearted one he knew would attract scant support, he offered a series of compromise resolutions directed to the Senate Committee of Thirteen. With these, and these alone, he was prepared to live as long as the Union remained intact: accepting the Fugitive Slave Laws up to a point, and calling for the repeal of local Personal Liberty laws that sought to override them. The question of slavery in the territories he conspicuously left unanswered:

Resolved:
That the fugitive slave clause of the Constitution ought to be enforced by a law of Congress, with efficient provisions for that

object, not obliging private persons to assist in it's execution, but punishing all who resist it, and with the usual safeguards to liberty, securing free men against being surrendered as slaves—

That all state laws, if there be such, really, or apparantly [sic], in conflict with such law of Congress, ought to be repealed; and no opposition to the execution of such law of Congress ought to be made—

That the Federal Union must be preserved.[66]

Lincoln handed this draft to an unlikely messenger. "Finding it not inconvenient to go West,"[67] New York State Republican boss Thurlow Weed had traveled across the country to meet the man who had shattered William H. Seward's White House dream. "Mr. Lincoln would be very glad to see you," Leonard Swett had advised him a few days earlier. "Your coming to Springfield may make newspaper talk, but he says he don't care for that, if you don't . . . go at once."[68]

Accompanied by two New York cronies, the "liege lord of the Albany lobby"[69] arrived on the 20th, the very day that South Carolina seceded. "The once almighty Weed," a Rochester newspaper exulted, had "migrated towards the rising sun."[70] At nine o'clock in the morning, Weed called on the president-elect at his home, in an effort to shield the meeting from press scrutiny. He spent the next six hours in Lincoln's parlor,[71] conferring with the president-elect, Judge Davis, and Leonard Swett, while outside, oblivious to the summit, the town buzzed over a different issue, "agog" over the bad news from Charleston.[72]

Although the boss his friends called "The Dictator"[73] arrived in Springfield committed to Crittenden's plan for "the reestablishment of the compact of 1820"[74]—meaning the Missouri Compromise—Weed quickly learned that Lincoln's opposition was not negotiable. The president-elect did not minimize "the dangers which threatened the safety both of the government and of the Union." But he would not yield on slavery extension, and "repudiated" Weed's sympathy for the Crittenden plan with "undisguised hostility."[75] Weed nonetheless concluded that while Lincoln "never underestimated the difficulties which surrounded him, his nature was so elastic, and his temperament so cheerful, that he always seemed at ease and undisturbed."[76] Despite the "loud threats and much muttering in the cotton States," Weed marveled, Lincoln still "hoped that by wisdom and forbearance the danger of serious trouble might be averted, as such dangers had been in former times."[77] Lincoln in turn grew to like the political leader, who despite his legendary political power, seldom spoke publicly because of a stammer.[78] The two men, Swett recalled, each "risen by their own exertions from humble relations to the control of a nation," simply "took to each other."[79]

Weed never admitted that Lincoln sent him back east armed with his handwritten alternate compromise resolutions. To guarantee its unmolested delivery, the president-elect made sure that all of Washington knew about it in advance, writing to Lyman Trumbull to predict it "would do much good, if introduced, and unanimously supported by our friends." Moreover, he knew precisely how they should be presented to the full Senate. "I think it would be best for Mr. Seward to introduce them," he ordered, making clearer than ever who was in charge of the debate, "& Mr. Weed will let him know that I think so." Continuing to spin his web behind the scenes, Lincoln let Trumbull know that he could share these latest instructions only with Hamlin—otherwise, he cautioned, "do not let my name be known in the matter."[80] (In the end, Seward protested against the alternative resolutions, insisting that, "in the form you give it, it would divide our friends." Southern "defiance," he added, "could not be arrested, even if we should offer all you suggest, and with it the restoration of the Missouri Compromise line.")[81]

Back in Springfield, believing he had shown good faith on compromise, Lincoln turned the discussions with Weed to the matter that had lured the political guru to town in the first place: the cabinet, especially Seward's "present unsettled views" on whether to accept a place in it.[82] Forming his official family, Lincoln willingly confided, had been "by no means as easy as he had supposed" when he was elected. The country was bigger than ever, but "great men were scarcer than they used to be." Revealing that he had settled on only the two leading places—Seward for State and Chase for the Treasury (this would have come as news to

Chase, with whom Lincoln had shared none of this)—he went on to flatter Weed by inviting his suggestions for the remaining departments.

This was just what the New Yorker wanted to hear. He had come to Springfield not just to discuss the Seward appointment, but to persuade Lincoln to grant the senator power to choose the rest of the cabinet, too.[83] The presumptuous scheme must be kept quiet. Seward himself acknowledged that "utter confusion would break out in the Republican party at once if it was understood or thought that I am or can be engaged in anticipating the dispensation of patronage next spring."[84] Lincoln, for his part, had no intention of ceding such power to the man the press had already dubbed the "Premier."

But Weed took the bait. When Lincoln mentioned Gideon Welles as a potential New England representative, the New Yorker countered that other local men seemed better qualified, including Charles Francis Adams, who had a better name, and far more money (not to mention less hostility to Seward). Unconvinced, Lincoln reminded Weed that his administration needed former Democrats like Welles, as well as ex-Whigs like Seward, Adams, and himself. The first lick went to the president-elect.

Undaunted, Weed went on to urge Lincoln to consider Southerners, and in reply Lincoln wondered aloud whether they could "be trusted" in case of disunion (though of course he had already concluded that some could). "Yes, sir," answered Weed, "the men whom I have in my mind can always be relied on."

"Well," replied Lincoln, "let us have the names of your white crows, such ones as you think fit for the cabinet."[85]

Weed was not shy about naming names. Such "white crows" as Congressman John M. Botts of Virginia ought to be considered, he advised, along with Judge Davis's relative, Henry Winter Davis of Maryland, former Congressman Balie Peyton of Tennessee, and "opposition party" representative John A. Gilmer of North Carolina. Gilmer's was just the name Lincoln wanted to hear; he had never completely abandoned his interest in the pro-slavery Greensboro congressman. Five days earlier, unbeknownst to Weed, the master puppeteer had quietly made him an overture. Concerned lest Gilmer "misconstrue my silence" after the Southerner reached out first, Lincoln clarified his views on the compromise proposals now before Congress.

To Gilmer, Lincoln stressed consistency: "Is it desired that I shall shift the ground upon which I have been elected? I can not do it." Then the president-elect added a familiar refrain: his previously printed speeches required no clarification anyway. "You need only to acquaint yourself with that ground, and press it on the attention of the South," he wrote. "It is all in print and easy of access," and should worry no Southerners about his plans. Besides, further explanations "would make me appear as if I repented for the crime of having been elected, and was anxious to apologize and beg forgiveness."[86]

Then, aggressively violating his own ban on further clarifications, Lincoln proceeded to offer precisely that on six hot issues raised by Gilmer—once again deftly inserting himself into the debate on constitutional amendments. No, as president he would not recommend abolishing slavery in the District of Columbia or prohibiting the interstate slave trade "among slave states." Even if he did, he pointed out, Congress would surely ignore him. He had never before heard of the idea of banning slavery in federal arsenals and dockyards, but saw no reason why the issue did not fall into the same category. And he would "be glad" to see the repeal of state liberty laws "in conflict with the fugitive slave clause," though he maintained, somewhat disingenuously: "I could hardly be justified, as a citizen of Illinois, or as President of the United States, to recommend the repeal of a statute of Vermont, or South Carolina."

On one point, however, he would not negotiate. "On the territorial question, I am inflexible. . . . On that, there is a difference between you and us; and it is the only substantial difference. You think slavery is right and ought to be extended; we think it is wrong and ought to be restricted. For this, neither has any just occasion to be angry with the other."[87]

Back at their Springfield summit, Weed could not muster much anger at Lincoln, either, even when the president-elect's baffling cabinet preferences became clearer. Coyly, the president-elect identified a Southern choice of his own, revealing that "Judge Blair has been suggested."

"What Judge Blair?" inquired Weed incredulously.

"Judge Montgomery Blair," answered Lincoln benignly, referring to the scion of the clan that traced its political roots to the age of Jackson.

"Has he been suggested by any one except his father, Francis P. Blair, Sr.?" Would not Henry Winter Davis fit the bill just as well?

Laughing, Lincoln guessed: "[David] Davis has been posting you up on this question. He came from Maryland and has got Davis on the brain. Maryland must, I think, be like New Hampshire, a good State to move from." Then he spun a story that Weed never forgot—that of an elderly witness at a trial who, asked his age, testified that he was sixty. Convinced he was lying, the judge repeated the question, got the same fantastic answer, then admonished the witness that the bench knew he was far older. "Oh," said the old man, "you're thinking about that fifteen year[s] that I lived on the eastern shore of Maryland; that was so much lost time and don't count." Weed concluded that Blair's appointment was a "fixed fact."[88] Indeed, Lincoln had quietly concluded that Blair should get a post. On Christmas Eve, he would advise Trumbull: "I expect to be able to offer Mr. Blair a place in the cabinet; but I can not, as yet, be committed on the matter, to any extent whatever."[89]

Weed tried one more time to urge Lincoln to look to the slave states for additional ministers. "But you object to Judge Blair, who resides in a slave State," protested Lincoln.

"I object to Judge Blair because he represents nobody, he has no following, and because his appointment would be obnoxious to the Union men of Maryland; and that, as I believe, while he can look into Maryland, he actually resides in the District of Columbia."

"Very well," Lincoln deflected this salvo. "I will now give you the name of a gentleman who not only resides in a slave State, but who is emphatically a representative man. What objection have you to Edward Bates of Missouri?"

To which Weed responded: "None, not a shadow or a shade of an objection. That is a selection, as Webster might have said, 'eminently fit to be made.' "

Closing their discussion of Southern representation, Lincoln craftily offered Weed a means of blocking Montgomery Blair after all: by enticing John A. Gilmer. "Now, if Mr. Gilmer should come in, somebody must stay out, and that other somebody must be either Judge Blair or Mr. Bates."

When Lincoln next turned the cabinet discussions to the possibility of appointing Simon Cameron, Weed cautiously acknowledged that the Pennsylvania senator had always treated him with "much kindness."

"But you do not say what you think about him for the cabinet," Lincoln noticed.

Weed explained that he thought the president-elect deserved the strongest possible cabinet, composed of men who had the "confidence of the people." Cameron, he suggested, did not.

"Pennsylvania, any more than New York or Ohio," Lincoln shot back, "cannot be overlooked. . . . Who is stronger or better than General Cameron?" Weed confessed he was unprepared to answer—or to object on specific grounds.

Counting heads, Weed did wonder whether there would, in the end, be too *few* former Whigs in Lincoln's final cabinet. "You seem to forget that *I* expect to be there," Lincoln corrected him, "and counting me as one, you see how nicely the cabinet would be balanced and ballasted." Weed left the session delighted with his host's "amusing but quaint manner . . . [his] stories, anecdotes, and witticisms."[90] On one matter Lincoln was altogether serious, reminding Weed: "I have not promised an office to any man."[91]

The two leaders parted company the next morning following a hearty breakfast of sausages. Bidding his visitor farewell, the president-elect gratefully admitted that allies had warned him the Albany political boss would come to town armed with unreasonable patronage demands. Most previous visitors, Lincoln admitted, "brought along an axe or two of their own to be ground."[92] The old rail-splitter appreciated the respite.

Back at Weed's home base, his Albany newspaper promptly confirmed the success of the meeting, hailing Lincoln for "his fitness for the high position he is to occupy," and "his enlightened appreciation of the difficulties and dangers" gripping the country. No doubt speaking for many Republicans, the *Evening Journal* added: "Our only regret is, that Mr. Lincoln could not have taken the helm of state, as successor to Mr. Buchanan, on the first Monday in December."[93] Writing from Pennsylvania, J. J. Lewis agreed that "If Mr Lincoln could now assume the administration of the government I feel assured that his wisdom and energy would conduct us safely thro' the perils of the crisis we have now reached. How it may be two months hence it is impossible to predict." Lewis had no doubt "Lincoln will be equal to his mission . . . and who shall say that the fame of Lincoln shall not rival that of Washington."[94]

Lincoln, too, yearned for Inauguration Day to arrive. "I would willingly take out of my life a period in years equal to the two months which intervene between now and my inauguration to take the oath of office now," he told his friend Joseph Gillespie. Gillespie, a veteran lawyer who had known the future president since their days as fellow volunteers in the Black Hawk War, asked why.

Relaxing at home "with his head lying upon his arms, which were folded over the back of his chair," Lincoln replied with "more bitterness" than Gillespie had ever heard him express. "Because every hour adds to the difficulties I am called upon to meet, and the present Administration does nothing to check the tendency toward dissolution. I, who have been called to meet this awful responsibility, am compelled to remain here, doing nothing to avert it or lessen its force when it comes to me."[95]

"I have read, upon my knees, the story of Gethsemane, where the Son of God prayed in vain that the cup of bitterness might pass from him. I am in the Garden of Gethsemane now, and my cup of bitterness is full and overflowing."

"Stay with me tonight," the emotional president-elect told his old friend with a "look of settled despondency" when Gillespie announced plans to depart after Christmas. "I have learned the value of old friends by making new ones."[96]

Yet enterprising "new friends" continued to make their way to Lincoln's headquarters in search of jobs, influence, and attention. Lincoln's open-door policy remained in full effect. Despite his new status, strangers could still march up the Capitol stairway unimpeded to request personal time with the president-elect. The latest arrivals included both intimates and enemies.

In the latter category, one damp and drizzly day, a "sensation" greeted the arrival of "a regular genuine secessionist,"[97] apparently the first ever glimpsed in Lincoln's hometown. With a "sullen air," one D. E. Ray of Yazoo, Mississippi, "stalked into Lincoln's reception room wearing a blue cockade [a rosette fastened with a gilt button] displayed upon his hat"—the emblem of disunion. After claiming the corner of a sofa, the visitor sat there silently for fifteen or twenty minutes, scowling, staring at Lincoln apprehensively, and manipulating his hat either to conceal the suggestive cockade or make sure "the object of his terror"[98] could not fail to notice it.

For a time, Lincoln ignored his strange guest, but then other visitors succeeded in engaging Ray's attention, and he overheard the visitor declare that "they were not afraid down South of Mr. Lincoln himself, but of those who followed him." Worried lest the confrontation escalate into violence, Lincoln plunged into the debate, reminding the Mississippian that, "although the republicans were anti-extensionists, they would not interfere with slavery where it existed, and that as to his own intentions, the slave States would find that their slave property would be as secure from encroachments as it had been under Buchanan." Though such assurances had failed to placate the Southern leadership, they seemed to relieve the visitor, who "softened" noticeably, and ended up asking the president-elect for a copy of the Lincoln-Douglas debates. Inscribing it to Ray, Lincoln joked that "he hoped its possession would not give him any trouble on his return to Mississippi."[99]

Ushering him to the door, Lincoln tried consoling him with a now familiar mantra: "The only difference between you and me is that I think Slavery wrong, and you think it right; that I am opposed to its extension, while you advocate it." He trusted his guest would so report his views, "so people were not afraid of getting hurt by him."

"No," was the secessionist's encouraging final word, "we aint." To which a "stout-looking yankee farmer" on the scene taunted: "Barking dogs never bite!"[100]

Soon thereafter, a genuine celebrity, Lincoln's dashing old friend, London-born Edward Dickinson Baker, followed into town—bringing with him an inescapable flood of bittersweet memories. The two men, fellow attorneys and Whig state legislators back in the 1830s, had once been close. But as aspiring politicians in the same party and the same town, they also, inevitably, became rivals. Both had once wanted to go to Congress, and each went on to serve a single term under a system of rotating Whig nominations with which neither ambitious man was entirely comfortable. Still, their affection for each other remained strong: while Baker was serving in Washington, the Lincolns honored him by naming their second-born son for the congressman. (Edward Baker Lincoln died tragically at age three in 1850.) When Baker finished his term, he dutifully handed off his House seat to Lincoln.

The peripatetic Baker later won a second House term from upstate Galena, then migrated to California, where he tried, but failed, to win election to the U.S. Senate. Heading north to Oregon and coasting on Lincoln's coattails in 1860, he was finally destined to win the Senate seat he so long coveted. Now, on Baker's first trip back to his old bailiwick since Election Night and his first extended visit to Springfield in a decade, Lincoln greeted his longtime ally and sometime rival "most cordially." A "host of relatives and acquaintances" happily surrounded the two men during their long, "purely private" reunion. "He is certainly a remarkable man," gushed Henry Villard. "Of restless ambition, indomitable energy, true English perseverance, fine natural parts, great elegance and popular manners, he could not well fail to make his mark."[101]

Lincoln and Baker probably took at least a few moments to recall the Wilmot Proviso, an old congressional resolution—which both antislavery congressmen, in their time, had supported avidly—that would have banned slavery from all federal territory acquired in the Mexican War. The measure never passed, but Lincoln once proudly reckoned he had cast more than forty votes in its favor.[102] Nine months before winning the presidency, between trains in Philadelphia en route to Cooper Union, Lincoln had tried paying an unannounced courtesy call on its author, Representative David Wilmot. He was disappointed to find Wilmot not at his hotel.[103]

Now, on Christmas Eve, at Lincoln's invitation, Wilmot himself arrived at Springfield's elegant St. Nicholas Hotel, offering to call on the president-elect "any hour of the day or evening that will suit your convenience."[104] According to one source, the famous Pennsylvanian became, after their five-hour meeting, "the recipient of the flattering offer of a place among Mr. Lincoln's Constitutional advisors."[105] Whether true or not, the Wilmot and Baker visits overlapped, and the three men at least got the chance to talk over old times—and doubtless discuss the portentous future as well. (Wilmot went on briefly to become a U.S. senator from Pennsylvania in 1861 after Simon Cameron resigned his seat to join Lincoln's cabinet.)

Lincoln found no real peace even on Christmas Day itself. On the morning of December 25, after briefly joining his sons in the family parlor to check Christmas stockings for gifts,[106] he left home to face a crowd of "country people" who surged into his reception room, holiday notwithstanding. Later, Lincoln settled down to political talks with a delegation from St. Louis.[107]

Then, a few days later, another old acquaintance, the celebrated Duff Green, joined the roster of distinguished visitors. Once a resident of the same rural Kentucky county where Lincoln was born, later married to a sister of Lincoln's brother-in-law—thus, by Kentucky standards, a relative—the sixty-nine-year-old Green had enjoyed a long career as an influential newspaper publisher, originally in support of Andrew Jackson and the Democrats, and later in sympathy with Whig presidential candidates Henry Clay and William Henry Harrison. He had gone on to serve in diplomatic posts in France, Texas, and Mexico, and now—sent west by President Buchanan himself—sought assurances from Lincoln that the South would truly remain unmolested under his administration. The press said nothing about Green's arrival, indicating the visit was conducted in secrecy.

"Duff Green is out here endeavoring to draw a letter out of me," Lincoln confided to Senator Trumbull on December 28. "I have written one, which herewith I inclose to you, and which I believe could not be used to our disadvantage." The letter to Green again made clear that Lincoln personally opposed any new constitutional amendments—"I do not desire any amendment of the Constitution," it began. But then Lincoln went on to agree to grant the American people "a fair opportunity of expressing their will" should the proposed Crittenden amendments ever reach the various state legislatures for ratification, an outcome that seemed increasingly unlikely. By then, with his own compromise counterproposal ignored, Lincoln likely knew that the likelihood that an alternative would be passed by Congress and sent on to the states was minuscule.

Conceding nothing that was not already part of the 1860 Republican platform, Lincoln reiterated "that the maintenance inviolate of the . . . right of each state to order and control its own domestic institutions according to its own judgment exclusively, is essential to that balance of powers on which the perfection, and endurance of our political fabric depends—and I denounce the lawless invasion, by armed force, of the soil of any State or Territory, no matter under what pretext, as the gravest of crimes."

Although Lincoln had privately confided his own intention to recapture any lost federal forts in South Carolina, here, not for the first time in these tense weeks, he now suggested the opposite. His letter ended with a deliciously Lincolnian offer: the consummate politician agreed to the publication of the Duff Green letter providing that six of the twelve senators from Georgia, Alabama, Mississippi, Louisiana, Florida, and Texas signed the document beneath his own name and consented to issue the manifesto whole.

Wisely, Lincoln did not entrust this combustible document to Green. Instead he sent it to Trumbull, with the caveat that "if, on consultation with our dearest friends, you conclude that it may do us harm, do not deliver it."[108] Thus, Lincoln's memorandum accomplished two goals at once. It got Green out of Springfield without concessions for President Buchanan. And it offered Lincoln's allies in Washington, already steeled by the president-elect to resist concessions, the opportunity to float an alternative proposal that gave the impression Lincoln was actually negotiating. In the end, Trumbull killed the Green memo. It was never made public.

Duff Green left town satisfied that Lincoln could be trusted "to administer the government in such a manner as to satisfy the South."[109] But after learning of Lincoln's memorandum, he wrote frostily: "I regret your unwillingness to recommend an amendment to the constitution which will arrest the progress of secession."[110]

ALTHOUGH CONGRESSIONAL MANEUVERING continued throughout the month in Washington, by late December the Crittenden proposals appeared doomed. "Compromise has gone up the spout," one newspaper reported on December 28, the day before a crucial vote, "the compromisers go about the street like mourners."[111] Any new constitutional amendment required approval of two-thirds of the House and Senate, and it seemed highly unlikely that without Lincoln's blessing, enough Northern Republicans would support the latest package to send it on to the states.[112]

Frustrated, Senator Stephen A. Douglas wrote home to Springfield: "The fact can no longer be disguised that many of the Republican Leaders desire war & Disunion under pretext of saving the Union. Th[e]y wish to get rid of the Southern Senators in order to have a majority in the Senate to confirm Lincolns appointments."[113] But some of these same Southern senators proved no more eager than the Republicans to support the Crittenden package. In their view, the measures did not go far enough. As Lincoln sadly put it, the South "has eyes but does not see, and ears but does not hear."[114]

The Senate Committee of Thirteen met four times in December, debating, and ultimately dismissing, several compromise blueprints. At one point the Republicans considered making a gesture to the South by supporting New Mexico's admission to the Union as a slave state—free state admission for Kansas was under consideration simultaneously—in the belief that slavery could not be sustained in the dry southwest, anyway. Even this idea foundered. Some politicians and editorial writers continued to advocate concessions, but Crittenden's compromise dream ended by year's end.

So too did Lincoln's seven-month-long occupancy of the Governor's Rooms. With the Illinois legislature about to gavel back into session on January 7, and with a new governor, Richard Yates, poised to assume office—along with his designated Capitol suite—Lincoln finally abandoned the State House headquarters he had occupied ever since his nomination in May.[115]

Just before New Year's, John Nicolay packed up the office and relocated to "a good room, about twenty feet square, newly painted papered and carpeted, and pretty well furnished" in the nearby Johnson Building, a commercial structure on the corner of Fourth and Washington Streets, across from the Republican-friendly Chenery House hotel.[116] Here the secretary would work and sleep until the trip to Washington, and here Lincoln would establish a new but truncated office routine. (Back in the State House, Governor Yates took one look at the trampled carpets and manhandled furniture Lincoln left behind, and ordered the historic pieces replaced.)[117]

Publicly, the president-elect made it known that he would spend the rest of the interregnum at home—though few of his confidants believed him. Nicolay fully expected to see him "when I need his advice or he my immediate assistance."[118]

LINCOLN MADE ONE final effort to look southward for sympathy—with a letter to Georgia senator Alexander H. Stephens. Although he would not consider him for the cabinet, after all, Lincoln wanted to make that sure his old congressional colleague knew he appreciated his recent pro-Union speech, and, more important, had nothing to fear from his presidency. "I fully appreciate the present peril the country is in," Lincoln told Stephens, "and the weight of responsibility on me." He marked his letter "*For your own eye only*," and Stephens later confirmed, "No 'eye' had ever seen his letters except my Private Secretaries."[119]

Then Lincoln got to the point: did the Southern people "really entertain fears that a Republican administration would, *directly*, or *indirectly*, interfere with their slaves, or with them, about their slaves? If they do, I wish to assure you, as once a friend, and still, I hope, not an enemy, that there is no cause for such fears."

"The South would be in no more danger in this respect, than it was in the days of Washington." Lincoln ended his appeal with a frank reiteration of a phrase he had used often, and it was not designed to make Stephens happy. "You think slavery is *right* and ought to be extended; while we think it is *wrong* and ought to be restricted. That I suppose is the rub. It certainly is the only substantial difference between us."

Stephens hastened to reply. "Personally, I am not your enemy—far from it," he assured Lincoln, "and however we may differ politically, yet I trust we both have an earnest desire to preserve and maintain the Union." But things had gone too far. Fanaticism and recklessness now prevailed, Stephens charged, and this time he did not mean the secessionists to whom he had appealed for moderation in Georgia. Rather, it was the likes of John Brown, whose 1859 abolitionist raid into Virginia, he fumed, had never elicited proper "condemnation" from Republicans. Now Stephens pleaded with Lincoln to "do what you can to save our common country." Like others before him, he advised Lincoln to speak out for conciliation: "A word fitly spoken by you now would be like 'apples of gold in pictures of silver.' "[120] Lincoln rejected the idea, but loved the closing phrase—from Proverbs 25:11. Within days, he would appropriate it for himself. But unwilling to debate Stephens, Lincoln offered no further reply. They had once stood side by side in Whig unity. Now the conversation ended. He and Stephens would not communicate again for four long years.[121]

One more Southern voice yearned to be heard—but remained muffled in frustrated, demented silence. In Philadelphia, a superbly gifted young actor from Maryland attended a midmonth "Grand Union Meeting." Lincoln had hoped the governors of all the Northern states would organize such rallies to mobilize public opinion against secession.[122] However, things did not go as hoped in Pennsylvania. Not all the speeches delivered in Independence Park that day sympathized with Lincoln's refusal to compromise. A banner held aloft among the throng proclaimed: "Concession Before Secession."[123]

The volatile actor in that crowd agreed. Eager to play a part on the national stage, he went on to draft a long, rambling, often incoherent speech he planned to deliver himself. Demanding "eaqual [sic] rights and justice to the South," it praised Philadelphians for acting "nobly," but insisted Southerners "cannot be reconciled . . . while the republican principals [sic] still exist . . . the South has been wronged. Ay wronged . . . O God what a dismal future have we before us." Its author never delivered the speech. Only later did he find a way to vent his anger.

His name was John Wilkes Booth.[124]

LINCOLN ENDED THE month of December—and the historic year of 1860—still hoping to damp down the secession crisis and solidify his cabinet options. He could not have been pleased if he calculated editorial reaction to secession: a surprising majority of writers had come down for the right of any state to leave the Union.[125] Encouragement came from odd sources—like the Beloit attorney-poet Charles Leland Porter, who dedicated his new verse, "Stand by the Right," to the beleaguered president-elect:

> Stand by the Right, and boldly struggle on,
> Plant on the rock thy foot and look before,
> Draw forth thy glittering sword, thou daring one,
> Though legion wrongs stand cowering at thy door:
> Stand by the Right! What though the Might be strong,

> *And towering lifts its haughty crest o'er all!*
> *Down it will come with thundering crash along,*
> *The ax is at its root and it must fall.*[126]

Lincoln certainly "struggled on" where cabinet-making was concerned. The final makeup of his official family still eluded him. Some of its vital pieces were in place—William H. Seward at State, if he accepted; Salmon P. Chase to represent Ohio, if he could be wooed; Edward Bates as attorney general; and very likely Montgomery Blair to represent the crucial border state of Maryland—but gaps remained.

Defeated presidential candidate John Bell of Tennessee briefly reentered the sweepstakes with a public letter condemning secession, predicting that Lincoln "will be powerless for mischief" because he lacked a Republican majority in Congress, and presumptuously hinting he was prepared to join the administration.[127] But with Bates on board, Lincoln felt he did not need another conservative Whig from the Upper South.

Who would satisfy Indiana: Schuyler Colfax or Caleb B. Smith?[128] Who might represent New England? Gideon Welles, or alternatives like Charles Francis Adams, George Fogg, or Nathaniel Banks? (Lincoln gave Hannibal Hamlin one last chance to choose for his region.)[129] And did he owe a place to Illinois's Norman Judd, to whom he admitted he was "more indebted" than to any other man for his nomination?[130] Seward still hoped the new president would name Hunt, Rayner, or Gilmer to represent the South, but Lincoln told him on the 29th that he had thought seriously only about Gilmer, who in any case had failed to respond to his recent request that he visit him in Springfield.[131] "I shall have a great deal of trouble," Lincoln confided to William Cullen Bryant about his struggle to form a cabinet, but "do the best I can."[132]

The most vexing challenge of all remained the claims of Pennsylvania, and the seemingly insoluble question of whether to appoint that state's controversial senator, Simon Cameron. "There has been delegation after delegation from Pennsylvania, hundreds of letters, and the cry is 'Cameron, Cameron!' " Lincoln moaned in desperation to Gustave Koerner. "The Pennsylvania people say: 'If you leave out Cameron you disgrace him.' Is there not something in that?"[133] Yet when Pennsylvania politicians Alexander Cummings and James K. Moorhead urged precisely the same thing, Lincoln showed he was still torn. "All through the campaign my friends have been calling me 'Honest Old Abe,' and I have been elected mainly on that cry," he protested. "What will be thought now if the first thing I do is to appoint Cameron, whose very name stinks in the nostrils of the people for his corruption?"[134]

On Sunday, December 30, although he insisted he did not want to come, and made the journey only when Leonard Swett importuned him, the saturnine Simon Cameron arrived in Springfield unexpectedly, accompanied by his trusted advisor, attorney John P. Sanderson, known by his critics as "the side-door man."[135]

"Shall I have the honor of waiting on you,—or will you do me the favor to call here?" he alerted the president-elect as soon as he registered at the Chenery House, enclosing Swett's recent summons encouraging his visit. Surprised by his presence, Lincoln opted to welcome Cameron to his house with his "customary artless Western heartiness."[136]

As the two launched their discussions, Lincoln rather mischievously summoned Edward Bates back from St. Louis, along with the vocal anti-Cameron Pennsylvanian Alexander K. McClure.[137] Bates arrived at 8:30 that same evening, in time to join Cameron and the president-elect for another two-hour-long "general conversation" in Cameron's hotel room. Perhaps Lincoln wanted to gauge for himself how two potential cabinet ministers might interact, not only with him, but also with each other. With their discussions focusing on national issues, not appointments, Bates never learned "what brought Cameron to Springfield," guessing only that he was a contender for Treasury. "I found him pleasant enough in conversation," the Missourian recalled, "but rather reticent about politics and parties. . . . I suppose he did not wish me to know the object of his visit."[138]

If we can believe Bates, Lincoln wanted him back in Springfield principally to tell him face-to-face that Seward planned to accept the State Department after all. After "due reflection and with much self-distrust," Seward had at last written to Lincoln on December 28 to tell him he would accept the post.[139] "I [think] that this is unfortunate," Bates believed, "and will complicate Mr. L's difficulties." The Missourian responded by offering to drop out of cabinet contention altogether, reminding the president-elect that he had agreed to take office only as "a *painful duty*." If Lincoln "could fill the places without me, It would be a relief rather than a disappointment." Suddenly, the cabinet plan seemed in jeopardy.

Lincoln would hear none of it. He still wanted Bates to serve as attorney general, and hoped the job was prestigious enough to lure him into the administration. "I cant do better than that," he explained. "State cant be pulled up."[140] Meanwhile, after "two long conversations" with his visitor from Pennsylvania, Lincoln told Cameron "he had made up his mind to give me either the Treasury or War Dept. he couldn't yet tell which."[141]

For his own use, Lincoln then prepared two extraordinary memoranda, meticulously summarizing the pros and cons of any Cameron appointment. In one he quoted three recent letters of warm endorsement, and carefully recorded the names of fifty other correspondents who had supported Cameron. For each man, Lincoln painstakingly noted whether he had written a "letter" or a "long letter." Yet in the other, equally dispassionate, memo, Lincoln enumerated various charges of corruption against Cameron: he had allegedly bribed legislators to win his Senate seat in 1857, became the object of an investigation in 1855, and bribed an entire *convention* (Lincoln underlined the word) back in 1849.[142]

One can almost visualize Lincoln patiently writing these documents, then reading and rereading each, weighing the evidence he had amassed. Ever lawyerly, he had imagined himself both Cameron's prosecutor and defense attorney. Now, he must serve as his judge and jury. Was Cameron "personally and politically an honest man"? he wrote on one of the pages. It is easy to imagine the president-elect working through the night to find the answer.

Finally, on New Year's Eve, Lincoln reached what he thought would be a final decision. Again taking up his pen, he composed a fresh letter, and handed it directly to Cameron before his departure: "I think fit to notify you now, that by your permission, I shall, at the proper time, nominate you to the U.S. Senate, for confirmation as Secretary of the Treasury, or as Secretary of War—which of the two, I have not yet definitely decided. Please answer at your own earliest convenience."[143]

Then Lincoln reached for a new sheet of paper and wrote one final letter before the year flickered to a close. "My dear Sir," he began a note to Salmon P. Chase. "In these troublous times, I would like a conference with you. Please visit me here at once."[144] At last, the key elements of the new administration seemed to be falling into place. Lincoln would have a cabinet, as nineteenth-century writer Allen Thorndike Rice later described it, of " 'all the talents' and all the popularities" in the nation.[145]

But not as expeditiously as the president-elect hoped. Even before the Pennsylvania senator left Springfield, the Washington newspapers announced that "Mr. Lincoln has appointed Hon. Simon Cameron as Secretary of the Treasury."[146] Within days, however, the appointment had unleashed such a "tremendous storm round Lincoln," gloated Henry Adams, that it collapsed in shambles.[147]

Chapter Six

Very Much Like the Critter

A S 1860 ENDED and 1861 began, Lincoln's attention briefly, but for him perhaps mercifully, returned to the subject of his public image.

He had been cultivating his new beard for five weeks, but after an initial flurry of interest, neighbors and journalists now hardly took notice. The president-elect must have envied the luxuriant white whiskers sported by his recent visitor, Edward Bates. His own were sprouting almost reluctantly, but growing they finally were. Now came a welcome opportunity to record his changing appearance—to remind both anxious Republicans and border state Unionists that "Honest Old Abe," the square-jawed but inexperienced rail-splitter-turned-politician, was evolving into "Uncle Abe,"[1] the wise-looking, bewhiskered statesman poised to face the secession crisis.

During the last week of December, an Ohio sculptor named Thomas D. Jones crossed the frozen prairie to Springfield, armed with a commission from patrons in Cincinnati, to execute a new portrait bust of Lincoln. Jones, a flamboyant little bohemian who enjoyed sporting wide-brimmed hats and slinging togalike shawls over one shoulder for effect, brought with him letters of endorsement from two of his state's most important Republican politicians, Salmon P. Chase and Thomas Ewing.[2]

Finding Lincoln still occupying his suite at the State Capitol on a "bitter, blustering, and freezing day," Jones approached him, presented his credentials—he had already sculpted Clay, Webster, Zachary Taylor, and Winfield Scott from life[3]—and invited the president-elect to join this distinguished roster. Lincoln, who admired all of Jones's previous subjects, also appreciated the fact that cabinet-size portrait sculptures could be mass-produced to decorate family parlors—a copy of his own bust by Leonard Wells Volk already graced his own. Through such "counterfeit presentments," mere politicians evolved into icons. With particular interest, Lincoln studied the introductory letter from Chase, whom he was hoping to lure into his cabinet, remarking to Jones that, "as strange as it may appear, I have never seen Gov. Chase. I look upon him as the Moses that brought us out of the land of bondage, but he has not been as lucky as some of us in reaching the promised land. I esteem him highly, very highly."[4]

Then, recalling the physical discomfort he had experienced posing for Volk seven months earlier, Lincoln closely questioned Jones about his own artistic methods, to which the sculptor offered "a brief description of my process." He would first sketch him from live sittings, then proceed to mold his likeness from clay.

"I like your mode," Lincoln replied after considering the idea, recalling that when Volk "made a bust of me, he took a plaster cast of my face, a process that was anything but agreeable."[5] The president-elect seemed relieved, Jones later remembered—probably with a dose of overdramatic hindsight—"that he was not to be assassinated through the custom of some sculptures [sic] in taking a cast of the face."[6]

Since Lincoln was about to abandon the Governor's suite for good, Jones proposed that the president-elect sit for him daily five blocks north at the sculptor's newly rented room on the top floor of the ornate St. Nicholas Hotel, Springfield's best.[7] Lincoln agreed to climb the four flights to Jones's makeshift studio each morning, if the press of official business allowed, and pose while he reviewed his daily mail. At their first appointment, probably on December 28 or 29, Jones was initially put off by the "hard and rugged lines upon his face," guessing from its "peculiar characteristics" that Lincoln "originated from the Hardshell Baptist persuasion,"[8] which his subject confirmed. To his relief, Jones found that "a good anecdote or story before commencing a sitting much improved the plastic character of his features." Thereafter, they "opened the ball in the morning with two or three anecdotes, each, and then went on with our work in silence."[9]

With daily access to Lincoln, Jones was uniquely positioned to observe the freshly dispossessed president-elect as he struggled to establish a new routine in the absence—for the first time since his nomination—of a capacious headquarters where he could receive callers and tend to his correspondence. Jones grew to believe that his hotel room became "Lincoln's only retreat from the pursuit of numerous applicants for office, where he could compose his addresses in peace."[10] As Jones labored on the bust, Lincoln worked away on letters and, later, orations—using pencils that he occasionally asked Jones to sharpen with his sculpting tools—writing on "a small portfolio and paper resting on his knee, with a copy of his published speeches lying beside him for reference."[11]

To his increasing annoyance, however, the sculptor faced frequent interruptions from visitors who somehow discovered Lincoln's new hideaway at the St. Nicholas. Early in January, the famed elocutionist James Murdoch came to town to perform two public readings—the first mainly Shakespearean, the second highlighted by recitations from Whittier and Dickens's *Pickwick Papers*.[12] Lincoln co-sponsored and attended the second show—he would continue to patronize the theater to escape temporarily from the pressures of office—laughing "heartily" at the comic turns. The morning after his triumph, Murdoch naturally paid a courtesy call on the president-elect at Jones's hotel room, where he delayed the sitting of the day by performing an impromptu "patriotic speech for the times."[13] In town for a Springfield performance of his own, an odd, Turkish-style entertainer named Oscanyan also beat a path to the studio to divert Lincoln's already whipsawed attention.[14]

Lincoln's son Robert barged in one typical day to ask his father for ten dollars. Another morning brought a surprise, extended visit from an old Indiana farmer named William Jones. As a boy, Lincoln had worked for him as a dollar-a-day hired hand, often borrowing books to feed his insatiable hunger for knowledge. As far back as 1828, Jones had told anyone who would listen: "Lincoln would make a great man one of these days." Now the two enjoyed a nostalgic reunion—but on Thomas Jones's valuable time.[15]

Having been "too frequently interrupted by some of Lincoln's curious friends and admirers," the exasperated artist tried to stem the tide. On one occasion he shooed yet another delegation down to the hotel lobby to wait until his subject finished his morning sitting. Visibly annoyed when he learned of their dismissal, Lincoln hurried downstairs to console them. It turned out that their spokesman, James Churchman, an old acquaintance, had come all the way from California just to present Lincoln with a gold-and-quartz-handled redwood cane worth $250. Even Jones sheepishly conceded it was "highly artistic and in very good taste."[16] Inscribed on the handle were the words: "To Abraham Lincoln. First Republican President of the U.S."[17]

Lincoln had been gratefully—and unashamedly—accepting gifts from admirers ever since his election. In the absence of laws and protocols that restricted such donations, or required public officials to declare their value, Lincoln saw nothing wrong with accepting every token that arrived, household goods and the occasional foodstuff included.[18] He seemed content to continue abiding by a rule he had articulated a quarter century earlier, when he admitted: "No one has needed favours more than I, and generally, few have been less unwilling to accept them."[19] Most of the presents, however, were homespun, not lavish.

The trickle of gifts that greeted Lincoln's election grew into a torrent around holiday time, 1860. Cleveland mill workers proudly forwarded a model T-rail, and Chicago city clerk Abraham Kohn, president of the synagogue Anshe Maariv (Men of the West), sent a flag beautifully decorated with a well-chosen Hebrew inscription from Deuteronomy 31: "Be strong and of good courage; be not afraid neither be thou dismayed for the Lord thy god is with thee whithersoever thou goest."[20]

Another admirer sent Lincoln a more secular, but equally evocative, gift. New York politician Daniel Ullmann had been waiting years to award the token to the "first citizen of the school of Henry Clay" to be elected president. Hailing Lincoln as "a true disciple of our illustrious friend," Ullmann dispatched a limited-edition bronze medal of the leader who had been known—unlike Lincoln so far—as the Great Compromiser. Touched by the gesture, Lincoln wrote "to express the extreme gratification I feel in possessing so beautiful a memento of him whom, during my whole political life, I have loved and revered as a teacher and leader."[21] Unfortunately, the donor ill-advisedly released Lincoln's acknowledgment to the press, and when the *Richmond Dispatch* got hold of the text it mocked: "*His* teacher! *His* leader. Henry Clay the teacher of Mr. Lincoln. What lesson of Henry Clay has he learned? Where does he follow his leader's footsteps?"[22] Even gifts could excite sectional discord.

Donations of clothing, however, piled up largely unnoticed. A Boston wholesaler offered what Lincoln appreciatively called "a very substantial and handsome overcoat," as an "elegant and valuable New Year's Gift." Lincoln apologized that he would have acknowledged it "sooner but for the multifarious demands upon my time and attention,"[23] perhaps a reference to the time-consuming sessions with sculptor Jones. The descendant of a New York delegate to the first American Congress sent a pair of well-fitting hats.[24] A Westerner sent a "Union grey shawl, made of California wool . . . together with a pair of family blankets" as samples of "Pacific State weaving." In thanking him, Lincoln paid politically astute tribute to the "forward state of California manufactures which those articles exhibit."[25]

A few weeks thereafter, as he stared into a mirror admiring the "texture and workmanship" of yet another elegant new topper, this one presented him by a Brooklyn hatmaker, Lincoln supposedly chuckled to Mary: "Well, wife, there is one thing likely to come out of this scrape, any how. We are going to have some *new clothes!*"[26] Evidently what he did not receive, Mary was expected to create. Mrs. Lincoln received an expensive gift of her own: a bejeweled sewing machine, "richly silver plated and ornamented with inlaid pearl and enamel . . . worthy [of] the possession of a duchess. An expert and enthusiastic seamstress, Mary proudly took it with her to Washington and used it in the White House.[27]

Not all gifts were meant to express admiration. To her horror, Mary opened an express package from South Carolina one day to find "a scandalous painting on canvass" depicting Lincoln "with a rope around his neck, his feet chained and his body adorned with tar and feathers."[28] Already fearful that her husband faced mortal danger on his upcoming trip to Washington, Mary found the caricature deeply unsettling. Some of Lincoln's friends responded by urging the future first lady to take the children and travel east separately, in advance of the official journey. But the "plucky" Mrs. Lincoln responded to the "rumors of intended attacks" by making "the spirited declaration . . . that she would see Mr. Lincoln on to Washington, danger or no danger."[29]

During one of his sittings with Jones at the St. Nicholas, Lincoln discovered a "suspicious" package of his own, wrapped in plain brown paper and barely held together by a loose string. Worrying the small express box might contain "an infernal machine or torpedo," the diminutive artist bravely offered to open it himself. The two men playfully considered instead soaking it in a tub of water or saying prayers over it. Finally "placing it at the back of the clay model on which I was at work, using it as an earthwork, so in case it exploded, it would not harm either of us," Jones recalled, he "cut the strings, and out tumbled a pig-tail whistle."[30]

Sent by an Ohio politician, the harmless device was meant to refute what journalist Henry Villard called the "time-honored saying, 'No whistle can be made out of a pig's tail.' " According to Villard, "Mr. Lincoln enjoyed the joke hugely. After practicing upon this masterpiece of ingenuity for nearly an hour . . . he jocosely remarked, that he had never suspected, up to this point, that 'there was music in such a thing as that.' "[31] Try as he did, Lincoln proved unable to make the novelty work, but his youngest son had more luck with it. Calling at the Lincoln home that evening, Jones "found Tad, making the house vocal, if not musical, with the pig-tail whistle, blowing blasts that would have astonished Roderick Dhu"—Dhu being the Highland leader in the musical version of Walter Scott's *Lady of the Lake* in whose honor, appropriately, the tune "Hail to the Chief" had been introduced.[32]

Although Jones enjoyed unprecedented exposure to his preoccupied sitter, the frustrated sculptor still found Lincoln "by far the most difficult subject that I have ever confronted"—and not just because he seldom sat still except when allowing Jones to take measurements of his head. Physically, Lincoln reminded the artist of "a rough block, of the old red primitive sand-stone—thoroughly tried by fire, and capable of enduring much more."[33] Finding it difficult to capture his shifting moods and expressions by the morning sun, Jones took to visiting Lincoln at his home "to study him by gas-light, and see whether I could discover any new phase of character since morning."[34] At a reception there one night, he finally saw him "for the first time to please me . . . surrounded by his nearest and dearest friends, his face illuminated, or in common parlance, lighted up."[35] (This probably occurred during the Lincolns' thronged New Year's Day levee at the family residence, at the end of which one guest showed such stubborn reluctance to leave that the president-elect was forced to beg the younger men in attendance to drag him home.)[36]

Ultimately, the artist concluded that he required further aid. Increasingly, painters and sculptors of the day were turning to the newer medium of photography to provide models that could supplement their life sittings with restless subjects.[37] So on January 13, Jones ushered Lincoln to the west side of the public square to the so-called national gallery of photographer Christopher S. German—in reality, a modest sky-lit studio above one of Springfield's drugstores—ostensibly "to pose him for some pictures the President-elect desired to present to a very dear friend."[38] Under Jones's expert guidance, German made a series of refined, three-quarter profiles against the elegant backdrop of a velvet curtain swathed with gold tassels. Wearing a handsome broadcloth suit, snug high collar, and small, neatly arranged tie, Lincoln looked calm and elegant, though understandably distracted—his faraway stare indicating his thoughts were elsewhere. Clearly visible at last was the "vigorously" flourishing[39] beard he had been cultivating for six weeks, as well as the bulging arms and strong chest that had convinced the sculptor that the "lean and muscular" Lincoln was "physically an athlete of the first order."[40] C. S. German published multiple copies of the pose for sale to the public, giving admirers a fresh look at the future president's changing appearance.[41] Jones retained an original for himself as a crutch to augment his sittings from life.

Only after making "considerable progress" on his clay bust did Jones finally summon the courage to invite Lincoln to examine it himself. He had earlier amused—and forewarned—his subject with the story of his final sitting with Winfield Scott years before. After telling the general he had been "working out the details of the face," Jones unveiled the work in progress to the old military hero, only to hear him roar: "Details? ——— the details! Why, my man, you are spoiling the bust!"[42] But Jones knew the day of reckoning in Springfield had to come. "Mr. Lincoln," he finally asked one day, "will you have the kindness to tell me what you think of the result thus far?"

Setting down his omnipresent pencil and paper, Lincoln walked over and "examined it very closely for some time," and finally, to the artist's delight, exclaimed, in quaint Western style: "I think it looks very much like the critter."[43]

The local newspaper agreed, predicting that though the bust would "yet require a number of 'sittings' more to complete the work . . . the artist has already so well succeeded in impressing the clay with the life and noble characteristics of his subject, that we hesitate not to pronounce it the best likeness of the President elect we have seen."[44]

A few days later, Jones supplied a rave review of his own to a friend. Dismissing recent photographs for giving "no idea of the man," he pronounced his own effort "the only likeness ever made of him." Considering "all the surrounding difficulties, and the character of my subject," he added with a flourish, "my bust of Lincoln is a triumph."[45]

His comment proved just a bit premature. As it turned out, Jones dawdled interminably over the sculpture, and Lincoln left Springfield for good before the artist completed it. As late as August 1861, in fact, Jones would still be in residence at the St. Nicholas, now watching Civil War regiments marching through town, continuing to labor over his clay head of Lincoln, and dreaming about a federal patronage job—the consulship in Rome.[46] The man who had deplored the "numerous applicants for office" who interrupted him so often at his studio now predictably joined their ranks. Only later did a copy of his magnificent draped bust—in the end, a true artistic triumph, just as he boasted—find an honored place in the Red Room of Lincoln's White House.[47]

WHEN JONES COMMENCED his project, he had found Springfield in the throes of a "glorious winter." Dazzled by the sight of snow-crusted streets whose half-visible foliage made them look like "a sandy desert," Jones joyfully reported "sleighing . . . moonlight nights, laughing girls—sweet voices."[48] But to another gifted, albeit distant, observer, the one voice *not* heard from Springfield was not only spoiling the season, but endangering the future of the nation.

Sometime in early 1861, Henry Adams, the brilliant son of Charles Francis, composed a long, critical essay entitled "The Great Secession Winter," which he planned to submit to the influential *Atlantic Monthly*.[49] Fortunately for Lincoln, Adams decided to withhold the piece, concluding it was "not worth printing."[50] It would not be published until the twentieth century. Although it remained unknown when it might have hurt Lincoln most, it nonetheless reflected the growing unease felt at the time by William H. Seward's ardent admirers. They had hoped—and still hoped—that the experienced New Yorker, not the supposedly ill-prepared Illinoisan, would be entrusted to manage the effort at conciliation needed to save the Union: to serve as Lincoln's "premier" even after the election.[51]

Lamenting that "the best ability of the party" had "exhausted its influence in advocating" compromise, Adams complained in his essay that, on the brink of Union-preserving success, Washington's Republican leaders had "hesitated, and turned for the decisive word to the final authority in Springfield." But "the word did not come. In its stead came doubtful rumors tending to distract public opinion still more." Although he expressed indignation enough over the South's "wild and suicidal" march toward disunion, and vented, too, about abolitionists who sought "a violent destruction of the slave power; perhaps by war, perhaps by a slave insurrection," Adams placed much blame on the president-elect. It was Lincoln's stubborn silence, he argued, that was principally responsible for undermining compromise advocates in Congress who held the key to preventing "separation":

> In spite of the assertions of newspapers and to the surprise of the country it became more and more evident that there was no concerted action between the President-elect and the Republicans at Washington, and that Mr. Seward had acted all winter on his own responsibility. The effect of this discovery was soon evident in the gradual destruction of party discipline in Congress, where every man began to follow an independent course, or commit himself against the measures proposed, from an idea that the President was against them.[52]

Young Henry, who thought of himself as "another Horace Walpole," the eighteenth-century English man of letters, was merely echoing the misgivings his influential father openly offered at the time to anyone who would listen. To the elder Adams, Lincoln's "mind had not even opened to the nature of the crisis. From his secluded abode in the heart of Illinois, he was only taking measure of geographical relations and party services, and beginning his operations where others commonly leave off, at the smaller end."[53] It was left to fellow New Englander Gideon Welles to defend him—years later—by insisting that Lincoln was neither "an inattentive or indifferent observer" nor "neglectful of the coming storm." Rather, Welles insisted, he "had a more correct knowledge and better appreciation of the condition of affairs—foresaw with more accurate perception the threatened difficulties—than the experienced politicians who predicted and promised peace."[54]

Moreover, what the Adamses regarded as frustrating silence in fact masked Lincoln's adroit behind-the-scenes maneuvering to scotch compromises that would extend slavery—an evil that the Adams family had opposed for generations. For the remainder of the interregnum, Seward's New England admirers nonetheless continued to agitate for the secretary of state–designate to display more independence on conciliating the South. And for a time, Seward believed it might still be possible for him to do so.

IRONICALLY, THOUGH HIS growing outspokenness in Washington owed something to Lincoln's continued, mute presence in remote Illinois, Seward sincerely believed the president-elect should hasten to the capital to assert his leadership as soon as possible. A newspaper there, as Seward knew, had recently revealed that both Lincoln and Hamlin had "received anonymous letters threatening violent opposition to their inauguration."[55]

The item was true enough—many times over. A self-proclaimed "Jackson Democrat" wrote to warn Lincoln directly: "Beware the Ides of March . . . the Suthron people will not Stand your administration," while a Virginian demanded he resign outright, darkly adding, "for your wife and children sake don't take the Chair" or risk being "murdered." Fearing a "servile rebellion," yet another anonymous correspondent predicted that if Lincoln did not relinquish the presidency, the South would surely "take your life." January brought more specific warnings from a Cincinnati admirer that "corrupt men" would "reach your plate with poison." A Pennsylvanian begged Lincoln to be alert not only about "what meat and drink you take" but about "poison in the ink" he used to write letters.[56]

Around the same time, the president-elect opened an equally chilling letter from yet another anonymous enemy in Washington: "Caesar had his Brutus. Charles the First his Cromwell. And the President may profit by their example." The letter was signed "Vindex"—the name of the first Roman governor to rebel against Nero—"one of a sworn band of 10, who have resolved to shoot you in the inaugural procession on the 4th of March, 1861."[57] Verifying these warnings, Lincoln's friend Abraham Jonas disclosed that "desperate characters . . . of the most violent character" planned on preventing the inauguration by "using violence on the person of Lincoln."[58] Even Salmon P. Chase agreed that reports "from Washington alarm me, though not easily alarmed" (although he pointedly called "Congressional attempts at Compromises" a "danger . . . greater still").[59] Similarly fearing "a *revolution*," and predicting to Lincoln that a secessionist army would invade Washington within weeks "to drive out the Republican members and to prevent your inauguration by force," Chicago editor Joseph Medill wondered, echoing Seward: "Would it not be a *coup d etat*[sic], were you to quietly, with only a carpet sack, get on the cars, and drop down in this city some day next week or very soon."[60]

It was no surprise that one New York journal reported "talk of his inauguration at Springfield" as a safety measure. Unsympathetically, the paper quickly added that "people will listen to no such cowardly suggestions," insisting "as a point of honor, that he be inaugurated as usual, in the usual place, just as if no traitor had ever dared to raise his parricidal hand against his country."[61] But Lincoln never entertained the idea of taking the oath at home. From his election onward, he had taken pains to show no fear.

Seward's proposal of an early, surprise arrival in Washington, therefore, had its appeal. Rather than delay the Springfield departure until the storm cooled, the senator proposed that Lincoln leave for the capital much sooner than expected. "Habit has accustomed the public to anticipate the arrival of the President elect in this city about the middle of February," he advised, "and evil minded persons would expect to organize their demonstrations for that time. I beg leave to suggest whether it would not be well for you keeping your own counsel to be prepared to drop into the city a week or ten days earlier. The effect would probably be reassuring and soothing."[62] The very next day, a worried Seward pressed Lincoln yet again to "renew my suggestion of your coming here earlier than you otherwise would—and coming in by surprise—without announcement." In case Lincoln had already selected secretaries of war and navy, Seward added darkly, they should come quickly as well.[63] (Paradoxically, he still harbored hopes that North Carolina's pro-slavery Gilmer would earn one of these plums.) Seward was so nervous he forgot to sign his second warning.

The president-elect did take the threats seriously. Either he or his friend, Illinois's new governor, Richard Yates—likely operating with Lincoln's consent—sent the state's adjutant general, Thomas Mather, to Washington to discuss the troubling rumors with Winfield Scott. In the bargain, Lincoln hoped that Mather might also learn definitively whether the ancient, Southern-born general could himself be relied upon to remain loyal to the Union in the event the secession crisis widened to include his native state of Virginia. In the capital, the "old warrior, grizzly and wrinkled . . . breathing [with] . . . great labor," wheezed in reply to Mather's inquiries that Lincoln could confidently "come to Washington as soon as he is ready." Scott promised to "plant cannon on both ends of Pennsylvania avenue, and if any of them [secessionists] show their faces or raise a finger I'll blow them to hell." Mather returned home to "assure Mr. Lincoln that, if Scott were alive on the day of the inauguration, there need be no alarm lest the performance be interrupted by any one."[64]

Clearly relieved, Lincoln now told Seward he felt secure enough to dismiss the rumored threat to his swearing in and to stay home until mid-February. But he did not minimize the danger of an earlier, and more worrisome, moment of potential crisis. "It seems to me the inaugeration [sic] is not the most dangerous point for us," he told Seward on January 3. "Our adversaries have us much more clearly at disadvantage, on the second Wednesday of February, when the [Electoral College] votes should be officially counted. If the two Houses refuse to meet at all, or meet without a quorum of each, where shall we be? I do not think that this counting is constitutionally essential to the election; but how are we to proceed in absence of it? In view of this, I think it is best for me not to attempt appearing in Washington till the result of that ceremony is known."[65]

Now feeling emboldened, Lincoln boasted to Henry Villard that he would not only journey to Washington in full public view, but might even take the southerly route, "doubtless to demonstrate how little fear he entertains for his personal safety."[66] Rejecting "ostentatious display and empty pageantry," moreover, he announced he would travel without a military escort.[67] "He knows," Villard reported, "that those who elected him, are anxious to see how he looks, and hence is willing to gratify this, their excusable curiosity."[68] Lincoln began telling friends he would remain in Springfield until mid-February, explaining lightheartedly: "I expect they will drive me insane after I get there, and I want to keep tolerably sane, at least until after the inauguration."[69] His show of bravado proved premature.

IF LINCOLN'S LIFE seemed "tolerably sane" at the time, it might just have been in part because Mary Lincoln had gone off to New York on a shopping spree, leaving the president-elect "keeping house alone," in the words of Henry Villard. "Whatever his other qualifications may be, it is well known that in the management of the kitchen and in other domestic concerns he is sadly destitute of both talent and experience."[70] Despite the inconvenience, the break may have done them both some good.

Ever volatile, Mary's anxieties grew more pronounced as the day of her family's departure from Springfield drew nearer. Historians have long focused sympathetically on Lincoln's pressure-filled preparations for Washington; but they have all but ignored the fact that his wife faced emotionally wrenching challenges of her own. Her obligations merely included packing up the memory-suffused home in which her family had lived for nearly seventeen years, deciding which cherished belongings to take and which to leave behind (including a horse, a cow, and a dog), preparing two young children for a potentially traumatic relocation to a large city, and making preparations to assume new duties as mistress of the White House. At the same time, she was expected to entertain the guests, distinguished and otherwise, who began flocking more regularly to their Springfield residence once Lincoln gave up his office at the State Capitol. Mary often served these visitors chilled water in a silver-plated pitcher.

Deciding that her future role as first lady should take precedence, Mary left Springfield in early January for a two-week vacation with a purpose. Arriving in New York, where she was joined by her college student son, Robert, she promptly opened an account with an exclusive Broadway dressmaker, ordered finery from a number of pricey stores, and hosted teas at the Astor House hotel, at one of which she was overheard confiding that her husband had named Seward as secretary of state "very reluctantly," and only in response to political "pressure."[71] One politician found it "very shocking" that the president-elect's wife was "kiting about the country and holding levees in which she indulges in a multitude of silly speeches."[72] But most of her press coverage was favorable; her days of true vilification were still before her. One Washington paper had described her earlier as "distinguished in appearance . . . conveying to the mind generally an impression of self-possession, stateliness and elegance." And the *Chicago Press and Tribune* called her "admirably calculated to preside over our republican court."[73] In New York, the *Times* treated her as a celebrity, reporting her visits to the Brooklyn Navy Yard and the Academy of Music.[74] (Robert meanwhile got celebrity treatment of his own, touring "the stock exchange, the Treasurer's office and other public places, where he was kindly received and shown the various objects of interest which might please the young gentleman from the Far West."[75]

Mary's occasionally embarrassing conduct on her trip—buying too many new clothes on the one hand, and talking politics with what seemed like unladylike candor on the other—arose from two warring aspects of her complex personality. First, chronically insecure, she frantically worried that she would be dismissed by Washington society as a Western parvenu. Always meticulous about her appearance, and a devoted reader of *Godey's Lady's Book*, the fashion bible of its day, she determined to dazzle the capital, even if it meant spending a small fortune on a new wardrobe in the process. Second, having been raised as a political insider from girlhood, she was also adamant that she would be more than a clotheshorse in Washington. She meant to show the federal capital that she had valuable opinions of her own and would continue in the role she truly, if delusionally, perceived she still occupied: that of her husband's closest advisor.

Few women of the time could have realized such contrary ambitions, and Mary began to show the strain of trying. Hearing rumors during her vacation that Lincoln was still considering Norman Judd for his cabinet, she even dashed off an astonishingly audacious letter from New York—not to her husband, but with Machiavellian ingenuity to his influential friend David Davis, to warn against the appointment. Claiming to have absorbed an intimate knowledge of New York financial affairs in just a few days, she wrote: "*Judd* would cause trouble & dissatisfaction, & if Wall Street testifies correctly, his business transactions, have not always borne inspection." Then she turned on the feminine charm, concluding: "Mr. Lincoln's great attachment for you, is my present reason for writing. I know, a word from you, will have much effect, for the good of the country, and Mr. Lincoln's future reputation, I believe you will speak to him on this subject & urge him, not to give him so responsible a place." In the end, Judd was not appointed—but only because Lincoln felt awkward naming a fellow Illinoisan, not because his wife opposed his elevation.[76]

Mary made many new friends in New York—unfortunately for her, chiefly among unctuous merchants who envisioned profit and publicity by snaring such a famous, and gullible, customer. After extending her stay without finding it necessary to notify her husband, she headed home weighed down with new outfits to complement ballooning debts and inflated notions of her own importance. In Buffalo, she erupted imperially when a railroad employee tried to charge her for her fare, forcing Robert to warn the ticket agent: "The Old Lady is raising hell about her passes."[77]

Yet while she was away, a lonely Lincoln pined for her. For three successive nights "stormy with snow," one newspaper reported, Lincoln walked to the town depot, "with an umbrella over him," to wait expectantly for "his better half," who failed to show up: "We should not be surprised," cracked the reporter, "if his conjugal fidelity has not inaugurated bronchitis, neuralgia, and diphtheria." Perhaps, it hoped, "if Mr. Lincoln will make such sacrifices for his own Union, he ought, as a patriot, to make some efforts to save the American Union."[78] Finally, to

Lincoln's delight, "Mrs. Lincoln returned in good health and excellent spirits," Henry Villard observed, adding: "whether she got a good scolding from Abraham for unexpectedly prolonging her absence, I am unable to say; but I know she found it rather difficult to part with the winter gayeties at New York."[79] The *New-York Illustrated News* thought the "touching picture" of the "model husband" waiting for three nights "in the cold . . . does not establish Mrs. Lincoln's claim to be a model wife."[80]

Back home as well for his own winter holiday, seventeen-year-old Bob proceeded to dazzle the local girls with the results of "the improving influences of genteel, well dressed and well behaved Boston." Villard observed the "heir apparent" walking the streets with the president-elect, "bringing up the rear of the 'old man.' " The "comparative elegance" of his appearance presented "a striking contrast to the loose, careless, awkward rigging of his Presidential father."[81] No presidential son since John Quincy Adams earned such attention from the press. But even if, at first, it made him popular with girls, Robert came to detest the scrutiny, expressing years later "a repugnance to what is called 'public life' that is almost morbid." To Abraham Lincoln's oldest son, life in the glare of presidential publicity came to resemble "a gilded prison."[82]

THE TRUTH WAS, Lincoln was having far more difficulty assembling his official family than reuniting his personal one. Just before the new year began, the *New York Herald* optimistically reported that "the work commenced in good earnest by the President elect immediately after the meeting of the electoral colleges, some three weeks, since, is nearly completed." Northerners took the report seriously; the *Herald*, after all, boasted a reporter "embedded" with Lincoln. Who would know better?

The cabinet seemed set, the paper declared—with Pennsylvania's David Wilmot certain to be secretary of the interior, John C. Frémont secretary of war, and either Moses H. Grinnell or George Opdyke as secretary of the treasury. The State Department would go to New En-

gland, while William H. Seward would go to *old* England—as ambassador to the Court of St. James. Save for the report that Edward Bates
would serve as attorney general, the *Herald*'s predictions proved not only
premature, but also inaccurate.[83]

A week later, reassessing "the Rail Splitter, as a Cabinet Maker," the
Herald caught on to the likelihood that Seward would accept State after
all, and Cameron the War Department—though it now reported that
William A. Graham of North Carolina would be awarded Interior and
Gideon Welles of Connecticut the job of postmaster general. "Simon
Cameron was . . . sound as Florida oak," the paper noted, torturing the
rail-splitting simile, and Seward well deserved the highest post though
he was "a rather crooked stick and desired that he should go abroad." As
for Welles, the paper asked: "Where in the name of all the departed
heroes and fossilized politicians, did they dig up that antique piece of
timber?" All in all, opined the *Herald*, the old rail-splitter had done a
fair piece of work "for a beginning," adding: "Whether the different elements, the Southern oak and the Northern maple, can be worked in
together, time will show."[84]

By the first week of January, the timbers buckled. Soon after Cameron departed Springfield, Lincoln welcomed the senator's Pennsylvania
enemy, Alexander K. McClure, to town on January 2. Predictably, Mc-
Clure had nothing good to say about the man Lincoln had invited to join
his cabinet. Lincoln, who knew the canny political operative well enough
to call him "Aleck,"[85] heard him out, ever "approachable," yet "reticent"
about encouraging intrigues.[86] Growing impatient after enduring the
usual litany of complaints and rumors, Lincoln demanded that his visitor
either prove the charges against Cameron or stop making them.[87] Prepared for this dramatic moment, McClure grandly replied that if "you
throw upon us the disagreeable duty of establishing his want of personal
& political integrity, it will be done with fearful fidelity."[88] He had
brought documents with him that he believed established Cameron as
morally and fiscally unfit for any cabinet post, especially the Treasury.

Evidently, McClure's proof took Lincoln's breath away. Swayed by
the disturbing evidence, Lincoln buckled, composing a brutal letter to

Cameron the following day, abruptly withdrawing his offer to appoint him to a key post.[89] As he bluntly advised the senator: "Since seeing you things have developed which make it impossible for me to take you into the cabinet"—not just the McClure charges, he hinted, but a "more potent matter . . . wholly outside of Pennsylvania," though, as Lincoln rather mysteriously put it, "I am not at liberty to specify it. Enough that it appears to me to be sufficient." Lincoln would offer Cameron no more than an opportunity for face-saving: "I suggest that you write me declining the appointment, in which case I do not object to it being known that it was tendered you. Better do this at once, before things so change, that you can not honorably decline, and I be compelled to openly recall the tender."[90]

Two days later on January 4, with the rebuff to Cameron en route, Salmon P. Chase finally made his own appearance in Springfield. Exhausted and disheveled from two days of travel on four different railroad lines, the fastidious Chase limped to the Chenery House, but barely had time to refresh himself before Lincoln broke protocol and respectfully came calling at his hotel, eager to meet the large-headed, nearsighted man he had a few days earlier called his party's "Moses."[91]

Chase arrived in town determined to exhibit no overt desire to join the administration, though his visit shouted otherwise. "I go to Springfield by request," he assured a friend ambitious for his appointment the day before his departure, "—simply for a conference. If it points where you wish I shall hardly know how to say yes."[92] Before long, however, Lincoln impressed him with "his clearsightedness, uprightness, fidelity to the principles he represents & firm resolve to administer the Govt in the most patriotic spirit and with the strictest regard to the rights of all the States and all their citizens." Chase proudly described their talks as "entirely free & unreserved."[93]

Lincoln quickly discovered, as Doris Kearns Goodwin has shown, that the surest way to Chase's heart was flattery. "I have done with you what I would not perhaps have ventured to do with any other man in the country," he told him, "—sent for you to ask you whether you will accept the appointment of Secretary of the Treasury, without, however,

being exactly prepared to offer it to you." As Lincoln described his pre-
dicament, he needed first to straighten out the political mess in Pennsylvania, to whose pro-tariff voters he still felt he owed a leading cabinet
position.[94] And Pennsylvanians, he admitted, would be displeased to
learn of an early appointment for Chase—whose free trade positions
they found obnoxious—before the Cameron situation resolved itself.
Somewhat testily, Chase replied that he "desired no position & could
not easily reconcile myself to the acceptance of a subordinate one."[95]
But slowly, Lincoln wore him down.

After a lengthy one-on-one conference that Friday, the two men
were joined Saturday at a second round of meetings by Amos Tuck, back
from New Hampshire for a final try for a post of his own in the administration.[96] Tuck could still remember the young Lincoln who first struck
him as a "good-natured . . . tall, awkward, genial" freshman congressman, demonstrating but "scanty preparation for influential position."[97]
Perhaps by sharing his colorful recollections with the starchy Ohio senator, Tuck may have contributed to softening Chase's formal veneer.

Early on the morning of Sunday the 6th, with the Cameron situation
still plaguing his mind, a visibly "distressed" Lincoln called on two other
Springfield visitors, Gustave Koerner and Norman Judd, at their hotel
and sought their counsel. Pennsylvania, he began, clearly deserved a
spot in the cabinet. To whom should it go? Almost in unison, the two
men replied: "Not Cameron!" Why not former Pennsylvania congressman David Wilmot or onetime Kansas territorial governor Andrew
Reeder (now practicing law in Easton) instead?

Losing patience, Lincoln reminded Koerner and Judd that he had
received hundreds of letters and scores of visitors endorsing Cameron,
not the other aspirants. If he was prepared to appoint to the cabinet
three of his four chief rivals at the Chicago convention—Seward, Chase,
and Bates—how could he omit the fourth? Koerner countered that
Cameron, however strong, was toxically corrupt. "I know," Lincoln sadly
replied, "but can I get along if that State should oppose my administration?" Even with his Cameron recall letter in the mail, he left the an-
guished session still unsure of what to do.[98]

Later that day, Chase was seen accompanying Mr. and Mrs. Lincoln to hear "a most excellent sermon" by minister John Howe Brown at Sabbath services at Springfield's First Presbyterian Church—a sure sign that the Ohio senator had already won Lincoln's respect, if not also a top job.[99] Privately, perhaps even while he sat in church that day, Lincoln weighed how he might reconcile Seward and Chase, each of whom selfishly opposed the other's appointment. Meanwhile, Cameron had not been heard from at all, certainly not to withdraw from contention gracefully as the president-elect had demanded.

Lincoln and Chase parted company with neither a specific offer nor a definite acceptance on the table, but Chase evidently left town believing he needed—and wanted—help to nail down the job that he supposedly did not crave. Writing to his friend Hiram Barney from the very train transporting him home, he urged the New Yorker, to whom Lincoln owed a debt for co-sponsoring his Cooper Union speech, to send "a deputation to Springfield" at once to further plead his case.[100]

Although he later told supporters he could serve the country as well from the Senate as the cabinet, and feared the "broken down" Treasury would require "the most toilsome drudgery almost without respite for four years,"[101] Chase could not disguise his newfound, if temporary, respect for the president-elect. Recalling their "very gratifying" Springfield meetings, he reported that Lincoln had "exhibited an integrity, capacity & firmness which gives me the best hopes of our future. He is a pensive patriot of the old school and loves the country & the Union with the devotion of a son." Most important of all to the vain Chase, Lincoln had "manifested a personal confidence which I would rather have than any official position."[102]

For his part, as soon as Chase was gone, Lincoln penned a new letter to Washington to his increasingly valuable advisor and sounding board, Senator Trumbull, to report on recent developments in Springfield. "Gen. C[ameron]. has not been offered the Treasury, and I think, will not be," reported Lincoln. "It seems to me not only highly proper, but a *necessity*, that Gov. Chase shall take that place. His ability, firmness, and purity of character, produce the propriety."[103] His appointment would solve a political problem, too. Chase alone could "reconcile" William Cullen Bryant "and his class" of anti-Seward New Yorkers to Seward's appointment to the State Department. Yet, as Lincoln knew, formidable complications still loomed, if nothing else because Seward favored Cameron and distrusted Chase.

But a Chase appointment, Lincoln fretted, brought with it "the danger that the protectionists of Pennsylvania will be dissatisfied, and, to clear this difficulty, Gen. C. must be brought to co-operate," Lincoln cautioned Trumbull. Cameron "would readily do this," he believed, in return "for the War Department"—although this solution carried pitfalls, too, for ". . . then comes the fierce opposition to his having any Department, threatening even to send charges into the Senate to procure his rejection by that body." If necessary, the new president consoled himself that he could use the patronage power to smooth things over: Cameron should stay out of the cabinet altogether and "retain his place in the Senate," and if his seat had been prematurely "promised to another, let that other take a respectable, and reasonably lucrative place abroad." Cameron's political friends—and Lincoln readily admitted that he had been "more amply recommended for a place in the cabinet, than any other man"—would, he promised, "with entire fairness" be "cared for in Pennsylvania, and elsewhere"[104] by federal appointments designed to keep their loyalty and limit their dissatisfaction.

There the Cameron matter rested—for all of one week. When the senator's friend J. P. Sanderson rushed back to Springfield on January 13, this time accompanied by Republican Senator-elect Edgar Cowan, Lincoln learned to his distress that Cameron felt mortally offended by Lincoln's letter withdrawing his offer, and what was worse, simply refused to abide by it.[105] Leonard Swett confirmed the "awkward fix," reporting to Lincoln that when Cameron was directly asked to "adopt the course you requested," he defiantly replied that "he could not[.]"[106] In effect, Cameron demanded that if Lincoln insisted on retracting his appointment, he must do so publicly and bear the political consequences.

Sharing Seward's dread at the thought of "the army of Camerons friends in hostility" against the new administration,[107] and rather priding himself on his own record of never willingly hurting other men, Lincoln tried yet another stratagem. He sat down and wrote not one but two fresh letters to the angry Pennsylvania senator, proposing an elaborate camouflage to soften the earlier rejection. Regretting that Cameron's "feelings were wounded by the *terms* of my letter," Lincoln now suggested: "Destroy the offensive letter, or return it to me," insisting he had written it "under great anxiety" and "intended no offence."[108] In its place, Lincoln offered yet another letter, deceptively backdated to January 3, in which he again removed Cameron from cabinet consideration, but this time in much softer terms.

In the second of these desperate new notes, Lincoln put it on record that Cameron had earlier traveled to Springfield "at my invitation, and not upon any suggestion of your own," and that once there, Lincoln had indeed offered him "a place in the cabinet." With "much pain," however, owing to an unspecified, "unexpected complication," rather than "any change of my view as to the ability or faithfulness with which you would discharge the duties of the place," Lincoln again asked "that you relieve me from great embarrassment by allowing me to recall the offer." Lincoln ended this elaborate subterfuge by declaring his intention to postpone the whole matter for a month. "I now think," he closed his new letter to Cameron, "I will not definitely fix upon any appointment for Pennsylvania until I reach Washington."[109]

Not satisfied that their enemy was merely injured, however, the forces arrayed against Cameron moved in for the kill. Following his own visit to Lincoln, *Chicago Tribune* editor Charles H. Ray wrote to Senator Trumbull suggesting Congress act to censure Cameron, sparing the president-elect the political embarrassment that might follow should the details of his indecision become public.[110] Congressman John Covode, of Cameron's own home state, warned Lincoln anew that Cameron lacked "the confidence of honest men generally."[111] And Harry Woods of Pittsburgh advised the president-elect that "the news . . . that Gen Cameron was not to be in your Cabinet was delightfully received by Republicans here."[112] Remarkably, little news of this internecine brawling, or of Lincoln's clumsy handling of the situation (though a good argument might be made that he proved as clumsy as a fox on the Cameron matter), leaked to the press. At a moment when he could least afford to be portrayed as indecisive, much less blind to malfeasance, Lincoln dodged a major crisis that might have crippled his presidency before it began. But fate alone was not responsible. Cameron continued to believe—correctly—that he might yet win the standoff, and as long as he remained a viable candidate for an appointment, he had nothing to gain from taking his hurt feelings to the newspapers. Lincoln, who would have been wise to ignore the overwhelming rush of pro-Cameron correspondence and look elsewhere to reward Pennsylvania, continued to believe that no substitute would convey the same degree of appreciation.

For the time being, understandably, Lincoln opted to keep his other likely cabinet choices to himself. On January 17, he saw to the announcement that he would make no further appointments until he arrived in Washington. This of course did nothing to inhibit candidates and their supporters from surging into town to stake their claims and reiterate their recommendations anyway. Over the next few days, delegations from both Indiana and California lay "close siege to the President elect."[113]

In short order came Republican leader George G. Fogg, determined to settle New England's claims, and Francis Preston Blair, Jr., to argue anew for a cabinet spot for his brother, Montgomery. One Springfield correspondent noted that "the presence of a man of Frank Blair's nerve and enthusiasm has a happy influence on the tone of feeling here," even when Blair provocatively told another journalist on the scene: "The day of compromise is gone, and the day of fighting come."[114]

Most of the fighting continued to swirl about Cameron. Two more of the Pennsylvanian's most ardent supporters, New York editor Alexander Cummings and Congressman James K. Moorhead, materialized in Springfield and cornered Lincoln there on January 21, telling him bluntly that the senator deserved—and expected—the appointment Lincoln had originally promised him. Perhaps feeling trapped, Lincoln penned yet another letter to the Pennsylvanian—"I shall be obliged if you will visit me again at this place"—but then either forgot or decided not to mail it.[115] At least it served to get rid of Cummings and Moorhead. Rumors swirled around town that, at Seward's urging, Thurlow Weed was expected to return to Springfield at any hour "to bring the Cameron business to a head."[116] But Cameron's backers had the last word. Days later, a leading Pennsylvania newspaper affirmed its belief "that Gen. Cameron will be in President Lincoln's Cabinet," adding: "we cannot think or believe that the wish of two hundred and sixty-seven thousand free men who cast their votes for a protective tariff policy in Pennsylvania will be slighted or overslaughed."[117]

As all this was transpiring, Chase's friends increasingly pressed him to join the administration if formally recruited. Voicing "a most earnest hope that if the Secretaryship of the Treasury has been tendered to you, you will accept it," Elihu Washburne wrote: "Will you permit me to say that in the present state of the country . . . and its finances, the country demands your services in the Treasury Department."[118] Charles Sumner similarly recommended "that you will accept the post," arguing that Chase would "help those principles for which we have so long labored together."[119] Back in New Hampshire, Amos Tuck wrote to affirm: "I esteem it necessary to our cause and to our friends to have you in the Cabinet."[120]

To Lincoln, Chase expressed no overt eagerness, confiding only his opposition to yet another cabinet aspirant, Caleb B. Smith, by arguing that the Hoosier's "reputation" in "railroad & other transactions" would make it difficult for Lincoln to "give the country a pure financial administration."[121] At least he was beginning to think like a treasury secretary. Like Seward, however, Chase not only wanted a cabinet position for himself, but veto power over others. Fortunately for Lincoln, Chase lacked Seward's self-confidence and could be more easily manipulated.

Lincoln was in no rush for Chase to show his hand, even when one supporter pressed him to "make the tender at once" and grant the Ohioan the same "delicacy of treatment"[122] he had afforded Seward and Bates—that is, an immediate, no-strings-attached appointment. Over the next month, as Chase continued to hint at his disinclination to serve in a cabinet headed by Seward, the exasperated but astute president-elect let matters run their course without further interference. His unerring political instincts told him that when Inauguration Day neared, and unless he felt the need before March to select someone altogether different, then Chase, so eager for "personal confidence" and "official position" alike, would join Bates and Seward in the cabinet he was having such difficulty in assembling.

Amid all this confusion and scheming, Gideon Welles, unable to journey west from Connecticut to stake his own claim—or perhaps, to his disappointment, uninvited—mounted his campaign for the New England cabinet appointment from afar. Although Welles would later claim, quoting the president, that Lincoln had decided to appoint him as early as Election Night, surviving written evidence suggests that he had a far harder time winning a spot.

The old Democrat surely did not endear himself to Lincoln when he proposed, in mid-December, that the president-elect issue "a document, in some form, that should appease the discontentive and violent portion of our countrymen who have been defeated."[123] Lincoln intended no such statement, and as far as we know, did not even bother replying to the suggestion.

More wisely, Welles turned to surrogates to make his own case for him. J. D. Baldwin of the *Worcester Daily Spy* replied on January 7 that he had begun applying pressure: "I have written to Mr. Lincoln to express to him my sense of your character and eminent fitness for a cabinet office, and to say how much it will heighten the very great satisfaction with which I remember my vote for him in the convention, (for I gave him my vote on the ballot that secured his nomination) to have him select you." Baldwin was not quite as smarmy in his actual letter to Lincoln, in which he merely praised Welles as "one of the very ablest and best men in the Republican party."[124]

The following day, Edward L. Pierce of Boston assured Welles that he, too, felt their region's place in the cabinet "should be conferred on you in preference to any New England man"—including Charles Francis Adams, who should stay in Congress, and Nathaniel Banks, dismissed as "too indifferent to principles."[125] George G. Fogg urged Welles to dispatch surrogates to Springfield to pressure Lincoln, and eventually took on the role himself.[126] On the other hand, New Yorker E. B. Hudson, asking that his name not be "exposed," alleged in a new letter to Lincoln that Welles had once mistreated female factory workers at a cotton mill he owned years before—and as a result was now "feared by every defenceless woman of this place."[127]

Endorsements and praise for Welles predominated, but Lincoln showed no urgency about announcing a decision, even after the *Chicago Tribune* reported that "it seems to be generally understood that the Hon. Gideon Welles, of Connecticut, would be a member of Mr. Lincoln's cabinet." Much as he needed former Democrats in his administration, Lincoln left the Connecticut editor in political limbo along with Chase and Cameron.

The Welles matter was probably settled earlier—but only privately—on December 29, when, from Maine, Vice President–elect Hannibal Hamlin offered his response to Lincoln's invitation to name the man to represent his region. "In reply to your enquiry," Hamlin wrote, "I have no hesitation in saying, that in my judgment, Mr. Wells [sic] is the better man for New England, and I feel confident it will give better satisfaction that either of the others named—That is my opinion."[128] Eventually, Lincoln came to share it. A month later, he finally confided to a gratified Fogg in Springfield that "if I were obliged to make a selection *today*, it would be Mr. Welles." Of course, Lincoln was not obliged to do so that day, and the offer remained unspoken.[129]

More than twenty years afterward, Illinois editor Jeriah Bonham would insist he had seen Welles himself at Lincoln's home during the first week of January. But Bonham must have confused him with Chase. Welles never went west. He remained in Hartford to await his future.[130]

"Poor Lincoln! God help him!" sympathized Lincoln's law partner, Billy Herndon, observing this endless parade of cabinet prospects, their supporters, and their enemies. "What angry looks & growls for bones that have fat & meat on them."[131]

• • •

MEANWHILE—FOR LINCOLN NEVER enjoyed the leisure, as president-elect, to deal with only one challenge at a time—the growling for compromise and conciliation from Washington intensified, too. According to the president-elect's own hometown newspaper—the pro-Democratic one—the South was more ablaze than ever "over the election of the abolitionist Lincoln and the free Negro Hamlin." What was worse, the paper exaggerated, the Republicans' obstinate resistance to conciliation had tragically encouraged premature slave uprisings that had unleashed horrific punishment. "They have been put down with great severity, some . . . burned at the stake, other[s] hung, others sold to go further south," and all "denied their usual Christmas indulgences." [132]

In an atmosphere of heightening danger to the Union, and growing concern in some quarters that the incoming president was not up to the crisis, renewed pressure built on Lincoln to compromise—at least to say something to communicate more than what Gideon Welles called his "unutterable distress." [133] There was wild talk in the press of replacing the new president with three chief executives, one from the South. [134] Showing a similar lack of confidence, a Brooklyn correspondent advised Lincoln to call an unorthodox "General Convention of the States . . . the earlier the better . . . to settle the 'vexed question' of Slavery." [135] With his own compromise plan moribund, Senator Crittenden threatened to bypass the Committee of Thirteen and submit the package to the full Senate as a personal bill or, somehow, directly to the nation's voters as an unprecedented public referendum—which some observers predicted would pass handily. [136]

The secessionists proved deaf to all overtures. One by one, Southern officials abandoned the Buchanan administration, leaving the incumbent's cabinet in far greater disarray than his successor's. Meanwhile, Georgia state militia defiantly captured a federal installation at Fort Pulaski outside Savannah. In short order, Florida seized control of the Apalachicola garrison, and Alabama troops occupied not only the federal arsenal at Mount Vernon, but Forts Morgan and Gaines, which guarded the entrance to Mobile Bay. Even without "violence and bloodshed," Lincoln's secretary John Nicolay fumed, the South had begun "levying actual war against the United States"[137] as President Buchanan stood by helplessly.

Some Northerners reacted much less indignantly. New York's Democratic mayor Fernando Wood—"either a wag or a lunatic," in the words of one Northern newspaper, "monstrous and treasonable" to another— proposed that his metropolis secede from the Union, too, and form a free port that could maintain its profitable commercial trade with the slaveholding South. "The joke would have been better," the *Boston Advertiser* shot back, "if he had planned to seize the forts in the harbor, to imprison Gen. Scott in the Tombs [the city jail], and to take possession of the State treasury and archives."[138]

Not everyone was laughing. Ascribing "incapacity, stupidity, imbecility, gross ignorance and habitual venality" to the stalemated Congress, the *New York Herald* angrily concluded that "no remedy whatever is to be looked for from their representatives." Sounding eerily like President Buchanan in his December annual message, it blamed not Southern extremism but "republican fanaticism" for the current "avalanche of destruction."[139] The editorial also bore echoes of Jefferson Davis's insistence that Southern discontent—even treason—should be blamed exclusively on "the stubborn refusal of a haughty majority" to "yield anything to the spirit of peace and conciliation."[140]

Surveying the worsening situation, even the anti-slavery poet John Greenleaf Whittier seemed to be urging conciliation with his latest offering in verse, "A Word for the Hour," published on January 16:

> The firmament breaks up. In black eclipse
> Light after light goes out. One evil star,
> Luridly glaring through the smoke of war,
> As in the dream of the Apocalypse,
> Drags others down. Let us not weakly weep
> Nor rashly threaten.

"Will You Paint Me with False Whiskers?"

Artists pressed Lincoln to sit for portraits after his election, but were foiled when the president-elect changed his image by growing a beard. G. P. A. Healy painted a handsome likeness (top) in November 1860, but by the time it went on exhibit in Chicago, the once clean-shaven subject had dramatically altered his appearance, rendering the painting obsolete. Itinerant artist Jesse Atwood faced a similar hurdle and ill-advisedly chose to update his canvas (bottom) by superimposing this unconvincing beard. *(Corcoran Gallery of Art, Washington; Lilly Library, Indiana University, Bloomington)*

The President-elect's Home and Office

Lincoln and his sons Willie and Tad pose on the front porch of their Springfield, Illinois, home in the summer of 1860, during the presidential candidate's non-campaign for the White House. Once elected, Lincoln continued to greet many callers in this house. Until January 1861, his official headquarters was the Governor's Suite in the nearby State Capitol. This Henri Lovie sketch of his second-floor reception room there was published in *Frank Leslie's Illustrated Newspaper* on November 24, 1860. The elaborate wood-link chain hanging in the corner of the room was a handmade gift from an admirer. (*The Lincoln Museum*)

Lincoln's Personal Aides

With no public funding, a nineteenth-century president-elect—particularly one of modest means like Lincoln—could afford scant office help. Despite mounting correspondence and an avalanche of visitors, Lincoln made do with: private secretary John George Nicolay (top left), and, later, assistant secretary John M. Hay (top right). Seeing to his personal protection—to push through the crowds on Election Day, for example, and later as bodyguards on the long journey to Washington—were: lawyer Ward Hill Lamon (bottom left); and celebrated young Zouave drillmaster Ephraim Elmer Ellsworth (bottom right), who was like a son to the Lincolns. Mary kept all these photos in her White House family album. (*The Lincoln Museum*)

His Last Photographs in Illinois

To satisfy growing public demand for new portraits, Lincoln—his beard beginning to fill in now—sat for the photograph at left at the Springfield gallery of Christopher S. German on January 13, 1861. Four weeks later—on February 9—Lincoln returned to German's studio at the request of sculptor Thomas D. Jones to sit for the widely distributed portrait on this book's title page, as well as this little-known profile, his final photographs in his hometown. (*Library of Congress*)

Famous Visitors to Springfield

Influential Republicans, among them cabinet aspirants, made their way to the president-elect's hometown during the secession winter to confer, lobby, and submit to the equivalent of job interviews. Among them were (clockwise from top left): Edward Bates of Missouri, who became attorney general; Salmon P. Chase of Ohio, Lincoln's choice for secretary of the treasury; Simon Cameron of Pennsylvania, a cabinet hopeful whose reputation for corruption bedeviled the incoming chief executive; and Thurlow Weed, the New York Republican boss and close advisor to Senator William H. Seward. (*Lincoln Museum [Cameron]; Library of Congress*)

Voices from the Press

Connecticut editor-turned-politician Gideon Welles (top left), a former Democrat, aspired to become New England's representative in the Lincoln cabinet. *New York Herald* correspondent Henry Villard (top right) was "embedded" in Springfield for most of the transition. *New York Tribune* editor Horace Greeley (bottom left) visited Lincoln in Springfield and later boarded his inaugural train unannounced to nag him on compromise and patronage appointments. And Frederick Douglass (bottom right), editor of his own abolitionist paper, unleashed a torrent of criticism. (*Greeley: New Castle Historical Society; Villard: Abraham Lincoln Presidential Library and Museum; others, Library of Congress*)

Administration Partners

Lincoln and incoming Vice President Hannibal Hamlin (left) had met only briefly before they were elected on the same ticket in 1860. After their victory, they conferred in Chicago, and later, in New York. Senator William H. Seward (right), who believed he, not Lincoln, should have won the presidency, corresponded with Lincoln, worried for his safety, and made suggestions for his inaugural address. Seward was Lincoln's first and only choice for secretary of state. *(Library of Congress; Lincoln Museum)*

Republican Confidants

At first, Lincoln relied on Illinois Republican friends to guide him through the interregnum—but later he distanced himself from many of them. U.S. Senator Lyman Trumbull (top left) accompanied the president-elect to Chicago after the election. Norman Judd (top right), chairman of the Republican State Committee, hoped for a Cabinet appointment he did not receive. Orville Hickman Browning (bottom left), who wanted ex-Democrat Judd kept out of the inner circle, later advised Lincoln on his inaugural address. And campaign manager David Davis (bottom right) accompanied Lincoln to Washington, but got no appointment of his own until Lincoln named him to the U.S. Supreme Court in October 1862. (*Lincoln Museum [Davis]; Library of Congress*)

The Democratic Opposition

Outgoing President James Buchanan (left), who had hoped his pro-slavery vice president would succeed him, nonetheless treated Lincoln cordially when he arrived in Washington to take office. Stephen A. Douglas (right), who ran unsuccessfully against Lincoln as a Northern Democrat, called on the president-elect several times when he reached the capital in an unsuccessful effort to persuade him to yield on compromise. The Lincolns owned this "autographed" Douglas *carte-de-visite*; it was signed by his widow three years after the Little Giant's death. *(Library of Congress; Lincoln Museum)*

Voices from the South

(Clockwise from top left): Secession agitator Edmund Ruffin hoped Lincoln would win so inflamed slave states would leave the Union. Former President John Tyler of Virginia became president of the Peace Convention, which tried to craft a binding compromise plan before Lincoln took office. Senator John J. Crittenden proposed his own failed congressional compromise package, but remained loyal to the Union. And Georgia's diminutive Alexander H. Stephens, Lincoln's onetime Congressional colleague, exchanged letters with president-elect Lincoln in an attempt to forestall disunion, but later became vice president of the Confederacy. (*National Portrait Gallery [Stephens]; Library of Congress*)

Lincoln Sits for a Sculpture

Ohio sculptor Thomas D. Jones created this handsome bust of Lincoln from daily, hour-long sittings in Springfield in January and February 1861. Lincoln posed for it in a local hotel after abandoning his State Capitol headquarters to make way for the 1861 Illinois legislative session. The last portrait of Lincoln to be made in his hometown, it combined neoclassical and modern elements and made Lincoln appear Jacksonian—precisely the way the artist saw his subject. Though the bust was later mass-produced in plaster and also widely copied for engravings, Jones earned only twenty dollars for it from his patron. (*Lincoln Museum*)

The New First Family

(Clockwise from top left): The Lincoln family never sat together for photographs, but occasionally posed individually or in groups. Before leaving for Washington, Mary Lincoln took Willie and Tad to the gallery of Preston Butler, a local Springfield photographer, to pose for this portrait—complete with a studio backdrop to suggest an outdoor setting. Eldest son Robert, an eighteen-year-old Harvard freshman, merrily drank and smoked his way to Washington and posed for his own photo in the capital a few months after his father became president. The president-elect made a final visit to his aged stepmother, Sarah Bush Johnston Lincoln, on the prairie before leaving Illinois for his inauguration. She posed for her only known photograph after her famous son's death. (*Lincoln Museum; Abraham Lincoln Presidential Library and Museum [Sarah]*)

An Affectionate Farewell

Neither artists nor photographers appeared on the scene to record Lincoln's emotional goodbye to Springfield on February 11, 1861. This crude but endearing nineteenth-century reimagining comes close to an informed illustration of the president-elect addressing the large crowd of neighbors that gathered for his departure. The small brick depot opposite Lincoln still stands, though it was later enlarged. (*Library of Congress*)

Face to Face with a Secessionist

Lincoln stares down New York Mayor Fernando Wood at a February 20, 1861, reception in the President-elect's honor at City Hall. Wood, who hoped to lead the metropolis out of the Union to safeguard trade with the South, offered Lincoln a tepid greeting from behind a desk once used by George Washington. This drawing appeared in *Frank Leslie's Illustrated Newspaper*. (*Library of Congress*)

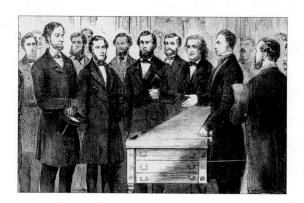

The Westerner in New York

An artist for *Harper's Weekly* made the sketch that inspired this newsworthy woodcut of President-elect Lincoln addressing well-wishers in New York from the second-floor balcony of the Astor House shortly after his arrival on February 19, 1861. In truth, Lincoln's welcome to the overwhelmingly Democratic city was chillier than the hat-waving uproar depicted here. *(Library of Congress)*

Raising the Flag at Philadelphia

Local photographer F. DeBourg Richards was perfectly positioned on the scene when Abraham Lincoln appeared on the grandstand to raise an American flag outside Independence Hall on February 22, 1861. The towering president-elect stands above the white star at far left, wearing his signature stovepipe hat. *(Library of Congress)*

Paying a Courtesy Call on the Incumbent

As President Buchanan reels at the sight of him, his successor appears unannounced at the Executive Mansion in a cloud of smoke—as revealed by prestidigitator William H. Seward—in this *New York Illustrated News* woodcut cartoon, "Awful Consternation of the Old Party at the White House, and Sudden Appearance of Lincoln—(Chief Magician, Mr. Seward)." *(New York State Library)*

Inauguration Day

As many as thirty thousand people—believed the largest crowd yet to witness a presidential swearing in—ringed the U.S. Capitol on March 4, 1861, to watch Lincoln take the oath of office and deliver his widely anticipated inaugural address. Although he is barely visible in this panoramic shot by photographer Alexander Gardner, Lincoln is likely the tallest figure standing beneath the square wooden canopy that straddles the base of the crowded East Portico. *(Library of Congress)*

Without authorization from Lincoln but encouraged by his own political friends, Seward had resumed his independent efforts to find common ground. New York businessman Moses H. Grinnell, a Seward ally,
set the stage by joining a group of influential Empire State Republicans
who petitioned the president-elect to demonstrate "action in advance of
power" and tender an "olive branch" to the South. Appealing to Lincoln's pride and sense of history, Grinnell and his co-signers predicted
that if Lincoln showed "the Sagacity of a Statesman and a Patriot," he
"would be hailed as the Savior of his Country and would deserve and
enjoy a place in the hearts of the people, second only to him, who is so
justly styled the Father of his Country." [141]

In a new letter of his own to Lincoln, Seward suggested the adoption
of compromise "principles" that included an amendment strictly guaranteeing that "the constitution shall never be altered so as to authorise
Congress to abolish or interfere with slavery in the states." [142] His proposal serves to remind the modern reader how history might have
changed had Seward, not Lincoln, won the 1860 election. But Seward
received no encouragement from the president-elect. Unwilling or unable to challenge him for the leadership of the party, Seward ultimately
voted against the Crittenden Compromise on December 28—and on
the same day, dispatched a letter to the president-elect finally, formally,
accepting the post of secretary of state. [143]

With the Crittenden proposals tabled, Lincoln saw no reason even
to affirm the Republican policy of noninterference with the slave states,
believing that reiterating this pledge now would smack of desperation.
He felt vindicated when conservative Republican senator James R.
Doolittle of Wisconsin advised him on January 10 that the secession
"disease" had grown "so deep seated" that an offer to compromise now
"would be treated with contempt as wrung from our fears." [144] In full
agreement, Lincoln rejected the contrary advice of Congressman John
A. Gilmer, whom he had been courting for the cabinet, but who, at the
moment, held the important post of chairman of the House Committee
on Elections. Sounding eerily like Seward, the North Carolinian believed that, with "the country in imminent peril," Lincoln's sole hope of

halting secession momentum was to support an amendment guaranteeing perpetual noninterference with slavery. "You may drive from you many party friends," Gilmer conceded, "but by the preservation of the peace of the country, you will nationalize yourself & your party—You would make to yourself deservedly a name, far beyond that of President."[145]

Similarly leaning to Seward's conciliatory position, the Herald agreed that "the concessions demanded by the South involve no sacrifice of Northern principles."[146] Such support no doubt encouraged Seward to ignore Lincoln's warnings and make one last attempt to conciliate the secessionists. With the Senate galleries packed to overflowing, Seward delivered a bravura speech to the chamber on January 12 that left Crittenden and others weeping in their seats. "If it be a Christian duty to forgive to the stranger even seventy times seven offenses," he implored his colleagues, "it is the highest patriotism to endure without complaint the passionate waywardness of political brethren so long as there is hope that they may come to a better mind." Urging his fellow senators to "discard" the hope "that the Union is to be saved by somebody in particular"—his only allusion to Lincoln—Seward begged them to act quickly "to redress any real grievances of the offended states," or at least to agree on a moratorium on secession.[147] To the New York Times, the performance at first seemed "free from every taint of partisan or sectional bitterness." The newspaper condemned both "dissatisfied" Republican zealots and "extreme" Southerners who ridiculed it.[148] In the end, the doubters prevailed. Shortly thereafter, the House Committee of Thirty-three met for the final time and deadlocked irreversibly. Thus ended what Charles Francis Adams called the "queer struggle" to devise a plan "sufficiently conciliatory to bridge over the chasm of rebellion."[149]

Lincoln was reportedly "not overpleased with Seward's oration, and not at all with any effort to abandon the Republican platform."[150] But eager to keep peace in the party, he nonetheless graciously told the New Yorker: "Your recent speech is well received here; and, I think, is doing good all over the country."[151] Seward proudly shared Lincoln's congratulatory note with his congressional colleagues. Back in Springfield, however, Lincoln irritably confided to Carl Schurz that "Seward made all his speeches without consulting him,"[152] perhaps a somewhat disingenuous attempt to have it both ways. Yet for a time, Lincoln did. By praising Seward, Lincoln hoped to demonstrate that Republicans were not insensitive to Southern concerns. But by concurrently keeping his closest allies aware of his own firmness, he made sure the party did not entertain deals involving the extension of slavery. As Schurz came to understand: "He himself will not hear of concessions and compromises, and says so openly to everyone who asks."[153]

With little visible prodding from Lincoln, the tide soon turned against Seward and his compromise initiative. The *National Anti-Slavery Standard* vigorously denounced the New Yorker's oration under the headline: "Senator Seward's Surrender," pronouncing it "a settled thing that all the demands the slaveholders have had the impudence to make . . . are to be granted, if they will be graciously pleased to pardon Abraham Lincoln for being elected and the North for having chosen him."[154] From Boston, Charles Russell Lowell termed Seward's speech "more worthy of a political dodger than a statesman."[155] Increasingly, strong anti-slavery men who had only recently questioned Lincoln's ability to deal with the emergency now looked to the president-elect to hold the line on conciliation with the South. Oliver Wendell Holmes, long worried that Republicans would bend "like a field of grain" on compromise, noted appreciatively that with each of Lincoln's assurances that he would execute the laws, "the backs of the Republicans stiffen again."[156]

The fiery Illinois congressman Owen Lovejoy was certain that Lincoln would never go back on his word about slavery extension, and so he told his colleagues. "I know he has too much regard for the common appellation by which he is familiarly known, of 'Honest Abe,' " he declared in a speech on the House floor, "ever to believe that he will betray the principles" of the party.[157] Back in Springfield, Billy Herndon remained equally confident that "Lincoln is as firm as a rock yet—opposed to all concessions that yield an iota of principle."[158] And in a rare interview, Lincoln told the *Missouri Democrat*—his words quickly picked up in other papers—that he would consent to no "compromising our diffi-culties" that involved "the victors put in the attitude of the vanquished, and the vanquished in the place of the victors." All he wanted, he in-sisted, was "a fair trial." [159]

Soon Frederick Douglass, otherwise increasingly dubious about Lin-coln, agreed that secession could succeed only "*by force, by treachery, or by negotiation*; and to neither [sic] will Abraham Lincoln succumb. To do so would be to put a razor to the throat of his party, write himself down a coward, make political platforms worse than a mockery, and to become the pliant tool of the very barbarism which he was elected to restrain, and"—quoting Lincoln—" 'place it where the public mind would rest in the belief in its ultimate extinction.' " [160]

Ultimately, even the *New York Herald* concluded that Seward had gone too far in suggesting Congress "wait for one, two or three years before anything is done to restore peace and harmony to the antagonis-tic sections." The senator's proposal, the paper now mocked, "suggests the picture of a man waiting on the bank of the Mississippi till its waters flowed off . . . in order to allow him to pass over." [161] Lincoln had sup-plied his party with "an infusion of backbone," Henry Villard wrote from Springfield. Once again, compromise died, and the secession winter continued, unthawed.

To Lincoln's relief, Villard's editors leveled scant criticism against him during this tense interlude, and what negative commentary did ap-pear was offset by the correspondent's friendly exclusives from Spring-field. Because the president-elect's quiet string-pulling to prevent compromise remained shrouded, his public silence served to cement his historical reputation as an inefficient transition leader. All but ignoring the president-elect, the widely read New York paper began directing its venom against the abolitionists, warning that if Lincoln's inauguration signaled "the beginning of a civil war," the fault would lie with "the fool-ish Bourbons of the republican party," [162] not the president-elect. At the time, such commentary usefully made Lincoln appear far more conser-vative than Republican extremists who might otherwise have won the White House had Lincoln never existed.

But this did little to assuage New York's powerful, but uneasy, commercial interests. On January 27, George Templeton Strong endured a diatribe from a particularly "lugubrious and despondent" dinner guest who bitterly complained that "those damned Republicans" seemed both unreasonable on compromise and blind to secession talk in the border states. Their intransigence threatened the entire economy. Southern debts would have to be written off, trade would come to an abrupt halt, and a depression was sure to follow.

In response, Strong tried speaking up in support of the incoming administration, wondering: "is any compromise or pacification desirable until we have ascertained whether we have or have not a government? Is not our first business now to see that the law of the land is executed and Abraham Lincoln, Esq., duly inaugurated March 4?" Sounding much like the president-elect himself, Strong added: "Would not 'concession' *now*, be an admission that what we have called the federal 'government' is and has been all along a mere sham, scarecrow, and practical nullity, unable to assert its own existence as against a seditious minority?"

Strong kept his own fears to himself. "Things look bad," he confided to his diary. Disunion—what had long been merely a "subject for college debating societies"—had become an "ugly spectre . . . risen—too soon."

Conceded Strong: "we have got to deal with the awful question of dissolution of the Union *now* and *here*."[163] Back in Springfield, Lincoln was preparing to do exactly that.

That very month, rebellious Democrats convened for a particularly riotous anti-Union mass meeting. Orator after orator rose to deliver "incendiary speeches," all "as favorable to the South as the most fiery secessionist could wish," and each "applauded to the echo." Had such a violent meeting occurred in Georgia or Alabama, few would have been surprised. But frighteningly, this one took place in Lincoln's own home town—inside the very same chamber where he had warned, only three years before: "A house divided against itself cannot stand." Now, not only was the house dividing; his own backyard seemed to be splitting as well. "It will be war in Chicago," warned one speaker that day, "—war in Springfield—war on the broad prairies of Illinois."[164]

The first photograph of President-elect Abraham Lincoln in Washington, taken by Alexander Gardner, Sunday February 24, 1861. (LIBRARY OF CONGRESS)

PART TWO

THE MOMENTOUS ISSUE OF CIVIL WAR

Chapter Seven

If We Surrender, It Is the End of Us

A S MORE AND more of his Springfield neighbors began noticing in the new year of 1861, Lincoln could no longer mask the "concerned expression" that overtook his "pallid features" as the crisis mounted. His mood supposedly lightened only when he learned of "Cameron's discomfiture" over recent headlines reporting his withdrawn appointment. "I am informed," Henry Villard confided, perhaps with some exaggeration, "that he laughed over it until the tears coursed down his cheeks. Bothered and perplexed as he is, the frequent application of such healthy medicine cannot but provide a relief and relaxation to him."[1] Most of the time, "the burden" seemed to be "taxing . . . his patience and power of endurance to the utmost."[2]

Burdened as he was, Lincoln continued to hold his ground—sacred ground, he maintained—on compromise involving slavery expansion, even as the next round of state secession conventions loomed. But an unexpected event occurred first, and it shocked Northerners and Southerners alike. Shortly after midnight on January 9, South Carolina artillery opened fire on the *Star of the West*, an unarmed merchant vessel that President Buchanan had secretly dispatched from New York to resupply Major Anderson's besieged garrison at Fort Sumter with food and reinforcements. The shipment, interpreted by South Carolina leaders as an act of aggression, might have triggered a civil war then and there, had the hapless outgoing president bothered to alert Anderson to the plan in advance. Instead, when mystified federal troops inside Sumter failed to return the fire from shore, the defenseless cargo ship wisely veered back out to sea and the crisis was postponed.

Later on that same tumultuous date, Mississippi predictably became the second state to secede from the Union. The very next day, Florida seceded, and the day after—specifically assigning blame for its decision on "the election of ABRAHAM LINCOLN . . . by a sectional party, avowedly hostile to the domestic institutions, and the peace and security of the state"—so did Alabama. Mocking Lincoln's "Eminence as a Rail Split-ter," one exuberant Alabama secessionist wrote to ask him tauntingly to recommend the most solid timber that might be used "in fencing in my South Carolina Georgia Alabama Mississippi Louisiana and Florida Lands."[3]

Then, on January 19—despite the opposition of the respected Alex-ander H. Stephens[4]—Georgia became the fifth southern state in a month to dissolve its relationship with the Union. Celebrating the revolt, the mayor of Savannah defiantly raised a toast that carried an implicit warn-ing to the incoming administration: "*Southern Civilization*—It must be maintained at any costs and at all hazards."[5]

A few days before these widely expected secession votes, Congress-man James T. Hale, a Pennsylvania Republican, had begged Lincoln to reconsider the idea of reviving and extending the Missouri Compromise line as a means of reversing the crisis. Yet the day after Alabama joined the "stampede," Lincoln rejected the idea more firmly than ever. Dis-union or no, he would oppose any gesture that allowed slavery to spread unimpeded across the West, perhaps even to the Caribbean. He would not "surrender." As Lincoln defiantly put it:

> We have just carried an election on principles fairly stated to the people. Now we are told in advance, the government shall be broken up, unless we surrender to those we have beaten, before we take the offices. In this they are either attempting to play

upon us, or they are in dead earnest. Either way, if we surrender, it is the end of us, and of the government. They will repeat the experiment upon us *ad libitum* [in accordance with desire]. A year will not pass, till we shall have to take Cuba as a condition upon which they will stay in the Union. They now have the Constitution, under which we have lived over seventy years, and acts of Congress of their own framing, with no prospect of their being changed; and they can never have a more shallow pretext for breaking up the government, or extorting a compromise, than now. There is, in my judgment, but one compromise which would really settle the slavery question, and that would be a prohibition against acquiring any more territory.[6]

Lincoln's powerful message to Hale arrived, like all his major policy letters at the time, marked "*Confidential.*" He supposedly meant for no one but the Pennsylvania congressman to see it, although he surely knew—perhaps even hoped—that it would make the rounds in Washington, freezing any revived compromise talk among Republicans. Even more secretively, Lincoln took up his pen around this same time to write a deeply felt manifesto of principle that he shared with absolutely no one, certainly not sculptor Thomas Jones, in whose presence he likely composed it.

Secret or not, it bracingly confirms Lincoln's steadfast determination to preserve—and ultimately, extend—not only the permanence of the Union, but also its guarantee of liberty. He had thought much about these questions in recent days, pondering concepts that went well beyond the planks of the Republican platform he so often cited. The result was an appeal not just to reason but also to emotion, a heartfelt justification for resisting any compromise that reneged on the original promise of American freedom. Apparently concluding that its publication would do little good, Lincoln proclaimed none of its sentiments publicly until he neared Washington a month later. One can imagine him struggling to apply his reverence for the founding fathers to the crisis that had percolated, in part, because of the seeming conflict between their two sacred documents. Over the past five years, the Declaration of Independence had held the preeminent place in Lincoln's rhetoric. Now, with the Union in jeopardy, the Constitution, flawed as it was on the subject of slavery, assumed vital new importance.

"Without the *Constitution* and the *Union*, we could not have attained the result," he began his text, referring not to his own recent election victory, but to the nation's steady growth, "but even these, are not the primary cause of our great prosperity. There is something back of these, entwining itself more closely about the human heart. That something, is the principle of 'Liberty to all'—the principle that clears the *path* for all—gives *hope* to all—and, by consequence, *enterprize*, and *industry* to all." Then he reiterated his belief that America, though founded on a promise only partly fulfilled, yet remained what years later he would call "the last best, hope of earth"[7]—inspirited by a declaration of principles, and then protected within a constitution of laws:

> The expression of that principle, in our Declaration of Independence, was most happy, and fortunate. Without this, as well as with it, we could have declared our independence of Great Britain; but without it, we could not, I think, have secured our free government, and consequent prosperity. No oppressed, people will fight, and endure, as our fathers did, without the promise of something better, than a mere change of masters.
>
> The assertion of that principle, at that time, was *the* word, "fitly spoken" which has proved an "apple of gold" to us. The Union, and the Constitution, are the picture of silver, subsequently framed around it. The picture was made, not to conceal, or destroy the apple; but to adorn, and preserve it. The picture was made for the apple—not the apple for the picture.
>
> So let us act, that neither picture, or apple shall ever be blurred, or bruised or broken.
>
> That we may so act, we must study, and understand the points of danger.[8]

Lincoln's persistent underlining for emphasis persuasively suggests that he intended this impassioned fragment as the draft of a speech—perhaps a jotting for the inaugural address he was scheduled to deliver in March. In the end, however, it remained a speech never given.[9] It is not hard to understand why Lincoln shelved it. Its imperfectly expressed but startling propositions—liberty to all, and path-clearing "enterprize" for all—by no means omitted African Americans; in fact, the very repetition of the world "all" strongly implied their inclusion. No American leader, particularly one facing a secession crisis over slavery, dared risk reminding his white constituents of his commitment to so advanced an ideal as equal opportunity. Even Americans opposed to slavery were anxious about what might happen to the slaves—and to themselves—if the institution died. Full integration into free society, and with it, competition with white workers for low-paying menial jobs, was not yet a political option in the Republican mainstream.

Then there was an additional irony. Lincoln had once called himself "a poor hand to quote Scripture."[10] But the idea for the principal metaphor in his manifesto was not only biblical, it had originated a few days earlier with Alexander H. Stephens of rebellious Georgia. If Lincoln now dared to appropriate it, Stephens might embarrassingly reveal himself as the source of the adaptation from Proverbs. It was a shame because Lincoln's ruminations went far beyond Stephens's unembellished scriptural reference. Every bit as brilliant an editor as he was a writer, he not only vastly improved its expression, but boldly reimagined its meaning.

No matter that a Southerner had brought it to his attention, the reanimated biblical image of an apple of gold preserved within the frame of silver comforted the beleaguered president-elect that it was not only legally possible, but morally imperative, to fulfill the promise of the Declaration of Independence, that all men were created equal, within the framework of the Constitution, which may have enshrined slavery, yet held the union of states perpetually sacred.[11] Therein lay the spirit of one of the greatest speeches Lincoln never gave.

• • •

TO "THE HOLY army of self-appointed Union savers" still plaguing the president-elect with demands for conciliatory declarations to the South, assistant secretary John Hay—desperate to safeguard his boss's time and privacy—composed an unequivocal response of his own and saw to its anonymous publication in the press late in January. "Mr. Lincoln will not be scared or coaxed into any expression of what everybody knows are his opinions until the will of the people and the established institutions of the Government are vindicated by his inauguration." Then, Hay vowed, "if anybody doubts his integrity, his liberality, his large-hearted forbearance and his conservatism, their doubts will be removed. Until then let them posses their souls in patience."[12]

Unfortunately, the country was not in a patient mood—least of all its office-seekers and influence-peddlers. Their relentless pilgrimage to Springfield had ebbed around holiday time, giving some local observers (especially Lincoln) the premature hope that the "severe and protracted strain"[13] would finally ease. But the herd resumed its migration in mid-month, making one final assault on Lincoln's hometown before he could escape for Washington. For weeks, Henry Villard chuckled, "the influx of politicians" became "so great that a large number are nightly obliged to seek shelter in sleeping cars."[14]

Though they lacked the extended access Lincoln had provided during his State House occupancy, the new regiment of favor-seekers was not to be deterred. They waylaid him on the street, accosted him when he stopped for meals or meetings at the city's hostelries, even paid uninvited calls at his unguarded home. Lincoln now restricted his official visitors' hours at the Johnson Building to just sixty minutes daily— "during which alone," the press reported with disgust, "the Presidential ear is open to their selfish, annoying whisperings." Nicolay tried to further limit his boss's exposure by granting few such callers private audiences; instead the entire crowd was "admitted into his office in bulk," preventing most of the job applicants "from making their desires and expectations known."[15]

Undaunted, patronage-hunters and political influentials sought other ways to gain special access. One such device was the celebrity endorsement. Editor Horace Greeley, for example, sent an office-seeker named John Deiffendorf to town on January 26, armed with a fulsome letter of introduction on *New York Tribune* letterhead, all but guaranteeing him an interview.[16] Major politicians who arrived in town to harass Lincoln on cabinet choices also got private time with the president-elect. Simon Cameron's tireless supporters were so often sighted in the vicinity that one local politician caustically observed that the aspiring cabinet minister "could be killed three times and yet would always come up anon."[17]

Cameron-boosters were not the only soldiers conducting this relentless siege. After another Hoosier delegation arrived to "agitate" further for Caleb B. Smith, Henry Villard denounced their "impudent obtrusiveness," concluding that "Indiana and Pennsylvania lived up to their reputations of breeding the most corrupt and rapacious politicians," adding: "All these gentlemen doubtless came to the conclusion from their experiences with Mr. Lincoln that it would have been better for them to have stayed at home."[18] But other delegations, too, violated what Villard called "his desire to be let severely alone during the remainder of his stay in Springfield."[19] Office-seekers from Massachusetts, Michigan, New York, and even Virginia competed for Lincoln's attention, the city's scarce lodgings, and the patronage jobs he had resolved to resist filling until after his inauguration.[20] Lincoln's own closest advisors, Norman Judd, David Davis, and Leonard Swett, made things more difficult still by converging in town and kicking up a huge "strife" of their own for "supremacy" within the inner circle, causing Lincoln "great tribulation."[21] Long hopeful that all—or at least one—of them would be rewarded for their loyalty and hard work with a major administration post, these frustrated confidants may have begun to sense they were destined for disappointment.

Swett, for one, though he had invested a small fortune in Lincoln's campaign, put on a game face. "Some of Mr. Lincoln's friends insisted that he lacked the strong attributes of personal affection which he ought to have exhibited," he later wrote. "I think this is a mistake. Lincoln had too much justice to run a great government for a few favorites, and the complaints against him in this regard when properly digested amount to this, and no more: that he would not abuse the privileges of his situation." As Swett admitted of his old friend, "He would be just as kind and generous as his judgment would let him be—no more."[22] Hiding his disappointment, Swett hurried off to Washington, loyally and usefully reporting back to Lincoln on political developments as they unfolded in the nation's capital.

As for Lincoln's equally ambitious campaign manager, David Davis, his longtime legal colleague Henry Clay Whitney insisted that "Lincoln never had any intention of appointing Davis to office at all & was disgusted at Davis' hoggishness after office for himself—for H[enry]. Winter Davis his cousin & for all his personal friends." Davis—whose reward would indeed come, but later (Lincoln named him to the U.S. Supreme Court in 1862), resigned himself to the belief that "Lincoln had . . . no Strong Emotional feelings for any person—Mankind or thing. He never thanked me for any thing I did."[23]

Equally hopeful and seemingly impossible to discourage or dodge, the unknown joined the familiar in the tireless quest for Lincoln's attention and reward. "Mother Robinson," a well-known "character" from Ohio who probably modeled herself on the maternal heroine of the popular *Swiss Family Robinson*, was one minor celebrity who placed herself on display in crowded Springfield. So did a young stranger who brought along "two wild fire eaters from the very blackest part of the South," but still earned a "jolly" handshake when they found Lincoln in his office, "seated beside a huge pile of letters as high as a mountain." The unusual delegation tried exchanging views with the president-elect, but claimed that "the old fellow went on talking so that one of us could hardly get a word in edgeways." In the end, Lincoln "almost converted the 'fire eaters' into black Republicans."[24] He similarly charmed visitors from South Carolina and Georgia, who "expressed themselves delighted with him"—probably because they wanted something.[25]

Meanwhile, as Henry Villard reported to the *Herald* on January 29:

"The pressure of place seekers from both at home and abroad continues unabated," discouraged by neither Lincoln's increasingly frequent displays of "coolness" and "anger" nor "the various devices he has resorted to within the last fortnight to keep the expectants at a safe distance." Strangers still appeared "at his private residence, and, if admission to the Presidential presence be denied them upon the first application they never fail to make a second, third, etc., one, until their wishes are . . . gratified by the object of their obtrusiveness." Worse, such callers were "hardly ever satisfied with the privilege of one interview. They either exact an invitation to call again by conversational tactics or persuade Mr. Lincoln to return their call at their hotels, where once got hold of, he is seldom able to cut himself loose without the loss of several hours' time."[26]

Villard acknowledged that "Lincoln's inexhaustible good naturedness is mostly at fault in this." He simply could not turn a visitor away. Only when he finally arrived at the realization that there was "no safety for him from this infliction either in his office or his house" did he occasionally escape to "other places of retreat, to which the irrepressible impudence of distinguished strangers would not follow him." Thomas D. Jones's studio became one such "secret haunt," and Villard confided that Lincoln now began spending "many a quiet hour," too, in the "sanctum" of the friendly *Illinois Daily State Journal*, two blocks from the Chenery House.[27] Here Lincoln had spent considerable time during the 1850s, discussing politics or proofreading his speeches before their publication.[28]

Once in a while, a truly important visitor managed to slip into town unexpectedly. On January 19, the Mexican chargé d'affaires in Washington, Matías Romero, stopped by on orders from Benito Juárez himself to assure Lincoln of his country's commitment to "cordial relations" with the United States and opposition to "the formation of an independent Southern confederacy," which it regarded as a potential threat to Mexican autonomy. In retrospect, Romero's visit was less surprising than its uniqueness. Though he was about to assume responsibility for American foreign policy, Lincoln received not a single caller from the

capitals of Europe between his election and inauguration. Understandably, John Hay was gratified to observe Romero's display of "deep respect
and consideration" for the president-elect.[29] In turn, on his first dip into
the waters of foreign diplomacy, Lincoln, the onetime opponent of the
Mexican War, received the diplomat "with great courtesy."[30]

Romero's friendly mission belied the skepticism growing for Lincoln
overseas. Horace Greeley believed that "foreign intrigue was already
hand-in-glove with domestic treason in sapping the foundations of our
Union,"[31] and may have told Lincoln so when he visited Springfield
himself the following week. And expatriate minister John McClintock
wrote from Paris to advise the president-elect to announce diplomatic
appointments promptly—to reassure French and English observers "be-
fogged on the American question."[32] One British writer smugly editorialized: "It does seem the most monstrous of anomalies that a government
founded on the 'sacred right of insurrection' should pretend to treat as
traitors and rebels" millions of people who were guilty of nothing more
than withdrawing from the Union and asking "to be let alone."[33] Indeed, the British foreign minister, Lord John Russell, had recently confided his belief that "the best thing now would be that the right to secede
should be acknowledged."[34] Recognizing a precious ally when he saw
one, the president-elect sent Romero off with a gushing letter thanking
him for his "polite call" and offering "sincere wishes for the happiness,
prosperity, and liberty" of the Mexican people.[35]

Most of Lincoln's January callers had less lofty goals in mind. On one
particularly "cold and dismal afternoon," Henry Clay Whitney knocked
on Lincoln's door at home, hoping to see him alone. Instead he found
his old friend "surrounded by five or six exceedingly small *bores*, and one
very disagreeable large *bore*: the latter trying to make himself solid with
the prospective dispenser of a large patronage, and all trying to air their
shrunken wit for their self-aggrandizement in this sublime presence. I
never listened with greater impatience to an aimless drivel of small
talk."[36]

Lincoln seemed "sad, abstracted and wearied" by this gaggle. Yet,
Whitney observed, "he responded to the flippant and inane remarks on

the political situation, with a jaded smile and a mechanical assent . . . and it was with great difficulty that I restrained myself from making a savage assault on their batteries of pointless jokes, aimed at the unresisting President." Only when the door had "closed on the last of the retiring *bores*" did Whitney irritably say to his old friend: "I wish I could take as rose-colored a view of the crisis as you seem to do." Lincoln replied "with no asperity, but with great sadness," declaring: "I hope you don't feel worse about it than I do: I can't sleep nights."

And then Lincoln showed a mortified Whitney his latest batch of mail: "editorials in pompous language, referring to him as the Illinois ape, a baboon, a satyr, a negro, a mulatto, a buffoon, a monster, an abortion, an idiot, etc. There were threats of hanging him, burning him, decapitating him, flogging him, etc. The most foul, disgusting and obscene language was used in the press which were the organs of the Southern *elite par excellence*. . . . Nor had the limner's art been neglected: in addition to several rude sketches of assassination, by various modes, a copy of Harper's Weekly was among the collection, with a full length portrait of the President-elect; but some cheerful pro-slavery wag had added a gallows, a noose and a black-cap, and had thus improvised him as a victim of Jack Ketch," the legendary executioner for Charles II of England whose name was now synonymous with death by hanging.

Yet the latest hate mail, Whitney recalled admiringly, "did not in the least intimidate him." Lincoln "exhibited no trace of either mock-heroism or cowardice, but simply firmness, resolution and self reliance." Confirming Villard's assessment of Lincoln's growing melancholy, Whitney noticed that the president-elect's customary "gloom, abstraction, absent-minded, misery" had intensified. "I don't think Lincoln enjoyed a single entire day of mental calm," he concluded, "after his election to the Presidency."[37]

Yet to other visitors Lincoln revealed an entirely different side of himself, and to some—particularly those to whom he was reluctant to let down his guard—he projected nothing but exuberant confidence. One such stranger remembered him dismissing the very same new round of threatening mail. "You would explode with laughter," the visitor reported, "to hear him tell about the southerners trying to assassinate him. He has got stacks of preserved fruit and all sorts of such trash which he is daily receiving from various parts of the south, sent to him as presents. He had several packages opened and examined by medical men who found them to be all poisoned."[38]

Threats were not the only missives with which Lincoln still had to contend. The job applicants who could not travel to lobby him in person continued to conduct their self-promotional campaigns through the mail, wanting to believe Lincoln had the time to pay individual attention to their claims. The sheer bulk of incoming correspondence made this impossible. Villard spied Lincoln at the post office one evening in late January, personally filling a "good sized market basket" with his latest heap of letters, then comically trying to keep it balanced as he toted it through the icy streets.[39] With little time to plow through so much correspondence during office hours, Lincoln was frequently observed distractedly reading letters in public, once even at the State House on the day he visited its chambers in January to witness the legislative re-election of Lyman Trumbull to the U.S. Senate. He was compelled to focus on his mail "constantly—at home—in the street—among his friends," John Hay remembered, adding the speculation: "I believe he is strongly tempted in church."[40]

Some of the individual letters proved literally too weighty to carry anywhere, "covering from twenty to thirty and more pages." The bulkiest treatises were almost always "transferred to the paper basket unnoticed." Neither Lincoln nor Nicolay was "equal to the task of opening, reading and answering" such lengthy "epistles."[41] Another class of letters was comically brusque. Typical of the latest requests for employment was one for a postmaster's job in Galesburg, whose author cited as his principal qualification the fact that his parents "look to me in their old age for sustience [sic]." A young Hoosier was encouraged to apply for the job of White House messenger based only on the fact that Lincoln had once "exchanged a few kind words" with him at a horse fair.[42] Citing his "Knowledge concerning the culinary business," and naming amply fed dignitaries like Edward Bates as references, a St. Louis chef applied for the position of "Chief Cook of the White House,"[43] while a Brattle-boro resident told Lincoln he was just the man to handle "all your me-chanical work" for "your premises at the Capital."[44]

Awkwardly, poor John Nicolay even had to deal with a letter propos-ing an applicant for the very job he already held. New York State legisla-tor Benjamin F. Manierre and his insurance business partner, Frank W. Ballard, actually sent Richard McCormick, one of the "young Republi-cans" who had helped arrange Lincoln's Cooper Union speech, all the way west to Springfield, to audition for the vacancy that did not exist. Praising him in their introductory testimonial as "liberally educated" and "quick witted," Ballard argued that the incoming president needed the best clerk he could get, and McCormick would be ideal for the post.[45] For himself, Nicolay was always proud, he recalled, that "Mr. Lincoln appointed me as his private secretary, without any solicitation on my part, or, so far as I know, anyone else."[46] For all his effort to promote Lincoln in New York, McCormick was turned away unrewarded. He likely did manage to get in a few words of support for the politician in whose interests the entire Cooper Union lecture series had been devised in 1860: Salmon P. Chase, who had inexplicably declined the same speaking invitation that Lincoln rode to prominence.[47]

Not that Lincoln objected to recommendations from influential politicians. But when New York factions began battling with each other over appointment perquisites that were Lincoln's alone to dispense, the president-elect made sure that the boss of bosses there, Thurlow Weed, remembered precisely who was in charge. "As to the matter of patron-age," he reminded him, "it perhaps will surprise you to learn, that I have information that *you* claim to have my authority to arrange that matter in N.Y. I do not believe you have so claimed; but still so some men say. On that subject you know all I have said to you is 'justice to all,' and I beg you to believe I have said nothing more particular to any one."[48]

Lincoln's vow of silence on "particulars" applied to the rest of the country as well. For the most part, he managed to suspend final decisions not only on his cabinet selections, but also on filling the thousands of lesser federal jobs at his disposal for which the multitude clamored so

eagerly. But his reluctance did not signal an aversion to the obligation—
and opportunity—of rewarding fellow Republicans and cleansing the
nation's bureaucracy of Democrats, even if he eventually agreed to tread
lightly in the South. One explanation for his reluctance to make immediate appointments arose from his belief that his future cabinet ministers deserved to play a major role in appointing subordinates. But the
official records of federal hiring under Lincoln demonstrate that though
the task was enormous, and took perhaps longer than expected, Lincoln
eventually did impose himself on the process, managing ultimately to
place hundreds of supporters, loyalists, friends, and even family members in civilian (and later military) government jobs.[49]

The federal bureaucracy, small as it was compared to today's behe-
moth, seemed vast to Lincoln and his contemporaries. To the new president went the responsibility of filling vacancies for federal judgeships
and marshals, and, if he chose, replacing incumbents in federal departments, agencies, post offices, ports, and territorial and Indian bureaus, as
well as diplomatic outposts.[50] For the foreign service alone, the register
for federal jobs in 1861 listed a total of 239 separate ministers and con-
suls, in postings from Acapulco to Zanzibar. Lincoln kept in his files a
newspaper article that held that "Among the first duties devolving on
the incoming Administration will be the complete restructuring of the
ministerial and consular appointments."[51] Lincoln took this responsibility seriously, armed with advice from the pastor of the Paris's American
Chapel "that *competent* men" should fill key consular posts in recognition of "capacity and adaptation," and not "as rewards . . . in order to
meet the needs of office seekers."[52]

The White House itself offered employment opportunities for stew-
ards, a gardener (each at $800 per annum), doorkeeper, assistant door-
keeper fireman (furnace operator), and two watchmen (all at $600), the
lot of them under the supervision of yet another presidential appointment, the commissioner of public buildings ($2,000 annually), who was
responsible as well for administering a staff of twenty-two additional
laborers, eight lamplighters, several Washington bridge "drawkeepers,"
a public gardener, and others.[53]

Postmaster jobs were perhaps the most plentiful, the most frequently sought, and the most often dispensed. For the sprawling Post Office Department, the names of postmasters, clerks, route agents, messengers, and outside contractors consumed 590 pages of the 1861 federal register, each page boasting an average of sixty-four names: a total of more than 37,000 positions, including outside vendors. A more conservative estimate—still staggering enough—held that the administration was empowered to fill a grand total of 40,651 civilian positions in 1861—22,700 post offices, 9,400 Navy Department positions, 4,000 places at Treasury, and 1,900 apiece for the Departments of War and Interior, the latter offering opportunities for accountants, surveyors, registers, receivers, patent examiners, librarians, clerks in the land offices, and Indian Division officials.[54]

For the healthy salary of $1,500, Chicago postmaster Isaac Cook was replaced by John L. Scripps, who not coincidentally had written an effective campaign biography of Lincoln—presumably his principal qualification for the job.[55] At the Lexington, Kentucky, post office, the $2,000-per-year Democratic holdover, Jesse Woodruff, lost his job by April 1861 to L. B. Todd—a relative of Lincoln's wife. And in the tiny Illinois hamlet of New Salem, a Pike County village that had taken the name of the abandoned frontier settlement where Lincoln himself had once served as a postmaster, another Buchanan incumbent, William L. Robison, was tossed out by 1861 in favor of Lincoln appointee Daniel Cover. That assignment paid just $74.10 per annum, which likely seemed princely in that infant outpost.[56] In the end, the administration replaced eight of every ten "presidential-class" postmasters nationwide by the end of 1861.[57]

The Treasury Department similarly offered a rich bounty of well-paid patronage jobs. In addition to the fourteen clerks assigned to work directly for the incoming cabinet secretary, the department employed bookkeepers, superintendents of lighthouses, and customs inspectors—among the most lucrative of all federal positions because of a prevailing system that allowed collectors to help themselves to a percentage of all fees and duties. When Lincoln appointed another Chase man, Hiram Barney, as collector of the Port of New York at $6,340 per annum, Barney not only increased his income exponentially via commissions, but as expected brought in a whole new slate of Republican auditors, clerks, and inspectors. The busiest port in the nation employed a total of 191 inspectors, of whom 131, or 68.5 percent, were quickly replaced by the new administration. They ranged from elite hires like James W. Roosevelt to the requisite number of loyal, foreign-born professionals needed for their ability to speak languages other than English—like Adam Schaepper of Germany and G. F. Secchi de Casali of Italy.[58] In March 1861 alone—Lincoln's first month in office—the U.S. Senate would receive for its advice and consent some sixty pages of names submitted for civilian and military appointments ranging from secretary of state to surveyor-general of Minnesota.[59]

The overhaul did not occur overnight. For months, even years, after his inauguration, Lincoln and his party could barely keep pace with the vast opportunities to reward political loyalists. A random examination of comparative pages in the 1859 and 1863 registers of federal jobs assigned to the state of Illinois alone, for example, shows that of fifty Buchanan-era postmasters from towns ranging from Tracy to Wauconda, twenty-six were replaced, while twenty-four were retained. A similar random sampling from another page listing postmasters from the towns of Argos to Blairsville in overwhelmingly Republican Indiana, reveals that the Lincoln administration replaced twenty-nine postmasters but kept on an equal number, twenty-nine. It had an even harder time filling jobs in Democratic New Jersey, where another set of random, one-page samples shows that in towns ranging from Penn's Grove to Somer's Point, the administration replaced seventeen postmasters but retained fifty-one. This accounting, however imperfect, does suggest how difficult it was for the new government to evaluate the hundreds of applicants for patronage appointments. It does not even take into account reasons for vacancies other than political, which might have included illness, death, or military service.[60] In many areas of the South, moreover, post offices slipped from federal control, not to mention patronage, with secession. The register continued to list a number of postmasters in Confederate states even after they stopped drawing their salaries.

Among the many classes of supporters Lincoln did reward quickly were newspapermen. In addition to bestowing the Chicago post office plum on Scripps, he named Joseph Lewis of Pennsylvania's pro-Republican *Chester County Times* to be commissioner of internal revenue, and Joseph Barrett of the *Cincinnati Commercial* as commissioner of pensions. Simeon Francis of the *Illinois Daily State Journal* eventually became a paymaster in the Union Army.[61] And Illinois editors John Nicolay and William O. Stoddard, of course, both went on the federal payroll, too, as White House clerks.[62] Most pro-Lincoln papers saw government advertising rise sharply. Both Thurlow Weed's *Albany Evening Journal* and William H. Bailhache and Edward L. Baker's *Illinois Daily State Journal* earned $94 in the first few months of 1861 from State Department advertising alone, while William Cullen Bryant's pro-Lincoln *New York Evening Post* and Henry Raymond's Republican *New York Times* went on the list for lucrative post office advertising after years of deprivation under Democratic presidents.[63]

One modern quantitative survey estimated that of the 1,520 federal appointments under direct presidential control, Lincoln replaced 1,194 incumbent office-holders[64]—a total of more than 78 percent. When an aspirant named L. P. Libby wrote to Illinois secretary of state Ozias Hatch in mid-February to ask "if there is any office within the gift of the President" he likely had not begun to imagine the vast opportunities.[65] But Lincoln certainly did.

Inevitably, there were more job-seekers than vacancies, and countless Republican loyalists and personal acquaintances ended up disappointed or angry when denied a place at the trough. Where patronage rewards were concerned, Henry Clay Whitney believed that "Lincoln neglected his friends" from his home state, because he worried that supporters from other areas would wonder whether "I'm going to fill up *all* the offices from Illinois."[66] This left many old colleagues embittered although the hope for influence undoubtley kept patronage-hungry, compromise-minded Republicans loyal to Lincoln. Even less generous in his reaction to Lincoln's equal treatment policy than Leonard Swett or Henry Clay Whitney, Jesse K. Dubois, an old friend of Lincoln's from their days in the Illinois state legislature, later complained that he "just used me as a plaything to accomplish his own ends: but the moment he was elevated to his proud position he seemed all at once to have entirely changed his whole nature and become altogether a new being—Knows no one and the road to favor is always open to his Enemies whilst the door is hymetically [sic] sealed to his old friends."[67]

Yet Dubois seemed stoic compared to another intimate who expected even more power and influence. Sometime before the family's departure from Springfield, Henry Villard's friend Hermann Kreismann called at Lincoln's home after the president-elect inexplicably failed to show up for a meeting downtown. The German-born visitor was, of course, seeking a patronage appointment for himself. When Kreismann arrived at the house, he found Lincoln sitting forlornly in his parlor. Mary, he was astonished to discover, "was on the floor in a sort of hysterical fit, caused by L's refusal to promise the position of Naval officer of the N. Y. Custom House to Isaac Henderson," an anti-Weed candidate proposed for the job by New York Evening Post editor William Cullen Bryant. Alarmingly, Henderson, who may have met Mary during her recent visit to the metropolis, had supposedly sent her a diamond brooch in anticipation of this plum reward. "Kreismann," Lincoln remarked despairingly to his guest, "she will not let me go until I promise her an office for one of her friends." Mary's "fit continued until the promise was obtained."[68]

Apparently, Lincoln preferred yielding to such demands to resisting them. As the endlessly patient husband explained of his volatile wife's outbursts some years later: "If you knew how little harm it does me, and how much good it does her, you wouldn't wonder that I am meek."[69] No admirer of Mary's, William H. Herndon later heard that Henderson was "afterward indicted . . . for defrauding the Government."[70] To "keep quiet in his house and to get the woman's fingers out of his hair," Herndon concluded, Lincoln "did the wrong thing" where the appointment was concerned, adding: "I suppose that in this case Lincoln did not know what to do. The devil was after him and he stumbled. Poor bedeviled fellow, unfortunate man!"[71]

• • •

BY THE END of January, far more bedeviling reports flowed across the president-elect's desk. New letters warned of "danger in the future" in teetering Maryland, a rapidly mounting "feeling of disunion in Texas," and the rise of a "mob Gvt" in the crucial border state of Kentucky under the influence of a "malignant" John C. Breckinridge and "an immediate *sum* of whiskey."[72]

"Instead of saving the Union," Henry Villard worried of Lincoln, "he may be called upon to bury it . . . the chances for utter wreck are equal to those for safe landing."[73] Yet even as the latest alarming news spread through Springfield, the president-elect was still reported for the most part "undisturbed in the midst of all the disastrous Southern revolutionary events."[74] Only his sorrowful expression, which thickening whiskers did little to conceal, betrayed his concerns to his neighbors and visitors. Lincoln held firm on conciliation even when his trusted old friend, Joseph Gillespie, came to town to plead that he address "the people of the Southern states, assuring them of his pacific intentions and imploring them to not make a *rumpus*." Gillespie was convinced that Lincoln's continued silence not only carried immense political risks, but exposed him to "personal danger of getting killed or hurt." As he shared these views, the Edwardsville jurist, who had known the president-elect for thirty years, lost his composure and began "sobbing like a child."

But Lincoln remained unmoved, patiently telling his emotional guest, as he had told countless others: "I should issue no address." He was still "a private citizen," he calmly pointed out, "having no authority over politics: my sentiments were well known [and] I could but reiterate them: if I should now avow any different views, they would not be believed and would be accepted as a mark of cowardice: and I was not going to back down from anything I had said."[75]

Lincoln repeated the very same vow to travel writer George Sumner, the globe-trotting younger brother of Senator Charles Sumner, who came to Springfield to lecture at the State House on his experiences in

Spain among the "*pronunciamientes* and secessions." Seeing "a running parallel between events there and with us," as he put it, Sumner, too, detoured to so advise the man he playfully referred to as "O.A."—for "Old Abe." After urging him not to appoint Cameron, and being told patiently in response, "We will try not to begin with a cloud," Sumner ornately warned the president-elect against compromise: "Be never seduced into suicide, by sacrificing in moments of panic, for an imaginary repose—for an illusory peace—those great principles which are the basis of all lasting prosperity, and the very essence of National life." In return, the lecturer got a lecture of his own from the president-elect, but as usual, Lincoln described the situation more succinctly than any of his self-appointed advisors. Assuring his visitor that "he looks with contempt on the whole pack of compromisers," he bluntly declared that "he did not wish to *pay* for being inaugurated."[76]

The harried Lincoln made clear to Sumner that he believed compromise would simply open the door for further demands and more concessions: "Give them personal liberty bills, and they will pull in the slack, hold on, and insist on the border-state compromises. Give them that, they'll again pull in the slack and demand Crittenden's compromise. That pulled in, they will want all that South Carolina asks." He "would sooner go out into his backyard and hang himself." Then Lincoln punctuated his resolve with a down-home pledge: "By no act or complicity of mine shall the Republican party become a mere sucked egg, all shell and no principle in it."[77] Impressed when he heard of, perhaps even witnessed, the exchange, Billy Herndon immediately dashed off a note to Lyman Trumbull in Washington to report with delight: "Lincoln said that he would rather be hung by the neck till he was dead on the steps of the Capitol, before he would buy or beg a peaceful inauguration. Lincoln is as firm as the base of the Rocky Mountains."[78]

Republican Congressman William Kellogg, Illinois's representative on the foundering House Committee of Thirty-three, encountered the same resolve when he returned to Springfield for a consultation of his own on January 21. Kellogg arrived "in a great deal of anxiety," Lincoln thought, no doubt because so many of the president-elect's supporters now viewed the pro-compromise Kellogg as a convert to "the most obnoxious wing of the Democratic party."[79] Determined to take his own measure of Lincoln's posture on "the vexed question" of conciliating the South, his visit set off yet another round of new rumors that Lincoln was indeed entertaining a reassessment.[80] Kellogg got an earful, too, and this time Lincoln's outburst quickly—no doubt with his compliance—found its way into more than one newspaper. As a show of good faith, Lincoln did offer what appeared to be two fresh, if minor, concessions. He would publicly oppose neither a convention "to remove any grievances complained of," Lincoln advised Kellogg, nor "new guarantees for the permanence of vested rights." But he also pointed out that such decisions were "not mine to oppose." They belonged to the Congress and the states, where, he well knew, compromise initiatives had stalemated.

In particularly emotional language, Lincoln added a statement of renewed resolve that he had never expressed for the public so passionately: "I will suffer death before I will consent or will advise my friends to consent to any concessions or compromise which looks like buying the privilege of taking possession of this government to which we have a constitutional right." However alluring others might regard the various compromise propositions still dangling before Congress, he added, "I should regard any concession in the face of menace the destruction of the government itself."[81]

Lincoln's widely published statement cheered reformer Carl Schurz, who promptly wrote home to his wife to applaud Lincoln's vow that "he would rather die than purchase the presidency at the cost of the surrender of a single plank of the Chicago platform. . . . Glory to him! (Long live Lincoln!) We live in a wonderful time."[82] Just to be certain, however, Schurz urged Lincoln just two days later to "tell the Republicans once more, that he, who will hold the helm of government will be true to his great trust, and that he will consider nobody a friend, whose fidelity is wanting in this supreme hour of danger. . . . Save us once more, I beseech you."[83] When he received no such promise, Schurz packed up and went to Springfield to see Lincoln himself, a measure of incurable public skittishness.

Anti-compromise leaders like Schurz, desperate for Lincoln to express his resolve in a public speech, remained disappointed. It was left to the comic weekly *Vanity Fair* to invent the oration the president-elect would not make. The journal filled the void by hilariously imagining Lincoln appearing before his Springfield neighbors to confide his views at long last.

Gentlemen, I *am* speaking. Now what do you want me to say? I suppose you want to know about my Cabinet, my policy, my appointments, my administration, &c., in advance. I will tell you. I mean to have Cabinet pictures in my house, the best I can get, and Cabinet champagne, the best that I can buy, and any other necessary Cabinet that may be required.

As to my policy—or policies—for I shall have several—I will have my two Life policies in two good companies for $5000, each in favor of MRS. ABE. Insurance policies upon my personal property in several staunch associations. Lottery policies I am opposed to. The best policy, Honesty, I am in favor of.

How as to my "appointments," like my "habit they will be costly as my purse can buy, though not expressed in fancy." MR. GREELEY, I shall not employ for my tailor. As to my "administration," I shall spank my children, and kiss my wife, and go to meeting as often as I please, and I shall pay all my bills as I go along, and exhort everybody else to do the same.

As to my "and so forth," that is nobody's business, and you need not ask me about it.

Now, fellow citizens, I trust that you are satisfied with my exposition of my principles. I have defined my position. But if you don't understand it fully, look up and see where I am.[84]

Heartily as he might have laughed at this parody, Lincoln soon turned his attention to a far more serious matter: a real speech he knew he must not only deliver soon, but make the finest of his career. The time for leaked statements and private letters was over. On January 28, a day after officially designating February 11 as the day of his family's departure for Washington,[85] Abraham Lincoln was reported to be working in seclusion on his inaugural address. Pleading for "the utmost privacy," he let it be known that "No further invitations will be issued to prominent politicians to visit" and "none are desired here."[86] Unimpressed, the opposition press doubted that seclusion would inspire eloquence. "We presume," the Washington Constitution sneered, "that Mr. Lincoln will try to rub his eyes and ears open about the fourth of March. He will then see and hear things not at present dreamed of in the romantic region of Springfield."[87]

WHILE LINCOLN MAINTAINED his "masterly inactivity," the political equilibrium in Washington changed dramatically. As each Deep South state seceded, it sent word to its United States senators officially recalling them from duty in Congress. One by one, they now packed their belongings and withdrew, but not before taking the floor to offer emotional, defiant farewell addresses to both their colleagues and to "crowded galleries," Henry Adams reported with dismay, whose occupants "broke into violent applause over disunion speeches." Adams feared that the rest of the city, undeniably pro-Southern and pro-slavery in its sympathies, plotted "an outbreak from day to day."[88]

"Shame upon this cowardly, guilty, and fantastical method of dealing with the stupendous crime and curse," railed an outraged Frederick Douglass.[89] In raw political terms, however, the departure of these Southern solons somewhat cheered the incoming administration by profoundly altering the Republican-Democratic congressional dynamic to their advantage. Their retirement, Elihu Washburne advised the president-elect from Washington, "weakens secession here very much."[90] Lincoln and his anti-compromise supporters no longer had to worry that a new, smaller, North-tilted Congress would provide the necessary votes to send a Crittenden-like concession package to the states for ratification as constitutional amendments. What was more, as Mississippi's Jefferson Davis further conceded, the mass resignation of pro-slavery Democrats effectively ended the possibility that Southerners might successfully stone-wall the confirmation of Lincoln's cabinet and thereby cripple the new government.[91] But there was no denying the painful void left by their empty desks, or the sparks ignited by their valedictories.

The warnings had been flowing for weeks. Senator Albert Gallatin Brown of Mississippi withdrew on January 12. Georgia's Robert Toombs, who had advised the Senate that his state would "trust to the blood of the brave and the Gods of battles for security and tranquility," resigned on February 4. The courtly Judah Benjamin of Louisiana, who withdrew the very same day, prophesied: "What may be the fate of this horrible contest no man can tell." And in a similar vein, Robert Hunter, whose home state of Virginia had yet even to consider secession, rose to predict ominously: "The South . . . will not shrink from war, if partisan madness makes *that* the price of independence."[92]

Few departures were more gravely received than that of Jefferson Davis. Disappointed that his labors "for adjustment" had proven fruit-less, his "functions terminated here" by his state's decision to secede, he took his leave from the Senate on January 21. With his wife, Varina, watching from the packed galleries, Davis, racked by painful neuralgia, delivered an emotional "final adieu," warning his fellow senators that his state's "safety" now required "that she should provide for the mainte-nance of her rights out of the Union."[93] Hoping to secede without war, Davis made clear where blame would lie if Mississippi was unable to do so: "I hope . . . for peaceable relations with you, though we must part. They may be mutually beneficial to us in the future, as they have been in the past, if you so will it. The reverse may bring disaster on every por-tion of the country, and if you will have it thus, we will invoke the God of our fathers, who delivered them from the power of the lion, to protect us from the raves of the bear."[94]

Davis was not the only senator to withdraw that historic day. David Yulee and Stephen R. Mallory of Florida, and Benjamin Fitzpatrick and Clement C. Clay, Jr., of Alabama offered their resignations, too. In-creasingly isolated in the lonely chamber, Kentucky's John J. Crittenden stubbornly, but hopelessly, argued for compromise. Alone among Southern senators, only Tennessee's Andrew Johnson countered with defiant pro-Unionism. In the face of considerable pressure—one Illinois farmer warned the Volunteer State Democrat that the Lincoln he knew was, despite "some cunning of a low, vulgar order . . . a whole hearted Abolitionist & yet without moral honesty or courage to admit it"—the senator refused to fall into line with the secessionist camp. "I voted against him; I spoke against him; I spent my money to defeat him," he declared of Lincoln, "but I still love my country; I love the Constitution; I intend to plant myself, with the confident hope and belief that if the Union remains together, in less than four years the now triumphant party will be overthrown."[95] (Four years later, in the midst of the Civil War, Johnson instead became Lincoln's running mate and, later, his vice president and White House successor.)

Johnson's caution went unheeded. Instead, from the deepest South came one more crushing episode in the worsening national nightmare. On January 26, just twelve days after its state troops had defiantly occupied Fort Pike near New Orleans, Louisiana voted overwhelmingly for secession and became the sixth Southern state to abandon the Union. Within a week, the state seized New Orleans's federal custom house and mint.[96]

But with the most virulent anti-Lincoln senators now heading south and Winfield Scott visibly increasing the federal military presence in Washington, Lincoln's relieved supporters at least foresaw less chance of an outright rebellion to block the inauguration. "The threat of the conspiracy to seize this city will be broken," Congressman Elihu Washburne predicted in a January 13 report to Lincoln, "by the preparations of Genl. Scott and the going away of the members from the seceding States. The retiring of Toombs, Jeff. Davis, Clay, Brown and others weakens session here very much. . . . It looks to me *now* more favorable for quiet here than it has done for *sometime*."[97] Lost in the premature euphoria was the unavoidable reality that quiet had come at an exorbitant cost: the apparent dissolution of the Union itself.

• • •

FOR A FEW precious days, Lincoln looked not to the "uncertain" future but to the "cherished past."[98] He decided to put down his initial inaugural jottings, escape Springfield, and return—if briefly—to the Illinois backwoods where he had come of age.

The first to learn of his plan was John Hanks, Lincoln's country cousin on his late mother's side. This thickly bearded Indiana pioneer could still recall his famous relative as "a bashful—Somewhat dull, but peaceable boy."[99] Hanks had chopped wood and manned flatboats alongside young Abe as far back as the 1820s. Later he had gone west to California, made a bit of money, and returned home a Democrat.

In 1860, however, he had made an invaluable contribution to the Republicans. That May, summoned (and paid) by Lincoln's handlers, Hanks had marched down the aisle at the Republican state convention at Decatur, bearing aloft two log rails and a banner proclaiming: "ABRAHAM LINCOLN The Rail Candidate for President in 1860[.] Two rails from a lot of 3,000 made in 1830 by John Hanks and Abe Lincoln." In response, the party faithful erupted in a "tempest of enthusiasm,"[100] and Lincoln emerged armed with not only the favorite-son designation for president, but also an indelible new image as a self-made man. Later that year, the fifty-eight-year-old Hanks officially changed his political affiliation and voted for his famous cousin for the White House.

For all this, Lincoln was undoubtedly newly grateful to his cousin, but from an early age he was said to "love this man, thought him beautiful, honest and noble."[101] Now, at the end of January 1861, contemplating one more trip to see his country relatives before departing for his swearing in, Lincoln asked Hanks to accompany him on a journey back to the prairie. One newspaper attributed his decision "to a desire for rest, not to be had in Springfield, where the incoming dispenser of place and pap is 'run to death' by eager and hungry crowds of patriots who 'carried the lamps' and split rails in the late canvass."[102] In truth, Lincoln decided to make the trip for a more sentimental reason: to say goodbye to his frail seventy-two-year-old stepmother at her log cabin home at Farmington, south of Charleston, Illinois. She had "expressed a strong wish to see him before he left Springfield for Washington,"[103] and Lincoln, probably fearing he would never lay eyes on her again, quickly agreed to visit.

"I now think I will pass Decatur, going to Coles, on the day after tomorrow," Lincoln alerted John Hanks on January 28. "Be ready," he instructed, "and go along."[104] Neither Mary nor the boys joined him. In fact, they had never set eyes on the family cabin or met Sarah Bush Johnston Lincoln, important as she was in her stepson's life. Mary no doubt thought it unseemly to bring such primitive relations into their lives.

Accompanied by state senator Thomas A. Marshall, Judge John Pettit, and, for part of the way, by Henry Clay Whitney, whom he ran into by chance at the Chenery House and invited along for the ride, Lincoln set off for Coles County on the morning of January 30, dressed for the journey more like a farmer than a statesman. Whitney thought his admirers "would have been extremely surprised to behold their President-elect" that day. Lincoln wore "a faded hat, innocent of a nap; and his coat was extremely short, more like a sailor's pea-jacket than any other describable garment. . . . A well-worn carpet-bag, quite collapsed, comprised his baggage." The trio reached the train depot by cutting across neighbors' back lots on foot, but as they neared the station, Lincoln, now accustomed to free rides on most lines, suddenly remembered; "My hat hain't chalked on this road now, so I reckon I must get a ticket." Whitney spared him the embarrassment by requesting a free pass from resident superintendent F. W. Bowen.[105]

When Lincoln unostentatiously took a seat in the men's waiting room, admires quickly surrounded him, and Bowen graciously offered his private office on the secluded mezzanine so the celebrity might wait in privacy. As Bowen approached him with the invitation, Lincoln appeared to be "industriously at work, tying the handles of his carpet-bag together with a string."[106]

Safely inside Bowen's room, the old railroad lawyer thoughtfully inquired about business on the Great Western line, and then commented: "You are a heap better off running a good road than I am playing President. When I first knew Whitney, I was getting on well—I was clean out of politics and contented to stay so; I had a good business, and my children were coming up, and were interesting to me: but now—here I am"—at which point, or so Whitney claimed, "he broke off abruptly, as if his feelings overpowered him" and changed the subject.[107] The train soon chugged into the station, and the group boarded and headed east.

As planned, John Hanks joined them along the route, and Lincoln spent the rest of the voyage regaling Judge Pettit with anecdotes, attracting a crowd of enthralled fellow passengers as he tirelessly spun yarn after yarn. Somehow, the traveling party missed its connection at Mattoon and did not arrive at Charleston until a freight train hauled them the final ten miles into town at 6 P.M. on January 30. The sun had already set.

By day or night, however, Lincoln knew this village well. Three decades earlier, he had first migrated to the region as a twenty-one-year-old, negotiating a stubborn oxcart laden with the family's crude belongings. Here he had returned in a triumphant carriage procession back in the fall of 1858 to battle Douglas at the fourth Lincoln-Douglas debate at the local fairgrounds.[108] Much had changed since the early days when railroads and Republicans were equally scarce here, and Lincoln was proud that Coles County now not only boasted "modern" transportation but tilted anti-slavery in the bargain.

No "formalities" greeted his arrival this time. A few curious locals braved the bitter freeze to gawk at him at the depot, but once the president-elect began hailing a few old friends, whatever "stiffness" inhibited these townspeople "disappeared like magic.[109] Later that evening, despite more "very cold" weather, hundreds of villagers, a few of whom could remember Lincoln as a youngster, and others as a senate candidate and orator, crowded into Senator Marshall's house to greet him more formally, as the local "Brass & Strings band" provided a serenade. There would be no new Charleston oration. Lincoln declined to speak, though the crowd offered "enthusiastic cheering" at the mere sight of him.[110] He slept that night at the Marshall home.

Early the next morning, in frigid weather, Lincoln set off to pick up another of his country cousins, the grizzled and incorrigible Dennis Hanks. This barely literate but inexhaustible tale-spinner, ten years Lincoln's senior, had lived with the family until 1830, and according to his own boast, "taught Abe to write with a buzzards quillen which I killed with a rifle."[111] After sharing breakfast, the two men boarded a two-horse buggy and headed off along frozen, rutted dirt roads for Sarah Lincoln's place—encountering "much difficulty" along the way fording the ice-choked Kickapoo stream, but no doubt enjoying their outing, which gave them the privacy and time to recall the old days. Finally disembarking at his stepmother's cabin, Lincoln and Sarah Bush Johnston Lincoln at last enjoyed a "very affectionate" reunion followed by a quiet family dinner in the home Sarah shared with her daughter's family.[112] Lincoln brought her a black dress or cape—reports disagree—and was observed at one point tenderly clasping the rocking chair on which she sat during the reunion.[113] She, in turn, "embraced and cried over him."[114] Sometime during the visit, Lincoln found time to visit his father's nearby, unmarked grave, and vowed to send money to erect a headstone there nearly ten years after his death.[115] He never did.

Lincoln probably spoke little of his father that day, except to recount the "old man's escape, when a boy," from an Indian attack.[116] Though he had named his own youngest son (later nicknamed "Tad") in his honor, they had become painfully estranged long before he died. The subject still distressed him. But he did talk "in the most affectionate manner" about his stepmother, proudly telling yet another cousin, Augustus H. Chapman, Dennis Hanks's son-in-law, that "she had been his best Friend in this world & that no son could love a Mother more than he loved her."[117] This remarkable pioneer "woman of great energy," sense, and industriousness, had first found her new family ill-clothed, and living alone in squalor in a dirt-floor cabin while their father was away courting her. She had convinced Thomas Lincoln to build a wood-plank floor, moved her fine furniture inside, and cleaned up and dressed the little boy and his sister. "She took an espical [sic] liking to young Abe," Chapman recalled, and "her love for him was warmly returned."[118] Sarah remembered Abe as "the best boy I ever saw," proudly but modestly explaining, "His mind & mine—what little I had seemed to run together—move in the same channel."[119]

This was not to be an altogether private day; no such days existed anymore for Lincoln. No sooner did he reach the village of Farmington, the local postmaster recalled, than news of his presence "spread like wild fire, the school was dismissed and teachers, scholars and villagers hastened to the house where he had stopped." When one old law client named John Rodgers heard that Lincoln had arrived in the neighborhood, he mounted his horse and galloped into town to see the president-elect for himself.

"Well Abe, I still own the mare you gained for me in the lawsuit a long time ago," Rodgers barked when they met, pointing to his steed. "I rode her to the election to vote for you and have rode her here." Lincoln "greeted him in the most cordial manner."[120]

Returning to Charleston along with his stepmother later that afternoon, Lincoln took dinner with all his Chapman relatives—including Harriet Ann Chapman, daughter to Dennis Hanks, granddaughter to Sarah Bush Johnston Lincoln, and not many years earlier, a live-in mother's helper at the president-elect's Springfield home—chatting happily about family matters.[121] Later they proceeded to the town hall for "an *impromptu* reception," crowded with people from the surrounding villages, "irrespective of party."[122] An observer reported that a "very large number of ladies and gentlemen took advantage of the opportunity to shake him by the hand."[123]

To one member of the "surging and admiring crowd," Lincoln seemed "comparatively cheerful,"[124] to another, "simplicity itself. He seemed to enjoy it so much that his face was continually lit up with a sunny smile."[125] When the onlookers called for a speech, however, Lincoln demurred as if solicited for a major policy statement by the secessionists, protesting "that the time for a public definition of the policy of his administration had not come, and that he could but express his gratification at seeing so many of his old friends and give them a hearty greeting."[126] He uttered a far more memorable response when one energized young supporter greeted his remarks by vowing he would shed his last drop of blood to save the Union. That reminded Lincoln of a little story. It seemed that when a young man announced he was going off to war, his sisters proposed making him a belt embroidered with the words, "Victory or Death." "No, no," protested the young soldier, "don't put it quite that strong. Put it 'Victory or get hurt pretty bad.' "[127]

For the amusement of another audience of old acquaintances he launched into another anecdote that promised to be far juicier. It concerned a girl whose daily chores included finding and herding home the family cow. "One day," Lincoln continued, "she rode a horse bareback to the woods. On the way home the horse, frightened by a dog or something which darted from behind a bus, made a wild dash ahead, the girl astride when suddenly—" at which point Lincoln was interrupted by a loud knock on the door. He never finished the story.[128]

Lincoln's emotional journey ended all too soon. Finally, on February 1, came the unavoidable, heart-wrenching goodbye between mother and son. "She embraced him when they parted," clung to him, and cried that "she would never be permitted to see him again." The old woman was sure that "his enemies would assassinate" him.

"No, no, Mama," Lincoln soothed her, "they will not do that[:] trust in the Lord and all will be well. We will see each other—again."[129]

"I did not want Abe to run for Pres[ident]t—did no want him Elected," Sarah Lincoln later recalled of that final visit, wiping tears from her old eyes as she remembered it. "Something told me that Something would befall Abe and that I should see him no more.[130] As it turned out, she was right.

Augustus Chapman spoke for all his old friends and relations when he concluded, with frontier simplicity: "Mr Lincoln appeared to enjoy his visit here remarkable well."[131] Though he departed for Springfield well before sunlight, and endured another long journey, the president-elect arrived home "much refreshed from his excursion into the woods," according to his assistant secretary. John Hay marveled that Lincoln seemed "one of those men who, having carried into middle age the stamina of a vigorous youth, always feel a new pulse of energy upon returning for a while, to the haunts of early exercise. . . . An earth-giant . . . he always gains strength by contact with his mother earth."[132]

On his first day home, Lincoln demonstrated that renewed vigor with a muscular letter to William H. Seward, ostensibly updating him on his recent conference with Congressman Kellogg on what he called the "vexed question" of compromise. More to the point, it was meant to reaffirm to his wavering secretary of state–designate that his own resolve to resist remained inflexible. Arriving in Springfield, Lincoln had found a message from Seward warning that "absent something of concession or compromise," more cotton states were certain to follow out of the Union. Dismissing Republicans who opposed compromise as "reckless," the secretary of state–designate had called on Lincoln to be "concilia-tory forbearing and patient, and so open the way for a rising Union Party in the seceding states which will bring them back into the Union." Seward thought he knew his man; longer than most, after all, Lincoln professed to believe that Union sentiment in the South was merely dor-mant, not dead.[133]

But the New Yorker had underestimated Lincoln—again. The president-elect told Seward he was willing enough to somewhat expand his list of acceptable points of concession. It represented a final, half-hearted gesture at conciliation without compromise of principle. He would make one last show of elasticity regarding issues on which he believed he was already on record, knowing full well that such "conces-sions" might douse him with the perfume of malleability while still prov-ing insufficient to lure the seceded states back into the Union fold.

On the subjects of Fugitive Slave Laws, the perpetuity of slavery in Washington, D.C., slave trade among the slave states, and "whatever springs of necessity from the fact that the institution is amongst us," he reiterated coldly, "I care but little." So great was the pressure for com-promise that even New Mexico's potential statehood with legalized slavery was not out of the question, he surprisingly added, as long as "further extension was hedged against." A deal along these generous lines—and in this latest iteration they actually embraced nearly all of the key Southern demands and Crittenden proposals, save for extending the Missouri Compromise line—would be acceptable to Lincoln, as long as a final legislative package was "comely, and not altogether outrageous."

As for slavery extension, however—what Lincoln intractably viewed as the slippery slope to extending the slave power west and south, delaying the ultimate extinction of an institution he regarded as immoral, violating the Republican platform, and upending the election result in the bargain—it remained off limits. And on this subject, Lincoln proclaimed one more time, he would never yield.

As Lincoln spelled it out for Seward that first day home from Charleston: "I say now . . . as I have all the while said, that on the territorial question—that is, the question of extending slavery under the national auspices,—I am inflexible. I am for no compromise which *assists* or *permits* the extension of the institution on soil owned by the nation. And any trick by which the nation is to acquire territory, and then allow some local authority to spread slavery over it, is as obnoxious as any other.

"I take it that to effect some such result as this, and to put us again on the high-road to a slave empire is the object of all these proposed compromises," he added with one final flourish. "I am against it."[134]

Chapter Eight

Will You Hazard So Desperate a Step?

B Y LATE JANUARY, with the date of his departure for Washington swiftly approaching, Lincoln could delay no longer devoting his full attention to the most important speech of his life: his inaugural address.

As Henry Villard saw it, with this "portentous undertaking" Lincoln "entered upon the discharge of a duty next in importance to the construction of his Cabinet."[1] Lincoln's inaugural message was all the more eagerly anticipated by virtue of the protracted silence that preceded it, and the likelihood that unless it offered major concessions, a whole section of the country might ignore it. The stakes were enormous and the pressure intense. Exactly when he threw himself into the work full time remains something of a mystery, and is guaranteed to remain so primarily because Lincoln the master craftsman seldom revealed the hard labor that went into his jewel-like narratives. Not surprising, he destroyed all of the early handwritten drafts of his oration.[2]

Admitting that even he did not know precisely "at what time Mr. Lincoln began the composition of his Inaugural Address," John Nicolay suspected the inveterate note-taker may have self-confidently begun the task even before he won the presidency. "While it is probable that he did not set himself seriously at this task until after the result of the November election had been ascertained beyond doubt," Nicolay guessed, "it is quite possible that not only had the subject been considered with great deliberation during the summer, but that sentences or propositions, and perhaps paragraphs of it had been put in writing." Lincoln, he explained, shedding light on his boss's creative process, "often resorted to the process of cumulative thought." Whenever he seized on "a forcible idea or an epigrammatic sentence," he would memorialize it on a scrap of paper, "seldom in the shape of mere rough notes, but almost always in the form of a finished proposition or statement"—then file it away "until further reasoning enabled him to add other sentences or additional phrases to supplement the first—to elaborate or to conclude his point or argument." Robert Lincoln, too, remembered his father crafting "many scraps of memoranda" before composing even a letter. And William Herndon concurred, recalling that his partner often deposited these fragments of "sentences & paragraphs . . . in his hat for safety." [3]

Of course, there was much more to Lincoln's speechwriting process than a quaint filing system. As Lincoln had shown at Cooper Union, he was capable of painstaking research, too. For the inaugural, his inquiries began early. On November 13, just a week after his election, though perhaps chiefly in anticipation of President Buchanan's impending annual message to Congress, Lincoln had borrowed from the Illinois State Library, located one flight below his Capitol office suite, a copy of Edwin Williams's indispensable two-volume 1848 reference work, the *Statesman's Manual*. Formally titled *Presidents' Messages, Inaugural, Annual, and Special, from 1789 to 1846*, it contained the full texts of the key utterances of all of Lincoln's predecessors. As Lincoln now discovered, its richly decorated title page also boasted inspiring visual symbols, including the scales of justice, the American eagle, and Columbia carrying her liberty pole. Included among these patriotic images, inexplicably, was a discordant engraving of the original Siamese Twins, Chang and Eng—their portrait now unwittingly serving, a dozen years after its publication, as a metaphorical reminder that North and South remained as inseparable as the famous Barnum attractions themselves. [4] Whether Lincoln contemplated these illustrations is not known. But a *New York*

Evening Post journalist did observe the president-elect leafing through the books as early as the day he first took them upstairs to his office, studying with particular interest Andrew Jackson's 1832 proclamation against South Carolina nullification. Although he returned them to the library on December 29 (as he cleared out of the Governor's Rooms for good), Lincoln enjoyed ample time—a full six weeks—to find inspiration from their pages for his own maiden public message as president.[5]

Around this same time—late December or early January—the president-elect and his aides began "with great diligence" assembling additional "historical and other researches" for Lincoln's further use in composing the inaugural.[6] His ability to borrow these sources was essential, for "aside from his law-books and the few gilded volumes that ornamented the centre-table in his parlor at home," William Herndon remembered, Lincoln possessed no library of his own. "He never seemed to care to own or collect books," his bibliophile law partner admitted, unable to disguise his envy that Lincoln seemed nonetheless able to memorize nearly everything he consulted with but one reading. Conveniently, Herndon owned an extensive personal library, so he was hardly surprised when Lincoln handed him a list of sources he hoped his partner might quickly retrieve for consultation. The only shock was its brevity. Lincoln asked Herndon only for a copy of "Henry Clay's great—his best speech in 1850," a fresh copy of Jackson's anti-Nullification proclamation, and the U.S. Constitution, "so as to be prepared," Nicolay recalled, "to give a definitive opinion" on the "laws relating to the question of secession."[7] From Herndon we also know that Lincoln turned, too, to Daniel Webster's 1830 Senate reply to South Carolina's Robert Hayne, which Lincoln had first read as a young postmaster in New Salem, and ever after, Herndon testified, "regarded as the grandest specimen of American oratory." Whether Lincoln needed a fresh copy now, or remained so "perfectly familiar" with it that he did not need to consult it anew, has never been ascertained.[8]

These old texts provided both inspiration and ammunition. Rather than offer direct concessions to the South at an earlier moment of sectional crisis over slavery, for example, Webster had long ago insisted he had never uttered "a single word which any ingenuity could torture into an attack on the slavery of the south." He had merely favored "legislating . . . to prohibit the introduction of slaves" into new territories—Lincoln's very own position three decades later. "Liberty *and* Union," Webster had famously proclaimed, "now and forever, one and inseparable!"[9] In reprinting the famous speech just a few weeks earlier, one Northern newspaper had declared of Webster: " 'Tho' dead he yet speaketh, Lincoln agreed.' "[10]

From Jackson's more prosaic but no less Union-affirming argument against the right of a state to nullify federal laws, Lincoln surely absorbed the old general's reassuring insistence that: "We are *one people* in the choice of President and Vice-President. Here the States have no other agency than to direct the mode in which the votes shall be given." South Carolinians' secession threat—now, as then, Lincoln likely concluded—was, as Jackson had put it, "fallacious" in its justifications and, "in direct violation of their duty as citizens of the United States, contrary to the laws of their country, subversive of its Constitution, and having for its object the destruction of the Union." As Jackson had bluntly concluded: "Disunion by armed force is *treason*."[11]

Finally, Lincoln could remind himself that a generation later, his idol Henry Clay had eloquently defended the right to question the spread of slavery. "The government has no right to touch the institution within the states," Clay had conceded in 1850, paving the road to Lincoln's current position, "but whether she has, and to what extent she has the right or not to touch it outside of the States, is a question which is debatable, and upon which men may honestly and fairly differ, but which, decided however it may be decided, furnishes, in my judgment, no just occasion for breaking up this happy and glorious Union of States."[12] Lincoln's inaugural text would bear echoes of these sentiments, too.

Not even journalist-in-residence Henry Villard knew precisely how long Lincoln took to absorb this material and develop his own arguments. Yet by January 29, even before Lincoln ventured off to see his frontier relatives, Villard convinced himself that after what seemed like only "two or three days" dedicated to the "delicate and difficult task"—in reality, weeks of research and note-taking—the president-elect had almost magically made remarkable progress on his text. "The ground from which the issues of the day will be viewed is already marked off. Abstract rights are ready to be asserted and wrongs to be pointed out, but the remedies to be recommended have not been determined upon, in view of the rapidity of events and the consequent dangers in the aspect of public affairs." Still, Villard predicted, "the erection of the argumentative structure can now be completed in a comparatively short period."[13]

As Lincoln himself revealed on February 2 in reply to a Louisville editor who, warning "against the murderous mutilations of the telegraph," made a premature request for an authorized copy of "the inaugeral"—a word Lincoln somehow never learned to spell—"I have the document already blocked out; but in the now rapidly shifting scenes, I shall have to hold it subject to revision up to near the time of delivery."[14] It was his first acknowledgment that he had come close to crafting an initial draft. A similar request for an advance copy a few days later, this from the London American, was similarly declined despite what its publisher insisted was "the custom of former Presidents to forward copies of their message to the Press."[15] It would not be Lincoln's custom. He was still far from ready to release his text.

No one—least of all Lincoln himself—doubted that he had much more work to do on his manuscript. As Villard revealed on February 4, "it is understood that during the remainder of Mr. Lincoln's stay in this place his time will be principally absorbed by it." So-called "Cabinet negotiations" were "altogether suspended for the time being, owing to the commencement of the message."[16] Visiting hours continued to be restricted, though they remained almost unreasonably generous: Lincoln would somehow continue to make himself available to the public daily, but "only" between 3:30 and 5:00 P.M.[17]

Unfortunately, Lincoln's most demanding speechwriting challenge arose at a bitterly ironic moment. Even as he labored over a policy statement designed to resuscitate the old Union, a new union declared its birth in the South. As he polished an address designed to reaffirm the

Constitution, the Confederacy approved a separate constitution of its own and named a chief executive—enshrining its revolution in a cloak of American-style legality. On February 4—precisely a month before his inauguration—thirty-eight representatives from the six seceded states convened in Montgomery, Alabama, and formally created a Southern confederacy "which will declare its independence of the late United States, as the Congress of the thirteen colonies declared their independence of Great Britain."[18] In Washington that same historic day, a "Peace Convention," attended by respected political luminaries north and south (including Ohio's Salmon P. Chase and Illinois's Stephen Trigg Logan, one of Lincoln's early law partners), gaveled itself to order in a highly publicized, last-minute effort to unite the country around a compromise plan that might yet lure the seceded states back and keep the border states from seceding. Fearing that some final, "desperate effort" was under way to "yield" on principle, Carl Schurz pleaded with Lincoln: "do not permit the cause of Liberty to sink ignominiously in the dust . . . do not fail us in this decisive hour."[19]

Against this roiling backdrop, Lincoln took up his pen to do what he did better than any politician of his day: express himself convincingly in writing. But, as always since his election, torn in different directions simultaneously, he was forced to tend to other business concurrently. On this same historic February 4, as Springfield plunged into an "intensely cold" spell of winter weather,[20] Lincoln warmly received an emissary from Pennsylvania's newly inaugurated Republican governor, Andrew Curtin. Knowing he must formally respond to invitations that he pause for official welcomes along the route to Washington, Lincoln sent the dignitary home with a letter confirming: "I expect, on my winding way to Washington, to make brief stops at Pittsburgh, Philadelphia, and Harrisburg; and I shall be glad to meet you at any or all those places; or in fact, at any other place."[21] That day he also agreed to New York governor Edwin D. Morgan's invitation to visit the Empire State, too, adding a postscript that reflected the mounting pressure he was feeling: "Please let ceremonies be only such as to take the least time possible."[22]

On that same exhausting day, Lincoln was again interrupted for another meeting with still another delegation of Simon Cameron detractors, who insisted that he be denied the Treasury Department.[23] Lincoln likely pledged little beyond what he had told a group of pro-Cameron Pennsylvanians less than two weeks earlier. On the one hand, he admitted: "I feel a strong desire to do something for your big State, and I am determined she shall be satisfied, if I can do it." On the other, as he cautioned, "I shall aim, as nearly as possible at perfection. Any man whom I may appoint to such a position, must be, as far as possible, like Caesar's wife, pure and above suspicion, of unblemished reputation, and undoubted integrity." If recent charges against Cameron were proven, he would not appoint him. And, he warned almost defensively in conclusion: "If, after he has been appointed, I should be deceived by subsequent transactions of a disreputable character, the *responsibility will rest upon you gentlemen of Pennsylvania who have so strongly presented his claims to my consideration.*"[24]

One other potentially explosive political matter required his attention: the upcoming legislative battle for the Republican-controlled U.S. Senate seat William Seward was set to surrender in order to join the cabinet. Powerful anti-Seward newspaperman Horace Greeley had emerged in late January as a leading candidate to succeed the senator whose presidential ambitions he had helped thwart. The editor seemed to take special pleasure in knowing that his candidacy aroused "the Fire-Eaters, who have been taught to believe me a decidedly vicious and dangerous Negro."[25] But Seward's vengeful admirers regarded Greeley's senatorial ambitions with no less horror, and Thurlow Weed plotted to block him by supporting lawyer William M. Evarts. Lincoln, determined to keep all local factions happy, wanted no part of the imbroglio. Nonetheless, a brazen Westchester state legislator had been busy promoting the president-elect as pro-Greeley. Weed, understandably irked, warned David Davis that "If Mr. Greeley gets into the Senate it will be because members are made to believe that Mr. Lincoln desires it!" and Davis, in turn, advised Lincoln to "set yourself right" on the matter.[26]

In a letter to Weed, Lincoln made clear that the Westchester official was accurate only in reporting his respect for the editor, not his endorsement. "The gentleman you mention did speak to me of Mr. Greely [sic], in connection with the Senatorial election, and I replied in terms of kindness towards Mr. Greely which I really feel; but always with the express protest that my *name must* not be used in the Senatorial election, in favor of, or against any one. Any other representation of me, is a misrepresentation."[27] As he wrote those very words, Lincoln would later learn, the crisis dissipated without his further intervention: New York Republicans caucused, deadlocked, and ultimately selected a compromise candidate to succeed Seward instead: Judge Ira Harris.[28]

As if nothing of consequence had occurred, the following day, February 5, Greeley himself turned up in Springfield to keep a lecture commitment—part of a tour that even the approaching party caucus in Albany had failed to interrupt. He had met Lincoln before—most recently at Cooper Union—but the twelve-year-long relationship between the two anti-slavery leaders had been rocky. Back in 1858, Greeley's Republican *Tribune* had briefly entertained the idea of endorsing Democrat Stephen A. Douglas over Lincoln for the Senate from Illinois as a gesture of hostility to President Buchanan. However much Lincoln prided himself on not holding grudges, part of him must have savored the news that New York had thrown cold water onto Greeley's own Senate ambitions three years later.[29]

The impetuous editor with the exuberant white side-whiskers had more than redeemed himself since his flirtation with the opposition. The *Tribune* had loudly cheered and skillfully promoted Lincoln's Cooper Union appearance. Then, after initially supporting Bates for president, chiefly as a means of blocking Seward's nomination in Chicago, Greeley returned to his New York office, displayed a souvenir woodcut of Lincoln, and declared: "There, I say, that is a good head to go before the people."[30] Subsequently, Greeley filled the *Tribune*'s columns with pro-Lincoln editorials.

Now repaying that support by courteously calling on the editor at the Chenery House, Lincoln devoted several valuable hours to a private interview, offering "gratifying assurances" in reply to the New Yorker's superfluous demands for "strict adherence to an anti-compromise policy."[31] These guarantees proved insufficient to satisfy Greeley, who left worried that the "genial, quiet, essentially peaceful" Lincoln, "trained in the ways of the bar and the stump . . . fully believed that there would be no civil war,—no serious effort to consummate Disunion." When Greeley inquired about the upcoming inaugural—whose writing his visit was serving to delay—Lincoln was equally sunny. "His faith in Reason as a moral force was so implicit," the editor concluded, "that he did not cherish a doubt that his Inaugural Address, whereon he had bestowed much thought and labor, would, when read throughout the South, dissolve the Confederacy as frost is dissipated by a vernal sun."[32]

Notwithstanding his self-imposed ban on cabinet discussions, Lincoln politely invited Greeley's views on prospective appointments, and was told, as expected, that Chase deserved to be in, and Cameron, out. If Seward, whom Greeley loathed, was discussed as well, neither man ever admitted it. According to Villard, the editor "did not ask anything either for himself or his friends."[33] This was hardly the case.

Villard never learned that, before leaving Springfield, Greeley wrote a long letter in his usual indecipherable scrawl, urging Lincoln "to do justice to the anti Weed Republicans of our state." Showing no absence of gall—despite his humiliating defeat for the Senate—the editor asked not only that several of his friends be appointed to plum officers, but that New York spoils be formally and equally divided among Lincoln, Seward, and anti-Seward men like Greeley. "Let a list be made of the offices local to New York," he presumptuously suggested, ". . . and from among these do you indicate such appointments as you choose to make of your own volition. Those being so made, let Gov. Seward or whoever may be chosen to represent that side select one office and name the person whom he recommends to fill it; then let the other side select an office from the list and name a person to fill it; and go on alternating till the list is completed."[34] Lincoln not only rejected the scheme, he never even replied to the outrageous letter.

With Greeley on the way to his next lecture venue, Lincoln could again turn his attention to his speech. Fortunately, he had a talent for effortlessly resuming discarded writing projects precisely where he left off—no matter how protracted or intense the diversion. "He had a wonderful facility in that way," testified his old friend Joshua Speed. "He might be writing an important document, be interrupted in the midst of a sentence, turn his attention to other matters entirely foreign to the subject in which he was engaged, and take up his pen and begin where he left off without reading the previous part of the sentence."[35]

There is no doubt that Lincoln drafted the address—all of it—alone. "I have often been asked if I did not write this or that paper for him; if I did not prepare or help prepare some of his speeches," Herndon reminisced years later. "To people who made such enquiries I always responded, 'You don't understand Mr. Lincoln. No man ever asked less aid than he; his confidence in his own ability to meet the requirements of every hour was so marked that his friends never thought of tendering their aid, and therefore no one could share his responsibilities. I never wrote a line for him; he never asked me to.[']"[36]

Not that he lacked for advice on the project. Whether he needed such help or not, Lincoln could find wildly discordant inaugural suggestions from ordinary Americans in his daily correspondence. Only days after his election, for example, James E. Harvey urged him not to make the same mistake as his two immediate predecessors by pledging to serve but one term in office—after which they "intrigued for another nomination."[37] Apparently, this admirer was already planning strategy for an 1864 reelection campaign!

From a political opponent in Beloit, on the other hand, came the advice that Lincoln should reject compromise ("medicines that momentarily allay present pain by destroying the vital energies of the patient"), yet concede that the federal government had no right "to discriminate against any species of property known to, and recognized by the laws of any of the original thirteen states." By reiterating such pledges "in an explicit manly manner," the writer prophesied, Lincoln would not only "surprise and pacify the country" but "give to its author a position in the hearts of his countrymen and on the page of history not second to that of any of his predecessors."[38]

A less prolix supporter from Cleveland simply quoted from Washington's Farewell Address—"But the Constitution which at any time exists, till changed by an explicit and authentic act of the whole people, is sacredly obligatory upon all"—and advised: "Would there not be a new freshness and force added to these words of Washington if transferred in an Inaugural Address?"[39]

The citation was useful. Washington had called the Union "the palladium" of the nation's "political safety and prosperity," and urged future generations to guard "its preservation with jealous anxiety . . . indignantly frowning upon the first dawning of every attempt to alienate any portion of our country from the rest, or to enfeeble the sacred ties which now link together the various parts."[40] Here at least was advice worth following. It would undoubtedly be more difficult to heed another correspondent's demand that the address somehow be not merely "comprehensively generous & magnanimous," but "Christ-like."[41]

Lincoln now had revisited all the history, precedent, and citizen exhortations he needed in order to complete his inaugural; soon he also had a precious implement with which to write it. A "veritable *eagle quill*" arrived from Pennsylvania, plucked back in 1844 in the hope that Henry Clay would use it to compose his own inaugural address. Ever since Clay's defeat that year, its owner had waited for a candidate of equal stature to win the White House. Now he wrote to Lincoln: "I . . . have the honor of presenting it to you in your character of President elect, to be used for the purpose it was originally designed. What a pleasing, and majestic thought!" The donor believed that, if properly publicized, an inaugural message "written with a pen made from a quill taken from the proud and soaring emblem of our liberties" would be "sufficiently potent to 'Save the the [sic] Union.' "[42] But Lincoln had long ago discarded scratchy quills for efficient steel-nibbed pens, and there is no evidence that he did more with the Clay-associated writing implement than receive it appreciatively.

For his final preparation, all Lincoln really needed was a secluded place to write. Neither sculptor Thomas Jones's hotel room, nor his own new, smaller, but still bustling office headquarters offered him the peace or privacy he required to reflect and compose. With only days left before his family's departure for Washington, his home was in a turmoil, too, busier and noisier than ever as Mary, the children, and the day servants packed their belongings. Lincoln finally found a new sanctuary in a crammed but isolated third-floor hideaway above his brother-in-law Clark M. Smith's grocery store, Yates & Smith, "Dealers in Staple & Fancy Dry Goods, Groceries, Boots and Shoes" on the south side of the public square.[43]

Looming from the large windows in its front room was the State Capitol, where he had first won national fame by pronouncing thoughts he could no longer apply to the crisis awaiting him in Washington: "A house divided against itself cannot stand." Those old words had only recently reminded a South Carolina secessionist that Lincoln was either "a fool, or a fanatic."[44] Lincoln would now be expected instead to advocate rebuilding a house dividing. He must somehow assure the South that he posed no threat to its sovereignty or its slaves, without abandoning the anti-slavery principles on which he had won the presidency or sacrificing the authority he was entitled to exercise as chief executive. He somehow had to reiterate Webster's commitment to liberty and union, as well as Jackson's warning that secession meant treason.

Offering his brother-in-law the small rear space above his back storeroom, the husband of Mary Lincoln's youngest sister, Ann, proudly cleared off his slant-front, pigeonhole desk for Lincoln's exclusive use.[45] In this "unromantic," claustrophobic aerie—a "dingy, dusty, and neglected back room," Herndon described it, "cut off from all communications and intrusion"[46]—Lincoln got down to serious work. As Herndon confirmed, Lincoln simply "went upstairs above Smiths . . . and then and there wrote his first Inaugural."[47]

To Nicolay, the chief virtue of this new "retreat" was that it was "completely safe from prying inquisition." The former journalist believed that with Springfield "full of both politicians and newspaper reporters who would have left no stone unturned to see even a scrap of his writing about the public questions of that day," it was "necessary to preserve the utmost secrecy in the preparation and transcription of the Inaugural." Lincoln had kept his silence too well, for too long, to risk a premature leak of his first formal address as president. The secretary admitted that the inelegant writing space above Smith's store was merely "a small counting-room" that "had been partitioned off," but added: "There he could hide himself," because "the way to it easily foiled inquiring pursuit." Here, Nicolay too attested, "withdrawing himself some hours each day from his ordinary receptions," the "Inaugural was written and copied, and nearly every surplus fragment of manuscript destroyed."[48]

In this room Lincoln probably first jotted down the words that, with but minor revisions, would ultimately constitute the opening sentence of his speech. Wisely, if in its earliest form, hesitantly, it sought to reassure, not alarm; it spoke not of unprecedented crisis but of unbreakable tradition. Whether or not they would prove sufficient to lure Union-loving Southerners back from the brink of disunion, the words Lincoln proposed to break his long silence would subtly but deftly serve to remind Americans that he was not the first president of the divided states, but the sixteenth president of the *United* States: As he wrote: "In compliance with a custom as old as the government, I appear before you to address you briefly, and, in your presence, to take the oath prescribed by the Constitution and laws by whomever enters upon [crossed out; replaced by 'assumes'] to discharge [crossed out; replaced by 'perform'] the duties of our national chief magistrate."[49]

From this starting point, Lincoln would use his message to reintroduce himself by reminding his hearing and reading publics that while he remained "bound by duty, as well as by inclination," to the principles of the Chicago platform, meaning opposition to the spread of slavery, he had, as he had guaranteed so often, "no lawful right" and "no inclination" to interfere with the institution "where it exists." In a gesture to the white South, he even pledged to "cheerfully" enforce the laws in all the states—including the Fugitive Slave Law—and attend to the potential revision of "hypercritical rules" later.[50]

The introduction behind him, Lincoln launched the next section of his draft by regretfully conceding the "peculiar difficulty" surrounding his inauguration, despite the national tradition established by the peaceful swearing in of fifteen previous "distinguished citizens." His own, he insisted, should be no different. But here the conciliatory tone shifted. Regardless of the "disruption" of secession, he insisted, both universal law and the Constitution must be regarded as "perpetual." It was unthinkable that some of the states could destroy a Union that all of the states had created. And since "no State, upon its own mere motion, can lawfully get out of the Union," Lincoln argued, "I therefore consider that the Union is unbroken; and, to the extent of my ability, I shall take care that the laws of the Union be faithfully executed in all the States." Plainly spoken, this meant that as president, he would use all the power at his disposal to ensure that security was maintained, the mails delivered, import duties collected, and where necessary, federal property not only held but reclaimed.

Though he hastened to add that this vow implied no "menace" to the South—that "there needs to be no bloodshed or violence; and there shall be none, unless it be forced upon the national authority," Lincoln's first draft left little room for compromise. To advance his case, Lincoln turned to a device he had employed so cleverly at Cooper Union—speaking to an absent audience, or, as the Greeks had called it, prosopopoeia—appealing not to those "who seek to destroy the Union at all events," but to those "who really love the Union": presumably pro-slavery antisecessionists in the Upper South. To them, he asked: "Will you hazard so desperate a step . . . while the certain ills you fly to, are greater than all the real ones you fly from? Will you risk the commission of so fearful a mistake?" Would they replace the honorable tradition of majority rule with "anarchy" and "despotism"?

Lincoln now added—in words similar to those he had recently shared privately with Alexander H. Stephens—his admission that one section of the country continued to believe slavery was *right*, and ought to be extended, "while the other believes it is *wrong*, and ought not to be extended." But he insisted that the Republican party had no avowed or secret desire "to destroy the property of the Southern people." Indeed, he pointed out, a separation caused by the advent of Republican rule would ironically mean that "fugitive slaves, now only partially surrendered, would not be surrendered at all."

The president-elect concluded this lawyerly appeal with a down-home aphorism that no subsequent editor with whom he shared the text could improve upon:

> Physically speaking, we cannot separate. We cannot remove our respective sections from each other, nor build an impassable wall between them. A husband and wife may be divorced, and go out of the presence, and beyond the reach of each other; but the different parts of our country cannot do this. They cannot but remain face to face; and intercourse, either amicable or hostile, must continue between them. Is it possible to make that intercourse more advantageous or satisfactory, *after* separation than *before?* Can aliens make treaties easier than friends can make laws? Can treaties be more faithfully enforced between aliens than laws can among friends? Suppose you go to war, you cannot fight always; and when, after much loss on both sides, and no gain on either, you cease fighting, the identical old questions, as to terms of intercourse, are again upon you.

What Lincoln composed next constituted a ringing defense of his reluctance to compromise on slavery expansion—"to shift the ground upon which I had been elected"—arguing that such a "surrender would not be merely the ruin of a man, or a party; but, as a precedent, would be the ruin of government itself." Admitting the possibility that "the people may err in an election," he maintained that "the true cure is in the next election; and not in the treachery of the party elected." But this section he would soon delete altogether, and patch it into a speech he hoped to deliver not in Washington but en route.

Now Lincoln addressed his full national audience to offer the most timeless phrases of his original draft: "Why should there not be a patient confidence in the ultimate justice of the people? Is there any better or equal hope, in the world?" And, a few sentences later, he inserted another sterling equivalent of the modern sound bite: "This country, with its institutions, belongs to the people who inhabit it. Whenever they shall grow weary of the existing government, they can exercise their *constitutional* right of amending it, or their *revolutionary* right to dismember or overthrow it," adding: "I shall place no obstacle in the way of what may appear to be their wishes." Until such time as a *genuine* revolution occurred—and, he implied, secession did not so qualify—his duty was "to administer the present government, as it came to his hands, and to transmit it, by him, to his successor."

Lincoln's first idea for a conclusion—later amended, at William Seward's suggestion, with a more conciliatory and sentimental peroration—was a stern warning against disunion:

My countrymen, one and all, take *time* and think *well*, upon this whole subject. Nothing valuable can be lost by taking time. Nothing worth preserving is either breaking or burning. If there be an object to *hurry* any of you, in hot haste, to a point where you would never go *deliberately*, that object will be frustrated by taking time; but no good object can be frustrated by it. Such of you who are now dissatisfied, still have the old Constitution unimpaired, and, on the sensitive point, the laws of your own framing under it; while the new administration will have no immediate power, if it would, to change either. If it were admitted that you who are dissatisfied, hold the right side in the dispute, there still is no single good reason for precipitate action. Intelligence, patriotism, Christianity, and a firm reliance on Him, who has never yet forsaken this favored land, are still competent to adjust, in the best way, all our present difficulty.

In *your* hands, my dissatisfied fellow countrymen, and not in *mine*, is the momentous issue of civil war. The government will not assail *you*, unless you *first* assail *it*. You can have no conflict, without being yourselves the aggressors. *You* have no oath registered in Heaven to destroy the government, while *I* shall have the most solemn one to "preserve, protect, and defend" it. *You* can forbear the *assault* upon it; *I* can *not* shrink from the *defense* of it. With *you*, and not with *me*, is the solemn question of "Shall it be peace, or a sword?"

With this startling challenge—couched as it was, as historian Douglas L. Wilson has shrewdly observed, with a purely Lincolnian reminder that war on such terms would be the South's fault, not his—Lincoln ended his prodigious first draft.[51] Only when he had filled as many as a dozen foolscap pages with his clear writing, did Lincoln finally emerge with the manuscript, confiding to journalist Ben Perley Poore that "a number of sentences had been reconstructed several times before they were entirely satisfactory" to him.[52] Such glimpses into his technique were rare coming from Lincoln, who almost never discussed his creative process with anyone, much less admitted a need to perform wholesale revisions on his texts.

Poore and Nicolay agreed on what happened next. Lincoln entrusted the finished handwritten draft to "his friend," as Poore described him, "the local printer."[53] This was William H. Bailhache, the unshakably loyal publisher of the pro-Lincoln *Illinois Daily State Journal*, in whose offices the president-elect had spent many secluded hours since moving from his suite at the State House. As Nicolay remembered, Bailhache then took "a trusty compositor and a case of type, locked himself in a room of the Journal office, and remained there until the document was set up, the necessary proofs taken, and the form secure in the office safe until Mr. Lincoln could correct and revise the proofs." Once the first galleys were in his hands, Lincoln proofread the results meticulously, returned the marked-up sheets to Bailhache for a second printing, then read and revised the second proofs as well, ordering his corrections incorporated into a third, and for the time being, final printed copy. "Perfect secrecy was maintained, perfect faith was kept," Nicolay testified. "Only the persons authorized knew that the work was done."[54]

Lincoln asked Bailhache to pull "about a dozen copies" of the third printing, these to share with his most trusted friends and advisors for comments and suggestions. Everything else associated with its production—even the racks of type that had been set up in the *Journal* office to print the speech—was, with almost paranoid stealth, discarded or destroyed. Almost immediately, Lincoln began revising these galleys himself, crossing out and substituting words in ink, and adding whole new paragraphs to the margins.

With only days to spare before his scheduled departure from Springfield, the president-elect was at last ready to invite outside readings. But he was pleased enough with his own work to preserve for posterity one clean, eight-page copy of the original typeset version printed by the *Journal*.[55] In a firm hand, he scrawled in pencil on the top, "First Edition." Then he filed it away with his most precious papers even as he continued scribbling on another set of proof. By February 9, Villard would confirm for the public: "The President-elect, having completed the first draft of his inaugural, is now busily engaged in arranging his domestic affairs."[56]

A KEEN STUDENT OF history, Lincoln no doubt took time as well during his last, hectic weeks in Springfield to make himself aware of how his predecessors had traveled to the federal capital for their own inaugurations. It was very much in his political interest, as he had suggested in his draft speech, to demonstrate that he was following tradition, just as if the country remained whole, and the threat to its indivisibility was but temporary.

As he knew, George Washington had established the tradition of inaugural travel, conducting a week-long, very public voyage from Mount Vernon to New York that cheering crowds transformed into a "prolonged coronation ceremony."[57] Lincoln, who as a youth had all but inhaled Mason Locke Weems's *Life of Washington*, knew from its pages that the Father of His Country had been welcomed to Trenton (a city Lincoln now planned to visit himself) with a "triumphal arch" erected to span the Sanpink Creek, and among the thousands of well-wishers, by a chorus of "young virgins" who sang a hymn of praise and threw flowers in his path.[58]

Lincoln could anticipate no such frenzy for himself, but he probably hoped to excite more emotion than his more recent predecessor, Martin Van Buren. As a sitting vice president, Van Buren was such a familiar figure in Washington that he neither sought nor expected a major welcome. On Inauguration Day, he was merely escorted to the Capitol, at least riding in a carriage hewn of wood from the USS *Constitution*.[59]

As for Van Buren's successor, after ignoring several of the factions clamoring for cabinet positions in his administration—Lincoln might have sought strength from this example—William Henry Harrison had made his way to the capital from his Ohio farm by way of Philadelphia and Baltimore, arriving in Washington to a frenzied public greeting on February 9.[60] Until the last possible minute, however, his vice president–elect, John Tyler, remained home in seclusion at his Virginia estate, Sherwood Forest, apparently in the throes of a religious reawakening too compelling to interrupt.[61] He ultimately arrived in the nick of time; the elderly Harrison lived for only a month after his swearing in and Tyler took over the presidency in April 1841.

Not all inaugural journeys proved triumphant. After dodging office-seekers, whom he found repugnant (a young Lincoln later became one of them),[62] the 1848 victor, Zachary Taylor, endured the most circuitous, mishap-cursed voyage in history. To reach Washington from Baton Rouge, he required half a dozen steamboats (aboard one of which a trunk fell on him from an upper deck), along with a march on foot through snow, a sleigh ride, and a train trip. By the time the old military hero staggered into the capital, he had come down with a bad cold. Taylor died sixteen months after taking office.[63]

Unwilling to submit himself to similar public exposure after losing his son in a January train wreck, Franklin Pierce made a furtive dash for Washington in mid-February 1853, taking such pains to enter New York incognito that when he tried to visit the widow of an old general on Bedloe's Island, guards refused him entry because he lacked a pass, then threatened him with bayonets when he refused to leave.[64]

Most recent, James Buchanan had been ushered to his village depot by local marching bands, then transported in a specially decorated train from his Lancaster, Pennsylvania, home for the brief ride to Washington. He chose to pass secretly through Baltimore when word reached him that a gang of Know-Nothing rowdies there planned to menace him. Here was one piece of information Lincoln must have digested, for he would soon face an eerily similar Baltimore threat of his own.[65] Lincoln discovered, too, that once Buchanan registered at Washington's National Hotel, a mysterious outbreak of "violent purging, inflammation of the large intestines and a swollen tongue" began afflicting its guests—including the president-elect himself.[66] Lincoln, whose mailbag still contained warnings of assassination by poison, wisely remained on guard. Reporting that "Mrs. L. objects to the National on account of the sickness four years ago," he asked Elihu Washburne to "select and engage quarters for us" elsewhere in Washington.[67]

Perhaps the best model of all for Lincoln was Andrew Jackson, who traveled the greatest distance (a mileage record Lincoln was destined to exceed) when he left the Hermitage in 1829. Though still mourning the recent death of his wife, "Old Hickory" made the journey with a private secretary, two military escorts, and a personal artist in tow, attracting massive crowds along the way "in every city and at every hotel." The general arrived in Washington on February 15 to find the city choked with place-seekers and speculators—"too many to be fed without a miracle" but all "hungry for office."[68] Lincoln had every reason to believe that, like Jackson—another Westerner ushering a new political party into power—he might excite similar enthusiasm en route, and an equally voracious appetite for favors, influence, and jobs once in town. The outpouring in Washington was likely to dwarf anything Lincoln had endured in Springfield.

Lincoln profited from all these examples. He would make himself visible to a public he had avoided for months, except at his own hometown headquarters. And he would at last feed his own undernourished hunger for exposure to ordinary Americans, for the ability to speak to them unfettered, to shake hands, to hear bands playing and cannons roaring, was mother's milk for nineteenth-century American politicians, particularly Lincoln.

He certainly paid no heed to Thomas Jefferson's old advice—reprinted a few weeks later under the mocking headline, "Mr. Lincoln on His Travels": "I confess that I am not reconciled to the idea of a Chief Magistrate parading himself through the several States as an object of public gaze, and in quest of public applause, which to be valuable should be purely voluntary. I had rather acquire silent good will by a faithful discharge of my duties, than owe expressions of it to my putting myself in the way of receiving them." By the time a New York paper republished those words, Lincoln was already in the midst of his journey. "Reader," the journal concluded, "was not Jefferson right!"[69]

LINCOLN ENJOYED THE unique additional benefit—as well as the potentially irritating burden—of more "guidance" than history alone could provide. No previous chief executive ever came to office with more ex-presidents alive, well, and seemingly unwilling to grant their successor the chance to lead without their advice. There were five hearty survivors on the scene in all: Van Buren, Tyler, Millard Fillmore, Pierce, and soon, Buchanan. Their admirable survival rate, Lincoln soon learned, was a prescription for trouble. None of these former White House occupants seemed ready to assume the mantle of silent elder statesman. Instead, revived by the disunion crisis, most attempted to exert new influence over policy. The most obvious culprit, incumbent chief executive Buchanan, continued to argue virtually until Inauguration Eve that the best way to save a country he had done so little to keep united was to shackle the incoming administration with legislative compromise, even if it included the extension of slavery.

But older ex-presidents proved no less vexing. After supporting fellow Northern Democrat Stephen A. Douglas for the White House, the seventy-eight-year-old Van Buren, though bowed down by gout and constant colds, still summoned the energy to vigorously support the Crittenden Compromise and to propose a constitutional convention to address the slavery issue. Lincoln could take some solace when he learned that "the Sage of Kinderhook" had drafted a resolution for the

New York state legislature asserting that secession "receives no countenance from the Federal Constitution and is founded neither on reason or justice."[70] Van Buren also admitted to the press that he had met Lincoln years earlier and believed him "endowed with talents to adorn the nation."[71]

Fillmore, who in 1856 had won 21 percent of the popular vote in a vain, third-party attempt at a comeback four years after leaving the White House, inexplicably began emphasizing the enforcement of the Fugitive Slave Law, a highly unpopular position in his native Buffalo (a mere boat ride away from the safe shores of Canada), not to mention an issue that Lincoln preferred to keep in the recesses of the national debate over compromise. Still open to conciliation, Fillmore nonetheless refused to attend the Peace Convention, and predicted it would fail.[72]

Democrat Pierce made no secret of his own disdain for Lincoln's Republicans, and in 1860 had briefly entertained hopes that the splintered Democrats would turn to him as a compromise candidate for the presidency. More recent, he had sent a message to the Alabama secession convention urging patience, but concluding: "If we cannot live together in peace, then in peace and on just terms, let us separate.[73] Lincoln could not be pleased that a New England–born former president, even a Democrat, was so openly willing to countenance secession.

But no former president did more to undermine the transition than John Tyler. As an accidental president two decades earlier, the proslavery Virginian could count few accomplishments save for validating the law of succession on the death of a chief executive. Now seventy, with two wives and fourteen children his most notable achievements, he reemerged onto the national stage in late 1860, praising Buchanan's dodgy leadership as a "wise and statesmanlike course" and supporting compromise even after Lower South states began declaring their independence from the Union.[74]

Tyler's efforts to shift the national conversation were just beginning. On January 19, he helped convince his home state to authorize a peace conference that would meet in Washington "to consider and, if practical, agree on some suitable adjustment" to national policies. The venture simply ignored the fact that, two months earlier, the nation's voters had already chosen to "adjust" policy by electing Lincoln. To no one's surprise, Tyler was named one of the five Virginia commissioners. Thereupon, sounding little like a conciliator, he warned his fellow Southerners that if the convention failed, "the conqueror will walk at every step over smouldering ashes and beneath crumbling columns. States once proud and independent will no longer exist and the glory of the Union will have departed forever.[75]

On February 4, the same day the Confederacy officially organized, the same day Lincoln published an open invitation to his Springfield neighbors to visit his home two days later for a final farewell reception, the Peace Convention gaveled into session at Willard's Hotel in the nation's capital. Its 132 sitting delegates from twenty-one states, many elderly and well past their political prime, elected Tyler not chairman but "president"—almost as if the thirty-day countdown to Lincoln's inauguration had not commenced. To one critic, Tyler had faded into a "tottering ashen ruin," and to another, he seemed nothing less than a traitor.[76] But even ex-President Franklin Pierce admitted he would have attended the convention, had not ill health—caused, some said, by his anxiety for civil war—made it impossible for him to travel."[77]

LEAVING NOTHING TO chance, Lincoln and his staff mapped his own travel schedule with exquisite care. He would leave Springfield a day before his birthday, perhaps to make sure that no unseemly celebration could be mounted that might appear frivolous or self-aggrandizing in a time of national crisis. And in recognition of the country's solemn mood, he would discourage long ceremonies and "established receptions" along the route (an aspiration nearly all of his hosts would ignore).[78]

Nevertheless, Lincoln would follow an itinerary arranged to bring him to the state capitals of Indiana, Ohio, New York, New Jersey, and Pennsylvania, and also to Philadelphia, the birthplace of the nation, on a far more important birthday, George Washington's, providing a perfect stage for a symbolic reaffirmation of national principles. Perhaps most significant of all, he would not wait anxiously at home until formally chosen president by the Electoral College; rather, he would depart two days before the scheduled February 13 vote tabulation, as if to demonstrate that he had not a doubt in the world that it would methodically affirm both the November popular vote and the December balloting by the various state electors. Unfortunately, Lincoln's input on these intriguing scheduling decisions cannot be confirmed by surviving evidence—merely surmised by how the itinerary unfolded. It is difficult to imagine that he did not ask and answer such questions before approving what he called his "winding way" to his inaugural.

To craft and manage the complex trip, Lincoln engaged one of the most mysterious figures to emerge that entire secession winter: an upstate New York hotel and railroad man named William S. Wood, of whom little was known then, and little more now. Wood had first ventured west to meet Lincoln in Springfield right after the election, armed with a letter from Thurlow Weed introducing him as "a reputable merchant" who desired only "to pay his respects to the President Elect."[79] It seems more likely that, egged on by Weed, he proposed himself at this initial interview as an ideal facilitator for the upcoming inaugural journey. Lincoln might as easily have turned to one of the railroad men he knew in Springfield, but probably saw no reason to reject so ardent a volunteer who, besides, was better acquainted with Eastern train and hotel amenities than anyone he knew at home.

Weed probably urged Wood on Lincoln during his own pilgrimage to the president-elect's hometown in December. Late the following month, as Henry Villard recalled, none too admiringly, "there appeared in Springfield, one W. S. Wood, a former hotel manager and organizer of pleasure excursions, I believe, from the interior of New York State, who, on the recommendation of Thurlow Weed, was to take charge of all the arrangements for the journey of the President-elect to Washington." Tellingly, before leaving to take up his new duties, Wood called on Weed in Albany to show him an advance copy of the "programme of Arrangements," an indication that he not only owed his job to the New York political boss, but had been working on the plan for some time. In return for his loyalty, the Seward-Weed machine harbored ambitions to place Wood in a permanent patronage job once he successfully ushered the president to Washington.[80]

The trouble was that Wood made as many enemies as timetables. Conceding only that he was "a man of comely appearance," Villard noted disdainfully that Wood seemed "greatly impressed with the importance of his mission and inclined to assume airs of consequence and condescension."[81] By the time the presidential party arrived in Washington, John Nicolay was probably dismayed to learn, one Southern newspaper was identifying Wood, rather than Nicolay, as Lincoln's secretary.[82] Though most historians subsequently ignored Wood, David Rankin Barbee described him in 1951 as a "scoundrel . . . who was sent to Springfield by the Eastern Railroads to entice Lincoln to make that roundabout journey to Washington for the inauguration. By lies and other propaganda he worked on the imagination of Lincoln until Uncle Abe actually imagined that if he took the direct route to Washington, he would be assassinated."[83]

This was said with considerable exaggeration, along with the benefit of hindsight—for though Wood ultimately did prove himself a scoundrel, he only did so later.[84] At the time of the inaugural journey, the *New York Times* probably described him best—though misidentifying him as W. S. *Wool*—as "*avant courier* to the President elect, making arrangements for special trains and apartments at hotels" (though two weeks later the paper referred to him instead as Lincoln's "business manager").[85] With more specificity, another paper reported that Wood would engineer "such arrangements as will insure both the comfort and safety of those under his charge," revealing: "He has provided special trains to be preceded by pilot engines all the way through."[86] Precautionary scout trains had similarly preceded the Prince of Wales during his recent cross-country tour. Once these pilot trains passed unharmed over a portion of track, switches would be "spiked and guarded" until the main engine followed through. Lincoln would ride in a brand-new "elegant . . . tastefully furnished and decorated" sleeping car equipped with an "improved ventilator," and pulled by swiftest and most modern locomotive.[87] As for the route, as the record shows, it was inspired by political obligations and Lincoln's own hunger to be seen by the public from whom he had been separated for so many months.

Initially, Wood proved a thorough, if somewhat overzealous, organizer. First he personally surveyed the complex array of railroad lines over which the presidential special would ride on the circuitous trip from Springfield to Washington.[88] Knowing better than most that the nation's rapidly expanding rail systems were still dizzyingly incompatible in terms of track gauge, equipment, even local time zones, Wood successfully chose a route that offered Lincoln ample time for full exposure in major cities without delaying his arrival in Washington. He wisely rejected, for example, a proposal that he accept the hospitality of a Canadian line that might speed him east via Detroit in the "most commodious passenger cars," even though Lincoln insisted: "Answer this respectfully."[89]

In the final days before the Lincoln family's departure from Springfield, Wood efficiently furnished the press with a detailed schedule of the trip, along with an authorized list of the traveling party—the "Family and Suite," as he ornately described it. The president-elect and Mrs. Lincoln would be accompanied, as he dutifully notified arrangements committees in every city and state preparing to receive them, by their three sons, along with Mary's cousin Lockwood Todd (who harbored hopes that his charming company would earn him a patronage job of his own in California), and as a sort of traveling medical aide, Mary's brother-in-law, Lincoln family doctor William S. Wallace.

The official "suite" would also include Nicolay and Hay as private secretaries; the Illinois politician Mary had tried to blackball from the cabinet, Norman Judd; Robert Lincoln's school chum George C. Latham (presumably to keep Bob company);[90] James M. Burgess, recently made a colonel by Wisconsin governor Alex Randall and ordered to accompany Lincoln all the way to Washington; and Lincoln's old law colleague, friend, and self-appointed bodyguard, Ward Hill Lamon. Along for the ride, too, would be a quintet of formidable military escorts whose presence would make an unusually public display of security. The Regular Army veterans would include the ominously named Captain George W. Hazzard (who voiced "the very highest regard for the integrity and abilities of your master of transportation, Mr. Wood").[91] Joining the party would be Captain John Pope of the Topographical Corps, a relative by marriage of the Todd family. Lincoln also summoned Major David Hunter, the paymaster of Fort Leavenworth, whose recent patriotic correspondence had so impressed Lincoln that he had sent him a personal invitation asking "the pleasure of your company" on what he expected would be "a circuitous and rather tedious journey."[92] Finally, reassuringly, there would be Colonel Edwin Vose "Bull Head" Sumner, so nicknamed because it was said a musket ball once bounced harmlessly off his skull, and who was now ready to rush to Springfield "in time to accompany him."[93*]

Joining the military ensemble, too, would be the celebrated young drillmaster and family friend, Colonel Ephraim Elmer Ellsworth, who originally hoped to bring along his entire regiment of sixty colorfully uniformed Zouaves—a show of force that might have looked a bit too bellicose. Fresh from an idealistic effort to lobby the Illinois legislature to ban liquor from armories and parade grounds, Ellsworth predictably now harbored dreams of patronage, hoping not only that his mentor Lincoln might appoint him chief clerk of the War Department, but that his boss there would not be Simon Cameron.[94] (Destined for disappointment on both counts, Ellsworth ultimately raised a regiment in Washington and became something of a surrogate big brother to the new president's younger sons once Robert returned to Harvard.)

Finally, Lincoln's personal valet, William H. Johnson, whom he described as an "honest, faithful, sober, industrious . . . colored boy . . . handy as a servant,"[95] would travel to Washington as well, though his

---

*These men would go on to both fame and criticism in the Civil War: Pope for losing the Second Battle of Bull Run; Hunter, for torching the Virginia Military Institute and issuing a precipitous 1862 emancipation order that Lincoln rescinded; and Sumner, for fighting through 1863 as the oldest active corps commander in Union ranks.

name did not appear on the manifest: African Americans were still considered nonpersons, even in the Northern state of Illinois. Bringing up the rear would be W. S. Wood himself, grandly identified as "Superintendent of Arrangements," along with his assistant superintendent, Burnett Forbes.

These well-laid plans would change before departure day. By the time Lincoln left for Washington, the "suite" would be augmented by a carload of friends and political cronies. Supporters of Stephen A. Douglas and John Bell would ultimately be invited, too. As a precaution, General Winfield Scott would assign Mrs. Lincoln and their younger boys to a separate train in case trouble broke out on the first leg of the journey; they would join the president-elect after his first stop in Indianapolis. For a time, Lincoln contemplated reducing the list further. Having earlier told the press he would travel without military escort, Lincoln was no doubt displeased to find a veritable regiment listed in his traveling party. Someone arranged a compromise: none of the Regular Army officers would be seen ushering Lincoln out of Springfield. Sumner, Hunter, Pope, and Hazzard were sent ahead to Indiana to meet the party there.

Usefully, the "Superintendent" provided a neatly printed set of rules and regulations meant to govern Lincoln's hosts en route on every aspect of his transportation, accompaniment, and accommodation. The handbill offered a level of specificity that would surely impress even the most paranoid twenty-first-century presidential advance men. In case anyone doubted the gravity of his task or the authority of his instructions, Wood began with a chest-thumping preamble: "Being charged with the responsibility of the safe conduct of the President elect, and his suite to their safe destination, I deem it my duty, for special reasons which you will readily comprehend," to specify arrangements to the smallest detail.

This he did. The president-elect would "under *no circumstances* attempt to pass through any crowd until such arrangements are made as will meet the approval of Col. Ellsworth." Accordingly, each local security chief was to consult with Ellsworth "immediately upon the arrival of the train." Wood dictated precisely who must ride in the first, second, and third carriages that met the group at each station. Lincoln and one or two members of the local escort committee would occupy the lead vehicle in every city—reassuringly accompanied by the menacing Ward Hill Lamon "or other members of his suite."[96]

Norman Judd, David Davis (inexplicably listed as a carriage occupant but not as a member of the official suite, perhaps because his elephantine size made him a suite unto himself), and military escorts Hunter and Sumner would follow close behind in the second carriage; Nicolay, Colonel Ellsworth, and Captain Hazzard would ride in the third; and Robert Lincoln and John Hay in the fourth. Two additional carriages would be required at each station "to convey Mrs. Lincoln and family and her escort from the cars." This was meant as no slight: in Victorian-era America, women were routinely excluded from official ceremonies and processions.

Wood handed each participant an official pass engraved with the words: "You are respectfully invited to participate in the courtesies extended to Hon. ABRAHAM LINCOLN, President elect, by the several Railway Companies, from Springfield to Washington."[97] Finally, Wood issued a list of requirements for the "Arrangement of Rooms." Each city was to provide sleeping quarters for the private secretaries "contiguous to the President elect"; Wood and his assistant must have a room nearby, and the other members of the suite would have rooms "as near as convenient." Each hotel was instructed to provide a "private dining room with table for six or eight persons." Anticipating complaints and bruised egos, Wood offered this guilt-inducing postscript: "Trusting, gentlemen, that inasmuch as we have a common purpose in this matter, the safety, comfort and convenience of the President elect, these suggestions will be received in the spirit in which they are offered."

Perhaps Wood's—and Lincoln's—most glaring oversight was in ignoring the embarrassing news (assuming they heard it in advance) that another American "president" would be simultaneously making his way to his own national capital for an alternative inauguration. For on February 9, 1861, after days of intense electioneering, delegates to the Mobile convention chose Jefferson Davis of Mississippi the provisional president of the new Confederate States of America. Now, just as Lincoln began his journey to Washington, his counterpart would be traveling to Alabama.

Though they were born only a few months apart, and within a hundred miles of each other in Kentucky, Davis and Lincoln were unmistakably different—one as stiffly formal as the other was relaxed and unpretentious[98]—and while history's hindsight has established Lincoln as far more sympathetic than his Confederate counterpart, an English observer of the day probably spoke for many contemporaries on both sides of the ocean in judging Davis at first the more presidential. "I appeal to the *cartes de visite* of both Lincoln and Davis," wrote Alexander J. Beresford-Hope, referring to the newly popular little photographs first introduced in France, "and I think all who see them will agree that Jefferson Davis bears out one's idea of what an able administrator and a calm statesman should look like better than Abraham Lincoln, great as he may be as a rail-splitter, bargee, and country attorney."[99]

Lincoln was probably more profoundly jolted by the news that his old congressional colleague, Alexander Stephens, would accept the post of vice president of the Confederacy, for Stephens had opposed Georgia secession only a few weeks earlier. A bit of consolation arrived in a report that same February 9 that voters in the crucial border state of Tennessee had rejected, by 68,272 to 59,449, a proposal to call a secession convention of their own. Tennesseans had faced Negrophobic warnings from local congressman John Vine Wright that "in his zeal for the negro, [Lincoln] has lost sight of the white man. Are you prepared, then, to have the negro set on your juries, represent you in your legislature and in Congress, marry your daughters, and in all things be the equals of yourselves and your families?"[100] The failure of such hysterical appeals offered Lincoln the first tangible evidence, however flimsy, to fuel his hope that he might yet hold the loyalty of the Upper South.[101]

EMERGING FROM HIS cocoon above Smith's grocery, Lincoln maintained his official silence on major issues, but unleashed a flurry of letters accepting more invitations to stop in various state capitals en route to Washington—Trenton, New Jersey; Columbus, Ohio; and Harrisburg, Pennsylvania. A "want of time" compelled him to turn down invitations to Dayton and Boston, but he decided he could afford a brief stopover at Cleveland, and of course, both New York City and Philadelphia would be granted visits as well. "Will not this rounabout [sic] way involve too much fatigue and exhaustion?" Salmon Chase wisely worried. But then, answering his own question, he told Lincoln: "I am glad you have relinquished your idea of proceeding to Washington in a private way. It is important to allow full scope to the enthusiasm of the people just now." [102]

Lincoln's major appearances would, not surprising, be devoted to places where he had won voter support in November, the better to draw friendly crowds: Indianapolis (51.4 percent in Marion County); Cleveland (62.5 percent in Cuyahoga County); Cincinnati (45.4 percent—a 1 percent plurality—in Hamilton County); Buffalo (53.3 percent in Erie County); and Philadelphia (50.8 percent in Philadelphia County). Only for his obligatory visits to Northern state capitals would he enter opposition territory: Columbus, Ohio (whose county he had lost by nearly 6 points); Trenton, New Jersey (51.8 percent); and Albany, New York (where the fusion ticket had outpolled him 53.2 percent to 46.8). He would stop in New York City, although he had been outpolled there by Douglas by 24,000 votes. Finally, there would be hostile but unavoidable Baltimore, the last stop before Washington, where only 3.6 percent of the voters had cast ballots for Lincoln, and nearly 50 percent for Southern Democrat John C. Breckinridge. [103]

Each moment on Lincoln's timetable would be allocated precisely, evidenced by the Trenton acceptance letter, which ended with a handwritten postscript rather brusquely insisting: "Please arrange no ceremonies that will waste time." [104] Still, it pained the old campaigner, so long muzzled, to turn down any summons to greet his supporters, and on the back of the Dayton invitation, he scrawled hopefully: "Mr. Nicolay will answer this that I will pass through Dayton, and bow to the friends there, if I can get to and from Columbus just as soon; otherwise not." [105] In the end, organizers could simply not impose the maneuver on the carefully structured itinerary. Absent a brief detour to his native Kentucky—which he desperately hoped he could manage—he would proceed as directly as possible to Washington, though frequent stopovers and refueling requirements would provide him much opportunity to see and be seen.

For just this reason, John Nicolay understandably worried about Lincoln's security. The secretary was amused—but probably not reassured—when a self-described former chemistry professor from Burlington, Iowa, offered to make Lincoln a chain-armor shirt of mail to wear for protection on his trip, "covered with silk" and "plated with gold, so that perspiration shall not affect it." Providing precise specifications for the undershirt to wear beneath his device, inventor A. W. Flanders urged haste, advising it would take ten or twelve days to craft it to the president-elect's unusual measurements. Lincoln need not be embarrassed, Flanders added: "I am told that Napoleon III is constantly protected in this way, and that his life was thus saved from small pieces of the Orsini shells which killed his horses and several persons. I shall be very happy to get this done for Mr. Lincoln if he will accept of it, and really hope he will not go to Washington without it." In the end, Lincoln proceeded to the capital without benefit of the gold-plated armor.[106]

On Wednesday, February 6, as advertised two days earlier, Abraham and Mary Lincoln opened the doors of their modest home for a "farewell soiree" for "their friends in this city"—and of course, enough journalists to make sure the levee was widely publicized. Describing the party as "the most brilliant affair of the kind witnessed here in many years," Henry Villard reported: "Hundreds of well dressed ladies and gentlemen gathered at the Presidential mansion to spend a last evening with their honored hosts. The occasion was a success in every respect, with the exception of a slight jam created by the limited dimensions of the building." Lincoln welcomed guests at the door, and Mary received them in the center of their parlor, but the visitors quickly pushed their way upstairs, and before long every room on "the first and second floor was densely packed with a fashionable multitude." To a Wisconsin visitor who squeezed his way in, Lincoln looked "several shades paler" than he remembered him, but joked, "it does not detract from his beauty."[107]

"Such a crowd," exulted Mary's friend Mercy Conkling, "I seldom, or ever saw at a private house. It took about twenty minutes to get in the hall door." When the Conklings finally elbowed their way toward their hosts, they observed Robert bursting good-humoredly into the receiving line, offering his hand to his father and wisecracking: "Good evening Mr. *Lincoln!*" In return for this performance, as Mrs. Conkling reported, "his father gave him a gentle slap in the face."[108]

Villard could not help noticing that "Mrs. Lincoln's splendid toilette gave satisfactory evidence of extensive purchases during her late visit to New York."[109] In the manner of a modern fashion reporter, a rival correspondent observed that Mary wore a "beautiful, full trail, white moire antique silk, with a small French lace collar. Her neck was ornamented with a string of pearls. Her head dress was a simple and delicate vine, arranged with much taste. . . . She is a lady of fine figure and accomplished address, and is well calculated to grace and do honors at the white house."[110] Another guest, aspiring young lawyer Henry Rankin, confirmed that the future first lady "endured the long and trying ordeal with admirable grace and poise," attended by her sisters. Scheduled from 7 P.M. to midnight, the "great occasion" lasted even later than expected, as what seemed to Rankin like "thousands" of well-wishers "hour after hour passed in and out.[111]

The next morning, as the Springfield weather turned "hard frozen and very cold," Lincoln, anxious about his fast-approaching departure, tried to warm a few more friends and associates to the idea of traveling east with him. On a break from last-minute chores, he collared Orville Browning during an apparent call to nature in the basement of the State Capitol—where the toilets were located. There the president-elect issued Browning "a very earnest invitation to go with him to Washington, where he starts on Monday." Browning expressed reluctance, but Lincoln was able to persuade him to join his party as far as Indianapolis.[112] Attorney General–designate Edward Bates turned down a similar invitation, explaining: "I have not yet fully completed my arrangements (professional & *pecuniary*—especially the latter) for a long absence."[113] Arriving for his own visit to town, Ward Hill Lamon proved easier to convince. Lamon remembered his old friend telling him: "Hill . . . I want you to go along with me . . . it looks as if we might have war. In that case I want you with me. In fact, I must have you. So get yourself ready and come along. It will be handy to have you around." Lamon probably embellished Lincoln's importuning, but go he did.[114]

Abraham Lincoln's life as a citizen of Springfield was coming to an end, and it made him "grave and reflective"—to the point of "grieving"—at the prospect of departing. Describing him as more "solemn" than ever, Villard noticed that "sadness pervades his conversation and restrains the wonted outbursts of humor." As the journalist sensed: "Parting with this scene of joys and sorrows during the last thirty years" and abandoning "the large circle of old and faithful friends apparently saddens him and directs his thoughts to his cherished past rather than the uncertain future." Most of his few remaining public hours were devoted to final "affectionate" visits "with the most intimate of his friends."[115]

But even the company of his "favored" confidants could not break through the sadness that overtook Lincoln in these final days at home. An alarmed John Hay admitted that Lincoln's usual "hilarious good spirits all but evaporated. "He does not attempt to conceal from himself or his friends his sense of the gravity of the mission which calls him in this troubled time," Hay reported, adding ominously, "nor that the future is one whereof the horoscope may not be cast."[116]

Chapter Nine

With a Task Before Me

LINCOLN STILL HAD much to do before departing his hometown. To finance the long trip—since his campaign coffers were bare and the government did not pay for a new president's transfer to Washington—he withdrew $400 from his account at the Springfield Marine and Fire Insurance Company, pocketed $100 in cash, and with the balance purchased three $100 bank drafts (the ancestors of modern traveler's checks), to see him through the journey east and his first days in Washington.[1]

Perhaps spying him that day in the bank, one Springfielder whispered that Lincoln was so impoverished he was reduced to borrowing money "in anticipation of the presidential salary."[2] This was not quite the case, though his balance after these withdrawals stood at just $600.[3] To Massachusetts congressman John B. Alley, Lincoln more believably confided that "when he came to Washington he was worth about $15,000"—though this estimate surely took into account land investments, outstanding loans, the value of his law practice, and of course the only home he ever owned.[4]

Ever careful with money, Lincoln had no intention of abandoning his most valuable asset without financial return. After paying local insurance agent James L. Hill $24 to purchase a $3,200 Hartford Life policy that covered his house, stable, and privy, he rented the property to Lucian Tilton, president of the same Great Western Railroad line that Lincoln would soon be taking out of town (with Tilton on board to supervise the sprint to Indiana).[5] The price was less than $30 per month—all of $350 a year (Lincoln would soon be earning around $2,100 a month, or $25,000 a year, as president)—a fair enough rent for what its new occupant described as "a plain, two-story wooden building . . . looking like the residence of a man neither poor nor rich."[6]

Apparently eager to recoup his relocation expenses and avoid storage costs, Lincoln also authorized his era's equivalent of the yard sale, no doubt further scandalizing his gossipy neighbors with this advertisement in the *Daily State Journal*:

> AT PRIVATE SALE—THE FURNITURE CONSISTING OF Parlor and Chamber Sets, Carpets, Sofas, Chairs, Wardrobes, Bureaus, Bedsteads, Stoves, China, Queensware, Glass, etc. etc., at the residence on the corner of Eighth and Jackson streets is offered at private sale without reserve. For particulars apply on the premises at once.[7]

Although, bowing to notions of propriety, the notice omitted Lincoln's name, Springfield residents well knew the dwelling it described, and its owner had no trouble selling his belongings to locals. Druggist Samuel Melvin made the biggest purchase, paying $82.25 for six chairs, a spring mattress, a wardrobe, a whatnot, a stand, nine and a half yards of stair carpet, and four comforters. Lincoln wrote out and signed an itemized receipt, recording the exact cost for each piece (listing his carpet at fifty cents a yard).[8] The remainder went to others. Widely dispersed were well-worn furnishings that future generations would come to venerate as relics.

Before departing, Lincoln deposited his financial records with local banker Robert Irwin for "safe-keeping, and to receive interest." They indicate just how robust a money-lending business Lincoln had maintained, listing as due to him more than $9,000 in outstanding loans and personal mortgages. Most collected 10 percent interest per annum, and some had been issued to unexpected recipients like his supposedly wealthier brother-in-law, Ninian Edwards, and his friend Norman Judd. Here, too, were six shares of a railroad stock, a scholarship certificate for Illinois State University, the record of a sole uncollected legal fee, and a Springfield city bond still payable at $666.67. Lincoln was worth more than most Springfielders knew.[9] A few weeks later, Irwin confidently posted a newspaper notice of his own, advising townspeople that he now held Lincoln's "notes and papers," and was empowered to remit any verifiable unpaid bills.[10]

On February 8, 1861, after dismissing a veteran of the Georgia secession convention who unexpectedly turned up in town to try one more time to elicit an eleventh-hour "positive committal" on compromise, the president-elect and his family vacated their home and moved temporarily into a second-floor suite at the two-dollar-per-day Chenery House.[11] Here they would spend their final three nights in Springfield.

Mariah Vance, an African American domestic who later claimed she had helped the Lincolns pack, remembered, many years later, that after doing a final cleaning of the now empty premises, she closed the windows, locked the doors, and brought the key to the hotel, where she turned it over to the proprietor. "I never saw Lincoln any more," she remembered, "until they brought him home dead."[12]

No one knows for certain how many of their personal documents and photographs the Lincolns discarded before moving. Mariah recalled that Mary did lovingly pack up the companion daguerreotypes that Nicholas H. Shepherd had taken in Springfield fifteen years earlier— the first photographic portraits for which either husband or wife had ever posed. "They are very precious to me," the servant overheard Mrs. Lincoln confiding as she removed them from the wall, "taken when we were young and so desperately in love. They will grace the walls of the White House."

To which Lincoln supposedly replied: "I trust that grace never slips a peg and becomes dis-grace."[13]

Other precious family records—photographic and written alike—were undoubtedly thrown away or burned and lost to history. The Lincolns did salvage and take to Washington a few album-sized photographs of their Todd family relations, along with a campaign-season *carte-de-visite* of their beloved dwelling, showing Lincoln standing inside its front gate with Willie and Tad. The boys took along a hastily arranged picture of the family dog Fido, who, Lincoln had decided, to his sons' bitter disappointment, to leave behind with neighbor boys John and Frank Roll. The Roll family got a horsehair sofa—Fido's favorite haunt—for their trouble.[14]

Ironically, even in the midst of discarding old pictures, Lincoln returned to C. S. German's gallery on Saturday, February 9, an unseasonably warm day, to pose for new ones—his very last before leaving the city. Unlike those first daguerreotypes, the fresh likenesses were designed not as personal keepsakes but as public portraits for his increasingly curious admirers. German exposed a disappointing profile that showed too much of the back of Lincoln's head, but also a more satisfying nearly full-faced image. The latter showed the president-elect sporting long hair cascading over his ear and, for the first time, a fully grown beard. He posed before the same tasseled drape that could be seen in the photograph German had taken three weeks earlier. The watch chain was the same, and so might have been the suit, shirt, and tie. But not the expression. A confident smile flickered across Lincoln's countenance, and though he looked careworn, his eyes shone bright with anticipation.[15] Here was not just a new portrait (see frontispiece), but a new persona. Lincoln's transfiguration from "Honest Abe" the rail-splitter to "Father Abraham" the confident statesman was complete—at least on the visible surface.

Later that same whirlwind of a day, Lincoln sat down with Orville Browning and predicted that "no good results" would come out of the distracting Peace Convention in Washington. The president-elect shared his old friend's belief that the convention would in fact produce "evil," since "increased excitement" was sure to "follow when it broke up without having accomplished any thing." Though Browning did much of the talking, he left the meeting convinced that Lincoln agreed that no concession "short of surrender" would be accepted by the South, that proposed compromise amendments should be rejected, and most important of all, "that far less evil & bloodshed would result from an effort to maintain the Union and the Constitution"—in other words, war, if it came to that—"than from disruption and the formation of two confederacies."[16]

Although he faithfully recorded these details in his diary, Browning neglected to mention that he also burdened his friend that same day with no fewer than four new requests for federal jobs, including one for Browning's brother-in-law.[17] Lincoln must have welcomed the chance that evening to escape from such friends, if only to submit to a final fitting for the recently delivered inaugural suit from the Chicago tailors Titsworth & Brother. The outfit had been on gaudy public display in a downtown shop window for two days.[18]

Lincoln's final distinguished guest in Springfield was Carl Schurz, who returned to town, he claimed, merely to say farewell—but doubtless as well to convince himself one last time that the president-elect would not yield on compromise. Lincoln received him "with the utmost distinction," devoted the afternoon and part of the evening to a frank discussion of "everything that was of common interest," generously urged Schurz to apply to the new administration "for a few offices" for his friends, and invited the German-born orator to join the traveling party headed for Washington. But Schurz had a speaking schedule to keep and was compelled to decline.

Bringing their long conversation to an abrupt halt, Lincoln offered to give his visitor " 'a mark of confidence which I have given to no other man.' Then he locked the door and read to me the draft of his inaugural address." John Nicolay and David Davis—and no one else—had seen the address earlier and it is likely their suggestions were already reflected in the printed version Lincoln now recited to Schurz. After the two men "discussed it point by point," Lincoln swore Schurz to secrecy, reminding him: "Now you know better than any man in this country how I stand, and you may be sure that I shall never betray my principles and my friends." To his wife, Schurz joyfully reported only that Lincoln remained *"fest wie eine mauer"*—firm as a wall.[19]

One more task still required Lincoln's attention—and it would be a wrenching one. On Sunday afternoon, February 10, he visited his old Capitol Square law office for the first time in months to go through the firm's outstanding case files with Billy Herndon. He had done no legal work at all for eight months—but felt obliged to discuss the backlog with the hard-drinking junior partner he was about to entrust with his practice.[20]

If we can believe self-described law student Henry Rankin, who claimed he witnessed part of this final visit, the president-elect's arrival could be heard before it was seen. Rankin, many of whose so-called recollections are questionable, believably claimed he was long accustomed to the sound of Lincoln's enormous boots clopping up the staircase several steps at a time; he always recognized his familiar tread. But this day he heard a slow shuffle thumping toward the office step by step, as if the caller was old and weary. Rankin remembered that he was flabbergasted when Lincoln entered the room. As the clerk watched quietly, Lincoln pulled from a shelf two scrapbooks, perhaps the very ones into which, over the years, he had pasted countless newspaper clippings, including reprints of his own speeches. Rankin wisely excused himself and left the two partners alone.[21]

Picking up the story, Herndon remembered: "We ran over the books and arranged for the completion of all unsettled and unfinished matters." Lincoln inquired after "certain legal matters in which he still felt some interest," and instructed his junior partner on "certain lines of procedure he wished me to observe." Lincoln supposedly offered Herndon a job in his administration, which the younger man declined. For a time, reminiscing merrily about their most "ludicrous" old cases on the circuit, Lincoln seemed more cheerful than Herndon had ever seen him. But then he crossed to the opposite side of the room and "threw himself down on the old office sofa," now literally on its last legs and wedged precariously against a far wall. There, Lincoln lapsed into a reverie, resting "for some moments, his face towards the ceiling." Neither man spoke.[22]

Finally Lincoln broke the silence to inquire: "Billy, how long have we been together?"

"Over sixteen years," came the answer.

"We've never had a cross word during all that time, have we?"

"No, indeed we have not," Herndon "vehemently" replied.

At that, Lincoln hauled himself up from the rickety couch, gathered the books and papers he had selected to take with him, and made one additional request—to have a last look at the old Lincoln-Herndon signboard that "swung on its rusty hinges at the foot of the stairway."

There, lowering his voice, the senior partner advised: "Let it hang there undisturbed. Give our clients to understand that the election of a President makes no change in the firm of Lincoln and Herndon. If I live I'm coming back some time, and then we'll go right on practising law as if nothing had ever happened."[23]

Lingering just a moment longer to cast one final glance toward the shabby quarters, Lincoln turned and walked slowly downstairs to the street. "I am sick of office-holding already," he confided in parting, "and I shudder when I think of the tasks that are still ahead." Not only was he sorrowful at the prospect of leaving home, he was convinced, he whispered, that he would never return alive. Herndon implored him to abandon such thoughts. It was not "in keeping," he argued, "with the popular ideal of a President."

"But," Lincoln replied icily before saying goodbye, "it is in keeping with my philosophy."[24]

Henry Villard shared Lincoln's anxiety about the "tasks that are still ahead." After keeping close watch on the president-elect for nearly three months, he believed he now faced the most "hazardous lot" any of his predecessors had ever confronted.

As Villard warned his readers in his final dispatch from Lincoln's hometown: "The path he is about to walk on may lead to success, glory, immortality, but also to failure, humiliation and curses upon his memory.

He may steer clear of the rock of disunion and the shoal of dissension among those that elevated him to the office he is about to assume, and safely conduct the Ship of State from amidst the turbulence of fanaticism and lawlessness to the port of peace and reunion. But he may, on the other hand, take his place at the helm of the craft only to sink with it." [25]

More than three full months after his election as president of the United States, and less than three weeks before his inauguration, Lincoln's future—together with the nation's—remained very much in question.

Not surprisingly, Abraham Lincoln's last full day in Springfield ended much as his first day as president-elect had begun: with one more annoying appeal from a job-seeker. Facing "pecuniary ruin," this February 10 letter-writer begged Lincoln to rescue him with "as good an office as your sense of what is right authorizes," implying that the president-elect's resistance to sectional compromise was to blame for his sour investments in the South. [26] Lincoln had been enduring such guilt-inducing pleas for months. The only surprise on this one was its signature. Just days earlier, Lincoln had put thoughts of office-seeking behind him for his retreat to Coles County. There he had enjoyed the hospitality of state senator Thomas A. Marshall. Apparently, barely a week later, his debt was now payable in full. The last of the Springfield office-seekers was the same Thomas A. Marshall.

THE CLOUDS AND drizzle that enshrouded Springfield at dawn on Monday, February 11, signaled in one sense an improvement over the frigid weather that had gripped the town in snow and ice for so many weeks. "Hard King Frost and soft Queen Thaw" had come "to a tussle," as *Harper's Weekly* put it, and for one morning at least, Queen Thaw prevailed. [27]

At around 7:30 A.M., after breakfasting at the hotel—and taking a moment to inquire thoughtfully about the health of the proprietor's wife—Lincoln casually strolled into the hotel office. There, calling on skills he had learned decades earlier as a flatboatman, he knotted a rope around the trunks packed with his family's transportable goods, and then, grabbing a handful of Chenery House note cards, flipped them over, marked each with characteristic simplicity in his own hand—"A. Lincoln, White House, Washington, D.C."—and tacked them to the trunks.[28] An African American porter named Jameson Jenkins then hauled them off to the train station in a drayman's cart.

This final chore accomplished, Lincoln climbed into an omnibus parked outside the back steps—Mary would follow later—and rode off through the muddy streets to the remodeled yet incurably "dingy" Great Western depot on the east end of town, just a few blocks from the family's recently surrendered home.[29] A knot of admirers followed them as they crept through town, and past the cluster of modest foundries, machine shops, mills, and lumberyards that ringed the tracks.[30] Lincoln said little. Nicolay believed the "stormy morning" added "gloom and depression" to their demeanor. Their mood was one of "subdued anxiety, almost of solemnity."[31]

Arriving at the station, Lincoln's spirits rose when he spied his gleaming three-car train hissing at the ready: a modern Rogers locomotive crowned by a towering, spark-retarding funnel stack, a baggage car, and bringing up the rear, a bright yellow passenger car "festively" adorned with patriotic bunting. Crowding the depot was a "vast concourse" of a thousand neighbors huddled against the mist and steam to properly see him off, "almost all of whom," Lincoln proudly testified, "I could recognize."[32]

When he first came into sight, the young men in the throng let out with "the most enthusiastic cheering." One of those who "shouted our farewell to Mr. Lincoln" explained, "we felt we were parting from a personal friend to whom we were deeply attached."[33] Visibly moved by this show of affection, Lincoln proceeded into the depot, where, flanked by Lamon and a uniformed Ellsworth, he bent to offer "an affectionate grasp of the hand" to each of the dozens of particularly dear friends who packed into the sky-lit gentlemen's waiting room to offer final, personal goodbyes[34] "His face was pale, and quivered with emotion," an onlooker observed, "so deep as to render him unable to utter a single word" to these neighbors.[35]

Near eight o'clock, it was time to bid farewell to his wife.[36] Then, preceded by Robert and his chum George Latham, by his secretaries Nicolay and Hay, and by their expanded "suite" of political associates and bodyguards, Lincoln followed William Wood and his assistant, Burnett Forbes, toward the tracks. The crowd parted respectfully as they passed, many offering final handshakes along the way.

John Hay joked that the guest list for the voyage had ballooned to such an extent it now embraced "members of all the political parties, with the exception of the secessionists."[37] Ozias Hatch, Newton Bateman, former Belleville legal colleague William H. Underwood, Quincy attorney Joseph Jackson Grimshaw, Democratic politician William Morrison, and longtime friend William Butler all joined the roster. So did Superintendent John J. S. Wilson, who had manned the telegraph office on Election Night and would now assume responsibility, using a portable telegraphy machine he planned to carry on board, for receiving messages confirming safe passage en route. And so did railroad superintendent F. W. Bowen himself, charged with overseeing the journey personally while it proceeded along his Great Western tracks. "This train will be entitled to the road, *and all other trains must be kept out of the way*," he announced in advance, laying out an elaborate system of danger signals and emergency procedures. "Carefulness is particularly enjoined."[38]

Joining the party, too, was banker Robert Irwin, evidently willing to abandon his newly conferred stewardship of Lincoln's accounts long enough to travel at least part of the way with his famous client. And crammed on board as well were two Republican governors: Richard Yates of Illinois, who had called out state militia to guard trestle bridges along the route;[39] and Oliver P. Morton of neighboring Indiana, where Lincoln's first day of travel would terminate. Lamon, Ellsworth, David Davis, Jesse Dubois, Orville Browning, and several other friends squeezed their way on board as well. As previously announced, they would be joined later not only by Mary and the children, but by Colonels Sumner and Burgess, along with Major Hunter, and Captain Pope. Lincoln's entourage dwarfed even Andrew Jackson's traveling circus a generation earlier. One of its dubious members, Norman Judd, worried that the roster was "very badly made up," and hoped it would "get through without especial discredit."[40]

If it did not, there were observers on board who would certainly make sure the entire country knew about it. "In common with other politicians," William Herndon observed, Lincoln ". . . never overlooked a newspaper man who had it in his power to say a good or bad thing of him."[41] Few were overlooked now. The pack of traveling journalists included not only Henry Villard, but Joseph Howard, Jr., of the *New York Times*, T. C. Evans of the *New York World*, O. H. Dutton of the *New York Tribune*, Henry M. Smith of the *Chicago Tribune*, Henri Lovie of *Frank Leslie's*, W. G. Terrell of the *Cincinnati Gazette*, Uriah Hunt Painter of the *Philadelphia Inquirer*, and no fewer than five correspondents from the Associated Press: J. R. Drake, S. D. Page, J. H. A. Boone, A. W. Griswold, and Theodore Stager.[42] John Hay, traveling principally as an aide to Lincoln, doubled as a correspondent, filing reports for the *Missouri Democrat* and the *Illinois Daily State Journal*, often grandly signing his dispatches "Ecarte"—after écarté, the popular card game favored by Rawdon Crawley in the novel *Vanity Fair*. Over the next eleven days, these reporters would provide a colorful, though sometimes contradictory, account of Lincoln's trip: a traveling Vanity Fair that would have inspired Thackeray himself.

Staying on schedule was crucial to William Wood's careful plan, and as the train bells sounded at 8 A.M. sharp, Lincoln mounted the steps of the rear passenger car, ascended to the platform, and then turned to face his neighbors. Doffing his top hat—a gesture the crowd promptly acknowledged by uncovering in response, even though by some accounts the drizzle had turned to snow—Lincoln raised his hands to call for silence. And then, even though he had prepared no written remarks for his departure, he began speaking, his voice choked with feeling:

Friends,
    No one who has never been placed in a like position, can understand my feelings at this hour, nor the oppressive sadness I

feel at this parting. For more than a quarter of a century I have lived among you, and during all that time I have received nothing but kindness at your hands. Here I have lived from my youth until now I am an old man. Here the most sacred ties of earth were assumed; here all my children were born; and here one of them lies buried. To you, dear friends, I owe all that I have, all that I am. All the strange, chequered past seems to crowd now upon my mind. To-day I leave you; I go to assume a task more difficult than that which devolved upon General Washington. Unless the great God who assisted him, shall be with and aid me, I must fail. But if the same omniscient mind, and Almighty arm that directed and protected him, shall guide and support me, I shall not fail, I shall succeed. Let us all pray that the God of our fathers may not forsake us now. To him I commend you all— permit me to ask that with equal security and faith, you all will invoke His wisdom and guidance for me. With these few words I must leave you—for how long I know not. Friends, one and all, I must now bid you an affectionate farewell.[43]

At least that is how the local *Daily State Journal* heard and reported Lincoln's last words in Springfield. When the *New York Times* and other newspapers published the text the following morning, however, they presented a slightly more refined version perhaps recorded by another stenographer on the scene. But the version left to posterity—the text Lincoln himself hoped would represent his parting words for all time— turned out to be neither of the above. Once inside his car, giving him hardly a moment to recover from the wrenching farewell, Henry Villard approached him and requested an authoritative text.

Only yesterday, Lincoln had sent word to correspondents that he would say "nothing warranting their attention" at his departure.[44] Now, after catching snippets of his unscheduled message, Villard and his colleagues believed the speech deserved publication. Lincoln agreed. Recognizing that his words could reach a reading audience far larger than his hearing audience, he promptly agreed to provide a text—even as the telegraph operators in Springfield prepared to wire his original remarks to newspapers throughout the country. If he wanted to modify the record, Lincoln needed to act quickly.

Coolly, he took a lined pad and pencil and began writing out a revised version of what became known as his Farewell Address[45]—a gem that rightly took its place as one of the greatest of his speeches, but that is seldom recognized for what it truly represents: a stunning example not of spontaneous eloquence, but of Lincoln's meticulous ability to edit and rewrite, even under pressure. Overcoming the emotional upheaval of his parting, Lincoln effortlessly focused on enshrining a revised text. As the firm, distinct penmanship of the first few lines suggests, he commenced writing even before his train pulled out of town. Then, as the presidential special picked up speed and began to jostle him, his hand trembled—for the next few words lurched into indecipherable blurs. Unable to continue after scrawling just four sentences, Lincoln handed the pad over to Nicolay, who took down more of the manuscript as Lincoln recited aloud, reconstructing and refining as he spoke. For the final thirty-two words, Lincoln asked for the pad and pencil back, and composed the remainder himself. Whether writing or dictating, Lincoln deftly condensed his thoughts from a colloquial if heartfelt goodbye into a compact hymn uniting elements of faith, appreciation, determination, and self-assurance within a neatly metered rhetorical structure featuring the device of ping-ponging parallel phrases, known formally as antiphony.[46]

This was Lincoln's final version of his Farewell Address:

My friends—No one, not in my situation, can appreciate my feeling of sadness at this parting. To this place, and the kindness of these people, I owe every thing. Here I have lived a quarter of a century, and have passed from a young to an old man. Here my children have been born, and one is buried. I now leave, not knowing when, or whether ever, I may return, with a task before me greater than that which rested upon Washington. Without the assistance of that Divine Being, who ever attended him, I cannot succeed. With that assistance I cannot fail. Trusting in

Him, who can go with me, and remain with you and be every where for good, let us confidently hope that all will yet be well. To His care commending you, as I hope in your prayers you will commend me, I bid you an affectionate farewell.[47]

Lincoln began scribbling this text of his farewell address to Springfield after his train left town, but handed the page to his secretary, John Nicolay, when it became too rocky to write. The president-elect took the manuscript back and wrote out the final words himself. (LINCOLN PAPERS, LIBRARY OF CONGRESS)

For years, Lincoln had made a conscious effort to apply logic and eschew emotion in his public addresses. "Passion has helped us; but can do so no more," he had lectured fellow Springfielders as early as 1838. "Reason, cold, calculating, unimpassioned reason, must furnish all the materials for our future support and defence."[48] But his departure had brought forth just the opposite: a deeply personal confession from the heart. "We have known Mr. Lincoln for many years; we have heard him speak upon a hundred different occasions," reported Edward L. Baker for the hometown State Journal, "but we never saw him so profoundly affected, nor did he ever utter an address which seemed to us so full of simple and touching eloquence, so exactly adapted to the occasion, so worthy of the man and the hour."[49]

Whichever iteration actually came from Lincoln's lips that morning, the words proved more than enough to move not only the audience, but also the speaker, to tears. John Hay confirmed that the farewell speech "left hardly a dry eye in the assemblage." "His exhortation to pray," Henry Villard reported, "elicited choked exclamations of 'we will do it; we will do it.'"[50] Eyewitness James C. Conkling agreed: "Many eyes were filled to overflowing as Mr. Lincoln uttered those few simple words. . . . His own breast heaved with emotion and he could scarcely command his feelings sufficiently to commence. He is now fairly on his way for weal or woe of the nation. God bless him and preserve him and nerve him for the terrible struggles and dangers which he may be called upon to meet and endure."

As Lincoln spoke his final words and turned to enter the train, the audience erupted with three rousing cheers. Then he passed from sight, the train bells sounded, its whistle screeched, the smokestack erupted with steam, engineer Elias Fralick kicked the brakes, and as John Hay testified, "the crowd stood silent as the train moved slowly from the depot."[51] Lincoln would never set foot in Springfield again.

But his farewell speech would resonate there—and throughout the North—for years. Lincoln broke his long, self-imposed silence with an ingeniously crafted little oration that began by conveying warm gratitude for twenty-five years of friendly support (though in fact his home-

ANTIPHONY ?

town remained evenly, and bitterly, divided politically). Here in Springfield, Lincoln volunteered, his heart would remain along with the remains of his beloved boy Eddie (deftly employing antiphony here: "my children have been born/and one is buried"). It was as close to raw personal observation as Lincoln ever allowed in public remarks.

From this confession, Lincoln shifted from the theme of gratitude to that of faith. His destiny, he declared, was now in God's hands—a powerful, omnipresent divinity capable of safeguarding his neighbors in Springfield even as He blessed his work in Washington. Lincoln was but a man; he could succeed only with divine intervention. He would surely fail without it (antiphony again: "go with me/remain with you"; "commending you/commend me"). Lincoln had so felt for years, though he had never summoned the nerve to say so publicly. "There is no contending against the Will of God," he had written in an 1858 jotting, "but there is still some difficulty in ascertaining it." Now Lincoln believed he had indeed identified—and identified *with*—God's will. Once again, these expressions were, for Lincoln, unprecedented. But read correctly, they signaled not only a suddenly manifested submission to fate, but a new recruitment of God's will to support the people's will—namely, his lawful election to the presidency. If God desired it—and Lincoln implied that He would—all would yet be well among mortals acting in His name.

Sandwiched between these ingeniously structured allusions to both the sentimental past and the portentous future, Lincoln introduced the novel suggestion that he faced a challenge equal to that which had confronted the nation's secular father: George Washington. In their original form—those heard and jotted down at the station—the words were awkwardly phrased, almost as if Lincoln had difficulty expressing them. Such might well have been the case, for it was a breathtakingly audacious claim. Through most of his life, and all of his political career, he had regarded George Washington as peerless—incomparable. To Lincoln, it made "human nature better to believe that one human being was perfect: that human perfection was possible."[52]

Now, remarkably, Lincoln dared to make just the kind of comparison he had long deemed unthinkable: to liken his own name to "the might-iest name on earth," by averring he faced a crisis not only equal to, but actually more dangerous than, the one the nation's founder had con-fronted nearly four score years earlier. Lincoln could not be clearer: he believed he now had "a task before me *greater* than that which rested upon Washington." This was an astonishing declaration. Did Lincoln genuinely believe he had already attained a status equal to his greatest hero? Perhaps not, but with Southern revolutionaries already comparing themselves to the founders, Lincoln was not about to cede the univer-sally revered symbol of George Washington to secessionists.

Precisely when the president-elect originated these themes remains a mystery, but if we can believe young Springfielder Robert H. Browne, Lincoln had expressed similar ideas to a group of friends shortly before leaving town. Lamenting that he felt all but overwhelmed, he admitted: "I feel that a burden such as few men have ever seen or borne is resting upon me. It seems greater to me that the task laid upon Washington, and I have no desire to compare myself with him; but the contest seems as definitely drawn, and the issues involved, in their relation to area, power, and people, are fully ten times as great. Alone I would be utterly powerless, but, sustained by the good people that love our country I will go forward . . . with the conviction firmly fixed in my mind that God will save and perpetuate the Nation if we but do our duty. . . . The des-tinies of nations are in his hands."[53]

On February 11, crystallizing these thoughts, he maneuvered God the Father together with the father of his country onto the side of the Union—with himself as the beneficiary of their blessings. Within only a few years, history would validate what might then have seemed like overreaching: Lincoln's name would indeed be permanently linked to America's hitherto "incomparable" hero Washington—as the founder and savior of the country, "Columbia's Noblest Sons."[54]

Now, as the inaugural special eased out of town, passing the home of a Springfield clergyman, the pastor unwittingly endorsed the conceit Lincoln had proposed only minutes before. "When the train bearing you passed my residence this morning," he confided, "my heart said, God bless Lincoln, & make him second to none but Washington."[55] Not everyone concurred, of course, especially in perennially divided Springfield. Reminding its readers that the president-elect had once told its citizens that the Union could not exist permanently half-slave and half-free, the local Democratic paper declared: "Accident has placed Mr. Lincoln in a position to enable him to do much towards verifying his prediction. It is hoped that he may prove less ambitious to be considered a prophet than a patriot."[56]

OVER THE NEXT nine hours, the big traveling party enjoyed what a relaxed John Nicolay called "a rather pleasant ride." Compared to the strain of the previous week, the long haul seemed like a vacation. "We have been so busy during several days previous to our departure," Nicolay explained, "there is not near so much physical fatigue in riding on railroads."[57] When things became dull, Ward Hill Lamon entertained passengers by singing and playing his banjo.

For miles, crowds could be seen lining the entire route in the rain. "Multitudes of spectators," assembled at stations at small villages all along the route in hopes of catching a fleeting glimpse of their president-elect, waving flags and handkerchiefs as his train sped through the prairie, past villages with names like Illiopolis, Niantic, and Summit.[58] "I never knew where all the people came from," recalled the train's brakeman, ". . . not only in the towns and villages, but . . . along the track in the country."[59] When the inaugural special "bowled" into Decatur to make its first stop for refueling, Lincoln disembarked to "enthusiastic cheers," incurring "embraces and blessings" from "several thousand people, gathered from the surrounding country." The president-elect inched happily through the throng, "shaking hands vigorously." John Hay believed that "No one could witness this frank, hearty display of enthusiasm and affection on the one side, and cordial, generous fraternity on the other, without recognizing . . . the tall, stalwart Illinoisan . . . as perfectly *en rapport* with its people now," adding: "Having spent his life in the very heart of the mighty West, having mingled with its people for a lifetime, the sympathy between the constituent and the elect is as perfect as that between near kindred."[60]

Then the train steamed off again, whistling through Oakley, Cerro Gordo, Bement, and Sadorus, the last of which hugged the banks of the same Okaw River where, not too many miles away, Lincoln and Dennis Hanks had once seen their oxcart nearly capsize in its swirling waters. After chugging past hundreds more onlookers—"all enthusiastic, vociferous, and fluttering with handkerchiefs and flags"—the train made its second stop in little Tolono, where Lincoln was welcomed with booming cannon and cheering well-wishers who, Hay reported, "bullied" him into a speech. It was but the first of many unrehearsed remarks Lincoln would find himself compelled to make during his long journey. "I am leaving you on an errand of national importance," he told the Tolono crowd, "attended, as you are aware, with considerable difficulties. Let us believe, as some poet has expressed it:—Behind the cloud the sun is still shining." Banal as it was, the greeting was enough to elicit "as wild an intensity of delight as if it had been a condensed embodiment of the substance of his inaugural."[61]

As the train hurtled next past Philo, Sidney, Homer, Salina, Catlin, and on toward the Indiana state line, Lincoln paused for only one more speech in his home state: a few plain-spoken words of greeting to "his good old friends" in Danville. Those on board who knew him best noticed that his mood darkened as he neared the border. "Something of the gloom of parting with neighbors and friends, bidding farewell to the community in which he has lived for a quarter of a century," Hay noted, "seemed to rest upon the President during the greater part of the journey. He was abstracted, sad, thoughtful." Moreover, though he was speeding toward his future, he would first be required to detour back to his Hoosier past, and it was making him wistful. "My childhood-home I see again," he had written years earlier in a long poem about the Indiana backwoods, "and sadden with the view." Now his childhood home was about to come into view again.[62]

Shortly after noon, right on schedule, the Great Western train crossed the state line, where the party paused for dinner while brakemen linked the cars to a new engine compatible with the Toledo & Wabash tracks—like many lines along the route, of a different gauge than the ones to which it was connected. "I am happy to meet you on this occasion, and enter again the state of my early life," Lincoln managed to declare. And then, promising a longer speech at Indianapolis, he resumed his journey, now accommodating a delegation of Indiana politicians further crowding the passenger cars.

At Lafayette, he marveled at the speed of modern transportation—his train had attained breathtaking speeds of up to thirty miles an hour—and addressing opponents as well as friends, expressed the hope that "upon the union of the States, there shall be between us no difference." At nearby Thorntown he apologized for not making a real speech, launching instead into an anecdote about an ambitious politician who rode a slow-moving horse to a county convention, making so many stops along the way that another candidate won the nomination he coveted before he could get there. Unfortunately, Lincoln's own train lurched off before he could supply the punch line, and the only laugh the audience offered came at the sight of the grinning speaker being hauled away before he finished his tale. At nearby Lebanon, however, he learned that some of his audience had followed the train all the way from the previous stop, "panting to hear the conclusion of the story." So Lincoln obligingly supplied it, explaining that, like the old county politician, "if he stopped at every station to make a stump speech, he would not arrive at Washington until the inauguration was over."[63]

Lincoln's 5 P.M. on-time arrival at Indianapolis triggered the most impressive welcome yet, unleashing cheers so "deafening" they could be heard "above the roar of cannon."[64] After Governor Morton ordered a thirty-four-gun salute, one blast for each state in the Union (including the newest state, Kansas), Lincoln responded with the eighth speech of this long day. Thanking the crowd at the station for "this magnificent reception," he modestly described himself as "an accidental instrument . . . of a great cause," adding to warm applause that "the salvation of this Union . . . needs but one single thing—the hearts of a people like yours. When the people rise in masses in behalf of the Union and the liberties of their country, truly may it be said, 'The gates of hell shall not prevail against them.' " He concluded with a question: "Shall the Union and shall the liberties of this country be preserved to the latest generation?" The crowd responded with "long and prolonged applause."[65]

Lincoln stood in an open barouche drawn by four white horses for the ride downtown, accompanied by marching bands, national guardsmen, Zouaves, and city firemen, bowing left and right to twenty thousand cheering spectators who lined the streets all the way to his hotel.[66] Otherwise, William Wood's meticulously crafted plan broke down in utter disarray. The carriages promised for the rest of the traveling party were nowhere to be found, and Robert Lincoln had to walk into town carrying his own carpetsack. Once the group arrived at the hotel, things were equally disorganized. "All the streets in front, and the halls and stairways of the house were so packed with an eager crowd," Orville Browning complained, "that we could scarcely make our way through them." Browning was further annoyed by his "poor accommodations." He was forced not only to share his room with Jesse Dubois, George Latham, and a pair of others, but "to sleep two in a bed." Henry Villard agreed that "the indoor arrangements" were "sadly deficient." Likening the Bates House to a "bee-hive," he reported that Lincoln was so "overwhelmed by merciless throngs" that "he only got in by wedging himself through."[67] Rowdy crowds made it impossible to retire until well past midnight.[68]

For Lincoln, the real challenge arose not inside the hotel but outside. Nicolay insisted that each of the "short speeches he might be required to make en route to Washington had been carefully written and placed in envelopes, each labeled to indicate the locality where they would probably be needed for delivery."[69] But when the president-elect stepped out onto the Bates House balcony to address a crowd huddled below, he offered a surprisingly clumsy and unexpectedly provocative challenge to the secessionists. In hindsight, it said too much, and did so far too soon. The tireless orator was tired, and it showed.

"The words 'coercion' and 'invasion' are in great use about these days," he began in a "clear sonorous voice." Cautioning that it was necessary to determine their "exact definitions," he asked: "What, then, is 'coercion?' What is 'invasion'? Would the marching of an army into South Carolina, for instance, without the consent of her people, and in hostility against them, be coercion or invasion?" Answering his own questions, he admitted that such an invasion would surely constitute both. "But if the Government, for instance, but simply insists upon holding its own forts, or retaking those forts which belong to it"—here he was interrupted by cheers—". . . or even the withdrawal of the mails where from those portions of the country where the mails themselves are habitually violated; would any or all of these things be coercion? Do the lovers of the Union contend that they will resist coercion or invasion of any State, understanding that any or all of these would be coercing or invading a State? If they do, then it occurs to me that the means for the preservation of the Union they so greatly love, in their own estimation, is of a very thin and airy character. [Applause.] If sick, they would consider the little pills of the homoeopathist as already too large for them to swallow. In their view, the Union, as a family relation, would not be anything like a regular marriage at all, but only as a sort of free-love arrangement, to be maintained on what that sect calls passionate attraction."[70]

Roars of laughter greeted these last two thoughts—an unexpected and ribald preview of the "husband and wife may be divorced" section from his forthcoming inaugural—and perhaps emboldened by the heartening response to it, Lincoln moved on to question the right of secession and the core issue of states' rights, issues probably better left until March 4. Plunging ahead, he inquired: "What is the particular sacredness of a State? . . . By what principle of original right is it that one-fiftieth or one-ninetieth of a great nation, by calling themselves a State, have the right to break up and ruin that nation as a matter of original principle?" By the time Lincoln concluded with the caveat—"I say I am deciding nothing, but simply giving something for you to reflect upon"—it was too late. The political bombshell detonated, he retreated back inside after offering yet another "affectionate farewell."[71] He had at least provided a first glimpse into his inaugural message, however clumsy the locution.

That Lincoln might have shown a firm hand prematurely was evident in some of the editorial reaction to his remarks. While the Democratic press condemned his line-in-the-sand avowals,[72] the Republican press endorsed them—"Mr. Lincoln maintains the right and the duty of the Government to enforce the laws," applauded the *New York Times*, adding "it is utterly impossible for any President of the United States to take any other view of his duty in the matter."[73] But the *Indiana State Guard* branded the speech as "inferior to what is delivered on many stumps by candidates for the lower house of the legislature," and the *Louisville Journal* called it "a singular indiscretion."[74] Alluding to his reference to hard-to-swallow pills, the *New York Herald* predicted that "Doctor Lincoln" would at least enjoy "the poor consolation of not being the only political quack who has killed his patient through combined stupidity and ignorance." In the cutting words of the *Cleveland Plain Dealer*, who predicted the cotton states would regard the speech "as the tocsin of war," Lincoln had "finally opened his mouth, and as Mrs. Partington [an Americanized Mrs. Malaprop] would say, got his foot in it."[75]

LINCOLN MAY HAVE sensed that he had done precisely that. Fighting his way past crowds thronging the hotel hallways after his speech, he was compelled to meet and greet "turbulent congregations of men" at an impromptu levee in the main parlor. It must have seemed to him that he had somehow accepted the invitation that local inmates had extended to visit to the city's insane asylum.[76] Finally liberated for a delayed fiasco of a supper, he was forced to wait half an hour more "for his slender share of the repast" while inept waiters spilled food on reporters or froze helplessly in mid-service.[77]

Irritably turning to his son—to whom he had entrusted what Robert described as "a small black hand-bag" containing not only his inaugural journey speeches but also the precious typeset copies of the inaugural draft itself—Lincoln asked him to produce the precious baggage,[78] probably intending to do some editing on the manuscripts. But Robert, distracted and bedazzled by the attention locals were bestowing on "The Prince of Rails"—and perhaps "tight" in the bargain, as one journalist hinted—no longer had possession of it.[79] He had blithely handed it off to a waiter, as he now sheepishly admitted to his father, and had no idea where it was. "My heart went up into my mouth," Lincoln recalled. John Nicolay witnessed the ensuing scene:

"A look of stupefaction passed over the countenance of Mr. Lincoln," he reported, "and visions of that Inaugural in all the next morning's newspapers floated through his imagination. Without a word he opened the door of his room, forced his way through the crowded corridor down to the office, where, with a single stride of his long legs, he swung himself across the clerk's counter, behind which a small mountain of carpetbags of all colors had accumulated. Then drawing a little key out of his pocket he began delving for the black ones, and opened one by one those that the key would unlock, to the great surprise and amusement of the clerk and bystanders, as their miscellaneous contents came to light." In one look-alike bag, Ward Hill Lamon testified, Lincoln discovered paper collars, a deck of cards, and a flask of whiskey—but no speeches.

Invariably, his panic reminded him of a funny story. "I feel," Lincoln confessed, "a good deal as the old member of the Methodist Church did when he lost his wife at the camp meeting, and went up to an old elder of the church and asked him if he could tell him whereabouts in hell his wife was." Then Lincoln added: "In fact, I am in a worse fix than my Methodist friend, for if it were only a wife that were missing mine would be sure to bob up somewhere." Eventually, Nicolay was relieved to report, "Fortune favored the President-elect, for after the first half dozen trials, he found his treasures."[80] Robert shrugged off the entire brouhaha, perhaps offering a glimpse into his father's chronic impatience with him when he confided: "the old man might as well scold about that as something else."[81]

Lincoln quickly recovered his poise—a good thing, since he was soon escorted out to the Bates House balcony to deliver yet another speech, this time wisely restricting his message to the hope that "we all might meet again under one flag of one Union." He had hardly enjoyed "a minute of rest" on his first day out of Springfield. "It is a severe ordeal for us," agreed Nicolay, "and increased about tenfold for him."[82]

The following morning, February 12—his fifty-second birthday, though no mention was made of it at the time—the demanding schedule resumed where it left off. After breakfasting with Oliver Morton at the Governor's Mansion, Lincoln paid a courtesy call on the state's legislators at the Capitol, then returned to the Bates House to deliver a third short speech from the hotel balcony to a fresh throng massed outside the window. Near 11 A.M., he was happily reunited with Mary, Willie, and Tad, tuckered out from their own breathless, overnight voyage from Springfield, arriving just in time to join the official traveling party to its next destination.

Just before departing, Lincoln ushered Orville Browning back to his room for one more quiet talk. There had been a purpose behind Lincoln's sudden desire to collect his gripsack the night before. Browning was scheduled to return home the following morning—a single day of presidential travel was "just about as much of that sort of thing as I want," he insisted—and Lincoln wanted his opinion of the inaugural address before they separated. The president-elect took his newly recovered gripsack, extracted a printed copy of the speech, and asked if Browning "would not read it over, and frankly tell him my opinion of it." After a quick reading, Browning's gratifying initial reaction was that it seemed "able, well considered, and appropriate." As he told Lincoln: "It is, in my judgment, a very admirable document." In turn, Lincoln permitted him to retain the copy "under promise" to keep it secret. His friend agreed to "take it back with me, and read it over more at my leisure," assuring him that "if I see anything in it that I think ought to be changed, I will write to you from home."[83] Browning proved true to his word on both counts.

Like Browning, many of Lincoln's friends planned to stay behind or scatter. Before leaving the Bates House, two of them, Ebenezer Peck and Jesse Dubois, enacted a "melodramatic" farewell in full public view. After attempting to "macadamize him with hydraulic embraces," they "told him to behave himself like a good boy in the White House." Then they "cut a lock off his head with which they rushed triumphantly out of the room."[84] In a more quiet vein, Dubois took Lamon aside and warned him: "We intrust the sacred life of Mr. Lincoln to your keeping; and if you don't protect it, never return to Illinois, for we will murder you on sight." The warning was issued in an amiable tone, Lamon remembered, but he had no doubt that if he proved remiss, "the President-elect's friends would have made good some part of their threat."[85]

Returning to the depot, Lincoln boarded a new, flag-draped, three-car train whose locomotive smokestack featured thirty-four white stars along with lithographic portraits of George Washington and all his White House successors.[86] Lincoln's picture was not among these icons, but even if it had been, it might not have satisfied his new friends in Indianapolis.

Although his visit there had stirred more controversy than he had planned, at least it had answered the burning question of what he looked like, no thanks to such widely circulated prints. "Until the visit of Old Abe to our city he was generally supposed to be horridly ugly," admitted the *Indiana Journal*, "but on acquaintance his looks improve greatly, and his expressive face shows how his pictures have belied him."[87]

RESUMING HIS JOURNEY east on what John Hay called "the crest of one continued wave of cheers,"[88] the president-elect went on to offer brief, inoffensive new speeches that day to the "wild multitudes" thronging the Indiana villages of Morris, Shelbyville, Greenburg, and finally, in Lawrenceburg.[89] At this, his last stop before crossing into Ohio, a wistful Lincoln told his audience: "I suppose you are all Union men here . . . in favor of doing full justice to all, whether on that side of the river (pointing to the Kentucky shore), or on your own." "We are!" came the reassuring reply. Lincoln closed with his increasingly familiar new refrain: "I have been selected to fill an important office for a brief period, and am now, in your eyes, invested with an influence which will soon pass away; but should my administration prove to be a very wicked one, or what is more probable, a very foolish one, if you, the people, are but true to yourselves and to the Constitution, there is but little harm I can do, *thank* God."[90]

On this, his birthday, Lincoln must have glanced across the Ohio River toward the shoreline of his native state with particular yearning that day. As Lincoln might have predicted, the *Louisville Journal* would soon denounce last night's Indianapolis speech as "a singular indiscretion."[91] Until the very eve of his departure from Springfield, the ever-confident politician had hoped he could squeeze in a personal visit to the place of his birth, and explain the case for Union there for himself. Before leaving Springfield he had even transposed several paragraphs from his inaugural draft for delivery to "an audience of my native state." To that slaveholding audience, teetering, he feared, on the brink of secession, he had planned to introduce this inaugural fragment by first insisting that it was useless to expect new words from him that might "restore peace to the country." Many of his words had long been before the public. Confirming them anew would be "useless repe[ti]tion." Contradicting them would be "dishonorable and treacherous."[92] (He could not know that across the continent, Charles Russell Lowell had just expressed the fear that Lincoln might yet "consult too nicely what is *acceptable* even to the Border States." Lowell probably spoke for many nervous Easterners who hoped Lincoln "will take his stand on the principles which the framers of the Constitution stood upon, and if there comes a collision, call upon the Border States *alone* to aid.")[93]

Lowell might have been cheered, however, by Lincoln's proposed argument to Kentuckians. "Is the speaking [of] the word a '*sine qua non*' to the inaugeration?" he asked. "Is there a Bell-man, a Breckinridge-man, or a Douglas man, who would tolerate his own candidate to make such terms, had he been elected? Who amongst you would not die by the proposition, that your candidate, being elected, should be inaugera-tred, solely on the conditions of the constitution, and laws, or not at all." And then he added, in what sounded like a dare couched in a down-home code of honor: "What Kentuckian, worthy of his birthplace, would not do this? Gentlemen, I too am a Kentuckian."

To this highly personal and unusually proud argument, Lincoln's draft now flowed into the three verbatim paragraphs he had clipped from the typeset version of his inaugural draft and pasted to the last of the five small pages of this new manuscript. Breaking pledges to his own party, this section asserted, would betray friends, and destroy the concept of "popular government." Acquiescence to "surrender," he insisted, "would not merely be the ruin of a man, or a party; but as a precedent they would ruin the government itself." He would not shift his ground, he said. So doing would "break the only bond of faith between public and public servant" and "distinctly set the minority over the majority."[94]

Lincoln never got the chance to offer the stirring message—an intriguing speech combining a rational appeal on the basis of majority rule with an emotional appeal to a notion of honor he imagined his Kentucky brethren shared. He had deleted these sentiments from his forthcoming inaugural, but the frustrated president-elect apparently still believed they were worth pronouncing—especially in a crucial Upper South state whose loyalty to the Union remained in the balance. Much as he had once hoped to campaign for the presidency there, much as he still believed he could change minds and win hearts en route to take office, Kentucky remained off limits.

The missed opportunity was not enough to cloud his improved spirits. Lincoln seemed "the merriest among the merry" on the trip into Ohio, chatting and laughing, and keeping "those around him in a continual roar." John Hay was relieved that his boss had apparently "shaken off the despondency which was noticed during the first day's journey; and now, as his friends say, looks and talks like himself."[95] Fatigued as she was by her overnight sprint to Indiana, Mary Lincoln "kept up a spirited conversation" of her own during the journey, while the sprightly Willie and Tad amused themselves at most of the brief stopovers by "asking outsiders, 'Do you want to see Old Abe?' and pointing out someone else."[96]

Shortly after 3 P.M., the presidential special pulled into Cincinnati for a gratifying welcome from the mayor before more "people assembled in winter weather," Lincoln marveled, than he had ever before seen. "I think what has occurred here to-day could not have occurred in any other country on the face of the globe," he proclaimed, "without the influence of the free institutions which we have unceasingly enjoyed for three-quarters of a century." Better still, Lincoln realized he might now have a Kentucky crowd in his grasp after all. The state was just an arrow's shot across the river. Even if he could not cross the water to see them, it was conceivable many had crossed the river to see *him*—and now he aimed his remarks in their direction, in a far more conciliatory tone than he intended to employ across the border.

Addressing these imagined Southern listeners before whom he would not have the opportunity to appear separately, specifically directing his prepared remarks to "Fellow citizens of Kentucky—friends" whom he believed had joined his audience, he vowed: "We mean to treat you, as near as we possibly can, as Washington, Jefferson, and Madison treated you. We mean to leave you alone, and in no way to interfere with your institution; to abide by all and every compromise of the constitution. . . . We mean to remember that you are as good as we are; that there is no difference between us, other than the difference of circumstances." And then, returning his attention to the assembled Ohioans, he asked: "Have you ever entertained other sentiments towards our brethren of Kentucky than those I have expressed to you[?]" When the crowd roared back with "Loud and continued cries of 'No,'" Lincoln took it "as the most reliable evidence that it may be so." The difficulties of the present were but temporary, he predicted. They would soon be "forgotten and blown to the winds forever."[97]

Lincoln maintained his rhetorical momentum when he appeared next to an exuberant ovation shortly thereafter at a nearby rally organized by Cincinnati's German-born workingmen. He had "earned their votes," they announced that day, "as the champion of free labor and free homesteads"—as the model "selfmade man."[98] To this audience, hungry now for tangible rewards after supporting Lincoln overwhelmingly, he now laid out an appetizing menu of pledges that included supporting a homestead law ("I am in favor of cutting up the wild lands into parcels, so that every poor man may have a home"), recommitting himself to American opportunity ("while man exists, it is his duty to improve not only his own condition, but to assist in ameliorating mankind"), rebuking oppression against foreigners ("I would do all in my power to raise the yoke than to add anything that would tend to crush them"), and even endorsing the notion of unfettered immigration ("it is not in my heart to throw aught in their way, to prevent them from coming to the United States"). Having entirely avoided discussing the sectional conflict while touching on pet issues dear to his audience, he departed to yet another round of robust cheers.[99]

Lincoln traveled to his hotel that day in an open carriage drawn by six white horses (two more than Indianapolis had provided!), riding past richly decorated public and private buildings. "The streets along the line were populous as the cities of the Orient," exclaimed John Hay. "Every window was thronged, every balcony glittered with bright colors and fluttered with handkerchiefs; the sidewalks were packed; even the ledges and cornices of the houses swarmed with intrepid lookers-on."[100] Along the way, the residents of a local orphanage sang a rousing "Hail Columbia." When a little girl rose above the masses on the arms of her German father to present a single flower to the president-elect, Lincoln responded with a kiss. Riding bareheaded, Lincoln "bowed his backbone sore, and his neck stiff, all the way to the hotel."[101]

All told, "A more magnificent ovation . . . was never witnessed west of the Alleghenies," claimed Henry Villard. "It was not the military pageantry, not the stateliness of civil dignitaries nor any other formal display that made the occasion a perfect success, but the spontaneous turnout of at least a hundred thousand people, comprising all classes, from the rich merchant and manufacturer down to the humblest day laborer to do honor to the man that will be called upon to save the Union."[102]

There was no sanctuary when Lincoln reached the swank Burnet House, where he and Mary had stayed in 1859. Uncontrollable admirers began "throwing their arms around him, patting him on the back, and almost wrenching his arm off," and Lincoln was obliged to respond with yet another speech. A family dinner followed, then another levee, even bigger than the one in Indianapolis, at which Lincoln "gravely" put up with much "affectionate . . . embracing," though it seemed clear to John Hay that "he wishes they wouldn't."[103] Guarded by Colonel Ellsworth, Colonel Sumner, and Major Hunter, Lincoln endured an onrush of well-wishers of "all classes, all sorts, all conditions, all employments, all ages, both sexes, all styles, all nations, and apparently all creation," a journal-ist in the crush reported. Calling him "Uncle Abe," "Old boy," "My friend," and "Old Cock," every guest "considered it his duty to shake 'Old Abe's' hand, as if it was a pump-handle." Whenever a "big-bellied, fob-chained, high-collared gentleman" tried to linger in his presence, "the surging crowd behind him, impatient of delay, would give him a boost which would send him irresistibly on, like a wad from a pop-gun." That night the journalist spied the president-elect's calfskin boots rest-ing outside "the Lincolnian door" to his suite, and calculated they were "as long as a sheet of foolscap paper."[104]

Resuming his journey at nine the next morning, February 13, in the glow of "magnificent weather," Lincoln's enthusiastic trackside wel-comes showed no signs of abating. As the inaugural special, now thronged by a hundred local politicians, crawled through the rest of the broad state of Ohio, crowds routinely greeted Lincoln with artillery sa-lutes, band music, and rousing cheers. He gamely offered lighthearted acknowledgment wherever "the iron horse stops to water himself,"[105] he joked at one such refueling spot. Now "stiffened in his limbs by his handshaking exertion," and beginning to exhibit the symptoms of a cold, Lincoln's voice began to fade on this "march of triumph,"[106] yet he continued obligingly croaking a few words at Milford, Loveland, Miami-ville, Morrow, Corwin, Xenia (where well-wishers "acted more like crazy people than American citizens,"[107]), and London.

As the inaugural special neared Columbus at 2 P.M., the now obligatory thirty-four-gun salute began erupting in cadenced welcome. A "deafening shout" greeted the Lincolns' first appearance, as all five family members alit from the train together, the president-elect bareheaded and bowing to the crowd. Some sixty thousand people—three times the city's population—offered another frenzied welcome as he paraded into town.[108]

Following dinner at the Governor's Mansion, Governor William Dennison escorted Lincoln to the newly built State Capitol. Lincoln looked "worn with travel and the fatigues of popularity," in the words of the local paper, but quickly "warmed to the cordiality of his reception."[109] Heading inside to address the legislature, his "great height was conspicuous . . . and lifted him fully in view as he walked down the aisle."[110] His official remarks touched on familiar themes—and just as in Indianapolis, he admitted, did so "altogether extemporaneously." This again proved unfortunate. Looking back to the past, he reiterated the boast of his Farewell Address, this time accompanied by a leavening dose of wonder, that "without a name, perhaps without a reason why I should have a name, there has fallen upon me a task such as did not rest even upon the Father of his country." Speaking of the present, he defended his longtime refusal to speak publicly, claiming "a degree of credit for having kept silence," and adding: "I still think that I was right." But then, looking to the future, he made another misstep. "I have not maintained silence from any want of real anxiety," Lincoln declared. "It is a good thing that there is no more than anxiety, for there is nothing going wrong. It is a consoling circumstance that when we look out there is nothing that really hurts anybody. We entertain different views upon political questions, but nobody is suffering anything."[111]

Hastening to criticize what seemed to be another gaffe, the *New York Herald* charged that after exhibiting "the obstinacy of an intractable partisan" at Indianapolis, Lincoln had now revealed "a most lamentable degree of ignorance" at Columbus. The "most charitable interpretation we can give to these 'assurances,' " added the paper, "is that Mr. Lincoln, under some embarrassment, spoke them at random, did not know what he was saying, or failed to catch the ideas flitting through his mind. In plainer terms, in finding himself the lion of the day, with all eyes and hopes turned upon him, he is bothered and makes a mess of it. 'Nothing going wrong'? Why, sir, we may more truly say there is nothing going right."[112]

Although one can reasonably imagine Lincoln intentionally testing these alternative messages of toughness and conciliation, then weighing the public response to each, the *Herald* had a valid point. In the span of just twenty-four hours, the president-elect had contradicted himself mortifyingly: first hinting at Indianapolis that in view of the national crisis he did not regard future efforts to reclaim federal property as coercion; then by declaring at Columbus that there was no real crisis after all.

Such details hardly seemed to matter in Republican Ohio. Moments after concluding his speech, Lincoln stepped outside the Capitol to another cataract of cheers from a crowd that had grown only larger anticipating his reappearance. Weary as he was, Lincoln summoned the strength to speak yet again, declaring he was "doubly thankful that you have appeared here to give me this greeting. It is not much for me," he insisted, "for I shall very soon pass away from you; but we have a large country and a large future before us, and the manifestations of good-will toward the government, and affection for the Union which you may exhibit are of immense value to you and your posterity forever." With thanks for "the exhibition you have given me," Lincoln ended with the warm coda that had closed many of his speeches since Springfield. To "deafening applause and cheers," he simply bid his audience another "affectionate farewell."[113]

But he was not going anywhere yet. Led back inside by a phalanx of soldiers, Lincoln found himself the center of attention at another public levee, swarmed by strangers rushing up to bless him, pledge their loyalty, or, their hats battered and their expressions blurred, merely to stare at him in a daze. At one point, Ward Hill Lamon, "a man of extraordinary size and herculean strength," in Nicolay's words, was compelled to rescue Lincoln from a throng so thick and eager that it threatened to crush him. After trying in vain to shake hands right and left from behind a pillar "little more than the thickness of his person," Lincoln finally retreated for safety to a staircase, and "contented himself with looking at the crowd as it swept before him."[114] As John Nicolay described it, such "immense" receptions had become so large, it had become a challenge "to prevent his being killed with kindness[.]"[115]

IN MOST BIOGRAPHIES that focus at all on Lincoln's inaugural caravan, the rest of American history seems to freeze in place as Lincoln is shown proceeding toward Washington. In fact, not every eye and ear in 1861 America focused on his journey east. On a parallel five-day train trip to his own inauguration, Jefferson Davis, too, attracted "the wildest enthusiasm," delivering no fewer than twenty-five speeches of his own to what a journalist described as "one continuous ovation."[116]

This was not precisely true. Because Southern railroad networks remained woefully underdeveloped, Davis was compelled to travel north to Memphis before heading south again to Atlanta and connecting to Montgomery. In thus far loyal Tennessee he was received icily. But the cheers, bonfires, and cannon salutes resumed when he reentered the new Confederacy, and in Jackson, Mississippi, he almost seemed to echo Lincoln's Ohio speech by assuring his audience that if the North would only "recognize the independence of the seceding states all would be well." At another stop he sounded more like Lincoln at Indianapolis, warning a local magistrate "there would be war, long and bloody."[117] However much Lincoln regarded Davis and his own coronation procession as illegitimate, the former senator's arrival in the new Confederate capital at least terminated press coverage of his competitive inaugural tour.

Back in Washington, meanwhile, the closely watched Peace Convention ponderously continued its deliberations, a show of independence that might have troubled the president-elect more greatly had not its "venerable old" delegates, in the New York Times's description, seemed "no more fit to be intrusted with . . . guidance than a bull is fitted to keep a china shop." Even so, Lincoln's New England friend Amos Tuck fretted that the conferees represented "a body unknown to the Constitution and the laws," while Connecticut's Roger Baldwin nervously branded the convention "a *revolutionary proceeding*" lacking "sufficient cause or justification."[118]

The most astute observers, however, understood that as long as the Peace Convention remained in session, debating endlessly on procedural matters without agreeing to a concrete compromise plan, the border states were likely to remain within the Union. Its representatives would continue occupying their seats in Congress, thus guaranteeing a quorum for the decisive session at which the Electoral College vote would be made official.[119] "Good nature and masterly inactivity," chuckled a delegate from Massachusetts, "is the policy till Lincoln is inaugurated."[120] Similarly hoping "to delay fatal action, until the dead points of danger, the counting [of] the votes, and the inauguration, were passed," Indiana governor Oliver Morton assured Lincoln: "time wears out revolutions."[121]

So, in General Winfield Scott's calculation, did muscular demonstrations of military might. As the Peace Convention dragged on, though increasingly favoring compromise Scott deployed federal troops throughout the city, and announced a massive, if provocative, military parade for Washington's birthday. The buildup signaled the general's resolve to keep Lincoln safe once he arrived in town—and perhaps to prevent an overt act from the South beforehand. "Thanks to Gen Scott," commented one relieved observer, ". . . the people feel as tho they were safe from 'invasion,' until after the 4th of March at least."[122]

On Wednesday, February 13, the most crucial pre-inaugural milestone of all "passed off with perfect quiet" in Washington: the formal decision of the Electoral College. Declaring it his duty "to suppress insurrection," Scott had warned that "any man who attempted by force or unparliamentary disorder to obstruct or interfere with the lawful count" would be "lashed to the muzzle of a twelve-pounder and fired out a window of the Capitol."[123] Taking his threat seriously, dissenters melted away. "*Unquestionably* it was at one time the purpose of the seceders to have prevented the counting of the votes for President," recalled D. W. Bartlett, "but finding that they would be ignominiously whipped if they attempted to execute their treason, they wisely concluded that it were better not to essay to do what they could not perform." [124]

With Winfield Scott's soldiers visibly stationed outside on Capitol Hill to guard against long-rumored outbreaks, Vice President John C. Breckinridge called the "imposing" joint session of Congress to order, his demeanor "dignified" and "graceful," the galleries above the House chamber notably devoid of "rowdies and ruffians." [125] Members of Congress marched down the aisle conspicuously paired off "with those of their own way of thinking"—Seward alongside Cameron, for example—looking to one reporter "like the animals in Noah's Ark." Then Breckinridge called for the reports of the various state electors, beginning with Maine, ordered them counted, and calmly proclaimed that "Abraham Lincoln, of Illinois, having received a majority of the whole of the electoral votes, is elected President of the United States, for four years, commencing on the 4th of March." [126]

The only interruption to the "solemn" ceremony occurred when Virginia congressman Muscoe Garnett stormed out of the hall during the chaplain's opening prayer, "stamping his feet with such emphasis as to attract the attention of the crowded galleries," and looking to one observer like "old [Junius Brutus] Booth in 'Richard III.'" Otherwise the result "was received in perfect silence, and, without any exhibition of gratification or disgust." [127] That in itself was a victory.

This was the moment Lincoln had awaited most anxiously of all—the event he worried the enemies of the Union would attempt to disrupt or prevent. Instead, right on schedule and in a remarkable, if somewhat overoptimistic, display of national continuity, the defeated Southern Democratic candidate for the White House dutifully announced the victory of his Northern Republican opponent. And for the third time since November, Abraham Lincoln was chosen president of the United States.

All of Washington seemed to exhale. Describing the mood of relief that permeated that deeply divided capital that historic day, Gideon Welles's friend John S. Williams joked that "every thing was as quiet as tho' a 'modern slave code Democrat' had been elected." [128] "This was the critical day for the peace of the capital," echoed New Yorker George Templeton Strong. "A foray of Virginia gents . . . could have done infinite mischief by destroying the legal evidence of Lincoln's election." Instead, he noted gratefully, "The electoral votes were counted today . . . in due form, and the result announced without disturbance."[129] Not until the following day—proof that genuine fear had reigned—did a select congressional committee report with relief that no "secret organizations hostile to the Government" existed in the district.[130]

All this transpired just at the time Lincoln was preparing to address the Ohio legislature at Columbus. "At this very hour," Governor Dennison acknowledged in introducing him, "the Congress of the United States will declare the verdict of the people." In responding, Lincoln evinced no particular anxiety about the outcome. Nonetheless, Villard admitted he had heard better speeches. As he explained it: "Mr. Lincoln was so profoundly moved as to be hardly able to do himself justice." Even Lincoln conceded he could summon no more than "a few broken remarks." But "the earnestness and conscientiousness that plainly shone on his face," Villard maintained, "effected more with the audience than words could."[131]

The telegram bearing the crucial news from the Electoral College vote in Washington arrived in Lincoln's hands at around 4:30 that afternoon, just as he was preparing to dive back into the surging crowd waiting for the levee to commence inside the newly opened Ohio State Capitol. Watching Lincoln tear open the dispatch, a journalist on the scene reported: "When he read it he smiled benignly and looking up, seeing everyone waiting for a word, he quietly put the dispatch in his pocket and said, 'What a beautiful building you have here, Governor Dennision.' "[132]

Chapter Ten

No Occasion for Any Excitement

BOARDING YET ANOTHER flag-bedecked inaugural special, Lincoln resumed his journey to Washington on Thursday morning, February 14. After an 8 A.M. farewell to Columbus "amidst the cheers of a few hundred Buckeyes" undeterred by the bad weather, the train, now overflowing with railroad officials and local politicians, zigzagged through eastern Ohio, past a ribbon of rural hamlets where "patient throngs" of well-wishers crowded the roadside to greet him, undaunted "by the shower above and the mud beneath."[1]

Saluted at each outpost by "songs, cheers, music, flying banners and the roar of artillery," Lincoln responded as often as his schedule and voice allowed. Growing hoarser by the mile, he offered little that was new or newsworthy, but seasoned his rain-soaked chats "with his irrepressible wit and humor," pleasing "his audiences hugely." In Newark, he regretted that his schedule had "deprived" so "many fair ladies assembled" of the opportunity "of observing my interesting countenance." Partaking of a home-cooked "dejeuner" during a stopover at Cadiz Junction, he teased that he was "too full for utterance." Others on board were reported full, too—not of food but of "things spirituous," the intake of which lubricated Ward Lamon enough to unleash his repertoire of rollicking songs, stimulating Robert Lincoln to join in while his father sat quietly in the rear of the car, reading newspapers, and resting his strained vocal cords.[2]

Then, after passing through tiny villages with formidable names—Frazeysburg, Dresden, Coshocton, Newcomerstown, and Uhrichsville—the president-elect turned serious when he once again reached the winding Ohio River at Steubenville. Now standing just across the shore from secession-minded Virginia, he told a crowd swelled by clearing skies: "We everywhere express devotion to the Constitution. I believe there is no difference in this respect, whether on this or on the other side of this majestic stream." Virginians, he acknowledged, wanted "their rights under the Constitution." But as to who was entitled to adjudge those rights, Lincoln left no doubt. It was the "voice of the people," as expressed in his own election. "If the majority does not control, the minority must—would that be right? Would that be just or generous? Assuredly not!"[3]

Back on the road, Lincoln's train now headed northward, hugging the Ohio River shoreline and, once the river diverted, turning back east toward Pennsylvania. But not before a comic scene unfolded at Wellsville, the final stop in Ohio. There, a drunken old Irishman staggered forward and dared Lincoln to shake hands with a Douglas Democrat. The president-elect not only seized the opportunity, but announced that "if he and the other friends of Mr. Douglas would assist in keeping the ship of state afloat, that perhaps Mr. Douglas might be selected to pilot it sometime in the future."[4]

The pilot of the inaugural special faced problems of his own. Not until past seven o'clock that evening, way behind schedule, did he finally ease the train into Allegheny City on the outskirts of Pittsburgh, much delayed by a derailed freight train blocking the way. Late as he was, and despite a "pelting rain," Lincoln still disembarked at a depot "literally jammed with people," according to John Nicolay. "We finally got Mr. Lincoln into a carriage," he reported, "but having accomplished that, it looked for a while as if we would never get the carriage out of the crowd that was pushing and pulling and yelling all around us."[5]

Obliged to stand on a chair and speak once he arrived inside the densely packed lobby of the Monongahela House, Lincoln thanked a crowd, "impatient to see Old Abe," for "the warm reception I have received." But "owing to his great fatigue," he begged them to allow him to retire for the evening and delay more extended remarks until the morning. Unwilling to liberate him, the crowd demanded, "Say it now, we are all attention," and relenting, Lincoln asked to be permitted to "procure a few notes that are in my overcoat pocket." Within minutes after retiring upstairs, he reappeared on the hotel balcony as promised, but asked to be excused after all. It was still raining and Lincoln was dead-tired. "I have made my appearance now," he declared with a smile, "only to afford you an opportunity of seeing, as clearly as may be, my beautiful countenance!"[6]

Not every American was amused. That same day, one of them, writing from an unknown location, unleashed a vile diatribe at "Mr Abe Lincoln," warning: "if you don't Resign we are going to put a spider in your dumpling and play the Devil with you you god or mighty god dam sundde of a bith go to hell and buss my Ass suck my prick and call my Bolics your uncle Dick god dam a fool and goddam Abe Lincoln . . . you are nothing but a goddam Black nigger." Such threats had become all too common. Testifying later that his boss's mailbag was "infested with brutal and vulgar menace," John Nicolay thought Lincoln had "a heart so kindly, even to his enemies, that it was hard for him to believe in political hatred so deadly as to lead to murder." This particular letter ended with a political warning that likely chilled Lincoln—if he saw it—more than its ugly personal threats: "Tennessee Missouri Kentucky Virginia N. Carolina and Arkansas is going to secede Glory be to god on high[.]"[7]

The next morning, Friday, February 15, brought no clearing to the persistently dark Pittsburgh skies, yet five thousand spectators massed outside Lincoln's hotel at 8:30 under "an ocean of umbrellas" in anticipation of his postponed speech. Reading from the manuscript retrieved from his coat the night before, Lincoln turned his attention to "national house-keeping" issues he knew to be of particular interest to Pennsylvanians, especially Cameron men. Reiterating his commitment to the protective tariff, he pledged support for the Morrill Tariff Act, which would increase some duties from 5 to 10 percent, vowing to sign the legislation if it came before his desk as president. But before getting to these platform-affirming prepared remarks, Lincoln first acknowledged—as if in surprise—that "every crowd through which I have passed of late" had demanded he address the secession crisis, too. He seemed almost reluctant to admit that the "condition of the country . . . fills the mind of every patriot with anxiety and solicitude."[8]

Their anxiety notwithstanding, Lincoln remained unwilling to admit of a national emergency. Repeating the self-confident message he had introduced at Columbus the day before, he again maintained: "In plain words, there is really no crisis except an *artificial one!*" The unpleasantness "over the river," he insisted, had been "gotten up" by "turbulent men, aided by designing politicians." And he refused to take their bait. "My advice, then, under such circumstances, is to keep cool. If the great American people will only keep their temper, on both sides of the line, the troubles will come to an end, and the question which now distracts the country will be settled." Lincoln departed the city later that morning after obligingly bending to kiss an assortment of proffered children, "amidst the laughter of spectators."[9] He would hold his own temper even as others' boiled over. Nonetheless, Henry Villard privately dismissed the Pittsburgh speech as "crude, ignorant twaddle, without point or meaning," a performance that "strengthened my doubts as to his capacity for the high office he was to fill."[10] Whether he could remove those doubts as he edged closer to the East Coast remained to be seen.

Before he could face this test, the convoy arranged one more major stop in Ohio. For the first time during its journey, the inaugural train now retraced its route and headed back west, making brief stops—with Lincoln pausing only to bow to and salute the crowds—at Staineville, Bayard, Alliance, Hudson, and Ravenna.[11] At 4:30 that afternoon, the train reached Cleveland in a snowstorm, to yet another outpouring of "soldiers, firemen, and citizens . . . on horseback, in carriages, and on foot," Villard reported. Their enthusiasm was controlled, Nicolay testified, only with the help of "the police and military."[12] Thanking the thousands who marched two miles into town "through snow, rain and deep mud" to usher him to the Weddell House, Lincoln interpreted the welcome as a tribute not to him but to the Union, evidence that "the cause of liberty can never be in danger." Besides, he insisted yet again, perhaps thinking wishfully, perhaps a bit out of touch, "I think that there is no occasion for any excitement."[13]

Speaking to "a sea of faces" massed below the hotel balcony "in such close proximity that one could but wonder if the owners of them all had bodies," Lincoln again dismissed Southern anger, inquiring: "Why all this excitement? Why all these complaints? As I said before, this crisis is all artificial. It has no foundation in facts. It was not argued up, as the saying is, and cannot, therefore, be argued down. Let it alone and it will go down of itself." He ended with his formulaic thanks "not for myself, but for Liberty, the Constitution, and the Union."[14] To the *Cleveland Morning Leader,* unaware that Lincoln had once hoped to employ the identical biblical metaphor himself, his words seemed "fitly spoken, like apples of gold in pictures of silver."[15]

Others disagreed. That day's edition of the *Cleveland Plain Dealer* led with a bitter "Epitaph for the Late American Republic: 'Here lies a people, who, in attempting to liberate the negro, lost their own freedom.' " The Democratic paper assailed Lincoln's recent speeches as "the first fruits of the triumphs of a sectional party in this country," predicting: "The next will be war, taxation and starvation."[16] Only reluctantly had the paper's editor, J. W. Gray, admitted after "a very quiet private interview with Mr. Lincoln and his lady" that he was "most favorably impressed with both." Then he added mischievously: "If mistakes do occur in the Executive Government of the country, we are satisfied they will not be chargeable to design."[17]

Departing Cleveland at ten the next morning, Lincoln and his entourage headed back east through the Ohio towns of Willoughby, Painesville, Geneva, and Madison. Lincoln offered only the briefest of remarks in each. Now reduced to a whisper, he bowed to the ladies, asked local bands to play music, and croaked that "the condition of my voice is such that I could not do more if there were time." Horace Greeley earned far more attention from Lincoln when he boarded unexpectedly at Girard, toting a yellow grip "labeled with his name and address," John Hay mocked, "in characters which might be read across Lake Erie."[18] Riding the twenty or so miles to the New York border, Greeley—described by a newspaper that week as the "drab-coated, white-hatted Philosopher . . . that made Lincoln President"—managed to snare a private audience with the president-elect while unconvincingly assuring fellow passengers that he had entered the unmistakably decorated special believing it was the regularly scheduled train[19]

More ordinary admirers made little secret of an equal determination to greet Lincoln as he passed through their towns, especially if they had job opportunities on their minds. Finding himself in tiny Wellsville, Ohio, for the second time in two days, Lincoln reached out adroitly to catch an apple tossed his way by an admirer, a gesture that one youngster perched on a lamppost derided by shouting to the "general merriment" of the crowd: "Mr. Lincoln, the man wants to be a Postmaster!"[20] If so, the apple-hurler was not the only one.

As the incident suggested, Lincoln was hardly immune while on the road to the incurable plague of both office-seekers and what William Herndon once called "cabinet-makers."[21] The contagion pursued him. Riding along on the train from Cleveland to Painesville, for example, Congressman-elect Albert Gallatin Riddle cornered Lincoln to warn him against Cameron, whose "influence in Pennsylvania," he insisted, "seemed way out of all proportion to his ability."[22] A group of Maine state senators petitioned Lincoln to appoint Schuyler Colfax postmaster general.[23]

Importuning letters from place-seekers were relentlessly forwarded to Lincoln, and eventually caught up with him.[24] Along with citizen petitions, new invitations to stop en route, newspaper clippings, and policy advice on both domestic and diplomatic matters, Lincoln's transportable correspondence boasted, more than any other class of mail, yet more personal pleas for jobs along with recommendations in behalf of others.[25]

The rapidly approaching swearing in seemed to embolden office-seekers more than ever. Ignoring propriety, the wife of one desperate patronage aspirant wrote directly to Mary Lincoln, hoping she would convince her husband to rescue her from a life of hard labor—as an embroiderer for hire—by naming her idle husband a postmaster. There is no evidence he got the job.[26] In similar end-run meaneuvers, others directed their pleas to Robert. These included Bob's Springfield schoolmate Harry Gourley, who asked that "his Royal Highness the Prince of Rails" use his influence to secure the post of register of the Land Office for a mutual acquaintance whose "imployment" as crier of the federal Court had been terminated "because he had the audacity to vote for 'Old Abe.' "[27]

No friendship was too sacred to risk in pursuit of office. Back on February 11, the day his train paused at Decatur, the president-elect had made a special point of publicly embracing both his old friend Richard Oglesby and his cousin John Hanks, as if to acknowledge, one more time, their earlier work in conceiving his "rail-splitter" image. Less than a week later, as Lincoln traveled between Ohio and New York, Oglesby asked the president-elect to award Hanks "a just recognition of old personal ties," adding: "No attribute of human nature is more beautiful when fitly illustrated—than the acknowledgment of former relations in life when one may be supposed to have forgotten them by reason of advancement to distinction and power in earthly matters." That Hanks could not read or write did not seem to matter. Surely Lincoln would "be able to confer upon him some position where the requirement may be dispensed with."[28]

In much the same way Lincoln learned that even his onetime frontier employer Denton Offutt—who thirty years earlier had hired him to pilot a flatboat to New Orleans, then invited him to work at his store in New Salem—now expected reward. He aspired to be named "Physiologist" of Louisiana, no less, in a seceded state whose federal patronage Lincoln no longer had much hope of controlling. Its "warm climate," Offutt naively justified in listing his so-called qualifications, would be "better for me." If that honor proved unattainable, he would gladly accept a "Pattent office or the office of Agriculteral Department or the

Commisary for Purchais of Horses Mules Beef for Army or Mail agent."[29] Although one historian later dubbed Offutt "the discoverer of Lincoln," there is no evidence that his old protégé offered him any federal job.[30]

BY NOW, THE long trip was starting to take its toll on all the weary travelers. Lincoln's ordeal was magnified by the persistent "hoarseness of his voice and soreness of his chest."[31] His son Robert pined for the pretty girls he successively met and left behind in cities along the route, mourning each loss with "sparkling Catawba" wine, reporters gossiped, "on the slightest provocation."[32] John Nicolay complained often of exhaustion. And the best that Norman Judd could report was that "Mrs. L. behaves quite well—and the children have been reasonably good considering what they are," adding: "I have kept at a respectful distance from the lady only paying my proper respects."[33]

In fact, Mary's equanimity was severely tested, and she bore up remarkably well. Expected to host levees for the ladies in most major cities, she proved a charming and tireless hostess, impressing Democrats as well as Republicans. In Alliance, Ohio, an artillery salute fired too close to Sourbeck's Hotel, where the Lincolns were dining, shattered a window and left her awash in a hail of broken glass. Frightened as she was, she quickly recovered.[34] By the time their train reached Ashtabula, crowds were calling for Mary as enthusiastically as for her husband. Lincoln used the occasion to joke that "he should hardly hope to induce her to appear, as he had always found it very difficult to make her do what she did not want to."[35]

For everyone else, the welcoming receptions, concerts, parades, and dinners grew stale, and the jaded traveling party increasingly showed signs of fatigue, especially Lincoln. As Joseph Howard, the New York Times correspondent, began to notice, when "listening to a prosy address, or shuddering at the brazen efforts of some country band, his eye is dull, his complexion dark, his mouth compressed and his whole appearance indicates excessive weariness, listlessness and indifference." To Howard, it seemed "a terrible ordeal through which to pass, when bound as he is, not to a place of rest and easeful quiet, but to a scene of discord, trouble and possible danger."[36]

Still, the endless trip occasionally brought out the best in Lincoln. On one of his last stops in Ohio, he rose to the occasion when a man in the audience shouted out: "Don't give up the ship!" Before reentering his train, the president-elect replied with a memorable sound bite: "with your aid I never will as long as life lasts."[37] But things quickly turned comical again when he reached Erie, Pennsylvania, where a "roof on which a large number of curious republicans had gathered" suddenly collapsed in a heap. "The sudden disappearance of the whole group, and the scramble among the ruins," Villard reported, "was most ludicrous."[38] Fortunately, no one was seriously injured. More important, Lincoln had finally reached the New York border.

His first stop there proved a sensation. "I am glad to see you," he began his greeting from the back of his railroad car when it pulled into the tiny village of Westfield beneath a banner that proclaimed: "Welcome Abraham Lincoln to the Empire State." "I suppose you are to see me; but I certainly think I have the best of the bargain." The joke was standard-issue Lincoln, but this was the hometown of the little girl who had advised him to grow a beard back in October, and he seized the unique opportunity.[39]

"Some three months ago," Lincoln told the crowd, "I received a letter from a young lady here; it was a very pretty letter, and she advised me to let my whiskers grow, as it would improve my personal appearance; acting partly upon her suggestion, I have done so; and now, if she is here, I would like to see her." Her name, Lincoln thought, was "Miss Barlly," or as another paper reported, "Burdell," probably coming closer to a phonetic re-creation of Lincoln's quirky Indiana accent.[40] Even though the visitor got this small detail wrong, a boy in the crowd instantly recognized the object of his inquiry, and shouted back, "there she is, Mr. Lincoln," pointing to "a beautiful girl, with black eyes, who was blushing all over her fair face." At that, the president-elect descended from his car, walked out onto the freight platform, reached down to Grace Bedell, and "gave her several hearty kisses."[41]

At least that is how a Philadelphia newspaper reported the encounter. Grace herself remembered it somewhat differently. In one of her accounts, written seventy years later, she arrived at the train station fully expecting to meet the president-elect. "In my hand was a bouquet of roses," she offered as proof. Lincoln did not walk to where she was standing; they met halfway. "I was conveyed to him," she recalled, by her older sister's beau as the crowd respectfully parted. Nor did Lincoln bend down to embrace her, but rather "lifted a somewhat frightened little girl into his arms and kissed her, and passed his hands over his newly started beard, remarking, 'You see, I let these whiskers grow for you, Grace.' " Then he "shook me cordially by the hand and, was gone." As she remembered: "It seemed to me . . . he looked very kind, yes, and sad."[42] Small details, to be sure; but not to an eleven-year-old who spent the next three-quarters of a century reliving her experience.

Grace never got to present her flowers to the president-elect that day. Embarrassed by the attention, she raced home and hid under a wagon, forgetting "the bouquet of roses that I was going to give to the great man to whom I had offered such rare advice, and when I arrived home I had the stems, all that remained of the bouquet, still tightly clutched in my hand."[43] Lincoln should have been gratified, at least, that the little girl asked him no favors—not just then, anyway. It took another three years for Grace Bedell to join the ranks of the office-seekers and petition Abraham Lincoln for a federal job.[44]

The kindly traveler's encounter with the little girl was widely reported, but not every commentator was captivated. "Old Abe is cultivating his whiskers and kissing the girls along the route," reported one Democratic paper, adding the vicious coda: "The telegraph, however, does not inform us what Mrs. Lincoln thinks of this kissing business, or what color the girls are."[45]

"There seems to be something supremely ridiculous in these troublous times," declared another hostile newspaper, "when our very national existence is imperiled, in having a President elect who devotes his energies to cultivating his whiskers, and otherwise improving his personal appearance."[46] Yet shortly before his arrival in Washington, the *New York Illustrated News* countered, albeit with tongue in cheek: " 'Honest Abe' has cultivated his whiskers and looks as handsome now as the best and greatest of his contemporaries . . . we hope all patriotic ladies will fall in love with him." The paper's enthusiasm was easy to explain. As it further "reported," Lincoln had turned to one of its very own advertisers, Bellingham's Stimulating Onguent, to help raise "the manly adornment." No evidence exists to confirm the brazen marketing claim. But before long, Bellingham's published updated notices that insisted that the dollar-a-box hair-growing ointment was directly responsible for Lincoln's "course of sprouts." [47]

Did Lincoln's fully cultivated beard accomplish more than to provoke chatter and consign his clean-shaven campaign likenesses to the junk heap? Much period testimony suggests it did. Seeing Lincoln for the first time with whiskers, Americans lining the inaugural route often found him better-looking than "his pictures"—and since all the pictures to which they made comparisons showed him clean-shaven, it is reasonable to conclude that his beard in fact markedly improved his appearance. As one contemporary put it, his beard gave the president-elect "a more sober and serene outlook . . . like a serious farmer with crops to look after, or a church sexton in charge of grave affairs." [48] In the past, Lincoln had striven to overcome his homeliness by offering beautiful words. Now, with the nation facing a graver crisis than Lincoln was so far willing to admit, his whiskers gave him something his words suddenly seemed to lack: gravitas. At least he *looked* up to the job.

As for the portraits he had so quickly rendered obsolete, Lincoln even did his share to reduce the stockpile. Just before his departure from Springfield, the American Bank Note Company, a currency printer in the what is now the Bronx, had sent Lincoln a batch of tiny proof engravings based on his beardless Cooper Union photograph by Mathew Brady. The adaptation presented Lincoln's head surmounted by a hero's laurel and flanked by American flags, a scroll marked "Constitution," and the scales of justice. Evidently the president-elect liked it. He took the pictures with him to Washington, autographing at least three copies for admirers along the way, one of them William M. Kasson, the man who designed the opulent railroad car in which he traveled. Though disagreeably heated by smoky stoves and illuminated by dim lamps "burning sperm oil," the car did feature walnut, horsehair-upholstered parlor furniture, including "an extra long sofa for Mr. Lincoln's ease." In thanking Kasson for providing these luxurious appointments, the designer's son later testified, "Mr. Lincoln reached down and into his carpetbag, took out a small engraved likeness, which, he remarked, was his favorite picture of himself, and gave it to my father, after having autographed it with the stub of lead pencil,—as you see, 'A. Lincoln.' "[49]

NOW PROCEEDING UP the Lake Erie shoreline and greeted everywhere by mammoth crowds, Lincoln responded briefly but memorably to fifteen thousand well-wishers in Dunkirk after his train passed under a triumphal arch suspended over the tracks. Stepping onto a velvet-carpeted platform erected around a flagpole, he vowed to a roaring audience: "Standing as I do, with my hand upon this staff, and under the folds of the American flag, I ask you to stand by me so long as I stand by it."[50]

Not long thereafter, at 4:30 P.M. on Saturday, February 16, Lincoln entered Buffalo to a hero's welcome. Among the ten thousand people surging into the station to receive him was the thirteenth president of the United States, Millard Fillmore, a show of respect that spoke volumes about the unbreakable continuity of the presidency. But it was not an altogether dignified encounter; boisterous crowds pressed in and jostled them alarmingly. The "perfect furor" grew so intense that neither local police nor Lincoln's seasoned military escorts were unable to restrain it, and "the wildest confusion ensued."[51] Major Hunter suffered a dislocated shoulder in the near-melee—he was forced to wear his arm in a sling for the remainder of the trip—and the president-elect "was safely got out of the depot only by the desperate efforts of those immediately around him." Only after struggling "with might and main for their lives" did the rest of the traveling party manage to find their way into carriages of their own. Others gave up and walked into town, joining the exuberant parade that ushered Lincoln up a Main Street "gaily draped with flags" to a "perfect ovation" from more large throngs.[52]

From the balcony of the American House, Lincoln launched into his now customary greeting, offering the rote messages he had been reciting at nearly every stop. Once again, he offered appreciation for the nonpartisan welcomes he was receiving "on my rather circuitous route to the Federal Capital." Again he confessed his continued reliance on "that Supreme Being who has never forsaken this favored land." And once more he shared his belief that Americans need only maintain their "composure" so "the clouds which now arise in the horizon will be dispelled." He spoke in a voice so hoarse he was "scarcely able to make himself heard," especially once a prankster in the audience began noisily sawing logs in payment of a pre-election wager to present a half-cord of firewood "to the poorest negro in the city" if Lincoln won.[53]

Gamely fighting the din, the president-elect managed also to allude to his forthcoming inaugural message, making clear that it was still a work in progress. He still hoped to shine on it "all the light I can," he declared, "so that when I do speak authoritatively I may be as near right as possible . . . to say nothing inconsistent with the Constitution, the Union, the rights of all the States, of each State, and of each section of the country, and not to disappoint the reasonable expectations of those who have confided to me their votes."[54] It was his first public admission that work on the text continued.

That night Lincoln greeted more enthusiastic well-wishers as guest of honor at a levee at his hotel. A large sign suspended from the Young Men's Christian Union across the street seemed to echo his recent calls for divine guidance: "We will pray for you." The message was especially appropriate. The next day was the Sabbath, and Lincoln rested—and did some praying of his own. He attended church twice that day, first as Fillmore's guest at Buffalo's First Unitarian Church, and later at another house of worship to hear the Indian minister Father John Beason. In between services, he and Mary dined at Fillmore's elegant home. (It was hard to imagine that only a year later Fillmore would denounce his famous guest as "a tyrant" who "makes my blood boil.")[55] This was a rare quiet day, and Lincoln may have used the downtime not only to rest his voice, but to think anew about the speeches he had yet to deliver—in particular the inaugural now little more than two weeks away.

It had become gratifyingly clear, at least, that his Farewell Address to Springfield had earned him much attention and praise. Noting its appreciation for "your earnest avowal of trust in God," an Oberlin, Ohio, prayer group declared that the speech "moved our hearts & strengthened our hopes of our country under your administration."[56] Calling the moment "The Dawn of Hope," one newspaper asked appreciatively: "Will not Christians throughout the land, with one accord, make daily supplications to God for the President who begins his Administration by invoking their prayers?"[57] And reporting from New York that "the people are alive, & patriotism and love of country and of our glorious Constitution, & of the Stars & Stripes, are yet living sentiments in true American hearts," Lincoln's old Cooper Union host James A. Briggs left no doubt that the excitement was attributable to "your beautiful & eloquent farewell remarks on taking leave of your neighbors and friends and fellow citizens at Springfield." It had "made a most profound sensation & impression on the hearts of all our people. Thousands and tens of thousands read them with tearful eyes."[58] Whether such accolades would prove enough to offset criticism of Lincoln's meandering and conflicting remarks since, however, remained very much in question.

Few hearts had been similarly moved by the president-elect's more recent speeches. After leaving his neighbors "in a lachrymose and pious frame of mind," the New York Herald venomously summarized the rhetorical record since, Lincoln "became jovial, and began to exercise his talent as a raconteur." In Indianapolis,

the seat of radical republicanism, the President made a rather clumsy speech on the delicate subject of coercion and State rights. The warmth of his reception had undoubtedly taken Mr. Lincoln off his feet, and turned his head. At Cincinnati, he patronized the Kentuckians, and began to find out that the crisis was only imaginary; that although trade had received a severe blow, public securities had been very seriously depreciated, the prestige of the nation lost so far as foreign Powers are concerned, the Union practically dissolved, the public treasury empty, and the public credit as bad as that of any kite flying jobber, a reign of terror existing over one-half the country, thousands of men in arms against the government—all this was nothing, only a bagatelle, a mere squall which would soon blow over.

"All this nonsense might be excused in a stump speaker," the paper concluded its tirade, "but it is to say the least, quite beneath any man of common sense who has been elected to a very high office, at a moment when the country needs more than at any other time in its history so far a first class man at the helm of State."[59] The New York Tribune was more succinct: Lincoln seemed like a "simple Susan."[60]

In Washington, Charles Francis Adams could only concur. Reporting that reprints of Lincoln's speeches "on his way here" were "rapidly reducing the estimate put upon him," the congressman lamented that these "givings out" were "growing more and more distracted in sentiment, and less likely to strike out any consistent policy." Especially worried about reaction in the Upper South, he reported that a Virginia friend had similarly complained about "Mr. Lincoln's actions in his round about tour toward this capital," the contemplation of which gave Adams a headache. "Nothing," he said, "has so much depressed my spirits as the account of these. They betray a person unconscious of his own position as well as of the nature of the contest around him. Good natured, kindly, honest, but frivolous and uncertain." Just a few days later, the Bay State Republican further confided: "I confess I am gloomy about him. His beginning is inauspicious. It indicates the absence of the heroic qualities which he most needs."[61]

Another important Massachusetts statesman was likewise dispirited. The same week as Adams recorded his concerns, Edward Everett, former pastor, congressman, Harvard president, ambassador, governor, senator, and, most recent, vice presidential candidate on the failed 1860 John Bell ticket, registered similar doubts. "The President-elect is making a zigzag progress to Washington," Everett complained, "called out to make short speeches at every important point. These speeches thus far have been of the most ordinary kind, destitute of everything, not merely of felicity and grace, but of common pertinence." Lamented the famous orator: "He is evidently a person of very inferior cast of character, wholly unequal to the crisis."[62] No American—least of all that master of "demonstrative oratory" and "fervid declamation"—would have imagined that less than three years later, Everett would be far outshone by that "inferior character" when the two men met to share the podium at Gettysburg.[63]

Not everyone agreed with these starchy New Englanders. Lincoln certainly earned his share of public and editorial praise for these very same speeches. For the most part, reaction to Lincoln's pre-inaugural messages reflected factional politics. Adams, for one, still nursed sore feelings about Lincoln's convention victory over Seward, Everett for his Election Day triumph over Bell (and himself). Nor was criticism from Democratic newspapers surprising in an era of unabashedly partisan journalism. Assailing "the trifling and flippant remarks indulged in by the President elect," the Democratic *Philadelphia Argus* condemned the "humiliating spectacle of the President elect of this great confederacy indulging in the merest clap-trap of the politician, thanking the people for voting for him, flattering their local pride, and appealing to their sectional animosities." The Democratic organ in Lincoln's own hometown chortled that its leading citizen's "speeches, jokes, etc." were "not of a character to elevate him in popular estimation."[64] And in a similar vein, the *New York Argus* charged that the "tone and frivolity, which characterizes the speeches of Mr. Lincoln, cause the hearts of our citizens to sink within them. They perceive already that he is not the man for the crisis, and begin to despond of any extrication from impending difficulties."[65]

But the stubborn myth that holds that his speeches proved a universal disappointment is simply untrue: many pro-Republican newspapers rose to Lincoln's defense. One such paper even reminded readers that it was "natural" for Democrats to "ridicule the little speeches made by Mr. Lincoln in acknowledging the welcomes he receives at different points."

Besides, it added: "Most of them don't know what is appropriate or sensible, and would ridicule it just the same if they did. Their ignorance both of the proprieties and duties of any station, is their warrant for laughing at anybody whose party name does not warn them that they may be hitting a friend." The man they called "Old Abe," the editorial concluded, was no "failure on the stump. . . . We . . . do not intend an apology for him, nor admit that any is required, for we have picked our teeth with the usual amount of pleasure after tasting his speeches, on this tour, notwithstanding they were hashed and served cold by the telegraphic reporters."[66]

Republican papers tended to cheer Lincoln's pre-inaugural statements, even the weakest of the lot. The *New York Times*, for example, argued that, however infelicitously expressed, he was "right in saying that the crisis is artificial . . . gotten up by disappointed demagogues."[67] Hailing his "great power of cool reserve," the *New York Sun* celebrated Lincoln's new and informal manner, noting he seemed "as much at his ease as if seated on a rail of his own splitting, describing the state of the nation with a fellow farmer." To this paper, his frank style meant he would "be no puppet of a cabinet master spirit, nor implement of faction, caucus or cabal," and that his inevitable success in Washington would "extinguish once more, for America at least, the assumption that erudite schooling, fastidious culture, and diplomatic manners, are important in the greatest ends and offices of human life."[68]

How then, amid the din of such conflicting period commentary, can the modern reader accurately assess Lincoln's inaugural journey speeches? Putting politics aside, the truth is that objections to Lincoln's rhetorical performances arose most often to the earlier of these speeches, many of which unquestionably deserved some of the criticism they elicited—for their inconsistency alone. At the same time, a case can also be made that Lincoln was feeling his way in these initial utterances for a safe, defensible ground between conciliation and coercion that might mollify Upper South Unionists and fill Northern Democrats with patriotic fervor, while reassuring anti-slavery Republicans that they had chosen the right leader.

Lincoln's remarks fall into two distinct categories: those he stumblingly offered at the beginning of his travels, in the West, where he was better known and perhaps let his guard down; and the more astute remarks he began pronouncing toward journey's end in the East, where he was in effect introducing himself with greater care. Lincoln seemed to gain in confidence and rhetorical momentum as he proceeded toward Washington—much as he would grow in stature once installed there— refining his message and finding his true voice. "Mr. Lincoln's speeches grow better as he comes Eastward," a Boston paper recognized.[69] As a result, ironically, he came to speak best where he was known least, and worst where he was known best.

In the sum of their parts, Lincoln's inaugural journey speeches were vastly undervalued—then and since. In many instances, they adroitly balanced the conflicting requirements that the incoming president demonstrate cordiality, confidence, and humility, without offending any of the constituencies on which he relied to maintain what would be left of the Union when he took office. He was not wrong to dismiss the crisis as the product of incendiary extremists, nor to remind dubious voters that if they felt they had made a mistake at the polls, they could reverse course four years down the road. I may not be beautiful to look at, Lincoln seemed to be reminding his hearers; but I have humility, a big heart, a reliance on God, and a belief in the American dream that made me what I am. Majority rule ensured liberty, and liberty guaranteed opportunity.

All through his thirteen-day speaking and listening tour, Lincoln skillfully avoided one subject entirely: that of slavery. While he occasionally vowed to protect existing institutions, and the relationship between the states and the federal government, he offered slavery neither specific support, which would have inflamed the North, nor overt condemnation, which would have aroused the Upper South.

Understandably reluctant to expound on any major policy issues (beyond Republican platform doctrine) before arriving in Washington to take personal measure of the secession crisis, assemble his final cabinet, and seek their advice, his greetings instead strove to rally confidence with vague assurances. They offered endearing flashes of his famous good humor. They boasted a reinvigorated defense of majority rule and a new reliance on divine blessing. They evinced a reassuring firmness coupled with a willingness to avoid further conflict, in sufficient doses to satisfy his Republican supporters and hopefully assuage wavering border state slaveholders. Above all, they revealed a Lincoln comfortable with himself, secure in the decision of the people, and particularly grateful for welcomes "without party distinction,"[70] well aware he might face a future in which he would need the support of pro-Union Northern Democrats. Unfortunately, the charm of such remarks, so pleasing to trackside audiences, was often lost in transcription when reprinted in the press.

What appeared to opposition readers as Lincoln's incoherence occurred at a particularly unpropitious moment, for many Americans of the time judged his words against reports of Jefferson Davis's speeches en route to his own presidential inaugural. Not that Davis should at first glance have offered formidable rhetorical competition. A ponderous orator, he was incapable of giving a brief or simply worded speech, and his formal style and rigid syntax were ill-suited to railroad depots. In print, however, his words could seem more dignified than Lincoln's colloquial remarks.

Acknowledging that Davis's war-mongering pre-inaugural speeches were "highly flavored with the odor of villainous saltpeter," the *Herald* nonetheless found it remarkable that "we do not hear that he told any stories, cracked any jokes, asked the advice of the young women about his whiskers, or discussed political platforms."[71] Cleveland's *Plain Dealer* agreed: "Of the positive character of the speeches" of each leader, it commented, "there is no chance for doubt." Davis's twenty-fifth and final address before his own swearing in, the paper worried, in a slap to Lincoln, offered "the unflinching, bold programme of a bold and too able man."[72] Unspoken was the fact that Davis was merely preaching to the converted—addressing crowds that had cast nearly all their votes for Democrats, while Lincoln was facing the far more delicate challenge of uniting regions where often nearly half the voters had supported others, even in states he had carried. In three areas through which Davis traveled, for example—Mississippi, Tennessee, and Alabama—Lincoln's name had not even appeared on the ballot. But among Lincoln's stops, Illinois and Indiana had been almost evenly divided, New Jersey and Maryland against him, and even in states where he had amassed strong majorities—Ohio, New York, and Pennsylvania—more than 731,000 men had cast their votes for others.

Anti-slavery journals appreciated this distinction. As the *New York Observer* pointed out, en route to his swearing in Davis had warned that Northerners would "smell Southern gunpowder and feel Southern steel." In marked contrast, Lincoln had insisted, "there need be no bloodshed or war." In the *Observer*'s judgment, the latter's sentiments were not only nobler, but left little doubt which man heaven and earth would hold responsible "if the country is plunged into the horrors of civil war."[73]

Late on the night of February 16, as Lincoln was being feted in Buffalo, Davis ended his triumphant, parallel inaugural tour through the South, arriving at Montgomery to the strains of the newly adopted anthem "Dixie." Welcoming him there with predictions of "prosperity, honor, and victory," the fiery Alabama secessionist William Lowndes Yancey confidently declared: "The man and the hour have met."[74] Among those on hand to greet him were two enthusiastic pro-secession women from Kentucky: the sisters-in-law of Abraham Lincoln told Davis they should not be held responsible for their sister Mary's choice for a husband.[75]

Two days later, on February 18, defying Northern predictions of a "gloomy phantom of an inauguration,"[76] Davis took the oath of office at ceremonies punctuated by cannon salutes and the cheers of exuberant spectators. "It is joyous in the midst of perilous times," Davis declared in his message, "to look around upon a people united in heart, where one purpose of high resolve animates and actuates the whole. Obstacles may retard, but they cannot long prevent, the progress of a movement sanctified by its justice and sustained by a virtuous people." The challenge was clear. As if responding to Lincoln's recent expressions of reliance on the Almighty, his Confederate rival now countered: "Reverently let us invoke the God of our Fathers to guide and protect us in our efforts to perpetuate the principles which by his blessings they were able to vindicate, establish, and transmit to their posterity."[77]

The battle between the dueling presidents for divine blessing thus commenced in earnest, and not all his fellow Northerners were prepared to give Lincoln the first lick. Noting that his speeches increasingly featured "references to his reliance upon the aid and protection of a Power higher than those of this mundane sphere," the increasingly hostile *New York Herald* advised: "He will do well to call in some supernatural aid, as it is quite evident that he has not sufficient mental calibre for the discharge of the duties he has undertaken." The people complained that Lincoln "has been almost killed with kindness, half smothered with endearments, and worshipped as a demigod by the western politicians, every mother's son of whom expects a fat office."[78] As the ever-critical Democratic newspaper back in Springfield worried: "We shall have the new president's inaugural next week, when we may learn something definite. Meanwhile, let us 'watch and pray' that he may not 'put his foot in it.'"[79]

On February 17, Lincoln's trusted friend Orville Browning wrote from Springfield to offer his considered reaction to the address everyone in the country was anticipating. "When I read your inaugural at Indianapolis, I did so in very great haste, and my attention was more attracted to the clear, bold and forcible statement of principles which are just and true than to considerations of policy, and expediency," Browning began. "Upon reading it with more deliberation since my return here, it occurs to me that there is one passage . . . which ought to be modified."

Browning raised particular objection to a sentence he believed would be regarded as unnecessarily provocative. It read: "All the power at my disposal will be used to reclaim the public property and places which have fallen; to hold, occupy and possess these, and all other property and places belonging to the government, and to collect the duties on imports; but beyond what may be necessary for these objects, there will be no invasion of any state."

"Would it not be judicious," Browning proposed, "to modify this" so as to read: "All the power at my disposal will be used to hold, occupy and possess the property and places belonging to the government, and to collect the duties on imports &c" omitting the declaration of the purpose of reclamation, which will be construed into a threat, or menace, and will be irritating even in the border states." The word "reclaim" would be dropped altogether, and so would the reference to "property and places which have fallen." Browning conceded that the "principle" behind Lincoln's thoughts remained "right." But, he hastened to add, could not the new president express the same resolve "as well, or even better, without announcing the purpose in your inaugural?" As he put it: "In any conflict which may ensue between the government and the seceding States, it is very important that the traitors shall be the aggressors, and that they be kept constantly and palpably in the wrong."[80]

Lincoln took Browning's suggestion to heart. He struck the section from his inaugural text. More important, perhaps imbued with a newly pacific mood, on the back of the third and final page of Browning's letter—though we cannot know precisely where or when he did so—he jotted down an original new thought of his own. This expression of conciliation looked to a more peaceful future by calling forth memories of the nation's blessed past: "Americans, all, we are not enemies, but friends—We have sacred ties of affection which, though strained by passions, let us hope can never be broken." In a few days more, Lincoln would explore this concept with William Seward, who would tease it into a proposed new inaugural peroration that the president-elect, in turn, would further massage into yet another oratorical masterpiece.[81]

There is no conclusive evidence to indicate that Lincoln made substantial revisions on his printed inaugural text before he reached Washington. But if he was true to his own creative habits, he continued to tinker throughout the journey. By the time he reached the capital, or shortly thereafter, he had cut and pasted entire sections of the speech into new order, and knowing he would soon come face-to-face with his old enemy, Chief Justice Roger B. Taney, boldly added new ruminations on the Supreme Court.

• • •

THE INAUGURAL CARAVAN reassembled before sunrise on Monday, February 18, with Lincoln's family mercifully assigned a rear sleeping car.[82] The "relentlessly executive" William S. Wood had compelled the traveling suite to awaken at the ungodly hour of 4 A.M. "Need I intimate that of the weird cluster of men, cloaked and muffled, who gathered gloomily in the dim corridors," complained John Hay, "not one but thirsted for the blood of Wood, as the hart thirsteth for the running brooks?"[83]

Under gray skies and through deep snow, the special chugged out of predawn Buffalo and coursed east along a path roughly parallel to the old Erie Canal—the nation's first great "internal improvement," Lincoln's favorite cause during his early political career. Now, the most modern of all such improvements, the railroad, raced—at some points attaining breathtaking speeds of sixty miles per hour—through Batavia, Rochester, and Clyde (where Lincoln and William Wood reportedly posed for a photograph that has never been located). Then it was on to exuberant welcomes in Syracuse (where a symbolic live eagle fluttered at a depot crowded with ten thousand onlookers), and Utica (where a "crazy man" dressed in flannel leggings waved his cane at Lincoln and tried to interrupt his speech in the midst of a snowstorm).[84] For most of this sprint, Lincoln occupied a passenger car boasting a portrait of Washington at one end, and a portrait of himself at the other—beneath a ceiling adorned with an American flag.[85]

The arrivals in Fonda and Schenectady attracted equally large crowds and more "fine" receptions.[86] Lincoln's response in Little Falls, whose local band played "Hail Columbia" when he first appeared in a thin coat and "shocking bad hat," was typical of the nondescript set speech so many Democrats were ridiculing: "I have no speech to make," he declared offhandedly, "and no sufficient time to make one if I had; nor have I the strength to repeat a speech, at all the places at which I stop, even if all the other circumstances were favorable. I have come to see you and allow you to see me and in this so far [as] regards the Ladies, I have the best of the bargain on my side."[87] Recognizing the painful truth in that statement, Mary ordered his servant William Johnson to produce a "handsome broadcloth overcoat" and "new hat-box" in Utica to replace her husband's threadbare outerwear, and thereafter, correspondent Joseph Howard reported, "Mr. Lincoln has looked fifty percent better." In Howard's view, "if Mrs. Lincoln's advice is always as near right as it was in this instance, the country may congratulate itself upon the fact that even its President elect is a man who does not reject, even in important matters, the advice and counsel of his wife."[88]

"Such crowds—" an exultant Hay described the trip across New York state, ". . . depots in waves, as if the multitudinous seas had been let loose, and its billows transformed into patriots, clinging along roofs and balconies and pillars, fringing loose embankments, swarming upon adjacent trains of motionless cars, shouting, bellowing, shrieking, howling" with an enthusiasm both "spontaneous and universal." The day's history, he exulted, could "be written in three words: 'Crowds, cannon, and cheers.'"[89]

To more of the same, Lincoln's train pulled into Albany at 2:30 that afternoon. Somehow, the tumult in this largely Democratic city seemed more irritating than elsewhere, perhaps because it had been preceded by widely reported squabbles over how best to welcome the president-elect. "All was confusion, hurry, disorder, mud, riot and discomfort," Henry Villard criticized. Not until soldiers belatedly burst onto the scene to clear a path did his bodyguards allow Lincoln even to leave the cars. Then, to make matters worse, his initial appearance elicited but a "faint cheer." Villard provided an explanation that in turn served to point out the crucial importance of Lincoln's time-consuming journey—for it helped introduce him to a nation that still regarded him as an unknown quantity. "Lincoln, tired, sunburned, adorned with huge whiskers, looked so unlike the hale, smooth shaven, red-cheeked individual who is represented upon the popular prints and dubbed the 'rail-splitter' that it is no wonder that the people did not recognize him. Only his extreme height distinguished him unmistakably."[90]

Beneath a muslin banner proclaiming, "Welcome to the Capital of the Empire State—No Compromise"—Albany, ironically, was home to compromise champion Thurlow Weed—Lincoln replied wanly to welcoming remarks by the mayor, and then, amid the usual skirmishes "between policemen and outsiders, more pushing and crowding, more mud, ill nature and bad language," squeezed his way into a horse-drawn barouche and rode into town in the customary cortege, greeted by "an immense throng . . . as enthusiastic as it was immense."[91] Heading up steep, rocky, wind-blown State Street toward the Capitol, he could be seen "swaying like a tall cedar in a storm."[92] A bedazzled law student watching the parade judged the crowd "quite as large as that which was present on the visit of the Prince [of Wales]. The streets & windows of the buildings for a distance of more than a mile were densely crowded. And as for getting inside or within twenty rods of the Capitol building it was impossible after the throng had once stationed themselves." The young man worried that Lincoln looked "much wearied & care worn," but added, characteristically, that "his pictures do not do him justice. He is both a smarter & pleasanter looking man than his pictures represent."[93]

John Wilkes Booth was said to have been in the crowd that day, too. He was certainly in the city, appearing to rave reviews in *The Apostate*, one critic commenting eerily that the actor "throws his whole soul into his sword." The night of Lincoln's arrival, Booth's zeal for athletic performing cost him: he fell on his own dagger on stage, inflicting a three-inch gash near his armpit. Booth recovered quickly enough to loudly condemn the president-elect to anyone who would listen[94]

To others in town, Albany's welcome seemed merely tepid. Offering his formal greeting in the Capitol Rotunda, Governor Edwin D. Morgan apologized: "If you have found your fellow citizens in larger numbers elsewhere, you have not found, and, I think, will not find, warmer hearts or a people more faithful to the Union, the constitution and the laws than you will meet in this time-honored city." Lincoln graciously agreed, saluting not only the city but "this great and glorious free country." Then, for the first time since his departure from home, having finally reached the capital of one of the original thirteen colonies, he again turned his thoughts to the founders. In a speech to the state legislature, Lincoln expressed both "diffidence" and "awe," explaining: "The history of this great State, the renown of those great men who have stood here, and spoke here, and been heard here, all crowd around my fancy, and incline me to shrink from any attempt to address you."[95]

Quickly overcoming this professed hesitancy, Lincoln proceeded to expound on familiar themes, but with new urgency and power. "It is true that while I hold myself without mock modesty, the humblest of all individuals that have ever been elevated to the Presidency, I have a more difficult task to perform than any one of them. You have generously tendered me the united support of the great Empire State. For this, in behalf of the nation, in behalf of the present and future of the nation, in behalf of the civil and religious liberty for all time to come, most gratefully do I thank you." Declaring once again that he would not speak on policy until "I shall have enjoyed every opportunity to take correct and true ground," he ended with his now familiar appeal to God. "I still have confidence," he concluded to applause and cheers, "that the Almighty, the Maker of the Universe will, through the instrumentality of this great and intelligent people, bring us through this as He has through all the other difficulties of our country." The Lord, he intimated, remained on the side of Union.[96]

That night, after putting "his long legs at will under the Executive mahogany" at a private dinner at the Governor's Mansion, a patient Lincoln allowed himself to be "crowded, jostled and pushed"[97] through a Delavan House levee in his honor "crowded to suffocation" by a thousand supporters, finding extra time to drop in on the ladies' reception dedicated to Mary.[98] By 7:45 the next morning, having successfully tiptoed around the political squabbles that marred his visit, Lincoln was ushered back to the depot by the city's elite Corps of Burgesses, and for the first time in his long journey to Washington, headed due south.[99] "Fatigued, unwell, ill at ease," sneered Villard, ". . . Mr. and Mrs. Lincoln left Albany with feelings of gratitude for their safe deliverance" as "several gunners made frantic attempts to explode a second hand cannon by way of salute."[100]

• • •

FOR DAYS, EACH successive railroad company that transported the president-elect had tried to outdo the others in speed and comfort. Now, for the journey to New York City, the Lincolns enjoyed the most opulent accommodations of the entire trip. Few of its passengers had ever seen anything to compare with the highly varnished, orange-colored passenger car flecked with exterior "ornamental flourishes" in black and brown, "gaily decorated" outside with national flags and streamers. Warmed by modern heaters, with lighting cast by elegant wax candle-burners under cut-glass globes, its interior featured a bright tapestry carpet in "pleasing contrast" to the four "splendid lounges . . . covered with a mazarine of dark blue cloth of fine texture, trimmed with tri-colored gimp braid and tassels; four cozy reading chairs, all converted with soft blue cloth . . . and a beautiful oblong table of black walnut and ebony."

But the car's most extraordinary feature was its curled-maple wall paneling set off by zebra-wood inlay, and finished with gilt moldings adorned with "dark crimson plush," and window panels upholstered in "heavy blue silk, each covered with thirty four silver stars, representing the States of the Union." At each end of the car stood a pair of crossed American flags, hung in festoons, with tricolored cords and tassels to match. Two "new and powerful" locomotives, the *Union* and the *Constitution*, would alternatively pull the "magnificent" vehicle. To ensure safety as well as comfort, the railroad activated more than five hundred employees of the line to safeguard its passage.[101] In this sumptuous, fiercely protected traveling hotel, Lincoln headed toward the metropolis whose heart he had won the previous winter at Cooper Union, but whose votes he had lost that fall in the presidential election.

First, as it happened, the train headed not south but north—unable to ferry across the ice-choked Hudson River as planned, and proceeding instead up to Waterford junction before making the crossing.[102]

Naturally enough, the experience reminded the inveterate tale-spinner of yet another story. It seemed a church committee needed an architect to build a bridge "over a very dangerous and rapid river." De-

signer after designer failed, until one boasted—to the horror of his prig-
gish benefactors—"I could build a bridge to the infernal regions, if
necessary." The chairman assured his shocked colleagues: "he is so honest a man and so good an architect that if he states soberly and positively
that he can build a bridge to Hades—why, I believe it. But," he admitted, "I have my doubts about the abutment on the infernal side!" Henry
Villard could not help noticing "Lincoln's facial contortions" as he
reached the story's moral: "So," he concluded, when "politicians said
they could harmonize the Northern and Southern wings of the democracy, why, I believed them. But I had my doubts about the abutment on
the Southern side.' "[103]

After steaming along the western shore of the Hudson, Lincoln
could harbor no such doubts about the sincerity of his welcomes. He
arrived at Cohoes to "solid phalanxes" of male and female factory workers liberated from work to greet him. Here, too, he saw the natural wonder, Cohoes Falls, so swollen by recent floods that its waters cascaded
violently over the precipices in "varying sheets of foam." As far as we
know, the furious scene inspired no further stories.[104]

At Troy, where the train paused to take on an extra car bulging with
local officials and railroad executives, Lincoln offered pleasantries to
another large gathering, declaring with his usual good humor: "I have
appeared only that you might see me and I you, and I am not sure but
that I have the best of the sight."[105] Downriver at the town of Hudson,
he declined to mount a speakers' platform erected to accommodate a
long speech, but jokingly cautioned that "you must not on this account
draw the inference that I have any intention to desert any platform I
have a legitimate right to stand on."[106]

Still further south at Poughkeepsie, he delivered the longest address
of the day to a crowd so vast it spread to the surrounding hills. "I do not
think that they have chosen the best man to conduct our affairs, now,"
he conceded. "—I am sure they did not—but acting honestly and sincerely, and with your aid, I think we shall be able to get through the
storm" and preserve "those institutions which have made us free, intelligent, and happy—the most free, the most intelligent and the happiest

people on the globe." Intelligent though they were, well-wishers could now be seen confidently standing directly on the frozen river as the train glided southward, waving handkerchiefs as Lincoln flashed by.

Such scenes proved especially fascinating to young Tad—up to a point. At Poughkeepsie, the imp finally succumbed to the stubborn streak for which he was infamous back home. There, Mary raised the window to wave at well-wishers, and to shouts of "Where are the children?" first produced Robert, whose appearance earned "a hearty cheer." "Have you any more on board?" someone in the crowd shouted. "Yes," Mary answered back, "here's another," and in the words of a reporter on board, "attempted to bring a tough, rugged little fellow, about eight years of age, into sight." This, undoubtedly, was Tad. "But the young representative of the house of Lincoln proved refractory, and the more his mother endeavored to pull him before the window the more he stubbornly persisted in throwing himself down on the floor of the car, laughing at the fun, but refusing to receive the proffered honor of a reception." Mary finally abandoned "the attempt to exhibit the 'pet of the household.' " [107]

Such comedy did little to restore Lincoln's good health or high spirits. But even weighed down by his stubborn cold, he remained impressive to Henry Villard, who observed him on this leg of the journey "towering above all, with his face and forehead furrowed by a thousand wrinkles, his hair unkempt, his new whiskers looking as if not yet naturalized, his clothes illy arranged." Even so, the reporter insisted, "no one can see Mr. Lincoln without recognizing in him a man of immense power and force of character and natural talent." [108]

At around 2 P.M. the special paused at Peekskill to change engines. A youngster in the crowd of 1,500 huddling around the town's modest brick depot recalled that "a man of tall sinewy form and smiling face" emerged and, to "cheers, and hurrahs," strolled to a nearby platform erected on a handcar, shaking hands all around as a twenty-one-gun tattoo reverberated from the surrounding hilltops. [109]

With "but a moment to stand before you," Lincoln's thanks were brief. "I will say in a single sentence, in regard to the difficulties that lie before me and our beloved country, that if I can only be as generously and unanimously sustained as the demonstrations I have witnessed indicate I shall be, I shall not fail; but without your sustaining hands I am sure that neither I nor any other man can hope to surmount those difficulties."[110] Unimpressed, the local paper described the ceremony as "orderly, but spiritless," noting that Lincoln's little speech "was probably not heard a dozen feet from the platform and to nearly all others presented the appearance of a pantomime, and without much stretch of the imagination, a rather ludicrous one."[111]

The journal did concede, echoing many others along the tour, that Lincoln appeared far "better looking than he is pictured," particularly with his "fine crop of dark whiskers." But even the new beard could not disguise the fact that he also appeared "jaded, fatigued, and as if just aroused from a nap." When Lincoln concluded his remarks, William Wood cried out, "Time's up," the train whistle shrieked, and amid more applause and handkerchief-waving, the special moved on, Lincoln as usual "remaining on the car platform, with uncovered head and bowing to both sides until the train was out of sight."[112] Then it was on toward Manhattan, with the train slowing down at intervening suburban stops like Dobbs Ferry and Manhattanville so Lincoln could offer his ritualistic bowing from the rear car—doing so even alongside Sing Sing, whose prisoners, wearing striped uniforms, saluted as the train passed by.[113]

Finally, at 3 P.M., seven long hours after its departure from Albany, Lincoln's opulent train rolled into the vast, recently built Hudson River Railroad terminal—so new it was still devoid of furniture—straddling 30th Street between Ninth and Tenth Avenues. Before alighting—at Mary's urging, Lincoln "allowed himself to be brushed, gave his hair an extra turn, arranged his whiskers . . . and tried to look his prettiest" before making his first appearance in the media capital of the nation—a city whose mayor had suggested it secede from the Union.[114] Mary steeled him to the task by giving him a kiss, and he happily lifted her out of her seat and ushered her from the train.[115]

Then, eliciting a loud cheer as he appeared on the sidewalk on this "mild and beautiful" afternoon, he, Judge Davis, Colonel Sumner, and

Nicolay boarded the first of thirty-five carriages parked outside to convey his suite and baggage downtown. Lincoln's was the same vehicle the Prince of Wales had used for his visit in 1860, an open coach drawn by six black horses. As he would learn, however, the royal conveyance did not guarantee the kind of unbridled welcome New York had given the future Edward VII. Turning down Ninth Avenue, Lincoln's procession followed a huge squad of policemen south to 23rd Street, east to Fifth Avenue—where the crowd thinned—south again to 14th Street, then down Broadway in a double line to the Astor House across the street from St. Paul's Chapel at Vesey Street.[116]

Flags did wave everywhere—"flung to the breeze" from hotels, stores, and private homes all along the route. One dressmaker hung a crinoline decorated with stars and stripes.[117] Banners strung across the broad thoroughfares, suspended from windows, and printed on hand-carried pennants, declared such sentiments as "Welcome Lincoln!" "Welcome, welcome, none too soon!" along with the occasional dissent: "We Beg for Compromise." One huge sign bore the telling words from Genesis: "Fear not, Abraham, I am thy shield and thy exceeding great reward." From Putnam's, the publishing house at 532 Broadway, hung a placard emblazoned with the words from Lincoln's 1860 Cooper Union speech: "Right makes might."[118]

Lincoln had stayed at the Astor House during that earlier visit to town, but on that occasion made the brisk walk from a ferry slip to the hotel in just a few minutes, alone and unrecognized, checking into an ordinary, street-level room. Now, hundreds accompanied his procession, a quarter of a million people lined the streets, the short trip consumed a full hour and a half, and Lincoln would occupy the same four-room, second-floor suite President Pierce once used.[119] Riding alongside Lincoln in the open carriage, Nicolay observed "a continuous fringe of humanity crowding "side streets, doors, balconies, windows," even rooftops.[120]

However vast the crowds—easily the largest of the trip so far, not entirely surprising in the nation's largest city—the "dense mass"[121] struck some observers as disquietingly subdued. One newspaper admitted that

Lincoln's arrival failed to "produce so much interest or excitement among our citizens . . . as such an event would naturally be supposed to create." Perhaps no more should have been expected from a city Lincoln and the Republicans had lost so overwhelmingly just a few months before. *Frank Leslie's Illustrated Newspaper*, whose artist Henri Lovie furiously sketched the caravan, was not alone in reporting "much respect" for Lincoln along the procession, but "little enthusiasm."[122]

Whatever the reason, in the *New York Herald*'s opinion, "there was nothing in the crowd to compare with the almost impenetrable *chevaux de frise* of humanity that lined roofs, walks, windows, ledges, awnings, lamp posts and every other tenable spot, on the arrival of the Prince of Wales"—to whose frenzied welcomes the president-elect's receptions were so often compared, usually unfavorably. Riding in the British heir apparent's carriage, the American heir apparent remained seated for most of the journey, rising only when a loud cheer caught his attention.

To be sure, many individuals viewed the reception more positively. George Templeton Strong encountered the "illustrious cortege" near St. Thomas's Church. "The great rail-splitter's face was visible to me for an instant," he happily confided, like so many others adding that it "seemed a keen, clear, honest face, not so ugly as his portraits." Strong heard "a torrent" of "hooraying," pointing out that any "signs of enthusiasm" were "unusual in the phlegmatic street gatherings of New York."[123]

"What do you think; I *have seen* 'Abe'—'Old Abe'—'Honest Old Abe,'" gushed one young woman after watching the procession pass from a balcony opposite the Fifth Avenue Hotel. "Abe" turned out to be "much better looking than is represented," agreed Lavinia Goodell, daughter of a prominent abolitionist, ". . . energetic looking, smiling and pleasant, frank and open. He looks young, his hair being perfectly black. Altogether I was quite favorably struck with him, and feel deeply interested in his welfare."[124]

From a nearby vantage point atop a trolley stalled outside the Astor House, another eyewitness worried for Lincoln's welfare, too, viewing what seemed to him a chilly welcome with portentous unease. Though the "broad spaces, sidewalks, and street in the neighborhood, and for some distance, were crowded with solid masses of people—many thousands," Walt Whitman remembered:

> The omnibuses and other vehicles had all been turn'd off, leaving an unusual hush in that busy part of the city. Presently two or three shabby black barouches made their way with some difficulty through the crowd, and drew up at the Astor House entrance. A tall figure stepp'd out of the centre of the barouches, paus'd leisurely on the sidewalk, look'd up at the dark granite walls and looming architecture of the grand old hotel—then, after a relieving stretch of arms and legs, turn'd round for over a minute to slowly and good-humoredly scan the appearance of the vast and silent crowds—and so, with very moderate pace, and accompanied by a few unknown-looking persons, ascended the portico steps. There were no speeches, no compliments, no welcome.

Whitman exaggerated, oblivious to the ceremonies planned later. "—As far as I could hear, not a word said. Still, much anxiety was concealed in that quiet."

As the poet melodramatically took note:

> All was comparative and ominous silence. The newcomer look'd with curiosity upon that immense sea of faces, and the sea of faces return'd the look with similar curiosity. In both there was a dash of something almost comical. Yet there was much anxiety in certain quarters. Cautious persons had fear'd that there would be some outbreak, some mark'd indignity or insult to the President elect on his passage through the city, for he possess'd no personal popularity in New York, and not much political. No such outbreak or insult, however, occur'd. Only the silence of the crowd was very significant to those who were accustom'd to the usual demonstrations of New York in wild, tumultuous hurrahs.[125]

For generations since, historians and literary critics alike have debated Whitman's recollection—particularly its climactic assertion that "I had no doubt (so frenzied were the ferments of the time) many an assassin's knife and pistol lurk'd in hip- or breast-pocket there—ready, soon as break and riot came." Written years later, after Lincoln had indeed succumbed to murder, Whitman's observations are of course less reliable than morning-after reports in the period press.[126] But even some of these agreed there "was perhaps some reason to anticipate much less creditable conduct" from the "untold thousands of idle and starving workmen . . . in curious attendance."[127] Ironically, the most crowded of all Lincoln's public welcomes en route to Washington also proved the least ardent. And Whitman was right: it might have been far worse.

Indifference did nothing to reduce the crowding and shoving in the Astor House lobby when Lincoln tried to ease his way to his four-room suite on the second floor. Nor did it lessen the calls for a speech once he disappeared inside. From the ledge of his parlor window, with all of lower Broadway spread out before him—including Barnum's museum, its gaudy facade emblazoned with depictions of a giant sea horse, a "man monkey," and a family of Aztec children—Lincoln protested good-naturedly that not only could he "not be heard by any but a very small fraction of you at best," he also had "nothing to say just now worth your hearing." Then he eased past a gauntlet of policemen into his formal reception room, where he greeted well-wishers so manhandled in the crush that they "emerged like pressed figs." Only then did Lincoln retreat to his ten-seat dining room for a sumptuous buffet dinner that included boiled salmon in anchovy sauce, goose liver, turkey, larded fillet of beef, sweetbreads with tomato sauce, oysters, roast fowl, and a variety of exotic pastries for dessert. Dominating the brilliantly decorated room was an evocative painting, *Washington Crossing the Delaware*.[128]

Afterward, called on to make a more substantial speech back in the adjacent reception room where Webster and Clay had once spoken, he apologized—though "rather an old man"—for feeling himself unable "to do something like those men, or do something unworthy of myself or my audience." His stellar audience included Wide-Awake leaders and Republican officials, the city's Republican presidential electors, led by venerable poet-editor William Cullen Bryant, and representatives of the Young Men's Republican Union who had hosted him at Cooper Union, Cephas Brainerd and Richard McCormick among them. Rumors abounded that the parlor was filled with men who wanted not only the chance to greet Lincoln, but to take credit for his victory, and reap the patronage rewards they now felt they deserved.[129] One paper noted that "the President elect did not appear to recognize them as important instruments in his election," staring down the composite "Mr. Blower . . . who has made speeches throughout the campaign, and has written several articles for the *Bugle of Freedom*, published in Cattaraugus county," with the same "cool and unspeculative an eye as if he were an obscure Democrat, with a dusty coat and a smashed hat."[130]

Ignoring the clamor, Lincoln simply attempted instead to justify his months of what historian Gabor Boritt has called his "intensely moral silence."[131] Admitting, "I have been occupying a position, since the Presidential election, of silence, of avoiding public speaking, of avoiding public writing . . . [not] from party wantonness, or from any indifference to the anxiety that pervades the minds of men about the aspect of political affairs of the country," he explained: "I have kept silence for the reason that I supposed it was peculiarly proper that I should do so until the time came when, according to the customs of the country, I should speak officially."[132]

Here, surprisingly, Lincoln was loudly heckled. "Custom of the country?" someone shot back. Acknowledging the query if not the sarcasm, Lincoln patiently replied: "I said several times upon this journey, and I now repeat it to you, that when the time does come I shall then take the ground that I think is right—the ground I think is right for the North, for the South, for the East, for the West, for the whole country." And after a few more nods to the Constitution, the Union, and the liberties of its people, he commenced greeting each member of the crowd individually, hand over hand, calling out "how d'ye do?" or "Glad to see you," as they mercifully passed from the overcrowded, overheated room. Lincoln may have shown how relieved he was that there had been none of the "outrage and violence" some had predicted in New York when a giant of a man neared him, and someone in the crowd cried out, "That's Tom Hyer," the retired prizefighter who had won fame with a 101-round victory years before. To which the president-elect replied, to much laughter: "I don't care, so long as he don't hit me."[133]

Chapter Eleven

I Would Rather Be Assassinated

ARLY THE NEXT morning, Wednesday, February 20, Lincoln joined Norman Judd, Thurlow Weed, editor James Watson Webb, and others for an 8:30 breakfast with a group of leading New York businessmen. The setting was luxurious enough to suggest bullish confidence in the future: the mansion of former congressman Moses H. Grinnell at Fifth Avenue and 14th Street.[1] Hiram Barney was there, too—Ohio's commercial representative in the city, who had once promoted Lincoln's Cooper Union speech in a failed effort to help his own White House choice, Salmon P. Chase.

This was by no means a social call: New York's commercial interests were extremely nervous about the untested president-elect, and the fluctuating markets reflected their anxiety over the possible termination of trade with the South, not to mention the prospect of new taxes to fund a war.[2] Lincoln surely tried assuring the businessmen that his administration would labor to protect their commercial interests.[3] But the effort fell flat. Barney thought the tense breakfast "a failure, nobody at his ease, and Mr. Lincoln least of all." Another guest, William Henry Aspinwall, confirmed that "Lincoln made a bad impression," especially after one of the wealthy guests tastelessly remarked that he "would not meet so many millionaires together at any other table in New York." To which Lincoln jested testily: "Oh, indeed, is that so? Well, that's quite right. I'm a millionaire myself. I got a minority of a million in the votes last November." (This recollection may have garbled the joke: Lincoln received a minority of the votes in 1860, but his total still exceeded 1.8 million.) A bristling Aspinwall thought Lincoln failed "to show any adequate sense of the gravity" of the crisis.[4]

Then it was back to the Astor House for a far less demanding obligation: greeting a ninety-four-year-old Lincoln supporter named Joshua Dewey, who had voted in every presidential election since Washington's. From there, escorted by city aldermen, Lincoln rode just across Broadway to City Hall for a potentially awkward public reception hosted by the most hostile New York audience yet: renegade mayor Fernando Wood.

The mayor, a pro-South Democrat, had recently intensified his calls to turn the city into some sort of independent free republic in order to guarantee "a continuance of uninterrupted intercourse with every section." Only weeks before, he had been branded a traitor for permitting the shipment of arms through the city to the South, then sent a "commission" to South Carolina, Georgia, Louisiana, and other seceded states to "pursue peace and secure the rights of the South."[5] Now, he ostentatiously greeted Lincoln from behind George Washington's writing desk in the building's high-ceilinged, second-floor Governor's suite. With little subtlety, Wood positioned himself beneath a painting of onetime Governor Seward, who, as everyone knew, now favored compromise. Acknowledging merely his "duty" to welcome the president-elect, Wood urged his visitor to use his "exalted powers" to return the country "to its former harmonious, consolidated and prosperous condition," bluntly warning that New York's "commercial greatness" was "endangered" by the crisis.

Lincoln neatly deflected the Democrat's insolent challenge. Facing the delicate task of conciliating the city without conciliating the secessionists, he simply expressed "gratitude" for the reception provided "by a people who do not by a majority agree with me in political sentiments." Declaring himself in agreement with the mayor's "sentiments," if not his manners or schemes, he offered that in his "devotion to the Union I hope I am behind no man," adding his new mantra: "I bring a heart devoted to the work."

"There is nothing," he craftily concluded, "that can ever bring me willingly to consent to the destruction of this Union, under which not only the commercial city of New York, but the whole country has acquired its greatness." Besides, he pointed out: "I understand a ship to be made for the carrying and preservation of the cargo, and so long as the ship can be saved, with the cargo, it should never be abandoned."[6] Privately, Lincoln dismissed Wood's outrageous New York secession plot with an equally efficient metaphor, drawling, "I reckon that it will be some time before the front door sets up housekeeping on its own terms."[7] The mayor, taunted the *Sun*, "got nothing.[8]

From the avalanche of citizens who thronged the suite to greet Lincoln that day, it was difficult to believe he had few friends in the city. As soon as policemen threw the doors to the Governor's Room open at 11:15,[9] people exploded inside as if "discharged by a piece of ordnance," shoving their way toward Lincoln to exclaim "God bless you," "Stand firm," or "How d'ye do, Uncle Abraham." Wood offered Lincoln the option of moving around the packed suite informally, but the president-elect chose to endure a long receiving line and shake hands at least until noon, standing beneath a symbol more to his liking: a statue of George Washington.[10] Thereafter he merely bowed, making exceptions of most of the ladies ("their hands don't hurt me"), grizzled War of 1812 survivors ("I must shake hands with the Veterans"), along with one male visitor who had journeyed all the way from Canada ("I suppose I must shake hands with the representatives of foreign nations").

Lincoln's droll comments delighted the crowd, even when he behaved like "a country clodhopper appearing in fashionable society."[11] When one bearded gentleman passed by the line and exclaimed, "Well, he looks like me," Lincoln was heard to observe: "I did not look at him, but I take it that he is a very handsome man." Meeting a gunpowder manufacturer burdened with the Dickensian name of "Hazard," he could not resist advising him to "keep his powder dry." And when one passerby solemnly lectured him, "the flag of our country is looking at you," Lincoln shot back: "I hope it won't lose any of its eyes."[12]

To the delight of the spectators, he offered to measure back-to-back with a huge Vermonter, bringing down the house when it turned out he was at least two inches the taller. "I saw he was stretching himself," Lincoln confided proudly, "so I thought I would try it," adding proudly when he won the competition: "I thought so; I'm hard to beat." He fared less well when a "mammoth" butter-dealer out-measured him after a similar test. When another visitor declared, "I hope you will take care of us. I have prayed for you," the guest of honor retorted, "But you must take care of me!"[13]

At 1 P.M., after nearly two hours of this tumult, during which some five thousand visitors shoved their way in and out of the suite, policemen shut the large doors, and Lincoln was importuned through a window onto the City Hall balcony to greet the disappointed crowds that had been turned away, and now massed in the plaza below. "I came merely to see you," he shouted to "tremendous cheers," adding his usual coda, "And I have to say to you, as I have said frequently to audiences on my journey, that, in the sight, I have the best of the bargain. Assuming that you are all for the Constitution, the Union, and the perpetual liberties of this people, I bid you farewell."[14]

That afternoon, except for a few private meetings, Lincoln managed to seize some time for much needed rest, rejecting P. T. Barnum's invitation to visit his showplace, though Mary and the boys eagerly accepted.[15] (Tad ultimately refused to go, insisting he had seen "plenty of bears" back home.) When Lincoln did emerge, he demonstrated that the tact he had shown at City Hall had not diminished. Presented new toppers by the city's competing hat-making titans, Knox and Leary (the latter occupied a storefront in the Astor House), Lincoln refused to say which he preferred, delicately suggesting: "They mutually *surpassed* each other."[16]

A few hours later, Lincoln welcomed Vice President–elect Hamlin to town, and for the first time since their meetings in Chicago two months earlier, the two took the opportunity to dine together with their wives and discuss their respective journeys—though policy matters were apparently avoided. Hamlin remembered only that when the hotel waiters served oysters on the half-shell, Lincoln stared at them "with a half-doubting, half-smiling look and said, as if he had never eaten such a dish before, 'Well, I don't know that I can manage these things, but I guess I can learn.'" He simply would not resort to "artifice," Hamlin noted, "even in the case of oysters."[17]

That night, a "very brilliant assemblage" packed the Academy of Music for a performance of Verdi's new opera, *Un Ballo in Maschera*, the story of the assassination of Gustav III of Sweden, a production that had proven so controversial in Europe that its setting had lately been switched to Boston, its martyred victim transformed from a king into a colonial governor. Whether Lincoln knew that the theme of the opera was political assassination is not known.

Shortly after the curtain rose, an unexpected "buzz and burr" stirred the audience, and, as one journalist reported, "one thousand opera glasses turned in one direction" to view the late arrival of "the largest amount of President the country has yet afforded." The observer thought "we saw seven feet of President—at least calculating from his knees upward," joking: "There was so much of him that we thought, if we could only divide him up, we could spare half for the new Confederacy, and the correspondence being perfect between the two halves of our omnipresent President, the most perfect harmony would ensue, and the Union would ultimately be made whole."[18]

No one seemed to hear the rest of Act I. "We all glared at Lincoln, we mentally devoured him," admitted the reporter, though "he did not seem to be in the least degree disturbed by this double-barreled opera glass attack." When the lights went up for intermission, cries of "Lincoln!" arose from the house, and the president-elect "commenced to uncoil himself, and as foot after foot unfolded itself before the public gaze more deafening became the noise and clamor. He bowed his acknowledgments and bowed them again," looking to the reporter "stern, rugged and uncompromising." When he smiled, however, "gentle, benevolent and kindly," his transformed face seemed to promise "that justice would be tempered with mercy, and stern principle would be leavened with that wisdom which springs from a knowledge of the human heart."

As the applause mounted, the orchestra struck up "Hail Columbia," an American flag unfurled from the summit of the proscenium, the principal singers returned to the stage to sing "The Star-Spangled Banner," and the crowd shouted itself "hoarse." Three cheers for Lincoln, three for the Constitution, and three more for the Union ended the president-elect's night at the opera. He left before Act II commenced, and never heard the accusatory Act III aria, *"Eri tu che macchiavi quell'anima."* Whether out of design or fatigue, Lincoln managed to avoid the horrific murder scene entirely.[19]

But the music did not end there. Back at the Astor House, 150 members of a Wide-Awake band greeted his return by launching into a blaring midnight serenade, pounding out the "Lincoln Quick Step," "Yankee Doodle," and even the new Confederate anthem "Dixie"—anything to rouse Lincoln into another appearance. But their cries went unheeded; he had gone from the opera straight to bed. For once, he did not appear. It was left to Hamlin to address the disappointed throng before it reluctantly dispersed at 1 A.M.—the last time the vice president–elect would fill in publicly for his chief.[20]

The following morning, as Lincoln prepared for the next leg of his journey, the ever-enterprising P. T. Barnum, notwithstanding his failure to lure the man of the hour to his sideshow, urged visitors to his museum anyway, not only to see its "great living black sea-lion" and Samson the two-thousand-pound bear, but to cram its windows for the best view of Lincoln "as he leaves the Astor House and passes down Broadway, Directly in front of the Museum." At no extra charge, the impresario offered a glimpse of "The Great Lincoln Turkey," now weighing forty pounds, which he vowed would grace the president's table at his inauguration.

"Farewell to President Lincoln. Farewell to President Lincoln," shouted Barnum's advertisements that day. "Who will not embrace the opportunity to look upon the Nation's Head, the Nation's deliverer, the People's Favorite and Friend?" During his two-day visit to New York, few had resisted the chance to do so, whether they regarded Lincoln a head or a pretender, a deliverer or a danger, a friend or an enemy. Now, his own menagerie moved on. One leading participant stayed put. Declaring himself "very sick of the 'travelling show,' " Henry Villard, the most astute of all the observers of Lincoln during that bitter secession winter, asked "to be relieved" of his duties and "remained behind."[21] As a result, he would miss the biggest story of the trip.

SOMETIME DURING ABRAHAM Lincoln's inaugural journey, the future Civil War nurse and social reformer Mary Livermore joined the multitudes who glimpsed him firsthand, standing one day "at the edge of an effervescing crowd," simply so she "might look in the rugged, homely face of our future President.

"Like many others on whose hearts the gradual disruption of the Union that dark winter lay like an agony of personal bereavement," she explained, "I longed to read in the face of our leader the indications of wisdom and strength that would compel the people to anchor in him and feel safe." She was not disappointed. Livermore, who had covered the 1860 Republican convention as a reporter—the only woman to do so—liked what she saw, and was reassured by what she heard in the warm responses from the crowd. From one voice came, "He *seems* like an honest man!" from another, "There is no spread-eagle nonsense about him—that is one consolation." "He is probably not much of a statesman, nor even a politician; but then he is a Northern man, an antislavery man, and he is honest and loyal, and perhaps we could not have done better than to elect 'Old Abe' President."[22]

Not every female shared Livermore's admiration. One Kentucky woman complained bitterly that Lincoln's election had encouraged "negros . . . beggers and Gipsies" to "poisoning and Incendiaryism" in the belief they would all soon be free. "*For God sake* Dear Sir," she demanded, "give us women some assurance that *you* will protect *us*, for we are the greatest *Slaves* in the South[.]"[23]

Ten days after Lincoln commenced his very public journey to Washington, and notwithstanding his welcomes without regard to party, Democrats continued to view "Old Abe" and his inaugural trip even less sympathetically. "We do not admire the taste and discretion of the President elect in making such an extended tour to reach Washington, and making so many speeches on the route," declared one opposition paper in faraway California. "It would have been better for him and the country to have gone directly to Washington."[24]

Southern opinion remained unified—against Lincoln. The mere sight of preparations to receive and protect the president-elect in Washington proved enough to outrage the correspondent for one South Carolina paper. Predicting almost ruefully that Lincoln would "be safe here under the strong arm of Federal Power," he fumed that "a thousand bayonets glisten before him, and loudmouthed cannon, imbedded in the earth, point to the homes of our citizens, proclaiming that the President of a portion of the Republic must be inaugurated within the confines of a military despotism."[25]

Even the nonpartisan comic weekly *Vanity Fair* weighed in, finding astringent humor not only in Lincoln's speeches but also in his imagined awkwardness before his urbane hosts. "Abe is becoming more grave," observed satirist Artemus Ward, one of Lincoln's favorite writers. "He don't construct as many jokes as he did. He fears that he will get things mixed up if he don't look out and sincerely as I regard myself competent to fill the Consulship of Liverpool, I fear he will. 'I am not so much a Washington as I was,' he touchingly remarked to me this morning. 'No,' I replied, 'George is dead . . .'

"It is popularly believed that Mr. Lincoln is not classically educated," Ward continued. ". . . but at the dinner at the Astor, where the bills of fare are printed in French, Mr. Lincoln unhesitatingly called for a *sine quanon* of beans and an *Ipsdixit* of pork, thus showing his thorough familiarity with deceased languages."[26] In a far graver tone, the high-minded New York journal *The Independent* called on "every Christian congregation" to offer up prayers to the president-elect, "that he may be so guided and strengthened by Divine Wisdom, that he may accomplish the great duty to which he is called."[27]

Neither complaint nor parody—not even supplication—seemed capable of dampening the mostly boisterous welcomes Lincoln continued attracting as he drew nearer to Washington. On Thursday, February 21, one New York paper went so far as to interpret his most recent greetings as "evidence that the popular mind is thoroughly aroused to the importance of his position, and disposed to maintain him in it." Admitting that the fervent demonstrations were mostly inspired by a mixture of "curiosity, party feeling, and the national love of excitement," the paper nonetheless predicted that their result would help Lincoln "enter upon his office with a stronger popular vote than that which raised him to the Presidency."[28] If so, the minority president's bold plan to put himself before the people would end in triumph. But he still had forty-eight hours of travel before him.

ON THE MORNING of February 21, Lincoln headed across the Hudson via the same Cortlandt Street ferry that had transported him to New York a year earlier to speak at Cooper Union. Then he had traveled alone and unnoticed. This time he was accompanied by his family, crowds of admirers, officials from Jersey City, and cannon salvos from the river, not to mention an exuberant valedictory from the *New York World*: "So far as the interval between a presidential election and the inauguration affords scope for the exercise of prudence, firmness and discreet reserve," it editorialized, "Mr. Lincoln has given the country no reason to distrust his good judgment."[29]

As soon as his carriage rolled onto the deck of the *John P. Jackson*, a band struck up the "Star-Spangled Banner," and as the ferry steamed across the Hudson, ships anchored near the Jersey City landing on the opposite shore unfurled the American colors.[30] Lincoln would do no more than bow in response to a formal greeting in the ladies' lounge—thus sparing his welcoming committee what otherwise would have been the only shipboard speech of his inaugural trip.

He did orate briefly at a hastily arranged ceremony when he reached the dockside. There, Lincoln thanked state attorney general William L.

Dayton—long rumored for a spot in Lincoln's cabinet—for greeting him with "sincere respect and high appreciation of your personal character." In response, Lincoln protested, "I am here before you care-worn," begging to be excused from further speaking. Only when crowds persisted with shouts of "Lincoln, Lincoln," did he reappear and issue his formulaic message: "There appears to be a desire to see more of me, and I can only say that from my position, especially when I look around the gallery (bowing to the ladies), I feel that I have decidedly the best of the bargain, and in this matter I am for no compromises here."[31] A ceremony John Hay judged "unexpectedly brilliant" was marred only when "a son of Erin" burst from the crowd to grab Lincoln's hand, only to be punched off the platform by a policeman's club "to the intense amusement of the crowd."[32]

Reaching Newark later that morning, Lincoln again offered not one but two speeches, the first at the city's Broad Street "lower depot," where, clearly showing signs of exhaustion, and perhaps boredom, he clumsily reiterated: "With my own ability I cannot succeed, without the sustenance of Divine Providence, and of this great, free, happy and intelligent people." Then, after taking a carriage through crowded streets for the half-mile ride to Newark's Chestnut Street "upper depot," he thanked townspeople "for their complimentary turnout" before boarding a new train. Crowd estimates varied, but as many as 75,000 enthusiasts probably turned out to greet Lincoln that day in a scene that, "for wild, crazy excitement," one reporter testified, "had not been equaled since we left Springfield." Though most people in the politically divided city cheered Lincoln energetically—he had lost Newark to the Democrats by only five hundred votes—the procession did at one point roll past a lamppost from which hung an effigy inscribed: "The Traitor's Doom." It was the only reminder that, after ten days of travel, Lincoln had only now entered a state whose voters had preferred one of his opponents. Further down the road, in welcome contrast, a thousand children lined up to sing "We Are a Band of Brothers," and Lincoln paused appreciatively and bowed.[33]

By 10:17 he was back on his train and again under way, now with

Hannibal Hamlin joining the official traveling party, along with Mary's sister Elizabeth Edwards, in whose parlor the Lincolns had married nearly twenty years before. Still, there was little time for nostalgic reunions. From the inaugural special's rear platform, Lincoln was obliged to stand in the cold and greet crowds of fifteen thousand at Elizabeth and three thousand more at Rahway, then to offer a "good morning" and "farewell" to five thousand spectators who massed at the depot in New Brunswick.[34] A loud cheer from the student body greeted him as the train slowed down in Princeton. Further south, as villages grew scarcer, "every farm house which could boast a gun or large pistol, had them out, and gave us a salute."[35]

Lincoln found renewed inspiration when, shortly before noon, he reached Trenton, the historic state capital where Washington had not only earned a rapturous welcome on his own inaugural journey in 1789 but where, back in 1776, he had won military glory against the Hessians. Now an "immense" crowd of twenty thousand offered his successor a rousing welcome of his own, punctuated by a thirty-four-gun artillery salvo at the depot. Lincoln's carriage plowed through the mud alongside a sloppy cavalcade of soldiers, musicians, and gaudily decorated politicians to the State House for separate speeches to the State Senate and Assembly. John Hay thought the "official display was embarrassingly elaborate," and "rather increased than mitigated the prevalent disorder."[36]

The lower chamber was in a jolly mood that day, offering a slew of mock resolutions while waiting for Lincoln to enter. When a Burlington County Republican proposed declaring Lincoln "a man six feet four inches in height," a Camden County Democrat countered by resolving that "when this House shall have seen Abraham Lincoln, they will have seen the ugliest man in the country." The speaker ordered both motions tabled.[37]

Unaware of the hilarity that preceded his arrival, Lincoln took the podium and did little more at first than unleash his stock repertoire of compliments and assurances, terming his reception a tribute to "the Union and the Constitution," acknowledging that a majority of the state "differ in opinion," protesting that he could not address policy matters until "I should avail myself of all the information and all the time at my command," yet vowing justice "to the North, the East, the West, the South, and the whole country."

Only then did Lincoln cause a genuine stir. Asserting that he bore "no malice toward any section"—words presaging his famous "malice toward none" inaugural four years in the future—he solemnly promised: "I shall do all that may be in my power to promote a peaceful settlement of all our difficulties. The man does not live who is more devoted to peace than I am." Then, Lincoln assumed "a subdued intensity of tone" to inject a breathtaking dose of bravado. "But it may be necessary to put the foot down firmly," he declared. For dramatic emphasis he lifted his huge boot "slightly" and pressed it "with a quick, but not violent, gesture upon the floor." The gesture unleashed "cheers so loud and long that for some moments it was impossible to hear Mr. L.'s voice." John Nicolay, who witnessed this scene, thought it proved that Lincoln "did not disguise to himself the significance" of Davis's recent inaugural at Montgomery.[38] This was his response: without dignifying that illegitimate event with a specific rebuke, he had hinted that it would not only go unrecognized, but perhaps be suppressed.

Not until quiet was restored could Lincoln continue: "And if I do my duty, and do right, you will sustain me, will you not?" To renewed cheers and shouts of "Yes! Yes! We will!" he concluded: "Received, as I am, by the members of a Legislature the majority of whom do not agree with me in political sentiments, I trust that I may have their assistance in piloting the ship of State through this voyage, surrounded by perils as it is; for, if it should suffer attack now, there will be no pilot ever needed for another voyage."[39]

Lincoln's iron-fisted Assembly oration would surely have captured the headlines and historical attention that day, had not it been preceded minutes earlier by one of the most remarkable speeches of Lincoln's entire journey—arguably one of the most intimate and personally revealing of his career. Inspired by his reverence for George Washington and his proximity to the scene of one of his triumphs—the old Hessian barracks stood just across the road—his words to the Senate that day were inflected as well by the experiences of his own prairie boyhood, far away, where he had first, and indelibly, absorbed the story of the place where he now stood. It came almost as a digression when Lincoln began searching his memory for the lessons history had taught him, and in a voice "as soft and sympathetic as a girl's," confided:

> May I be pardoned if, upon this occasion, I mention that away back in my childhood, the earliest days of my being able to read, I got hold of a small book, such a one as few of the younger members have ever seen, "Weem's [sic] Life of Washington." I remember all the accounts there given of the battle fields and struggles for the liberties of the country, and none fixed themselves upon my imagination so deeply as the struggle here at Trenton, New-Jersey. The crossing of the river; the contest with the Hessians; the great hardships endured at that time, all fixed themselves on my memory more than any single revolutionary event; and you all know, for you have all been boys, how these early impressions last longer than any others. I recollect thinking then, boy even though I was, that there must have been something more than common that those men struggled for. I am exceedingly anxious that that thing which they struggled for; that something even more than National Independence; that something that held out a great promise to all the people of the world to all time to come; I am exceedingly anxious that this Union, the Constitution, and the liberties of the people shall be perpetuated in accordance with the original idea for which that struggle was made, and I shall be most happy indeed if I shall be an humble instrument in the hands of the Almighty, and of this, his almost chosen people, for perpetuating the object of that great struggle.[40]

In a sense, it was Lincoln's most original address since the marathon at Cooper Union. There, employing a dryer style, he had appealed for unity by citing law and precedent. Now Lincoln was on to something much deeper and far more emotional—proposing, for him, an entirely

new definition of American "civil religion." This concept he had introduced a generation earlier by stressing "cold, calculating, unimpassioned
reason."[41] Now, twenty-three years later in Trenton, Lincoln's notion of
civil religion and what he had earlier called "gratitude to our fathers"[42]
approached a messianic belief in American exceptionalism—the idea
that God shone special grace on the land conceived in liberty and dedicated to the proposition that all men are created equal.

To frame this new interpretation, Lincoln wove together threads he
had barely hinted at in his Farewell Address. Back in Springfield, just
two weeks before, he had boldly imagined himself Washington's heir,
calling for divine guidance to sustain the conceit. Now he went further,
binding the two notions into one, suggesting that Washington's struggle,
and the entire American experiment, had been divinely blessed, its
founding generation "almost chosen people," as singularly ordained as
the Hebrews of the Old Testament. Invoking divine will and the founders within a new exceptionalist paradigm, Lincoln did nothing less than
direct God and public memory toward a renewed justification for the
perpetuity of the Union. And if Americans were still but "almost chosen
people," it was perhaps only because they had not yet endured the pain
required to sanctify what He had granted them. That test, Lincoln implied, was yet to come. And to face it, he surely meant to imply, the
"almost chosen people" had chosen their next leader wisely.[43]

For any orator, even Lincoln, it would have proven impossible to
maintain these rhetorical heights. Two daring speeches behind him, he
headed off to what was to be a "splendid collation" at the nearby Trenton House, but which in John Hay's words turned into a "tedious and
irritating" affair at which guests armed with forks had no food, and din-
ers "surrounded by all the luxurious varieties of cold cut had no forks."[44]
With the first course comically delayed, Lincoln, his energies spent,
could do no better than offer an anticlimactic greeting from the front
balcony, in which he clumsily asserted that it "would be disgusting to my
friends around me" to deliver yet another oration. As he had hinted to
the "hungry and tired" guests at the banquet, "speech-making, while
very good in itself, was becoming rather a bore."[45]

The whirlwind visit at an end in less than three hours, Lincoln departed New Jersey's capital city by 2:30 P.M.[46] "No man could look upon Lincoln's face, and hear his voice," concluded the city's Republican paper, "without becoming thoroughly satisfied that he was an honest man, and that he had no thought but what was in consonance with the good of his *whole* country." The journal reported "several prominent Democrats" admitting that, "though they had come here with strong prejudices against Mr. Lincoln, they would return to their homes fully satisfied that he was 'the right man for the right place.' " It was not only what he said, the paper concluded, but "the *manner* of his saying it."[47]

Two hours later, at 3:45, again to the roar of cannon fire, Lincoln's train pulled into the Kensington depot in another historic city, Philadelphia, to a reception the local paper asserted, "surpassed everything which he had yet experienced in the way of popular demonstration." Here, 100,000 "old men and young men, wives and maidens, matrons and children, all anxious for a sight of the hero of the hour," choked the flag-festooned streets all the way to Lincoln's hotel, the Continental House, cheering and waving handkerchiefs as Lincoln stood in an open carriage pulled by four plumed white horses.[48]

With the inaugural journey finally nearing its conclusion, incident-free, the local Republican newspaper took pains to salute all its participants, commiserating with Major Hunter over his injured arm, saluting Captain Hazzard for his cultivated manners, acknowledging that Captain Pope had "endeared himself" to Lincoln with his "strongly expressed devotion to the Union," and lauding Colonel Ellsworth for managing "to protect the President elect from the importunities of curious crowds." Even the harried William Wood earned a share of the plaudits. "Had it not been for his experience, energy, firmness and tirelessness," the paper declared, "the trip would have proved an intolerable annoyance to the Presidential party, owing to the stupidity, laziness and jealousy of the members of the local Committees in the different stopping places."[49] Little did any of these characters—or the reporter—realize that their gravest challenge was yet before them.

First, appearing on the hotel balcony—thickly bearded now, predict-

ably looking to one reporter "much more prepossessing than his portraits," and likewise to an eighteen-year-old schoolgirl visiting from
Illinois, "better looking than his pictures"[50]—Lincoln acknowledged
an official welcome from Mayor Alexander Henry, who assured the
president-elect: "Your fellow countrymen look to you in the earnest
hope that true statesmanship and unalloyed patriotism may with God's
blessing restore peace and prosperity to this distracted land."[51] To this,
Lincoln yet again insisted that "the crisis, the panic, the anxiety of the
country at this time is artificial." Perhaps deciding he had gone too far,
he hastened to add: "I do not mean to say that this artificial panic has
not done harm. That it has done much harm I do not deny."[52]

Lincoln's response was to pledge himself anew to "peace and harmony and prosperity." But then, his thoughts again straying to the founding fathers whose spirit reigned strongest here in Philadelphia, he added
a vow to honor "those breathings rising within the consecrated walls
where the Constitution of the United States and, I will add, the Declaration of American Independence was originally framed"—Independence
Hall, the American shrine sitting only blocks away. With considerable
passion, he assured the crowd "that I shall do nothing inconsistent with
the teachings of those holy and most sacred walls. I have never asked
anything that does not breathe from those walls. All my political warfare
has been in favor of the teachings coming forth from that sacred hall."
Then, quoting Psalms with almost fire-and-brimstone zeal, he vowed:
"May my right hand forget its cunning and my tongue cleave to the roof
my mouth, if ever I prove false to those teachings." Though a reporter
stationed in the street insisted "that not one person in the crowd below
heard one word of Lincoln's speech," it was widely reprinted—serving
well as a prelude to the next morning's widely anticipated events at the
revered historic site.[53]

Lincoln's long day was not yet done, however, and after dining with
Mary at the hotel, he was obliged to perform receiving line duty along
its main staircase beginning at 8:30 P.M., greeting well-wishers, beaming
good-naturedly at repeated shouts of "Honest Old Abe," and enduring
the usual shoving, gape-mouthed stares, and endless small talk. Then at

ten, together with crowds still ringing the hotel, he watched in awe as a dazzling fireworks show illuminated the Philadelphia night, highlighted by the eruption of silvery letters within a red, white, and blue wall of fire, miraculously forming the words "Welcome, Abraham Lincoln. The Whole Union."[54]

Once this marvel evaporated in the cold winter sky, Lincoln retreated for a secret conference that not only generated fireworks of its own, but also abruptly changed the spirit of the entire inaugural journey.

AT NORMAN JUDD'S urgent request, the president-elect agreed to visit his friend's hotel room after the pyrotechnics and meet there with a Scottish-born sleuth named Allan Pinkerton. The detective had convinced himself—and Judd—that he possessed evidence of a well-planned scheme to murder Lincoln when he arrived at Baltimore on the 23rd.[55]

Judd had known about the plot as far back as Cincinnati, had received confirmation from Kate Warne, one of Pinkerton's female agents, while in New York, and now, frantic with worry, wanted Pinkerton himself to lay out the facts for the president-elect, who had remained stubbornly oblivious to concerns about his safety. The detective, who operated under the aliases E. I. Allen, J. H. Hutcheson, or the code name "Plums," had initially shared his discovery with his client Samuel M. Felton, president of the Philadelphia, Wilmington & Baltimore Railroad, who had hired him a month earlier to investigate rumors that secessionists might try to sabotage "our road." Lincoln knew of Pinkerton's reputation, Judd added, and "had the utmost confidence in him."[56]

The president-elect made his way to Judd's room at around 10:15 P.M., deploying Colonel Ellsworth to guard the door against intruders. Eventually, Lamon joined the meeting. While the men huddled there, Pinkerton remembered, a large crowd milled noisily in the hallway outside, adding to the palpable tension. As Lincoln listened "very attentively," his expression betraying no emotion, asking questions only "occasionally," Pinkerton methodically laid out the details of what he had learned:[57] Once the inaugural special pulled into Baltimore's Calvert Street station, a gang of well-armed pro-secession "Bullies" planned to stage a diversionary brawl outside just as Lincoln entered the narrow vestibule leading out into the street. When policemen rushed out to investigate, as surely they would, Lincoln would be left "entirely unprotected and at the mercy of a mob of Secessionists who were to surround him at that time" and take his life. Members of the gang had enthusiastically drawn straws to determine which of them would enjoy the "honor" of striking the fatal blow. "Calm and self-possessed" as he absorbed this distressing report, Pinkerton recalled, Lincoln's "only sentiments appeared to be those of profound regret." The detective was adamant: Lincoln must avoid a public appearance in Baltimore. This was "the only way to save the country from Bloodshed."[58]

Before the president-elect could respond, Norman Judd injected an additional concern: the probable political fallout should Lincoln choose to heed this warning and alter his itinerary. Much as he believed the assassination threat genuine, Judd predicted that dodging it would elicit "sneers and scoffs" from "friend & foe alike." This was especially likely since the justification for any change of plan would have to be withheld so as not to endanger the Pinkerton operatives who had infiltrated secessionist hotbeds. Without proof, the press and public were bound to be skeptical about "the existence of so desperate a plot." As Lincoln and Judd both knew, ridicule was, to a politician, a fate nearly as awful as death itself. Charges of cowardice were perhaps worse. Judd did not want his friend to do anything to "bring you into ridicule, because you are to bear the burthen of the thing." Assuring Judd that he "appreciated these suggestions," Lincoln replied without "agitation" that he "could stand anything that was necessary."[59]

Threats were nothing new to Lincoln—especially over the last few weeks, when his correspondence had been filled with warnings of "midnight and noonday assassin[s]" prepared to "destroy many lives to reach your plate with poison."[60] But he long believed that assassination was not in the American character. "I never attached much importance," he insisted, to rumors of "people who were intending to do me mis-

chief . . . never wanted to believe any such thing."[61] Essentially corrob-
orating Pinkerton's version of the meeting, Lincoln admitted a few years
later: "Pinkerton informed me that a plan had been laid for my assassination, the exact time when I expected to go through Baltimore being
publicly known. He was well informed as to the plan, but did not know
that the conspirators would have the pluck to go execute it. He urged
me to go right through with him to Washington that night."[62]

Leaving town immediately, however, was out of the question. "I cannot consent to this," Lincoln declared. "I shall hoist the Flag on Independence Hall to-morrow morning and go to Harrisburg to-morrow,
then I have fulfilled all my engagements, and if you"—addressing Judd—
and "you Allan"—meaning Pinkerton—"think there is positive danger
in my attempting to go through Baltimore openly according to the publicized programme . . . I shall endeavor to get away quietly from the
people at Harrisburgh [sic] to-morrow evening and shall place myself in
your [hands]." Lincoln's "firmness of tone" indicated to Pinkerton "that
there was no further arguing."[63] For tonight, the matter was closed. The
president-elect rose to leave and the meeting ended.

Reentering the hallway and elbowing his way back through the persistent throng to return to his own suite, Lincoln found another shock
awaiting him in his bedroom. There sat William H. Seward's son, Frederick, who had been ushered there secretly by Lamon after seeking out
Robert Lincoln on the hotel landing and asking him to arrange an audience. Young Seward, too, desperately needed a moment of Lincoln's
time.

Now, as Lincoln listened, Frederick reported that he had raced to
Philadelphia from Washington at his father's urgent request, armed with
an important letter from the senator. Lincoln took it, sat down at a
table, and began reading its contents under the gaslight. There were
actually three letters in the package Frederick Seward brought with him.
First was a note from Frederick's father, bearing the astonishing news
that, based on an altogether separate and independent investigation,
General Scott, too, believed Lincoln should "reconsider" his arrangements out of fear for his personal safety.[64] Enclosed with Seward's brief

letter was another, from Scott to Seward, introducing "my friend" Colonel Charles P. Stone, "a distinguished young officer" who had served under the old general in Mexico. Lincoln probably took note of Scott's tone—"my friend," he had written with uncharacteristic informality. Scott usually took pains to write of himself in the third person; here it was clear he was rushing, worried, neglecting to inject the usual ceremonial flourish. This was because Stone, as Scott explained, had "an important communication to make."[65]

Completing the package was Stone's report. It quoted a New York "detective officer" who had been on duty in Baltimore for three weeks and now believed "there is serious danger of violence to and the assassination of Mr Lincoln in his passage through that city should the time of that passage be known." A band of "rowdies holding secret meetings" there had expressed "threats of mobbing and violence." The peril, the detective concluded, was not only "imminent," but "one which the authorities & people in Baltimore cannot guard against[.]" Colonel Stone's proposed solution eerily echoed Pinkerton's: "All risk might be easily avoided by a change in the travelling arrangements which would bring Mr Lincoln & a portion of his party through Baltimore by a night train without previous notice."[66]

Unmentioned—it would have meant little at the time, but a great deal just a few months later—was the fact that the "detective officer" in question, John A. Kennedy, superintendent of the New York Metropolitan Police, had taken his discoveries to Captain Stone only after considering, then rejecting, the notion of sharing the incendiary secret with a different officer: Virginia-born Robert E. Lee, who had captured abolitionist John Brown in 1859 but would earn his greatest fame fighting against Lincoln, not for him. Instead, in a matter of hours—for all the correspondence now in Lincoln's hands bore today's date, February 21—Stone had rushed Kennedy's warning to Scott, an alarmed Scott had shared it with Seward, and Seward had summoned his son and entrusted him to speed it to Lincoln "wherever he is."[67]

The president-elect "made no exclamation" as he digested this new evidence, and Frederick could detect "no sign of surprise in his face."

The young visitor remembered only that Lincoln's looked a bit more careworn than in his recent pictures, a defect more than compensated by a warm smile. But Lincoln stopped smiling soon enough. Suddenly, he unleashed a barrage of questions. "Did you hear any thing about the way this information was obtained? Did you hear any names mentioned . . . such a name as Pinkerton?" No, Frederick insisted, he had heard the news from his father, through Scott. Only then did Lincoln confide that, just moments before, another source had issued precisely the same warning—about "an attempt on my life in the confusion and hurlyburly of the reception at Baltimore."

"Surely, Mr. Lincoln," young Seward replied, "that is strong corroboration of the news I bring you." Lincoln merely smiled again, admitting there might be "something in it" if "different persons, not knowing of each other's work," had uncovered "separate clues that led to the same result. But," he cautioned, "if this is only the same story, filtered through two channels, and reaching me in two ways, then that don't make it any stronger. Don't you see?" It was getting late—he need not make a final decision that night—and thanking his visitor for his concern, Lincoln assured him, "I shall think it over carefully and decide it right, and I will let you know in the morning."[68] Only later did Lincoln convince himself that Seward and Scott "knew nothing of Pinkerton's movements," concluding that the threat was indeed genuine. "I now believed such a plot to be in existence."[69]

As well he should have. There is strong additional evidence to support the belief that Lincoln knew about the Baltimore plot even before he began the first of that night's disquieting meetings—weeks, in fact, before either Pinkerton's or Kennedy's separate investigations ever reached his ears. He surely retained his remarkable composure at the hotel that evening because neither revelation came as a particular surprise.

Back on February 5, Henry C. Bowen, editor of the New York antislavery weekly The Independent, first brought the outlines of such a scheme to Lincoln's attention in a confidential mailing. Lincoln undoubtedly received Bowen's communication while still in Springfield.

Enclosed within was a letter Bowen had received that same day from one Charles Gould, reporting that "traitors" planned to "kill Mr Lincoln on his way to Washington," and advising that it would be "impossible" for him to "go in safety to the Capital when his progress is known to the public." Gould had learned this from none other than Samuel Felton! The same railroad executive who hired Pinkerton evidently leaked the preliminary results of his investigation to Gould more than two weeks before Judd learned of it and took the report officially to Lincoln. Weeks before the Pinkerton meeting, Gould was already adamant that the president take the needed precautions, pointing out "he is no longer simply Mr Lincoln. We have elected him to the office of President; and on his life and his inauguration rests the question of government or revolution. We must not run a risk for the car which carries him to Washington, carries the welfare of a great nation."[70]

If Bowen and Gould were unable to persuade the president-elect through the mail, there is reason to believe they made their case again in person when Lincoln visited New York; Bowen told Lincoln he would do so, and likely tried. A year earlier, Lincoln had called on Bowen at his newspaper office to chat about the upcoming Cooper Union engagement. Busy as he was, the president-elect would have certainly made time for a reciprocal visit. But even if the editor did not turn up at the Astor House as promised, Lincoln would soon have the opportunity to read about the supposedly secret threat—on the pages of Bowen's newspaper. On February 21, the same day as the nighttime Pinkerton-Judd meeting, Horace Greeley published his opinion that Lincoln was "in peril of outrage, indignity, and death," and that "substantial cash rewards" had been "openly proffered in the Cotton States to whomsoever" would kill Lincoln "before the 4th of March." Sounding an eerily prescient note, Greeley concluded: "Only begirt with a mighty army or disguised like a fugitive felon or spy, could the elected Chief Magistrate of Thirty Millions of Freemen pass through eight or ten of the States which he has been chosen to lead."[71]

Thus the warnings Lincoln was asked to digest in Philadelphia were in a way not revelations at all, merely confirmations. Moreover, though he told his friends and advisors on February 21 that he would delay a final decision about how to confront the Baltimore threat, Lincoln already knew that, at best, his visit there would not unfold as planned. The press had announced that he would arrive the next day around 1 P.M., head to the Eutaw House hotel in an open carriage, and after dining there, would return to the southbound depot at 2:30 for the final leg of the trip to Washington. But the same paper reported that plans to greet Lincoln with marching bands had been scuttled for fear that mere music would "produce a disturbance of the most violent and dangerous character to the President and all who are with him." [72] A few days earlier, while in Albany, Governor Morgan had handed Lincoln a letter from loyal Maryland Republican Worthington Snethen, further alerting him that Baltimore's mayor and council refused to extend formal hospitality. Under the circumstances, Snethen now felt it "inadvisable" to "attempt any organized public display on our part." [73]

Taking such threats ever more seriously, Lincoln had already conceded one point in the name of security. He had changed his mind about the accommodations required for the nine nights his family would spend in Washington before moving into the Executive Mansion. Montgomery Blair had offered "a spare room" at his famous home across from the White House—the very chamber Jackson once occupied. [74] Although Lincoln declined his hospitality, he briefly entertained the idea of taking over an entire dwelling until Inauguration Day. Horrified when he learned in Albany that Lincoln was considering such a plan, Thurlow Weed had insisted, "it will never do. . . . He is now public property, and ought to be where he can be reached by the people until he is inaugurated." Lincoln not only agreed, but seized Weed's clever phrasing as justification and, as usual, improved on it. Choosing a hotel would "give mortal offense to our friends," he conceded, and for this he was sorry. But as he had come to realize: "The truth is, I suppose I am now public property; and a public inn is the place where people can have access to me." [75]

On February 15, writing from Cleveland, Lincoln had advised Congressman Elihu Washburne that he had "decided to stop at a public, rather than a private house when I reach Washington." He neither elaborated nor explained—except to alert Washburne that Mary objected to the National Hotel "on account of the sickness four years ago"—the outbreak of intestinal complaints that had afflicted Buchanan while he waited there for his own inauguration.[76] Washburne protested, insisting "a furnished house" serviced by "the most reliable and trustworthy servants (colored)," would help keep things "much better controlled."[77] Lincoln held firm—like a chain of steel. The congressman ended up booking Lincoln a suite of rooms at the very hotel where the Peace Convention was now deadlocked over procedural trifles: Willard's.

Still, the question of how—and when—Lincoln would arrive remained unsettled as of 11 P.M. on February 21. As Lincoln retired for the night at Philadelphia's Continental House, Judd and Pinkerton, now in concert with railroad and telegraph officials, worked hours longer to hash out a blueprint to spirit him safely through Baltimore. Frederick Seward was sent back to Washington, Lamon testified, "with just enough information to enable his father to anticipate the exact moment of Mr. Lincoln's surreptitious arrival in Washington."[78] Aside from this, the advisors agonized over whom to tell and whom to exclude, worrying anew even about his "superintendent of arrangements," William Wood, especially after Lincoln confessed to Pinkerton that, in fact, he had known nothing at all about him until William Seward's friends recommended him to organize the trip. With danger lurking, everyone now fell under suspicion. Meanwhile, totally unaware of these developments, the rest of Philadelphia continued to celebrate well into the night.

SHORTLY AFTER SUNRISE the next morning, his fully exposed open carriage preceded by a marching band and an elite cadre of aging Mexican War veterans, Lincoln calmly left the Continental House for his first visit in years to Independence Hall.[79] He would make two speeches that cold, crystal-clear day, one inside, and one outside the "sacred hall" where America had been born and where pro-Compromise demonstrators had rallied just two months before.

Here, the spirit of place again inspired Lincoln to new explorations of the meaning of the American experiment—and he offered a fresh, history-suffused argument for why the country was worth saving. This was the site, Lincoln told the City Council and other dignitaries gathered inside, "where were collected together the wisdom, the patriotism, the devotion to principle, from which sprang the institutions under which we live." Once again aligning himself with the founders, Lincoln reminded his audience that "all the political sentiments I entertain have been drawn, so far as I have been able to draw them, from the sentiments which originated, and were given to the world from this hall in which we stand. I have never had a feeling politically that did not spring from the sentiments embodied in the Declaration of Independence."

What were those feelings? What specifically were those sentiments? Lincoln was now ready to offer a definition, a new way to express his long-held belief that political freedom generates economic opportunity.[80] "It was not the mere matter of the separation of the colonies from the mother land; but something in that Declaration giving liberty not alone to the people of this country, but hope to the world for all future time. It was that which gave promise that in due time the weights should be lifted from the shoulders of all men, and that *all* should have an equal chance." Put another way, revolution for revolution's sake—like Southern secession, based not on liberation but on enslavement—defied this requisite spirit.

"Now, my friends," he asked in conclusion, "can this country be saved upon that basis? If it can, I will consider myself one of the happiest men in the world if I can help to save it. If it can't be saved upon that principle, it will be truly awful. But, if this country cannot be saved without giving up that principle"—and here he paused, surely thinking now of the threats facing him in Baltimore, and suddenly interjected— "I was about to say I would rather be assassinated on this spot than to surrender it." Norman Judd was convinced that the startling "reference to sacrificing himself for his country" was "induced by the incidents of the night preceding."[81]

Then it was outside to the plaza in front of the building, where a large wooden platform stood awaiting the dignitaries for a flag-raising ceremony. Another giant banner lay draped across the length of the front railing, facing a line of soldiers, rifles on their shoulders. As boys clung to tree branches for good views, local photographer F. DeBourg Richards exposed the only known Lincoln pictures of this entire inaugural journey. Blurred and indistinct, the shots nonetheless reveal the unmistakably tall figure, stovepipe hat in hand as he arrives on the platform, then later as he begins to speak, the edge of the flag lowered to expose the lectern. Here, however imperfect, were the first known photographs of an American president-elect.[82]

Now Lincoln spoke of "cherishing that fraternal feeling which has so long characterized us as a nation, excluding passion, ill-temper and precipitate action on all occasions." Noting proudly that the flag now boasted thirty-four stars—the last of which represented Kansas, admitted to the Union as a free state less than a month before—he boldly predicted that "we may promise ourselves that not only the new star placed upon that flag shall be permitted to remain there to our permanent prosperity for years to come, but additional ones shall from time to time be placed there, until we shall number as was anticipated by the great historian, five hundred millions of happy and prosperous people."[83]

Lincoln had come a long way since his stumbling tariff speech at Pittsburgh. After days of alternating between messages of conciliation and near-coercion, he had used his visit to the cradle of American freedom to probe the moral basis for the founding—and to find new urgency in its promise that all men were created equal. To Lincoln, he had been trying merely "to harmonize and give shape to the feelings that had been really the feelings of my whole life." Perhaps so, but one savvy eyewitness understood immediately the revolutionary character of what Lincoln was now saying: by here and now reiterating the promise of opportunity, he was in effect pledging to extend freedom to every "individual man . . . white, red, yellow or black," offering "nothing less than the progressive steps of African emancipation."[84]

As the crowd gaped, Lincoln then proceeded to hoist the huge new flag to the top of the pole "by the strength of my own feeble arm," watching it "flaunting gloriously to the wind without an accident, in the bright glowing sun-shine of the morning." A man who believed in signs and wonders, Lincoln convinced himself that "there was in the entire success of that beautiful ceremony, at least something of an omen of what is to come." So he wished to believe. A loud cheer erupted from the ten thousand men and women who had braved the early hour and frigid weather to pack Chestnut Street all the way from Fifth to Sixth.[85] The local paper reported that Lincoln drew the halyards "with a firm hand," and then joined the onlookers in gazing tearfully at the unfurled banner as a band let out with a patriotic air and the Washington Greys fired a salute. Its report ricocheted smartly over the hallowed square.[86]

After returning briefly to his hotel, then riding in yet another procession through still crowded streets toward the West Philadelphia depot, where Lincoln boarded the Prince of Wales car and after pausing briefly for another artillery salute, commenced his detour to Harrisburg by 9:30. The festively decorated train slowed down at Haverford to acknowledge a crowd of college students, then stopped at Leaman Place long enough only for Lincoln to bring the diminutive Mary out to the platform—having concluded to offer the crowd "the long and the short of it!" If he was anxious, he showed no outward signs.

Yet it would prove difficult to surpass his performance in the City of Brotherly Love. Arriving under "sharp and bracing" sunshine at Lancaster, Lincoln declined to orate at length at the town's Cadwell House by explaining "it is well known that the more a man speaks the less he is understood—the more he says one thing, his adversaries contend he meant something else."[87] The feeble joke fell on unsympathetic ears. Hay thought it unusual that a city with so substantial a Quaker population should be filled with such "rough, unruly, and ill bred" crowds, among whom "not one man in a hundred cheered." For most of the day, unaware Lincoln might be troubled by last night's news about Baltimore, Hay reported that the president-elect was "so unwell he could hardly be persuaded to show himself." Lincoln did manage to summon the strength to gaze out the train window in time to enjoy a fleeting view of Wheatland, the Lancaster estate President Buchanan would soon reoccupy once he ceded the White House to his successor.[88]

Sometime during this four-and-a-half-hour, hundred-mile ride west, Judd laid out for Lincoln the elaborate plan he, Pinkerton, and a few loyal railroad and telegraph executives had concocted late the previous night to get him safely to Washington. Lincoln would quietly leave Harrisburg on a special train around six that evening, arriving back in Philadelphia by eleven and secretly transferring there to the regular overnight train to Baltimore, then Washington. Only one person—yet to be determined—would accompany him on this final leg of the trip. Pinkerton would meet the party back in Philadelphia and escort it all the way to the capital. As a precaution, the cars speeding Lincoln to Baltimore would enjoy unimpeded right-of-way: every other train along the road would be sidetracked, the telegraph lines in and out of Harrisburg cut to preclude leaks. William Wood would be told nothing. Mary and the boys would follow out of Harrisburg the following morning as if nothing had occurred.[89]

These whispered conferences on board the Harrisburg-bound special aroused considerable suspicion that morning. "Judd there is something up," Nicolay observed at one point, perhaps recalling Bowen's February 5 warning letter, which habit suggests he had surely read even before Lincoln did. "George," replied Judd, "there is no necessity fore your Knowing & one man can keep a secret better than two."[90] Like the secretary, Lamon and Ellsworth, too, concluded that "something was on foot" but "judiciously refrained" from asking questions. "I reckon they will laugh at us, Judd," Lincoln finally remarked. "You had better get them together." Judd arranged to brief the entire party before that evening's dinner in Harrisburg.[91]

Arriving at the state capital at 1:30 P.M., Lincoln calmly assured Governor Curtin—and the masses of people gathered at the Jones House hotel—that "I am quite sure I do not deceive myself when I tell you I bring to the work an honest heart." Even in the face of a "drunken, fighting, noisy crowd,"[92] Lincoln seemed in a pacific mood, telling the region's "Friends" that there was no "more devoted lover of peace, harmony and concord than my humble self." Then, reacting to a spruce display of military precision by units of the National Guard, local Zouaves, and other companies, he expressed "the hope that in the shedding of blood their services may never be needed." He concluded with a vow he soon would find himself hard-pressed to keep: "With my consent, or without my great displeasure, this country shall never witness the shedding of one drop of blood in fraternal strife."[93]

Finally came the promised speech to the Pennsylvania State Assembly. Acknowledging his appearance occurred "upon the birthday of the Father of his Country," repeating his hope that no blood would ever be spilled in a brother-against-brother war, Lincoln provided in this, the final public utterance of his journey, one last justification for the controversial "no crisis" sentiments he had offered days before at Pittsburgh. "I now wish only to say, in regard to that matter, that the few remarks which I uttered on that occasion were rather carefully worded. I took pains that they should be so. I have seen no occasion since to add to them or subtract from them. I leave them precisely as they stand."[94] In other words, he assured this city, this state, and the entire country one more time—"*there is no crisis*, excepting such a one as may be gotten up at any time by turbulent men, aided by designing politicians."[95] With that anticlimactic summary of the situation, Lincoln's long, eventful, pre-inaugural speaking tour came to an end at last.

For endurance alone, the journey was a resounding triumph of absolutely unprecedented proportions. To this point, Lincoln had traversed more than 1,900 miles on eighteen different railroad lines, through seven states and uncountable towns and villages. In total, he had delivered no fewer than 101 known speeches—orating from the back of his trains, at rail depots, hotels, state houses, municipal buildings, and historic sites, indoors and outdoors alike; from legislative chambers, hotel lobbies, parlors, restaurants, windows, and balconies; on wooden platforms, bridges, and roadsides—thirty-five speeches in Ohio, twenty-six in New York, sixteen in Pennsylvania, eleven in Indiana, and ten in New Jersey, to add to the three with which he had launched his journey back in Illinois. On two different days of this eleven-day marathon he had spoken no fewer than a staggering thirteen separate times; on three other occasions, twelve times. He had addressed the state legislatures in five state capitals, mayors in several major cities. He had ridden in at least twenty-four parades and processions to and from his major destinations, shaken thousands of hands at more than a dozen formal receptions, greeted female admirers at ten or more ladies levees, raised or grasped flags, watched fireworks, received bouquets, nosegays, fruit baskets, new hats, kisses, back-slaps, and salutes, and heard more martial music and artillery fire than most seasoned military veterans. Though precise crowd counts are impossible to estimate, Lincoln probably appeared in the flesh before at least three-quarters of a million people—surely more than had ever cast their eyes on any president of the United States in all of American history.[96]

Lincoln's oratorical performances had certainly varied—ranging from colloquial greetings (not always delivered flawlessly) to stern warnings to unconvincing assurances to achingly beautiful sentiments applauded by his contemporaries and destined to live in history. Crucially, his words had reintroduced the old campaigner to his hungry, and now national, public, expanded his fame exponentially, and done little to give away the official policy he planned to unveil at his swearing in.

It is little wonder that, looking back on the journey, glad as he was when it came to an end, John Nicolay believed that "Mr. Lincoln gave his hearers the reflection and outline of his character and policy—his candor, forbearance, and liberality—his desire to remove misunderstanding; but his determination to defend the government. Most of all," he summarized of Lincoln's speeches, "they manifest[ed] his leading political trait—his reliance upon the people, and his faith that they would maintain their own cause and maintain their own liberties."[97]

BY 3 P.M. THAT unforgettable Washington's Birthday, right on schedule, Lincoln returned to Harrisburg's Jones House, ostensibly to rest before dinner. Instead, he joined Judd and slipped into the hotel parlor to finally confide the details of the new security plan to their fellow travelers. Lincoln said little at the meeting, but to no one's surprise, Bull Head Sumner loudly protested the scheme. Sneaking through Baltimore, the battle-toughened colonel bellowed, "will be a d——d piece of cowardice." Allow him instead, he implored, to "get a Squad of Cavalry Sir, cut our way to Washington Sir." But Judd advised Sumner, "that view of the Case has already been presented to Mr. Lincoln" and ruled out. Nonetheless another military man in the group, George W. Hazzard, proposed Lincoln should either "yield yourself unreservedly to the protection" of fifty thousand soldiers, follow a new route across the Potomac River at Hagerstown, or leave Harrisburg "disguised."[98]

With the group fully briefed, David Davis took the floor to ask a few probing questions of his own, then turned to Lincoln and suggested he render the final judgment. The judge knew better than to venture an opinion of his own. Lincoln, he bitterly remembered, "never asked my advice on any question." Today would be no different. Lincoln's reply was definitive: "Unless there are some other reasons besides ridicule," he replied, almost sadly, "I am disposed to carry out Judd's plan."[99] The most public inaugural journey in the nation's history would end in total secrecy.

The big decision made, the subject turned to who would accompany and guard the president-elect en route. Not surprising, arguing he had been ordered "to see Mr Lincoln to Washington" safely, Sumner demanded the job go to him. Pinkerton was hardly surprised that Lincoln's "Military men were anxious," worried that a stranger "might be leading him into a trap and selling him to the Secessionists."[100] Even Lincoln's loyal young acolyte Ellsworth would be excluded. Sumner had a point: if this was a Pinkerton plot instead of a Baltimore plot, Lincoln would be sealing his own doom.

Lincoln believed his wife would be satisfied with no other protector than Ward Hill Lamon.[101] To prove he was up to the task, the self-confident Lamon flashed his formidable personal arsenal: a "brace of fine pistols, a huge bowie knife, a black-jack and a pair of brass knuckles,"[102] and even offered some of the weapons to Lincoln. But Pinkerton protested. The president-elect must not enter Washington armed, he insisted, arguing that "if fighting had to be done, it must be done by others." The weary Lincoln concurred, assuring his friends that "he wanted no arms . . . had no fears," and was confident Pinkerton's plans "would work right."[103]

For years, no one else in the nation knew that any of these secret meetings occurred. Yet the pro-secessionist humor writer George Washington Harris—creator of an illiterate fictional mountaineer named Sut Lovingood—would soon, and hilariously, imagine his character as a participant in just such delicate deliberations about the president-elect's safety. "Sutty," Harris had Lincoln imploring at this session, "what had I best do in this orful emergency? The party can't spare me now, besides I ain't fit tu die, an my whiskers hev just begin tu grow an I want tu try the vittils in Washington City; hit won't du tu let me be made a sefter by these sececshun bullits just at this time." Sut pledges to put the worried traveler "safe tu bed with Missis Linkhorn" and constructs an elaborate disguise of "hogshead fur the body, an a par ove telegraph poles for the laigs." They part with Lincoln exacting a final promise from his benefactor. "Sutty, my sun, if Alex Stephens kills me I want you tu go tu Illinoi an tell em that I died game an that my las wurds wer the Declerashun ove Independence."[104] As so often was the case with the cornpone, dialect-suffused humor so popular at that time—and Lincoln was one of the literature's biggest fans—it bore the ring of painful truth.

"Tomorrow we enter slave territory," John Hay warned a friend that holiday, trying hard to maintain his own sense of humor. "There may be trouble in Baltimore. If so, we will not go to Washington, unless in long, narrow boxes."[105]

NOT IF PINKERTON and Lamon could help it. That evening at around 5:45, someone—either Judd or Sumner or perhaps both—interrupted Governor Curtin's reception at the Jones House right on schedule, and tapped Lincoln on the shoulder to signal that the time had come for his early departure.

Fearing he might attract too much attention by leaving so soon, Lincoln at first hesitated. Only after several more reminders did he finally rise, take Curtin by the arm, and stroll out the back door of the hall "without exciting any curiosity." He was still dressed in his evening clothes. The governor, to whom the president-elect had now confided details of the Baltimore conspiracy and his revised itinerary, remembered that Lincoln only "seemed pained and surprised that a design to take his life existed, and although much concerned for his personal safety as well as for the peace of the country," but "neither in his conversation or manner exhibited alarm or fear."[106]

By some accounts, Lincoln then detoured to his room to get his coat. By others, he headed directly outside, where Pinkerton's cohort G. C. Franciscus, superintendent of the railroad line that ran between Harrisburg and Philadelphia, handed the president-elect an old overcoat. Either way, Lincoln now donned it; the night air was chilly. But he would not wear his signature silk stovepipe hat tonight—the instantly recognizable trademark would make him the tallest target in the country. Instead he drew from his pocket the wide-brimmed model he had received as a gift in New York just days before. As Lincoln remembered: "I put on the soft hat and joined my friends"—Lamon and others awaited him in a carriage—"without being recognized by strangers, for I was not the same man."[107]

Before they left, Sumner stubbornly made one last attempt to join them. At the last possible minute, Judd audaciously tapped him on the shoulder to get his attention, and when the colonel whirled round, Lincoln's carriage sped away. "A madder man," Judd admitted, "you never saw."[108] Accompanied only by Lamon, Franciscus, a few railroad officials, and a telegraph operator, Lincoln sped to the depot, boarded the two-car train that awaited them there, and headed east for Philadelphia. As soon as the train chugged out of the depot, a Pinkerton operative wired an update to his boss, using the agreed-upon, irreverent code word for the president-elect: "Nuts left at six—Everything as you directed—all is right."[109]

Enjoying unimpeded right-of-way, this first leg of the secret trip ended much sooner than anyone had predicted. The train pulled into the West Philadelphia depot at 10 P.M., nearly an hour before the sleeper was scheduled to leave a nearby station for Baltimore. After rendezvousing with Pinkerton and his operatives, Lincoln and Lamon stepped into another carriage, and with time to spare, occupied the intervening time rolling aimlessly through the streets of the city. During the carriage ride, Lincoln shared the news that William Seward believed that fifteen thousand men were preparing "to blow up the railroad tracks" or "fire the train," to prevent his safe arrival in Washington. "Here was a plot," Lamon believed, "big enough to swallow up the little one."[110]

Just minutes before the Baltimore train was scheduled to pull away, Lincoln's carriage slipped into the depot, pulled all the way up to the back of the sleeping car, and deposited its precious cargo through a rear door. Wearing his wide-brimmed felt hat and wrapped in a "Gentleman's shawl"—another eyewitness described it as a "muffler"—Lincoln would have gone unrecognized even if he were noticed.[111]

Once on board, the president-elect was put to bed in a rear berth, the curtains securely drawn, and the train left on schedule. But Lincoln got little rest, "so very tall that he could not lay straight in his berth." Besides, the travelers were all too excited to sleep. Lincoln "talked very friendly" during the voyage, whispering the occasional joke "in an undertone," recalled Pinkerton agent Kate Warne, posing on board as the mysterious passenger's sister. Otherwise the group maintained perfect silence. The only one among them who moved about was Pinkerton, who walked to the rear platform at regular intervals to look for "all safe" signals from operatives stationed with lanterns all along the route to Maryland.[112]

Some four hours later, at around 3:30 A.M., the overnight train from Philadelphia steamed into Baltimore's Calvert Street station. Kate Warne quickly left for Pinkerton's nearby safe house. It would hardly do for the press or the jealous Mary Lincoln to learn that the president-elect had traveled to the city in a sleeping car accompanied by a woman.

Now would come perhaps the most delicate part of the journey. While the other passengers inside remained asleep "as if Lincoln had never been born," rail workers uncoupled the sleeping car from its engine and hitched it to a team of horses, which hauled it, creaking and groaning, to the nearby Camden depot, there to link to an engine of the Baltimore & Ohio line for the final haul to Washington. Not a voice was heard until a drunken night watchman suddenly began pounding his club against a trackside box, shouting, "Captain, it's four o'clock." His effort to rouse some drowsy or absent ticket agent unanswered, he kept up his cry—and his pounding—for at least twenty minutes, never varying his time estimate, never succeeding in doing more than rousing all the slumbering passengers. A mirthful Lincoln, said Pinkerton, seemed to enjoy the scene, "and made several witty remarks, showing that he was as full of fun as ever."[113]

With Lincoln now fully awake and much amused, the trains were noisily coupled. But its departure was delayed for a time, and as dawn neared, the station began springing to life. Pinkerton remembered hearing "the usual bustle and activity" outside, and the president-elect "joking with rare good humor" at the sounds around them. His mood changed only when music began floating in the air—"snatches of rebel harmony," claimed Pinkerton—first the strains of the toxic anthem "Maryland My Maryland," (which had yet to be written!), then the popular tune "Dixie." Lincoln turned grimly to the detective and observed: "No doubt there will be a great time in Dixie by and by."[114] Finally, just after 4 A.M., the Washington-bound train left Baltimore for the last two hours of Lincoln's trip.

Two hours later, at 6 A.M. on Saturday, February 23, Allan Pinkerton, Ward Hill Lamon, and their famous charge slipped into the capital of the United States unrecognized—that is, nearly unrecognized. One man in the crowd inside the vast, ugly depot seemed to take note of the tall passenger who emerged from the cars and ambled across the terminal, looking "more like a well-to-do farmer . . . than the President of the United States."[115] After the president-elect passed him by, the stranger suddenly strode up, "looked very sharp at him," lunged for Lincoln's hand, and exclaimed: "Abe, you can't play that on me."

Reacting quickly, Pinkerton—or perhaps Lamon; the record is unclear—made as if to strike him. By one account, Pinkerton actually landed a blow with his elbow—"staggering him back," and then raised a fist to strike the intruder again—when Lincoln declared something like: "Don't strike him! don't strike him! It is Washburne. Don't you know him?"[116]

And then, arm in arm with the Congressman Elihu B. Washburne of Illinois—the man Lincoln had instructed, weeks earlier, to "hold firm, as with a chain of steel" and who now represented the sum and substance of his official welcoming delegation—Abraham Lincoln left the depot, and before the sun rose on a "mild and cloudy" day, boarded the horse-drawn carriage Washburne had ordered to wait, and "drove rapidly" off to the 14th Street side entrance of Willard's Hotel, safely in Washington at last.[117]

Exhausted, Lincoln asked nothing of proprietor Henry A. Willard when he arrived, except whether he might have a spare pair of bed-slippers: he had misplaced his own. Glancing at his distinguished guest's enormous boots, and realizing his own small-size footwear would never do, Willard quickly sent someone to fetch the pair owned by his wife's long-limbed grandfather. Lincoln wore old William C. Bradley's slippers for the rest of his stay.[118]

To his colleagues, Pinkerton wired the good news: "Plums arrived here with Nuts this morning—all right."[119]

Artist Thomas Nast made this sketch of the "Flag drawn to the top of the Staff by Mr. Lincoln" at Independence Hall on Washington's Birthday. Lincoln appeared in full public view knowing a murder plot awaited him the next day. (JOHN HAY LIBRARY, BROWN UNIVERSITY)

Chapter Twelve

Plain as a Turnpike Road

LINCOLN'S SUDDEN, CLANDESTINE arrival shocked Washington—triggering a public "Furore," as even Allan Pinkerton admitted—and subjected the president-elect to a barrage of deeply wounding personal criticism.[1] The secret trip undid weeks of careful reputation-building, embarrassed many Republican supporters, and provided both Democrats and Southerners with an irresistible excuse for ridicule. "How unfortunately was Mr. Lincoln advised!" smirked one Marylander. "How deplorably did he yield to his advisors!"[2]

Some placed the blame squarely on Lincoln himself. Hinting he had shown the white feather, the *Albany Atlas & Arugus* derisively attributed his "Underground Railroad" trip to fear of "ASS-ASS-IN-ATION," a charge seconded by the *Baltimore Sun*, which similarly labeled its report: "The 'Underground Railroad' Journey."[3] Readers of the day would immediately have understood the slur. In case they did not, Frederick Douglass spelled it out a bit more sympathetically in his own newspaper. Though it was likely "galling to his very soul," he pointed out, Lincoln had "reached the Capital as the poor, hunted fugitive slave reaches the North, in disguise, seeking concealment, evading pursuers by the underground railroad . . . crawling and dodging under the sable wing of night."[4]

After so confidently submitting to "formal receptions" in "all the large cities and towns of the country," predicted the *Cincinnati Enquirer*, Lincoln's "avoidance" of Baltimore was moreover sure to "subject Mr. Lincoln to imputations of fear, which will be injurious to him."[5] Baltimore's own leading daily wickedly reported the city's loyal citizens so perplexed by his failure to appear as scheduled that they cheered a suitcase bearing the initials "A.L." According to the mock dispatch, a crowd followed the unclaimed luggage all the way to the next depot, assuming "the lost President-elect might have been stowed" inside "to be smuggled through," until reminders of "his great reputed length at once dissipated the idea."[6]

Journalists outdid each other in exaggerating reports and inventing allusions. Pointing out that "Mohammedans compute time from the Hegira or flight of their Prophet from Mec[c]a to Medina, which took place July 15, 622," the *Ohio Statesman* cleverly observed: "We suppose Republicans will reckon their era from the remarkable and secret elopement of 'Old Abe' on the 23d of February, 1861, from Harrisburg to Washington." And noting that history also abounded with "remarkable instances of sudden and disguised flights *from* power"—citing the examples of Charles II fleeing Cromwell, and Louis Philippe escaping revolutionaries in France—the *New York Evening Post* announced: "Abraham Lincoln has given us the first instance of a flight *to* power [emphasis added]."[7] To the *New York Herald*, Lincoln had simply "crept into Washington" like "a thief in the night."[8]

What was worse, warned the incisive, anonymous writer who billed himself as the "Public Man, "when we have reached a point at which an elected President of the United States consents to be smuggled through by night to the capital of the country, lest he should be murdered in one of the chief cities of the Union, who can blame the rest of the world for believing that we are a failure?"[9] Such reactions threatened to unravel the message Lincoln so earnestly conveyed at Philadelphia: that the rest of the world looked to America to preserve hope for people everywhere by preserving democracy here. As a result of his Baltimore "escapade," one Washington correspondent reported, Lincoln had "but few defenders here."[10] And a pro-Lincoln Indiana paper reported that news of the president-elect's secret nighttime ride had been received by local Republicans "with deep humiliation."[11] Even the ardently pro-Lincoln *New York Tribune* expressed the hope that "this is to be the last sacrifice of the kind required of him." A Louisville paper went so far as to charge that Lincoln had exchanged clothing with his wife at Harrisburg and stolen through Baltimore in a dress—an eerie preview of the libels that his counterpart, Jefferson Davis, would endure during his flight *from* his capital four years later. The same journal printed a new version of *Yankee Doodle* with new words to the air inspired by the president-elect's nighttime journey:[12]

> Uncle Abe had gone to bed,
> The night was dark and rainy—
> A laurelled night-cap on his head,
> 'Way down in Pennsylvany.
>
> They went and got a special train
> At midnight's solemn hour,
> And in a cloak and Scotch plaid shawl,
> He dodged from the Slave-Power.
>
> Refrain:
>
> Lanky Lincoln came to town
> In night and wind, and rain, sir
> Wrapped in a military cloak,
> Upon a special train, sir.

Not unexpected, Southern newspapers were the most unrestrained in their abuse, with the Washington correspondent for the *Charleston Mercury* reporting: "Everybody here is disgusted at his cowardly and undignified entry." Hints of "Railway plots, powder plots, [and] assassination plots," the paper judged to be insufficiently credible to "relieve the tall person . . . of the imputation of the most wretched cowardice."[13]

The most fevered assaults erupted not in words but in pictures—and these proved even more indelible than the cavils in the papers. Rarely did the nation's dailies take the trouble to publish woodcut illustrations. But two days after Lincoln's incognito arrival in Washington, the Baltimore incident inspired the Democratic *Cleveland Plain Dealer* to unveil a scathing front-page caricature depicting Lincoln on the run, the tails of his exaggerated muffler dangling in the wind as he flees. Entitled " 'Hail to the Chief!' 'Old Abe' in his late traveling costume between Harrisburgh [sic] and Washington. The Fright and Flight of the President Elect,"[14] it proved the first, but by no means the last, pictorial assault. Cartoonists went on to subject Lincoln to the most merciless barrage of lampooning since the no-holds-barred days of the 1860 campaign. In those introductory images, pro and con alike, Lincoln had typically appeared in an open-necked linsey-woolsey shirt, clutching a log rail, representing the self-made man. Now he was outfitted in humiliating garb designed to brand him as a coward.

Elihu Washburne, the man who met the president-elect at the Washington depot, testified that Lincoln appeared in "a soft, low-crowned hat, a muffler around his neck, and a short bob-tailed overcoat." But on February 25, *New York Times* traveling correspondent Joseph Howard, no doubt irked at being stranded in Harrisburg without the man he was assigned to cover, filed a report asserting that Lincoln had fled toward the capital wearing "a Scotch plaid Cap and very long military cloak so that he was entirely unrecognizable."[15] Howard's barb may have cloaked a retributive payback for being abandoned: having perhaps heard of Pinkerton's involvement and surely noticed Lamon's disappearance, his choice of description amounted to a symbolic taunt that at least Lincoln's inner circle would recognize: "Colonel" Lamon—he had held an official Illinois commission as Colonel of Artillery for days now—was represented by the military cloak, and the Scottish-born cop became the "Scotch Cap."

In the cartoonists' spirited exaggerations, with no more evidence at hand than Howard's libel, Lincoln's slouch hat and long overcoat morphed into a plaid-accented tam and voluminous greatcoat. The dignified gentleman hailed in recent articles for parading bravely through the nation's cities disintegrated into a quaking sneak. *Vanity Fair*, for one, portrayed "The New President of the United States" as a giant apparition submerged in an overcoat, his face completely masked. And *Harper's Weekly* mocked him in a hilarious four-panel cartoon called "The Flight of Abraham," in which a spindly-legged Lincoln initially rejects the plan to evade Baltimore ("Run—no—nev-a-r-r—let em Shoo-o-t"), then, relents, and races toward Washington disguised in a cape and tam.[16]

Once such interpretations gained visual currency, Lincoln could even be shown by the widely read *Vanity Fair* in the ultimate humiliation: bare-kneed in a kilt and feathered cap, dancing a bow-legged "McLincoln Highland Fling"[17] at the Harrisburg station, a caricature that came perilously close to depicting Lincoln as a cross-dresser.[18] The only fortunate aspect of this bombardment for its victim was that perhaps the most scathing of all these image-shattering caricatures remained unknown until after the Civil War except to a small number of the artist's fellow Baltimore "Copperheads"—antiwar Democrats who lived within the Union. The work of Adalbert Volck, a gifted anti-Union etcher, the inspired composition showed the door of a freight car sliding open to reveal a wide-eyed Lincoln, adorned in a double-breasted, ankle-length coat, a Scotch cap low on his head, recoiling at the mere sight of a hissing cat. To identify the cargo on board, Volck imposed the dismissive label: "freight[:] Bones/cap[acit]y 000."[19]

Insisting that Lincoln had worn nothing more concealing than "an overcoat thrown loose over his shoulders without his arms being in the sleeves, and a black Kossuth hat"—the very hat given him in New York—Pinkerton later branded "the story of the Scotch cap" as "a falsehood made out of whole cloth," apparently unaware of the pun.[20] Washburne agreed, dismissing the "Scotch cap" and "big shawl" story as "mere stuff."[21] And John Hay tried, too, to "dispel the picturesque illusion," yet admitted it was "too dramatic to be squelched."[22] In its day, the calumny had longer legs than the president-elect himself. For years to

Baltimore etcher Adalbert Volck portrayed Lincoln passing through his city as a coward cringing from a freight car, alarmed by a hissing cat. (LINCOLN MUSEUM)

come, anti-Lincoln cartoons—using the Scotch cap as a trenchant background prop—would periodically revive the indignity by including oblique, damning visual references to "The Flight of Abraham."[23]

Not surprising, Lincoln quickly came to regret his entrance. So he confided to his Illinois friend Henry Clay Whitney, admitting, "I do not think I should have been killed, or even that a serious attempt would have been made to kill me," but adding: "It ain't best to run a risk of any consequence for looks' sake."[24] To Pennsylvania Republican Alexander K. McClure, however, even conceding "reasonable grounds for apprehension," Lincoln later sighed that the trip was "one of the grave mistakes in his public career."[25]

In the full light of history, scholars and skeptics have continued to wonder: was the "Flight of Abraham" justified? Was the danger genuine? Although detectives hyperbolically identified the would-be assassin as a mysterious Corsican-born barber (who sounds rather too much like the stereotyped gangster-villain of 1930s films), verifiable evidence strongly suggests that some kind of threat did exist.[26] One Baltimore Republican wrote Lincoln that while his detour "fell like a thunder clap upon the community," a genuine attack was "*meditated and determined*," adding: "By your course you have saved *bloodshed* and a *mob*."[27] Still, Lincoln and his counselors might have devised a means of confronting it that held less potential for humiliation. A massive military or police presence, for example, might have sufficed to deter the plotters, though some insisted that, if tested, local security forces may well have betrayed their trust.

Only later, after Lincoln did fall victim to an assassin after all, did early doubts about his decision to avoid Baltimore evaporate. The force that took his life, one orator pointed out at a memorial service held in his honor at Philadelphia, was "one and the same spirit that organized a band of murderers to take the life of Abraham Lincoln while on his way to the seat of Government, to assume the duties of the Presidential office, to which the American people had called him." Early post-assassination biographies—like that written by Henry J. Raymond, the *New York Times* editor who later chaired Lincoln's 1864 reelection cam-

paign—loyally reiterated the prevailing belief that there was "full justification" for "precaution" in 1861.[28]

For a time, participants in the actual Baltimore adventure echoed
this view, outdoing each other in the effort to seize credit for saving the
president-elect from premature death. Learning that Lincoln's old law
partner was writing his biography, for example, Pinkerton lent William
H. Herndon his agency case file in August 1866, trusting he would vindicate him. Before he could do so, however, Police Superintendent Kennedy's account of his own parallel Baltimore Plot investigation appeared
in the New York Times under the headline "Who Saved Mr. Lincoln's
Life in 1861?"[29] Not surprising, the answer was: Kennedy. Rushing to
stake his claim, Pinkerton solicited testimonials from participants like
Norman Judd and Andrew Curtin, and published the results in a little
book of his own, from which, unsurprisingly, he emerged its hero.[30] The
battle for credit raged for years, obscuring the threshold question of
whether Lincoln truly faced death by assassination in Baltimore.

Baltimore Plot historiography changed seismically when Herndon
experienced both cash flow problems and writer's block, and opted to
sell his research material—the Pinkerton file included—to none other
than Ward Hill Lamon, who had decided to issue a Lincoln biography,
too. Lamon's utter lack of writing ability hardly slowed him down. In his
1872 ghostwritten book, Lamon, whom Pinkerton regarded as "a fool,"
surprised readers by raising doubts about the 1861 escapade. Admitting
he had "believed in the reality of the atrocious plot" for years, he now
concluded that "there was no conspiracy . . . of a hundred, of fifty, of
twenty, of three . . . of even one man to murder Mr. Lincoln in Baltimore," merely an inflated reaction to an "ambitious" detective's effort
"to shine by furnishing "tangible proofs of an imaginary conspiracy."[31]
Whether Lamon's skepticism was his own, or that of his Democratic,
Lincoln-debunking collaborator, remains hard to know.

In their own magisterial biography of the Lincoln administration,
published as the nineteenth century came to a close, John Nicolay and
John Hay elected to sidestep the controversy, conceding only that "the
fate of the government" had required Lincoln "to shun all possible and

unnecessary peril."[32] The last word, for a time, belonged to Lamon—from beyond the grave. Three years after his death, his daughter posthumously published his supposedly more authentic memoirs. The 1895 volume not only reiterated Lamon's belief that the Baltimore danger never existed, but echoed McClure's contention that Lincoln "soon learned to regret the midnight ride to which he had yielded under protest." By "Lamon's" account, Lincoln "frequently upbraided me for having aided him to degrade himself at the very moment in his life when his behavior should have exhibited the utmost dignity and composure."[33] But paradoxically, the same Lamon book also claimed, "there never was a moment from the day he crossed the Maryland line, up to the time of his assassination, that he [Lincoln] was not in danger of death by violence."[34]

Just two months after Lincoln's nightmarish passage through the city, the citizens of Baltimore supplied ugly proof of their own that the threat of violence there had indeed been genuine. On April 19, as troops from the Sixth Massachusetts Infantry, heading to the defense of Washington, left the Calvert Street station—the same depot through which their future commander-in-chief had planned to make his own public appearance back in February—a furious mob attacked them with stones. When the ensuing riot finally subsided, four soldiers lay dead and thirty-nine wounded. It was a manifestation of the "same spirit," Norman Judd maintained, that had made the threat against Lincoln so credible. In Judd's view, the riot furnished positive proof that he was right to circumvent the city.[35]

Four years thereafter, yet another band of conspirators hatched a scheme to kill Lincoln. This time it was John Wilkes Booth—the same actor who had attended the pro-compromise rally in Philadelphia, composed a lengthy screed damning the incoming president, then found himself in Albany a few months later, fuming as Lincoln visited New York's capital en route to his inauguration—who conceived the plot. And this time it would end in murder at Ford's Theatre. Booth originated the homicidal idea in Baltimore.

• • •

EARLY ON SATURDAY morning, February 23, a servant was observed quietly entering the Peace Convention meeting at Willard's Hotel and delivering a note to delegate James A. Seddon of Virginia. Seddon read it silently, then passed it on to Missouri's Waldo Porter Johnson. The message announced the breathtaking news: "Mr. Lincoln is in this hotel."

Perhaps betraying more knowledge of the assassination plot than he should, Johnson blurted out: "How the devil did he get through Baltimore?" Fellow delegate Lucius Chittenden, who witnessed this outburst, believed for the rest of his life that it testified convincingly that the threat there had been both genuine and serious.[36]

Upstairs, though fatigued by his sleepless overnight journey, Lincoln chose to plunge immediately and energetically into the daunting task of restoring his prestige, perhaps anticipating the derisive news coverage that would greet his arrival. Nine days remained before his swearing in—a period nearly as long as the entire inaugural journey just ended—to undo the damage unleashed on a single night. First he greeted and thanked New York's Peace Convention delegate William Dodge, who had vacated his choice rooms adjoining Parlor Six to make way for the president-elect. "Mr. Lincoln," Dodge generously assured him, barely awake himself, "the prayers of many hearts were with you before you started upon this journey, they accompanied you all the way here, and they will follow you as you enter upon your administration." Hearing the sentiment, Lincoln choked back tears.[37]

Certainly the newly arrived "public property" could have chosen no more visible public property to domicile himself, and the locale ultimately served as the perfect stage from which to restore his image of accessibility. Washington's busiest hotel fronted Pennsylvania Avenue just down the street from the Executive Mansion and the hulking Treasury Department. Sprawling, ideally situated Willard's, the largest hotel in the city—and the country—anticipated housing no fewer than three thousand guests for the inauguration, perhaps something of an exaggeration, but not by much. "The numbers here since the arrival of Mr. Lincoln is unprecedented," commented one visitor from Philadelphia. "The avenues and passages in Willards Hotel are so crowded that it is difficult to enter," for "the 'labourers in the cause,' flock to head quarters for the spoils of victory." Ezra Cornell agreed about the crowds, reporting to his wife on March 3 that the hotel's "halls and parlors" were "radiant nightly with ladies," but also thronged with curiosity seekers "hoping to get a look at Mr. Lincoln," increasing "the jamb to an intolerable degree." Cornell confided that "Mr. Willard told me today that he had 1,500 guests booked. I asked him how many rooms he had in the house. He answered, about five hundred. Thus you see he averages three to a room, which is just the number I have in my room—a gent. From Jamestown, N.Y., one from Fort Wayne, Ind., and myself."[38]

To an earlier visitor, Nathaniel Hawthorne, Willard's could "be much more justly called the centre of Washington and the Union than either the Capitol, the White House, or the State Department." Nowhere else, the author claimed, could be found "such a miscellany of people" enveloped in a "constant atmosphere of cigar smoke." Among its denizens milled "governors of Sovereign States . . . illustrious men . . . generals . . . statesmen and orators speaking in their familiar tones . . . loafers," and so many "office-seekers, wire-pullers, inventors, artists, poets, prosers . . . clerks, diplomatists, mail contractors, railway-directors," all fueled by mint juleps, whiskey-skins, gin cocktails, and brandy smashes, that "your own identity is lost among them."[39]

Lincoln's identity, however, would never be in doubt. Only minutes after registering for Parlor Six "and the magnificent suite of apartments attached to it"[40] on the hotel's second floor, he greeted his secretary of state–designate, William H. Seward, who had raced to the hotel in advance, and was observed anxiously lingering there, "solitary and alone . . . evidently looking for someone to arrive," by Washburne's account "much out of breath and somewhat chagrined to think he had not been up in season to be at the depot on the arrival of the train." "I am . . . out of direct responsibility," he had grandly written home a few days earlier. "I have brought the ship off the sands, and am ready to resign the helm into the hands of the Captain whom the people have chosen."[41] In truth, determined to demonstrate his influence by seizing control of the president-elect's schedule, Seward took breakfast with Lincoln, then, after allowing him a few hours to rest, accompanied him on an unscheduled 11 A.M. visit to his future home, the Executive Mansion.

Located just down the block from Willard's, America's largest and best-known residence looked "palace-like" from the outside, as "spotless as snow" when Walt Whitman glimpsed it on another February day a few years later, the "White House of future poems, and of dreams and dramas."[42] From the inside, however, another observer thought the mansion had assumed "the soiled aspect" of a "deserted farmstead" after a "hard winter."[43] On this unseasonably warm February morning, in what one reporter jokingly labeled a *"coup d'etat,"* Lincoln and Seward drove up to pay an unannounced courtesy call on James Buchanan.[44] Though "greatly surprised," the outgoing president obligingly interrupted a cabinet meeting to receive his successor for fifteen minutes in a first-floor parlor, then ushered both men upstairs to inspect his office and meet his ministers. The cabinet officers likewise received Lincoln "in a very cordial manner."[45]

Observing him as he moved about the city that day and the next, one Washington newspaper described Lincoln as looking "physically much weakened by the constant labor and excitement of the popular ovations forced upon him since leaving Springfield."[46] (Seward hardly noticed, predictably observing only how Lincoln treated *him:* "He is very cordial and kind toward me—simple, natural and agreeable."[47]) Also acknowledging he looked "pale and haggard at night," another journalist marveled that Lincoln somehow "awakened the next day restored and ready for its most unwelcome toils." The *Times*'s Joseph Howard, too, commented admiringly on Lincoln's recuperative powers, noting: "Strong-limbed, strong-boned and sinewy, rather than muscular, he can endure great fatigue with wonderful ease. To many he seems ill, or, at best, greatly worn. This is not the case. He sleeps well, eats regularly, and relishes the constant labor that is put upon him. The multitudinous hand-shakings, the incessant bending of his body, the everlasting small-talk, and the long, long ride from Springfield, though temporarily wearying him, have put flesh upon his bones, and he stands to-day a heavier man than when he left his Western home." Howard noticed something else: a growing shrewdness. " 'Honest Old Abe' was all very well for an electioneering rally, but shrewd Old Abe is much more to the purpose about these days. He cannot be fooled, he cannot be led unwillingly, and he cannot be swerved from an opinion of the honesty and policy of which he is convinced."[48]

What Lincoln honestly thought of Washington remained unreported. The vast city of 75,000, if one included Georgetown and environs, was home to 61,000 whites, 3,185 slaves, and 11,100 free blacks (all of these second-class citizens required by law to carry residence permits). In many ways, the capital had changed little in the decade since Lincoln had last lived here as a congressman, growing larger but neither calmer nor healthier. The city's boulevards remained unpaved and mired in mud, its fetid swamps and filthy river still exuded repulsively foul odors, its grand public buildings towered anomalously over both brick houses and wooden shanties, and black slaves still toiled, without wages, liberty, or hope here in the seat of government of the freest country on earth. The most ambitious structure of all, the long-planned Washington Monument whose dedication Lincoln had attended years earlier, stood half-finished, an eyesore whose abandonment, many believed, constituted a metaphor for the lost spirit of Union. Even the imposing U.S. Capitol remained incomplete, though at least its new steel dome was now rising into the sky under a web of scaffolding. Yet the city also boasted attractions like the Smithsonian Institution, overflowing with enough curiosities "to write a book about," gushed Julia Maria Buel, a twenty-year-old visitor from Detroit. "I am perfectly delighted with the capital," she wrote home after arriving for the inauguration, "and my *American heart* beats with a feeling of *pride, righteous pride,* as I walk through its frescoed chambers and noble halls."[49]

Not everyone agreed. A dyspeptic traveler named A. D. White, who first encountered the capital ten years earlier, found it difficult to believe that this "forlorn, decaying, reeking city was the goal of political ambition."[50] Newly arrived to serve as secretary to his congressman father,

Henry Adams sadly concluded that there was nothing to learn in Washington but "bad temper, bad manners, poker, and treason."[51] And Lincoln's old friend Leonard Swett dismissed the city as "the worst place in the world," warning that "a ship might as well learn its bearings in the Norway Maelstrom."[52] Reports still abounded that would-be assassins lurked among its thousands of Southern sympathizers, determined that the man who had survived his nocturnal passage through Baltimore should never live to be inaugurated in Washington. One New Yorker who believed these rumors worriedly offered Lincoln "*One hundred able bodied Men*," not one shorter than five-foot-six, "to proceed to Washington . . . and defend your person."[53]

Optimistic newcomers like young John Hay found the city more exhilarating than dangerous, unrolling "its dusty magnificence" through "stupendous harmonies" of design, like the "broad avenues, which converge upon the capitol as all the roads of the Roman empire converged upon the golden milestone by the Pincian gate." So Hay gushed after a thrilling climb to the top of the construction site that would become the Capitol's new dome. His friend Robert Lincoln paid a visit to another tourist attraction, the federal Patent Office, where he got to see the little wooden model his father had submitted years before: his invention to lift large boats over sandbars.[54] The president-elect, Hay knew, had little time for such sightseeing, "pulled hither and thither, alternatively by the conservatives and the ultraists" within his own party, until Hay wondered whether "in his inner heart, he does not wish himself back in the quiet village of Springfield again." It was, of course, too late for such a retreat. Within days, Hay reported, Lincoln had seamlessly "exchanged the minor tribulations of hand-shaking and speech-making for the graver woes which attach to the martyr toasted between two fires."[55]

Wisely, the president-elect determined to take the pulse of the roiling capital in other ways, greeting its leading citizens and allowing himself to be seen as openly and frequently as if he had returned to Indianapolis, Buffalo, or New York. Together with Seward, his putative "prime minister," the president-elect left the White House on the 23rd and headed immediately to the headquarters of General Winfield Scott to meet the man who had kept the city safe for the counting of the electoral votes a few weeks earlier, and whose recent warnings helped influence Lincoln to bypass Baltimore. Of course it was impossible to call ahead, and Scott was not there to receive them.

Instead, Lincoln retreated to Willard's for some much needed additional sleep, and Scott returned the call later that afternoon, his "majestic form . . . grandly rising" on the stairway "as if solemnly lifted by noiseless machinery."[56] Ohio congressman Albert G. Riddle never forgot the sight of the general, "in full dress sword, plumes, and bullion," come "to pay his respects" to the quintessentially civilian Lincoln. Riddle believed anyone who thought "the gentlemanly art of bowing" lost should have witnessed "the profound grace of the old hero's acknowledgment of the President-elect, as he swept his instep with his golden plumes of his chapeau."[57] Another eyewitness testified that Lincoln, self-confident as always, did most of the talking, "flashing with anecdote and story . . . [the] complete master of himself and of all who came within the magic of his presence."[58] The president-elect thanked Scott "for the many marks of attention" he had paid him, and Scott, in turn, congratulated him for leaving Harrisburg "unattended by any display, but in a plain, democratic way"—rather an extraordinarily understated way of describing the Baltimore evasion.[59] (Within days, Scott, increasingly favorable toward compromise, would advise that Lincoln's military options—that is, if he "passed through all personal dangers" and survived the inaugural—were "limited" to but four unattractive choices: accept compromise; blockade Southern ports; "Conquer the seceding states by invading armies"; or tell them, "*wayward sisters, depart in peace!*"[60])

Giving some much needed attention as well that first day to the still unsettled subject of assembling a cabinet, Lincoln huddled with candidate Montgomery Blair of Maryland, accompanied by his father, editor Francis Preston Blair, Sr. Lincoln had refused the powerful Blair family's offer of Washington hospitality. Now he would consider its quest to situate the younger Blair in his cabinet. Lincoln probably took advantage of the opportunity to share all or parts of his draft inaugural address with the wily old Jacksonian-era editor.

To Lincoln's likely relief, Mary and the boys arrived in town beneath a heavy rain shower late that afternoon, met at the depot by a somber William H. Seward.[61] It was nothing like the welcomes Mary had received along the way, but her disappointment probably faded out of concern for her husband. If Lincoln, in turn, was concerned about his family's safety as it fulfilled the schedule he had abandoned, he never so admitted to anyone. (He had seemed far more worried about assuring his wife that his own trip had ended safely, telegraphing Mary in Harrisburg when he reached the capital at 6 A.M.[62]) The Charleston Mercury was quick to criticize him for leaving "his family to follow him in the very train in which he himself was to be blown up, or blown over!"[63]

Recollections of the family's actual traveling experience vary. Some reports suggested that crowds of up to fifteen thousand treated it respectfully in Baltimore, only a few "ruffians" shouting mockingly "for old Jeff. Davis," disappointed though everyone was that the president-elect failed to appear. A large police force closely guarded the party.[64] But a contrary report held that Mary was "grossly insulted by a rabble which surrounded" her car.[65] After witnessing the "shocking abuse . . . oaths, obscenity, disgusting epithets and unpleasant gesticulations" that greeted Mary,[66] Joseph Howard of the New York Times, inventor of the Scotch cap story, atoned by admitting that it was "well Mr. Lincoln went as he did." The full truth may never be known.

Safely ensconced at Willard's, Mary took up occupancy in the handsome chambers adjoining Parlor Six, while Nicolay and the rest of the traveling party had to make do with "sorry accommodations," in many cases, as usual, doubling up.[67] While Mary commenced rummaging through her baggage to pick out clothes to wear at a reception planned for later that night, a happy Lincoln relaxed in an armchair, Willie and Tad "climbing joyously" over him. But when a young Pennsylvania woman who had accompanied Mary from Harrisburg asked if he would like to hear a song, the mercurial Lincoln abruptly shifted moods and requested a sad one. Margaret Williams chose the appropriate ballad, "Alone." It was every bit as gloomy as Lincoln's expression—"among the saddest I have ever seen," the chanteuse remembered.[68]

Mary soon headed off on her own White House tour, welcomed by the bachelor incumbent's niece and official hostess, Harriet Lane. Apparently neither of the Lincolns impressed the current residents, although they kept their impressions largely to themselves. Harriet confided only that she thought Lincoln looked like the "tall, awkward Irishman who waits at the door" of the White House, and predicted his wife would prove "awfully *western*, loud & unrefined."[69] Publicly, Harriet remained unfailingly courteous, welcoming Mary for several additional visits, "unrelenting in her attentions."[70]

Lincoln's unendurably long first day in the capital did not end with his family's arrival. Important ceremonial duties remained on his crowded agenda. At 2:30 that afternoon he welcomed to his suite the entire congressional delegation from his home state of Illinois. Conspicuously leading the group, which included his Republican friends Senator Browning and Congressman Washburne, was its senior senator, Democrat Stephen A. Douglas, the very man he had defeated for the presidency. Their reunion was reported to be "particularly pleasant."[71]

At 7 P.M., Lincoln dined with Seward at his F Street residence, then returned to find Willard's hallways so choked with well-wishers that, a newspaper clucked, he forgot to remove his hat in the lobby—the very space that, according to the tradition, later gave rise to the word "lobbyist."[72] Two hours later, learning that members of the Peace Convention desired an audience of their own, Lincoln received a hundred of them, with delegate and likely cabinet designee Salmon P. Chase handling the introductions. Here, at long last, the compromise advocates came face-to-face with the nation's uncompromising new leader. What the visitors encountered was a lively wit and a spectacular memory, one observer astonished that, "in nine cases out of ten, Mr. Lincoln would promptly recall their entire name, no matter how many initials it contained."[73]

There would be no confrontation if Lincoln could help it. His cordial greetings to each delegate broke the tension and established the kind of informal mood in which he always shone. "You are a smaller man than I supposed," he playfully greeted Virginia's William C. Rives, quickly acknowledging the contrast to the "greatness of your intellect."

Lincoln meets the members of the Peace Convention at Willard's Hotel on the night of his arrival in Washington, February 23, 1861. This unpublished sketch from life was made by artist Thomas Nast. (JOHN HAY LIBRARY, BROWN UNIVERSITY)

Introduced to his hero's son, James B. Clay of Kentucky, he declared: "Your name is all the endorsement you require. From my boyhood the name of Henry Clay has been an inspiration to me." And to an old House colleague, Virginia Whig George W. Summers, he proclaimed: "You cannot be a disunionist, unless your nature has changed since we met in Congress!" This was not the "boor" or "clown" that Southerners like John Tyler and James Seddon expected to encounter. "They saw a tall, powerful man whose grand face overlooked them all," remembered Vermont delegate Lucius Chittenden, "whose voice was kindly, who greeted every one with dignity and a courteous propriety of expression." If a Southerner ventured a rude comment, Lincoln only "seemed to grow loftier," responding "with a ring to his voice and a flash from his eyes."[74]

Not that Lincoln remained unchallenged. When a Pennsylvania delegate insisted that compromise "must be done sooner or later," Lincoln tartly replied: "Perhaps your reasons for compromising the alleged difficulties are correct, and that now is the favorable time to do it; still, if I remember correctly, *that* is not what *I* was elected for!"[75] Picking up the argument, Rives warned the president-elect that "the clouds" hanging over the Union had grown "very dark," and that saving it "now depends upon you."

"I cannot agree to that," Lincoln shot back. "My course is as plain as a turnpike road. It is marked out by the Constitution. I am in no doubt which way to go. Suppose now we all stop discussing and try the experiment of obedience to the Constitution and the laws. Don't you think it would work?"

To this, James Seddon had a retort of his own, protesting in his "sepulchral voice": "It is not of your professions we complain. It is of your sins of omission—of your failure to enforce the laws—to suppress your John Browns and your [William Lloyd] Garrisons, who preach insurrection and make war upon our property!" (Seddon would later serve as the Confederacy's secretary of war.)

Lincoln would hear none of it. "I believe John Brown was hung and Mr. Garrison imprisoned," he calmly retorted. "You cannot justly charge the North with disobedience to statutes or with failing to enforce them. You have made some which were very offensive, but they have been enforced, notwithstanding." When Seddon persisted that Republicans refused to enforce Fugitive Slave Laws, Lincoln finally exploded: "You are wrong in your facts again." Though Northerners indeed hated serving as "tip-staves or bum-bailiffs," he insisted: "Your slaves have been returned, yes, from the shadow of Faneuil Hall in the heart of Boston."

Finally, it was the turn of delegate William Dodge, perhaps more irritable now after losing his choice rooms to make way for the Lincolns.[76] "It is for you, sir," the New Yorker declared in a loud voice, "to say whether the whole nation shall be plunged into bankruptcy; whether the grass shall grow in the streets of our commercial cities."

"Then I say it shall not," Lincoln replied, with "a merry twinkle" of the eye. "If it depends upon me, the grass will not grow anywhere except in the fields and the meadows."[77]

According to Chittenden, Lincoln ended the hour-long session with one final objection to any compromise that embraced slavery extension. Slavery, he told the delegates who remained after Southern ultras peeled away, "must be content with what it has. The voice of the civilized world is against it." So, he added, was the voice of God, at least according to Chittenden, one of many memoirists who suggested retrospectively—and not always convincingly—that as president-elect, Lincoln invoked heavenly intervention. "Those who fight the purposes of the Almighty will not succeed. They have always been, they always will be, beaten."[78] Such conviction in divine guidance undoubtedly helped Lincoln endure the calumnies that greeted his secret trip to Washington. Republican delegates left the reception "encouraged and strengthened" by Lincoln's "presence," the Baltimore stories notwithstanding; secessionists departed "discouraged and depressed," sensing perhaps that they had met their match.[79]

Even then, Lincoln's protracted debut day in the capital was still not over: not before the president-elect staged an impromptu, late-night public levee for congressmen and other dignitaries surging through the hallways and lobby for the chance to greet him, and not until the Buchanan cabinet returned his earlier courtesy call with a visit of its own. Congressman Riddle found the inexhaustible Lincoln at the former reception still "in wonderful spirits, surrounded by twenty or thirty admiring adherents, standing at his full height," his expression "radiant, his wit and humor at flood tide."[80]

The following day, Sunday the 24th, somehow waking refreshed and reenergized, Lincoln breakfasted with his wife and children. Then, braving a "wind that swept over the city with mighty power,"[81] he joined Seward for a worship service at St. John's Episcopal Church, which stood within sight of the White House at Lafayette Square. There, "not a dozen persons" present seemed "aware of the presence of the President elect," not even the pastor, Dr. Smith Pyne. Lincoln wore "plain black clothes, with black whiskers and hair well-trimmed . . . a different man entirely from the hard-looking pictorial representations seen of him."[82]

As the president-elect listened from Seward's pew, the rector read a psalm that sounded as if it had been lifted chapter and verse not from

Scripture but from Lincoln's own recent speeches: "Depend on God, and Him obey; So thou within the land shall stay; / Secure from danger and from want."[83] After the service, Lincoln and Hamlin sat down with Seward at his home for another long conference. Here Lincoln may have handed Seward a copy of his inaugural address and for the first time invited his comments. Supposedly—at least according to the senator—Lincoln also used the occasion to assure his host he would enjoy complete authority over one aspect of administration policy: diplomacy. "Governor Seward," Lincoln reportedly promised, ". . . I shall have to depend upon you for taking care of these matters of foreign affairs, of which I know so little, and with which I reckon you are familiar." Such concessions sound out of character for Lincoln, but by the time the reminiscence appeared, the president was dead and no better testimony existed to refute it.[84]

Among the callers at Willard's later this day was another recent election opponent, Vice President John C. Breckinridge, along with the veteran senator whose recent compromise initiatives had defied Lincoln's opposition to slavery extension, John J. Crittenden. Representative Thomas Corwin and fiery Senator Ben Wade arrived to pay their respects, along with the stuffy abolitionist hero Charles Sumner. Lincoln at least managed to squeeze some fun out of Sumner's visit. Taking note of the Bostonian's impressive height, Lincoln could not resist playfully inviting the senator "to measure with me," and seemed tickled when a horrified Sumner indignantly replied that "this was a time for uniting our fronts and not our backs before the enemies of the country." The speech, Lincoln recalled with "an indescribable glimmer" on his face, was "very fine. But I reckon the truth was . . . he was—afraid to measure!" Gazing rather appreciatively at his own long limbs, he told his other laughing visitors: "I have never had much to do with bishops down where I live; but, do you know, Sumner is just my idea of a bishop."[85]

Finally came the Massachusetts congressman who had been so privately critical of Lincoln's pre-inaugural oratory, Charles Francis Adams. "Mr. Lincoln is a tall, ill-favored man, with little grace of manners or polish of appearance," he observed, bristling because he had to "wait a good while" before gaining entrance. But Adams was won over by Lincoln's "plain, good natured, frank expression which rather endears one to him." The two men—one the descendant of a founding father, the other the son of a semiliterate farmer—spoke mainly of Lincoln's nighttime trip from Baltimore. Adams left believing: "that such schemes are still in agitation no one can doubt." [86]

On this Sunday, Lincoln also, wisely, found the time to visit the Pennsylvania Avenue gallery operated by Mathew Brady, the photographer who had made his enormously influential 1860 Cooper Union portrait a year earlier in New York. That dignified photograph had served, in a sense, to "illustrate" a seminal speech, providing vital pictorial accompaniment to an oratorical triumph. What Lincoln most needed now was a pictorial rebuttal—an equally powerful image capable of reassuring the public he was nothing like the caricature in a Scotch cap and military cloak. Fortuitously, *Harper's Weekly*, even as it prepared to publish merciless cartoons of Lincoln in disguise, commissioned Brady to take these distinguished-looking portraits "expressly for this paper." [87]

Brady himself was not behind the camera that day; the honor went, ironically, to a Scot—probably the last nationality Lincoln wanted to encounter at that moment—named Alexander Gardner. To the Glasgow-reared photographer, Brady had dispatched a note two days before the sitting, succinctly notifying him: "President Elect Lincoln will visit the Gallery on the 24th. Please ready equipment." [88] Realizing he had a historic opportunity to create the first portraits of Lincoln in Washington, Gardner sent word upstairs to one of the boarders in Brady's building, a painter named George Henry Story, hoping the artist might come down and help him arrange the pose.

Story quietly entered the gallery to find Lincoln already sitting in the studio's sturdy chair, a prop pillar, suggesting authority, meaningfully situated to one side. The subject's left forearm rested wearily on a scallop-edged wooden table on which he had plopped his large silk top hat, upside down; his right hand, swollen from a fortnight's worth of handshaking, remained tightly clenched and resting in his lap. Patiently waiting for the camera exposure, the distracted Lincoln had drifted into a trance of private thoughts, staring vacantly into the distance, his eyes lowered, his un-barbered hair, the longest he would ever wear, swept back high on his head and cascading over his ears. To Story, the solemn giant seemed "absolutely indifferent to all that was going on about him, and he gave the impression that he was . . . overburdened with an anxiety and fatigue and care."

But the artist did not dare attempt to improve the mise-en-scène. Seeing him "wholly absorbed in deep thought, and apparently oblivious to his immediate surroundings," Story whispered "in an undertone" to Gardner: "Bring your instrument here and take the picture."[89] Gardner did more: shunning close-ups, he exposed not one but a series of five glass plates of the full-length seated figure, between which a confident-looking Lincoln hardly moved at all, turning but once to stare blankly at the camera as if awakened from a dream. The results could hardly have been better. Lincoln's massive form, though folded into a chair, looked formidable enough to evoke awe, his expression somber enough to suggest nobility. Gardner's poses (for one, see page 218) were quickly mass-produced as *cartes-de-visite*—the small photographs that had suddenly become a national collecting rage for display in family albums[90]—and they became best-sellers. Soon thereafter, a pose was adapted not only for the pages of *Harper's Weekly* (as "the first accurate portrait of him"), but by engravers and lithographers for separate-sheet display prints—not only domestically but across the ocean in Europe. The array of handsome, almost heroic likenesses provided admirers with just the pictorial response Lincoln needed to combat the comic portrayals of his flight through Baltimore.[91]

OVER THE NEXT few days, Lincoln's schedule remained mercilessly hectic, his suite crowded with visitors, the hotel lobby and streets outside flooded with admirers, serenaders, and the perennially unavoidable job-seekers.

Without directly responding to the crushing new charges of cowardice, Lincoln effectively managed to restore political equilibrium and some degree of public confidence by remaining feverishly active and highly visible. "His presence in Washington this week is timely and salutary," observed the anti-slavery *New York Independent* once the Baltimore brouhaha subsided, predicting that Lincoln's "unwavering fidelity to freedom, will invigorate the wavering, confirm the feeble, and embolden the faithful."[92] Massachusetts congressman Henry L. Dawes agreed that glimpses of Lincoln's "kindly homeliness of manner" "began early to overcome the dislike and break through the prejudices created by the manner of his entry into the capital."[93]

Whether Lincoln so presented himself in a calculated effort to revive his image as an accessible man of the people, or merely fell back into the routine patterns of his entire public life, the result proved a balm to the recent injury to his reputation. That he accomplished a resurrection absent the benefit of advice from trusted old friends made his recovery all the more remarkable. True, Lincoln quickly made it his business to engage with most of the distinguished Republicans, and many of the leading Democrats, in Washington. But for a while he had few hometown counselors in whom to confide. Lincoln not only arrived in Washington without the comforting retinue that had accompanied him from Springfield to Harrisburg, but also spent his early days, indeed months, in the city with few trusted colleagues beside him for advice or relaxation. On the other hand, Lincoln was accustomed to leaving one set of acquaintances behind as he moved higher up the ladder of prominence. And incoming presidents who rely exclusively on old friends usually come to regret it. By quickly establishing a rapport with Seward and then welcoming longtime allies like David Davis and Norman Judd to town, Lincoln probably grew quickly and fully comfortable in this challenging environment even though he had not held public office in Washington since 1849.[94]

Finally, Lincoln always particularly enjoyed the company of loyal young acolytes, and of this class of companionship he was never deprived. Nicolay, Hay, and Ellsworth, all in their twenties, arrived in Washington just hours after their boss, joining up with thirty-three-year-old Lamon to provide just the support structure the president-elect needed to prepare calmly and efficiently for his inauguration.

Nor should it ever be forgotten that Lincoln seldom lacked for self-assurance, even in solitude. Dressed in his handsome new black broadcloth suit, a gold watch chain draped elegantly from his waistcoat, looking seven feet tall when wearing his stovepipe hat, he quickly came to dominate the capital. He seemed to turn up everywhere: at churches and banquet halls, at the White House and Capitol Hill, riding about in carriages, or strolling freely through the city's streets, the observed of all observers.

Opening his parlor doors at 11 A.M., Lincoln resumed his activities with renewed vigor on Monday the 25th, welcoming such dignitaries as Lewis Cass, the old Michigan senator who had served as Buchanan's first secretary of state; Republican senators Preston King of New York and James Doolittle of Wisconsin; and delegations of pro-Lincoln electors from Ohio and Pennsylvania.[95] Shortly after noon, President Buchanan himself paid a fifteen-minute courtesy call.[96] Seward was seldom far from Lincoln's side.

That afternoon, in a breathtaking demonstration of political authority and personal confidence, Lincoln introduced himself to all three branches of the federal government.[97] First came a session at Willard's with the clerks of the executive departments, all of whom undoubtedly arrived for the meeting fully aware that their jobs were in jeopardy at the hands of the first-ever Republican president. Then, at 3 P.M., accompanied by Seward, Lincoln rode down Pennsylvania Avenue to the Capitol, following much the same route he would be taking to his inauguration a week later. His mission this day was to pay courtesy calls on Congress and the Supreme Court.

Provoking a huge stir as he entered and took a seat in the rear of the Senate chamber on the Republican side of the aisle, Lincoln received "a cordial and friendly shake of the hand" not only from members of his own party, but from Democrats like Stephen Douglas of Illinois and Tennessee's Andrew Johnson. Only ardent secessionists like Louis Wigfall of Texas made a show of ignoring the guest, and when Seward decided to escort the president-elect to the Democratic side, even Joseph Lane of Oregon greeted him, though one observer reported that the failed Democratic vice-presidential candidate, now in his final days as a legislator, looked "nervous, as if he thought Old Abe was after him with a fence rail." Then it was over to the House, Lincoln's old political base, where his ten-minute appearance created nothing less than a "sensation." The speaker suspended business and onlookers in the galleries rose and craned their necks for a closer look. Republican congressmen in the chamber rushed to greet him, along with most of the Democrats, their resistance less pronounced than in the upper house.[98]

The visit to the Supreme Court's nearby Capitol Building chambers provided the day's most extraordinary drama. Here to welcome him, his emotions rigidly masked, stood doddering Chief Justice Roger B. Taney, the eighty-three-year-old Maryland Democrat whose 1857 pro-slavery *Dred Scott* decision had inspired Lincoln's eloquent denunciation—and refueled his meteoric political comeback. Nicolay and Hay remembered, in markedly tortured prose, that the "venerable chief and associate justices extended to him an affable recognition as the lawful successor in constitutional rulership," perhaps even remembering—or being reminded—that Lincoln had appeared before his court as a lawyer several times beginning back in 1849. Between the lines, nonetheless, it is easy to infer that their "reunion" proved awkward in the extreme. Neither man left a personal record of the historic encounter, but no one ever disputed the secretaries' official view that at least it had been dignified and free of rancor.[99]

That night, Lincoln and Mary hosted separate levees at Willard's, the future mistress of the White House earning critical glances from the snobbish Washington elite, and her husband so "backed up in a corner and so button-holed by successive squads of eager individuals—each of whom, by his earnest gesticulations, had something of vital importance to communicate," that most visitors had to content themselves "with a bow and a look at the coming man."[100]

The president-elect began the next day, Monday the 26th, strolling the avenues of Washington before dawn in the company of his son Robert and John Nicolay, his face still not "familiar enough to be popularly recognized."[101] Then it was back to Willard's to welcome Horace Greeley, who burst in "like a shot out of a hot shovel" in a last-ditch effort to influence cabinet choices.[102] Following another long walk outdoors on Wednesday the 27th, Lincoln met with the third of his three election opponents, John Bell, who left "impressed with the conservative tone of Mr. Lincoln's mind."[103] Later that day he proudly received a congressional committee, Trumbull and Washburne among the group, officially reporting the results of the recent Electoral College. Lincoln took the ceremonial event seriously, dictating two drafts of his official thanks, and using the occasion to reiterate his "firm reliance on the strength of our free government, and the ultimate loyalty of the people to the just principles upon which it is founded, and above all an unshaken faith in the Supreme Ruler of nations."[104]

That same day, Lincoln made his maiden public speech in Washington, replying in his parlor to the city's official greeting from Mayor James G. Berret. Noting pointedly (for he had spoken often in town as a congressman), that this was "the first time in my life, since the present phase of politics has presented itself in this country, that I have said anything publicly within a region of country where the institution of slavery exists," he adopted his most conciliatory tone yet to assure his new neighbors: "I have not now any purpose to withhold from you any of the benefits of the constitution, under any circumstances, that I would not feel myself constrained to withhold from my own neighbors." He hoped that "when we shall become better acquainted—and I say it with great confidence—we shall like each other the more."[105] Viewing the talk as a fitting conclusion to his inaugural journey orations, John Nicolay thought it clearly defined both "his character and policy": his "desire to remove misunderstanding" coupled with "his determination to defend the government." Above all, Nicolay believed, the greeting manifested "his leading political trait—his reliance upon the people, and his faith that they would maintain their own cause and protect their own liberties."[106] Whether Lincoln was too optimistic Nicolay did not mention.

The next morning, Thursday, February 28, began with Lincoln receiving John Crittenden to discuss the fading hopes for compromise, and welcoming the seventy-seven-year-old commander of the army's Department of the East, John Wool, another dissatisfied delegate to the Peace Convention.[107] At a dinner that night, New Yorkers seized the opportunity to harangue Lincoln about the potentially ruinous threat that disunion posed to the economy—and their own future profits. He disarmed these critics, too. When one of them pointed out that Georgians had recently vowed to wear no clothes made under Republican rule, Lincoln merrily remarked that he should be delighted to see Georgia men clad only in what could be produced in their home state— namely shirt collars and spurs.[108]

Late that night, from the boulevard outside his hotel, the Marine Band serenaded Lincoln for the first time with "Hail to the Chief," and the president-elect's now familiar face appeared at the window of Parlor Six to express his thanks to the crowd below. To loud cheers, he again insisted that he wanted only to be a good friend to his new neighbors, had no plans to "deprive you of any of your rights under the constitution of the United States or even narrowly to split hairs with you in regard to these rights."[109] Several onlookers shouted back expressions of their confidence. His informal words proved the last that Lincoln would speak publicly in Washington before his inaugural address. Following precisely the pattern he had established on his journey from Springfield, once again conciliation would set the tone for something tougher.

Even silent, however, Lincoln remained in the spotlight. On Friday, March 1, he dominated a diplomatic reception given by Bremen's minister resident, Rudolph Schleiden, at his opulent Sixth Street residence. Among the dignitaries on hand were General Scott, British minister Lord Lyons, and cabinet hopefuls Seward, Chase, and Cameron.[110] Saturday, March 2, found the president-elect happily riding through the city streets in a brand-new, maroon-colored, $1,600 "full-dress coach," complete with a speaking tube, given him as a gift by carriage-makers from New York.[111] Whether at formal galas or un-self-consciously flourishing about in exotic conveyances, the old rail-splitter now seemed fully at home amid the trappings of a head of state.[112]

• • •

As LINCOLN LABORED to reestablish himself socially and politically, pressure had meanwhile intensified on him to bend to compromise. According to one fantastic press report, his unscheduled overnight trip to Washington had actually been "brought about by the condition of things in the Peace Convention." Though such was hardly the case, the rumor persisted that with secessionists about to prevail there, Republicans had issued an urgent call that Lincoln rush to town and accept the idea of extending slavery in an effort to save the Union.[113]

In truth, Lincoln's private resolve to "hold firm" on extension never wavered, however graciously he publicly proffered friendship to slaveholding Washingtonians. In a more private setting at Willard's on February 26, Maryland governor Thomas Hicks had gotten no encouragement when he joined Stephen A. Douglas in another effort to get him to change his mind. The following day, Douglas returned to Lincoln's suite alone to press him further, warning that the only alternative to conciliation was war, darkly reminding him that they both had sons old enough to fight—and die. The senator implored his old rival "in God's name, to act the patriot, and to leave our children a country to live in."[114]

Patiently, Lincoln replied to his longtime rival's "agitated and distressed" proposals for yet another national convention "respectfully and kindly," growing animated only when Douglas vowed not to "make political capital out of secession and whatever might follow."[115] Pennsylvanian James Pollock, another old congressional colleague of Lincoln's, heard Douglas offer this assurance. Lincoln, he remembered, "could not withhold the tears that slowly coursed down his manly cheeks, and, seizing Mr. Douglass' [sic] hand with both of his and giving it a most heartfelt pressure, said in tones that bespoke the fullness of his heart: 'God bless you Douglass! With such pledges and such assurances from my political opponents, and with God's help we must succeed.'"[116]

On February 27, a group of moderate Peace Convention delegates from the Upper South had returned to Willard's to make one final appeal on compromise. The sole record of the meeting was kept by Charles

S. Morehead, a former governor of Kentucky who had also served with the future president in the House. Morehead did little to disguise his current hostility, though he did concede that Lincoln greeted the group "very kindly." The once clean-shaven young Illinois congressman had aged—though his irrepressible personality seemed unchanged. "He had placed himself in a chair with rounds to it, with his feet upon the highest round," Morehead recalled, sitting "with his elbows upon his knees, and his hands upon the sides of his face." Whenever he spoke, he would "drop his hands and raise his face."

The atmosphere at the meeting quickly turned icy. After Lincoln recited his now familiar, modest declaration that he was "accidentally elected President of the United States," Morehead unexpectedly agreed, pointing out that more voters had opposed than favored him. At this, Lincoln bristled that if he were indeed "a minority President he was not the first, and that in all events he had obtained more votes than we could muster for any other man."

Trying a different approach, Lincoln endeavored to charm his visitors with funny stories. Asked to pledge not to coerce the South—by which his visitors meant agreeing in advance not to reenforce Southern forts or collect revenue—Lincoln spoke of an old man who had once asked him to bring a lawsuit. It seemed a good case at the start, but when his client heard the arguments piling up against him in court, he worriedly whispered into his lawyer's ear: "Guv it up."

"Now," Lincoln said. "Wouldn't this be 'guvin it up'?"

Undaunted, Morehead insisted that by simply withdrawing federal troops from the South, Lincoln could guarantee peace and harmony. This, too, reminded Lincoln of a story. "It is from Aesop's Fables," he patiently explained, "and doubtless in your schoolboy days you have read it"—as had he as early as age twelve, his cousin Dennis Hanks later testified.[117] The tale concerned a lovesick lion who proposed to a beautiful woman. Her fearful parents demanded that he first consent to have his sharp claws and teeth removed so as not to injure their "frail and delicate" daughter. The lion submitted, but as soon as his "claws were cut off and his tusks drawn . . . they took clubs and knocked him on the head." The moral was clear enough: Lincoln would not allow himself to be defanged and clubbed into submission before his own big day.

Lincoln's "jests" only served to irritate his guests, and one of them, the Virginia delegate William Rives, finally rose from his seat to fume that such stubborn unwillingness to declare against coercion would almost guarantee his state's secession. At that, Lincoln supposedly "jumped up" from his own chair, advanced a step toward the Virginian, and allegedly declared: "Mr. Rives! Mr. Rives! If Virginia will stay in, I will withdraw the troops from Fort Sumter." Taken aback, Rives could only mumble that he had no authority to enter into such an agreement, but would do everything in his power to "promote the Union."

It was not enough for a deal—if one was ever really proffered. Lincoln endured some more hectoring, then ended the meeting by observing irritably: "Well, gentlemen, I have been wondering very much whether, if Mr. Douglas or Mr. Bell had been elected President you would have dared to talk to him as freely as you have to me."

To which, Morehead claimed—though he did not hear it distinctly at the time—that Kentucky delegate James Guthrie insisted he would have assumed the same tone with "General Washington" himself.[118] The man who had taken to comparing his burden to Washington's, however, remained unmoved and somewhat insulted. Lincoln possessed much more dignity than most of his first-time guests appreciated. The insensitive ones learned this lesson too late.

After a hiatus, the Peace Convention had reconvened downstairs at Willard's on February 25, with Northerners joining militant Southerners to defeat most new proposals aimed at breaking its frustrating deadlock. Then, in the predawn hours of February 27, after yet more haggling on language defining slave territory, a dramatic moment arrived. In a climactic vote—one that Lincoln evidently did nothing to encourage or block—the Illinois delegation switched from "no" to "yes," enabling a final, if watered-down, compromise plan to pass by a vote of 9–8. Illinois's Thomas J. Turner quickly wrote to assure Lincoln the delegates had made the decision "of our own volition."[119]

To Senator Crittenden's rekindled delight, the Peace Convention sent Congress a proposed Thirteenth Amendment to the Constitution. Section 1 prohibited slavery north of the Missouri Compromise line, but guaranteed it would remain perpetual "in all the present territory south of that line," though leaving enforcement to common law. By the provisions of Section 2, no future territory could be acquired, even by treaty, without separate majority votes by free- and slave-state senators alike. Section 3 barred Congress from regulating or abolishing slavery where it existed, but banned the slave trade in the District of Columbia. Section 4 reenforced the Fugitive Slave Laws, and Section 5 reiterated the ban on the foreign slave trade.[120]

Surely reflecting Lincoln's own reaction, Nicolay and Hay judged this result to be "as worthless as Dead Sea fruit."[121] But Crittenden quickly substituted the new proposals for his own dormant compromise plan, and rushed the measure to the Senate floor, where its fate was never much in doubt. With a two-thirds vote required to send it on to the states for adoption, and the remaining Southern senators as opposed to compromise as Northern abolitionists, the amendment never stood a chance. Lincoln prudently kept his silence. Just hours before his inaugural ceremonies were scheduled to commence, the amendment went down to defeat by a lopsided vote of 28–7.[122] That very night, the president-elect publicly paid his respects to the process he had done so little to encourage by visiting the Senate galleries to listen attentively to Senator Crittenden's farewell message—the Kentuckian was retiring to take a seat in the House of Representatives. Describing the country as "inflamed," the seventy-four-year-old leader capped his futile months of work on compromise by insisting his only goal had been "to quench the destroying fire." Though he was leaving without success, he surely cheered the president-elect when his final, unequivocal advice resounded through the chamber: "Hold fast to the Union."[123]

Congress's last-gasp effort at good-faith, if toothless, compromise resulted in another tepid substitute Thirteenth Amendment obliquely guaranteeing that no future amendment could ever grant it "the power to abolish or interfere, within any state, with the domestic institutions thereof, including that of persons held to labor or service by the laws of said state." Known as the Corwin Amendment after its sponsor, Ohio congressman Thomas Corwin, this resolution passed the House by a vote of 133–65 on February 28, and by the Senate, 24–12, three days later. (Optimistically the ever-Machiavellian Thurlow Weed promptly wired his broker "to buy stocks.")[124] Both tallies represented two-thirds of the members present, precisely so in the upper chamber, but with so many secessionist Southerners absent, the "ayes" did not amount to two-thirds of the elected bodies—and doubters immediately called the result into question.[125]

Nonetheless, with President Buchanan's enthusiastic approval—an endorsement he was not required to make—the amendment was duly prepared for consideration by the States, three-quarters of which needed to approve it to make the Corwin Amendment law. Ironically, with Buchanan leaving office, the obligation to forward the resolution to the nation's governors fell to Lincoln, who dutifully performed the task even after the rebellion began. Perhaps out of respect for Corwin, Ohio's legislature passed it in May 1861, and Maryland's followed in January 1862—by which time the nation was fully embroiled in civil war. The measure also received an endorsement at a state convention in Lincoln's own Illinois, but this vote was considered unofficial. There the amendment stalled, to be supplanted in 1865 by a Thirteenth Amendment that, conversely, ended slavery everywhere. But not before Lincoln dutifully transmitted the Corwin Amendment to the various states, signing his name to form letters that managed to point out that Buchanan, not he, had approved it. He urged neither passage nor rejection of the strange amendment, which by then made absolutely no difference to war, peace, union, or history.[126]

Constitutional scholars today refer to the Corwin initiative as the "Shadow Amendment"—not only because it was superseded by another Thirteenth Amendment that ironically affirmed freedom instead of bondage, but because technically it remains alive and eligible for ratification after nearly a century and a half. For, in the view of many legal scholars, there was in 1861 no statute of limitations on constitutional amendments.[127]

Chapter Thirteen

The Ultimate Justice of the People

ONE OF LINCOLN'S last, but most stubbornly elusive, challenges before taking the reins of government was the long-delayed task of finalizing his official family. "The struggle for Cabinet portfolios," the *Washington Evening Star* reported on March 1, "waxes warmer hourly."[1] Only three days remained until the inauguration.

William H. Seward appeared to be not only on board but ubiquitous. Edward Bates was firm for attorney general, and Gideon Welles a certainty for a major post, too. Summoned to Washington, with special cars arranged by William S. Wood himself, an exhausted Welles arrived from Connecticut to find Willard's distastefully thick with "the quadrennial revel of the office seekers." Still believing he might get the Post Office Department, Welles would not learn for certain that he had earned the Navy portfolio until the day before the inauguration.[2]

Meanwhile, delegations continued to beat a path to Lincoln's headquarters with last-gasp importunings for and against Salmon P. Chase, Schuyler Colfax, and other aspirants.[3] Rumors held that Montgomery Blair, not Gideon Welles, would likely become postmaster general, with Caleb Smith, not the far younger Colfax, the likely choice for Interior. Lincoln liked Nathaniel Banks and "tried to find a place for him," but as he admitted to Banks's fellow Massachusetts Republican George B.

Loring, "I am afraid I shall not quite fetch it."[4] That left only the delicate, still vexing matter of how to bring both Chase and Cameron together in one administration without offending either man, or insulting Seward in the bargain.

Lincoln summoned Cameron to Willard's on the night of February 28, and the Pennsylvanian returned the following day, March 1, to continue their interview as a "high wind" blew "the dust about in great quantities" outside.[5] This was their final chance to damp down the dust that still muddled their own relationship. With no time left, Lincoln realized he must once and for all balance the need to satisfy Pennsylvania and the high tariff lobby against Cameron's poisonous reputation for dishonesty. Even after their eleventh-hour sessions, Lincoln simply could not make up his mind.

For some reason, the Cameron mess always seemed to drive Lincoln to his desk to write out his options—just as he had done after the senator left their initial conference at Springfield. Now, to help himself sift through his dilemma, Lincoln meticulously wrote out a list of nineteen important Republican senators on a single sheet of paper. Next to each name he jotted down the individual senator's cabinet recommendations. Trumbull favored Chase, as did James R. Doolittle of Wisconsin, Maine's William Pitt Fessenden, and several others. Lincoln's old friend Edward D. Baker wanted Cameron, along with Michigan senator Zachariah Chandler and Connecticut's James Dixon. Lafayette Foster, the other Connecticut senator, still held out hope for New Jersey's William L. Dayton, and remained "against Chase & Cameron" alike.[6] Notwithstanding Welles's insistence that the matter of appointments was settled back in Springfield on Election Night, the document proves that Lincoln remained torn, continuing to poll senators with just days left before he took office.

The situation came to a head quickly. On Friday, March 1, having been assured in recent days that leading Pennsylvanians had withdrawn their long-standing objections to their controversial native son,[7] Lincoln finally promised Cameron a post—not the Treasury, to which the senator had hungrily aspired, but the War Department.[8] Disappointed, though relieved that his agonizing wait for redemption was over at last, Cameron accepted. (He would serve for less than a year. With the Pennsylvanian bedeviled by unceasing charges of corruption, Lincoln would banish him to Russia in 1862 as the American minister.)

Matters then took an unexpected and potentially devastating turn. The very next day, anticipating that Chase was about to be awarded the Treasury post, William H. Seward shockingly threw the entire selection ritual into turmoil by advising Lincoln he was himself no longer willing to serve. For days, rumors had circulated that because of Seward's "endeavors to adjust sectional differences"—in other words, to defy his chief and continue pressing for compromise—Lincoln was preparing to dump him and replace him at State with Chase. In truth, Lincoln had tossed one petition calling for Seward's rejection into the fire.[9] Nonetheless Seward now decided to dump himself. Lincoln's "acts of kindness and confidence" toward the New Yorker no longer mattered, as Seward wrote him on March 2. "Circumstances which have occurred since I expressed to you in December last my willingness to accept the office of Secretary of State, seem to me to render it my duty to ask leave to withdraw that consent."[10]

Lincoln might understandably have reacted to this lightning bolt by yielding to the New York senator. Ever since Lincoln had arrived in Washington, Seward had worked to help Lincoln restore his bearings, demonstrating his own indispensability in the process. But the president-elect refused to panic. When Seward's New York ally Simeon Draper led a cleverly timed delegation into Lincoln's suite at Willard's to protest the appointment of Chase, Lincoln called its bluff by offering to reshuffle the cabinet deck altogether, suggesting an entirely new slate of ministers—without Seward included at all. The delegation, many of whose members had job aspirations of their own, hurriedly beat a retreat.[11] For the time, Lincoln said nothing further, and again effectively using the weapon of silence, just as he had done to dampen enthusiasm for compromise, effectively stood his ground. As he told his secretaries: "I can't afford to let Seward take the first trick."[12]

The following morning, the recalcitrant New York senator returned to Willard's to reopen discussions. Lincoln held firm on Cameron and Chase. Seward would either have to join the cabinet as Lincoln shaped it, or risk injuring the party and the incoming administration with a refusal that would, moreover, undoubtedly be judged an act of selfish pique. Whatever their sudden differences, the two men likely found time to discuss the inaugural message this day. The matter of Seward's inclusion in the still unstructured administration, however, remained unsettled.

The uncertainty and confusion had done little to inhibit all the cabinet hopefuls from putting on their bravest faces and gathering together for a gala dinner hosted by Buffalo, New York, congressman Elbridge Spaulding at the National Hotel on the night of February 28. Joining a constellation of celebrities that included Lincoln, General Scott, Thurlow Weed, Peace Convention delegate Dodge, Senators King, Chandler, and Crittenden, and Congressmen Washburne and Adams, along with Judge David Davis and his cousin Henry Winter Davis (who still hoped for a cabinet place of his own), was the full roster of future administration ministers: Chase (Treasury); Cameron (War); Welles (Navy); Blair (Post Office); Smith (Interior); Bates (Attorney General)—and, inevitably, William H. Seward (State).

In a delicious complication, they were joined at the table by Ira Harris, the New Yorker already designated to succeed Seward in the Senate once he joined the administration, and John Sherman, the Ohioan recently chosen to succeed Chase in that same body. Their presence sent a strong message that their predecessors were indeed destined to leave one branch of government for another. Ignoring this real news, the press blandly heralded the glittering affair as "one of the most agreeable entertainments given this season," filled with "some of the most distinguished men of the day," while Adams dismissed it with equal blindness as "quite formal and a little dull."[13] Few observers seemed to notice that it signaled the first public appearance of the entire Lincoln government, even though Inauguration Eve came, and passed, without Lincoln officially informing "a living soul as to whom he designs offering the Cabinet portfolios"—including at least "several" of the aspirants at the banquet.[14]

Lincoln successfully kept his secretary of state–designate in his orbit simply by ignoring his request to be dropped from the cabinet. In the end, every nominee at the National Hotel fete would join Lincoln's official family, though Seward would keep the new president guessing for a day or two more, finally countermanding his withdrawal only after Lincoln wrote Seward on March 4 that both his "personal feelings" and the "public interest" demanded "that you should."[15] Of crucial importance in defining their future relationship, Seward failed to elicit from Lincoln the kind of despairing plea he likely hoped his change of heart would provoke. Nor did Chase earn the kind of effusive assurance of his own value that he so desperately desired. After their meeting with the rest of the peace commissioners on Lincoln's first night in town, the president-elect avoided Chase entirely; the Ohio senator's warnings of the "dreadful consequences" of a Cameron appointment went unheeded.[16]

The man who, some of the public believed, had been too frightened to appear publicly in Baltimore, was not too frightened once he reached Washington to juggle the egos that dwelled within Seward, Chase, and other far more experienced statesmen. Under Lincoln's patient stewardship, ex-Whigs and ex-Democrats, Northerners and border state men, progressives and conservatives, ultimately all came together to serve the Union—and the new president. Lincoln the master political puppeteer—self-effacingly maneuvering the wires—skillfully molded a unity government composed of "an equal number of men of opposing parties in the past," in John Nicolay's admiring assessment.[17] Chicago editor Joseph Medill later offered the opinion that Lincoln fearlessly included "the strongest men of the party" in the cabinet because he felt he had "no right to deprive the country of their service." But as Doris Kearns Goodwin has astutely added, Lincoln was also supremely confident that he was the strongest of them all.[18]

THAT STRENGTH WAS sorely tested by those who still quested insatiably for minor offices and favors big and small, right up until the final hours before Lincoln's inauguration as president. Their letters had begun pouring into Willard's from the moment he checked in, and showed no signs of abating as February ended and March began. Strangers continued questing for influence, even money—one stranger, an Italian opera singer, begged Lincoln to help her pay her "Mortgag"—unconcerned that the president-elect had far more important priorities on his mind.[19] Equally inconsiderate, old friends and political associates alike pelted him with last-minute advice and warnings about ministerial selections.[20] Self-aggrandizement aside, some of the pressure was inspired by genuine fears that Lincoln might grant too many appointments to one wing of the party or another. Salmon P. Chase, for example, believed that abandonment of "the great body of men who elected him"—in other words granting supremacy to conciliators in Seward's camp—represented an "imminent danger."[21]

Augmenting this correspondence was an endless flow of visitors offering unsolicited in-person advice on secession, conciliation, coercion, and cabinet. A clever cartoon created during this period aptly depicted the beleaguered Lincoln as a Gulliver assaulted by "Lilliputian Office-Seekers" swarming over him like insects, whispering in his ears, tugging at his coattails, and clinging to his sleeves. The caricature came astonishingly close to literal truth.[22] As mundane as the patronage process may appear, compared with the dramatic intrigues surrounding slavery compromise, disunion, and cabinet selection, the quest for other offices was never far from Lincoln's mind—or hotel suite—during these hectic days in Washington.

On February 27, one journalist spied "the hungriest-looking crowd with which the President elect has ever been bored." This included the so-called "Dutch element"—German-born Republicans—who "poured in thick and fast," armed with their petitions, until they "vamoosed" in disappointment, unable to corner their prey.[23] John Hay similarly claimed Lincoln was "violently besieged" by the "rabble of office seekers." That he was not "torn in pieces, like Actaeon"—the mythical hunter transformed into prey and killed by his own hounds—Hay attributed to "the vigor of his constitution, and the imperturbability of his temperament.[24]

Arriving in Washington to cover the inauguration, *New York Herald* correspondent Henry Villard was equally astounded to find Willard's overrun by these eager throngs. "Yes," the president-elect shrugged, "it was bad enough in Springfield, but it was child's play compared with this tussle here. I hardly have a chance to eat or sleep. I am fair game for everybody of that hungry lot." But he could still find humor in this situation, too. Learning that one candidate for a military appointment planned to eliminate a rival by challenging him to a fight and killing him, Lincoln was heard to remark: "If the custom could be generally introduced, it might lubricate matters in the way of making political appointments."[25]

Most of the spurned job-seekers and influence-peddlers failed to find humor in the situation. "I have waited some 6 hours with the view of having a five minute interview with thee," one frustrated Marylander penned in a huff from Willard's lobby on February 26, "but all to no purpose." As a "hard worker in the Republican cause," the irate caller believed he more than deserved a private audience. In claiming his "rights," the faithful loyalist neatly summed up the presumptuous determination exhibited by so many office-seekers: "I am unwilling to give up."[26]

Nor, apparently, was Mary Lincoln herself. So new to the capital that she gratefully accepted the gift of a guidebook called *Philp's Washington Described,*[27] Mary nonetheless plunged spiritedly into the patronage morass with which she was equally unfamiliar. "She meddled not only with the distribution of minor offices," Villard complained, "but even with the assignment of places in the Cabinet. Moreover, she allowed herself to be approached and continuously surrounded by a common set of men and women, who, through her susceptibility to even the most barefaced flattery, easily gained a controlling influence over her."[28]

Not until only hours remained before his swearing in did Lincoln's staff finally limit public access to the next president of the United States, terminating his routine of nightly two-hour public levees and posting signs in the hallway that announced he would no longer welcome visitors to Parlor Six.[29] His wife, one assumes, remained exempt from the new restrictions. With or without her cooperation, nonetheless, it was time for Lincoln to focus on polishing his inaugural message.

ALL THAT REMAINED now were the words. To Lincoln, words always mattered most. Newspaper stories lived but a single day, caricatures flamed into view and just as quickly faded, and even the most flattering photographs inevitably receded behind the thick covers of family albums. But words lived forever. Writing, Lincoln believed, was "the great invention of the world."[30]

"Everybody longing for the inaugural," George Templeton Strong reported from New York at the beginning of March. "Feverish anxiety in Wall Street." Grateful to God that "the disgraceful reign of James Buchanan" was at last drawing "near its close," Strong believed the nation's future might well hinge on "the tone of Lincoln's Inaugural."[31]

As for Lincoln, he likely understood that while he still had "a task before me greater than that which rested upon Washington"—as he had boasted on leaving Springfield—he first faced an inaugural challenge more like that which had confronted Thomas Jefferson. The third president's bitterly won 1800 victory had fractured the country, but inspired one of the most conciliatory inaugural addresses in history. Lincoln had drafted his own rather defiant speech weeks earlier, in the absence of knowledge gleaned since. It now cried out for revision, perhaps to lighten its bellicose original tone. He had composed it in the seclusion of a makeshift hideaway back in Springfield, reasonably free from interruption—or advice. Here in Washington, as the clock ticked away and the hour of his swearing in drew near, he turned to the task of perfecting his text with no similar hope of quiet or privacy.

Instead, wisely taking advantage of the proximity of—and frequent visits by—so many distinguished statesmen, Lincoln began sharing printed drafts with a widening body of readers. Editor Francis Preston Blair, Sr., was one of the first in the capital asked to review the text. The Marylander "highly commended it, suggesting no changes."[32] Other leading Republicans likely earned glances or recitations of their own, though the record remains murky.

One reader was almost certainly Lincoln's onetime law partner Stephen Trigg Logan, "almost a father to me," as Lincoln described him, serving now as an Illinois delegate to the Peace Convention.[33] At the very least, Lincoln shared with him the crucial passage that began with the vow: "All the power at my disposal will be used to reclaim the public property and places which have fallen."[34] Logan begged Lincoln to damp down the provocative language. "I have great respect for your opinion," the president-elect replied, "but the statements you think should be modified were carefully considered by me—and the probable consequences, as far as I can anticipate them." If there was "patriotism enough in the American people," he insisted, "the Union will be saved; if not, it will go down, and I will go with it."[35] In the end, however, Lincoln recast the sentence after all. The phrase, "All the power at my disposal" became the far more benign: "The power confided to me."[36]

Springfield editor William H. Bailhache was emboldened to write home on March 3 that he believed Lincoln's "original draft has been modified every day to suit the views of the different members of the Cabinet" as well. Bailhache, whose printers had committed Lincoln's first draft to type, and therefore was familiar with its contents, had just arrived in Washington from Springfield to witness its delivery in person. There, he learned enough to accurately predict a "softening [of] some of the words & elaborating more at length some of the ideas contained in the original draft."[37] The Bailhache correspondence persuasively suggests that Lincoln in fact relied on a wider circle of advisors than previously imagined—Bailhache himself likely among them.

Lincoln may even have included at least one Democrat among his reviewers: none other than Stephen A. Douglas, to whom Lincoln evidently read the same passage he had shared with Stephen Logan, or perhaps the edited version that superseded it. Somewhat encouraged by what he heard, Douglas conveyed its "spirit and intent" to at least one confidant before the March 4 ceremony.[38] But he may still have hoped for a yet more conciliatory rewrite. As late as Inauguration Day, the pro-

Douglas *New York Herald* predicted that Lincoln would be "holding out the sword and not the olive branch."[39]

Clinging to the opposite view, George Templeton Strong confided to his diary that New York banker Robert Lenox Kennedy had "seen private dispatches assuring him it would be a conciliatory and emollient paper" instead. For himself, Strong still agreed with the more "general belief" that the speech would "announce Lincoln's intention to uphold the law; to reinforce Fort Sumter . . . to retake the other forts now in the hands of the rebellion; and to collect federal revenue, by blockade or otherwise, at every Southern port." The attorney hoped this was so, pointing out: "How can Lincoln say anything else, if he allude to the subject of secession at all, and how can he ignore it without shame? The logic of the situation is inexorable, and war is the only possible deduction from the premises." Besides, as the perceptive Strong noted, nothing Lincoln could say was likely to prevent civil war, "however pacific, fair, and reasonable" his inaugural address might be.[40]

Ever hopeful for compromise, William H. Seward maintained otherwise, and it was he who in the end exacted the greatest influence over the pugnacious draft Lincoln shared with him shortly after his arrival in Washington. It was Seward, still vowing to "adhere" to him faithfully even if he would not serve in his cabinet,[41] who contributed the most to making his address more "pacific" than Lincoln originally intended.

Along the way to Washington, Lincoln had continued to labor on his text—progressively toning it down around the edges, heeding the advice of advisors like Orville Browning, and perhaps concluding that with compromise proposals still floating in the air, he could hardly enter the capital armed with blustering ultimatums. Thus the entire section defiantly upholding an elected president's right to rule—or risk betraying those who elected him—ended up on the cutting room floor. Though Lincoln had once hoped to adopt some of it for a speech to Kentuckians, the opportunity had never gelled. He had paraphrased the notion at other venues en route to the capital and perhaps felt that reiterating it now was unnecessary. Smaller handwritten editorial alternations—

changing "repeating" to "re-stating," or modifying the "execution" of patronage power to its "exercise"—now littered the typeset pages.[42]

Lincoln had also scrawled longer handwritten inserts. He would, for example, add a pledge that he would not "attempt to force obnoxious strangers" on the South. This seems at first glance trivial: after all, the six new Confederate states had not seceded over the prospect of enduring an influx of Republican postmasters. But for Lincoln, who prized his patronage-dispensing prerogatives, it was no small concession to "forego for the time, the uses of such offices." Lincoln also discarded altogether a scolding reference to the "melancholy mistake" of any effort to "break up the government" for what he believed to be an "imaginary cause."

In a different vein, he added a provocative new section on the judiciary, praising its faithful attention to duty, but warning that "if the policy of the government, upon vital questions, affecting the whole people, is to be irrevocably fixed by decisions of the Supreme Court, it is plain that the people will have ceased to be their own rulers, having turned their government over to the despotism of the few life-officers composing the Court." Relying on unelected "life officers," he added, was an invitation to "despotism" (he later substantially softened this argument, too). Weighing the pattern of all these alterations, historian Douglas L. Wilson has convincingly argued that after carefully reconsidering his early drafts, Lincoln chose to use his inaugural not to rebut others' arguments for the right to secede but to affirm his own belief in the inviolability of the Union.[43]

We do not know precisely when the president-elect first shared his printed text with his secretary of state–designate and asked for his input: it might have been as early as Lincoln's first day in Washington, Saturday, February 23, but more likely occurred at Seward's home the following day over luncheon after church. If so, Hannibal Hamlin, who joined them that day as well, probably found himself brought into the widening circle of advisors and editors that already included David Davis, Carl Schurz, Orville Browning, and Francis Preston Blair.

Much to his credit, Seward took to his task passionately, restricted only by the limits of his own writing ability. Within hours, he took the seven-page typescript and methodically numbered each of its 225 lines of copy—this to facilitate reference to the corrections, additions, and deletions he would propose. This was a good start: Lincoln liked to make lists himself, and probably admired people who liked to make them as well.

By nightfall, Seward forwarded more than four dozen proposed revisions to Lincoln. "I have suggested many changes of little importance severally," he explained in his cover note, "but, in their general effect tending to soothe the public mind." Overall, he advised Lincoln not to fear the "displeasure" of fellow Republicans should he recalibrate his message toward conciliation, reminding him: "They will be loyal, whatever is said." Like Jefferson sixty years earlier, he urged, Lincoln should practice "the magnanimity of a victor." The third president, Seward noted, "sank the partisan in the patriot in his inaugural address."[44] Lincoln should do likewise.

Apparently convinced of their efficacy, and no doubt hopeful that his enthusiasm for them might persuade Seward back into the cabinet, Lincoln adopted, by scholar Ronald C. White's careful count, twenty-seven of the forty-nine proposed editorial changes contained in the four-page report.[45] These included Seward's impassioned recommendations that Lincoln both soften his pledge to adhere to the principles of the 1860 Republican platform, and substantially soften his vow to reclaim and hold federal property in the South. The latter declarations, Seward predicted, even if edited, would "give such advantages to the Disunionists that Virginia and Maryland will secede, and we shall within ninety, perhaps within sixty, days be obliged to fight the South for this capital, with a divided North for our residence, and we shall not have one loyal magistrate or ministerial officer south of the Potomac." Should he fail to delete these paragraphs, Seward warned, "the dismemberment of the republic would date from the inauguration of a Republican Administration."[46]

Seward's modest assessment that his suggestions carried "little importance" to the speech understated their overall impact: the cumulative effect was to markedly palliate its tone. Lincoln's most recent draft, for example, argued that a "disruption of the Federal Union" had not only been "menaced" but "already effected." Seward urged him to replace the phrase with "heretofore only menaced is now formidably attempted." Perhaps against his better judgment—for Lincoln typically shunned words like "heretofore"—he agreed. Similarly, Lincoln had planned to warn of the consequences should the minority refuse to "submit." Seward preferred "acquiesce." Later in the text, "submission" would be replaced by "acquiescence." In this manner "rule" became "practice," and the notion that "the moral sense of the people is against" the Fugitive Slave Laws was supplanted by the fact that "it imperfectly supports" the law itself. Lincoln went along with all these changes.

Further, Seward advised Lincoln to delete his thundering reference to "the despotism of the few life officers" of the Supreme Court. Lincoln agreed even to this change, retaining only the warning against turning government over entirely to "that eminent tribunal."[47] Satisfied with his contributions, Seward could not help telling a group of ten men at dinner on March 3 that the address was "a very sensible paper" and predicted it would "give general satisfaction." While he refused to share details, he did concede Lincoln's impressive intellect, confiding he sensed "a vein of imagination and sentiment running through Mr. Lincoln's mind" that he thought "outweighed all his other qualities."[48]

The most substantive of all William Seward's inaugural suggestions was that Lincoln conclude his speech on a more uplifting, less threatening, note than the harsh words that originally constituted its final phrase: the dare, "Shall it be peace or a sword?" Seward believed Lincoln's overarching argument was "strong and conclusive and ought not to be in any way abridged or modified." But he argued that "something besides or in addition to argument is needful—to meet and remove the prejudice and passion in the South, and despondency in the East." To accomplish this goal, Seward proposed "Some words of affection—some of calm and cheerful confidence."[49]

A surviving sheet of paper in what appears to be the handwriting of Seward's son and secretary, Frederick, indicates that he had just such an ending in mind. Labeled "Suggestions for a closing paragraph" and enclosed along with his line-by-line edits, it was an earnest, but lumbering, recapitulation of thoughts Lincoln had expressed along the journey to Washington: his loyalty to all sections of the country, his adherence to the Constitution; and his reliance on the spirit of the founders. But in Seward's hands, the sentiments emerged far too ponderously to fit Lincoln's concise argumentation and muscular narrative structure.

As Nicolay and Hay delicately explained: "The literary styles of Mr. Seward and Mr. Lincoln differed essentially. Mr. Seward was strongly addicted to long, sonorous sentences," while "Mr. Lincoln liked to condense his idea[s]." Seward wanted Lincoln to sacrifice "brevity and force" in order to gain "greater ambiguity," and this Lincoln would never do.[50] This is the blunderbuss paragraph that Seward originally submitted as a peroration for Lincoln's inaugural address:

> However unusual it may be at such a time to speak of sections or to sections, yet in view of the misconceptions & agitations which have strained the ties of brotherhood so far, I hope it will not be deemed a departure from propriety, whatever it may be from custom, to say that if in the criminations and misconstructions which too often imbue our political contests, any man south of this capital has been led to believe that I regard with a less friendly eye, his rights, his interests or his domestic safety and happiness or those of his State, than I do those of any other portion of my country or that I would invade or disturb any legal right or domestic institution in the South, he mistakes both my principles and feelings, and does not know me. I aspire to come in the spirit, however far below the ability and the wisdom, of Washington, of Madison, of Jackson and of Clay. In that spirit I here declare that in my Administration I shall know no rule but the Constitution, no guide but the laws, and no sentiment but those of equal devotion to my whole country, east, west, north and south.[51]

We do not know exactly how Lincoln responded to this bloated mess, although stylistic incongruities aside, one imagines that, having taken to comparing himself to George Washington, the president-elect certainly did not now intend confessing that he lacked his ability. We can only marvel that he encouraged Seward to try anew. Perhaps this was the very moment Lincoln conceived or shared the captivating sentence he wrote on the back of Orville Browning's earlier comments on the inaugural—"Americans all, we are not enemies, but friends"—although it is equally possible that Lincoln jotted down this line later, working in solitude, all of the suggestions from all of his advisors arrayed before him as he labored to unite them into a master text.[52] Despite his original failure, Seward went back to work, and this time came back with a shorter and, for him, more condensed, expression whose prose sounded at least a bit more Lincolnian:

> I close. We are not we must not be aliens or enemies but fellow countrymen and brethren. Although passion has strained our bonds of affection too hardly they must not, I am sure they will not be broken. The mystic chords which proceeding from so many battle fields and so many patriot graves pass through all the hearts and all the hearths in this broad continent of ours will yet again harmonize in their ancient music when breathed upon by the guardian angel of the nation.[53]

The notion of harmonizing broad continents or appealing to "brethren" to avoid alienation still sounded clankingly discordant, but "mystic chords" and "patriot graves" appealed to Lincoln's ear for bold imagery. This time he accepted his advisor's suggestions in principle, and agreeing to excise his "peace or a sword" ending entirely, went to work massaging Seward's latest draft into perfection. With extraordinary deftness, Lincoln took Seward's paragraph in hand and improved it almost magically. The subtle but transformative changes that Lincoln imposed demonstrated, as historian Don E. Fehrenbacher has pointed out, a gift for editing nearly as formidable as his gift for writing.[54] Rather than merely heralding his intention of closing his speech, for example, Lincoln would announce that he was loath to do so—as if reluctant to tear himself away from his fellow countrymen. Seward's long, ponderous sentences became short bursts of Lincolnian emotion. Flaming "hearths" became comforting "hearthstones." The fatuous word "proceeding" became the evocative one, "stretching." The deadly reference to "ancient music" was vivified into a throbbing "chorus." The nation's "guardian angel" became its "better angels"—although Seward deserves credit for this expression: he had ill-advisedly crossed the phrase out of his draft, and Lincoln wisely resurrected it.

Lincoln's revision not only affirmed his ability to write and rewrite in his own, singularly original, quintessentially American voice, but demonstrated his remarkable feel for dramatic expression, not to mention an uncanny ability to rise to great occasions under pressure. By significantly altering Seward's peroration, Lincoln transformed a reasonably good closing paragraph into something sublime and unforgettable. This is how Lincoln decided to close his inaugural address:

> I am loth [sic] to close. We are not enemies, but friends. We must not be enemies. Though passion may have strained, it must not break our bonds of affection. The mystic chords of memory, stretching from every battle-field, and patriot grave, to every living heart and hearthstone, all over this broad land, will yet swell the chorus of the Union, when again touched, as surely they will be, by the better angels of our nature.[55]

To the tolling of bells on Sunday morning, March 3, crowds massed outside Willard's in the hope of catching a glimpse of the president-elect when he headed to church. But if Lincoln said any prayers that final Sabbath before his inauguration, he did so privately. On his very last day as a private citizen, he remained indoors, still hard at work polishing the speech he knew would end the interregnum, either prevent or provoke revolution, and perhaps define his entire presidency on its very first day. Back on the streets, his public had to make do with brand-new lithographs of " 'Uncle Abe,' damp from the press—a good likeness, with the new crop of whiskers sported by the new President brought out in fine relief." For a few hours more, such "counterfeit presentments" would have to suffice.[56]

IF THE PHILADELPHIA *Inquirer* was right—in predicting that the "vast vista of the future will take its color from the sunshine or clouds which will mark the political horizon after noon today"[57]—then the nation's prospects seemed splendid indeed by late Monday morning, March 4. After waking to "leaden skies, tornadoes of dust," and "a slight fall of rain," one spectator testified, "the clouds disappeared and the sun came out gloriously bright." As another, equally superstitious newspaperman exulted, these "auguries" thrilled "those who put faith upon such omens."[58] "At last," an excited Charles Francis Adams exhaled, "the long expected day dawned upon us . . . mild and clear." He was about to witness his first presidential inauguration.[59]

So was Abraham Lincoln. Anxious and virtually sleepless, he got out of bed at 5 A.M., quietly breakfasted with his family, then excused himself "to his closet" to gird for the momentous day. Sometime during the morning, Seward came to call for final discussions about the closing words of the inaugural. Later that morning, as the weather outside turned "cool and bracing," Lincoln decided he must hear—rather than speak—the address for himself. He asked his son Robert to do the honors, and for half an hour the president-elect, perhaps the most discerning and demanding of all his audiences, listened to his own words read back to him one final time.[60]

Outside his windows, meanwhile, Washington sprang to life, bedecked with stars and stripes, reverberating to patriotic music, and the relentless sound of drum and fife, and looking unusually clean, laborers having worked for days to clear mud and debris from the roads between the White House and Capitol—and with it, drunks, rowdies, and pickpockets. "All business, public and private, was suspended, and the display of the national flag from innumerable buildings gave great liveliness to the scene," a journalist reported.[61]

But there was no ignoring the added, clanking presence of the military. Mary Lincoln's cousin Elizabeth Todd Grimsley observed "files of cavalry, troops of infantry, riflemen, and a battery of artillery" deployed along the streets, "all betokening the feeling of unrest and possible danger."[62] To the mysterious observer, a Public Man, "Nothing could have been more ill-advised or more ostentatious than the way in which the troops were thrust everywhere upon the public attention, even to the roofs of the houses on Pennsylvania Avenue, on which little squads of sharpshooters were absurdly stationed."[63]

But few other civilians seemed to mind. By daybreak, celebrants began lining Pennsylvania Avenue on foot and in carriages, and as early as 8 A.M. "the streets adjacent to . . . the Capitol were nearly impassable from the crowds of people."[64] By noon, "Every available spot was black with human beings; boys and men clinging to rails and mounting on fences and climbing trees until they bent beneath the weight."[65] By the time Lincoln stepped outside for the ceremony, more than 25,000 people stood waiting for his arrival—and his speech.

Shortly after noon, an elegant liveried carriage rolled up to the side entrance of Willard's Hotel. As an eyewitness testified: "A large, heavy, awkward-moving man, far advanced in years . . . head curiously inclined to the left shoulder," wearing "a low-crowned, broad-brimmed silk hat, an immense white cravat like a poultice," and a "swallow-tail coat not of the newest style," emerged and lumbered into the building. "It was President Buchanan," delayed by last-minute bill-signings, "calling to take his successor to the Capitol."[66] (By prearrangement, Senators James Dixon and John P. Hale had called for Mary and escorted her to the Capitol at 11:15.[67])

A few minutes later, Lincoln and Buchanan emerged onto crowded 14th Street to the first applause of the day, as soldiers surrounding the entrance snapped to a smart salute and a band struck up "Hail to the Chief." The two men then took their seats side by side in the open brett, facing Edward Dickinson Baker of Oregon and James A. Pearce of Maryland, attending them as the official Senate escort committee.[68] Lincoln looked resplendent. He wore his new, Chicago-made cashmere suit, a high silk hat perched on his head, and "to cap the climax of novelty," gripped an incongruous gold-tipped ebony cane.[69] In all the excitement, he had neglected to pay his $773.75 hotel bill. Not until he was dunned for the balance six weeks later did an "annoyed" president acknowledge the embarrassing discrepancy and order his secretary to make good the outstanding balance.[70]

Followed by floats, marching bands, swarms of politicians, and regiments of uniformed soldiers—by nineteenth-century tradition the ritual inaugural parade occurred before, rather than after, the swearing in— the head carriage now clattered slowly onto broad Pennsylvania Avenue, and turned left toward Capitol Hill. That was the signal for the rest of the long procession to come to life and follow. Marching into lockstep behind the presidential barouche came squadrons of Wide-Awakes, the "mounted marshals four files deep," and delegations representing all the loyal states, along with grizzled veterans of both the War of 1812, their ranks sparse, and of the more recent Mexican War, which Lincoln had once opposed. Then came a richly decorated "tableau car" drawn by six white horses, crowded with thirty-four seated young women to represent each of the states, their float "surmounted by a handsome gilt eagle."[71] A snide reporter could not help noticing that "the pretty girls who represented the North and the South were quarreling typically." This did not prevent Lincoln from later bestowing kisses on all of them.[72]

However imposing the procession, however well behaved the crowds, there was no denying the restless, crackling tension that lurked behind the pomp. One cavalry officer who hovered near the presidential barouche admitted he used his spurs unflinchingly—by design—to keep all the nearby steeds "in an uneasy state, so that it would have been very difficult for even a very good rifle shot to get an aim at one of the inmates of the carriage between the dancing horses."[73] As a result, it grew increasingly difficult for onlookers on Pennsylvania Avenue to "distinguish Mr. Lincoln" behind the wall of troops. In the words of one observer: "It seemed more like escorting a prisoner to his doom than a President to his inauguration."[74]

Watching the scene, an outraged Southern journalist fumed: "I have seen today such a sight as I could never have believed possible at the capital of my country. An inauguration of a President surrounded by armed soldiery, with loaded pieces and fixed bayonets. The President himself hid from public view . . . did not look either to the right or the

James Buchanan and Abraham Lincoln ride down Pennsylvania Avenue in the hour-long parade that preceded that March 4, 1861, inauguration. This woodcut stressed unity and showed no sign of the military presence that dominated the procession. (LIBRARY OF CONGRESS)

left, and it was only occasionally that he raised his hat," instead fixing his stare "vacantly at the bottom of the carriage." The reporter insisted that there was "no enthusiasm exhibited—no cheering—and with but very few exceptions the ladies remained motionless at the windows, and looked upon the pageant without manifesting the slightest feeling."[75] But as Frederick Douglass pointed out, "No mean courage was required to face the probabilities of the hour." Lincoln, the African-American leader declared, "stood up before the pistol or dagger of the sworn assassin, to meet death from an unknown hand, while upon the very threshold of the office to which the suffrages of the nation had elected him."[76]

Even the highly partisan *Baltimore Sun* acknowledged the presence of thousands of "enthusiastic Lincolnites . . . who thronged the avenue on each side as far as the eye could reach."[77] Marshal-in-chief Benjamin Brown French believed: "No more imposing or more orderly pageant ever passed along Pennsylvania Avenue,"[78] and a local journalist agreed, calling it "the most brilliant and imposing pageant ever witnessed" in the entire capital.[79] At one point along their tense ride, legend holds, a beaming Buchanan turned to his successor and reportedly exclaimed: "My dear sir, if you are as happy in entering the White House as I shall feel on returning to Wheatland, you are a happy man indeed." To which Lincoln supposedly replied: "Mr. President, I cannot say that I shall enter it with much pleasure, but I assure you that I shall do what I can to maintain the high standards set by my illustrious predecessors who have occupied it."[80] It nearly amounted to a compliment.

When the procession finally arrived at the north doors of the Capitol about an hour later, Lincoln took Buchanan's arm in a gesture of unity, and together they entered the building along an extemporized wood-plank walkway to watch the swearing in of the new vice president, Hannibal Hamlin, in the Senate chamber. To accommodate the crowd there, its desks had been cleared, and additional seating installed. Above, its galleries were "crowded to repletion." An onlooker noticed that after their long ride, both the incoming and outgoing chief executives appeared to be covered with dust." To eyewitness Charles Francis

Adams, the incumbent "looked old and worn out," his successor, "awkward and out of place."[81]

Taking seats in the front row facing the vice president's desk, a flushed Buchanan "sighed audibly and frequently." Not a sound was heard from Lincoln, who remained as "grave and impassive as an Indian martyr" during the "solemn" and "memorable" ceremony.[82] Once Hamlin swore his oath, all the dignitaries formed a line and proceeded through the Capitol Rotunda and out onto the East Portico, led by Marshal of the District of Columbia French, and the justices of the Supreme Court, and then followed down the stairs by the president and the president-elect.[83] Lincoln's first appearance outdoors at the top of the Capitol steps unleashed "a most glorious shout of welcome" from the throngs below him in the plaza—"immense cheering," according to another description—as the Marine Band struck up the national anthem.[84]

One by one, senators, congressmen, and the entire diplomatic corps in "gorgeous" full court dress, descended in a line toward the square-roofed wooden canopy hastily erected at the portico's base "to protect the President Elect from possible rain."[85] On the bottom step, beneath this makeshift structure, stood a "miserable little rickety table" that someone had evidently salvaged from a storage room to serve as a rostrum; it held only a water pitcher and drinking glass.

To one well-placed onlooker, Lincoln appeared "pale and very nervous"[86] as he took a seat in the front row under the canopy near Buchanan and Taney, but there was no denying he looked young and vigorous alongside the two elderly Democrats. From deep in the crowd, an excited spectator was "much surprised at Lincoln's youthful looks," adding: "Instead of being a long, lean, lank, clumsy individual, he is very genteel, easy and graceful."[87]

Even from the outskirts of the vast crowd, larger than had ever attended a presidential inaugural, the spectacle must have looked dazzling. Elbow-to-elbow in seats to the left of the canopy crowded diplomats, members of Congress, robed associate justices, and scores of assorted dignitaries. To the immediate right sat a proud Robert Lincoln,

John Nicolay, and John Hay, along with various uniformed officers, their eyes fixed on the "many thousand citizens assembled in the grounds, filling the square and open space, and perching on every tree, fence, and stone affording a convenient point from which to see or hear." Ladies "by the score," Mary Lincoln included, huddled in a separate section behind the men.[88]

Tradition dictated that inaugural addresses precede, rather than follow, the oath-taking. In effect, Lincoln would speak before officially becoming president. So at precisely 1:30 P.M., with everyone successfully assembled, Senator Edward Dickinson Baker—the man who had journeyed to Springfield to congratulate Lincoln on Election Day, and for whom, years earlier, the Lincolns' late son had been lovingly named—moved to the base of the portico and in a "silvery" voice launched the ceremony with this simple announcement: "Fellow-citizens: I introduce you to Abraham Lincoln, the President-elect of the United States of America!"[89] (Tragically, just seven months later, Baker would become one of the most prominent early casualties of the Civil War.)

To a "slight ripple of applause,"[90] by one account, Lincoln untangled himself from his chair, rose to his full height, and approached the central table, still grasping his hat and cane. As he began searching awkwardly for a place to store them, Stephen Douglas, of all people, came to the rescue from his seat at the far left, reaching over and offering to take possession of the accessories. Lincoln gratefully surrendered his silk topper. "If I cannot be President," the Little Giant supposedly whispered to his lifelong political foe, "I can at least be his hat-bearer."[91] It was, an eyewitness admitted, "a trifling act, but a symbolical one, and not to be forgotten."[92] (No one would have suspected that an exhausted Douglas would be dead within months, after a fruitless national tour to advocate reunion.)

Now, at last, Lincoln stood alone and bareheaded, facing the vast audience, bowing low to renewed applause and cheers. Then, calmly placing his cane on the table, he reached into his breast pocket and produced his freshly revised inaugural address, some of it pasted together with glue from a series of drafts and inserts, several of its paragraph indentations now highlighted by small pointed fingers that Lincoln had sketched himself. With slow-motion deliberation, he methodically lay the papers on the little table before him, and placed his cane on top of the sheaf to hold it fast in the March breeze. Still utterly composed, he extracted his spectacles from his trousers and slowly adjusted them on his nose, every little gesture drawing either "wild cheers" or deadly silence—the varying recollections tinged by political bias. One insisted that Lincoln "could not make a movement, however slight, which did not elicit rounds of applause." But another held that the audience remained so noiselessly transfixed by Lincoln's methodical preparations that it could hear the loud snap of his steel eyeglass case as he closed it shut, and then responded with laughter as Lincoln fumbled with his spectacles. This eyewitness claimed that someone far back in the crowd hissed, "Look at old goggles!" before police moved in to make an arrest.[93] Hours earlier, plainclothesmen had "scattered through the mass" to "strike down any hand which might raise a weapon." Sensitive to the slightest danger, they would not even tolerate heckling.[94]

Whether applauded or not, the *New York Tribune* maintained that Lincoln's bearing remained "deliberate and impressive" at this solemn moment, though Henri Mercier, the elegant French minister, caustically likened this plain American's appearance amid the "marble and gilt" of the Capital to inaugurating "a Quaker in a Basilica."[95] Buchanan and Taney leaned forward and gazed intently to listen for his introductory words.

"Fellow citizens of the United States!" Lincoln began. He gave pronounced emphasis to the word "united," to an eruption of "loud cheers."[96]

Lincoln opened with the sentence he had first composed in Springfield and changed little since: "In compliance with a custom as old as the government itself, I appear before you to address you briefly, and to take, in your presence, the oath prescribed by the Constitution of the United States, to be taken by the President 'before he enters on the execution of his office.' " Charles Francis Adams, who appraised the ceremony as "grand in its simplicity," noted that Lincoln spoke "in a clear, distinct voice which was heard by every body."[97] Agreeing that Lincoln's voice was "loud and distinct," the *Washington Intelligencer* was less sanguine

7

improved, I make no recommendations of amendments. I am, rather, for the old ship, and the chart of the old pilots. If, however, the people desire a new, or an altered vessel, the matter is exclusively their own, and they can move in the premises, as well without as with an executive recommendation. I shall place no obstacle in the way of what may appear to be their wishes.

The Chief Magistrate derives all his authority from the people, and they have conferred none upon him to fix terms for the separation of the States. The people themselves can do this *also* if they choose; but the executive, as such, has nothing to do with it. His duty is to administer the present government, as it came to his hands, and to transmit it, unimpaired by him, to his successor.

Why should there not be a patient confidence in the ultimate justice of the people? Is there any better or equal hope, in the world? In our present differences, is either party without faith *of being* in the right? If the Almighty Ruler of nations, with his eternal truth and justice, be on *on your side of the North, or on* *yours of the South,* that truth and that justice, will surely prevail, by the judgment of this great tribunal, the American people.

By the frame of the government under which we live, this same people have wisely given their public servants but little power for mischief; and have, with equal wisdom, provided for the return of that little to their own hands at very short intervals. While the people *retain their virtue, and vigilence, no administration* by any extreme of wickedness or folly, can very seriously injure the government, in the short space of four years. My countrymen, one and all, *think calmly and* well, upon this whole subject. Nothing valuable can be lost by taking time. If there be an object to *hurry* any of you, in hot haste, to a step which you would never take *deliberately*, that object will be frustrated by taking time; but no good object can be frustrated by it. Such of you as are now dissatisfied, still have the old Constitution unimpaired, and, on the sensitive point, the laws of your own framing under it; while the new administration will have no immediate power, if it would, to change either. If it were admitted that you who are dissatisfied, hold the right side in the dispute, there still is no single good reason for precipitate action. Intelligence, patriotism, Christianity, and a firm reliance on Him, who has never yet forsaken this favored land, are still competent to adjust, in the best way, all our present difficulty.

In *your* hands, my dissatisfied fellow countrymen, and not in *mine*, is the momentous issue of civil war. The government will not assail *you.* You can have no conflict, without being yourselves the aggressors. You have no oath registered in Heaven to destroy the government, while *I* shall have the most solemn one to "preserve, protect and defend" it.

7744

I am loth to close. We are not enemies, but friends— We must not be enemies. Though passion may have strained, it must not break our bonds of affection. The mystic chords of memory, streching from every battle-field, and patriot grave, to every living heart and hearthstone, all over this broad land, will yet swell the chorus of the Union, when again touched, as surely they will be, by the better angels of our nature.

The final page of the manuscript Lincoln read on Inauguration Day. The printed text has been cut and pasted, and bears a final paragraph in the president-elect's own hand. Lincoln drew the hand-shaped paragraph indentation mark himself.
(LINCOLN PAPERS, LIBRARY OF CONGRESS)

about its carrying power: in the days before electronic amplification it reported that he was heard by "at least ten thousand persons before him"—if so, perhaps half of the vast throng that ringed the plaza—still no small accomplishment for an outdoor speaker.[98] Most of the special guests seated behind Lincoln caught only a smattering of his words.

As always, Lincoln read slowly, disdaining gesture, enunciating as clearly as he could to make sure his words cut through the chill air and penetrated the huge audience. He wanted this crowd to hear every sentence: wanted it to fully digest his assurance to the South there was no reason for "apprehension"; his vow to uphold the Constitution and the laws, even those requiring "the delivering up" of fugitive slaves; his immutable belief in the perpetuity of the Union; the declaration of his "simple duty" to make certain the government would "defend, and maintain itself"; and his assertion that, "Physically speaking, we cannot separate. We cannot remove our respective sections from each other, nor build an impassible wall between them . . . ."

"Intelligence, patriotism, Christianity, and firm reliance on Him, who has never yet forsaken this favored land," he assured the country, "are still competent to adjust, in the best way, all our present difficulty." And mere mortals could hardly overcome divine intervention. "While the people retain their virtue, and vigilance," he insisted, "no administration, by any extreme of wickedness or folly, can very seriously injure the government, in the short space of four years."

"I never listened to a speaker whose enunciation was so clear and distinct," remembered an awe-struck eyewitness named Charles Aldrich. ". . . You not only heard every word that he uttered, but every sentence was most clearly expressed. I believe his voice was perfectly audible to every one of the people who occupied the acres before and around him." Yet a Virginian in the audience thought Lincoln must be "consumptive" because of the way his voice trailed off enunciating long words like "Constitution." In "making use of the word reiterate," the onlooker added, "he pronounced it—re-*i*-te-rate," complaining "perhaps it is proper, but it don't sound right to me, in making use of the word 'national' he—calls it "*naa*-ti-on-al. . . ." Stephen A. Douglas did not seem to mind. Lincoln's old rival was heard more than once responding to the speech in a low voice, "Good," "That's so," and "no coercion," sounding much like the partisans who had once shouted encouragement to both orators during their spirited 1858 debates."[99]

To some, not surprising, Lincoln sounded unyielding. "Physically speaking," he made clear, "we cannot separate." The Union was older than the Constitution: it was "perpetual" and could not be dissolved. These sentiments he softened by vowing, "there will be no invasion— no using of force against, or among the people anywhere," unless, that is, quickly shifting his tone yet again, "current events, and experience, shall show a modification, or change, to be proper." In any case, "the laws of the Union" would be "faithfully executed in all the states." To this indistinct pledge he added his "patient confidence in the ultimate justice of the people" and his assurance that "there needs to be no blood- shed or violence"; that he could do no harm in four years that voters could not correct by electing someone else later; and that the country, "with its institutions, belongs to the people who inhabit it." But he left little doubt that slaves would never inhabit America's new territories. The federal government, he assured those who would read his words in the South, would "never interfere with the domestic institutions of the States, including that of persons held to service." To do so would violate the Constitution.

That did not mean Lincoln was prepared to extinguish the moral lights that had always guided him. "One section of our country believes slavery is *right*, and ought to be extended," he declared, repeating virtu- ally word for word the message he had sent to Georgia's Alexander H. Stephens months before, "while the other believes it is *wrong*, and ought not to be extended. That is the only substantial dispute." Perhaps so, but no American president had ever publicly declared slavery to be a "wrong." Few alert listeners could have been shocked to hear such a pronouncement from the nation's first Republican chief executive. But it made history nonetheless.

Then came his penultimate paragraph—still constituting a roar of challenge, even in the absence of its "peace or sword" climax: "In *your* hands, my dissatisfied fellow countrymen, and not in *mine*, is the momentous issue of civil war. The government will not assail *you*."—at Seward's suggestion, he had cut the provocative antiphony "unless you *first* assail *it*"—"You can have no conflict, without being yourselves the aggressors. *You* have no oath registered in Heaven to destroy the government, while *I* shall have the most solemn one to 'preserve, protect and defend' it." And finally he pronounced the coda he had honed from William Seward's clumsy draft: surely "the chorus of the Union" would swell anew, he concluded, his ringing voice finally faltering with emotion, "when again touched, as surely they will be, by the better angels of our nature."[100]

No one could quite agree on how the massive crowd responded. Aldrich remembered that when he spoke the climactic closing words, Lincoln was "greeted with deafening cheers, which seemed to carry with them an expression of highest confidence." The *Times* added that the final passage "broke the watering pot" among many in the crowd deeply moved by the emotional closing. But eyewitness Stephen Fiske insisted that Lincoln's appeal to "the better angels of our nature" evoked "no response" at all. The disappointed orator, he remembered, "bowed his head as if in silent prayer," and "sighed wearily as if he knew that he had failed to touch the Southern heart."[101] The truth probably lies somewhere in between these two partisan recollections.

When Lincoln was done, a visibly "agitated" Chief Justice Taney, trembling now either "with age or with anxiety," his "cadaverous countenance" reminding one observer of "a galvanized corpse,"[102] shuffled toward the central table to administer his eighth presidential oath. Raising his head uncomfortably high in order to face the gigantic man who had just denounced the judiciary he had led for decades,[103] Taney dutifully invited him to repeat the traditional declaration. In measured tones, Lincoln pronounced the timeworn words: "I Abraham Lincoln, do solemnly swear that I will faithfully execute the office of President of the United States, and will to the best of my ability, preserve, protect, and defend the Constitution of the United States." In an uncharacteristically extravagant gesture, Lincoln took the tattered Bible from Taney's hands and kissed it.[104]

He was ready at last to serve. The long interregnum—the cold winter of secession—the frustration of responsibility without power—was finally over. The crisis of the Union was beginning in earnest. Lincoln had successfully maintained a masterly inactivity and public silence to prevent the spread of slavery, privately fought a bare-knuckle political battle to bar unprincipled compromise, and brilliantly introduced himself to the press and people of the North with a new look, new images, and a new style of informal oratory along a triumphant voyage to the capital. And then, despite a giant step backward at Baltimore that might have crippled less agile leaders, he had recaptured public confidence while harmonizing a balanced and brilliant cabinet. And he had crafted one of the nimblest and most eloquent of all inaugural addresses, one that not only reiterated his devotion to the rule of law and invoked the emotional power of national tradition, but maintained that slavery could be contained without compromising founding principles. But of course, the greatest challenge—"the tug," as Lincoln had called it—was yet to come.

If he lifted his gaze from Taney's at this, the greatest moment of his life, but the most dangerous in the nation's, Lincoln would have noticed, beyond the "sea of upturned faces"—reflecting "every shade of feeling: hatred, discontent, anxiety, and admiration"[105]—the mammoth marble statue of George Washington sitting at the edge of Capitol Plaza. Its arm was cast heavenward, very much like his own at the very moment he swore his oath. Looking beyond that comforting icon, he could have glimpsed the streets and fields that led all the way to the river, across which loomed Virginia, the rebellious South, and the portentous, unknowable future that would surely test the better angels he had just summoned.

As the new president of the United States turned to stride back up the portico steps, a "battery on the brow of the hill thundered"[106] a salute, as if in belated echo of the cannon fire that had greeted his Election Day triumph in Springfield four long months before. It would not be the last artillery round to explode in America during the presidency of Abraham Lincoln.

Mystic Chords of Memory

L ONG OVERSHADOWED BY his subsequent masterpiece, the elegiac second inaugural, Abraham Lincoln's first such message also deserves to be remembered as one of the greatest of all his speeches, and one of the finest inaugural orations ever delivered by any president. It was certainly the most breathlessly awaited, so much so that some newspapers rushed the first portions of the speech into their late editions only hours after its delivery.[1] Yet it by no means pleased all its hearers or readers.

Lincoln worked tirelessly—with the help of many editors and advisors—to strike the perfect tone: to make certain that the speech he began writing in Illinois, and completed in Washington, left no doubt about his constitutional obligation to reunite the country, while offering neither impatient threats nor line-in-the sand deadlines to states that had already seceded. In style, Lincoln crafted the text to appeal both to ordinary and sophisticated audiences: a homey reference comparing disunion to divorce, for example, was soon followed by a majestic contemplation on the "ultimate justice of the people." But in some sections of the text, Lincoln's customarily muscular prose style yielded to the cautious editing of his secretary of state–designate William H. Seward—and some of its language became uncharacteristically indirect and flabby.

In many ways, Abraham Lincoln's inaugural message reflected the dilemma facing his regime: it was at once pliant and tough, exasperated but understanding, assertive and soothing. Not surprising, it pleased most Northern Republicans, displeased many Northern Democrats, and outraged Southerners. But in its emphasis on forbearance and the rule of law rather than political advantage and belligerence, it may at least have coalesced Northern resolve to preserve the Union—a resolve destined for a severe and bloody test during the entire four years of Lincoln's administration.

Press reaction to the speech predictably broke along party and sectional lines. The *Albany Evening Journal* declared: "No Message was ever received with greater favor. It is universally conceded to be alike clear, compact, and impressive—equally firm and conciliatory." That very same day, however, the *Richmond Times Dispatch* countered: "The Inaugural Address of Abraham Lincoln inaugurates civil war. . . . The sword is drawn and the scabbard thrown away."[2] And while New York's anti-slavery *Independent* called it "the wisest state-paper issued to the American people since the Declaration of Independence," the pro-secession *Charleston Mercury* assailed it as an example of "impotence and perversity of thought . . . judgment which blinds, and that impulse that hastens to the precipice."[3]

National fissures—and political divisions—were on equally stark view in Chicago, where the Democratic *Daily Times* assailed the speech as "a loose, disjointed, rambling affair," while the Republican *Press & Tribune* countered: "No document can be found among American state papers embodying sounder wisdom and higher patriotism."[4]

Eyewitnesses to the event were equally divided. One reported home four days after the speech: "His inaugural is variously received here. The Republicans are jubilant; the Unionists, or old Whigs, are encouraged to hope; while the Secessionists see nothing but threats of war, blood and fury."[5] The writer known by the nom-de-plume a Public Man spoke for the disenchanted, insisting: "The address has disappointed everyone, I think . . . as was to have been expected from a man whose whole career has been that of an advocate in his private affairs, and who has had absolutely no experience of an executive kind."[6] Complaining that the address "abounds in traits of craft and cunning" bearing "marks of indecision, and yet of strong coercion," the querulous *New York Herald* added: "It would have been almost as instructive if President Lincoln would have contented himself with telling his audience, yesterday, a funny story, and let them go." To the newspaper, the address "would have caused a Washington to mourn, and would have inspired a Jefferson, Madison, or Jackson with contempt."[7]

On the other hand, Benjamin Brown French, the chief marshal of the inaugural ceremonies, thought "words could not have been selected & framed into sentences that could better express the ideas of those who elected Abraham Lincoln to the Presidency. The Inaugural is conciliatory—peaceable—but firm in its tone, and is exactly what we, Union men, want."[8] Reading the speech breathlessly in New York, George Templeton Strong—who acknowledged that the stock market fell in response to it—hoped on one hand that the speech would prove "pacific" enough "to prevent collision," but perceptively recognized: "I think there's a clank of metal in it."[9] Yet to Henry Watterson, a reporter hailing from Tennessee, Lincoln had not gone far enough toward conciliation: "To me it meant war."[10] The ardent secessionist Edmund Ruffin could not have agreed more. "Lincoln, in his message, denied any possible right of a state to secede," he happily recorded, eager for an excuse for open rebellion. The "tenor of the President's speech" not only meant "war speedily begun here" but "great gratification that things would now be brought to an issue."[11]

Reflecting the challenges that whipsawed Lincoln from all sides of the political spectrum, abolitionist conscience Frederick Douglass was no less critical, assailing the new president's "human coldness" in declaring he lacked not only constitutional authority but personal "*inclination*" to interfere with slavery where it existed. To an outraged Douglass, Lincoln had begun his address by "prostrating himself before the foul and withering curse of slavery," then added a "revolting declaration" admitting to a willingness to enforce the Fugitive Slave Act, and finished by offering "immunity to traitors." Douglass concluded his withering critique by predicting: "With such declarations before them, coming from our first modern anti-slavery President, the Abolitionists must know what to expect during the next four years, (should Mr. Lincoln not be, as he is likely to be, driven out of Washington by his rival, Mr. Jeff. Davis, who has already given out that should Mr. Lincoln attempt to do, what he has sworn to do—namely, execute the laws, fifty thousand soldiers should march upon Washington!)."[12]

Beyond politics and philosophy, Lincoln's unique style of expression caught notice as well. "His quaint logic" was "absolutely irresistible," Ohio congressman Albert Gallatin Riddle enthused after hearing the speech at the Capitol. "His vocabulary was limited, he used mainly the simple words that one learns in childhood, which are always the most serviceable, and which arrange themselves easily, delivering their burden of thought with certainty and force to the minds to which they are addressed. Perhaps there never was a more immediately effective address delivered to men than this quaint, masterly performance."[13]

Perhaps the wisest comment of all came from Senator Charles Sumner. Riding back from the ceremony at the Capitol, he was asked his opinion. Strongly applauding the speech, the Massachusetts Republican observed that it epitomized the old simile: "a hand of iron in a velvet glove."[14] But not even all New Englanders concurred. Another Bay State dignitary to weigh in on the new president's first public address was the distinguished former senator Edward Everett. After reading not only the speech but the initial reviews, the nation's most acclaimed orator sniffed: "It is almost universally spoken of as feeble, unequivocal, and temporizing." Less than three years later, Everett would find himself face-to-face with Lincoln at Gettysburg—he to give the principal address, the president to deliver "a few appropriate remarks." Afterward, Everett would be forced to take full measure of Lincoln as a speechmaker, generously—and accurately—admitting to him: "I should be glad, if I could flatter myself that I came as near to the central idea of the occasion, in two hours, as you did in two minutes."[15]

● ● ●

THIS IS THE final text of Abraham Lincoln's first inaugural address. It is composed of the typescript (with handwritten emendations) that Lincoln carried with him to the U.S. Capitol on March 4, 1861. The words and paragraphs that Lincoln deleted have been retained here, with lines struck through to indicate precisely which words and sections he eliminated. Those incorporated or cut at William H. Seward's suggestion have been rendered in bold. Lincoln's inserts are noted with ^ to begin each phrase and to end it. His characteristic misspellings ("oppertunity," "guarranties") have been retained throughout. In the final draft, the salutation—"Fellow Citizens of the United States"—was added to the official press copy by Lincoln's secretary, John G. Nicolay. Apparently this rousing opening—in which Lincoln placed intentionally dramatic emphasis on the word "United"—was entirely extemporaneous.

This text shows how, under Lincoln's sure hand, a complex message with many editors, but one ingenious author, painstakingly evolved into a masterpiece.

Abraham Lincoln's Inaugural Address
Washington, March 4, 1861

In compliance with a custom as old as the government itself, I appear before you to address you briefly, and to take, in your presence, the oath prescribed by the Constitution of the United States, to be taken by the President "before he enters on the execution of his office."

~~The more modern custom of electing a Chief Magistrate upon a previously declared platform of principles, supercedes, in a great measure, the necessity of re-stating those principles in an address of this sort. Upon the plainest grounds of good faith, one so elected is not at liberty to shift his position. It is necessarily implied, if not expressed, that, in his judgment, the platform which he thus accepts, binds him to nothing either unconstitutional or inexpedient.~~

~~Having been so elected upon the Chicago Platform, and while I would repeat nothing in it, of aspersion or epithet or question of motive against any man or party, I hold myself bound by duty, as well as im-~~

pelled by inclination to follow, within the executive sphere, the principles therein declared. By no other course could I meet the reasonable expectations of the country.

I do not consider it necessary at present for me to say more than I have, in relation to those matters of administration, about which there is no special excitement.

^I do not consider it necessary, at present, for me to discuss those matters of administration about which there is no special anxiety, or excitement.^

Apprehension seems to exist among the people of the Southern States, that by the accession of a Republican Administration, their property, and their peace, and personal security, are to be endangered. There has never been any reasonable cause for such apprehension. Indeed, the most ample evidence to the contrary has all the while existed, and been open to their inspection. It is found in nearly all the published speeches of him who now addresses you. I do but quote from one of those speeches when I declare that "I have no purpose, directly or indirectly, to interfere with the institution of slavery in the States where it exists. I believe I have no lawful right to do so, and I have no inclination to do so." Those who nominated and elected me did so with full knowledge that I had made this, and many similar declarations, and had never recanted them. And more than this, they placed in the platform, for my acceptance, and as a law to themselves, and to me, the clear and emphatic resolution which I now read:

"*Resolved*, That the maintenance inviolate of the rights of the States, and especially the right of each State to order and control its own domestic institutions according to its own judgment exclusively, is essential to that balance of power on which the perfection and endurance of our political fabric depend; and we denounce the lawless invasion by armed force of the soil of any State or Territory, no matter under what pretext, as among the gravest of crimes."

I now reiterate these sentiments: and in doing so, I only press upon the public attention the most conclusive evidence of which the case is susceptible, that the property, peace and security of no section are to be in anywise endangered by the now incoming Administration. I add too, that all the protection which, consistently with the Constitution and the laws, can be given, will be cheerfully given to all the States ^when lawfully demanded, for whatever cause^—as cheerfully [Seward proposed adding "in every case and under all circumstances"] to one section^,^ as to another.

There is much controversy about the delivering up of fugitives from service or labor. The clause I now read is as plainly written in the Constitution as any other of its provisions:

"No person held to service or labor in one State, under the laws thereof, escaping into another, shall, in consequence of any law or regulation therein, be discharged from such service or labor, but shall be delivered up on claim of the party to whom such service or labor may be due." [Quoting the U.S. Constitution, Article IV, Section 2—ed.]

It is scarcely questioned that this provision was intended by those who made it, for the reclaiming of what we call fugitive slaves; and the intention of the law-giver is the law. All members of Congress swear their support to the whole Constitution—to this provision as much as to any other. To the proposition, then, that slaves whose cases come within the terms of this clause, "shall be delivered up," their oaths are unanimous. Now, if they would make the effort in good temper, could they not, with nearly equal unanimity, frame and pass a law, by means of which to keep good that unanimous oath?

There is some difference of opinion whether this clause should be enforced by national or by state authority; but surely that difference is not a very material one. If the slave is to be surrendered, it can be of but little consequence to him, or to others, by which authority it is done. And should any one, in any case, be content that his oath shall go unkept, on a merely unsubstantial controversy as to how it shall be kept?

Again, in any law upon this subject, ought not all the safeguards of liberty known in civilized and humane jurisprudence to be introduced, so that a free man be not, in any case, surrendered as a slave? ^And might it not be well, at the same time, to provide by law for the enforcement of that clause in the Constitution which guarranties that "The citizens of each State shall be entitled to all previleges and immunities of citizens in the several States"?^

I take the official oath to-day, with no mental reservations, and with no purpose to construe the Constitution or laws, by any hypercritical rules. And while I do not ~~think proper~~ ^choose^ now to specify particular acts of Congress as proper to be enforced, I do suggest, that it will be much safer for all, both in official and private stations^,^ to conform to, and abide by, all those acts which stand unrepealed, than to violate any of them, trusting to find impunity in having them held to be unconstitutional.

It is ~~now~~ seventy-two years since the first inauguration of a President under our national Constitution. During that period fifteen different and greatly distinguished citizens, have, in succession, administered the executive branch of the government. They have conducted it through many perils; and, ~~on the whole,~~ ^**generally,**^ with great success. Yet, with all this scope for precedent, I now enter upon the same task for the brief constitutional term of four years, under great and peculiar difficulty. A disruption of the Federal Union ~~is menaced, and, so far as can be on paper, is already effected. The particulars of what has been done are so familiar, and so fresh, that I need not to waste any time in recounting them.~~ **heretofore only menaced, is now formidably attempted.**

I hold, that in contemplation of universal law, and of the Constitution, the Union of these States is perpetual. Perpetuity is implied, if not expressed, in the fundamental law of all national governments. It is safe to assert that no government proper, ever had a provision in its organic law for its own termination. Continue to execute all the express provisions of our national Constitution, and the Union will endure forever—it being impossible to destroy it, except by some action not provided for in the instrument itself.

Again, if the United States be not a government proper, but an association of States in the nature of contract merely, can it, as a contract, be peaceably unmade, by less than all the parties who made it? One party to a contract may violate it—break it, so to speak; but does it not require all to lawfully rescind it?

Descending from these general principles, we find the proposition that, in legal contemplation, the Union is perpetual, confirmed by the history of the Union itself. The Union is much older than the Constitution. It was formed in fact, by the Articles of Association in 1774. It was matured and continued by the Declaration of Independence in 1776. It was further matured ~~and expressly declared and pledged, to be~~ ^and the faith of all the then thirteen States expressly plighted and engaged that it should be perpetual, by the Articles of Confederation in 1778^. And finally, in 1787, one of the declared objects for ordaining and establishing the Constitution, was "*to form a more perfect union.*"

But if destruction of the Union, by one, or by a part only, of the States, be lawfully possible, the Union is *less* perfect than before, ~~which contradicts~~ the Constitution, ~~and therefore is absurd.~~ ^having lost the vital element of perpetuity.^

It follows from these views that no State, upon its own mere motion, can lawfully get out of the Union,—that *resolves* and *ordinances* to that effect are legally ~~nothing;~~ ^**void;**^ and that acts of violence, within any State or States, against the authority of the United States, are insurrectionary or ~~treasonable~~ ^**revolutionary,**^ according to circumstances.

~~I therefore consider that the Union is unbroken; and, to the extent of my ability, I shall take care that the laws of the Union be faithfully executed in all the States.~~ ^I therefore consider that, in view of the constitution and the laws, the Union is unbroken; and, to the extent of my ability, I shall take care, as the constitution itself expressly enjoins upon me, that the laws of the Union be faithfully executed in all the states.^ [This line was scrawled on the verso of this page, meaning Lincoln would have turned it around to read it, then turned it around again to read the next sentence—ed.] Doing this I deem to be only a simple duty on my part; and I shall perform it, so far as practicable, unless my rightful masters, the American people, shall withhold the requisite means, or, in some ~~tangible way~~ ^**authoritative manner,**^ direct the contrary. I trust this will not be regarded as a menace, but only as the declared purpose of the Union that it *will* ~~have its own, and *defend* itself.~~^**constitutionally defend, and maintain itself.**^

In doing this there needs to be no bloodshed or violence; and there shall be none, unless it be forced upon the national authority. ~~All the power at my disposal will be used to reclaim the public property and places which have fallen; to hold, occupy and possess these, and all other property and places belonging to the government, and to collect the duties on imposts; but beyond what may be necessary for these objects, there will be no invasion of any State.~~ ^**The power confided to me, will be used** to hold, occupy, and possess the property, and places belonging to the government, and to collect the duties on and imposts; but beyond what may be necessary for these objects, there will be no invasion—no using of force against, or among the people anywhere.^ [Lincoln handwrote the previous sentence and pasted it where the deleted sentence had stood in print—ed.] Where hostility to the United States, in any interior locality, shall be so great and so universal, as to prevent competent resident citizens from holding the Federal offices, there will be no attempt to force obnoxious strangers among the people for that object. While the strict legal right may exist in the government to enforce the exercise of these offices, the attempt to do so would be so irritating, and so nearly impracticable with all, that I deem it better to forego, for the time, the uses of such offices.

The mails, unless ~~refused~~ ^repelled^, will continue to be furnished in all parts of the Union. So far as possible, the people everywhere shall have that sense of perfect security which is most favorable to calm thought and reflection. ~~This course will be pursued until current experience shall show a modification or change to be proper.~~ ^The course here indicated will be followed, unless current events, and experience, shall show a modification, or change, to be proper; and in every case and exigency, my best discretion will be exercised, according to circumstances actually existing, and with a view and a hope of a peaceful solution of the national troubles, and the restoration of fraternal sympathies and, affections.^

That there are persons ^**in one section, or another**^ [Lincoln modified Seward's more condescending proposal: "in one section as well as another"—ed.] who seek to destroy the Union at all events, and are glad of any pretext to do it, I will neither affirm or deny; but if there be such, I need address no word to them. To those, however, who really love the Union, may I not speak?

Before entering upon so grave a matter as the destruction of our national ~~Union,~~ ^fabric, with all its benefits, its memories, and its hopes,^ would it not be wise to ascertain precisely why we do it? Will you hazard so desperate a step, while there is any possibility that any portion of the ills you fly from, have no real existence? Will you, while the certain ills you fly to, are greater than all the real ones you fly from? Will you risk the commission of so fearful a mistake?

All profess to be content in the Union, if all constitutional rights can be maintained. Is it true, then, that any ~~distinct~~ right, plainly written in the Constitution, has been denied? I think not. Happily the human mind is so ~~constructed,~~ ^constituted,^ that no party can reach to the audacity of doing this. Think, if you can, of a single instance in which a plainly written provision of the Constitution has ever been denied. If, by the mere force of numbers, a majority should deprive a minority of any clearly written constitutional right, it might, in a moral point of view, justify revolution—certainly would, if such right were a vital one ~~;—b~~ ^. B^ut such is not our case. All the vital rights of minorities, and of individuals, are so plainly assured to them, by affirmations and negations ^**guarranties and prohibitions,**^ in the Constitution, that controversies never arise concerning them. But no organic law can ever be framed with a provision specifically applicable to every ~~possible~~ [Seward had asked Lincoln to retain "possible"—ed.] question which may occur in practical administration. No foresight can anticipate, nor any document of reasonable length contain express provisions for all possible questions. Shall fugitives from labor be surrendered by national or by State authority? The Constitution does not expressly say. *May* Congress prohibit slavery in the territories? The Constitution does not expressly say. *Must* Congress protect slavery in the territories? The Constitution does not expressly say.

From questions of this class spring all our constitutional controversies, and we divide upon them into majorities and minorities. If the minority will not ~~submit~~ ^acquiesce,^ the majority must, or the government must cease. There is no other alternative; for continuing the government, is ~~submission~~ ^acquiescence^ on one side or the other. If a minority, in such case, will secede rather than ~~submit~~ ^acquiesce,^ they make a precedent which, in turn, will divide and ruin them; for a minority of their own ~~number~~ will secede from them, whenever a majority refuses to be controlled by such minority. ~~For instance, why may not South Carolina, a year or two hence, arbitrarily, secede from a new Southern Confederacy, just as she now claims to secede from the present Union? Her people, and, indeed, all secession people, are now being educated to the precise temper of doing this.~~ ^For instance, why may not any portion of a new confederacy, a year or two hence, arbitrarily secede again, precisely as portions of the present Union now claim to secede from it. All who cherish disunion sentiments are now being educated to the exact temper of doing this. [The previous lines were handwritten between printed paragraphs that had been clipped and pasted together—ed.] Is there such perfect identity of interests among the States to compose a ~~Southern~~ ^new^ Union, as to produce harmony only, and prevent renewed secession? Plainly, the central idea of secession, is the essence of anarchy. ^A majority, held in restraint by constitutional checks, and limitations, and always changing easily, with deliberate changes of popular opinions and sentiments, is the only true sovereign of a free people. [The previous sentence was also handwritten—ed.] Whoever rejects it, does, of necessity, fly to anarchy or to despotism. Unanimity is impossible; the rule of a minority, as a permanent arrangement, is wholly inadmissable; so that, rejecting the majority principle, anarchy^,^ or despotism in some form^,^ is all that is left.

I do not forget the position assumed by some, that constitutional questions are to be decided by the Supreme Court; nor do I deny that such decisions must be binding in any case, upon the parties to a suit, as to the object of ~~the~~ ^that^ suit, ^**while they are also entitled to a very high respect and consideration, in all paralel cases, by all other de-**^

partments of the government^ [Seward's suggestion inserted by hand—ed.] And while it is obviously possible that such decision may be erroneous in any given case, still the evil effect following it, being limited to that particular case, with the chance that it may be over-ruled, and never become a precedent for other cases, can better be borne than [the following handwritten on a separate sheet—ed.:] ~~could the greater evils of a different rule~~ ^practice.^. ~~But if the policy of the government, upon vital questions affecting the whole people, is to be irrevocably fixed by decisions of the Supreme Court, it is plain that the people will have ceased to be their own rulers, having turned their government over to the despotism of the few life officers composing the Court. Nor is there, in this view, any assault upon the Court or the judges. It is a duty from which they may not shrink, to decide cases properly brought before them; and it is no fault of theirs if others seek to turn their decisions to political purposes.~~

~~The Republican party, as I understand, have avowed the purpose to prevent, if they can, the extension of slavery, under the national auspices; and upon this arises the only dispute between the sections.~~ ^could the evils of a different practice. At the same time the candid citizen must confess, that if the policy of the government, upon vital questions, affecting the whole people, is to be irrevocably fixed by decisions of the Supreme Court, the instant they are made, in ordinary litigation between parties, in personal actions, ~~it is plain that~~ the people will have ceased, ~~to~~ to be their own rulers, having, to that extent, **practically resigned their government, into the hands of that eminent tribunal.** Nor is there, in this view, any assault upon the Court, or the judges—It is a duty, from which they may not shrink, to decide cases properly brought before ~~brought before~~ them; and it ^is^ no fault of theirs, if others seek to turn their decisions to political purposes.

One section ^**of our country**^ believes slavery is *right*, and ought to be extended, while the other believes it is *wrong*, and ought not to be extended. This is the only substantial dispute. The fugitive slave clause of the Constitution, and the law for the suppression of the foreign slave trade, are each as well enforced, ^**perhaps**^ as any law can ever be in a community where the moral sense of the people ~~is against~~ ^**imperfectly**^ supports the law itself. The great body of the people abide by the dry legal obligation in both cases, and a few break over in each. This, I think, cannot be perfectly cured; and it would be worse in both cases *after* the separation of the sections, than before. The foreign slave trade, now imperfectly suppressed, would be ^**ultimately**^ revived without restriction, in one section; while fugitive slaves, now only partially surrendered, would not be surrendered at all, by the other.

Physically speaking, we cannot separate. We cannot remove our respective sections from each other, nor build an impassable wall between them. A husband and wife may be divorced, and go out of the presence, and beyond the reach of each other; but the different parts of our country cannot do this. They cannot but remain face to face; and intercourse, either amicable or hostile, must continue between them. Is it possible ^~~possible~~^ then to make that intercourse more advantageous, or more satisfactory, *after* separation than *before?* Can aliens make treaties easier than friends can make laws? Can treaties be more faithfully enforced between aliens^,^ than laws can among friends? Suppose you go to war, you cannot fight always; and when, after much loss on both sides, and no gain on either, you cease fighting, the identical old questions, as to terms of intercourse, are again upon you.

This country, with its institutions, belongs to the people who inhabit it. Whenever they shall grow weary of the existing government, they can exercise their *constitutional* right of amending it, or their *revolutionary* right to dismember, or overthrow [it.—word inadvertently cut by scissors—ed.] ~~As I am not much impressed with the belief that the present Constitution can be~~ [the following handwritten—ed.] I can not be ignorant of the fact that many worthy, and patriotic citizens are desirous ~~that~~ ^of having^ the national constitution ~~shall be~~ amended. While I make no recommendation of amendments, I fully recognize the rightful authority of the people over the ^whole^ subject, to be exercised in either of the modes prescribed in the instrument itself; and I should, under existing circumstances, favor, rather than oppose, a fair oppertunity being afforded the people to act upon it.

~~improved, I make no recommendations of amendments. I am, rather, for the old ship, and the chart of the old pilots. If, however, the people desire a new, or an altered vessel, the matter is exclusively their own, and they can move in the premises, as well without as with an executive recommendation. I shall place no obstacle in the way of what may appear to be their wishes.~~[16] [This section was handwritten—ed.:] I will venture to add that, to me, the Convention mode seems preferable, in that it allows amendments to originate with the people themselves, instead of ~~allowing~~ ^only permitting^ them ~~merely~~ to take, or reject, propositions, originated by others, not especially chosen for the purpose, and which might not be precisely such, as they would wish to either accept or ~~reject.~~ ^refuse.^ I understand a proposed amendment to the constitution which amendment, however, I have not seen, has passed ~~the House of Representatives~~ ^Congress,^ [By Inauguration Day Corwin's proposed Thirteenth Amendment had indeed passed both houses—ed.] to the effect that the federal government, shall never interfere with the domestic institutions of the States, including that of persons held to service. To avoid misconstruction of what I have said, I depart from my purpose not to speak of particular amendments, so far as to say that, holding such a provision to now be implied Constitutional law, I have no objection to it's being made express, and irrevocable.

The Chief Magistrate derives all his authority from the people, and they have conferred none upon him to fix terms for the separation of the States. The people themselves can do this ^also^ if they choose; but the executive, as such, has nothing to do with it. His duty is to administer the present government, as it came to his hands, and to transmit it, unimpaired by him, to his successor.

Why should there not be a patient confidence in the ultimate justice of the people? Is there any better, or equal hope, in the world? In our present differences, is either party without faith ^of being^ in the right? If the Almighty Ruler of nations, with his eternal truth and justice, be on ~~our side, or on yours,~~ ^on [sic] your side **of the North,** or on yours **of** the South,^ that truth, and that justice, will surely prevail, by the judgment of this great tribunal, the American people.

By the frame of the government under which we live, this same people have wisely given their public servants but little power for mischief; and have, with equal wisdom, provided for the return of that little to their own hands at very short intervals.

While the people ~~remain patient, and true to themselves, no man, even in the presidential chair~~ ^retain their virtue, and vigilance^, no administration ~~can~~, by any extreme of wickedness or folly, can very seriously injure the government ^,^ in the short space of four years.

My countrymen, one and all, ~~take *time* and think~~ ^think calmly^ and *well*, upon this whole subject. Nothing valuable can be lost by taking time. ~~Nothing worth preserving is either breaking or burning.~~ If there be an object to *hurry* any of you, in hot haste, to a step which you would never take *deliberately*, that object will be frustrated by taking time; but no good object can be frustrated by it. Such of you as are now dissatisfied, still have the old Constitution unimpaired, and, on the sensitive point, the laws of your own framing under it; while the new administration will have no immediate power, if it would, to change either. If it were admitted that you who are dissatisfied, hold the right side in the dispute, there still is no single good reason for precipitate action. Intelligence, patriotism, Christianity, and a firm reliance on Him, who has never yet forsaken this favored land, are still competent to adjust, in the best way, all our present difficulty.

In *your* hands, my dissatisfied fellow countrymen, and not in *mine*, is the momentous issue of civil war. The government will not assail *you* ~~unless *you* first assail it.~~ You can have no conflict, without being yourselves the aggressors. *You* have no oath registered in Heaven to destroy the government, while *I* shall have the most solemn one to "preserve, protect and defend" it. ~~You can forbear, the assault upon it, I can not shrink from the defense of it. With you, and not with me, is the solemn question of "Shall it be peace, or a sword?"~~

I am loth to close. We are not enemies, but friends—We must not be enemies. Though passion may have strained, it must not break our bonds of affection. The mystic chords of memory [originally ~~"memories"~~—ed.], stretching from every battle-field, and patriot grave, to every living heart and hearthstone, all over this broad land, will yet swell the chorus of the Union, when again touched, as surely they will be, by the better angels of our nature.

⊶ WHAT BECAME OF . . . ? ⊷

A cast of characters that includes Thurlow Weed and Samuel Weed, William Wood and Fernando Wood, John Crittenden and Lucius Chittenden, Edward D. Baker and Edward L. Baker, Charles Sumner and "Bull Head" Sumner, cries out for a dramatis personae. The following postscript recalls some of these figures, and details their post-inaugural careers:

Charles Francis Adams, the Seward admirer who doubted President-elect Lincoln's abilities, became America's minister to the Court of St. James in 1861, and later led the Union Pacific Railroad. He died in 1886.

John Bell, who ran against Lincoln for president, retired from public life after the 1860 election, and made a small fortune running a Tennessee ironworks. He died in 1869.

John C. Breckinridge, Lincoln's 1860 election opponent on the Southern Democratic ticket, turned against the Union after Lincoln's victory, became a Confederate general and briefly served as Jefferson Davis's secretary of war. He died in 1875.

Orville Hickman Browning, who suggested changes in Lincoln's inaugural message, became U.S. senator from Illinois after Stephen Douglas's death in 1861. He and his wife remained close to the Lincolns, and helped them through their mourning for their son Willie, who died in 1862. Browning later fell out with the president over emancipation, which he opposed. He later served under Lincoln's successor, Andrew Johnson, as secretary of the interior. Lincoln denied him his great ambition: a place on the Supreme Court. Browning became a Democrat and died in 1881.

John J. Crittenden, leader of the compromise forces in Congress from 1860 to 1861, returned to his native Kentucky long enough to help keep the state from seceding from the Union. His career in the Senate over, he returned to Washington in May 1861 as a member of the House of Representatives, where he opposed the war, emancipation, and black enlistment. One of his sons fought for the Union, the other for the Confederacy. Crittenden was seeking a second term in the House when he died in July 1861.

David Davis was appointed associate justice of the U.S. Supreme Court by his old friend Lincoln in 1862. In 1866 he wrote the majority decision in the famous case *Ex parte Milligan,* which found that the Lincoln administration had exceeded its authority in suspending the writ of habeas corpus during the Civil War. Davis left the court after fifteen years in 1877 to become a U.S. senator. He died in 1889.

Stephen A. Douglas, senior senator from Illinois, and Lincoln's chief opponent for the presidency in 1860, died only three months after his archrival's inauguration as president, after undertaking an exhausting speaking tour in behalf of the Union. He was only forty-eight. Lincoln ordered the White House draped in black in his honor.

Ephraim Elmer Ellsworth, the law student and drillmaster who accompanied Lincoln to Washington as a bodyguard, hoped for a patronage job in the War Department, but after Fort Sumter was attacked he organized a Zouave regiment. On May 24, 1861, he led troops into Virginia to remove a Confederate flag hanging conspicuously from an Alexandria hotel, and visible all the way to the White House. But after seizing the banner, Ellsworth was fatally shot by the proprietor. The first Union officer killed in the Civil War, Ellsworth earned an East Room funeral and inspired a famous condolence letter from a grieving Lincoln, who called the martyred young soldier "the best talent" in military matters "I ever knew."

Alexander Gardner, who took the crucially important photographs of a dignified President-elect Lincoln after his controversial secret arrival in Washington in February 1861, eventually left the employ of Mathew Brady, opened his own gallery, and made a justifiably famous photographic record of the Civil War, along with countless iconic portraits of Lincoln. He died in 1882.

Horace Greeley continued his extraordinary career as quixotic but influential editor of the *New York Tribune*, pressing Lincoln on emancipation and later advocating peace talks with the Confederacy. He caused an uproar by signing the bail bond for Jefferson Davis in 1865, and challenged Ulysses S. Grant for the presidency in 1872 as a Democrat. After a huge Election Day loss, he died before the Electoral College ratified his defeat.

Hannibal Hamlin, vice president–elect during the Great Secession Winter, seemed destined for a close relationship with the new president after emerging as an influential advisor at their pre-inaugural meetings in Chicago and New York. But Hamlin's influence on the president faded—principally because, by custom, the job of vice president was legislative, not executive. Lincoln either ordered or tolerated his removal from the ticket when he sought a second term in 1864. Hamlin returned to the U.S. Senate from Maine, and then ended his career as America's minister to Spain. He died in 1891.

John M. Hay, Lincoln's assistant private secretary, went on to a distinguished diplomatic career, serving as ambassador to Great Britain, and

U.S. secretary of state under William McKinley and Theodore Roosevelt, negotiating the Hay-Pauncefote Treaty, which led to construction of the Panama Canal. His entertaining diary of his White House service during the Civil War became a primary source for historians. He lived until 1905.

William H. Herndon, Lincoln's junior law partner, spent the rest of his life writing and lecturing on his famous colleague, with little financial success or critical acclaim. *Herndon's Lincoln: The True Story of a Great Life*, published in 1889, is today valued less highly than the notes and interviews he recorded for its preparation, now considered the principal resource on Lincoln's early life. Herndon died in poverty in 1891.

Ward Hill Lamon served in the Lincoln administration as marshal of the District of Columbia, enjoying his proudest moment as grand marshal of the Gettysburg cemetery dedication in 1863. To some Lincoln's intimate friend, to others merely a self-aggrandizing bodyguard, Lamon, who frequently slept on the floor outside Lincoln's bedroom door at the White House, fully armed, always regretted being away from Washington the night the president went to Ford's Theatre and met his death. He believed he would have saved him. Lamon's controversial 1872 Lincoln biography outraged Lincoln's son Robert, who exacted revenge by blocking a later federal appointment for him in Colorado. Lamon lived until 1893.

Robert T. Lincoln, the president's eldest son, who won fame as the "Prince of Rails" during the secession winter, was the only one of his children to live to maturity. He became U.S. secretary of war, minister to Great Britain, and president of the Pullman Company following brief service on General Grant's staff at the end of the Civil War. Though frequently mentioned as a Republican candidate for president, Robert shunned electoral politics. He later brought his mother to trial in a successful effort to have her committed for insanity. Robert died an extremely wealthy man at age eighty-four in 1926.

John George Nicolay, private secretary to the president-elect, served in the same role in the White House, and later became marshal of the U.S. Supreme Court. In 1890 he and John Hay co-authored a magisterial ten-volume biography of Lincoln. He died in 1901.

John Pope, who served with the military team that accompanied Lincoln to Washington on his inaugural journey, became a Civil War general. After early successes in the West, he led the Army of the Potomac to a disastrous rout at the Second Battle of Bull Run in 1862, and Lincoln relieved him of command. Pope died in 1892.

Edmund Ruffin, the fire-eating secessionist who applauded Lincoln's election and inaugural address, convinced they would provoke Southern independence, was given the "honor" of firing the first shot on Fort Sumter in April 1861. Four years later, the Confederacy vanquished, he turned his gun on himself and committed suicide.

Carl Schurz, the prominent German-American leader, became Lincoln's minister to Spain, then returned to the United States to become a general in the Union Army. He later served as a U.S. senator, secretary of the interior, and as a journalist and editor. He died in 1906.

George Templeton Strong, the New York lawyer who recorded acute observations on the Lincoln era in his famous diary, became active in the U.S. Sanitary Commission during the Civil War, helped found the Union League Club and the New York Philharmonic, and remained active at his alma mater, Columbia University. He died of cancer in 1875.

Roger Brooke Taney, the ancient chief justice of the U.S. Supreme Court who swore Lincoln into office, attempted in 1861 to block the new president's efforts to prevent the secession of his home state of Maryland. Lincoln largely ignored him. Taney died in 1864, and Lincoln replaced him with his anti-slavery secretary of the treasury, Salmon P. Chase.

Lyman Trumbull, who accompanied Lincoln on his post-election trip to Chicago, remained in the U.S. Senate until 1873, and is credited with introducing the resolution that became the Thirteenth Amendment to the Constitution abolishing slavery. Yet his once close relationship with Lincoln cooled during the Civil War. Trumbull returned to the Democratic party late in his life and died in 1896.

John Tyler, the Virginia-born ex-president who returned to Washington to preside over the ill-fated 1861 Peace Convention, later advocated his state's secession. He served briefly that year in the Provisional Confederate Congress, and was about to take a permanent seat in its House of Representatives in 1862 when he died.

Henry Villard left the *New York Herald* for the *New York Tribune* shortly after Lincoln's inauguration, then abandoned journalism altogether to become a railroad entrepreneur. He proved enormously successful, taking over the Northern Pacific Railroad and eventually feeding his old passion for newspapers by buying the *New York Evening Post.* Married to the daughter of abolitionist William Lloyd Garrison, he lived until 1900.

Thurlow Weed, political guru to Secretary of State William H. Seward, never gave up his quest for Lincoln administration patronage, but proved highly useful to Lincoln during his reelection campaign in 1864. The political boss died at the age of eighty-five in 1882.

Fernando Wood, the seventy-second and seventy-fourth mayor of New York City, rallied to the defense of the Union after the April 1861 attack on Fort Sumter, but his show of patriotism came too late to save him from the wrath of voters, many of whom never forgave him for his early show of sympathy for the South, his scheme for New York secession, or his halfhearted reception for president-elect Lincoln at City Hall. Wood left office in 1862, but returned to Congress, where he served as an antiwar Democrat from 1863 to 1865, then again from 1867 until his death in 1881.

William S. Wood, manager of Lincoln's inaugural journey, enjoyed Mary Lincoln's fervent and, some believed, unseemly support when, after the inauguration, he sought as his reward the prestigious federal post of commissioner of public buildings. Lincoln reluctantly nominated him, but with Wood embroiled in controversy for allegedly encouraging the first lady to overspend on clothes and decorations, the Senate refused to confirm him. Lincoln nominated a replacement, and the mysterious Wood faded into obscurity.

⊰ ACKNOWLEDGMENTS ⊱

A LIST THAT ADEQUATELY acknowledged all the benefactors, colleagues, friends, and family whose help was essential to the creation of this book would fill more pages than my incomparable editor Alice Mayhew—about whom more later—could possibly allocate.

Making best use of the space at my disposal, I must begin with my deepest gratitude to Norman Peck and the Peter Jay Sharp Foundation for generously providing the seed research grant to launch this project. Another foundation, which prefers anonymity, provided crucial additional support, and I am equally grateful for its crucial help.

In researching the book, I was fortunate to benefit from a wonderful experience with the Hertog Research Assistantship Program in the Writing Division of the School of the Arts at Columbia University, which assigns graduate students to working historians. Under the guidance of its director (and professor in the writing program), the historian Patricia O'Toole (and with the generous support of philanthropists Roger and Susan Hertog), the school assigned the gifted young writer Brendan Hughes to my project. Except for his inexcusable loyalty to the Boston Red Sox, which I not only tolerated but permitted to culminate in a New York Yankees defeat during the 2007 playoffs, Brendan proved a resourceful, intelligent, and committed research assistant and in the process became a friend as well. I am grateful not only for his help, but also for the archival and computer research skills, not to mention tolerance and good humor, repeatedly demonstrated under deadline pressure by my full-time assistant Kraig Smith, as well as the additional help provided by researchers Win Rutherfurd and Avi Mowshowitz.

My great friend, Rhode Island Chief Justice Frank J. Williams, Chairman of the Lincoln Forum, as always repeatedly took time from his own demanding schedule to identify, locate, copy, and ship pamphlets, broadsides, and book chapters from his vast personal library. I cannot count the times he came to the rescue with material that was unavailable elsewhere. Similarly, my friends Daniel Weinberg, the knowledgeable proprietor of Chicago's Abraham Lincoln Book Shop, and Louise Taper, the boundlessly generous Lincoln collector from Beverly Hills, unearthed, e-mailed, or j-pegged important pieces of Lincolniana whose inclusion in this book is due entirely to their thoughtfulness.

An especially huge debt is owed to historian Doris Kearns Goodwin. When I hesitantly asked if she might share a transcript of a particular William Seward letter she had cited in her magisterial study, *Team of Rivals*, Doris immediately offered to send her entire research file from the secession winter period—folder upon folder of diary entries, correspondence, newspaper clippings, and notes, which might otherwise have taken months to accumulate. With her usual combination of generosity and modesty, she added, "This is the one period I wish I'd written about in more detail. I'm happy you're the one who's doing it." No one could be happier than I to have such a treasured friend and selfless colleague to provide both raw material and crucial encouragement.

My own research itinerary took me from Los Angeles to Washington, and many places in between—Chicago, Springfield, Richmond, Philadelphia, Albany, Trenton, Fort Wayne, Los Angeles, and Boston, to name but a few—and all along the way, for a period of more than two years, institutions threw open their doors and provided large doses of expertise and patience to handle my countless requests.

I particularly thank Illinois State Historian Thomas F. Schwartz at the Abraham Lincoln Presidential Library and Museum in Springfield for providing access, guidance, and much appreciated hospitality in Lincoln's hometown. At the library, I also enjoyed help from former Lincoln specialist Kim Bauer, now Director of the Lincoln Heritage Project for the city of Decatur, from Byron Andreason, and from the skillful staffs of the library (Donna Dougherty, Kathryn Harris, Gwen Podeski, and Dennis Suttles), the periodicals and manuscript collections (especially Cheryl Schnirring, Glenna Schroeder-Hamm, and Debbie S. Hamm), and from Jennifer Ericson on illustrations.

I spent more time at the Library of Congress than at any other repository, and thanks to John R. Sellers, knowledgeable Chief of Nineteenth-Century Manuscripts, enjoyed not only advice and direction, but priceless access to the Abraham Lincoln Papers collection. These old letters—mostly the incoming correspondence now housed in oversize binders—are easily available today on both microfilm and the World Wide Web. But there is nothing to compare with examining the originals: seeing and touching the very envelopes and hand-scrawled letters that Lincoln once held, studied, and often jotted notes upon. For additional help, I am also grateful to Clark Evans, Head of Reference and Reader Services at the Library's Rare Book and Special Collections Division, and to librarian Joan Sullivan and the other patient professionals who staff the Manuscripts Section.

Nearby, the National Archives provided equally open access to its own vital records. I thank the Archivist of the United States, Allen Weinstein, for taking an interest in this project, and the head of the National Archives Foundation, Thomas Wheeler, for additional encouragement. I am particularly indebted to the institution's most priceless nondocumentary assets, volunteers extraordinaire Budge Weidman and her husband, Russ, who took much time from their own important research on Civil War pension records to guide me through the relevant holdings. Thanks to Budge, Russ, and their colleague Richard (Rick) Peuser, I had the opportunity to examine the original, handwritten electoral vote records from 1860, many of which looked as if they had not been opened since the day they were read aloud in Congress a century and a half ago. Further thanks go to Budge and Russ for the sanity-preserving after-hours blasts that they hosted at the Army & Navy Club and elsewhere, and individually to Russ (and the late Charles D. Platt) for handling the bookkeeping for the Sharp Foundation grant, and to Budge for inspiringly fighting the hard fight and winning.

At Fort Wayne, Indiana, Joan Flinspach, director and CEO, and Cindy VanHorn, Registrar, of the Lincoln Museum gave me unlimited access to its peerless picture and clipping files, and Sara Gabbard provided her usual encouragement and help. The regrettable March 2008 announcement that the institution would close its doors only makes me value my most recent experiences there the more. All Lincoln scholars will miss this resource—and its superb staff—enormously. Further help with pictorial resources came from: Samuel Streit at the John Hay Library, Brown University, Ila Furman, assistant registrar at the Corcoran Gallery of Art, Lizanne Garrett at the National Portrait Gallery, and the staff of the Lilly Library at Indiana University. Ellen H. Fladger, Head of Special Collections at Union College in Schenectady, New York, pointed me to some little known information about its famous alumnus, William H. Seward. And at the New York State Archives in Albany, both Judy Hohmann (upon whom I imposed at a most challenging time) and Jo-Anne Burnside provided expert help, while Chris Ward and Robert Bullock offered their usual friendship and support.

I'm indebted to John Coski, Historian and Director of Library and Research at the Museum of the Confederacy in Richmond, and to his colleague, Library Manager Teresa Roane, for help well beyond the call of duty in searching Southern newspapers for reaction to Lincoln's election; to Peter J. Mazzei, Manager of Library and Information Technology Services for the New Jersey Legislature (along with his colleagues David Price and Peter R. Manoogian) for so generously reproducing newspaper accounts of Lincoln's visit to Trenton; to Edouard L. Deschrochers, Assistant Librarian and Academy Archivist at Phillips Exeter for his customary help in accessing Robert Lincoln's student records; to April Hunt and Roy Eddey at the New-York Historical Society for sharing much valuable information about Lincoln's visit to the big city; as well as to Olga Tsapina, Norris Foundation Curator of American Manuscripts (and staff member Susi Krasnoo) at the Huntington Library in San Marino, California, for providing a number of hard-to-find documents.

Thanks for guidance and information go, also, to: Thomas Mason, Paula Corpuz, Erin Kelley, and the research staffs of the Indiana Historical Society in Indianapolis; the research staffs of the Minnesota Historical Society in St. Paul and the Library of Virginia in Richmond; Judy Birdsell of the Stephenson County Historical Society (and also George Buss of the Lincoln-Douglas Society) in Freeport, Illinois; Paul Martin III of the Lincoln Club of Peekskill; Director Daniel Stowell and Associate Director/Associate Editor John Lupton of the Lincoln Legal Papers (and Presidential Papers) projects in Springfield; and Director Seth Bongartz and Curator Brian Knight at Hildene.

I am grateful as well to: historian Jason Emerson for sharing a number of outstanding letters and articles that he unearthed during the course of his own research on both Mary and Robert Lincoln; Wendell Garrett, the former editor of the *Magazine Antiques* and now a consultant to Sotheby's, who sent many interesting clippings; Revolutionary War expert Thomas Fleming for sharing his knowledge of presidential inaugural tradition; Justin Lyons, then of the Mariners' Museum in Newport News, Virginia, and John E. Schultz, a formidable expert on the nineteenth-century military telegraph (whom I met on the museum's grounds); and both writer Christopher Dickey and historian Darrel Bigham, director of Historic Southern Indiana, for offering sound advice and answering perplexing questions. I also thank Richard Fox, professor of history at USC, for pointing me to an important archive at the Western Historical Manuscript Collection at the University of Missouri–Columbia; Jean Soman of Pinecrest, Florida, for advice and materials on her distinguished ancestor, Lincoln photographer Samuel Alschuler; and author-filmmaker Phillip Kunhardt for providing a much appreciated copy of yet another elusive document. My hero Mario Cuomo offered his usual valuable insight into the tradition of political debate (as well as diverting phone calls to discuss the 2008 presidential campaign). To John O'Keefe and Tim Mulligan I send heartfelt thanks, knowing full well that my debt to them can never be adequately repaid.

The opportunity to meet occasionally and correspond often with fellow historians is almost as valuable as original research, and I benefited much from in-person and e-mail explorations with many colleagues: David Long, Assistant Professor of History at East Carolina University in Greenville, regarding Lincoln's cabinet obligations to Pennsylvania; James Horton, Benjamin Banneker Professor of American Studies and History at George Washington University, and David W. Blight, Director of the Gilder Lehrman Center for Slavery and Abolition at Yale University, on the subject of Frederick Douglass; Garry Wills, from whom I benefited from sound advice on Henry Adams; Paul Finkelman, the President William McKinley Distinguished Professor of Law and Public Policy at Albany Law School, who shared his knowledge of the Constitutional amendment process; Michael Vorenberg of Brown University, who provided additional advice on the Constitutional amendment process; and the two reigning experts on Lincoln's writings, Ronald C. White, Jr., Professor of American Intellectual and Religious History at the San Francisco Theological Seminary, and Douglas L. Wilson, Co-director of the Lincoln Studies Program at Knox College in Galesburg, Illinois, who engaged on the subject of Lincoln's first inaugural address. Of course, up-close and personal discussions are best, and our favorite Washington research trips were those we spent laptop-to-laptop with Craig and Marylou Symonds of Annapolis.

Every new book should be vetted by experts before it is read by the public, and I was fortunate to enlist several brilliant readers to review the early drafts. The first, fastest, and most crucial reading was provided by Wayne C. Temple, the miraculous longtime Chief Deputy Director of the Illinois State Archives, who took on the manuscript chapter by chapter, almost as quickly as the pages emerged from my word processor. No one has a more thorough knowledge of Lincoln's life in Springfield, and Wayne devoted uncountable hours of personal time subjecting the material to his thorough scrutiny. I shudder to think of how many blunders I would have made had it not been for Wayne's catches, and I sincerely thank him for once again proving an incomparable resource and terrific friend.

I am also deeply grateful to Lincoln scholars Matthew Pinsker, the Brian Pohanka Chair for Civil War History at Dickinson College; Gerald Prokopowicz, Assistant Professor of History at East Carolina State University; and Craig Symonds, Professor of History Emeritus at the U.S. Naval Academy; and of course Frank Williams, all of whom read all or part of the manuscript and offered highly useful advice. Any errors that remain, of course, are mine alone.

Offering their good offices to bring the book to a wide audience even before it was completed were a number of organizations and publications devoted to Abraham Lincoln. For these expressions of confidence, I am most grateful to Gabor Boritt and Tina Grim of the Civil War Institute at Gettysburg College; Frank Williams, Russ Weidman, John Y. Simon, and Betty Anselmo of the Lincoln Forum; Louise Mirrer, Linda Ferber, Roy Eddey, Dale Gregory, Laura Washington, and their staff at the New-York Historical Society; Joseph E. Garrera of the Lincoln Group of New York; Patrick Falci and Len Rehner of the Civil War Round Table of New York; Dana Shoaf of *Civil War Times*; and Ed Grosvenor and John Ross of *American Heritage*.

At the Abraham Lincoln Bicentennial Commission, which I am privileged to co-chair, I have enjoyed the rewarding opportunity to work closely with my co-chairs, Senator Dick Durbin and Congressman Ray LaHood, and with commissioners Jean T. D. Bandler, Darrel Bigham, Gabor Boritt, Hon. Jim Bunning, Julie Cellini, Joan L. Flinspach, James O. Horton, Hon. Jesse Jackson, Jr., Lura Lynn Ryan, Louise Taper, Tommy Turner, and Frank Williams, along with Executive Director Eileen Mackevich, staff members Jennifer Rosenfeld, David Early, and Suresh Venkitaraman (plus former staff members Michael Bishop, Jackie Williams, and Roberta Schutz). Their tireless work in behalf of the Lincoln field has raised all scholarly boats and made the years 2008 and 2009 the most conducive ever for writers and readers of Civil War–era history.

I owe an especially strong expression of gratitude to my colleagues at The Metropolitan Museum of Art, an institution I have been privileged to serve for sixteen years. It remains endlessly stimulating to enjoy opportunities to discuss Lincoln art with the likes of curators Morrison Heckscher, Carrie Rebora Baratt, Thayer Tolles, and Peter Kenney.

Above all I am grateful to our peerless Director, Philippe de Montebello—whom I will miss enormously when he begins the retirement he announced (against my advice) in January 2008—and our amazing President and my loyal friend, Emily K. Rafferty, for their unfailing tolerance (even when accompanied by a leavening dose of teasing) for my avocational preoccupation with all things Lincoln.

At Simon & Schuster, I much enjoyed the opportunity to work again with Senior Editor Roger Labrie and Director of Public Relations Victoria Meyer, along with Senior Production Editor Lisa Healy, Karen Thompson, Julia Prosser, and many others. Above all, I benefited more than I can express from the guidance of Editorial Director Alice Mayhew. Her constant encouragement and incisive suggestions made the book and its author much better than they could have been absent her crucial input. Through it all, my indefatigable agent, Geri Thoma, as always proved not only an advocate but a valuable advisor.

My final, and as always my deepest, thanks go to my precious family. My daughters, Meg, a gifted attorney, and Remy, an astute film historian, were unfailingly generous, as always, with their support and love. As this book was coming to life, Remy and her husband, writer Adam Kirsch, brought to life a new generation: their son, and our first grandchild, the magnificent Charles Ezra Kirsch. If the book was delayed, B.C.: Blame Charlie. He's irresistible, and since most spare moments away from the book were devoted to him, I'm frankly amazed it got done at all.

My partner in both life and grandparenting, my wonderful wife, Edith, played the biggest role of all in this book. She has always been my most important and perceptive critic, but for the first time, she also accompanied me on my travels as a research assistant, and her patience, initiative, professionalism, and endurance not only made our research adventures more enjoyable, but doubled their effectiveness. Even though this book is dedicated to others—the newest member of the family, along with the man for whom he is named, my beloved father—in the end this was our choice, just as, in so many ways, this is our book.

⊰ NOTES ⊱

Abbreviations Used in the Notes:

ALPLC   Abraham Lincoln Papers, Library of Congress. (available at http://memory.loc.gov/ammem/alhtml/alhome.html)

ALPLM   Abraham Lincoln Presidential Library and Museum, Springfield, Illinois.

NPLC   Papers of John G. Nicolay, Library of Congress.

CW   Roy P. Basler et al., eds., *The Collected Works of Abraham Lincoln*, 8 vols. New Brunswick, N.J.: Rutgers University Press, 1953–1955.

Lincoln Day by Day
   Earl Schenck Miers, ed., *Lincoln Day by Day: A Chronology, 1809–1865*, 3 vols. Washington, D.C.: Lincoln Sesquicentennial Commission, 1960.

Introduction

1. Charles Eugene Hamlin, *The Life and Times of Hannibal Hamlin*, 2 vols. (Cambridge, Mass.: Riverside Press, 1899), 2:393.
2. William O. Stoddard, *Abraham Lincoln: The True Story of a Great Life . . .*, rev. ed. (New York: Fords, Howard, & Hulbert, 1884), 185.
3. Noah Brooks, *Abraham Lincoln and the Downfall of American Slavery* (New York: G. P. Putnam's Sons, 1894), 236.

4. Mrs. P. A. Hanaford, *Abraham Lincoln; His Life and Public Services* (Boston: B. B. Russell & Co., 1866), 57, 64. For the latter quote, Hanaford cited a book entitled *The Secret Service—the Field, Dungeon, and Escape*, by A. D. Richardson.

5. L. P. Brockett, *The Life and Times of Abraham Lincoln, Sixteenth President of the United States* . . . (Philadelphia: Bradley & Co., 1865), 199.

6. J. G. Holland, *The Life of Abraham Lincoln* (Springfield, Mass.: Gurdon Bill, 1866), 249, 252

7. Isaac N. Arnold, *The Life of Abraham Lincoln*, orig. pub. 1884, 10th ed. (Chicago: A. C. McClurg, 1906), 178.

8. David M. Potter, *Lincoln and His Party in the Secession Crisis* (New Haven: Yale University Press, 1942), 315.

9. Allan Nevins, *The Emergence of Lincoln*, 2 vols. (New York: Charles Scribner's Sons, 1950), 2:437, 450–51.

10. J. G. Randall, *Lincoln the President: Springfield to Gettysburg*, 2 vols. (New York: Dodd, Mead, 1945), 1:247.

11. James M. McPherson, *Battle Cry of Freedom: The Civil War Era* (New York: Oxford University Press, 1988), 261.

12. Mark E. Neely, Jr., *The Abraham Lincoln Encyclopedia* (New York: McGraw-Hill, 1982), 159.

13. Richard Carwardine, *Lincoln: A Life of Purpose and Power* (New York: Alfred A. Knopf, 2006), 140.

14. Phillip Shaw Paludan, *The Presidency of Abraham Lincoln* (Lawrence: University Press of Kansas, 1994), 35, 45.

15. Doris Kearns Goodwin, *Team of Rivals: The Political Genius of Abraham Lincoln* (New York: Simon & Schuster, 2005), 310.

16. See, for example, Thomas Di Lorenzo, *The Real Lincoln: A New Look at Abraham Lincoln, His Agenda, and an Unnecessary War* (Roseville, Cal.: Forum/Prima Books, 2002), esp. Chapter 5, "The Myth of Secession as 'Treason.' "

17. CW, 5:537.

18. Hamlin, *Hannibal Hamlin*, 2:394.

1. The Government Is About to Fall into Our Hands

1. The cannon fire and "roving bands of music" were reported by the *New-York Daily Tribune*, November 7, and November 10, 1860. The Republicans had fired their "little cannon" on Election Eve as well, disrupting a concert at a local church with "deafening noise." See Octavia Roberts Corneau and Georgia L. Osborne, eds., "A Girl in the Sixties. Excerpts from the Journal of Anna Ridgely (Mrs. James L. Hudson) . . .", *Journal of the Illinois State Historical Society* 22 (October 1929): 418.

2. [St. Louis] *Daily Missouri Democrat,* November 7, 1860, *New-York Daily Tribune,* November 12, 1860.

3. *Charleston Mercury,* November 3, 1860.

4. James S. Thayer, quoted in *New York World,* November 3, 1860.

5. *New-York Daily Tribune,* November 10, 1860.

6. Memorandum by John G. Nicolay, October 25, 1860, NPLC.

7. John Coyle to Lincoln, November 1860, ALPLC.

8. Ward Hill Lamon to Lincoln, October 10, 1860, ALPLC.

9. Lincoln to John M. Read, *CW,* 4:127. Read, a Pennsylvania judge, had recently commissioned a Philadelphia artist to travel to Springfield and paint a flattering portrait for adaptation into an engraving designed to allay local concerns that Lincoln was too homely to be president.

10. Lincoln to William H. Seward, October 12, 1860, *CW,* 4:126–27.

11. Joshua Wolf Shenk has convincingly described Lincoln's agonies during this period. See Shenk, *Lincoln's Melancholy: How Depression Challenged a President and Fueled His Greatness* (Boston: Houghton Mifflin, 2005), esp. 168–70.

12. *Douglass' Monthly,* December 1860, in Philip S. Foner and Yuval Taylor, eds, *Frederick Douglass: Selected Speeches and Writings* (Chicago: Lawrence Hill, 1999, 413.

13. Lincoln to Anson G. Henry, September 22, 1860, *CW,* 4:118.

14. William W. Freehling, *The Road to Disunion, Volume 2: Secessionists Triumphant, 1854–1861* (New York: Oxford University Press, 2007), 338. Freehling has estimated that with just under 50 percent of states, Southerners would exert far more influence in a House vote than in the Electoral College, where they had just under 40 percent of the representatives. Lincoln, a student of political history, surely remembered that the 1824 presidential election had gone to the House of Representatives. There, ignoring Democrat Andrew Jackson's 10-percentage-point victory over Whig John Quincy Adams, the chamber awarded the presidency to Adams. Like the Lincoln-Douglas-Breckinridge-Bell race, the 1824 contest had included four candidates, not two. The 238-member 36th Congress, which served from 1859 to 1861, had 116 Republicans, ninety-eight Democrats, five American (know-Nothing) party members, and nineteen others. One hundred twenty votes were needed for a majority. See http://clerk.house.gov/histHigh/Congressional_History/index.html.

15. Douglas to Charles H. Lanphier, July 5, 1860, in Robert W. Johannsen, ed., *The Letters of Stephen A. Douglas* (Urbana: University of Illinois Press, 1961), 498. A canny political veteran from the crucial border state of Missouri not only believed no candidate would win an electoral majority; he predicted the House would award the presidency to none of the above—but, rather, to Edward Everett, the venerable Massachusetts politician now

running for the vice presidency with Bell. See Samuel Treat to Thomas Reynolds, in "Missouri in the 1860 Campaign: Correspondence of Thomas C. Reynolds," *Moorsfield Antiquarian* (November 1937): 18–19.

16. *New York Times*, November 5, 1860. See also David M. Potter, *The Impending Crisis, 1848–1861* (New York: Harper & Row, 1976), 438.

17. *New York World*, November 1, 1860. Moreover, banker August Belmont flatly predicted that "the election of Lincoln would lead to dissolution and civil war."

18. *The* [New York] *Independent*, November 1, 1860. The newspaper was one of the few weeklies Lincoln read regularly.

19. Winfield Scott, the Whig presidential candidate in 1852, had campaigned in his own behalf, and was defeated by Franklin Pierce, who did not.

20. Frederick Douglass, *Life and Times of Frederick Douglass*, in Henry Louis Gates, Jr., ed., *Frederick Douglass: Autobiographies* (New York: Library of America, 1994), 767.

21. William Cullen Bryant to Lincoln, June 16, 1860, ALPLC.

22. Lincoln to Samuel Haycraft, June 4, 1860, *CW*, 4:69–70.

23. Lincoln clipped the offending August 8, 1860, news item and pasted it into a letter to George G. Fogg on August 16, 1860. See *CW*, 4:96.

24. For turnout numbers, see Glenn C. Altschuler and Stuart M. Blumin, *Rude Republic: Americans and Their Politics in the Nineteenth Century* (Princeton: Princeton University Press, 2000), 70. In fairness, the authors contend that Americans in fact were less consumed by politics than previously believed. But a powerful response was provided in Mark E. Neely, Jr., *The Boundaries of American Political Culture in the Civil War Era* (Chapel Hill: University of North Carolina Press, 2005).

25. Lincoln to Samuel Galloway, June 19, 1860, *CW* 4:80. Galloway had urged Lincoln to proofread a new campaign biography, but Lincoln refused, claiming that if he agreed "to send forth, by my authority, a volume of hundreds of pages, for my adversaries to make points upon without end . . . the convention would have a right to reassemble, and substitute another name for mine."

26. Thomas J. McCormack, ed., *Memoirs of Gustave Koerner, 1809–1896*, 2 vols. (Cedar Rapids, Iowa: Torch Press, 1909), 2:104.

27. Undated typescript in John G. Nicolay's scrapbook, 1856–1870, Library of Congress. Nicolay attested: "Mr. Lincoln appointed me as his private secretary, without any solicitation on my part, or, so far as I know, of anyone else; and I presume simply on account of the acquaintanceship" the two had enjoyed when Nicolay worked as chief clerk in the office of Illinois secretary of state Ozias M. Hatch. His salary was paid out of a $5,000 fund raised by ten Sangamon County Republicans contributing $500 apiece. See Sunderine (Wilson) Temple and Wayne C. Temple, *Abraham Lincoln and Illi-*

nois' Fifth Capitol, rev. ed. (Mahomet, Ill.: Mayhaven Publishing 2006), 245.

28. "I can not answer all I am receiving," Lincoln confessed to one correspondent. Lincoln did not even acknowledge the gift of a new anti-slavery oration from Republican icon Charles Sumner of Massachusetts; see Lincoln to Sumner, June 14, 1860; Lincoln to Mordecai Mobley, June 4, 1860, *CW,* 4:76, 70.

29. Speech at Chicago, March 1, 1859, in *CW,* 3:366, 370. Voters could find Lincoln's views on these questions in the best-selling editions in circulation of both the Lincoln-Douglas debates and the Cooper Union address.

30. For "tolerate," see Cooper Union address, *CW,* 3:535; for "ultimate extinction," Lincoln's address at Chicago, July 10, 1858, *CW,* 2:492.

31. John G. Nicolay and John Hay, *Abraham Lincoln: A History,* 10 vols. (New York: The Century Co., 1890), 3:280–281.

32. Lincoln to William S. Speer, October 23, 1860, *CW,* 4:130.

33. Lincoln to George T. M. Davis, October 27, 1860, *CW,* 4:132–33.

34. Lincoln to George D. Prentice, October 31, 1860, *CW,* 4:135.

35. The eclipse was described in advance in *The Evening Journal 1860 Almanac* (Albany: Weed, Parsons & Co., 1860). Its publisher, Thurlow Weed, failed to predict the political eclipse of his favorite Republican, William Seward, who lost to Lincoln at the Republican National Convention two months earlier.

36. "Election Day with Mr. Lincoln," *Concord* (New Hampshire) *Independent Democrat,* November 22, 1860.

37. His assistant private secretary John Hay recorded for biographer William H. Herndon President Lincoln's affection for toast and eggs for breakfast. See Wayne C. Temple, *"The Taste Is in My Mouth a Little . . .": Lincoln's Victuals and Potables* (Mahomet, Ill.: Mayhaven Publishing, 2004), 101, 116.

38. *New York World,* November 8, 1860.

39. Theodore Calvin Pease, ed., *The Diary of Orville Hickman Browning,* 2 vols. (Springfield: Illinois State Historical Library, 1925), 1:434.

40. Bloomington, Illinois, *Daily Pantagraph,* November 7, 1860. To the Bloomington-based Lincoln campaign manager, David Davis, this was "the only pleasant election day that we have had for years."

41. *Sacramento Daily Union,* August 15, 1860; David W. Davis to Mrs. Davis, November 11, 1860, David Davis Papers, ALPLM. I am indebted to state historian Thomas F. Schwartz and curator Cheryl Schnirring for locating this letter.

42. *Frank Leslie's Illustrated Newspaper,* December 22, 1860.

43. *New York World,* November 8, 1860.

44. *Diary of Orville Hickman Browning,* 1:415.

45. One reason Lincoln felt he did not need to speak anew was that the Lincoln-Douglas debates had sold thirty thousand copies, and reprints of the Cooper Union address another 26,870. For the best-selling status of the former, see Jay Monaghan, "The Lincoln-Douglas Debates," *Lincoln Herald* 45 (June 1943): 2; for the latter, see *Report. Young Men's Republican Union . . .* , ca. November 1860, brochure in the ALPLC. The authors of *Report* calculated they had distributed 864,000 "pages" of Lincoln's New York speech. Since the pamphlet was thirty-two pages in length, the total number of publications distributed is calculated to be 26,870.

46. Douglas L. Wilson and Rodney O. Davis eds., *Herndon's Lincoln* by William H. Herndon and Jesse W. Weik, orig. pub. 1889 (Urbana: University of Illinois Press, 2006), 261.

47. Temple and Temple, *Abraham Lincoln and Illinois' Fifth Capitol*, 258. An accidental chief executive—a lieutenant governor who had succeeded to the state's highest office in March upon the death of Lincoln's friend William H. Bissell—Wood had seemed almost relieved to cede his suite to the Republican presidential candidate.

48. Newton Bateman, *Abraham Lincoln: An Address*, orig. pub. 1899, 2nd ed. (Gardena, Cal.: H. E. Barker Spanish-American Institute, 1932), 21.

49. Ibid., 15.

50. "Lincoln in 1860. His Humor and Homely Philosophy on the Campaign," undated clipping in the Lincoln Museum, Fort Wayne, Indiana.

51. Samuel R. Weed, "Hearing the Returns with Mr. Lincoln: The Unpublished Story of a Reporter Who Spent Election Day of 1860 in Springfield with the Candidate," *New York Times*, February 14, 1932. Weed served as a visiting correspondent for the [St. Louis] *Daily Missouri Democrat*, and filed two stories from the scene. He wrote these reminiscences in the 1880s.

52. *New-York Daily Tribune*, November 10, 1860.

53. Ibid.

54. "Lincoln in 1860," undated clipping in the Lincoln Museum, Fort Wayne, Indiana.

55. *New-York Daily Tribune*, November 12, 1860; [Concord, New Hampshire] *Independent Democrat*, November 22, 1860, quoted in Michael Burlingame, ed., *Abraham Lincoln: The Observations of John G. Nicolay and John Hay* (Carbondale: Southern Illinois University Press, 2007), 17–18; Weed, "Hearing the Returns with Mr. Lincoln."

56. Weed, "Hearing the Returns with Mr. Lincoln."

57. [St. Louis] *Daily Missouri Democrat*, November 7, 1860.

58. *New York Times*, November 7, 1860.

59. *New York World*, November 7, 1860.

60. *Frank Leslie's Illustrated Newspaper*, November 17, 1860.

61. Allan Nevins and Milton Halsey Thomas, eds., *The Diary of George Templeton Strong*, 4 vols. (New York: Macmillan, 1952), 2:58–59.

62. Edmund Ruffin, *Anticipations of the Future, to Serve as Lessons for the Present Time. In the Form of Extracts of Letters from an English Resident in the United States, to the London Times, from 1864 to 1870* (Richmond: J. W. Randolph, 1860), viii–ix.

63. William Kauffman Scarborough, ed., *The Diary of Edmund Ruffin*, 2 vols. (Baton Rouge: Louisiana State University Press, 1972), 1:481–83.

64. Diary of Charles Francis Adams, November 5 and 6, 1860, Adams Papers, Massachusetts Historical Society. Nearby Boston was still reeling from the recent visit of England's Prince of Wales. See *Frank Leslie's Illustrated Newspaper*, November 10, 1860, 385.

65. Ulysses S. Grant, *Personal Memoirs*, 2 vols. (New York: Charles L. Webster, 1892), 2:222. Grant was referring to his preference for Douglas in the 1858 campaign for the U.S. Senate.

66. John Y. Simon, ed., *The Papers of Ulysses S. Grant*, 28 vols. (Carbondale: Southern Illinois University Press, 1967–2005), 1:357.

67. Grant, *Memoirs*, 1:224. Galena is well described in Jean Edward Smith, *Grant* (New York: Simon & Schuster, 2001), 95–96.

68. Herschel Johnson, quoted in Johannsen, *Stephen A. Douglas*, 784.

69. Lincoln to Hamlin, July 18, 1860, CW, 4:84.

70. Lincoln to Hamlin, September 4, 1860, CW, 4:110.

71. The platform was widely published. This text comes from the eighth plank, as printed in *The National Republican Chart*, a large campaign engraving published by H. H. Lloyd in New York, a copy of which is in the author's collection.

72. See, for example, Douglas's remarks at the Lincoln-Douglas debate at Freeport, Illinois, on August 27, 1858, CW, 3:55–56.

73. Douglass was, as historian James Oakes has pointed out in his excellent study, "a reformer at heart," who viewed Lincoln as but "a politician." See Oakes, *The Radical and the Republican: Frederick Douglass, Abraham Lincoln, and the Triumph of Antislavery Politics* (New York: W. W. Norton, 2007), 131–32. Oakes opens his excellent chapter, "I Cannot Support Lincoln," imagining Douglass considering whether he should "reserve his vote for those with the highest abolitionist principles" (87).

74. *Douglass' Monthly*, September 1860.

75. David W. Blight, *Frederick Douglass' Civil War: Keeping Faith in Jubilee* (Baton Rouge: Louisiana State University Press, 1989), 60. The *New York Herald* charged on November 9, 1860, that "white-skinned" Republicans had abandoned the amendment, while "the negroes themselves who have votes in virtue of possessing property with $250 voted against their colored brethren."

76. In the end, fewer than 14 percent of New York's eligible voters cast ballots in favor of the amendment; it went down by more than 55,000 votes. For results see *The Tribune Almanac for the Years 1838 to 1864, Inclusive* . . . (New York: New York Tribune, 1868), 41.

77. Harry E. Pratt, *Springfield's Public Square in Lincoln's Day, 1861 and 1941* (Springfield, Ill.: Williamson Printing & Publishing Co., [1941]), 3.

78. The process of printing and distributing party tickets is well described in Richard Franklin Bensel, *The American Ballot Box in the Mid-Nineteenth Century* (Cambridge, U.K.: Cambridge University Press, 2004), 30–31. Hardly an acquisitive man, Lincoln nonetheless obtained, and kept in his files, such curiosities as a Douglas ticket decorated with an emblematic engraving of a bantam rooster, a Breckinridge ballot crested by an eagle clutching a flag, and a Bell ticket that featured a roaring railroad locomotive. See D. H. Wood to Lincoln, November 6, 1860, enclosing three ballots, ALPLC. Lincoln himself had been involved in disputes about ballot tickets from his earliest days as a politician. See Hawkins Taylor's reminiscence of an 1834 campaign, "How Lincoln Won His First Election to Office," in Rufus Rockwell Wilson, ed., *Intimate Memories of Lincoln* (Elmira, N.Y.: Primavera Press, 1945), 9–10.

79. *New-York Daily Tribune*, November 10, 1860.

80. William H. Herndon, *Herndon's Lincoln: The True Story of a Great Life*, orig. pub. 1889, 3 vols. (Springfield, Ill.: The Herndon's Lincoln Publishing Co.), 3:467

81. *New-York Daily Tribune*, November 7, 1860.

82. William H. Herndon to Jesse Weik, November 14, 1885, Herndon Papers, Library of Congress.

83. *Frank Leslie's Illustrated Newspaper*, August 11, 1860. The newspaper called Ellsworth an "incentive to our young men to follow his example, and, like him, scorn enervating delights and live laborious days."

84. Herndon, *Herndon's Lincoln*, 3:467.

85. Herndon embellished the tale in his Lincoln biography, claiming Lincoln agreed to vote only at his junior law partner's urging. See ibid., [St. Louis] *Daily Missouri Democrat*, November 7, 1860; *Chicago Daily Tribune*, November 10, 1860; Herndon to Weik, November 14, 1885, Herndon Papers, Library of Congress.

86. Michael Burlingame, ed., *Lincoln's Journalist: John Hay's Anonymous Writings for the Press, 1860–1864* (Carbondale: Southern Illinois University Press, 1998), 14.

87. [St. Louis] *Daily Missouri Democrat*, November 7, 1860; Herndon to Weik, November 14, 1885, Herndon Papers, Library of Congress.

88. *New-York Daily Tribune*, November 7, 1860.

89. [St. Louis] *Daily Missouri Democrat*, November 7, 1860.

90. *New-York Daily Tribune*, November 7, 1860.

91. Herndon, *Herndon's Lincoln*, 3:467.

92. An original Republican ballot for November 6, 1860, is in the ALPLM. A copy was printed the previous day in the *Illinois Daily State Journal*. The author is indebted to Illinois state historian Thomas F. Schwartz for bringing both copies to his attention. Lincoln voted that day only for fellow Republicans contending for state and local office: Richard Yates for governor (as he had pledged at the post office), Francis A. Hoffmann for lieutenant governor, Henry Case for Congress, Ozias M. Hatch for another term as secretary of state, and Jesse K. Dubois for reelection as state auditor. With his single preprinted ballot, Lincoln also voted for William Jayne for state senator, Shelby M. Cullom and George R. Weber for state representatives, Stephen S. Whitehurst for clerk of the Circuit Court, John W. Smith for sheriff, and John Hopper for coroner. Earning Lincoln's vote for state treasurer was his old friend and fellow Kentucky native William Butler, for whom he had done farm work back in 1824, "breaking up prairie." (Butler later gushed to the press that Lincoln had "not been known to utter an oath, or taste a drop of any intoxicating liquor for twenty years.") For superintendent of public instruction, Lincoln voted for another term for Newton Bateman, whose State House office sat next to Lincoln's headquarters at the Springfield State House. It was as straight a Republican ticket as anyone in Springfield could vote—save for Lincoln's refusal to include the presidential electors pledged to himself.

93. *New York Times*, November 10, 1860.

94. Ibid., and *New-York Daily Tribune*, November 10, 1860. Herndon later claimed it had been his idea for Lincoln to cut his own name from his ballot. See Herndon to Weik, November 14, 1885, Library of Congress, and Herndon, *Herndon's Lincoln*, 3:467.

95. [Concord, New Hampshire] *Independent Democrat*, November 22, 1860.

96. *New-York Daily Tribune*, November 7, 10, 12, 1860.

97. Weed, "Hearing the Returns with Mr. Lincoln."

98. *New-York Daily Tribune*, November 7, 10, 12, 1860.

99. Ibid.

100. *New York Times*, November 8, 1860.

101. John G. Nicolay to Therena Bates, November 8, 1860, NPLC. The crowd estimate was published in the *New-York Daily Tribune*, November 8, 1860.

102. Weed, "Hearing the Returns with Mr. Lincoln."

103. Ibid.

104. Hay, quoted in Burlingame, *Lincoln's Journalist*, 15.

105. *New-York Daily Tribune*, November 8, 1860.

106. C. F. McIntire to Lincoln, November 5, 1860, ALPLC.

107. CW, 3:357. The best book on the subject is Tom Wheeler, *Mr. Lincoln's*

T-Mails: The Untold Story of How Abraham Lincoln Used the Telegraph to Win the Civil War (New York: HarperCollins, 2006). Lincoln's chief rival, Stephen Douglas, similarly called the newfangled Morse code messages "intelligence by lightning." See Lincoln-Douglas debate at Alton, October 15, 1858, in *CW*, 3:323. Lincoln was first exposed to the new technology at Tazewell, Illinois, in 1857. See Wheeler, *Mr. Lincoln's T-Mails*, 31.

108. This boast was emblazoned on its blank telegraph forms. Originals in ALPLC, esp. November 6, 1860.

109. *New-York Daily Tribune*, November 10, 1860; *New York Herald*, November 10, 1860.

110. *New-York Daily Tribune*, November 12, 1860.

111. The author is grateful to the "Signal Corps of the James," a group of reenactors who use period instruments in recreating telegraph tents at Civil War battle reenactments, for a personal demonstration of these authentic instruments at the opening of the USS *Monitor* Center at the Mariners' Museum in Newport News, Virginia, on March 9, 2006. The group also published an informative brochure, *Telegraph in the US Civil War*.

112. John G. Nicolay and John Hay, *Abraham Lincoln: A History*, 10 vols. (New York: The Century Co., 1890), 3:345.

113. *New-York Daily Tribune*, November 12, 1860.

114. Ibid. Eastern Division superintendent Wilson and telegraph operator C. F. McIntire are identified in C. S. Williams, *Williams' Springfield Directory, City Guide, and Business Mirror, for 1860–1861* (Springfield, Ill.: Johnson & Bradford, 1860), 42.

115. Nicolay and Hay, *Abraham Lincoln*, 3:346.

116. Ibid.

117. *New York Times*, November 8, 1860.

118. B. J. F. Hanna to Lincoln, November 6, 1860, ALPLC.

119. Weed, "Hearing the Returns with Mr. Lincoln."

120. [St. Louis] *Daily Missouri Democrat*, November 8, 1860.

121. Weed, "Hearing the Returns with Mr. Lincoln."

122. Nicolay and Hay, *Abraham Lincoln*, 3:346.

123. Original, ca. November 1, 1860, in ALPLC. A meticulous vote-counter, Lincoln had been following and analyzing state and local election results for nearly thirty years, first serving as a clerk in a village contest as early as 1832. He was long accustomed to tabulating and interpreting such numbers, and using them to calculate the expanding potential for Whig and, later, Republican advantage as Illinois grew more populous and diverse. Lincoln oversaw elections for constable in 1832, Congress and sheriff in 1834. See *CW*, 1:13–14, 23–24, 25–26.

124. A. H. Conner to Lincoln, November 6, 1860 (telegraph), November 6, 1860, ALPLC.

125. George Hamersly to Lincoln, November 6, 1860 (telegraph), November 6, 1860, ALPLC.

126. James E. Harvey to Lincoln, November 6, 1860 (telegraph), November 6, 1860, ALPLC.

127. Election Day telegrams in ALPLC. The surviving collection of his incoming Election Day correspondence boasts more than twenty such wires, all of them once studied by Lincoln himself.

128. Michael Burlingame, ed., *A Reporter's Lincoln: Walter B. Stevens* (Lincoln: University of Nebraska Press, 1998), 64.

129. Weed, "Hearing the Returns with Mr. Lincoln."

130. Ibid., Cameron to Lincoln, November 6, 1860, ALPLC.

131. Simeon Draper to Abraham Lincoln (telegraph), November 6, 1860, ALPLC. For the assessment of Chairman Draper as "impulsive," see Thurlow Weed Barnes, ed., *Memoir of Thurlow Weed*, 2 vols. (Boston: Houghton Mifflin, 1884), 2:483.

132. Weed, "Hearing the Returns with Mr. Lincoln," and Burlingame, *A Reporter's Lincoln*, 64.

133. Weed, "Hearing the Returns with Mr. Lincoln."

134. "Lincoln in 1860. His Humor and Homely Philosophy in the Campaign." Undated clipping in the Lincoln Museum, Fort Wayne, Indiana.

135. Mrs. James C. Conkling to Clinton L. Conkling, November 6, 1860, in Harry E. Pratt, ed., *Concerning Mr. Lincoln: In Which Abraham Lincoln Is Pictured as He Appeared to Letter Writers of His Time* (Springfield, Ill.: Abraham Lincoln Association, 1944), 28. The *New York Times* reported that Lincoln visited the "Chen[er]y" House, a local hotel. See *New York Times*, November 8, 1860. For Watson's, see *Williams' Springfield Directory*, 140, which described the gathering place as "manufacturers and dealers in Candies, Confectionary, Fruits, etc."

136. Nicolay to Bates, November 8, 1860, NPLC.

137. [St. Louis] *Daily Missouri Democrat*, November 8, 1860.

138. Weed, "Hearing the Returns with Mr. Lincoln."

139. [St. Louis] *Daily Missouri Democrat*, November 8, 1860.

140. Weed, "Hearing the Returns with Mr. Lincoln."

141. *New York Times*, November 8, 1860; *New-York Daily Tribune*, November 12, 1860.

142. *New-York Daily Tribune*, November 12, 1860.

143. *New-York Daily Tribune*, November 8, 1860, quoted in Robert S. Harper, *Lincoln and the Press* (New York: McGraw-Hill, 1951), 65.

144. Mary Lincoln to Hannah Shearer, October 20, 1860, in Justin G. Turner and Linda Levitt Turner, eds., *Mary Todd Lincoln: Her Life and Letters* (New York: Alfred A. Knopf, 1972), 66.

145. *New-York Daily Tribune*, November 8, 1860. Mrs. Lincoln's attendance was

confirmed by Mrs. James C. Conkling in a letter to her son on November 12. See Pratt, ed., *Concerning Mr. Lincoln*, 29.

146. Bateman, *Abraham Lincoln: An Address*, 21.

147. Preston H. Bailhache, "Abraham Lincoln as I Remember Him," undated typescript in the Lincoln Museum, Fort Wayne, Indiana. See also "Lincolniana Notes: Recollections of a Springfield Doctor," *Journal of the Illinois State Historical Society* 47 (June 1954): 62.

148. Bateman, *Abraham Lincoln: An Address*, 21.

149. *New York Times*, November 8, 1860.

150. Mrs. James C. Conkling to Clinton L. Conkling, November 12, 1860, in Pratt, ed., *Concerning Mr. Lincoln*, 27–28.

151. "Election Day with Mr. Lincoln," *Concord* (New Hampshire) *Independent Democrat*, November 22, 1860. The reporter was referring to public demonstrations he had witnessed for, among others, William Walker, a "filibuster"— meaning an American insurrectionist in Latin America—who had established rogue outposts in both Lower California and Nicaragua; and Peter Cooper, who promoted and financed the laying of the Atlantic Cable before he founded the Cooper Union in New York in 1859.

152. Weed, "Hearing the Returns with Mr. Lincoln."

153. *New-York Daily Tribune*, November 12, 1860.

154. Bailhache, "Abraham Lincoln as I Remember Him."

155. *Chicago Tribune*, October 2, 1893; *New York Tribune*, November 12, 1860.

156. Weed, "Hearing the Returns with Mr. Lincoln."

157. Ibid. Weed's original 1860 reports suggest a slightly different chronology; it remains unclear whether Lincoln attended the ice cream parlor celebration before or after this scene occurred.

158. [St. Louis] *Daily Missouri Democrat*, November 8, 1860.

159. Anonymous to Lincoln [telegraph], November 6, 1860, ALPLC.

160. New Jersey eventually awarded Lincoln three of its seven electoral votes even though Douglas won the popular tally there.

161. Weed, "Hearing the Returns with Mr. Lincoln." The best source for easy-to-consult election tables is Stefan Lorant, *The Glorious Burden*, rev. ed. (Lenox, Mass.: Author's Edition, 1976), 1,066.

162. Missouri boasted the largest foreign-born population of any Southern state: 160,525. With the Missouri vote subtracted, Lincoln received fewer than ten thousand votes in the entire South. Census records (transcripts) in Albert Beveridge Papers, Library of Congress, Container 196, 1922–1927.

163. Washington *Constitution*, November 7, 1860.

164. Conkling to Conkling, in Pratt, ed., *Concerning Mr. Lincoln*, 28–29.

165. *New York Times*, November 12, 1860.

166. John G. Nicolay to Therena Bates, November 8, 1860, NPLC.

167. *New-York Daily Tribune*, November 12, 1860, reported Lincoln's 1:30 A.M. departure; for 2 A.M., see Gideon Welles to Isaac Newton Arnold, November 27, 1872, Arnold Papers, Chicago Historical Society. I am indebted to historian Doris Kearns Goodwin for making this, and many other documents, available to the author.

168. *New-York Daily Tribune*, November 12, 1860.

169. The Sangamon and Springfield results can be found in Paul M. Angle, *"Here I Have Lived": A History of Lincoln's Springfield, 1821–1865*, rev. ed. (Chicago: Abraham Lincoln Book Shop, 1971), 253. For complete Illinois returns, county by county, see Howard W. Allen and Vincent A. Lacey, eds., *Illinois Elections, 1818–1990: Candidates and County Returns for President, Governor, Senate, and House of Representatives* (Carbondale: Southern Illinois University Press, 1992), 144–45.

170. *New-York Daily Tribune*, November 12, 1860.

171. *Washington Constitution*, November 22, 1860.

172. Weed, "Hearing the Returns with Mr. Lincoln." According to the wife of John M. Palmer, Lincoln said: "Well, I must go home and tell Mary," *Chicago Tribune*, October 2, 1893.

173. Nicolay and Hay, *Abraham Lincoln*, 3:346–47.

174. Gideon Welles, *Lincoln and Seward* (New York: Sheldon & Co., 1874), 38.

175. Ward Hill Lamon, *Recollections of Abraham Lincoln, 1847–1865*, ed. Dorothy Lamon (Chicago: A. C. McClurg, 1895), 180.

176. Henry Guest McPike quoted in Stevens, *A Reporter's Lincoln*, 65.

177. Recollection of Henry C. Bowen, reprinted in Wayne Whipple, *The Story-Life of Lincoln* (Philadelphia: John C. Winston, 1908), 345.

178. Memorandum by Frederic W. Sutton (Mayor Goyn Sutton's son), April 7, 1926, copy enclosed with correspondence from Lincoln biographer Albert Beveridge to Lincoln collector Oliver R. Barrett, July 11, 1926, Albert J. Beveridge Papers, Library of Congress, Barrett File, "Lincoln Correspondence B," Container 286. The younger Sutton described Lincoln placing his hand on his father's knee before making these remarks, "much affected with emotion." But he alternately described the event as taking place on the evening of Lincoln's election, and nomination. Although the reminiscence was composed sixty-six years after these events, when memories might well be clouded by time, the context makes it clear that Frederic Sutton was referring to Election Night.

2. My Troubles Have Just Commenced

1. R. Bunyan to Samuel Williams, November 9, 1860, transcript in the Lincoln Museum, Fort Wayne, Indiana.
2. *Richmond Dispatch*, November 9, 1860. Abolitionist John Brown's unsuccessful raid on Harpers Ferry, Virginia, in 1859, remained a campaign issue through 1860.
3. Edward A. Pollard, *Southern History of the War*, 2 vols., orig. pub. 1866 (New York: Fairfax Press, 1990), 41.
4. *Fayetteville North Carolinian*, November 17, 1860, in Donald E. Reynolds, *Editors Make War: Southern Newspapers in the Secession Crisis* (Carbondale: Southern Illinois University Press, 2006), 141.
5. *Charleston Mercury*, November 8, 1860, reprinted in David M. Potter [and Don E. Fehrenbacher], *The Impending Crisis, 1848–1861* (New York: Harper & Row, 1976), 485.
6. Edmund Ruffin, "Consequences of Abolition Agitation," *De Bow's Review* 23 (September 1857): 271.
7. *Richmond Dispatch*, November 9, 1860.
8. Jefferson Davis, *The Rise and Fall of the Confederate Government*, 2 vols., orig. pub. 1881 (New York: Da Capo Press, 1990), 1:57–59.
9. Quoted in Allan Nevins, *The Emergence of Lincoln*, 2 vols. (New York: Charles Scribners' Sons, 1950), 2:321.
10. Quoted in Robert W. Johannsen, *Stephen A. Douglas* (New York: Oxford University Press, 1973), 808.
11. Secretary of War John B. Floyd's diary, November 8, 1860, quoted in John G. Nicolay and John Hay, *Abraham Lincoln: A History*, 10 vols. (New York: The Century Co., 1890), 2:316, 324, 326.
12. *Richmond Dispatch*, November 8, 1860. The celebration is exquisitely detailed by historian William W. Freehling, who saw the mutually reenforcing celebrations as one of the small coincidences that propelled both states toward secession. See William W. Freehling, *The Road to Disunion, Volume 2: Secessionists Triumphant, 1854–1861* (New York: Oxford University Press, 2007), 406–12.
13. Reprinted in the *New York Herald*, November 29, 1860. That day the paper was filled with similarly anti-Union verse supposedly printed in Southern newspapers.
14. *Richmond Dispatch*, November 14, 1860.
15. *New York Herald*, November 9, 1860.
16. Ibid.
17. C. Vann Woodward, ed., *Mary Chesnut's Civil War* (New Haven: Yale University Press, 1981), 4. Former Judge Andrew Gordon Magrath later became a delegate to the South Carolina secession convention.

18. *New York Times*, November 9, 1860.
19. Leonard L. Richards, *The California Gold Rush and the Coming of the Civil War* (New York: Alfred A. Knopf, 2007), 4–6, 228. The September 13, 1859, duel was between "Chivalry" Democrat David S. Terry, chief justice of the California Supreme Court, and Senator David Broderick, an antislavery Democrat.
20. *New York Herald*, November 20, 1860.
21. Milton H. Shutes, *Lincoln and California* (Stanford: Stanford University Press, 1943), 48. Though more than sixty years and flawed by the absence of formal sourcing, Shutes's remains the standard study.
22. *Newark Mercury* and *Newark Journal*, quoted in Betsy Moriarity, "Newark Newspaper Editorials, in Journalistic Style of Period, Reflected Tense Feeling Campaign Aroused," *Newark Evening News*, February 12, 1949.
23. *Chicago Daily Press & Tribune*, November 7, 1860; [Springfield] *Illinois Daily State Journal*, November 10, 1860, in *Annals of Sangamon County, 1942* WPA ms., in collection of the ALPLM; *Daily Illinois State Register*, November 7, 1860.
24. Undated clipping in the Lincoln Museum, Fort Wayne, Indiana.
25. *Boston Advertiser*, ca. November 1860, undated clipping in the Lincoln Museum, Fort Wayne, Indiana.
26. Draft of a letter by Franklin Pierce to an unknown correspondent, November 24, 1860, quoted in Peter A. Wallner, *Franklin Pierce: Martyr for the Union* (Concord, N.H.: Plaidswede Publishing, 2007), 332. The author provides valuable insights into Pierce's post-election fears, but perhaps errs when he claims, quoting historian Richard Carwardine, that Lincoln "misjudged" disunion sentiment in the South, and "knew better" than Lincoln the seriousness of the crisis.
27. *Boston Atlas*, reprinted in the *New York Times*, November 9, 1860.
28. *Boston Traveller*, quoted in David C. Mearns, *The Lincoln Papers: The Story of the Collection with Selections to July 4, 1861*, 2 vols. (Garden City, N.Y.: Doubleday, 1948), 1:8.
29. *Boston Herald*, November 9, 1860, reprinted in Osborn H. Oldroyd, *Lincoln's Campaign: The Political Revolution of 1860* (Chicago: Laird & Lee, 1896), 146–48.
30. James A. Bayard to S. L. M. Barlow, October 4, 1860, Barlow Papers (Box 31), Huntington Library, San Marino, California.
31. *Philadelphia Bulletin*, reprinted in the *Richmond Dispatch*, November 12, 1860.
32. *Boston Herald*, November 12, 1860.
33. *Harper's Weekly*, November 10, 1860.
34. Allan Nevins and Milton Halsey Thomas, eds., *The Diary of George Templeton Strong*, 4 vols. (New York: Macmillan, 1952), 3:61.

35. *New York World*, November 7, 1860.
36. *New York World*, November 8, 1860.
37. Ibid.
38. *New York Times*, November 10, 1860. The paper had once been partial to Salmon P. Chase. See Augustus Maverick, *Henry J. Raymond and The New York Press, for Thirty Years* (Hartford, Conn.: A. S. Hale, 1870), 151.
39. *New York Times*, November 9, 1860.
40. Quoted in the *Alexandria Gazette & Virginia Advertiser*, November 8, 1860.
41. *Memphis Daily Appeal*, November 10, December 11, 1860, in Reynolds, *Editors Make War*, 151. The phrase "irrepressible conflict" had been introduced—to his political detriment—by William H. Seward.
42. *Memphis Daily Appeal*, November 9, 1860.
43. Ibid.
44. From his speech at Springfield on June 26, 1857, CW, 2:405.
45. Woodward, *Mary Chesnut's Civil War*, 3.
46. *Charlotte Daily Bulletin*, November 27, 1860, in Richard Bardolph, "Malice Toward One: Lincoln in the North Carolina Press," *Lincoln Herald* 53 (Winter 1952): 35.
47. *Waynesboro [Georgia] Gopher*, n.d., clipping ca. November 1860, ALPLC.
48. From Douglass's speech in Glasgow, March 26, 1860, in John W. Blassingame et al., eds., *The Frederick Douglass Papers, Series One: Speeches, Debates, and Interviews*, 5 vols. (New Haven: Yale University Press, 1979–92), 3:365.
49. See Don E. Fehrenbacher and Ward M. McAfee, *The Slaveholding Republic: An Account of the United States Government's Relations to Slavery* (New York: Oxford University Press, 2001), 301–4.
50. Message to the People of Georgia, December 6, 1860, in *Annual Report of the American Historical Association, for the Year 1911* (Washington, D.C: n.p., 1913), 513–14.
51. Letter to 96 New Orleans citizens, November 13, 1860, in Robert W. Johannsen, ed., *The Letters of Stephen A. Douglas* (Urbana: University of Illinois Press, 1961), 499.
52. Ibid., 500–501.
53. Ibid, 502.
54. *New York Herald*, November 22, 1860.
55. Undated 1860 clipping in the Lincoln Museum, Fort Wayne, Indiana.
56. Noah Brooks, *Washington in Lincoln's Time* (New York: The Century Co., 1895), 220–22.
57. Ward Hill Lamon, *Recollections of Abraham Lincoln, 1847–1865*, ed. Dorothy Lamon (Chicago: A. C. McClurg, 1895), 111–12.
58. See, for some examples, ibid., 109–21.
59. Gideon Welles, *Lincoln and Seward* (New York: Sheldon & Co., 1874), 38.

60. Gideon Welles, *Diary of Gideon Welles: Secretary of the Navy Under Lincoln and Johnson*, 2 vols. (Boston: Houghton Mifflin, 1911), 1:82. The quote, "men on whom he could depend," is from Welles, *Lincoln and Seward*, 38. For Lincoln's undated list, see entry 6495c, [November 7, 1860], ALPLC. The list is reprinted and discussed as original in David Herbert Donald, *Lincoln* (New York: Simon & Schuster, 1996), 261–62; and see Doris Kearns Goodwin, *Team of Rivals: The Political Genius of Abraham Lincoln* (New York: Simon & Schuster, 2005), 280.

61. Nicolay and Hay, *Abraham Lincoln*, 3:345.

62. William O. Stoddard, *Abraham Lincoln: The True Story of a Great Life* (New York: Fords, Howard & Hulbert, 1884), 85.

63. Goodwin, *Team of Rivals*.

64. Nicolay and Hay, *Abraham Lincoln*, 3:374.

65. *Concord* [New Hampshire] *Independent Democrat*, November 22, 1860.

66. *St. Louis Globe Democrat*, February 7, 1909, quoted in Michael Burlingame, *The Inner World of Abraham Lincoln* (Urbana: University of Illinois Press, 1994), 58.

67. *New York Times*, November 14, 1860.

68. *Frank Leslie's Illustrated Newspaper*, November 24, 1860.

69. *Philadelphia Inquirer*, November 8, 1860.

70. Samuel R. Weed, "Hearing the Returns with Mr. Lincoln: The Unpublished Story, of a Reporter Who Spent Election Day of 1860 in Springfield with the Candidate," *New York Times*, February 14, 1932.

71. David Davis to his wife, November 11, 1860, ALPLM.

72. Mrs. James C. Conkling to Clinton L. Conkling, November 12, 1860, in "Lincoln Described in Family Letters," *Lincoln Centennial Association Bulletin* 7 (June 1, 1927): 2.

73. [St. Louis] *Daily Missouri Democrat*, November 7, 1860.

74. Ibid.

75. Ibid.

76. Ibid., and *New-York Daily Tribune*, November 10, 1860.

77. *The* [New York] *Independent*, November 13, 1860.

78. Weed, "Hearing the Returns with Mr. Lincoln."

79. Octavia Roberts Corneau and Georgia L. Osborne, eds., "A Girl in the Sixties: Excerpts from the Journal of Anna Ridgely . . . ," *Journal of the Illinois State Historical Society* 22 (October 1929): 418.

80. John McConnell quoted in Don E. Fehrenbacher and Virginia Fehrenbacher, *Recollected Words of Lincoln* (Stanford: Stanford University Press, 1996), 319.

81. "Public sentiment is everything," Lincoln had said in 1858. "With public sentiment, nothing can fail; without it nothing can succeed." See *CW*, 3:27.

82. The poet was Park Benjamin, who wrote from New York to express his hope that Lincoln would value "among the thousands of congratulations that will pour in upon you from all parts of our country . . . that of a literary man and not a party-politician." See Benjamin to Lincoln, November 7, 1860, ALPLC.

83. *New York Times*, November 15, 1860.

84. This went on for months. See, for example, the recently discovered Lincoln to B. Perking, February 6, 1861: "Herewith I send you my autograph, which you requested. Yours Truly, A. Lincoln." Swann Galleries (New York), *Catalogue of Autographs, Public Auction Sale 2123*, October 11, 2007, Lot 149.

85. John G. Nicolay to Therena Bates, November 14, 1860, NPLC.

86. Salmon P. Chase to Lincoln, November 7, 1860, ALPLC.

87. Carl Schurz to Lincoln, November 7, 1860, ALPLC.

88. George G. Fogg to Lincoln, November 7, 1860, ALPLC.

89. Cyrus M. Allen to Lincoln, November 8, 1860; Helen Haskell to Lincoln, November 10, 1860; James Shoaff to Lincoln, November 14, 1860, ALPLC.

90. "Abes boys" to Lincoln, November 9, 1860, ALPLC.

91. William F. Smith to Lincoln, November 7, 1860, ALPLC; G. C. Neumeister of La Crosse, Wisconsin, wrote to Lincoln a few weeks later to inquire about Mrs. Lincoln's given name, noting that "My wife get on Election day a little Girl, and I made the proposition that if it is a girl to give your wifes name." Neumeister to Lincoln, November 27, 1860, ALPLC.

92. H. Jeffords to Lincoln, November 1860, ALPLC.

93. C. H. Moore to Lincoln, November 14, 1860, ALPLC.

94. Lincoln to Hamlin, November 8, 1860, CW, 4:136; Lincoln to James Comstock, November 9, 1860 (thanking him for a barrel of flour), CW, 4:137; Lincoln to Park Benjamin, November 19, 1860 (thanking him for his "kind note of congratulation"), CW, 4:140.

95. Alexander Jenkins to Lincoln, November 7, 1860, ALPLC.

96. Mary E. Raikes to Lincoln, November 1860, ALPLC.

97. Samuel Haycraft to Lincoln, November 9, 1860, ALPLC.

98. Lincoln to Haycraft, November 13, 1860, CW, 4:139.

99. Joshua Speed to Lincoln, November 14, 1860, ALPLC.

100. Lincoln to Speed, November 19, 1860, CW, 4:141.

101. Lacking an electoral majority, Jefferson was chosen by the House of Representatives on February 17 and inaugurated March 4. See Merrill D. Peterson, *Thomas Jefferson and the New Nation*, 2 vols. (New York: Oxford University Press, 1970), 651.

102. Book of Isaiah, 25:5.

103. As recently as 2007, historian William C. Harris argued in an excellent new study that Lincoln took "a sanguine view of the impact of his election

on Southerners." See Harris, *Lincoln's Rise to the Presidency* (Lawrence: University Press of Kansas, 2007), 248. Richard Carwardine similarly wrote of "Lincoln's larger misreading of the southern surge toward secession," though he conceded that "Lincoln's general policy of silence was not unwise." See Richard Carwardine, *Lincoln: A Life of Purpose and Power* (New York: Alfred A. Knopf, 2006), 140–41.

104. Mason Brayman to Adaline Brayman Bailhache, November 10, 1860, Hatch Papers, ALPLM, Box 2.

105. See, for example, M. J. Thomas to Lincoln, October 16, 1860; and Zenas Wood to Lincoln, November 5, 1860, ALPLC.

106. George W. Hazzard to Lincoln, November 5, 1860, ALPLC. Hazzard wrote that "it would afford me pleasure to be near your person."

107. "Maine" to Lincoln, after November 6, 1860, ALPLC.

108. A. W. H. to Lincoln, November 10, 1860; Joseph I. Irwin to Lincoln, November 12, 1860, ALPLC. So-called Border Ruffians were Missourians who had migrated to Kansas in the 1850s and intimidated local residents to ensure it voted to enter the Union as a slave state.

109. Unsigned, undated letter to Lincoln, filed with November correspondence in ALPLC.

110. "A Citizen" to Lincoln, November 8, 1860, ALPLC.

111. *New-York Daily Tribune*, November 9, 1860.

112. Harry E. Pratt, *The Personal Finances of Abraham Lincoln* (Springfield, Ill.: Abraham Lincoln Association, 1943), 153, 160, 169.

113. Several important Lincoln & Herndon legal cases were still pending when the campaign began, including *The Columbus Machine Manufacturing Co. v. Edward R. Ulrich et al.* See *Reports of the Cases Determined in the Supreme Court of the State of Illinois at April and November Terms, 1860, and January and April Terms, 1861* (Chicago: E. B. Myers, 1862), 169. An appeal decision on the case of *The State of Illinois v. The Illinois Central Railroad Company* was not handed down until the November term in 1861. See *Reports of the Cases Determined in the Supreme Court . . . 1861 and 1862* (Chicago: E. B. Myers, 1863), 65–70, with "A. Lincoln" still listed as attorney for the railroad. Some important new books have been published on Lincoln's twenty-five-year-long legal career but none deals specifically with the nature of his practice after May 1860. See: Mark E. Steiner, *An Honest Calling: The Law Practice of Abraham Lincoln* (Dekalb: Northern Illinois University Press, 2006); and Brian Dirck, *Lincoln the Lawyer* (Urbana: University of Illinois Press, 2007). John M. Palmer believed the last case for which Lincoln appeared in court was for the defense in *David J. Baker v. Faculty of Shurtleff College.* See John J. Duff, *A. Lincoln Prairie Lawyer* (New York: Brahall House, 1960), 365. And Walter B. Stevens, chief Washington correspondent of the *St. Louis Globe-Democrat*, concluded in 1909 after

twenty-three years of research that Lincoln had visited Bloomington, Illinois, after his election, "to make disposition of the cases in which he was retained. See Walter B. Stevens, *A Reporter's Lincoln*, ed. Michael Burlingame (Lincoln: University of Nebraska Press, 1998), 32.

114. Conceding that Lincoln's previously published speeches should be "sufficient proof of his moderation and conservatism," for example, the *New York World* nonetheless recommended that Lincoln issue a "conciliatory" new statement of his views." Reprinted in the *Philadelphia Inquirer*, November 9, 1860.

115. W[illia]m H. Price to Lincoln, November 9, 1860, ALPLC.

116. *New-York Daily Tribune*, November 10, 1860

117. Truman Smith to Lincoln, November 8, 1860, ALPLC.

118. Smith to Lincoln, November 7, 1860, ALPLC; Lincoln to Smith, November 10, 1860, *CW*, 4:138.

119. Views on Commercial and Financial Uneasiness," *CW*, 4:138

120. *New-York Daily Tribune*, November 10, 1860.

121. Nathaniel P. Paschall to Lincoln, November 18, 1860, ALPLC.

122. *New York Times*, November 7, 1860.

123. *Daily Illinois State Register*, November 10, 1860.

124. *New-York Daily Tribune*, November 10, 1860.

125. Lincoln to Nathaniel P. Paschall, November 16, 1860, *CW*, 4:139–40.

126. *Diary of George Templeton Strong*, 3:62.

127. Ibid., 3:64–66.

128. Gabor S. Boritt, *Lincoln and the Economics of the American Dream* (Memphis, Tenn.: Memphis State University Press, 1978), 198.

129. William Marvel, *Mr. Lincoln Goes to War* (Boston: Houghton Mifflin, 2006), 4.

130. Memorandum by Winfield Scott, October 29, 1860, copy in ALPLC. General Scott sent copies to President Buchanan, the secretary of war, and an assortment of newspaper editors and "conservative" Southern politicians. The copy to the president-elect was marked: "For the Hon. A. Lincoln with the respects of Winfield Scott."

131. James Buchanan, *Mr. Buchanan's Administration on the Eve of the Rebellion* (New York: D. Appleton & Co., 1866), 99, 106.

132. Lincoln to Winfield Scott, November 9, 1860, *CW*, 4:137.

133. Report from Springfield, November 14, 1860, *New York Evening Post*, reprinted in the *Boston Advertiser*, November 21, 1860.

3. We Won't Jump That Ditch

1. "Wide-Awake Head-Quarters," undated circular, ca. November 1860, ALPLM.

2. John G. Nicolay to Therena Bates, November 11, 1860, NPLC.

3. John G. Nicolay to Therena Bates, November 14, 1860, NPLC.

4. *New-York Daily Tribune*, November 12, 1860.

5. Francis B. Carpenter, *Six Months at the White House with Abraham Lincoln: The Story of a Picture* (New York: Hurd & Houghton, 1866), 281.

6. *Illinois Daily State Journal*, November 13, 1860.

7. Harold G. Villard and Oswald Garrison Villard, *Lincoln on the Eve of '61: A Journalist's Story by Henry Villard* (New York: Alfred A. Knopf, 1941), 13.

8. Henry Villard, *Memoirs of Henry Villard, Journalist and Financier, 1835–1900*, 2 vols. (New York: Houghton Mifflin, 1904), 1:141. The *Herald*'s editor, James Gordon Bennett, apparently determined to treat Lincoln fairly during the four-month interregnum—at least in its news coverage.

9. Alexandra Villard de Borchgrave and John Cullen, *Villard: The Life and Times of an American Titan* (New York: Nan A. Talese/Doubleday, 2001), 125.

10. Villard, *Memoirs of Henry Villard*, 1:146–47.

11. *Illinois Daily State Journal*, November 26, 1860.

12. H. W. Master, "Lincoln's Last Law Partner—William H. Herndon as I Knew Him," typescript in the Albert Beveridge Papers, Library of Congress, container 296; F. A. Dallam to Ozias M. Hatch, November 11, 1860, Hatch Papers, ALPLM, Box 2.

13. Ward H. Lamon, *The Life of Abraham Lincoln: His Birth to His Inauguration as President* (Boston: James R. Osgood; 1872), 457.

14. Villard, *Lincoln on the Eve of '61*, 13–14.

15. Newton Bateman, *Abraham Lincoln: An Address* (Galesburg, Ill.: Cadmus Club, 1899), 22–23.

16. Villard, *Lincoln on the Eve of '61*, 14.

17. Villard, *Memoirs of Henry Villard*, 1:143.

18. Reprinted in the *Daily Ohio Statesman*, November 20, 1860. I am indebted to Doris Kearns Goodwin for bringing this whimsical report to my attention.

19. *Illinois Daily State Journal*, November 26, 1860.

20. *Westliche Post*, November 18, 1860, reprinted in Thomas J. McCormack, ed., *Memoirs of Gustave Koerner, 1809–1896*. 2 vols. (Cedar Rapids, Iowa: Torch Press, 1909), 2:104.

21. Bateman, *Abraham Lincoln*, 21.

22. Villard, *Memoirs of Henry Villard*, 1:147.

23. *New York Herald*, November 20, 1860.

24. Donn Piatt in Allen Thorndike Rice, ed., *Reminiscences of Abraham Lincoln by Distinguished Men of His Time* (New York: North American Publishing, 1888), 480–81.

25. Villard, *Memoirs of Henry Villard*, 1:147.

26. *New York Herald*, November 22, 1860.

27. Ibid.

28. Rice, *Reminiscences of Lincoln*, 480.

29. Mrs. William Bailhache to Mrs. Mason Brayman, November 20, 1860, in Pratt, *Concerning Mr. Lincoln*, 32.

30. Villard, *Lincoln on the Eve of '61*, 16–17.

31. Ibid., 16.

32. Quoted in Charles Hamilton and Lloyd Ostendorf, *Lincoln in Photographs: An Album of Every Known Pose* (Norman: University of Oklahoma Press, 1963), 87. The story was corroborated in the diary of Mrs. Sam Cowell, quoted in Katharine McCook Knox, "Healy's Lincoln No. 1," catalogue of the Thrift Shop Washington Antique Show (1956), 12.

33. *Lexington* [Illinois] *Globe*, November 22, 1860, quoted in CW, 4:414n.

34. *Albany Argus*, reprinted in the *Boston Post*, February 7, 1861.

35. Villard, *Lincoln on the Eve of '61*, 16. The joke may have originated with the *Illinois Daily State Journal*, which reported on November 17: "Our English friends say that President Lincoln is putting on airs. They think so we suppose because Mr. Lincoln is raising a pair of whiskers."

36. Thomas B. Bryan to Abraham Lincoln, November 10, 1860, ALPLC.

37. George P. A. Healy, *Reminiscences of a Portrait Painter* (Chicago: A. C. McClurg, 1894), 69–70.

38. Healy's glowing thirty-inch-by-twenty-five-inch oil portrait is in the collection of the Corcoran Gallery of Art in Washington. For a reproduction, see Harold Holzer, "Some Contemporary Paintings of Abraham Lincoln," *Magazine Antiques* 107 (February 1975): 278.

39. "True Republicans" to Lincoln, October 12, 1860, ALPLC.

40. Grace Bedell to Abraham Lincoln, October 15, 1860, reprinted in CW, 4:130.

41. Grace Bedell to "L. R. Herndon" [William H. Herndon], December 14, 1866, in Douglas L. Wilson and Rodney O. Davis, eds. *Herndon's Informants: Letters, Interviews, and Statements About Abraham Lincoln* (Urbana: University of Illinois Press, 1998), 517.

42. Lincoln to Grace Bedell, October 19, 1860, CW, 4:129.

43. Undated manuscript in NPLC.

44. John Hay, January 7, 1861, quoted in Michael Burlingame, ed., *Lincoln's Journalist: John Hay's Anonymous Writings for the Press, 1860–1864* (Carbondale: Southern Illinois University Press, 1998), 17.

45. *Illinois Daily State Journal*, October 26, November 1, 1860.

46. *Illinois Daily State Journal*, November 14, 1860.

47. For one of its rare reproductions, see Rufus Rockwell Wilson, *Lincoln in Portraiture* (New York: Press of the Pioneers, 1935), 141.

48. See Harold Holzer, "The Bearding of the President, 1860: The Portraitists Put on Hairs," *Lincoln Herald* 78 (Fall 1976): 95–101.

49. *Leslie's* full-page Lincoln portrait, which ran on March 9, 1861, was surrounded by smaller engravings depicting "scenes and incidents in his life," all—like the sketches of the young man splitting rails and chopping corn—were meant to burnish his emerging legend as a self-made American success story. One picture gilded the lily; it showed "Lincoln's father killed by the Indians." Actually, Thomas Lincoln had died in bed. The president-elect's grandfather, not his father, had been slain by Indians.

50. *New York Herald*, November 24, 1860.

51. "His Whiskers Are a Great Improvement," *Journal of the Illinois State Historical Society* 48 (Summer 1954): 186.

52. Villard, *Lincoln on the Eve of '61*, 17.

53. John G. Nicolay, autograph memorandum, NPLC.

54. *New York Herald*, December 4, 1860.

55. The three-dollar estimate is based on a $6.50 receipt Ozias Hatch received for a thirteen-day stay at the Chenery House, one of Springfield's best hotels, in December 1860. Hatch Papers, February 1, 1861, ALPLM.

56. *New York Herald*, December 4, 1860.

57. Ibid.

58. Villard, *Lincoln on the Eve of '61*, 19–20.

59. "Wide-Awake Headquarters, Springfield, Illinois," undated circular ca. November 1860, ALPLM.

60. Medill to Ozias M. Hatch, November 16, 1860, Hatch Papers, ALPLM.

61. *CW*, 4:142–43.

62. The audience response was reported in the *New York Times*, November 21, 1860.

63. Reprinted in the *Illinois Daily State Journal*, December 3, 1860.

64. *New York Times*, November 21, 1860.

65. *Harper's Weekly*, November 20, 1860.

66. *New York Herald*, December 4, 1860.

67. Paul M. Angle, *"Here I Have Lived": A History of Lincoln's Springfield, 1821–1865*, rev. ed. (Chicago: Abraham Lincoln Book Shop, 1971), 256; Octavia Roberts Corneau and Georgia L. Osborne, eds., "A Girl in the Sixties. Excerpts from the Journal of Anna Ridgeley . . ." *Journal of the Illinois State Historical Society* 22 (October 1929): 418–19.

68. Mrs. William H. Bailhache to Mrs. Mason Brayman (her mother), November 20, 1860, in Pratt, *Concerning Mr. Lincoln*, 31–32.

69. *New York Herald*, December 4, 1860.

70. *CW*, 4:141–42.

71. Different versions appeared in the *New York Times* and *Illinois Daily State Journal*, November 21, 1860.

72. *New York Times*, November 21, 1860.

73. *New York Herald*, December 4, 1860.

74. *CW*, 4:142.

75. Obituary of Louise Piatt (who wrote for the *Home Journal* and other publications under the nom de plume Bell Smith), *New York Times*, October 7, 1864, reprinted in Piatt Family Newsletter 7 (1992): 103. I am indebted to Laverne Ingram Piatt for information about her ancestors.

76. James E. Harvey to John G. Nicolay, November 25, 1860, NPLC. Harvey was referring to Simon P. Hanscom of the *New York Herald*, with whom Lincoln remained on good terms, warning notwithstanding, during the Civil War. Evidently Hanscom traveled with Lincoln to Chicago, while Villard remained behind in Springfield.

77. Villard, *Lincoln on the Eve of '61*, 21.

78. Mary Lincoln to Hannah Shearer, June 26, 1859, in Justin G. Turner and Linda Levitt Turner, *Mary Todd Lincoln: Her Life and Letters* (New York: Alfred A. Knopf, 1973), 57; for details about the relationship between Mary Todd and Julia Jayne, see ibid., 43–44.

79. Roswell B. Mason to Lincoln, November 26, 1860, ALPLC.

80. *New York Herald*, November 26, 1860.

81. Rice, *Reminiscences of Lincoln*, 71.

82. Lawrence B. Stringer, *History of Logan County* (Chicago: Pioneer Publications, 1911), 178.

83. *CW*, 4:143. The speech was reprinted in the *New-York Daily Tribune*, November 23, 1860.

84. *CW*, 4:143–144.

85. *New York Herald*, November 22, 1860.

86. Historians, myself included, continue to be vexed by the mysterious fact that Lincoln, a spellbinding lawyer before juries and incomparable orator when armed with prepared texts, was never a brilliant spontaneous speaker. See Harold Holzer, " 'Avoid Saying Foolish Things': The Legacy of Lincoln's Impromptu Oratory," in Holzer, *Lincoln Seen and Heard* (Lawrence: University Press of Kansas, 2000), 162–78.

87. *New York Times*, November 23, 1860.

88. *New York Herald*, November 23, 1860.

89. The conversation, as Hamlin reconstructed it for his grandson and biographer, was published in Charles Eugene Hamlin, *The Life and Times of Hannibal Hamlin*, 2 vols., orig. pub. 1899 (New York: Kennikat Press Scholarly Reprints, n.d.), 2:367.

90. Delegate George William Curtis caught one such print and so inscribed it. The original is in the Lincoln Museum, Fort Wayne, Indiana.

91. *New York Herald*, November 23, 1860; *Harper's Weekly*, December 1, 1860.

92. *New-York Daily Tribune*, November 23, 1860.

93. *New York World*, November 23, 1860. The *World* reported that the reception lasted until noon.

94. *New York Herald*, November 24, 1860.

95. *Chicago Daily Press & Tribune*, November 24, 1860; Reminiscence by James Grant Wilson, orig. pub. 1909, in Rufus Rockwell Wilson, ed., *Intimate Memories of Lincoln* (Elmira, N.Y.: Primavera Press, 1945), 421.

96. A. K. McClure, *Lincoln's Own Yarns and Stories* (Chicago: Thomas J. Cooper & Co., 1901), 2–6.

97. *Chicago Daily Press & Tribune*, November 24, 1860; "dignity" quote from the *New York Herald*, November 24, 1860.

98. *Chicago Daily Press & Tribune*, November 24, 1860.

99. *New York Herald*, November 24, 1860.

100. "Won a Sobriquet by Shaving Mr. Lincoln: Philadelphia Hair Cutter Attended the Great Statesman, and Is Known as 'Lincoln's Little Barber,'" undated clipping, ca. 1900, *Chicago Tribune*, Lincoln Museum, Fort Wayne, Indiana.

101. *Chicago Daily Press & Tribune*, November 24, 1860.

102. *New York Herald*, November 24, 1860.

103. *Chicago Journal*, November 23, 1860, quoted in Wayne C. Temple, *"The Taste Is in My Mouth a Little . . .": Lincoln's Victuals and Potables* (Springfield, Ill.: Mayhaven Publishers, 2004), 128.

104. *Chicago Daily Press & Tribune*, November 7, 1860; description comes from a report on the suit when it went on display in Lincoln's hometown on February 7, 1861—see *Illinois Daily State Journal*, February 8, 1861. I am grateful to Wayne C. Temple for identifying this newspaper article.

105. *New York Herald*, November 24, 1860. The newspaper further claimed, also erroneously, that Henry was David Davis' nephew, not his cousin.

106. John G. Nicolay to Therena Bates, November 16, 1860, NPLC.

107. Gideon Welles, *Diary of Gideon Welles, Secretary of the Navy Under Lincoln and Johnson*, 3 vols. (Boston: Houghton Mifflin, 1911), 2:388–89.

108. Ibid., 2:389. Other evidence points to the fact that Lincoln later sent the Seward appointment letter to Hamlin in Washington.

109. Letter to Martin Van Buren, quoted in Larry Gara, *The Presidency of Franklin Pierce* (Lawrence: University Press of Kansas, 1991), 46.

110. *New York Herald*, November 23, 1860.

111. Ibid.

112. *New York World*, November 24, 1860. For the anecdote—told as he approached the fallen Confederate capital of Richmond in 1865—see David D. Porter, *Incidents and Anecdotes of the Civil War* (D. Appleton & Co., 1885), 294–95.

113. Donn Piatt, *Memories of the Men Who Saved the Union* (New York and Chicago: Butler Brothers, 1887), 33.

114. Ibid., 30; Rice, *Reminiscences of Lincoln*, 483–84.

115. Piatt, *Memories of the Men Who Saved the Union*, 156.

116. *New York Herald*, November 24, 1860.

117. Charles Eugene Hamlin, quoted in William E. Baringer, *A House Dividing: Lincoln as President Elect* (Springfield, Ill.: Abraham Lincoln Association, 1945), 84. There is little evidence to suggest that Lincoln made good on his promise. In Lincoln's day, vice presidents did not attend all-important cabinet meetings, and Hamlin would be no exception. As Hamlin later put it, delicately: "I did not obtrude upon or interfere with the Presidential duties," admitting he enjoyed "no power to wield, and no influence to exert." See Michael Burlingame, ed., *An Oral History of Abraham Lincoln: John G. Nicolay's Interviews and Essays* (Carbondale: Southern Illinois University Press, 1996), 68.

118. *New York Herald*, November 29, 1860. Hamlin soon decided to go home to Maine for the holidays, limiting his usefulness and perhaps dooming his future as an important Lincoln advisor.

119. *New York Herald*, November 20, 1860.

120. *New York Herald*, November 26, November 29, 1860.

121. Rice, *Reminiscences of Lincoln*, 485.

122. Lincoln to Davis, May 26, 1860, Roy P. Basler, ed., *The Collected Works of Abraham Lincoln, Supplement, 1832–1865* (Westport, Conn.: Greenwood Press, 1974), 54.

123. See, for example, William C. Harris's excellent *Lincoln's Rise to the Presidency* (Lawrence: University Press of Kansas, 2007), 257.

124. An excellent description of this process can be found in Phillip Shaw Paludan, *The Presidency of Abraham Lincoln* (Lawrence: University Press of Kansas, 1994), 35–36.

125. Charles E. Hamlin and Thurlow Weed, quoted in Baringer, *A House Dividing*, 88.

126. One writer, a Kinsey-trained sex therapist, caused a sensation in 2005 when he offered the Lincoln-Speed cohabitation as "evidence" the two were lovers, but aside from other arguments, it is difficult to believe Lincoln, without embarrassment, would have jumped into Speed's bed in Chicago to chat while their wives chatted in the next room. See C. A. Tripp, *The Intimate World of Abraham Lincoln* (New York: Free Press, 2005), esp. 126–27.

127. William H. Herndon, notes from an interview with Joshua Fry Speed, ca. 1865–66, in Wilson and Davis, eds., *Herndon's Informants*, 475.

128. Ibid.

129. *New York Herald*, November 26, 1860; Wayne C. Temple, *Abraham Lincoln: From Skeptic to Prophet* (Springfield, Ill.: Mayhaven Publishing, 1995), 86.

130. *Chicago Journal*, November 26, 1860, quoted in *Lincoln Day by Day*, 2:299.

131. Theodore J. Karamanski, *Rally Round the Flag: Chicago and the Civil War*, orig. pub. 1983 (Lanham, Md.: Rowman & Littlefield, 2006), 57–58; Richard K. Curtis, *They Call Him Mister Moody* (Grand Rapids, Mich.: William Eeerdmans, 1962), 83; James L. Findlay, *Dwight L. Moody, American Evangelist, 1837–1899* (Chicago: University of Chicago Press, 1969), 76–80.

132. See Lincoln to Henry C. Whitney, November 26, 1860, *CW*, 4:145. Wrote Lincoln: "Your note in behalf of Mr. Alshuler [sic] was received. I gave him a sitting."

133. Horace White recollections in Wilson and Davis, eds., *Herndon's Informants*, 698.

134. Samuel G. Alschuler to Lincoln, November 28, 1860, ALPLC. I am grateful to Alschuler's descendant Jean Soman of Florida for taking the time to discuss her ancestor with me in 2007.

135. Hamilton and Ostendorf, *Lincoln in Photographs*, 67. Under different circumstances, Lincoln might instead have visited the gallery of Chicago's premier photographer, Alexander Hesler, who had made superb campaign likenesses of the candidate back in June. But according to local newspapers, Hesler was deeply involved at the time in organizing the first Chicago Art-Union Distribution, and exhibition and sale by lottery of artwork by local painters and sculptors. See *Chicago Daily Times*, December 29, 1860.

136. *Chicago Daily Press & Tribune*, November 17, 1860.

137. Bryan to Lincoln, November 22, 1860, ALPLC; Lincoln's undated endorsement in *CW*, 4:144.

138. *New York Herald*, November 26, 1860.

139. *New-York Daily Tribune*, November 27, 1860.

140. Robert T. Lincoln to Mary Lincoln, December 2, 1860, Collection of Phillips Exeter Academy Library. The author is indebted to historian Jason Emerson for pointing him to the original letter, and to Phillips's assistant librarian and academy archivist Edouard Desrochers for supplying a copy.

141. Villard, *Lincoln on the Eve of '61*, 21. The local *Illinois Daily State Journal* thought, on the other hand, that Lincoln returned "in excellent health, and quite refreshed by the visit to Chicago," November 27, 1860.

142. *New York Times*, November 22, 1860; Mississippi report in the *New York Herald*, November 28, 1860.

143. *New York Times*, November 10, 1860.

144. Lincoln to Henry J. Raymond, November 28, 1860, *CW*, 4:146.

145. *Chicago Daily Press & Tribune*, November 17, 1860.

146. Villard, *Lincoln on the Eve of '61*, 30.

147. Letter from Benjamin Welch, Jr., to Lincoln (with clipping), ca. Nov 8, 1860, ALPLC.

4. A Masterly Inactivity

1. One local newspaper reported an equal frenzy over the imminent publication in *Harper's Weekly* of Charles Dickens's latest novel, *[Great] Expectations*. See *Illinois Daily State Journal*, November 28, 1860.

2. *Thanksgiving Day. Proclamation. By His Excellency, John Wood, Governor of the State of Illinois*. Broadside, November 12, 1860. The copy in ALPLM is signed at the bottom, "written by John Hay," in his own handwriting. As president, Lincoln would institutionalize the annual Thanksgiving holiday we celebrate today.

3. *Illinois Daily State Journal*, November 27, 1860.

4. *New-York Daily Tribune*, December 1, 1860. The sermon that day was preached by minister John Howe Brown, who led the church from 1856 until 1864, when he resigned to become a druggist. Lincoln scholar Wayne C. Temple constructed his biography for his *Abraham Lincoln: From Skeptic to Prophet* (Springfield, Ill.: Mayhaven Publishing, 1995), 86, 78n.112.

5. Harold G. Villard and Oswald Garrison Villard, eds., *Lincoln on the Eve of '61: A Journalist's Story by Henry Villard* (New York: Alfred A. Knopf, 1941), 27–28.

6. Ibid., 28.

7. *Washington Constitution*, November 22, 1860.

8. Newton Bateman, *Abraham Lincoln: An Address*, orig. pub. 1899, 2nd ed. (Gardena, Calif.: H. E. Barker Spanish-American Institute, 1932), 15.

9. John G. Nicolay to Therena Bates, November 25, 1860, NPLC.

10. John Hay to Mrs. A. E. Edwards, November 29, 1860, in Michael Burlingame, ed., *At Lincoln's Side: John Hay's Civil War Correspondence and Selected Writings* (Carbondale: Southern Illinois University Press), 3.

11. John G. Nicolay to Therena Bates, November 26, 1860, NPLC.

12. See, for example, John Hickman to Lincoln, November 8, 1860, introducing Thomas Webster of Philadelphia as a hardworking Republican party loyalist "worthy of confidence and esteem," original in ALPLC.

13. *Washington Constitution*, November 22, 1860.

14. *New York Herald*, December 4, 1860.

15. Lincoln played a version of the game known as "fives," and according to a contemporary, " 'Old Abe' was always the champion, for his long arms served a good purpose in reaching and returning the ball from any angle." See Preston H. Bailhache, "Abraham Lincoln As I Remember Him," copy of typescript in the Lincoln Museum, Fort Wayne, Indiana. Urbana acquaintance Henry M. Russell similarly attested that Lincoln "liked out-of-door sports, especially ball-playing, up to the time he was elected president." Walter B. Stevens, *A Reporter's Lincoln*, ed. Michael Burlingame (Lincoln: University of Nebraska Press, 1998), 25.

16. *Illinois Daily State Journal*, November 27, 1860.

17. Statement by Henry Clay Whitney for William H. Herndon, 1887 [?], in Douglas L. Wilson and Rodney O. Davis, eds., *Herndon's Informants: Letters, Interviews, and Statements About Abraham Lincoln* (Urbana: University of Illinois Press, 1998), 648. In transcribing his interview with Whitney, Herndon spelled out the full word. Much has been written recently about Lincoln's allegedly promiscuous use—at least by today's standards—of the "N" word. See, for example, Lerone Bennett, *Forced into Glory: Abraham Lincoln's White Dream* (Chicago: Johnson Publishing, 2000), 96 ("The words n——r, darky, and colored boy came early to his lips. . . . Harold Holzer, who edited a collection of the Lincoln-Douglas debates, was surprised that Lincoln used the N-word twice in the first"). In fact, however repellent, the word was in use at the time even among anti-slavery abolitionists. The definitive historical study of the odious word, and its various meanings and implications, has yet to be written, though a compelling start, not at all sympathetic to Lincoln, was made by Jabari Asim, *The N Word: Who Can Say It, Who Shouldn't, and Why* (Boston: Houghton Mifflin, 2007), esp. 86–88. For a good summary of Lincoln's use of the "n" word, see Gerald J. Prokopowicz, *Did Lincoln Own Slaves? And Other Frequently Asked Questions About Abraham Lincoln* (New York: Pantheon, 2008), 170–71.

18. Villard, *Lincoln on the Eve of '61*, 29.

19. Ibid., 40.

20. Bateman, *Abraham Lincoln*, 15.

21. Among the nineteen churches listed in the Springfield city directory for 1860, two were identified as "African." See C. S. Williams, *Williams' Springfield Directory: City Guide and Business Mirror for 1860–61* (Springfield, Ill.,: Johnson, Bradford, 1860), 20–21.

22. *New York Herald*, December 1, 1860.

23. *New York Herald*, December 9, 1860.

24. *New York Herald*, December 4, 1860. Henry Villard speculated that Fogg and Lincoln discussed a possible "manifesto" by the RNC, presumably on the secession crisis.

25. *A Memorial of George Gilman Fogg . . . at the Funeral Services, October 8, 1881* (Concord, N.H.: Republican Press Association, 1882), 3, 18. Fogg became U.S. minister to Switzerland.

26. Thomas J. MacCormack, ed., *Memoirs of Gustave Koerner, 1809–1896: Life Sketches Written at the Suggestion of His Children*, 2 vols. (Cedar Rapids, Iowa: Torch Press, 1909), 2:114–15.

27. *New York Herald*, December 4, 1860.

28. Amos Tuck to Joshua Giddings, November 26, 1860, Giddings Papers, Ohio Historical Society.

29. *New York Herald*, December 9, 1860.

30. Villard, *Lincoln on the Eve of '61*, 32.

31. *New York Herald*, December 6, 1860; Villard, *Lincoln on the Eve of '61*, 30–31.

32. *Illinois Daily State Journal*, November 26, 1860.

33. Diary of Charles Francis Adams, November 25, 1860, Adams Papers, Massachusetts Historical Society.

34. The first and best book on the subject is Harry J. Carman and Reinhard H. Luthin, *Lincoln and the Patronage* (New York: Columbia University Press, 1943). The authors' account of the "clever" and "clumsy . . . requests and demands, moderate and extravagant," the "appeals to pity and charity," the demands for "reward for party services . . . some re-enforced with bribes" (4–5) remains unparalleled, though a new study has long been needed.

35. Ward H. Lamon, *The Life of Abraham Lincoln: His Birth to His Inauguration as President* (Boston: James R. Osgood, 1872), 457.

36. Clipping entitled "True Story of a Great Life," by J.H.C. & M.M.M., 366, Box 8, NPLC.

37. See, for example, Thomas L. Friedman, "Clinton Selects Diverse Team of Advisers," *New York Times*, November 13, 1992; Ben White, "Bush Administration Picks Transition Chiefs," *Washington Post*, December 21, 2000.

38. See, for example, George W. Franklin to Hatch, November 10, 1860, Hatch Papers, ALPLM.

39. The Lyman Trumbull Papers at the Library of Congress are filled with such application. See, for example, letters from William Jerome (seeking the postmastership of Carbondale), December 26, 1860 (Jerome argued that "no man in Jackson County exercised a greater influence in procuring Mr. Lincoln's election than myself"); and George J. Allen of Alton, December 27, 1860, seeking a postmaster's job in Kansas for his nephew.

40. Lincoln to Seward, December 8, 1860, *CW*, 4:149.

41. William O. Stoddard, Jr., ed., *Lincoln's Third Secretary: The Memoirs of William O. Stoddard* (New York: Exposition Press, 1955), 93.

42. Stoddard to William H. Herndon, December 17, 1860, Herndon Papers, Library of Congress.

43. Stoddard to Herndon, December 27, 1860, Herndon Papers, Library of Congress.

44. Stoddard to Trumbull, December 27, 1860, Trumbull Papers, Library of Congress.

45. The federal government authorized Lincoln to employ only two staff secretaries, so Stoddard was hired as a clerk for the Interior Department, and loaned permanently to the White House.

46. For the May 4, 1859, editorial endorsement in the *Central Illinois Gazette* (at least one 1858 editorial had suggested Lincoln for president), see Har-

old Holzer, ed., *Lincoln's White House Secretary: The Adventurous Life of William O. Stoddard* (Carbondale: Southern Illinois University Press, 2007), 208–10.

47. Henry Fawcett to Lincoln, November 7, 1860, ALPLC.

48. Charles Balance to Lincoln, November 13, 1860, ALPLC.

49. A. R. Hyde to "a friend," Abner H. Hyde Collection, Folder 1, Indiana Historical Society.

50. Henry F. Johns to Lincoln, December 1860, ALPLC.

51. John J. Hendee to Lincoln, December 3, 1860, ALPLC.

52. "Artemus Ward on His Visit to Abe Lincoln," *Vanity Fair*, December 8, 1860. On Christmas Day, Ward was reported en route to Springfield "on the express invitation of Mr. Lincoln to assist in the construction of his cabinet." According to the *Daily Illinois State Register* (December 25, 1860), he advised the president-elect to fill up the cabinet "with showmen, as showmen ain't got nary darned principle."

53. "Unterified" to Lincoln, November 30, 1860, ALPLC.

54. Villard, *Lincoln on the Eve of '61*, 23.

55. Philip S. Foner and Yuvall Taylor, eds., *Frederick Douglass: Selected Speeches and Writings* (Chicago: Lawrence Hill, 1999), 419 (speech at Tremont Temple, December 3, 1860), 414–15 (*Douglass' Monthly*, December 1860).

56. McCormack, ed., *Memoirs of Gustave Koerner*, 2:105.

57. *New-York Daily Tribune*, December 9, 1860.

58. *New York Times*, December 3, 1860, December 1, 1860.

59. *New York World*, December 4, 1860.

60. All the quotes, including *"whatever it might be,"* are from Lincoln's "House Divided Address," delivered at the Springfield State House on June 16, 1858; see *CW*, 2:461, 465–67. In fact Buchanan's inaugural plea was, at best, disingenuous: he already knew the Supreme Court decision and hoped it would insulate his new administration from the slavery issue.

61. An excellent account of Buchanan's stubborn support for the Lecompton Constitution can be found in James A. Rawley, *Race and Politics: "Bleeding Kansas" and the Coming of the Civil War*, orig. pub. 1969 (Lincoln: University of Nebraska Press, 1979), esp. 236–37.

62. This and the above quotes, from James Buchanan, *Mr. Buchanan's Administration on the Eve of the Rebellion* (New York: D. Appleton & Co., 1866), 108–9.

63. Jefferson Davis, *The Rise and Fall of the Confederate Government*, 2 vols., orig. pub. 1881 (New York: Da Capo, 1990), 1:51 Notwithstanding the Mississippi senator's displeasure, the *New York Times* (December 5, 1860) saw "the crafty hand of Jeff. Davis" in the president's message.

64. Buchanan, *Mr. Buchanan's Administration*, 106–7.

65. Ibid., 119–20.

66. Ibid., 113–14.

67. Ibid., 127.

68. Winfield Scott to James Buchanan, December 15, 1860, copy in ALPLC.

69. *New York Times*, December 5, 1860.

70. *Boston Post*, November 22, 1860. The Supreme Court moved into the chamber left vacant when the Senate relocated.

71. *Congressional Globe*, 1860, 9.

72. Quoted in Frederick Seward, ed., *William H. Seward: An Autobiography . . .* (New York: Derby & Miller, 1891), 480. Historian James M. McPherson has astutely pointed out that Republicans were no better able to come up with a plan of their own to prevent disunion. See McPherson, *Battle Cry of Freedom: The Civil War Era* (New York: Oxford University Press, 1988), 241.

73. Diary of Charles Francis Adams, December 4, 1860, Adams Papers, Massachusetts Historical Society.

74. Historian Jean Baker has made a compelling counterargument that Buchanan deserves credit for resisting further acquiescence—insisting the president showed strength by making clear that "no government installed an entitlement to its own suicide." See Jean H. Baker, *James Buchanan* (New York: Times Books, 2004), 124.

75. Buchanan, *Mr. Buchanan's Administration*, 110, 133.

76. *Boston Daily Advertiser*, December 7, 1860.

77. *New York Times*, December 5, 1860.

78. *The* [New York] *Independent*, December 20, 1860.

79. *New York Herald*, December 10, 1860, Buchanan Annual Message.

80. *Illinois Daily State Journal*, December 5, 1860.

81. William Hunt to Lincoln, December 13, 1860, ALPLC.

82. Buchanan's full message and this reaction were both published in the *New York Times*, December 5, 1860.

83. *New York Herald*, December 11, 1860.

84. George N. Eckert to Lincoln, November 23, 1860, ALPLC.

85. Elihu D. Washburne to Lincoln, November 29, 1860, ALPLC.

86. *New York Herald*, December 9, 1860.

87. Ibid.

88. *New York Herald*, December 10, 1860.

89. Herbert Wells Fay, then curator of the Lincoln Tomb in Springfield, offered a pioneering account, "Lincoln Presidential Electors," published in *Week by Week*, April 22, 1933, copy in the Lincoln Museum, Fort Wayne, Indiana.

90. In Boston, John Greenleaf Whittier was one of the thirteen Massachusetts electors to vote for Lincoln at 11 A.M. George Morey, who chaired the meeting, used the occasion to assure the audience of Lincoln's continued silence on doctrinal issues. "His mouth will be shut with regard to the par-

ticular manner he may purpose to discharge the duties of his high office until he shall have taken the required oath," Morey declared, ". . . and he be able to speak as one having authority, and under official responsibility: and then the American people may expect to hear from him words of wisdom, moderation, firmness and prudence." Undated clipping in the Lincoln Museum, Fort Wayne, Indiana. See also John G. Nicolay to Therena Bates, December 5, 1860, NPLC.

91. *New York Herald*, December 10, 1860. A onetime colleague of Lincoln's at the bar, Swett once observed of him: "Any man who took Lincoln for a simple-minded man would very soon wake up with his back in a ditch." See William H. Herndon, *Herndon's Lincoln*, 3 vols. (Springfield, Ill.: Herndon's Lincoln Publishing Co., n.d.), 2:334.

92. Affidavits recording the Illinois electoral voting, December 5, 1860, National Archives and Records Administration, Sen. 36-A-K1/Electoral Votes. I am grateful to Budge and Russ Weidman for arranging my access to these remarkable documents.

93. John G. Nicolay to Therena Bates, December 5, 1860, NPLC.

94. *New York Herald*, December 9, 1860.

95. *New York Herald*, December 10, 1860; James C. Conkling to Clinton Conkling, December 20, 1860, in Harry E. Pratt, *Concerning Mr. Lincoln* . . . (Springfield, Ill.: Abraham Lincoln Association, 1944), 33.

96. For location of the shop, see *Williams' Springfield Directory City Guide and Business Mirror, for 1860–61* (Springfield Ill: Johnson & Bradford, 1860), 144. For Lincoln's purchase, see Harry E. Pratt, *The Personal Finances of Abraham Lincoln* (Springfield, Ill.: Abraham Lincoln Association, 1943), 163, 170–71.

97. *Illinois Daily State Journal*, December 6, 1860.

98. *Frank Leslie's Illustrated Newspaper*, December 15, 1860. The photograph on which the woodcut was modeled showed Mary with their younger sons, Willie and Tad. *Leslie's* identified the boys as "Robert and Thomas [Tad]"; Robert was not only much older, he was away at school. For the original Preston Butler photograph on which the woodcut was modeled, see Lloyd Ostendorf, *The Photographs of Mary Todd Lincoln* (Springfield; Illinois State Historical Society, 1969), 10–11.

99. *Chicago Daily Press & Tribune*, November 27, 1860.

100. *Scientific American* 13 (December 1, 1860). The same journal had published the patent on June 2, 1849.

101. Gaius Paddock, "Is the Sangamon River Navigable?," *Journal of the Illinois Historical Society* 13 (April 1920): 48–50, quoted in Jason Emerson, "Abraham Lincoln's Mechanical Mind, and the Completer Story of His Invention and Patent," 2007 ms.

102. Lincoln paid thirty dollars to secure his patent on March 10, 1849. See

Louis A. Warren, "Congressman Lincoln's Patent," *Lincoln Lore* 843 (June 4, 1945). Noting that "it has fallen to his lot to be in command of a ship of uncommon burden on a voyage of uncommon danger," *Harper's Weekly* (April 6, 1861) later suggested: "We trust that the President will set the fashion of using his own patent. He must throw some of his cargo overboard, and buoy up his craft on all sides." The best account of his invention is Wayne C. Temple, *Lincoln's Connections with the Illinois Michigan Canal, His Return from Congress in '48 and His Invention* (Springfield, Ill.: Illinois Bell, 1986).

103. "The President Elect's Mode of Buoying Vessels. Patented May 22, 1849," *Scientific American* 3 (December 1, 1860): 356.

104. The calculation of prevailing Democratic sympathy among Springfield's ministers was made by Lincoln scholar nonpareil Wayne C. Temple, in correspondence with the author, July 16, 2007, accompanied by a list. There is no surviving indication that these preachers made their views known from the pulpit. Lincoln put the number at twenty-three in October 1860, noting "all of them are against me but three." Newton Bateman quoted in Francis B. Carpenter, *Six Months at the White House: The Story of a Picture* (New York: Hurd & Houghton, 1866), 193.

105. Stephen A. Douglas to William H. Prentice, December 5, 1860, in Robert W. Johannsen, ed., *The Letters of Stephen A. Douglas* (Urbana: University of Illinois Press, 1961), 503.

106. Carpenter, *Six Months at the White House*, 194. Historian Don E. Fehrenbacher later dismissed Bateman's recollections as but a "well-known contribution to the apotheosis of Lincoln" to be "regarded as dubious biographical material." See Don E. Fehrenbacher and Virginia Fehrenbacher, *Recollected Words of Lincoln* (Stanford: Stanford University Press, 1954), 26.

107. *The Assertions of a Secessionist. From the Speech of A. H. Stephens, of Georgia, November 14th, 1860* (New York: Loyal Publication Society, 1864), 2.

108. Lincoln to Stephens, November 30, 1860, CW, 4:146. The *New York Herald* (December 4, 1860) reported Lincoln engaged in "protracted conversation" about the Stephens oration.

109. *Illinois Daily State Journal*, December 15, 1860. Four years later, Republicans recirculated excerpts of the address to remind voters that not all Southerners had considered secession logical. See, for example, *Southern Testimony*, a broadsheet published by the *Waltham* [Mass.] *Free Press*, and available for fifty cents per hundred. Original copy in ALPLM.

110. John D. Defrees to Lincoln, November 25, 1860, ALPLC.

111. *Speech of Hon. Robert Toombs, on the Crisis, Delivered Before the Georgia State Legislature, December 7, 1860* (Washington, D.C.: Lemuel Towers, 1860), 13.

112. Lincoln to E. B. Pease, December 7, 1860, CW, 4:147.

113. John G. Nicolay to Therena Bates, December 9, 1860, NPLC.

114. John G. Nicolay to Therena Bates, December 2, 1860, NPLC.

115. Hannibal Hamlin to Lincoln, December 4, 1860, ALPLC.

116. Lincoln to Hannibal Hamlin, December 8, 1860, CW, 4:147; Lincoln to William H. Seward, December 8, 1860, CW, 4:148.

117. Ibid.

118. Elihu B. Washburne to Lincoln, December 11, 1860, ALPLC.

119. William H. Seward to Lincoln, December 13, 1860, ALPLC.

120. *Illinois Daily State Journal*, December 14, 1860.

121. William P. Prince to Lincoln, December 7, 1860, ALPLC.

122. William Cullen Bryant to Lincoln, November 9, 1860, ALPLC.

123. Lyman Trumbull to Lincoln, December 8, 1860, ALPLC.

124. Lincoln to Hamlin, December 8, 1860, CW, 4:147; Hannibal Hamlin to Lincoln, December 14, 1860, ALPLC.

125. Nathan Sargent to Lincoln, November 12, 1860, ALPLC. Ultimately it was Sargent, not Ewing, who got a federal job. In 1861, Lincoln named him commissioner of customs.

126. Charles Billinghurst to Lincoln, November 14, 1860, ALPLC.

127. Francis W. Kellogg to Lincoln, November 16, 1860, ALPLC.

128. Charles F. Fletcher to Lincoln, December 10, 1860, ALPLC.

129. John N. Purviance to Lincoln, November 22, 1860, ALPLC.

130. Anonymous letter to Lincoln, December 12, 1860, ALPLC.

131. Fennelon Hasbrouck to Lincoln, November 9, 1860, ALPLC.

132. George W. Waite to Lincoln, December 1, 1860, ALPLC.

133. John Edgar Thomson to Lincoln, November 16, 1860, ALPLC.

134. John D. Defrees to Lincoln, December 15, 1860, ALPLC.

135. Alexander H. Stephens, *Constitutional View of the Late War Between the States; Its Causes, Character, Conduct, and Results . . .*, 2 vols. (Boston and Atlanta: Ziegler, McCurdy & Co., 1870), 265.

136. "All Kentucky" to Lincoln, December 2, 1860, ALPLC. Ohio's Thomas Hutchison similarly insisted, "You will need some southern men as advisers, and the cooperation and influence of still more." See Hutchison to Lincoln, December 12, 1860, ALPLC.

137. John D. Defrees to Lincoln, December 15, 1860, ALPLC. The letter added that several Republican colleagues, including Ewing of Ohio and Covode of Pennsylvania, endorsed the idea of offering an appointment to Stephens.

138. Hannibal Hamlin to Lincoln, December 4, 1860, ALPLC.

139. John Nicolay to Therena Bates, December 9, 1860, NPLC. The phrase "Disunion Rampant!" had been seen in town a month earlier, in the Springfield *Illinois Daily State Journal*, November 13, 1860.

140. *Illinois State Daily Journal*, December 12, 1860; reprinted in CW, 4:150.

141. *New York Herald*, December 18, 1860. The paper emphasized that only

"two or three Southern gentlemen" were "alluded to"—keeping the door open for the inclusion of Upper South moderates.

142. The *Cincinnati Commercial*, for one, quickly speculated that Lincoln wrote the editorial, and the *Illinois Daily State Journal* rather proudly republished the comment on December 15. Springfielders were thus aware of the president-elect's authoritative hand almost immediately. A copy in Lincoln's handwriting exists in the ALPLC, settling the question.

143. Lincoln to William H. Seward, December 29, 1860, CW, 4:164; Gilmer's response reprinted CW, 4:153.

144. R. P. King to Lincoln, November 24, 1860, ALPLC.

145. James H. Campbell and others to Lincoln, December 12, 1860, ALPLC. A similar Cameron endorsement came from New Jersey's G. L. Vliet ("his [Cameron's] well known views on finance and business, indicated in a life of varied experience, inspires confidence"). See Vliet to Lincoln, November 29, 1860, ALPLC.

146. "one who desires your Good" to Lincoln, n.d., ca. January 1861, ALPLC.

147. G. Rush Smith to Lincoln, November 15, 1860, ALPLC.

148. John D. Defrees to Lincoln, November 25, 1860, ALPLC.

5. The Tug Has to Come

1. *New York Herald*, December 15, 1860; *Illinois Daily State Journal*, December 1, 1860.

2. *Daily Illinois State Register*, December 15, 1860.

3. Joseph Medill to Lincoln, December 18, 1860, ALPLC. Medill did recommend a number of potential cabinet ministers from the Upper South states of Missouri, Kentucky, Tennessee, Virginia, and Maryland, adding, "and that is enough."

4. *Lincoln Day by Day*, 2:300; Harry E. Pratt, *The Personal Finances of Abraham Lincoln* (Springfield, Ill.: Abraham Lincoln Association, 1943), 112.

5. Howard K. Beale, ed., *The Diary of Edward Bates, 1859–1866*, Volume IV of the Annual Report of the American Historical Association for 1930 (Washington, D.C.: U.S. Government Printing Office, 1933), 164.

6. Blair apparently facilitated the Bates meeting as well. On December 13, he wrote Lincoln to alert him of Bates's arrival in Springfield. Original in ALPLC.

7. John D. Defrees to Lincoln, December 15, 1860, ALPLC; Lincoln to Defrees, December 18, 1860, CW, 4:155.

8. The Springfield directory listed the Chenery House as Nicolay's official residence. See C. S. Williams, *Williams' Directory: City Guide and Business Mirror for 1860–61* (Springfield, Ill.: Johnson, Bradford, 1860), 115.

9. John G. Nicolay memorandum, December 15, 1860, NPLC.

10. *Philadelphia Evening Bulletin*, December 14, 1860, reprinted in the *New York Times*, December 20, 1860.

11. Ibid.

12. Bates, *Diary*, 164–65.

13. David Davis to Thurlow Weed, December 10, 1860, in Thurlow Weed Barnes, *Life of Thurlow Weed Including His Autobiography and a Memoir*, 2 vols. (Boston: Houghton Mifflin, 1884), 2:302.

14. Edward Bates to Lincoln, December 18, 1860, ALPLC.

15. Lincoln to Edward Bates, December 18, 1860, CW, 4:154.

16. Republished in the *Illinois Daily State Journal*, December 22, 1860.

17. Some newspapers speculated that Bates would be named to another spot— perhaps secretary of the interior. See *Boston Post*, December 17, 1860.

18. *Daily Illinois State Register*, December 22, 1860.

19. "G. A." to Lincoln, December 11, 1860; *New York Herald*, November 24, 1860.

20. Horace White to Lincoln, December 11, 1860, ALPLC.

21. Anonymous to Lincoln, December 13, 1860; "Alabam" to Lincoln, December 22, 1860, ALPLC.

22. David Hunter to Lincoln, December 18, 1860, ALPLC.

23. Lincoln to Hunter, December 22, 1860, CW, 4:159. A letter confiding "similar apprehensions" arrived nine days latter from P. W. Curtenius of Kalamazoo, who offered to lead a "well equipped—well organized and well officered" citizen army to Washington to guard Lincoln's "personal safety either at your inauguration or immediately following it" (Curtenius to Lincoln, December 31, 1860, ALPLC).

24. "Yours in 'Israel' " to Lincoln, December 10, 1860, ALPLC.

25. J. B. McClure, ed., *Anecdotes of Abraham Lincoln* (Chicago: Rhodes & McClure, 1879), 80.

26. The Melvin story was unearthed and expertly told in Wayne C. Temple, *Abraham Lincoln: From Skeptic to Prophet* (Springfield, Ill: Mayhaven Publishing, 1995), 97–99. Four months later, Dr. Melvin sent President Lincoln five boxes of the laxatives.

27. *New York Herald*, December 20, 1860.

28. Harold G. Villard Oswald Garrison Villard, eds., *Lincoln on the Eve of '61: A Journalist's Story by Henry Villard* (New York: Alfred A. Knopf, 1941), 41.

29. Henry J. Raymond to Lincoln, December 18, 1860, CW, 4:156.

30. Lincoln to Raymond, December 18, 1860, CW, 4:156.

31. At the time, some reporters were busily rebutting a spurious 1858 Lincoln speech in which he had purportedly called for equal rights. The *Albany Atlas & Argus* called it "a forgery, out and out." See *New York Times*, December 28, 1860.

32. Lyman Trumbull to Lincoln, December 4, 1860, ALPLC.

33. A fine brief analysis of their work can be found in Sean Wilentz, *The Rise of American Democracy: Jefferson to Lincoln* (New York: W. W. Norton, 2005), 780; see Lincoln to John J. Chittenden, November 4, 1858, CW, 3:335.

34. Worthington G. Snethen to Lincoln, December 8, 1860, ALPLC.

35. *New York Herald*, December 17, 1860.

36. An expert account of this crisis can be found in Kenneth Stampp, *The Imperiled Union: Essays on the Background of the Civil War* (New York: Oxford University Press, 1980), esp. 180.

37. Ibid., 167.

38. Lincoln to Lyman Trumbull, December 10, 1860, CW, 4:149–50.

39. William Kellogg to Lincoln, December 6, 1860, ALPLC.

40. Lincoln to Kellogg, December 11, 1860, CW, 4:150. Unbeknownst to Lincoln, who did not meet him until after writing these letters, Edward Bates had expressed the same view (privately, to his diary) a few weeks earlier on November 22: "If we must have civil war, perhaps it is better now than at a furture date." It is reasonable to assume the two men discussed the potential for war when they conferred in Springfield. See Bates, *Diary*, 158.

41. Elihu Washburne to Lincoln, December 9, 1860, ALPLC.

42. Lincoln to Washburne, December 13, 1860, CW, 4:151.

43. Washburne to Lincoln, December 18, 1860, ALPLC.

44. Lincoln to Trumbull, December 17, 1860; to John D. Defrees, December 18, 1860, CW, 4:153, 155.

45. Lincoln to Thurlow Weed, December 17, 1860, CW, 4:154.

46. *Philadelphia Bulletin*, reprinted in the *New York Times*, December 20, 1860.

47. Ibid.

48. John A. Gilmer to Lincoln, December 29, 1860, ALPLC.

49. Lincoln to Peter H. Silvester, December 22, 1860, CW, 4:160.

50. *New York Times*, December 22, 1860.

51. William Kauffman Scarborough, *The Diary of Edmund Ruffin, Volume 1: Toward Independence . . .* (Baton Rouge: Louisiana State University Press, 1972), 512–13. Ruffin also noted the rainy weather in Charleston, despite which celebratory fireworks lit the skies.

52. Joseph H. Gillespie quoted in Rufus Rockwell Wilson, ed., *Intimate Memories of Lincoln* (Elmira, N.Y.: Primavera Press, 1945), 334.

53. Original, undated copy, now rag-backed, in ALPLC. For another illustration of the ordinance, see Bell Irvin Wiley and Hirst D. Milhollen, *Embattled Confederates: An Illustrated History of Southerners at War* (New York: Harper & Row, 1954), 11.

54. *New York Herald*, December 27, 1860.

55. An excellent discussion can be found in William C. Davis, *Look Away! A*

History of the Confederate States of America (New York: Free Press, 2002), esp. 23–30.

56. David M. Potter (and Don E. Fehrenbacher), *The Impending Crisis: 1848–1861* (New York: Harper & Row, 1976), 491–96. Based on a study by Michael P. Johnson—"A New Look at the Popular Vote for Delegates to the Georgia Secession Convention," *Georgia Historical Quarterly* 56 (1972): 259–75—Potter and Fehrenbacher estimated that popular support for secession amounted to only 50 to 51 percent.

57. A. Toomer Porter, *Led On! Step by Step*, orig. pub. 1898, quoted in Davis, *Look Away!*, 31.

58. Lincoln to David Hunter, December 21, 1860, CW, 4:159.

59. Lincoln to Elihu Washburne, December 21, 1860, CW, 4:159.

60. Lincoln to Peter H. Silvester, December 22, 1860; to Lyman Trumbull, December 24, 1860, CW, 4:160, 162.

61. Memorandum by John G. Nicolay, December 22, 1860, NPLC.

62. Ibid.

63. John G. Nicolay to Therena Bates, December 30, 1860, NPLC.

64. Article V, which grants two U.S. senators to each state, is similarly protected from modification. For details of the amendments see *Congressional Globe, 36th Congress, 2nd Session*, 114.

65. *Chicago Daily Times*, December 29, 1860.

66. CW, 4:156–57. Within days, Seward reported to Lincoln, the proposals were submitted, discussed, proposed, debated, amended—and rejected. See William H. Seward to Lincoln, December 26, 1860, ALPLC.

67. Davis to Thurlow Weed, December 10, 1860, in Barnes, *Life of Thurlow Weed*, 2:301; William H. Seward to Lincoln, December 16, 1860, ALPLC.

68. Leonard Swett to Thurlow Weed, December 10, 1860, in Barnes, *Life of Thurlow Weed*, 2:301.

69. *New York Herald*, December 25, 1860. The two aides were Judge Slosson and J. H. Vanalin (*New York Times*, December 20, 1860).

70. Undated clipping in the Thurlow Weed Papers, quoted in Doris Kearns Goodwin, *Team of Rivals: The Political Genius of Abraham Lincoln* (New York: Simon & Schuster, 2005), 287.

71. *Boston Daily Advertiser*, December 22, 1860, reported that the men met from 9 A.M. until 3 P.M. Lincoln recorded that they met "all day." CW, 4:158.

72. *New York Herald*, December 25, 1860.

73. Glyndon G. Van Deusen, "Thurlow Weed: A Character Study," *American Historical Review* 49 (April 1944): 427.

74. Barnes, *Life of Thurlow Weed*, 2:314.

75. *New York Times*, December 20, 1860 ("repudiated"); *New York Herald*, December 27, 1860 ("hostility").

76. Harriet A. Weed, ed., *Autobiography of Thurlow Weed* (Boston: Houghton Mifflin, 1883), 603.

77. Ibid., 603–5.

78. Horatio Seymour, "Recollections of Weed," *Washington Post*, February 4, 1883. The ex–New York governor revealed that it took the political boss a while before his "hesitancy in conversation" was replaced by "an easy flow of language."

79. Barnes, *Life of Thurlow Weed*, 2:294–95.

80. Lincoln to Lyman Trumbull, December 21, 1860, CW, 4:158. Seward and other Republicans on the committee ultimately concluded that Lincoln need not declare his resolve to enforce the hated Fugitive Slave Laws, arguing that "the duty of executing" those provisions "belongs to the States, and not at all to Congress." Seward to Lincoln, December 26, 1860, ALPLC.

81. Frederick Seward, *William H. Seward: An Autobiography from 1801 to 1834, with a Memoir of His Life and Selections from His Letters*, 3 vols. (New York: Derby & Miller, 1891), 484–85.

82. Seward to Lincoln, December 16, 1860, ALPLC.

83. Henry Adams believed Weed would advocate his father, Charles Francis Adams, for the Treasury Department. See Adams to Charles Francis Adams, Jr., January 11, 1861, in J. C. Levenson et al., eds., *The Letters of Henry Adams*, 3 vols. (Cambridge: Harvard University Press, 1982), 1:220. By this time, Henry knew Lincoln preferred Welles, believing him "jealous of C.F.A., as too Sewardish."

84. William H. Seward to Worthington Snethen, November 29, 1860, Original in the William H. Seward Papers, Rochester University, Rochester, New York.

85. *Autobiography of Thurlow Weed*, 605–6.

86. Lincoln to John A. Gilmer, December 15, 1860, CW, 4:151–52

87. Ibid. Gilmer wrote to Lincoln on December 10, original in ALPLC.

88. *Autobiography of Thurlow Weed*, 606–7.

89. Lincoln to Lyman Trumbull, December 14, 1860, CW, 4:162.

90. *Autobiography of Thurlow Weed*, 608–11. These dialogues are adapted from the text. Quotes within quotes have been eschewed but, otherwise, nothing is changed from Weed's own recollections.

91. Ibid., 612. Lincoln made one exception: he told Weed he would offer the highest paying job at his disposal, collector of the Port of New York, to anti-Seward Republican Hiram Barney, who had been one of his hosts at Cooper Union the previous February.

92. Ibid., 612–13.

93. Reprinted in *New York Times*, December 25, 1860.

94. Joseph J. Lewis to Jesse W. Fell, January 15, 1861, Herndon–Weik Papers, Library of Congress.

95. Wilson, *Intimate Memories of Lincoln*, 333.

96. Ibid., 332–33.

97. John G. Nicolay to Therena Bates, December 19, 1860, NPLC.

98. *Cincinnati Commercial*, reprinted in *New York Times*, December 27, 1860.

99. Villard, *Lincoln on the Eve of '61*, 42–43.

100. *New York Times*, December 27, 1860; John G. Nicolay to Edward Bates, December 19, 1860, NPLC.

101. Villard, *Lincoln on the Eve of '61*, 44.

102. Mark E. Neely, Jr., "Lincoln's Theory of Representation: A Significant New Lincoln Document," *Lincoln Lore* 1683 (May 1978).

103. Lincoln to Simon Cameron (with whom he also attempted a visit on February 26, 1860), *CW*, 3:521. Lincoln enclosed a letter to the former congressman that has never been located.

104. *New York Herald*, December 25, 1860; David Wilmot to Lincoln (accepting invitation), December 12, 1860, and December 24, 1860, ALPLC.

105. Villard, *Lincoln on the Eve of '61*, 43. Baker, too, was rumored for a cabinet spot after his visit. *New York Herald*, December 25, 1860.

106. Wilson, *Intimate Memories of Lincoln*, 334.

107. Villard, *Lincoln on the Eve of '61*, 44.

108. Lincoln to Lyman Trumbull, December 28, 1860, and draft letter to Duff Green, December 28, 1860, *CW*, 4:162–63.

109. *New York Herald*, January 8, 1861. Green later wrote Lincoln to say he regretted his "unwillingness to recommend an amendment," indicating that when he returned to Washington, Trumbull did show him the memorandum. See Roy P. Basler's comments in *CW*, 4:162n1. Lincoln never lost his fancy for secret memos. In 1864, convinced he would lose his bid for reelection, he asked his entire cabinet to sign, sight unseen, a memo pledging cooperation with the incoming Democratic administration. See *CW*, 7:514.

110. Duff Green to Lincoln, January 7, 1861, ALPLC.

111. *Springfield* [Massachusetts] *Daily Republican*, December 28, 1860, quoted in Carroll C. Arnold, "The Senate Committee of Thirteen, December 6–31, 1860," in J. Jeffery Auer, ed., *Antislavery and Disunion, 1858–1861: Studies in the Rhetoric of Compromise and Conflict* (New York: Harper & Row, 1963), 327.

112. Seward, *An Autobiography*, 479.

113. Douglas to Charles H. Lanphier, December 25, 1860, in Robert W. Johannsen, ed., *The Letters of Stephen A. Douglas* (Urbana: University of Illinois Press, 1961), 504.

114. Villard, *Lincoln on the Eve of '61*, 34.

115. Just before he moved from the Capitol, Lincoln signed a petition advocat-

ing a separate Supreme Court building. Its home in the State House had become too small, the building itself too crowded. If anyone sympathized with overcrowding in the Capitol, it was Lincoln, whose long occupancy there had filled lobbies and choked stairways since the previous spring. The petition, which was never formally submitted to the legislature, was discovered by Wayne C. Temple. See Sunderine (Wilson) Temple and Wayne C. Temple, *Abraham Lincoln and Illinois' Fifth Capitol*, rev. ed. (Mahomet, Ill.: Mayhaven Publishing, 2006), 264.

116. John G. Nicolay to Therena Bates, December 30, 1860, NPLC. Nicolay gave the date of the move as December 29; other sources give December 27.

117. Temple and Temple, *Abraham Lincoln and Illinois' Fifth Capitol*, 265.

118. John G. Nicolay to Therena Bates, December 30, 1860, NPLC.

119. Lincoln to Alexander H. Stephens, CW, 4:160; Alexander H. Stephens, *A Constitutional View of the Late War Between the States; Its Causes, Character, Conduct and Results . . .* , 2 vols. (Philadelphia: Zeigler, McCurdy & Co., 1870), 2:296.

120. Alexander H. Stephens to Lincoln, December 30, 1860, copy in Myrta Lockett Avery, ed., *Recollections of Alexander H. Stephens . . .* (New York: Doubleday, Page, 1910), 60.

121. In 1863, Lincoln blocked Stephens's attempt to visit Washington with a communication from Confederate president Jefferson Davis. "You will not permit Mr. Stephens to proceed to Washington," he ordered Rear Admiral Samuel P. Lee, "or to pass the blockade." CW, 6:314. The two men did not see each other again until March 1865, when they met at a futile peace conference in Hampton Roads, Virginia.

122. In New York, exultant Wide-Awakes organized "republican rejoicings" that included dancing in the streets. *New York Times*, December 21, 1860.

123. *New York Times*, December 14, 1860.

124. John Rhodehamel and Louise Taper, eds., *"Right or Wrong, God Judge Me"*: *The Writings of John Wilkes Booth* (Urbana: University of Illinois Press, 1997), 55–64.

125. Howard Cecil Perkins, *Northern Editorials on Secession* (Glouscester, Mass.: Peter Smith, 1964), esp. 10, 18.

126. "Stand by the Right. Inscribed to Abraham Lincoln by his brother at the bar, Chas. Leland Porter," *The Independent*, December 27, 1860.

127. *New York Observer*, December 20, 1860. Tennessean William S. Speer wrote Lincoln a few days later to report that Bell would accept a cabinet post; see Speer to Lincoln, December 26, 1860, ALPLC.

128. David Davis urged Lincoln to choose Smith, whom he called "the ablest man in the state." See Davis to Lincoln, November 19, 1860, ALPLC.

129. "I need a man of Democratic antecedents," Lincoln wrote Hamlin on December 24. "This stands in the way of Mr. Adams. I think of Governor Banks, Mr. Welles, and Mr. Tuck. Which of them do the New England delegation prefer? Or shall I decide for myself?" *CW*, 4:161.

130. Recollection by Simon Cameron, February 20, 1875, NPLC. Reprinted in Michael Burlingame, ed., *An Oral History of Abraham Lincoln: John G. Nicolay's Interviews and Essays* (Carbondale: Southern Illinois University Press, 1996), 43. Cameron told Lincoln that Davis and Swett had done more for him, for they "bought all my men . . . stole all my men." Ibid.

131. William H. Seward to Lincoln, December 25, 1860, ALPLC; Lincoln to Seward, December 29, 1860, *CW*, 4:164.

132. Lincoln to William Cullen Bryant, December 29, 1860, *CW*, 4:163.

133. Thomas J. MacCormack, ed., *Memoirs of Gustave Koerner, 1809–1896 . . .*, 2 vols. (Cedar Rapids, Iowa: Torch Press, 1909), 2:279–80. One typical, anonymous, correspondent urged Lincoln: "do not be led astray by corrupt Politicians, do your duty, fear 'God rather than man,' " and reject Cameron because he sought "Honor and Profit." See "One who desires your good" to Lincoln, January [?], 1861, ALPLC.

134. Statement to John G. Nicolay, May 12 and May 13, 1880, in NPLC. Reprinted in Don E. Fehrenbacher and Virginia Fehrenbacher, *Recollected Words of Lincoln* (Stanford: Stanford University Press, 1996), 333.

135. John Allison to Lincoln, quoted in Elwin L. Page, *Cameron for Lincoln's Cabinet* (Boston: Boston University Press, 1954), 19.

136. *New York Herald*, January 7, 1860.

137. *New York Times*, December 31, 1860.

138. Bates, *Diary*, 171.

139. Seward, *An Autobiography*, 486–87.

140. This and the previous quotes, from Bates, *Diary*, 172.

141. Simon Cameron in Burlingame, ed., *An Oral History of Abraham Lincoln*, 42.

142. *CW*, 4:165–67.

143. Lincoln to Simon Cameron, December 31, 1860, *CW*, 4:168.

144. Lincoln to Salmon P. Chase, December 31, 1860, *CW*, 4:168. Cameron testified in 1875 that Lincoln volunteered to give Cameron the letter "before you go," and did so. See Burlingame, ed., *An Oral History of Abraham Lincoln*, 42.

145. Allen Thorndike Rice, ed., *Reminiscences of Abraham Lincoln by Distinguished Men of His Time* (New York: North American Review, 1886), liii.

146. *National Intelligencer*, January 1, 1861.

147. Henry Adams to Charles Francis Adams, Jr., January 11, 1861, in Levenson et al., *Letters of Henry Adams*, 1:220.

6. Very Much Like the Critter

1. The *Washington Constitution* used the moniker "Uncle Abe" as early as November 22, 1860—albeit mockingly.

2. Jones's reminiscences were published in the *Cincinnati Commercial*, October 18, 1871, and the *Sacramento Weekly Union*, November 4, 1871; reprinted in Thomas D. Jones, *Memories of Lincoln*, ed. Rufus Rockwell Wilson (New York: Press of the Pioneers, 1934), 4,5. A contemporary who knew him in later years said the sculptor, despite his full name—Thomas Dow Jones—"lacked the money-getting instinct," in Jones, 3.

3. *Illinois Daily State Journal*, July 2, 1861.

4. Thomas D. Jones to William Linn McMillen, December 30, 1860, Lincoln Collection, Indiana University at Bloomington; reprinted in Wayne C. Temple, "Lincoln as Seen by T. D. Jones," *Illinois Libraries* 58 (June 1976): 448.

5. Jones, *Memories of Lincoln*, 5.

6. Ibid, 5–6. Lincoln was making reference to Leonard Wells Volk, who had cast Lincoln's face in wet plaster in May 1860. Volk recalled that "it hurt a little" when he removed the dried mask from his subject's face. See Leonard Wells Volk, "A Lincoln Life-Mask and How It Was Made," orig. published in *Century Magazine*, December 1881, in Rufus Rockwell Wilson, ed., *Intimate Memories of Lincoln* (New York: Primavera Press, 1945), 243.

7. See Wayne C. Temple, *Abraham Lincoln and Others at the St. Nicholas* (Springfield, Ill.: St. Nicholas Corp., 1968), 7. One guest had exclaimed, "from the Revere House in Boston, to the St. Charles Hotel of New Orleans, you can find no better accommodation." Rooms cost two to three dollars per night.

8. Jones, *Memories of Lincoln*, 9.

9. Ibid., 7, 15.

10. Ibid., 14.

11. Ibid., 8.

12. *Illinois Daily State Journal*, January 7, 1860; John G. Nicolay attended, too, and "enjoyed" the performance "very much," because Murdoch's recitations were "accompanied with a kind of running criticism of the play." Nicolay to Therena Bates, January 9, 1861, NPLC.

13. Murdoch later performed patriotic readings in the U.S. Senate chamber in Washington, which Lincoln attended in January 1863; *Washington Chronicle*, January 11, 20, 1863.)

14. Jones, *Memories of Lincoln*, 8–9, 12–13.

15. Douglas L. Wilson and Rodney O. Davis, eds., *Herndon's Informants: Letters, Interviews, and Statements About Abraham Lincoln* (Urbana: University of Illinois Press, 1998), 133.

16. *New York Times*, January 14, 1861; Jones, *Memories of Lincoln*, 7–8.

17. *New York World*, January 26, 1861.

18. Ronald Reagan set off a small furor in 1982 when it was revealed that while he was donating gifts from foreign sources to the State Department, he retained gifts sent by domestic admirers. See *New York Times*, May 18, May 27, 1982.

19. Lincoln to Robert Allen, June 21, 1836, *CW*, 1:49. In fairness, Lincoln made this statement in the course of *refusing* a favor, noting: "In this case, favour to me, would be injustice to the public."

20. Victor Searcher, *Lincoln's Journey to Greatness* (Philadelphia: John C. Winston, 1960), 152; Harold Holzer, *Lincoln and the Jews: The Last Best Hope of Earth* (Los Angeles: Skirball Cultural Center, 2002), 6.

21. Daniel Ullmann to Lincoln, January 25, 1861, ALPLC; Lincoln to Ullmann, February 1, 1861, *CW*, 4:184. Donor Ullmann had been the American party (Know-Nothing) candidate for governor of New York in 1854.

22. *New York Times*, February 4, 1861; *Richmond Dispatch*, February 13, 1861. The story appeared in the *Chicago Tribune* the following day.

23. Lincoln to Isaac Fenno, January 22, 1861, *CW*, 4:179.

24. Louisa Livingston Siemon to Lincoln, December 10, 1860, ALPLC; *Boston Daily Courier*, December 29, 1860.

25. Donald McClennan to Lincoln, January 31, 1861, ALPLC; Lincoln to McClennan, March 20, 1861, *CW*, 4:296. See also, Louis A. Warren, "Gifts for the President," *Lincoln Lore* 401 (December 14, 1936).

26. G. B. Lincoln, quoted in Francis B. Carpenter, *Six Months at the White House with President Lincoln: The Story of a Picture* (New York: Hurd & Houghton, 1866), 113.

27. *Chicago Daily Press & Tribune*, January 24, 1861. For Mrs. Lincoln's sewing machine, see Mark E. Neely, Jr., and R. Gerald McMurtry, *The Insanity File: The Case of Mary Todd Lincoln* (Carbondale: Southern Illinois University Press, 1986), 165; Catherine Clinton, "Wife Versus Widow: Clashing Perspectives on Mary Lincoln's Legacy," *Journal of the Abraham Lincoln Association* 28 (Winter 2007): 15.

28. *New York Herald*, January 20, 1860.

29. Harold G. Villard and Oswald Garrison Villard, *Lincoln on the Eve of '61: A Journalist's Story by Henry Villard* (New York: Alfred A. Knopf, 1941), 53.

30. Jones, *Memories of Lincoln*, 8.

31. Villard, *Lincoln on the Eve of '61*, 69–70.

32. Jones, *Memories of Lincoln*, 8. The whistle was sent by A. R. Russell.

33. Ibid. 7; Jones to McMillen, December 30, 1860.

34. Jones, *Memories of Lincoln*, 13.

35. Ibid., 15.

36. Paul M. Angle, *Lincoln, 1854–1861, Being the Day-by-Day Activities of Abraham Lincoln* (Springfield, Ill.: Abraham Lincoln Association, 1933), 366.

37. See Van Deren Coke, *The Painter and the Photograph: From Delacroix to Warhol* (Albuquerque: University of New Mexico Press, 1964), esp. 25–35. In 1867, pioneer art critic Henry Tuckerman suggested that the availability of photographs had helped "to banish mediocrity in portraiture," quoted on p. 22.

38. Jones, *Memories of Lincoln*, 14. For the location of German's studio, see *Campbell & Richardson's Springfield City Directory & Business Mirror . . .* (Springfield, Ill.: Johnson, Bradford, 1863), 3. See also Wayne C. Temple, "C. S. German: Photographer to President-elect Lincoln," *Illinois History* 4 (July–August 2006): 9–10. What is likely the original pose was sold by Chrsitie's auction gallery in 2007, but offered no clues as to its original recipient. The inscription said only: "A. Lincoln—Springfield, Ill. January 26, 1861 [.]" See *The Jerome Shochet Collection of Signed Historical Photographs, Tuesday, 19 June 2007* (New York: Christie's, 2007), 65. The photograph was the first of Lincoln to be engraved for currency; see Fred Reed, "Did Abraham Lincoln's Icon Image on Money Influence His Public Perception?" *Lincoln Herald* 109 (Winter 2007): 206.

39. John G. Nicolay quoted in Michael Burlingame, ed., *Lincoln's Journalist: John Hay's Anonymous Writings for the Press, 1860–1864* (Carbondale: Southern Illinois University Press, 1998), 17, entry for January 7, 1861.

40. Jones, *Memories of Lincoln*, 15.

41. Charles Hamilton and Lloyd Ostendorf, *Lincoln in Photographs: An Album of Every Known Pose* (Norman: University of Oklahoma Press, 1963), 68.

42. Carpenter, *Six Months at the White House*, 34–35.

43. Jones, *Memories of Lincoln*, 12.

44. *Illinois Daily State Journal*, January 29, 1861.

45. Thomas D. Jones to William Linn McMillen, February 11, 1861, in Temple, "Lincoln as Seen by T. D. Jones," 451.

46. Jones to John G. Nicolay, August 11, 1861, ALPLC.

47. Carpenter, *Six Months at the White House*, 35. As late as 1865, Lincoln was still considering a consular appointment for Jones. He died before he could fulfill the sculptor's ambition. See Lincoln to William H. Seward, March 6, 1865, CW, 8:337.

48. Jones to McMillen, December 30, 1860.

49. Michael O'Brien, *Henry Adams and the Southern Question* (Athens: University of Georgia Press, 2005), 7.

50. George Hochfield, ed., *The Great Secession Winter of 1860–1861 and Other Essays by Henry Adams* (New York: Sagamore Press, 1958), 1.

51. Henry Adams to Charles Francis Adams, Jr., January 2, 1861, in J. C. Levenson et al., eds., *The Letters of Henry Adams*, 6 vols. (Cambridge: Belkap Press of Harvard University, 1982), 1:217.

52. Henry Adams, "The Great Secession Winter of 1860–1861," *Proceedings of the Massachusetts Historical Society* 43 (June 1910): 681–682. See also Hoch-

field, ed., *The Great Secession Winter*, 2–20. For an excellent essay on Adams's views on Lincoln, see Garry Wills, "Henry Adams on Lincoln," in John Y. Simon, Harold Holzer, and Dawn Vogel, eds., *Lincoln Revisited: New Insights from the Lincoln Forum* (New York: Fordham University Press, 2007), 297–310.

53. Charles Francis Adams, *An Address on the Life, Character, and Services of William Henry Seward* (New York: Weed, Parsons, 1873), 48. See also, Garry Wills, *Henry Adams and the Making of America* (Boston: Houghton Mifflin, 2005), 40, 411n8. Adams actually denied he was another Walpole, but in dismissing the comparison, succeeded in inviting it.

54. Gideon Welles, *Lincoln and Seward. Remarks Upon the Memorial Address of Chas. Francis Adams, on the Late Wm. H. Seward . . .* (New York: Sheldon & Co., 1874), 42–43. Welles produced this book to refute the Adams lecture. To Adams's claim that Seward possessed "higher culture and scholastic attainments," for instance, Welles argued that Lincoln "was greatly superior in intellectual strength and vigor" (34).

55. *Washington Star*, January 2, 1861.

56. "A. Jackson Democrat" to Lincoln, January 20, 1860; R. A. Hunt to Lincoln, January 18, 1861; "J——a. J——s" to Lincoln, all ALPLC. The two letters on poison—John F. Wright to Lincoln, January 24, 1861, and David Wylie to Lincoln, January 25, 1861, are in the Lincoln Museum, Fort Wayne, Indiana.

57. Ernest Ferguson, *Freedom Rising: Washington in the Civil War* (New York: Alfred A. Knopf, 2004), 59.

58. Abraham Jonas to Lincoln, December 30, 1860, ALPLC.

59. Salmon P. Chase to Lincoln, January 28, 1860, ALPLC.

60. Joseph Medill to Lincoln, December 30, 1860, ALPLC.

61. *New York Times*, January 4, 1861.

62. William H. Seward to Lincoln, December 28, 1860, ALPLC.

63. William H. Seward to Lincoln (unsigned), December 29, 1860, ALPLC.

64. Thomas Mather, quoted in Wilson and Davis, eds., *Herndon's Informants*, 709.

65. Lincoln to William H. Seward, January 3, 1861, CW, 4:170.

66. Villard, *Lincoln on the Eve of '61*, 49.

67. *New York Herald*, February 4, 1861.

68. Villard, *Lincoln on the Eve of '61*, 49–50.

69. *Philadelphia Evening Bulletin* (dateline December 14, 1860), reprinted in *New York Times*, December 20, 1860.

70. Villard, *Lincoln on the Eve of '61*, 50.

71. Herman Kreismann to Charles H. Ray (of the *Chicago Tribune*), January 16, 1861, Huntington Library, San Marino, Cal., quoted in Ruth Painter Randall, *Mary Lincoln: Biography of a Marriage* (Boston: Little, Brown, 1953), 193.

72. *Baltimore Sun*, quoted in Jean H. Baker, *Mary Todd Lincoln: A Biography* (New York: W. W. Norton, 1987), 166. For its balance, scholarship, and humanity, Baker's biography remains unsurpassed.

73. *Washington Evening Star*, November 10, 1860; *Chicago Daily Press & Tribune*, November 13, 1860.

74. *New York Times*, January 23, 1861.

75. *New-York Daily Tribune*, January 23, 1861.

76. Mary Lincoln to David Davis, January 17, 1861, in Justin G. Turner and Linda Levitt Turner, *Mary Todd Lincoln: Her Life and Letters* (New York: Alfred A. Knopf, 1972), 71. On January 3, Judd himself admitted he believed he was "substantially played out" as a cabinet aspirant. See Judd to Lyman Trumbull, January 3, 1861, Trumbull Papers, Library of Congress.

77. Quoted in Baker, *Mary Todd Lincoln*, 166.

78. *New York Illustrated News*, February 23, 1861.

79. Villard, *Lincoln on the Eve of '61*, 54–55.

80. *New York Illustrated News*, February 23, 1861.

81. Villard, *Lincoln on the Eve of '61*, 55.

82. Robert Lincoln to unknown correspondent, June 28, 1887, Lincoln Museum, Fort Wayne, Indiana; "Highest Office was 'Prison' to Robert Lincoln," unidentified newspaper article in the Lincoln Museum clipping files.

83. *New York Herald*, December 26, 1860. The rival *New York Tribune* countered that two Southerners, Robert E. Scott of Virginia, and William A. Graham of North Carolina, would get the Navy and Interior Departments, respectively, reprinted in the [Washington] *Evening Star*, January 7, 1861.

84. *New York Herald*, January 6, 1861.

85. Charles A. Dana, in Allen Thorndike Rice, ed., *Reminiscences of Lincoln by Distinguished Men of His Time* (New York: North American Publishing Co., 1886), 368.

86. Alexander K. McClure, *Recollections of Half a Century* (Salem, Mass.: Salem Press, 1902), 9.

87. The precise date of the McClure visit remains uncertain, but a David Davis letter to Lincoln on December 31 stated that McClure would be in Springfield the next day, and "for no good purpose." ALPLC.

88. Willard L. King, *Lincoln's Manager David Davis* (Chicago: University of Chicago Press, 1960), 165.

89. Elwin L. Page, *Cameron for Lincoln's Cabinet*, (Boston: Boston University Press, 1954), 13. Correspondent R. V. Johnson advised Lincoln around the same time that McClure was "a good talker but a more treacherous man never lived," Johnson to Lincoln, January 5, 1861, ALPLC.

90. Lincoln to Simon Cameron, January 3, 1861, CW, 4:169–70. Lincoln's change of heart was leaked to the *New York Herald*, January 16, 1861.

91. For a good physical description of Chase, see J. W. Schuckers, *The Life and Public Services of Salmon Portland Chase* . . . (New York: D. Appleton & Co., 1874), 619.

92. Salmon P. Chase to George G. Fogg, January 3, 1861, Salmon P. Chase Papers (microfilm), ed. John Niven (Frederick, Md.: University Publications of America, 1987)

93. Salmon P. Chase to Nathaniel Banks, January 7, 1861; Chase to James Shepherd Pike, January 10, 1861, Chase Papers.

94. See, for example, Rep. John W. Killinger to Lincoln, January 15, 1861, ALPLC: "I beg leave to protest against the selection of a gentleman with so offensive a tariff record as Mr. Chase for the Treasury."

95. The conversations were recalled in Schuckers, *Salmon Portland Chase*, 201. See also Chase to George Opdyke, January 9, 1861, Chase Papers, Library of Congress.

96. Back on November 29, Tuck had sent a long letter to Illinois governor-elect Richard Yates, stressing that "it will be vital with Mr. Lincoln, to have some true and loving friends near his person—in his Cabinet," and proposing himself. The letter ended up in the Lincoln Papers, suggesting Yates forwarded it to the president-elect. See Tuck to Yates, November 29, 1860, ALPLC. Between December 19 and 22, Tuck's New Hampshire supporters pelted Lincoln with letters of endorsement. See, for example, state political leaders to Lincoln, December 19; Dartmouth faculty to Lincoln, December 19; New Hampshire citizens to Lincoln, December 19; and Joseph G. Hoyt and Edwin D. Sanborn to Lincoln, December 22, all ALPLC.

97. Amos Tuck, *Autobiographical Memoir of Amos Tuck* (Paris, N.H.: Clarke & Bishop, 1902), 83. Tuck eventually "accepted a government office in Boston, tendered me by President Lincoln" (56).

98. Thomas J. MacCormack, ed., *Memoirs of Gustave Koerner, 1809–1896* . . . , 2 vols. (Cedar Rapids, Iowa Torch Press, 1909), 2:114.

99. William H. L. Wallace to Ann Wallace, January 6, 1861 in Harry E. Pratt, *Concerning Mr. Lincoln* (Springfield, Ill.: Abraham Lincoln Association 1944), 35.

100. Salmon P. Chase to Hiram Barney, January 8, 1860, Chase Papers, Library of Congress. Barney had helped organize the February 1860 Cooper Union lectures, believing they would hurt Seward's chances at the presidency and help Chase's. But Chase declined the invitation, Lincoln accepted, and emerged the leading alternative to Seward for the Republican nomination.

101. Salmon P. Chase to John Jay, January 16, 1861, Chase Papers.

102. Salmon P. Chase to James Worthington, January 14, 1861, Chase Papers.

103. Lincoln to Lyman Trumbull, January 7, 1861, *CW*, 4:171.

104. Ibid.

105. *Washington Star*, January 15, 1861, quoted in *Lincoln Day by Day*, 3:5.

106. Leonard Sweet to Lincoln, January 14, 1861, ALPLC.

107. William H. Seward to Lincoln, January 15, 1861, ALPLC.

108. Lincoln to Simon Cameron, January 13, 1861, *CW*, 4:174.

109. Lincoln to Simon Cameron, January 3, 1861, *CW*, 4:174.

110. Horace White, *Life of Lyman Trumbull* (Boston: Houghton Mifflin, 1913), 148.

111. John Covode to Lincoln, January 15, 1861, ALPLC.

112. Harry Woods to Lincoln, January 14, 1861, ALPLC.

113. *Lincoln Day by Day*, 3:6–7.

114. *Cincinnati Daily Gazette*, January 24, 1861; *New York Herald*, January 24, 1861.

115. Lincoln to Simon Cameron, January 21, 1860, *CW*, 4:177. Nicolay found it in Lincoln's files seventeen years later, and inscribed the envelope: "Found sealed and opened by me Sept 26th 1878."

116. *New York Herald*, January 25, 1861.

117. *Harrisburg Daily Telegraph*, January 24, 1861.

118. Elihu Washburne to Chase, January 10, 1861, Chase Papers, Library of Congress.

119. Charles Sumner to Chase, January 19, 1862, Chase Papers, Library of Congress.

120. Amos Tuck to Chase, January 14, 1861, Chase Papers, Library of Congress.

121. Salmon P. Chase to Lincoln, January 11, 1861, ALPLC.

122. George Opdyke to Lincoln, January 24, 1861, ALPLC. In the manner of an endorsement, Opdyke cited Chase's "purity of character, his eminent abilities, his great experience." He also warned Lincoln that Ohio Republicans would need time to find a successor for the Senate.

123. Welles to Lincoln, December 10, 1860, Welles Papers, Box 2, Library of Congress. I am indebted to historian Craig Symonds for bringing this letter to my attention.

124. J. D. Baldwin to Lincoln, January 7, 1861, ALPLC.

125. J. D. Baldwin to Welles, January 7, 1861; Edward L. Pierce to Welles, January 8, 1861, in Papers of Gideon Welles, ALPLM. The fact that an entire box of Welles correspondence turned up in, and remains, in Springfield, indicates that much of it was shared with Welles's supporters among Lincoln's inner circle there. J. D. Baldwin to Welles, January 7, 1861, Welles Papers, Library of Congress.

126. George G. Fogg to Welles, January 5, 1861, Welles Papers, Library of Congress.

127. E. B. Hudson to Lincoln, January 5, 1861, ALPLC.

128. Hannibal Hamlin to Lincoln, December 29, 1861, ALPLC.

129. George G. Fogg to Welles, January 27, 1861, Papers of Gideon Welles, ALPLM.

130. Jeriah Bonham, *Fifty Years' Recollections with Observations and Reflections on Historical Events . . .* (Peoria, Ill.: J. W. Franks & Sons, 1883), 184.

131. William H. Herndon to Lyman Trumbull, January 27, 1861, in Pratt, *Concerning Mr. Lincoln*, 45.

132. *Daily Illinois State Register*, January 5, 1861.

133. Welles, *Lincoln and Seward*, 39.

134. *New-York Daily Tribune*, December 11, 1860.

135. J. Bryant to Lincoln, December 14, 1860, ALPLC.

136. See James A. Hamilton, J. J. Astor, Jr., Hamilton Fish, Moses H. Grinnell, and other New York Republicans to Lincoln, January 29, 1861. This letter included the warning that, in New York, "the compromise would be supported in our judgment, by a vote of over four hundred thousand."

137. John G. Nicolay, *The Outbreak of the Rebellion*, orig. pub. 1881 (New York: Da Capo, 1995), 16.

138. *Boston Advertiser*, January 8, 1861; *New York World*, January 8, 1861.

139. *New York Herald*, January 5, 1861. The New York paper's editorial attack was particularly painful. Although it had backed Stephen A. Douglas for president, its ongoing publication of Henry Villard's friendly reports from Springfield suggested editor James Gordon Bennett's growing sympathy for Lincoln, to go along with his strong belief in the sanctity of the Union. His editorial criticism, however, grew harsher.

140. Jefferson Davis, *The Rise and Fall of the Confederate Government*, 2 vols., orig. pub. 1881 (New York: Da Capo, 1990), 1:65. Even the *Boston Post*, December 3, 1860, had wondered: "Northern Agitation—Is It to Stop?" Like the *Herald*, the *Post* was a Democratic paper.

141. James A. Hamilton et al. to Lincoln, January 29, 1861, ALPLC.

142. William H. Seward to Lincoln, December 26, 1860, ALPLC. At around this time, defeated presidential candidate Stephen A. Douglas proposed his own alternative: that no decision on slavery for *any* territory be made until its population totaled fifty thousand, and together with John J. Crittenden, implored influential Georgians: "Don't give up the Ship." See Douglas to Alexander H. Stephens, December 25, 1860, and Douglas and John J. Crittenden to William Ezzard and others, December 29, 1860, in Robert W. Johannsen, ed., *The Letters of Stephen A. Douglas* (Urbana: University of Illinois Press, 1961), 506.

143. William C. Harris, *Lincoln's Rise to the Presidency* (Lawrence: University Press of Kansas, 2007), 286; James M. McPherson, *Battle Cry of Freedom: The Civil War Era* (New York: Oxford University Press, 1988), 254.

144. James R. Doolittle to Lincoln, January 10, 1861, ALPLC.

145. John A. Gilmer to Lincoln, December 29, 1860, ALPLC.

146. *New York Herald,* January 8, 1861.

147. George E. Baker, ed., *The Works of William H. Seward,* 5 vols. (Boston: Houghton Mifflin, 1884), 4:651–52, 654.

148. *New York Times,* January 13, 1861.

149. Diary of Charles Francis Adams, January 21, 1861, Adams Papers, Massachusetts Historical Society.

150. George G. Fogg to Gideon Welles, Welles Papers, ALPLM.

151. Lincoln to William H. Seward, January 19, 1861, *CW,* 4:176.

152. Seward to Charles Francis Adams, quoted in Doris Kearns Goodwin, *Team of Rivals: The Political Genius of Abraham Lincoln* (New York: Simon & Schuster, 2005), 304; Carl Schurz to Mrs. Schurz, February 9, 1861, in Carl Schurz and Joseph Schafer, eds., *Intimate Letters of Carl Schurz* (Madison: State Historical Society of Wisconsin, 1928), 247.

153. Schurz, *Intimate Letters of Carl Schurz,* 247.

154. [New York] *National Anti-Slavery Standard,* January 19, 1861.

155. Edward W. Emerson, ed., *The Life and Letters of Charles Russell Lowell, Captain Sixth United States Cavalry, Colonel Second Massachusetts Cavalry, Brigadier-General United States Volunteers* (Boston: Houghton Mifflin, 1907), 192–93.

156. John T. Morse, *Life and Letters of Oliver Wendell Holmes,* 2 vols. (Boston: Houghton Mifflin, 1869), 2:154.

157. *Congressional Globe,* January 23, 1861, Appendix, 86–87, reprinted in William F. Moore and Jane Ann Moore, *His Brother's Blood: Owen Lovejoy—Speeches and Writings, 1838–64* (Urbana: University of Illinois Press, 2004), 257.

158. Herndon to Trumbull, January 27, 1861, in Pratt, *Concerning Mr. Lincoln,* 46.

159. *New York Times,* January 14, 1861.

160. *Douglass' Monthly,* January 1861, in Philip S. Foner and Yuval Taylor, eds., *Frederick Douglass: Selected Speeches and Writings* (Chicago: Lawrence Hill, 1999), 428.

161. *New York Herald,* January 13, 1861.

162. *New York Herald,* January 29, 1861.

163. Allan Nevins and Milton Halsey Thomas, eds., *The Diary of George Templeton Strong,* 4 vols. (New York: Macmillan, 1962), 2:94. All three quotes are from the diary, but one can reasonably infer that Strong recorded the arguments he had advanced at his December 27 dinner.

164. Recollection of Franklin Blades, in Paul M. Angle, ed., *Abraham Lincoln—By Some Men Who Knew Him* rev. ed., (Bloomington, Ill.: Pantagraph Printing, 1910), 122–126.

7. If We Surrender, It Is the End of Us

1. Henry G. Villard and Oswald Garrison Villard, *Lincoln on the Eve of '61: A Journalist's Story by Henry Villard* (New York: Alfred A. Knopf, 1941), 47–48.

2. *New York Herald*, January 20, 1861.

3. "A. Jackson Democrat" to Lincoln, January 20, 1861, ALPLC.

4. *New York Times*, January 21, 1861.

5. Quoted in William C. Davis, *Look Away! A History of the Confederate States of America* (New York: Free Press, 2002), 37. Daniel W. Crofts has made a compelling case for Georgia Unionism as a "lifeless shadow." See Crofts, *Reluctant Confederates: Upper South Unionists in the Secession Crisis* (Chapel Hill: University of North Carolina Press, 1989), 380.

6. James T. Hale to Lincoln, January 6, 1861, ALPLC; Lincoln to Hale, January 11, 1861, CW, 4:172.

7. From Lincoln's annual message to Congress, December 1, 1862, CW, 5:537.

8. CW, 4:168–69. The fragment is undated, and some scholars have assigned it to December 31, 1860. More likely, Lincoln crafted it a few weeks later, as he began seriously pondering the composition of his inaugural address.

9. See Allen C. Guelzo, *Abraham Lincoln: Redeemer President* (Chicago: William B. Eeerdmans, 1999), esp. Chapter 5, "Moral Principle Is All That Unites Us."

10. CW, 2:501. Lincoln made his remark during his speech at Chicago on July 10, 1858.

11. Earlier, Lincoln had admitted the Constitution's imperfections, conceding at one point, "we could not get our constitution unless we permitted . . . slavery." See his speech at Chicago, July 10, 1858, CW, 2:501. Historian Mark E. Neely, Jr., has maintained, "In truth, the Constitution stood as an embarrassment to the antislavery cause." See Neely, *The Fate of Liberty: Abraham Lincoln and Civil Liberties* (New York: Oxford University Press, 1991), 216.

12. Michael Burlingame, ed., *Lincoln's Journalist: John Hay's Anonymous Writings for the Press, 1860–1864* (Carbondale: Southern Illinois University Press, 1998), 21.

13. Douglas L. Wilson and Rodney O. Davis, eds., *Herndon's Lincoln* by William H. Herndon and Jesse W. Weik, orig. pub. 1889 (Urbana: University of Illinois Press, 2006), 282.

14. Villard, *Lincoln on the Eve of '61*, 62.

15. Ibid., 51.

16. Horace Greeley to Lincoln, January 26, 1861, ALPLC

17. *New York Herald*, January 26, 1861.

18. *New York Herald,* February 16, 1861.

19. Ibid.

20. *New York Herald,* February 1, 1861. In one example, A. W. Campbell secretary of the Virginia State Republican Committee, journeyed to Springfield to ask Lincoln to appoint Virginian Alfred Caldwell to the cabinet. For his trouble, Campbell, editor of the *Washington Intelligencer,* got the postmaster's job in Wheeling; Caldwell earned appointment as U.S. consul in Honolulu. See J. M. Pumphrey to Lincoln, February 4, 1861, and notes in transcription by Lincoln Studies Center, Knox College, Galesburg, Illinois, on http://memory.loc.gov/cgi-bin/query/r?ammem/mail:@field(DOCID+@lit(d0711800)). The *New York World* erroneously reported on January 8, 1861, that Lincoln had offered a cabinet post to Southerner William A. Graham, who declined it.

21. *New York Herald,* February 1, 1861

22. Douglas L. Wilson and Rodney O. Davis, eds., *Herndon's Informants: Letters, Interviews, and Statements About Abraham Lincoln* (Urbana: University of Illinois Press, 1998), 166. Lincoln did finally offer a post to Swett during his inaugural journey, but nothing came of this. See Robert S. Eckley, "Lincoln's Intimate Friend: Leonard Swett," *Journal of the Illinois State Historical Society* 92 (Autumn 1999): 280.

23. Wilson and Davis, eds., *Herndon's Informants,* 627, 348.

24. Joshua Allen to his mother, January 26, 1861, Louise and Barry Taper Collection, Beverly Hills, California.

25. *New York World,* January 22, 1861.

26. Villard, *Lincoln on the Eve of '61,* 56–57.

27. Ibid., 57–58.

28. The only major book on this subject, charming but maddeningly unsourced, is Andy Van Meter, *Always My Friend: A History of the State Journal-Register and Springfield* (Springfield, Ill: Copley Press, 1981).

29. John Hay quoted in Burlingame, ed., *Lincoln's Journalist,* 20.

30. *New York Herald,* January 26, 1861; Francisco Ocampo to Matias Romero, December 22, 1860, ALPLC. Minister Romero undoubtedly handed this letter to Lincoln, hence its preservation in the Lincoln Papers.

31. Horace Greeley, *The American Conflict: A History of the Great Rebellion in the United States of America* (Hartford: O. D. Case & Co., 1864), 335.

32. John McClintock to Lincoln, February 5, 1861, ALPLC.

33. "American Crisis," *Quarterly Review* (July–October 1861), quoted in Charles Adams, *When in the Course of Human Events: Arguing the Case for Southern Secession* (Lanham, ed.: Rowman & Littlefield, 2000), 13.

34. Belle Becker Sideman and Lillian Friedman, eds., *Europe Looks at the Civil War* (New York: Orion, 1960), 19.

35. Lincoln to Matias Romero, January 21, 1861, CW, 4:177–78.

36. This and subsequent quotes are from Henry C. Whitney, *Life on the Circuit with Lincoln* (Boston: Estes & Lauriat, 1892), 491–92.

37. Ibid., 492–93.

38. Allen to his mother, January 26, 1861.

39. Villard, *Lincoln on the Eve of '61*, 51–52.

40. John Hay quoted in Burlingame, ed., *Lincoln's Journalist*, 18.

41. *New York Herald*, February 4, 1861.

42. Samuel Bernstein to Lincoln, January 15, 1861, ALPLC.

43. See job-seeking letters to Lincoln from H. M. Moyers, February 4, 1861; Edward Fenno, February [?], 1861, Daniel D. Mattice, February 9, 1861; Charles Pfefferling, January 25, 1861, all ALPLC.

44. Leonard Worcester to Lincoln, January 28, 1861, ALPLC.

45. Frank W. Ballard to Norman B. Judd, December 22, 1860, ALPLC.

46. Statement by John G. Nicolay, undated typescript in Nicolay scrapbook, 1856–1870, "dictated to H. M. N," NPLC.

47. The invitations to Chase—dated September 26, 1859, and October 26, 1859—are in the collection of the Lincoln Shrine in Redlands, California. This author detailed the story of Chase's inexplicable refusal in *Lincoln at Cooper Union: The Speech That Made Lincoln President* (New York: Simon & Schuster, 2004), 82.

48. Lincoln to Thurlow Weed, February 4, 1861, CW, 4:185.

49. A classic example was the case of Lincoln's brother-in-law Ninian W. Edwards, a Democrat who nonetheless secured a wartime appointment as commissary of subsistence in August 1861, claiming "pecuniary embarrassment"—and then proceeded to embarrass Lincoln when Springfield leaders reported that he had appropriated money. Lincoln eventually transferred him to Chicago. See Mark E. Neely, Jr., and Harold Holzer, *The Lincoln Family Album: Photographs from the Personal Collection of a Historic American Family*, orig. pub. 1990 (Carbondale: Southern Illinois University Press, 2006), 4.

50. Carol Blanchard and Harold W. Ryan, *Letters of Application and Recommendation During the Administrations of Abraham Lincoln and Andrew Johnson, 1861–1869* (Washington, D.C.: National Archives and Records Service, 1970).

51. Undated clipping enclosed with Frank Blair, Jr., to Lincoln, January 25, 1861, ALPLC. Blair worried that in the interregnum, Buchanan appointees in the foreign service were capable of "turpitude, misrepresentation, financial transgressions, and offensive language."

52. John McClintock to Lincoln, February 5, 1861, ALPLC.

53. *Register of Officers and Agents, Civil, Military, and Naval, in the Service of the United States, on the Thirtieth September 1861* . . . (Washington, D.C.: General Printing Office, 1862), v–viii, 95–99. See also "Data on White House Expenditures from Files of General Accounting Office," notes from the Na-

tional Archives in the Papers of James G. Randall, Box 71, Library of Congress.

54. Paul Van Riper and Keith A. Sutherland, "The Northern Civil Service: 1861–1865," *Civil War History* 11 (December 1965): 351–69.

55. See [John Locke Scripps], *Life of Abraham Lincoln* (Chicago: Chicago Press & Tribune, 1860).

56. *Register of officers and Agents* . . . , 251 (Lexington), 346 (New Salem), 358 (Chicago).

57. In addition, seven thousand lower-level postmasters were relieved and replaced by 1863. See Don E. Fehrenbacher, "Political Uses of the Post Office," in *Lincoln in Text and Context: Collected Essays* (Stanford: Stanford University Press, 1987), 31–32. For another view, see Mark E. Neely, Jr., *The Union Divided: Party Conflict in the Civil War North* (Cambridge: Harvard University Press, 2002), 22.

58. *Register of Officers and Agents for 1861* . . . , 43, 49, 55–57

59. *Journal of the Executive Proceedings of the Senate of the United States of America, 1858–1861,* 291–364, National Archives and Records Administration.

60. Federal registers, 74 (Illinois 1859), 77 (Indiana 1859), 220 (New Jersey); *Register of Officers and Agents* . . . *1863,* 352–53 (Illinois), 355–56 (Indiana), 494–95 (New Jersey), National Archives.

61. Richard Carwardine, "Abraham Lincoln and the Fourth Estate: The White House and the Press During the American Civil War," *American Nineteenth Century History* 7 (March 2006): 6.

62. Nicolay became a White House appointment, but because Lincoln's personal staff was limited to two secretaries, Stoddard was appointed to the Interior Department, assigned to signing the president's name on land patents, but assigned to work in the Executive Mansion.

63. *Register of Officers and Agents* . . . *1861,* 199, 205.

64. See Phillip Shaw Paludan, *The Presidency of Abraham Lincoln* (Lawrence: University Press of Kansas, 1994), 35.

65. L. P. Libby to Ozias M. Hatch, February 14, 1861, Hatch Papers, ALPLM.

66. Wilson and Davis, eds., *Herndon's Informants,* 618–19.

67. Ibid., 620.

68. Ibid., 701; Harry J. Carman and Reinhard H. Luthin, *Lincoln and the Patronage* (New York: Columbia University Press, 1943), 62. Kreissmann himself won an appointment from Lincoln as secretary to the Berlin legation. The tantrum story has occasionally been portrayed as occurring on the very day the Lincolns left for Washington—with Mrs. Lincoln's fit delaying their departure until her husband gave in (see, for example, Villard, *Lincoln on the Eve of '61,* 70). But there is insufficient evidence to take this assertion seriously. The position involved was not insignificant; Lincoln later called it "so high an office." See Lincoln to Salmon P. Chase, May 18, 1861, *CW,* 4:373.

69. Margartia Spalding Gerry, ed., *Through Five Administrations: Reminiscences of Colonel William H. Crook, Bodyguard to President Lincoln* (New York: Harper & Bros., 1916), 10.

70. Horace White to William H. Herndon, January 26, 1891, Wilson and Davis, eds., *Herndon's informants*, 701.

71. William H. Herndon to Jesse W. Weik, February 5, 1861, in Emanuel Hertz, *The Hidden Lincoln: From the Letters and Papers of William H. Herndon* (New York: Viking, 1938), 260–61. Hertz's transcripts are notoriously imperfect, but this is the only source for this interesting letter.

72. A. K. McClure to Lincoln, January 15, 1861, J. G. Hornberger to Lincoln, January 22, 1861, C. F. Mitchell to Lincoln, January 27, 1861, ALPLC.

73. Villard, *Lincoln on the Eve of '61*, 52.

74. *New York Herald*, January 28, 1861.

75. Whitney, *Life on the Circuit with Lincoln*, 492.

76. George Sumner to Andrew Curtin, January 21, 1861, in Harry E. Pratt, *Concerning Mr. Lincoln . . .* (Springfield, Ill.: Abraham Lincoln Association, 1944), 40–41.

77. Quoted in Don E. Fehrenbacher and Virginia Fehrenbacher, *Recollected Words of Lincoln* (Stanford: Stanford University Press, 1996), 436.

78. William H. Herndon to Lyman Trumbull, January 28, 1861, in Pratt, *Concerning Mr. Lincoln*, 47.

79. *Illinois Daily State Journal*, February 14, 1860.

80. For "anxiety" and "vexed question," see Lincoln to William H. Seward, February 1, 1861, *CW*, 4:183. The *New York Times* reported (January 22) that "with Mr. Lincoln's sanction," Kellogg favored a national convention and extension of the Missouri Compromise. The next day, the paper speculated that perhaps Kellogg's real mission was to urge Lincoln's "immediate departure for Washington."

81. *CW*, 4:175–76. The remarks were reprinted in the *New-York Daily Tribune* and *Chicago Daily Press & Tribune* the following week.

82. Carl Schurz to Mrs. Schurz, January 29, 1861, Joseph Schafer, ed., *Intimate Letters of Carl Schurz, 1841–1869* (Madison: State Historical Society of Wisconsin, 1928, Publications of the Historical Society, 30), 240.

83. Carl Schurz to Lincoln, January 31, 1861, ALPLC.

84. *Vanity Fair*, January 12, 1861. The "speech" was an imagined response to *New York Herald* editor James Gordon Bennett's frequent urgings that Lincoln offer a public statement on the secession crisis.

85. On January 27, John Nicolay told his fiancée that Lincoln had set February 11 as his departure date. See Nicolay to Therena Bates, January 27, 1861, NPLC.

86. *New York Herald*, January 28, 1861; *New-York Daily Tribune*, January 29, 1861.

87. *Washington Constitution*, January 3, 1861.

88. George Hochfield, ed., *The Great Secession Winter of 1860–61 and Other Essays by Henry Adams* (New York: Sagamore Press, 1958), 14.

89. *Douglass' Monthly*, February 1861, in Philip S. Foner and Yuval Taylor, *Frederick Douglass: Selected Speeches and Writings* (Chicago: Lawrence Hill, 1999), 430.

90. E. B. Washburne to Abraham Lincoln, January 13, 1861, ALPLC.

91. Jefferson Davis, *The Rise and Fall of the Confederate Government*, 2 vols., orig. pub. 1938 (New York: Da Capo, 1990) 1:194–95.

92. *Washington Constitution*, January 9, 1861, January 15, 1861. Hunter would resign from the Senate on March 28. All the resignation dates are documented in *Biographical Directory of the United States Congress, 1774–2005* . . . (Washington, D.C.: U.S. Government Printing Office, 2005), 641 (Benjamin), 1304 (Hunter), 2053 (Toombs).

93. Frank H. Alfriend, *The Life of Jefferson Davis* (Cincinnati and Chicago: Caxton Publishing, 1868), 221, 227. A good description of Davis's departure is given in William C. Davis, *Jefferson Davis: The Man and His Hour—A Biography* (New York: HarperCollins, 1991), 289–96. For Mrs. Davis's role, see Joan E. Cashin, *First Lady of the Confederacy: Varina Davis's Civil War* (Cambridge: Belknap Press/Harvard University Press, 2006), 101.

94. *Congressional Globe*, January 21, 1861.

95. Leroy P. Graf and Ralph W. Haskins, eds., *The Papers of Andrew Johnson*, 15 vols. (Knoxville: University of Tennessee Press, 1976), 4:43, 85.

96. *New York Times*, February 4, 1861.

97. Elihu B. Washburne to Lincoln, January 13, 1861, ALPLC.

98. Villard, *Lincoln on the Eve of '61*, 67.

99. Wilson and Davis, eds., *Herndon's Informants*, 454.

100. Ibid., 463; see also, Wayne C. Temple, *Lincoln the Railsplitter* (La Crosse, Wis.: Willow Press, 1961).

101. Notes by William H. Herndon on his interview with John Hanks, reprinted in Mark E. Neely, Jr., *The Abraham Lincoln Encyclopedia* (New York: McGraw-Hill, 1973), 138.

102. *Illinois Daily State Journal*, January 3, 1861.

103. Villard, *Lincoln on the Eve of '61*, 55.

104. Lincoln to John Hanks, January 28, 1861, CW, 4:181.

105. Whitney, *Life on the Circuit with Lincoln*, 494–95.

106. Ken Kirgan and Mary Reynolds, *Great Western Depot Interpretive Manual* (Springfield, Ill.: privately printed, 1995), 3.

107. Whitney, *Life on the Circuit with Lincoln*, 496.

108. Harold Holzer, ed., *The Lincoln-Douglas Debates: The First Complete Unexpurgated Text*(New York: HarperCollins, 1993), 186. Charleston was also the setting for the most retrograde of Lincoln's debate speeches, in which

he denied that he favored "a perfect equality between the negroes and the white people" (189).

109. Jesse W. Weik, *The Real Lincoln: A Portrait* (Boston: Houghton Mifflin, 1922), 295.

110. Wilson and Davis, eds., *Herndon's Informants*, 136.

111. Ibid., 37.

112. The 1860 Coles County census listed Sarah as part of the family of her son-in-law John J. Hall. At least six people lived in the cabin. See [Rose Talbott], *U.S. 1860 Census Coles Co. Ill.* (Charleston, Ill.: Coles Co. Genealogical Society, 1990), 261.

113. *St. Louis Globe-Democrat*, December 12, 1933, reprinted in Charles H. Coleman, *Abraham Lincoln and Coles County, Illinois* (New Brunswick, N.J.: Scarecrow Press, 1955), 206.

114. John J. Hall quoted in Wilson and Davis, eds., *Herndon's Informants*, 693.

115. Wilson and Davis, eds., *Herndon's Informants*, 136.

116. Ward Hill Lamon, *The Life of Abraham Lincoln, from His Birth to His Inauguration as President* (Boston: James R. Osgood, 1872), 464.

117. Wilson and Davis, eds., *Herndon's Informants*, 136.

118. Ibid., 99.

119. Ibid., 107.

120. Ibid., 594.

121. The relationships probably seem more complicated today than they did in pioneer days, when such commingling was common. Dennis Hanks had married his stepcousin Sarah Elizabeth Johnston, Lincoln's stepsister (Sarah Lincoln's daughter by her first marriage). Their daughter Harriet Ann Hanks lived in the Lincoln home around 1844, when she was eighteen. In 1947, Harriet married Champman. See Wayne C. Temple, *"The Taste Is in My Mouth a Little . . .": Lincoln's Victuals and Potables* Mahomet, Ill.: Mayhaven Publishing, 2004), 31.

122. *Illinois Daily State Journal*, February 1, 1861; Wilson and Davis, eds., *Herndon's Informants*, 137.

123. *Illinois Daily State Journal*, February 1, 1861.

124. Eli Wiley, scrapbook article, February 8, 1888, reprinted in Coleman, *Abraham Lincoln and Coles County*, 208.

125. O. H. Osborne reminiscences, in *Lerna Weekly Eagle*, February 1928, reprinted in Coleman, *Abraham Lincoln and Coles County*, 205.

126. *New York Herald*, February 4, 1861, reprinted in CW, 4:182.

127. Coleman, *Abraham Lincoln and Coles County*, 198–99.

128. James A. Connolly, quoted in Weik, *The Real Lincoln*, 296–97.

129. Wilson and Davis, eds., *Herndon's Informants*, 137.

130. Ibid., 108. Sarah outlived her stepson by four years, dying in 1869.

131. A. H. Chapman to William H. Herndon, October 8, 1865, in ibid., 137.

132. Burlingame, ed., *Lincoln's Journalist*, 22–23.

133. William H. Seward to Lincoln, January 27, 1861. A good discussion of this exchange, and the events leading up to it, can be found in Russell McClintock, *Lincoln and the Decision for War: The Northern Response to Secession* (Chapel Hill: University of North Carolina Press, 2008), 171.

134. Lincoln to William H. Seward, February 1, 1861, *CW*, 4:183.

8. Will You Hazard So Desperate a Step?

1. *New York Herald*, February 4, 1861.

2. Douglas Wilson, *Lincoln's Sword: The Presidency and the Power of Words* (New York: Alfred A. Knopf, 2006), 2006.

3. Robert T. Lincoln to Isaac Markens, June 18, 1918, in Paul M. Angle, ed., *A Portrait of Abraham Lincoln by His Oldest Son* (Chicago: Chicago Historical Society, 1968), 62; John G. Nicolay, "Some Incidents in Lincoln's Journey from Springfield to Washington," in Michael Burlingame, ed., *An Oral History of Abraham Lincoln: John G. Nicolay's Interviews and Essays* (Carbondale: Southern Illinois University Press, 1996), 107. Historian Burlingame found the complete, unpublished essay in the NPLC, though it was generously paraphrased nine decades earlier in Nicolay, *Short Life of Abraham Lincoln* (New York: The Century Co., 1902), 167–68. See also Helen Nicolay, *Lincoln's Secretary: A Biography of John G. Nicolay* (New York: Longmans, Green, 1949), 63; William H. Herndon, "Facts Illustrative of Mr. Lincoln's Patriotism and Statesmanship: A Lecture by William H. Herndon," *Abraham Lincoln Quarterly* 3 (December 1944): 186.

4. For the record, the conjoined brothers were credited with a rather sad public statement of their own endorsing the "union as it is," whatever the flaws in its original conception. See *Vanity Fair*, January 21, 1861.

5. Amy Louise (Sutton) Kellerstrass, "Lincoln and Son Borrow Books," *Lincoln Herald* 69 (Spring 1967): 15; Marion D. Pratt, "Some New Salem Finds in the State Archives," *Illinois History* 12 (February 1959): 112. The original set that Lincoln consulted, now rebound, is in the collection of the Illinois State Archives; a reproduction of the decorative title page can be found in Amy Louise Sutton's original published study in *Illinois Libraries* 48 (June 1966): 450. The *Statesman's Manual* is curiously missing from a comprehensive recent account of books Lincoln read. See Robert Bray, "What Abraham Lincoln Read—An Evaluative and Annotated List," *Journal of the Abraham Lincoln Association* 28 (Summer 2007): 28–81.

6. *New York Herald*, February 4, 1861.

7. John G. Nicolay, Memorandum, December 15, 1860, NPLC.

8. Douglas L. Wilson and Rodney O. Davis, eds., *Herndon's Lincoln*, by Wil-

liam H. Herndon and Jesse Weik, orig. pub. 1889 (Urbana: University of Illinois Press, 2006), 286–87. In this excellent annotated edition, the editors point out that Herndon had failed to mention supplying the Webster text on two previous occasions, acknowledging only that Lincoln admired the speech. See p. 448n.7, and "Facts Illustrative of Mr. Lincoln's Patriotism and Statesmanship," *Abraham Lincoln Quarterly* 3 (December 1944): 194. Quoted here, too, is Herndon to Jesse Weik January 1, 1886, Herndon–Weik Papers, Group 4, Library of Congress.

9. *Speeches of Hayne and Webster in the United States Senate, on the Resolution of Mr. Foot, January, 1830* (Boston: Redding & Co., 1852), 42, 84.

10. *Daily Minnesotan*, December 2, 1860.

11. Francis Newton Thorpe, ed., *The Statesmanship of Andrew Jackson as Told in His Writtings and Speeches* (New York: Tandy-Thomas Company, 1909), 254.

12. Samuel Bannister Harding, ed., *Select Orations Illustrating American Political History* (New York: Macmillan, 1909), 275.

13. *New York Herald*, February 4, 1861.

14. George D. Prentice (editor of the *Louisville Daily Journal*) to Lincoln, quoted in David C. Means and C. Percy Powell, "Abraham Lincoln: Bibliographer; Some Notes on the First Inaugural," typescript in the Manuscript Collection, Library of Congress; Lincoln to Prentice, February 2, 1861, CW, 4:184.

15. John A. Knight to Lincoln, February 12, 1861, ALPLC.

16. *New York Herald*, February 4, 1861.

17. *Illinois Daily State Journal*, February 4, 1861.

18. *New York Herald*, February 4, 1861. The arguments at this convention—over the choice of a new national flag and seal, for example—are richly detailed in Scott Nelson and Carol Sheriff, *A People at War: Civilians and Soldiers in America's Civil War* (New York: Oxford University Press, 2008), 51.

19. Carl Schurz to Lincoln, January 31, 1861, ALPLC.

20. *Daily Illinois State Register*, January 26, 1861.

21. Lincoln to Andrew Curtin, February 4, 1861, CW, 4:184. The emissary was Meadville lawyer Solomon N. Pettis, who may have used his visit to request a favor of his own: Lincoln later appointed him associate justice for Colorado Territory.

22. Lincoln to Edwin D. Morgan, CW, 4:185. The letter—except for the postscript—is in Nicolay's hand.

23. *New-York Daily Tribune*, February 5, 1861; *Lincoln Day by Day*, 3:9.

24. Remarks to a Pennsylvania delegation, January 24, 1861, CW, 4:179–81.

25. Don C. Seitz, *Horace Greeley: Founder of the New York Tribune* (Indianapolis: Bobbs-Merrill, 1926), 186.

26. Thurlow Weed to David Davis, January 28, 1861; David Davis to Lincoln, February 2, 1861, ALPLC.

27. Lincoln to Thurlow Weed, February 4, 1861, CW, 4:185–86.

28. The balloting for the Republican nod came down to Greeley and Evarts, with one Albany newspaper warning that Greeley was "too emotional for Statesmanship." See Evening Standard, February 5, 1861. When Weed realized his candidate would not prevail, he ordered the Evarts men to switch to Harris to prevent Greeley's election. For the official vote for Harris (22–9 against Democrat Horatio Seymour), see Journal of the Senate of the State of New York: At Their Eighty-fourth Session . . . January 1861 (Albany: Charles Van Benthuysen, Printer to the Legislature, 1861), 137.

29. Lincoln Day by Day, 3:9; Lloyd A. Dunlap, "President Lincoln and Editor Greeley," Abraham Lincoln Quarterly 5 (June 1948): 96. Dunlap erroneously gives the date of the visit as February 4.

30. Recollection by Thomas Hicks in Allen Thorndike Rice, ed., Reminiscences of Lincoln by Distinguished Men of His Time (New York: North American Publishing Co., 1886), 593.

31. Harold G. and Oswald Garrison Villard, eds., Lincoln on the Eve of '61: A Journalist's Story by Henry Villard (New York: Alfred A. Knopf, 1941), 62–63.

32. Horace Greeley, Recollections of a Busy Life: Including Reminiscences of American Politics and Politicians . . .(New York: J. B. Ford & Co., 1858), 404. Greeley believed that "Disunion, should it befall, may be a calamity but complicity in Slavery extension is a guilt, which the Republicans must in no case incur." See Greeley, Recollections of a Busy Life, 397.

33. Villard, Lincoln on the Eve of '61, 62–63.

34. Horace Greeley to Lincoln, February 6, 1861, ALPLC. Lincoln obliged by naming one of Greeley's specific choices, Rufus D. Andrews, surveyor of the Port of New York. Andrews repaid Lincoln by plotting against his renomination in 1864, prompting the president to remove him.

35. Joshua F. Speed, Reminiscences of Abraham Lincoln and Notes of a Visit to California. Two Lectures (Louisville: John P. Morton, 1884), 25. I am indebted to historian Douglas L. Wilson for reminding me of this Lincolnian talent at a discussion at the New-York Historical Society, November 8, 2007.

36. Wilson and Davis, eds., Herndon's Lincoln, 287.

37. James E. Harvey to Lincoln, November 8, 1860, ALPLC.

38. DeLorma Brooks to Lincoln, January 25, 1861, ALPLC.

39. A. Penfield to Lincoln, February 15, 1861, ALPLC.

40. Washington's Farewell Address, September 17, 1796, in William Trufant Foster, Washington's Farewell Address to the People of the United States and Webster's First Bunker Hill Oration (Boston, Houghton Mifflin, 1909), 27.

41. Julius Bing to Lincoln, March 3, 1861, ALPLC.

42. E. P. Oliphant to Lincoln, December 10, 1860, ALPLC.

43. C. S. Williams, *Williams' Springfield Directory: City Guide and Business Mirror for 1860–61* (Springfield, Ill: Johnson, Bradford, 1860), 144. Yates & Smith was one of fifty-four Springfield grocers listed in that year's town directory (see pp. 150–51).

44. John Townsend, *The South Alone, Should Govern the South. And African Slavery Should Be Controlled by Those Only, Who Are Friendly to It.* (Charleston: 1860 Association and Evans & Cogswell, 1860), quoted in Richard B. Harwell, "Propaganda for Secession: The 1860 Association and the Secession Convention of 1860," *Lincoln Herald* 54 (Winter 1952): 32.

45. Harry E. Pratt, *Springfield's Public Square in Lincoln's Day, 1861 and 1941* (Springfield: Williamson Printing. and Publishing Co., 1941), [5–6]. Perhaps Smith owed Lincoln a favor: although his famous brother-in-law's hand was nowhere evident, Illinois's Republican-controlled State Senate had only two years earlier awarded C. M. Smith the lucrative contract to install new carpeting in its chamber. See Sunderine (Wilson) Temple and Wayne C. Temple, *Abraham Lincoln and Illinois' Fifth Capitol*, rev. ed. (Mahomet, Ill.: Mayhaven Publishing, 2006), 236. The original, surviving desk is now on exhibit on the third floor of the restored Tinsley Building, now known as the Lincoln-Herndon Law Office.

46. Wilson and Davis, eds., *Herndon's Lincoln*, 287.

47. Herndon to Weik, January 1, 1886, Herndon Papers, Library of Congress.

48. Burlingame, ed., *An Oral History of Abraham Lincoln*, 107–8; Nicolay, *A Short Life of Lincoln*, 168.

49. Either a jotting, or an opening sentence clipped from an early draft, rewritten, but retained, this is likely the first surviving draft of Lincoln's introductory inaugural paragraph. The original is in ALPLC.

50. All these and subsequent quotes are from the first printed draft of the inaugural address, ALPLC.

51. Wilson, *Lincoln's Sword*, 50.

52. Ben: Perley Poore, in Rice, ed., *Reminiscences of Lincoln by Distinguished Men of His Time*, 224.

53. Ibid.

54. John G. Nicolay, "Some Incidents in Lincoln's Journey from Springfield to Washington," in Burlingame, ed., *An Oral History of Abraham Lincoln*, 108.

55. David C. Mearns (Chief, Manuscript Division, Library of Congress) to Arthur Swann (Vice President, Parke-Bernet Galleries), October 31, 1951, Manuscript Collection, Library of Congress.

56. *New York Herald*, February 9, 1861.

57. W. W. Abbot, Dorothy Twohig, and Philander D. Chase, eds., *The Papers of George Washington*, Presidential Series, 2 vols. (Charlottesville: University Press of Virginia, 1987), 2:60. A contemporary described the precedent-setting "public effusions of gratitude" as the "*voluntary* honours of a free and

enlightened people." See John P. Kaminski and Jill Adair McCaughan, *A Great and Good Man: George Washington in the Eyes of His Contemporaries* (Madison, Wis.: Madison House, 1989), 24.

58. Mason L. Weems, *The Life of George Washington*, orig. pub. 1809, 9th ed., reprint (Cambridge: Belknap Press, 1962), 132–33.

59. Ted Widmer, *Martin Van Buren* (New York: Times Books, 2005), 94.

60. Dorothy Burne Goebel, *William Henry Harrison: A Political Biography* (Indianapolis: Indiana Library and Historical Department, 1926), 369–70. Among the groups of office-seekers Harrison "overlooked" were conservative Democrats and anti-Masons, even though the later group had handed the Whig nomination to Harrison over Henry Clay.

61. Oliver Perry Chitwood, *John Tyler: Champion of the Old South* (New York: D. Appleton-Century Co., 1939), 435.

62. Lincoln aspired to be commissioner of the Land Office, but was instead offered the post of governor of Oregon Territory, which he declined.

63. K. Jack Bauer, *Zachary Taylor: Soldier, Planter, Statesman of the Old Southwest* (Baton Rouge: Louisiana State University Press, 1985), 249–53.

64. Roy Franklin Nichols, *Franklin Pierce: Young Hickory of the Granite Hills* (Philadelphia: University of Pennsylvania Press, 1931), 220–21, 232–33.

65. Philip Shriver Klein, *President James Buchanan: A Biography* (University Park: Pennsylvania State University Press, 1962), 270–71.

66. *New York Times*, May 2, 1857.

67. Lincoln to Elihu Washburne, February 15, 1861, CW, 4:217. Lincoln wrote the letter from Cleveland.

68. A. S. Collyer, *Life and Times of Andrew Jackson: Soldier, Statesman, President*, 2 vols. (Nashville: Marshall & Bruce, 1904), 598–99. The mileage comparison—calculated as the crow flies—was gleaned from www.maps.google.com.

69. [Peekskill, New York] *Highland Democrat*, February 23, 1861.

70. Niven, *Martin Van Buren*, 610.

71. *New York World*, January 10, 1861.

72. *New York World*, January 22, 1861.

73. Peter A. Wallner, *Franklin Pierce: Martyr for the Union* (Concord, N.H.: Plaidswede Publishing, 2007), 328–30, 333–34.

74. Chitwood, *John Tyler*, 436.

75. Ibid., 437, 440.

76. Edward P. Crapol, *John Tyler: The Accidental President* (Chapel Hill: University of North Carolina Press, 2006), 262.

77. Wallner, *Franklin Pierce*, 335.

78. *New York World*, February 8, 1861.

79. Thurlow Weed to Lincoln, November 9, 1860, ALPLC. Herndon believed it was Seward who engineered Wood's appointment. See Wilson and Davis, eds., *Herndon's Lincoln*, 290.

80. Thurlow Weed to Lincoln, January 28, 1861, ALPLC; Wilson and Davis, eds., *Herndon's Lincoln*, 290. One of the problems associated with Wood is that he has often been confused with one William P. Wood, who figured in the Lincoln assassination story, and wrote several reminiscences for the Washington *Sunday Gazette* in 1867.

81. Henry Villard, *Memoirs of Henry Villard: Journalist and Financier, 1835–1900*, 2 vols. (Boston: Houghton Mifflin, 1904), 1:148.

82. *Charleston Mercury*, February 24, 1861.

83. David Rankin Barbee to Mrs. J. G. Randall, April 27, 1951, James G. Randall Papers, Box 71, Library of Congress.

84. After endearing himself to Mary Lincoln, Wood became interim superintendent of public buildings at the start of the Lincoln administration. A trip with Mrs. Lincoln to New York to choose furnishings for the White House triggered ugly rumors about their relationship and, according to Speaker of the House Schuyler Colfax, the president and his wife had a fight about it and did not speak for days. Although Lincoln submitted his name to the Senate for confirmation, the nomination bogged down over another scandal, and Wood was replaced. Mary later called him "a very bad man." See Michael Burlingame, *The Inner World of Abraham Lincoln* (Urbana: University of Illinois Press, 1994), 292.

85. *New York Times*, February 6, 1861, February 18, 1861.

86. *Saturday Evening Post*, February 16, 1861.

87. *Buffalo Express*, reprinted in the *New York World*, February 12, 1861.

88. There are no scholarly accounts of the journey, but the liveliest popular book is still Victor Searcher, *Lincoln's Journey to Greatness: A Factual Account of the Twelve-Day Inaugural Trip* (Philadelphia: John C. Winston, 1961). For Wood's arrangements, see 8–9.

89. Thomas Reynolds to Lincoln, January 29, 1861 with endorsement, ALPLC.

90. Lincoln had recently urged young Latham to try again, after failing his first exams, to test for entrance to Harvard. His famous letter to Latham ("you *can* not fail, if you resolutely determine, that you *will* not"), July 22, 1860, is in *CW*, 4:87. Latham eventually matriculated instead at Yale. For the story, see Harold Holzer, ed., *"In the end you are sure to succeed": Lincoln on Perseverance* (New York: Gilder Lehrman Institute of American History, 2001).

91. George W. Hazzard to Lincoln, [January 1861], ALPLC.

92. Lincoln to David Hunter, January 26, 1861, *Presidential and other American Manuscripts from the Dr. Robert Small Trust*, Sotheby's April 3, 2008, 125.

93. E. V. Sumner to John G. Nicolay, January 20, 1861, NPLC; *New York World*, January 16, 1861.

94. Charles A. Ingraham, *Elmer E. Ellsworth and the Zouaves of '61* (Chicago: University of Chicago Press, 1925), 116. Despite his fame as a Zouave

drillmaster—he had even earned praise from President Buchanan (p. 97)—Ellsworth was already considered virtually a member of Lincoln's staff. John R. Turner Ettlinger, "A Young Hero—Elmer Ellsworth, 1837–1861," *Books at Brown* 19 (May 1963), 42–44. "I believe I have Mr. Lincoln's confidence and respect," Ellsworth wrote on January 7.

95. CW, 4:277. Johnson was assigned to the White House as a "fireman" at a salary of $600 per year. He had been with Lincoln since the spring of 1860. Johnson later accompanied the president on another of his famous train journeys—to Gettysburg in 1863—and when Lincoln came down with smallpox on the way home, faithfully attended him, caught the disease himself, and died. See John E. Washington, *They Knew Lincoln* (New York: E. P. Dutton, 1942), 107, and Gabor Boritt, *The Gettysburg Gospel: The Lincoln Speech That Nobody Knows* (New York: Simon & Schuster, 2006), 170.

96. *To the Committee of Arrangements for the RECEPTION OF THE PRESIDENT ELECT*, handbill, Box 2, NPLC.

97. Correspondent Joseph Howard, Jr., reported receiving this pass in the *New York Times*, February 18, 1861.

98. Historians Herman Hattaway and Richard E. Beringer, who labeled Davis "stiffly formal," believed he "lacked the passion and eloquence that seems necessary in revolutionary leaders." But the same description would fit an earlier revolutionary leader—George Washington—and image makers, particularly print publishers, were not reluctant to make the comparison. See Hattaway and Beringer, *Jefferson Davis: Confederate President* (Lawrence: University Press of Kansas, 2002), 21; Harold Holzer, Gabor S. Boritt, and Mark E. Neely, Jr., *The Confederate Image*.

99. Belle Becker Sideman and Lillian Friedman, eds., *Europe Looks at the Civil War* (New York: Orion, 1960), 33.

100. *Washington Constitution*, December 29, 1860.

101. In a pro-Union political pamphlet if the time, a former Maryland congressman reminded border state citizens that "Mr. Lincoln was both nominated and elected by what may be called the moderate, conservative division of the Republican party . . . and that he will enter into office not only with the determination, but with the desire to render his administration one of impartial justice to the South." See John P. Kennedy, *The Border States: Their Power and Duty in the Present Disordered Condition of the Country* (Philadelphia: J. B. Lippincott, 1861), 46.

102. Salmon P. Chase to Lincoln, January 28, 1861, ALPLC.

103. Michael J. Dubin, *United States Presidential Elections, 1788–1860* (Jefferson, N.C.: McFarland, 2002), 165, 171, 176, 178, 181. For the New York City vote, see *The Tribune Almanac for the Years 1838 to 1864, Inclusive* . . . (New York: New York Tribune, 1864), 41.

104. Lincoln to Charles S. Olden, governor of New Jersey, February 6, 1861; to John A. Andrew, governor of Massachusetts, February 7, 1861; to William Dennison, governor of Ohio, February 7, 1861; to John G. Lowe and others (Dayton), February 7, 1861, to Pennsylvania state senator Darwin A. Finney and others, February 8, 1861; to Cleveland city councilman George B. Senter and others, February 8, 1861, *CW*, 4:184–88.

105. Endorsement on verso of John G. Lowe and others to Lincoln, ALPLC, reprinted in *CW*, 4:187.

106. Quoted in Helen Nicolay, *Lincoln's Secretary: A Biography of John G. Nicolay* (New York: Longmans, Green, 1949), 60.

107. *Janesville* [Wisconsin] *Gazette and Free Press,* February 15, 1861.

108. Mrs. James C. Conkling to Clinton L. Conkling, February 12, 1861, in Harry E. Pratt, *Concerning Mr. Lincoln* (Springfield, Ill: Abraham Lincoln Association, 1944), 48.

109. *New York Herald,* February 16, 1861.

110. [St. Louis] *Daily Missouri Democrat,* February 7, 1861.

111. Henry B. Rankin, *Intimate Character Sketches of Abraham Lincoln* (Philadelphia: J. B. Lippincott, 1924), 255–56. Rankin's recollections have been called into question by many observers, who note that his name never appeared in the Springfield census during the time of Lincoln's residence— nullifying his alleged "intimate" observations of him. But as many of his uncanny reports show, either his powers of recollection and skill at research were extraordinary, or his doubters have been too hard on him.

112. Theodore Calvin Pease, ed., *The Diary of Orville Hickman Browning,* 2 vols. (Springfield: Illinois State Historical Library, 1925), 1:452–53.

113. Edward Bates to John G. Nicolay, February 9, 1861, ALPLC.

114. Ward Hill Lamon, *Recollections of Abraham Lincoln, 1847–1865,* ed. Dorothy Lamon (Chicago: A. C. McClurg, 1895), 28–29.

115. Villard, *Lincoln on the Eve of '61,* 64, 67.

116. Burlingame, ed., *Lincoln's Journalist,* 24.

9. With a Task Before Me

1. Harry E. Pratt, *The Personal Finances of Abraham Lincoln* (Springfield, Ill.: Abraham Lincoln Association, 1943), 123, 175.

2. Mrs. Benjamin Edwards, quoted in the *St. Louis Globe-Democrat,* February 21, 1909, reprinted in Walter B. Stevens, *A Reporter's Lincoln,* ed. Michael Burlingame (Lincoln: University of Nebraska Press, 1998), 160.

3. Pratt, *Personal Finances of Abraham Lincoln,* 123, 175.

4. Allen Thorndike Rice, ed., *Reminiscences of Lincoln by Distinguished Men of His Time* (New York: North American Publishing, 1886), 587.

5. J. L. Hill was one of thirty insurance brokers in Springfield at the time, in-

cluding agents for Aetna, Springfield Fire Insurance Co., and Hartford Fire Insurance Company. See C. S. Williams, *Williams' Springfield Directory: City Guide and Business Mirror for 1860–61* (Springfield, Ill: Johnson, Bradford, 1860), 22–23, 91. A copy of the policy itself is in ALPLM. See also, Wayne C. Temple, *By Square and Compass: Saga of the Lincoln Home*, orig. pub. 1984 (Mahomet, Ill.: Mayhaven Publishing, 2002), 139–53.

6. Theodore Tilton to Elizabeth Tilton, January 5, 1865, in Temple, *By Square and Compass*, 145.

7. *Daily Illinois State Journal*, January 30, 1861, quoted in Thomas J. Dyba and George L. Painter, *Seventeen Years at Eighth and Jackson: The Lincoln Family in Their Springfield Home* (Lisle, Ill.: Illinois Benedictine College, 1985), 65.

8. *CW*, 4:189. The receipt is dated February 9, 1861.

9. Receipt countersigned by Robert Irwin, *CW*, 4:188–89.

10. Jesse W. Weik, *The Real Lincoln: A Portrait* (Boston: Houghton Mifflin, 1922), 314.

11. See Chenery House invoice, April 28, 1859, Thomas L. Harris Papers (SC 655), ALPLM. James N. Chenery had to sue the Harris estate to recover a bill of $48.35 for five weeks and five days of lodging, laundry, and three bottles of ale—from which bill the two-dollar-per-day lodging price has been extrapolated. Conceivably, prices had increased due to the demand for rooms that surely followed Lincoln's election and the resulting onslaught of office-seekers.

12. *Daily Illinois State Journal*, July 13, 1903, reprinted in Wayne C. Temple, "Mariah (Bartlett) Vance[,] Daytime Servant to the Lincolns, Part 3," *For the People: A Newsletter of the Abraham Lincoln Association* 7 (Summer 2005): 4–5. Few of Ms. Vance's recollections have been universally accepted. Allegedly related orally to a later employer, transcribed, later imbued with "Negro" dialect, then altered yet again to deflect criticism that they were politically incorrect, they ignited a firestorm of criticism when they were edited and republished in 1995. See Lloyd Ostendorf and Walter Oleksy, *Lincoln's Unknown Private Life: An Oral History by His Black Housekeeper Mariah Vance, 1850–60* (Mamaroneck, N.Y.: Hastings House, 1995).

13. Quoted in Ostendorf and Oleksy, *Lincoln's Unknown Private Life*, 276.

14. It is impossible to know for certain whether the tattered, family-owned Fido picture in the Lincoln family's own collection was taken before the Lincolns left Springfield, or after the assassination, when portraits of the dog—along with images of everything else Lincoln knew and touched— were widely published and sold to an eager public. Lincoln photo historian Dorothy Meserve Kunhardt believed that Springfield photographer F. W. Ingmire took the dog's picture in 1861 specifically so the Lincoln boys could

take it to Washington as a keepsake. See Mark E. Neely, Jr., and Harold Holzer, *The Lincoln Family Album*, orig. pub. 1990, rev. ed. (Carbondale: Southern Illinois University Press, 2006), 97; Dorothy Meserve Kunhardt, "Lincoln's Lost Dog: It Turns Out He Was a Frisky Mongrel Who Came to a Tragic End," *Life* (February 15, 1954): 83–85.

15. Charles Hamilton and Lloyd Ostendorf, *Lincoln in Photographs: An Album of Every Known Pose*, orig. pub. 1963, rev. ed. (Dayton: Morningside Books, 1985), 70–71; Wayne C. Temple, "C. S. German: Photographer to President-elect Lincoln," *Illinois Heritage* 9 (July–August 2006), 9–13.

16. Theodore Calvin Pease, ed., *The Diary of Orville Hickman Browning*, 2 vols. (Springfield: Illinois State Historical Library, 1925), 1:453. Indiana governor Oliver P. Morton had recently written to Lincoln to explain why his state had chosen to send delegates to the Peace Convention: "It was not that I expected any positive good to come of it, but to prevent positive evil." Lincoln evidently adopted the phrase for himself. See Morton to Lincoln, January 29, 1861, ALPLC.

17. Orville H. Browning to Lincoln (four letters), February 1861. The patronage bombardment that day culminated in a plea from an unemployed Illinois teacher who demanded a postmastership "in consequence of my Vote at the Nov Election." See D. D. Mattice to Lincoln, February 9, 1861, ALPLC.

18. *New York Herald*, February 16, 1861.

19. Michael Burlingame, ed., *John Hay's Anonymous Writings for the Press, 1860–1864* (Carbondale: Southern Illinois University Press, 1998), 24; Schurz to his wife, February 10, 1861, in Frederic Bancroft, ed., *Speeches, Correspondence and Political Papers of Carl Schurz*, 2 vols. (New York: G. P. Putnam's Sons, 1913), 1:179; Schurz quoted in German in Robert Gray Gunderson, *Old Gentlemen's Convention: The Washington Peace Conference of 1861* (Westport, Conn.: Greenwood Press, 1961), 21.

20. Daniel W. Stowell, editor of the comprehensive Lincoln Legal Papers Project, provided the author with the authoritative date of June 14 as the last known day on which Lincoln actively practiced law.

21. Rankin further claimed that Lincoln also asked him to gather a pile of magazines on the floor—the *Southern Literary Messenger*—have them bound, and "keep them until his return." See Henry B. Rankin, *Intimate Character Sketches of Abraham Lincoln* (Philadelphia: J. B. Lippincott, 1924), 258–59; see also Weik, *The Real Lincoln*, 298. Rankin, who said he adjourned to a nearby jewelry store while the partners enjoyed their last conference, actually claimed Lincoln made not one but two visits to the law office that day, the first to pack his books, the second to chat further with Herndon. (Mary Lincoln later claimed her husband not only left most of his books behind, but that Herndon stole them!) For a brief history of

the *Southern Literary Messenger*, see entry by John A. Lent and Kohava Simhi in Richard N. Current, ed., *Encyclopedia of the Confederacy*, 4 vols. (New York: Simon & Schuster, 1993), 3:986.

22. Douglas L. Wilson and Rodney O. Davis, eds., *Herndon's Lincoln* (Urbana: University of Illinois Press, 2006), 289, 290n. Herndon testified: "He asked me if I desired an appointment at his hands, and, if so, what I wanted. I answered that I had no desire for a Federal office," but hoped Lincoln would use his influence with Illinois governor Yates to keep his job as state banking commissioner. According to Herndon, Lincoln complied.

23. Jesse Weik—who later polished Herndon's reminiscences for *Herndon's Lincoln*—reprinted Herndon's original, slightly different account of this encounter in *The Real Lincoln*, 298–99.

24. Wilson and Davis, eds., *Herndon's Lincoln*, 289–90.

25. Harold G. Villard and Oswald Garrison Villard, *Lincoln on the Eve of '61: A Journalist's Story by Henry Villard* (New York: Alfred A. Knopf, 1941), 66–67.

26. T. A. Marshall to Lincoln, February 10, 1861. The letter was written in Springfield, so Lincoln surely saw it before he left town. Marshall remained unrewarded until the outbreak of war, when he became a colonel in the First Illinois Cavalry. Lincoln finally gave him a job—as postmaster in Vicksburg, Mississippi—in 1864.

27. *Harper's Weekly*, February 16, 1861.

28. Weik, *The Real Lincoln*, 300, 307.

29. The station was upgraded in 1857, when freight and passenger areas were separated, gas lighting installed, and railroad offices placed in an upstairs mezzanine. See *Illinois Daily State Journal*, April 28, 1857. The article was reprinted in James T. Hickey, "History of Great Western Railroad Depot," in Ken Kirgan and Mary Reynolds, *Great Western Depot Interpretive Manual* (Springfield, Ill.: privately printed, 1995); Wayne C. Temple, "Lincoln as Seen by T. D. Jones," *Illinois Libraries* 58 (June 1976): 450, 456.

30. *New York Times*, February 12, 1861; Kirgan and Reynolds, *Great Western Depot Interpretive Manual*, 2.

31. John G. Nicolay and John Hay, *Abraham Lincoln: A History*, 10 vols. (New York: The Century Co. 1890), 3:290. On the other hand, Lincoln confessed to his first law partner—and cousin-in-law—John T. Stuart, that while he always hoped to return to his hometown, "Mary does not expect ever to go back there, and don't want to go." See John T. Stuart to John G. Nicolay, July 4, 1875, NPLC.

32. From Lincoln's speech at Lafayette, Indiana, February 11, 1861, *CW*, 4:192.

33. William B. Thompson, quoted in Stevens, *A Reporter's Lincoln*, 100.

34. John Hay, report filed February 11, 1861, in Michael Burlingame, ed., *Lin-*

coln's Journalist: John Hay's Anonymous Writings for the Press, 1860–1864 (Carbondale: Southern Illinois University Press, 1998), 24.

35. *New York Herald*, February 12, 1861.

36. Years later, Robert T. Lincoln confused matters by insisting that "my father and his entire family left Springfield together." But on this count, Lincoln's eldest son was almost certainly in error. See RTL to Horace White, January 19, 1911, Herndon–Weik Collection, Library of Congress. I am grateful to Jason Emerson for bringing this letter to my attention.

37. Burlingame, ed., *Lincoln's Journalist*, 24.

38. *Wabash Formerly the Great Western Railroad. Time Card for a Special Train, Monday, Feb. 11, 1861. with His Excellency Abraham Lincoln, President Elect*, broadside, ALPLM.

39. Adin Baber and Mary E. Lobb, "How a Railroader Saw Lincoln Leave Illinois in 1861," *Lincoln Herald* 68 (Fall 1966): 122.

40. Norman B. Judd to his wife, February 14, 1861, ALPLM.

41. Wilson and Davis, eds., *Herndon's Lincoln*, 231.

42. Burlingame, ed., *Lincoln's Journalist*, 24, 353n. The author is also indebted to Robert Hoffman of Rochester, New York, and photographica detective extraordinaire Joseph Buberger of North Haven, Connecticut, who supplied him with a photocopy of John Hay's original scrapbook of his newspaper reports during the inaugural journey, from which much of this information was gleaned.

43. *CW*, 4:190–91. Lincoln expert Wayne C. Temple believes the speech may have been recorded at the depot by Robert Roberts Hitt, the Republican "phonographic reporter" at the 1858 Lincoln-Douglas debates, and since 1859 the official shorthand recorder for the Illinois State Senate. See Temple, *Abraham Lincoln: From Skeptic to Prophet* (Mahomet, Ill.: Mayhaven Publishing, 1995), 120–21.

44. Weik, *The Real Lincoln*, 311.

45. According to Villard, he "prevailed on Mr. Lincoln, immediately after starting, to write it out . . . on a 'pad.' " See Henry Villard, *Memoirs of Henry Villard*, 2 vols. (Boston: Houghton Mifflin, 1904), 1:149. Villard also claimed he had possession of the text, but lost it during the Civil War. But in fact the text survived in the Nicolay Papers. Villard's version of the story was passed on to his son—and biographer: see Mrs. O. S. Kimberly [secretary to Oswald Garrison Villard] to David C. Mearns, February 1, 1949, David C. Mearns Papers, Box 82, Manuscript Division, Library of Congress.

46. See Ronald C. White, *The Eloquent President: A Portrait of Lincoln Through His Words* (New York: Random House, 2005), 20.

47. *CW*, 4:190.

48. From Lincoln's address to the Springfield Young Men's Lyceum, January 27, 1838, *CW*, 1:115.

49. Weik, *The Real Lincoln*, 314.

50. *New York Herald*, February 12, 1861.

51. Burlingame, ed., *Lincoln's Journalist*, 24; James C. Conkling to Clinton L. Conkling, February 12, 1861, in Harry E. Pratt, *Concerning Mr. Lincoln* (Springfield: Abraham Lincoln Association, 1944), 50.

52. Henry C. Whitney, *Life on the Circuit with Lincoln* (Boston: Estes & Lauriat, 1892), 45–46.

53. Robert H. Browne, *Abraham Lincoln and the Men of His Time* (Cincinnati: Jennings & Pye, 1901), 408–9.

54. For iconographic examples, see Harold Holzer, *Washington and Lincoln Portrayed: National Icons in Popular Prints* (Jefferson, N.C.: McFarland, 1993), esp. 173–236.

55. Francis Springer to Lincoln, February 11, 1861, ALPLC; Millard Fillmore to S. Chamberlain, March 3, 1862, *Presidential and Other American Manuscripts from the Dr. Robert Small Trust*, Sotheby's catalogue, April 3, 2008, 118–19.

56. *Daily Illinois State Register*, February 12, 1861.

57. John G. Nicolay to Therena Bates, February 11, 1861, NPLC.

58. [Washington] *National Intelligencer*, February 14, 1861.

59. Thomas Ross, quoted in John W. Starr, Jr., *Lincoln and the Railroads: A Biographical Study* (New York: Dodd, Mead, 1927), 180.

60. *New York Herald* February 12, 1861; Burlingame, ed., *Lincoln's Journalist*, 25.

61. Burlingame, ed., *Lincoln's Journalist*, 25, and *CW* 4:191.

62. *CW*, 4:191–92; Burlingame, ed., *Lincoln's Journalist*, 25; *CW*, 1:367

63. *CW*, 4:192; *Indianapolis Daily Sentinel*, February 12, 1861.

64. [Indianapolis] *Indiana Daily Journal*, February 12, 1861.

65. *CW*, 4:193–94.

66. [Indianapolis] *Indiana Daily Journal*, February 11, February 12, 1861; Burlingame, ed., *Lincoln's Journalist*, 25.

67. Villard, *Lincoln on the Eve of '61*, 78.

68. Browning, *Diary*, 1:454.

69. Weik, *The Real Lincoln*, 313.

70. Burlingame, ed., *Lincoln's Journalist*, 25; *CW* 4:195.

71. *CW*, 4:195–96.

72. See Winfred A. Harrison, "Lincoln and Indiana Republicans, 1861–1864," *Indiana Magazine of History* 33 (September 1937): 279.

73. *New York Times*, February 13, 1861.

74. [Indianapolis] *Indiana State Guard*, February 16, 1861.

75. *New York Herald*, February 13, 1861; *Cleveland Plain Dealer*, February 12, 1861, *Indiana Daily Journal*, February 16, 1861. The *Indianapolis Star*, Febru-

ary 13, 1861, reported an "unprecedented . . . rush on our newsboys" for copies of the issue reporting on Lincoln's visit.

76. [Indianapolis] *Indiana Daily Journal*, February 13, 1861; Perry Hall was one of the citizens who never forgot that he enjoyed "a fair view of him while Gov. Morton addressed him & he replied," and got to "shake him by the hand" at the Bates House. See Diary of Perry Hill for February 11, 1861, Indiana Historical Society.

77. Burlingame, ed., *Lincoln's Journalist*, 26. Villard, *Lincoln on the Eve of '61*, 78.

78. Robert T. Lincoln to Judd Stewart, January 8, 1920, Henry Huntington Library, San Marino, Cal. I am grateful to Jason Emerson for bringing this letter to my attention. Eyewitnesses have variously placed this incident in both Cleveland and Harrisburg, though Nicolay and Robert convincingly agreed on Indianapolis. For Cleveland, see Ben: Perley Poore, *Perley's Reminiscences of Sixty Years in the National Metropolis*, 2 vols. (Philadelphia: Hubbard Bros., 1886), 2:65–66; for Harrisburg, see James T. Sterling, "How Lincoln 'Lost' His Inaugural Address," *Lincoln Herald* 45 (February 1943): 23–25.

79. *Rochester Union*, quoted in *New York Illustrated News*, March 9, 1861.

80. John G. Nicolay, "Some Incidents in Lincoln's Journey from Springfield to Washington," in Michael Burlingame, ed., *An Oral History of Abraham Lincoln: John G. Nicolay's Interviews and Essays* (Carbondale: Southern Illinois University Press, 1996), 107; Poore, *Reminiscences*, 2:65–66; Lamon quoted in Alexander K. McClure, *"Abe" Lincoln's Yarns and Stories: A Complete Collection of the Funny and Witty Anecdotes That Made Lincoln Famous as America's Greatest Story Teller* (Philadelphia: International Publishing Co., 1891), 111–12. Like many others, McClure (and Lamon) situated this near-disaster in Harrisburg.

81. *Boston Post*, February 23, 1861.

82. CW, 4:196; Villard, *Lincoln on the Eve of '61*, 78; John G. Nicolay to Therena Bates, February 11, 1861, NPLC.

83. Browning, *Diary*, 1:455–56; written record of a conversation with Browning at the Leland Hotel, Springfield, June 17, 1875, in the John Hay Collection, John Hay Library, Brown University. This statement, recorded fourteen years after the events of February 1861, differs only slightly with the version Browning recorded in his diary a few days after they occurred.

84. Burlingame, ed., *Lincoln's Journalist*, 29; Villard, *Lincoln on the Eve of '61*, 79.

85. Ward Hill Lamon, *Recollections of Abraham Lincoln, 1847–1865*, ed. Dorothy Lamon (Chicago: A. C. McClurg, 1895), 33.

86. [Indianapolis] *Indiana Daily Journal*, February 13, 1861; *New York Herald*, February 13, 1861.

87. [Indianapolis] *Indiana Daily Journal*, February 13, 1861.

88. Burlingame, ed., *Lincoln's Journalist*, 29.

89. *New York Herald*, February 13, 1861.

90. CW, 4:197.

91. *Louisville Journal*, February 16, 1861.

92. CW, 4:193.

93. Charles Russell Lowell to John M. Forbes, February 11, 1861, in Edward W. Emerson, *The Life and Letters of Charles Russell Lowell, Captain Sixth United States Cavalry* . . . (Boston: Houghton Mifflin, 1907), 193.

94. CW, 4:200–201.

95. *New York Herald*, February 13, 1861, February 14, 1861; Burlingame, ed., *Lincoln's Journalist*, 27.

96. *New York Herald*, February 13, 1861.

97. CW, 4:197–99. Lincoln's handwritten three-page draft of part of this speech is in ALPLC.

98. *Der Deutsche Republikan* [Cincinnati], February 12, 1861, clipping in the Lincoln Museum, Fort Wayne, Indiana.

99. CW, 4:202.

100. Burlingame, ed., *Lincoln's Journalist*, 29.

101. *New York Times*, February 18, 1861.

102. Villard, *Lincoln on the Eve of '61*, 80.

103. *Boston Transcript*, February 13, 1861; Burlingame, ed., *Lincoln's Journalist*, 30. The original bed, chest of drawers, and table Lincoln used at the Burnett House are now in the Abraham Lincoln Museum, Lincoln Memorial University, Harrogate, Tennessee.

104. *New York Times*, February 18, 1861.

105. Remarks at London, Ohio, February 13, 1861, CW, 4:204.

106. Burlingame, ed., *Lincoln's Journalist*. 80–82.

107. *Frank Leslie's Illustrated Newspaper*, March 2, 1861.

108. *Lincoln Day by Day*, 3:13.

109. *Ohio State Journal*, February 14, 1861, quoted in William T. Coggeshall, *Lincoln Memorial: The Journeys of Mr. Lincoln, from Springfield to Washington, 1861, as President-Elect* . . . (Columbus: Ohio State Journal, 1865), 48.

110. *Ohio State Journal*, quoted in Robert S. Harper, *During Two Journeys* (Columbus: Ohio Lincoln Sesquicentennial Commission, 1959), 3.

111. CW, 4:204–5.

112. *New York Herald*, February 15, 1861.

113. CW, 4:205–6.

114. Coggeshall, *The Journeys of Mr. Lincoln*, 43–45; Chase to AL, March 7, 1861, original in ALPLM.

115. John G. Nicolay to Therena Bates, February 15, 1861, Nicolay Papers,

NPLC; Nicolay, "Some Incidents in Lincoln's Journey from Springfield to Washington," manuscript, NPLC.

116. *New York Herald*, February 18, 1861; William Cooper, Jr., *Jefferson Davis* (New York: Alfred A. Knopf, 2000), 328.

117. Herman Hattaway and Richard E. Beringer, *Jefferson Davis, Confederate President* (Lawrence: University Press of Kansas, 2002), 20–21; [Washington] *National Intelligencer*, February 14, 1861.

118. Robert Gray Gunderson, *Old Gentlemen's Convention: The Washington Peace Conference of 1861* (Westport, Conn.: Greenwood Press, 1961), 13, 46–47.

119. Reports of imminent compromise approval also helped. See, for example, "Likelihood of an Agreement by the Peace Conference," *New York Times*, February 15, 1861.

120. J. Z. Goodrich to John A. Andrew, February 7, 1861, quoted in Gunderson, *Old Gentlemen's Convention*, 51.

121. Oliver Morton to Lincoln, January 29, 1861, ALPLC.

122. John S. Williams to Gideon Welles, February 17, 1861, ALPLM.

123. L. E. Chittenden, *Recollections of President Lincoln and His Administration* (New York: Harper & Bros., 1891), 38.

124. *New York Independent*, February 21, 1861.

125. Ibid.; [Washington] *National Intelligencer*, February 14, 1861.

126. [Washington] *National Intelligencer*, February 14, 1861. Stephen Douglas made sure the session was mercifully brief when he moved without objection that the names of the individual electors not be read aloud. See [Pittsfield, Mass.] *Berkshire County Eagle*, February 14, 1861, clipping in the Lincoln Museum, Fort Wayne, Indiana.

127. *New York Times*, February 15, 1861. Junius Brutus Booth was the father of John Wilkes Booth.

128. Williams to Welles, February 17, 1861, Welles Papers, ALPLM.

129. Allan Nevins and Milton Halsey Thomas, eds., *The Diary of George Templeton Strong*, 4 vols. (New York: Macmillan, 1952), 3:99.

130. *Congressional Globe*, 36th Congress, 2d Session, 1860–1861, 572.

131. Villard, *Lincoln on the Eve of '61*, 83; *CW*, 4:205.

132. Quoted in Gilder Lehrman Institute Web site, www.abrahamlincolnsclassroom.org / Library/newsletter.asp?ID, section on Ohio, 31.

10. No Occasion for Any Excitement

1. *New York Herald*, February 15, 1861. There are several highly readable sources about this part of the trip. See, especially, Victor Searcher, *Lincoln's Journey to Greatness* (Philadelphia: John C. Winston, 1960), perhaps most valuable of all for its research on the rail lines Lincoln rode, but flawed

because of its lack of sourcing; and, more recently, Larry D. Mansch, *Abraham Lincoln, President-Elect: The Four Critical Months from Election to Inauguration* (Jefferson, N.C.: McFarland, 2005).

2. *CW*, 4:206; *New York Herald*, February 15, 1861.

3. *CW*, 4:207. Lincoln did not mention Virginians by name, but just a few miles from their territory, he left little doubt he alluded specifically to them.

4. *CW*, 4:208. Lincoln himself identified the man as "a certain Irish friend" when he recalled the incident the next day in Ravenna, Ohio. See *CW*, 4:217.

5. *New York Herald*, February 15, 1861; John G. Nicolay to Therena Bates, February 15, 1861, NPLC.

6. *CW*, 4:208–9; *New York Herald*, February 15, 1861.

7. A. G. Frick to Lincoln, February 14, 1861, original discovered in the Chicago Historical Society. See Harold Holzer, ed., *Dear Mr. Lincoln: Letters to the President* (New York: Addison-Wesley, 1993), 341; John G. Nicolay, *A Short Life of Abraham Lincoln* (New York: The Century Co., 1904), 533.

8. Outgoing President Buchanan signed the Morrill Tariff Act two days before he left office, on March 2, 1861. See *New York Herald*, February 15, 1861; *CW*, 4:210–11.

9. *CW*, 4:210–13; *New York Herald*, February 15, 1861.

10. Henry Villard, *Memoirs of Henry Villard, Journalist and Financier*, 2 vols. (Boston: Houghton Mifflin, 1904), 1:152.

11. *Cincinnati Commercial*, February 16, 1861.

12. Harold G. Villard and Oswald Garrison Villard, *Lincoln on the Eve of '61: A Journalist's Story by Henry Villard* (New York: Alfred A. Knopf, 1941), 86; John G. Nicolay to Therena Bates, February 17, 1861, NPLC.

13. *CW*, 4:215–16.

14. *Elgin* [Ohio] *Democrat*, February 20, 1861; *CW*, 4:215–16.

15. *Cleveland Morning Leader*, February 16, 1861.

16. *Cleveland Plain Dealer*, February 20, 1861.

17. *Cleveland Plain Dealer*, February 15, 1861.

18. *CW*, 4:218; Michael Burlingame, ed., *Lincoln's Journalist: John Hay's Anonymous Writings for the Press, 1860–1864* (Carbondale: Southern Illionis University Press, 1998), 32.

19. *Cleveland Plain Dealer*, February 14, 1861.

20. Villard, *Lincoln on the Eve of '61*, 87; *New York Herald*, February 16, 1861.

21. Douglas L. Wilson and Rodney O. Davis, eds., *Herndon's Lincoln*, orig. pub. 1889 (Urbana: University of Illinois Press), 282.

22. Albert Gallatin Riddle, *Recollections of War Times: Reminiscences of Men and Events in Washington, 1860–1865* (New York: Putnam, 1895), 179.

23. Joseph Granger and others to Lincoln, February 20, 1861, ALPLC.

24. Though he was too ill to greet him personally when Lincoln arrived in his city, Buffalo mayor F. A. Allberger sent his "compliments" along with "letters which have been received for you." See Allberger to Lincoln, February 16, 1861, ALPLC.

25. See, for example, John Lorton to Lincoln, S. L. Carlton to Lincoln, both February 14, 1861, John N. Lindsey to Lincoln, February 15, 1861, ALPLC.

26. C. A. Meriweathetr to Mary Lincoln, February 15, 1861, ALPLC.

27. Harry W. Gourley to Robert T. Lincoln, February 22, 1861. Robert received a second request to secure the job for A. R. Robinson from Presco Wright on the same day. Both letters are in ALPLC.

28. Richard Oglesby (endorsed by Isaac Pugh) to Lincoln, February 17, 1861.

29. Denton Offutt to Lincoln, February 11, 1861, ALPLC.

30. Benjamin P. Thomas, *Lincoln in New Salem* (Springfield, Ill.: Abraham Lincoln Association, 1934), 61.

31. *New York Times*, February 19, 1861.

32. *New York Herald*, February 14, 1861; *Frank Leslie's Illustrated Newspaper*, March 2, 1861; *Boston Post* February 16, 1861.

33. Norman Judd to his wife, February 14, 1861, Manuscript Collection, ALPLM.

34. *Lincoln Day by Day*, 3:15; *New York Herald*, February 16, 1861; *Cincinnati Commercial*, February 16, 1861.

35. CW, 4:218.

36. *New York Times*, February 18, 1861.

37. CW, 4:218–19.

38. *New York Herald*, February 18, 1861.

39. CW, 4:130, 219.

40. *Cleveland Plain Dealer*, February 13, 1861.

41. *Philadelphia Inquirer*, February 20, 1861; CW, 4:219. Most village depots of the day—including Springfield's—combined freight and passenger areas in a single building.

42. Grace Bedell Billings to John E. Boos, January 24, 1934, *The Forbes Collection of American Historical Documents, Part Six* (Catalogue, New York, May 22, 2007), 63; Grace Bedell Billings to Herbert Wells Fay, July 28, 1922, *Seaport Autographs* Catalogue No. 107 (Fall 2007), 7; Grace Bedell to William H. Herndon, December 14, 1866, in Douglas L. Wilson and Rodney O. Davis, eds., *Herndon's Informants: Letters, Interviews, and Statements About Abraham Lincoln* (Urbana: University of Illinois Press, 1998), 517.

43. Grace Bedell Billings to the Lincoln National Life Foundation, February 11, 1931, original in the Lincoln Museum, Fort Wayne, Indiana; R. Gerald McMurtry, "Mr. Lincoln's Whiskers," *Lincoln Lore* 1557 (November 1967);

Bedell also quoted in "Why Abe Put on (H)airs," *Dayton Daily News*, February 7, 1960.

44. Grace Bedell to Lincoln, January 14, 1864, National Archives. Though only a teenager, Grace asked for a job in the Treasury Department. But White House clerks, evidently failing to realize who she was, forwarded her letter to the department, and her request went unfulfilled. The long-lost letter was unearthed in 2007 by researcher Karen Needles. Grace Bedell Billings died in 1936 at age eighty-eight.

45. [Peekskill, N.Y.] *Highland Democrat*, February 23, 1861.

46. *Orleans Republican*, reprinted in the *Atlas & Argus*, February 23, 1861, and quoted in an undated clipping in the files of the Lincoln Museum, Fort Wayne, Indiana.

47. *New York Illustrated News*, March 2, 1861; *New York Herald*, March 3, 1861.

48. Quoted in R. Gerald McMurtry, "Mr. Lincoln's Whiskers," typescript in the Lincoln Museum, Fort Wayne, Indiana.

49. Typescript by Mahon O. Kasson, September 30, 1937, copy in the Lincoln Museum, Fort Wayne, Indiana. For illustrations, see Harold Holzer, Gabor S. Boritt, and Mark E. Neely, Jr., *The Lincoln Image: Abraham Lincoln and the Popular Print* (New York: Charles Scribner's Sons, 1984), 31; Mark E. Neely, Jr., *The Last Best Hope of Earth: Abraham Lincoln and the Promise of America* (Cambridge: Harvard University Press, 1993), opp. 118.

50. *Philadelphia Inquirer*, February 20, 1861; CW, 4:219–20.

51. *New York Herald*, February 17, 1861.

52. *New York Times*, February 18, 1861; *New York Herald*, February 17, 1861.

53. CW, 4:220–21; *New York Herald, February*, 17, 1861.

54. CW, 4:221 *New York Times*, February 18, 1861.

55. Millard Fillmore to S. Chamberlain, March 3, 1862, *Presidential and Other American Manuscripts from the Dr. Robert Small Trust*, Sotheby's Auction Catalogue, April 3, 2008, 118–19. *New York Times*, February 18, 1861; *Lincoln Day by Day*, 3:16.

56. John Keep and Henry Cowles to Lincoln, February 14, 1861, ALPLC.

57. The [New York] *Independent*, February 14, 1861.

58. James A. Briggs to Lincoln, February 17, 1861, ALPLC.

59. *New York Herald*, February 19, 1861.

60. *New-York Daily Tribune*, February 15, 1861.

61. Diary of Charles Francis Adams, February 16, February 18, February 20, February 21, 1861, Adams Papers, Massachusetts Historical Society.

62. Paul Revere Frothingham, ed., *Edward Everett, Orator and Statesman* (Boston: Houghton Mifflin, 1925), 414.

63. The descriptions of Everett's oratorical style are from *Wells' Illustrated National Campaign Hand-Book for 1860* (New York: J. G. Wells, 1860), 25.

64. *Philadelphia Argus*, reprinted in the *Baltimore Sun*, February 18, 1861; *Daily Illinois State Register*, February 25, 1861.

65. *Baltimore Sun*, February 18, 1861.

66. [Indianapolis] *Indiana Daily Journal*, February 23, 1861.

67. *New York Times*, February 22, 1861.

68. *New York Sun*, February 18, 1861.

69. *Boston Post*, February 22, 1861.

70. CW, 4:205.

71. *New York Herald*, February 19, 1861.

72. *Cleveland Plain Dealer*, February 18, 1861.

73. "Who Talks of War?," *New York Observer*, February 28, 1861.

74. *Montgomery* [Alabama] *Weekly Post*, February 20, 1861, quoted in Eric H. Walther, *William Lowndes Yancey and the Coming of the Civil War* (Chapel Hill: University of North Carolina Press, 2006), 295. Yancey quoted in James McPherson, *Battle Cry of Freedom: The Civil War Era* (New York: Oxford University Press, 1988), 259.

75. *Boston Post*, February 21, 1861; *Selma* [Alabama] *Weekly Times*, February 19, 1861, quoted in William C. Davis, *"A Government of Our Own": The Making of the Confederacy* (New York: Free Press, 1994), 167.

76. *Pittsburgh Press*, quoted in *Richmond Dispatch*, February 13, 1861.

77. For details of the Davis inaugural, see William C. Davis, *Jefferson Davis: The Man and His Hour* (New York: HarperCollins, 1991), 308–10; for the text of the inaugural, see Jefferson Davis, *The Rise and Fall of the Confederate Government*, 2 vols., orig. pub. 1881 (New York Da Capo, 1990), 1:203.

78. *New York Herald*, February 19, 1861.

79. *Daily Illinois State Register*, February 26, 1861.

80. Orville H. Browning to Lincoln, February 17, 1861, ALPLC.

81. I am grateful to the two leading experts on Lincoln's oratory, Douglas L. Wilson and Ronald C. White, for exploring this matter with me in e-mail correspondence in December 2007. Neither scholar is convinced that Lincoln conceived this thought during the inaugural journey. Neither is willing to abandon the long-held view that William Seward created the idea, and gave it to Lincoln to edit. But neither historian is willing to rule out the possibility, either. How else to explain this jotting?

82. *New York Times*, February 19, 1861.

83. Burlingame, ed., *Lincoln's Journalist*, 36–37.

84. *Albany Evening Standard*, February 18, 1861. Villard estimated the throngs at eight thousand in Rochester, ten thousand in Syracuse, and thousands more "standing in a snowstorm" at Utica; *New York Times*, February 19, 1861.

85. Unidentified clipping dated November 16, 1887, files of the Lincoln Museum, Fort Wayne, Indiana; *Frank Leslie's Illustrated Newspaper*, March 2, 1861.

86. Villard, *Lincoln on the Eve of '61*, 91.

87. *CW*, 4:223.

88. *New York Times*, February 19, 1861.

89. Burlingame, ed., *Lincoln's Journalist*, 37–38.

90. *New York Herald*, February 19, 1861.

91. *Albany Evening Journal*, February 19, 1861.

92. *New York Herald*, February 19, 1861.

93. Adoniram J. Blakely to Dan Blakely, February 18, 1861, in Pratt, *Concerning Mr. Lincoln*, 53.

94. The newspaper rave, and a description of Booth's injury, is from Michael W. Kauffman, *American Brutus: John Wilkes Booth and the Lincoln Conspiracies* (New York: Random House, 2004), 113; for an evocative account of the near-meeting of future assassin and victim, see William Kennedy, *O Albany!* (New York: Viking, 1983), 11.

95. *New York Herald*, February 19, 1861; *CW*, 4:225.

96. *CW*, 4:226.

97. *New York Times*, February 19, 1861; *New York Herald*, February 20, 1861.

98. *Frank Leslie's Illustrated Newspaper*, February 23, 1861.

99. Technically, the sprint from Lafayette to Cincinnati had moved southeast.

100. *New York Herald*, February 20, 1861. The *New York Times*, February 20, 1861, also reported that Lincoln "felt far from well" that morning.

101. *New York Herald*, February 18, 1861.

102. *New York Evening Post*, February 19, 1861.

103. *New York Herald*, February 20, 1861.

104. Ibid. A visit to Niagara Falls years earlier had inspired Lincoln to write a long fragment about its "mysterious power" that he never published. See *CW*, 2:10–11. Historians have long suggested that Lincoln saw the falls in 1848; Wayne Temple, among others, believes he may not have paid his visit until 1857.

105. *CW*, 4:227.

106. *CW*, 4:228.

107. Ibid; *New York Times*, February 20, 1861; *Frank Leslie's Illustrated Newspaper*, March 2, 1861.

108. *New York Herald*, February 20, 1861.

109. Henry S. Free quoted in *Lincoln in Peekskill* (Peekskill, N.Y.: Lincoln Society in Peekskill, 1925), 8; [Peekskill] *Highland Democrat*, February 23, 1861; *Mrs. Harriet Smith, Eighty-eight Year Old Peekskill Citizen Who Shook Hands with Abraham Lincoln When He Spoke in Peekskill, February 19, 1861, Is Honored . . .* (Peekskill, N.Y.: Friendly Town Association, 1932). The Lincoln Society in Peekskill recently erected a life-size sculpture of Lincoln at the site, created by Richard Masloski.

110. CW, 4:229.

111. [Peekskill] *Highland Democrat*, February 23, 1861.

112. Ibid.

113. *New York Herald*, February 20, 1861.

114. Ibid.

115. Rufus Rockwell Wilson, ed., *Lincoln Among His Friends: A Sheaf of Intimate Memories* (Caldwell, Idaho: Caxton Printers, 1942), 305.

116. With its handsome facade and interior courtyard fountain, the Astor House became "among hotels, that which Niagara is among waterfalls." By 1860 it was no longer the most elegant of New York's hotels, but still popular. See David W. Dunlap, *On Broadway: A Journey over Time* (New York: Rizzoli, 1990), 21.

117. *New York Sun*, February 20, 1861.

118. *New York Herald*, February 20, 1861; *New York Times*, February 20, 1861.

119. *New York Times*, February 19, 1861.

120. John G. Nicolay, "Some Incidents in Lincoln's Journey from Springfield to Washington."

121. *New York World*, February 20, 1861. Most accounts give the city's 1860 population at 800,000; another population estimate, of one million, based on the Eighth Census of the United States, is reprinted in George Rogers Taylor, *The Transportation Revolution, 1815–1860*, orig. pub. 1951 (Armonk, N.Y.: M. E. Sharpe, 1977), 389.

122. *New York Herald*, February 20, 1861; *Frank Leslie's Illustrated Newspaper*, March 2, 1861.

123. *New York Herald*, February 20, 1861; Allan Nevins and Milton Halsey Thomas, eds., *The Diary of George Templeton Strong*, 4 vols. (New York: Macmillan, 1952), 3:101.

124. Lavinia Goodell to Maria Goodell Frost, February 25, 1860 [1861], Berea College Library, Berea, Kentucky, reprinted in Elisabeth S. Peck, "Abraham Lincoln in New York," *Lincoln Herald* 60 (Winter 1958): 129. Her father was William Goodell.

125. Walt Whitman, *Specimen Days*, orig. pub. 1883, in *Memoranda During the War*, ed. Peter Coviello (New York: Oxford University Press, 2004), 39–40n.

126. Daniel Mark Epstein believes Whitman's analysis was "suffused with dread," pointing out that Lincoln "had carried New York on election day." But while winning the state, Lincoln had in fact lost badly in New York City, and it is not beyond the realm of reason that he had many enemies among the crowds that "welcomed" him to the city in 1861. See Epstein, *Lincoln and Whitman: Parallel Lives in Civil War Washington* (New York: Ballantine, 2004), 66, 68

127. *New York Times*, February 20, 1860. A few months later, ships in the New

York harbor could be observed displaying Lincoln effigies hanging from the rigging, wearing signs that declared: "Abe Lincoln, dead and gone to hell" and "Abe Lincoln, the Union breaker." See Ernest A. McKay, *The Civil War and New York City* (Syracuse: Syracuse University Press, 1990), 45.

128. *New York Herald*, February 20, 1861; *New York Times*, February 20, 1861; CW, 4:230.

129. *New York Evening Post*, February 20, 1861.

130. *Boston Courier*, February 27, 1865.

131. G. S. Boritt, *Lincoln and the Economics of the American Dream* (Memphis: Memphis State University Press, 1978), 193.

132. CW, 4:230–31.

133. Ibid.; *New York Times*, February 20, 1861.

11. I Would Rather Be Assassinated

1. The breakfast group included Rhode Island's rich young governor William Sprague, William M. Evarts, Robert Bowne Minturn, and other "representatives of the mercantile wealth of the Metropolis," according to the *New York Times*, February 21, 1861.

2. Thomas Kessner, *Capital City: New York City and the Men Behind America's Rise to Economic Dominance, 1860–1900* (New York: Simon & Schuster, 2003), 31.

3. *New York Tribune*, February 21, 1861.

4. "The Diary of a Public Man, Part III: Unpublished Passages of the Secret History of the American Civil War," *North American Review* 129 (August 1879): 135.

5. See "To the People of Louisiana, Their Executive and Representatives, Greetings," broadside, January 28, 1861, in the New-York Historical Society collection. Wood quoted in Ernest A. McKay, *The Civil War and New York City* (Syracuse, N.Y.: Syracuse University Press, 1990), 33. According to the *New York Evening Post* (February 20, 1861), Wood also paid—or at least planned—a courtesy call on Lincoln the day before. Just a few weeks earlier, Wood had aroused outrage by objecting when his police superintendent tried seizing munitions from a ship, nestled in New York's harbor, bound for Savannah. Wood apologized to Georgia's Robert Toombs and was charged with supplying weapons to traitors. See Barnet Schecter, *The Devil's Own Work: The Civil War Draft Riots and the Fight to Reconstruct America* (New York: Walker, 2005).

6. CW, 4:233.

7. Harold Holzer, ed., *State of the Union: New York and the Civil War* (New York: Fordham University Press, 2002), 8.

8. *New York Sun*, February 21, 1861.

9. Lincoln would lie in state on the other side of those very doors in 1865.

10. *New-York Daily Tribune*, February 21, 1861.

11. Henry Villard, *Memoirs of Henry Villard, Journalist and Financier, 1835–1900*, 2 vols. (Boston: Houghton Mifflin, 1904), 1:152.

12. *New York World*, quoted in the *Boston Post*, February 21, 1861.

13. *New York Herald*, February 21, 1861; *New York Times*, February 21, 1861; *Baltimore Sun*, February 22, 1861; *Boston Post*, February 21, 1861.

14. *CW*, 4:233.

15. Undeterred, Barnum advertised on February 20, "President Abraham Lincoln has promised Mr. Barnum that he will positively visit the museum this day." See *New York Times*, February 20, 1861.

16. *New York Herald*, February, 21, 1861; *New York World*, February 21, 1861.

17. Charles Eugene Hamlin, *The Life and Times of Hannibal Hamlin*, 2 vols. (Cambridge, Mass.: Riverside Press, 1899), 2:387–88.

18. *Frank Leslie's Illustrated Newspaper*, March 2, 1861.

19. Robert Lincoln stayed behind and actually appeared on stage, disguised, in the climactic masked ball scene. See *New York Evening Post*, February 21, 1861.

20. *New York World, New York Herald*, February 21, 1861. Mary Lincoln, who loved opera, nevertheless remained at the Astor House to preside over a ladies' levee, looking to one reporter "fine-looking but not beautiful" in a ribbon-trimmed brocade dress, fastened at the collar by a diamond brooch (*New-York Daily Tribune*, February 21, 1861). Willie and Tad attended a performance that night at Laura Keene's theater—the same Laura Keene who would appear on stage at Ford's Theatre in Washington on April 14, 1865, the night Lincoln was assassinated there.

21. Villard, *Memoirs*, 1:152.

22. Mary A. Livermore, *My Story of the War: A Woman's Narrative of Four Years Personal Experience as Nurse in the Union Army* . . . , orig. pub. 1887 (New York: Da Capo, 1995), 553–54. Livermore never named the city where she saw Lincoln, but it was almost certainly New York or Philadelphia.

23. Sue H. Burbridge to Lincoln, January 20, 1861, Lincoln Museum, Fort Wayne, Indiana.

24. *Sacramento Daily Union*, quoted in Milton Shutes, *Lincoln and California* (Stanford: Stanford University Press, 1943), 53.

25. *Charleston Daily Courier*, February 15, 1861.

26. Reprinted in Herbert Mitgang, ed., *Lincoln as They Saw Him* (New York: Rhinehart, 1956), 229–30.

27. *The* [New York] *Independent*, February 28, 1861.

28. *The* [New York] *Independent*, February 21, 1861.

29. *New York World*, February 21, 1861.

30. *New-York Daily Tribune*, February 22, 1861.

31. *New York Times*, February 22, 1861; CW, 4:233–34.

32. Michael Burlingame, ed., *Lincoln's Journalist: John Hay's Anonymous Writings for the Press, 1860–1864* (Carbondale: Southern Illinois University Press, 1998), 39; *Philadelphia Inquirer*, February 22, 1861.

33. *Philadelphia Inquirer*, February 22, 1861.

34. *New York World*, February 22, 1861; CW, 4:234–35; *Lincoln Day by Day*, 3:19.

35. *Philadelphia Inquirer*, February 22, 1861.

36. *New York Times*, February 22, 1861; [Trenton, N.J.] *Gazette & Republican*, February 22, 1861; Burlingame, ed., *Lincoln's Journalist*, 39.

37. New Jersey *Assembly Minutes*, 1761, 500–503. I am grateful to Peter J. Mazzei for sharing this hilarious archive.

38. CW, 236–37; John Nicolay, "Some Incidents in Lincoln's Journey from Springfield to Washington," ms., NPLC.

39. CW, 4:237.

40. CW, 4:235–236; Burlingame, ed., *Lincoln's Journalist*, 40.

41. Address to the Springfield Young Men's Lyceum, January 27, 1838, CW, 1:115.

42. CW, 1:108.

43. Historian Ronald C. White, Jr., provides an interesting alternative interpretation, suggesting that Lincoln's reference to "almost chosen people" showed that, in an era of absolutism and a tradition of American exceptionalism, he continued to demonstrate he could "live comfortably with the uncertainties facing the nation." See White, *The Eloquent President: A Portrait of Lincoln Through His Words* (New York: Random House, 2005), 54.

44. Burlingame, ed., *Lincoln's Journalist*, 40–41.

45. *Philadelphia Inquirer*, February 22, 1861.

46. *New York Times*, February 22, 1861; Wayne C. Temple, "Lincoln in Trenton, N.J.," *Lincoln Herald* 95 (Fall 1993), 87–90.

47. [Trenton, N.J.] *Gazette & Republican*, February 23, 1861.

48. *Philadelphia Inquirer*, February 22, 1861.

49. Ibid.; *New York Times*, February 22, 1861.

50. *Philadelphia Press*, February 22, 1861, quoted in Charles William Heathcote, "Lincoln in Philadelphia, Part I," *Lincoln Herald* 46 (Fall 1944): 36; Elizabeth Taylor to her mother, ca. February 1861, original in the Stephenson County (Illinois) Historical Society. Young Miss Taylor hailed from the Lincoln-Douglas debate town of Freeport.

51. *New York Times*, February 22, 1861.

52. CW, 4:238.

53. CW, 4:238–39; *Baltimore Sun*, February 22, 1861.

54. *Philadelphia Inquirer*, February 22, 1861.

55. Douglas L. Wilson and Rodney O. Davis, eds., *Herndon's Informants: Let-*

ters, Interviews, and Statements About Abraham Lincoln (Urbana: University of Illinois Press, 1998), 312.

56. Ibid., 433–34; S. M. Felton to Allan Pinkerton, December 31, 1867, in [Allan Pinkerton] *History and Evidence of the Passage of Abraham Lincoln from Harrisburg, Pa., to Washington, D.C. on the 22d and 23d of February, 1861* (Privately printed, 1868), 15.

57. Allan Pinkerton, quoted in Wilson and Davis, eds., *Herndon's Informants*, 312.

58. Allan Pinkerton, *The Spy of the Rebellion; Being a True History of the Spy System of the United States Army During the Late Rebellion* (Philadelphia: H. W. Kelley, 1883), 85, and in report provided to William Herndon, reprinted in Wilson and Davis, eds., *Herndon's Informants*, 312.

59. Wilson and Davis, eds., *Herndon's Informants*, 433; N. B. Judd to Allan Pinkerton, November 3, 1867, in [Pinkerton], *History and Evidence of the Passage of Abraham Lincoln*, 19.

60. John F. Wright to Lincoln, January 24, 1861, original in the Lincoln Museum, Fort Wayne, Indiana.

61. Frederick W. Seward, *Seward at Washington as Senator and Secretary of State: A Memoir of His Life . . .* , 2 vols. (New York: Derby & Miller, 1891), 1:510.

62. Benson J. Lossing, *Pictorial History of the Civil War in the United States of America*, 2 vols. (Philadelphia: G. W. Childs, 1866), 1:279–80. Historian Norma B. Cuthbert accepted Lossing's testimony, which neatly corresponded with other contemporary recollections, but Lincoln scholar Don E. Fehrenbacher doubted its authenticity. See Cuthbert, ed., *Lincoln and the Baltimore Plot 1861: From Pinkerton Records and Related Papers* (San Marino, Cal.: Huntington Library, 1949), xv; Don E. Fehrenbacher and Virginia Fehrenbacher, *Recollected Words of Lincoln* (Stanford, Calif.: Stanford University Press, 1996), 305–7.

63. Judd to Pinkerton, November 3, 1867, [Pinkerton], *History and Evidence of the Passage of Abraham Lincoln*, 19–20; Wilson and Davis, eds., *Herndon's Informants*, 313.

64. Frederick W. Seward, "How Lincoln Was Warned of the Baltimore Assassination Plot," in William Hayes Ward, ed., *Abraham Lincoln: Tributes from His Associates . . .* (New York: Thomas Y. Crowell, 1895), 60–63; William H. Seward to Lincoln, February 21, 1861, ALPLC.

65. Winfield Scott to William H. Seward, February 21, 1861, ALPLC.

66. Memorandum from Charles P. Stone, February 21, 1861, ALPLC.

67. Frederick W. Seward, *Reminiscences of a War-Time Statesman and Diplomat, 1830–1915* (New York: G. P. Putnam's Sons, 1916), 135; *New York Times*, October 31, 1867. The *New York Evening Post* this same day (February 21, 1861) praised Kennedy and "his well-drilled forces" for "admirably" managing the crowds during Lincoln's visit to New York City. Just weeks

earlier, Kennedy had incurred Mayor Wood's wrath for attempting to seize the munitions on board the *Monticello*.

68. Seward, *Seward at Washington*, 1:509–11.

69. Lossing, *Pictorial History of the Civil War*, 1:279–80.

70. Henry C. Bowen to Lincoln, February 5, 1861; Charles Gould to Henry C. Bowen, February 5, 1861, ALPLC.

71. *The* [New York] *Independent*, February 21, 1861. Greeley made no mention of his personal interview with Lincoln aboard the inaugural train just days before.

72. See the *New York Herald*, February 22, 1861.

73. Worthington G. Snethen to Lincoln, February 15, 1861, ALPLC.

74. Montgomery Blair to Lincoln, December 8, 1860. "Blair House," as it came to be known, now serves as a guest residence for distinguished visitors to the city—just as Blair hoped in Lincoln's case.

75. Ward Hill Lamon, *Recollections of Abraham Lincoln, 1847–1865*, ed. Dorothy Lamon (Chicago: A. C. McClurg, 1895), 34–35.

76. Lincoln to Elihu B. Washburne, February 15, 1861, CW, 4:217.

77. Elihu B. Washburne to Lincoln, February 19, 1861, ALPLC.

78. Lamon, *Recollections of Abraham Lincoln*, 40.

79. Recollection by eyewitness Henry J. Snyder in "Old Philadelphian, Civil War Veteran, Eyewitness of Lincoln's Memorable Visit to Philadelphia in 1861 . . . Recalls and Describes Details of that Historic Event," undated clipping in the Lincoln Museum, Fort Wayne, Indiana.

80. See Daniel Walker Howe, *Making the American Self: Jonathan Edwards to Abraham Lincoln* (Cambridge, Mass.: Harvard University Press, 1997), 9.

81. CW, 4:240; Judd to Pinkerton, November 3, 1867, in [Pinkerton], *History and Evidence of the Passage of Abraham Lincoln*, 20.

82. Lloyd Ostendorf, *Lincoln's Photographs: A Complete Album* (Dayton: Rockywood Press, 1998), 73, 396. The book was the third, and final, edition of the Ostendorf (and Hamilton) study.

83. CW, 4:241–42.

84. CW, 4:244; *New York Herald*, February 22, 1861.

85. James B. Nicholson recollection, in "He Saw Lincoln Raise Old Glory," undated clipping ca. 1933, Lincoln Museum, Fort Wayne, Indiana; CW, 4:244–45.

86. *Philadelphia Inquirer*, February 23, 1861.

87. *Philadelphia Inquirer*, February 23, 1861; CW, 4:242, H. Frank Eshelman, "Lincoln's Visit to Lancaster in 1861," *Papers of the Lancaster County Historical Society* 13 (1909): 63, 67.

88. Burlingame, ed., *Lincoln's Journalist*, 41; Eshelman, "Mr. Lincoln's Visit to Lancaster," 74.

89. Wilson and Davis, eds., *Herndon's Informants*, 314, 434.

90. Ibid., 434.

91. Judd to Pinkerton, in [Pinkerton] *History and Evidence of the Passage of Abraham Lincoln*, 21. Writing to William Herndon in November 1866, Pinkerton had a somewhat different recollection of this detail, suggesting Lincoln was indifferent about sharing the plan with the others, commenting, "You can do what you like about that." See Wilson and Davis, eds., *Herndon's Informants*, 434.

92. Burlingame, ed., *Lincoln's Journalist*, 42; CW, 4:243.

93. *Philadelphia Inquirer*, February 23, 1861; CW, 4:243–44.

94. CW, 4:244–45.

95. CW, 4:211.

96. The calculations are derived from *Lincoln Day by Day*, and the Web version, www.thelincolnlog.org. See also W. H. Bunce railroad map in Victor Searcher, *Lincoln's Journey to Greatness* (Philadelphia: John C. Winston, 1960), flyleaves.

97. John G. Nicolay, "Lincoln's Speeches on the Journey to Washington," pencil copy written for the book *Outbreak of the Rebellion*, original in the Library of Congress. I am grateful to Doris Kearns Goodwin for alerting me to this manuscript.

98. George W. Hazzard to Lincoln, [January 1861], ALPLC.

99. Davis quoted in Wilson and Davis, eds., *Herndon's Informants*, 346; Judd to Pinkerton, November 3, 1867, [Pinkerton], *History and Evidence of the Passage of Abraham Lincoln*, 22.

100. Cuthbert, ed., *Lincoln and the Baltimore Plot*, 78; Wilson and Davis, eds., *Herndon's Informants*, 390, 431.

101. Wilson and Davis, eds., *Herndon's Informants*, 290.

102. Curtin quoted in Clement Clay Tilton, "Pinkerton and the Baltimore Scare," *Lincoln Group Papers, Report Number 9* (Chicago: Home of Books, 1939), 136.

103. Wilson and Davis, eds. *Herndon's Informants*, 290.

104. [George Washington Harris], "Sut Lovingood Travels with Ole Abe," *Nashville Union and American*, reprinted in Ben Harris McClary, "Sut Lovingood Views 'Abe Linkhorn,' " *Lincoln Herald* 56 (Fall 1954): 44–45.

105. John Hay to "Annie," February 22, 1861 (from Harrisburg), original in the John Hay Papers, John Hay Library, Brown University.

106. Lossing, *Pictorial History of the War*, 1:279–80; Andrew G. Curtin to Pinkerton, December 8, 1867, [Pinkerton], *History and Evidence of the Passage of Abraham Lincoln*, 37.

107. Lossing, *Pictorial History of the Civil War*, 1:279–80; Margaret D. Williams, "A Brief Reminiscence of the First Inauguration of Abraham Lincoln as President," typescript in Robert Todd Lincoln Papers, File A, ALPLM; Wilson and Davis, eds., *Herndon's Informants*, 322.

108. Wilson and Davis, eds., *Herndon's Informants*, 435.

109. Enoch Lewis to Allan Pinkerton, November 7, 1867, [Pinkerton], *History and Evidence of the Passage of Abraham Lincoln*, 31; George H. Burns to "Hutcheson" [Pinkerton], February 22, 1861, in Wilson and Davis, eds., *Herndon's Informants*, 289.

110. Ward H. Lamon, *The Life of Abraham Lincoln from His Birth to His Inauguration as President* (Boston: James R. Osgood, 1872), 523–24.

111. Lamon, *Recollections of Lincoln*, 43; Enoch Lewis to Pinkerton, November 7, 1867, John Pitcairn to Pinkerton, November 23, 1867, in [Pinkerton], *History and Evidence of the Passage of Abraham Lincoln*, 32–33, 36.

112. Wilson and Davis, eds., *Herndon's Informants*, 291; Lamon, *Life of Lincoln*, 524.

113. Lamon, *Recollections of Lincoln*, 44; Lamon, *Life of Lincoln*, 525.

114. Pinkerton, *The Spy of the Rebellion*, 97.

115. E. B. Washburne, "Abraham Lincoln in Illinois," *North American Review* 141 (November 1885): 457.

116. In Pinkerton's February 23, 1861 report, in Wilson and Davis, eds., *Herndon's Informants*, 286, Lincoln shouts, "Don't strike him, Allan!" Lamon's account is in *Life of Abraham Lincoln*, 426. Washburne remembered Lincoln shouting: "This is only Washburne!" See Washburne, "Abraham Lincoln in Illinois," 457.

117. Weather noted in Diary of Charles Francis Adams, February 23, 1861, Adams Papers, Massachusetts Historical Society. Washburne later claimed that Lamon, not Pinkerton, menaced him at the Washington terminal, suggesting that the detective embellished his role as a bodyguard—the assignment that in fact belonged to the Danville, Illinois lawyer. Yet it is difficult to believe that Lamon would not have recognized the Galena congressman. Lamon's memoir left the subject unsettled. He wrote only that "the detective and Col. Lamon were instantly alarmed. One of them raised his fist to strike the stranger." See Lamon, *Life of Abraham Lincoln*, 526.

118. Henry Kellogg Willard, "Henry Augustus Willard: His Life and Times," *Records of the Columbia Historical Society* 20 (Washington, D.C.: Columbia Historical Society, 1917): 249–50).

119. Wilson and Davis, eds., *Herndon's Informants*, 291.

12. Plain as a Turnpike Road

1. Pinkerton quoted in Douglas L. Wilson and Rodney O. Davis, eds., *Herndon's Informants: Letters, Interviews, and Statements About Abraham Lincoln* (Urbana: University of Illinois Press, 1998), 287.

2. *Cleveland Plain Dealer*, February 25, 1861.

3. *Albany Atlas & Argus*, February 28, 1861; *Baltimore Sun*, February 25, 1861.

4. *Douglass' Monthly*, April 1861, in Philip S. Foner and Yuvall Taylor, eds., *Frederick Douglass: Selected Speeches and Writings* (Chicago: Lawrence Hill, 1975), 432–33.

5. *Cincinnati Enquirer*, February 25, 1861.

6. *Baltimore Sun*, February 25, 1861.

7. *Ohio Statesman*, quoted in *Cleveland Plain Dealer*, February 26, 1861; *New York Evening Post*, February 25, 1861.

8. *New York Herald*, February 25, March 5, 1861.

9. "The Diary of a Public Man, Part II," *North American Review* 129 (September 1879): 260. The article dismissed the plot as a "cock-and-bull story" and branded Lincoln's response "weak and vulgar."

10. *Boston Post*, February 26, 1861.

11. *St. Joseph Valley Register*, February 28, 1861, quoted in Winfred A. Harrison, "Lincoln and Indiana Republicans, 1861–1864," *Indiana Magazine of History* 33 (September 1937): 280.

12. *New-York Daily Tribune*, February 25, 1861; *Louisville Courier*, reprinted in *The* [Columbus, Ohio] *Crisis*, March 7, 1861, quoted in Robert S. Harper, *Lincoln and The Press* (New York: McGraw-Hill, 1951), 91.

13. *Charleston Mercury*, February 26, 1861, quoted in Herbert Mitgang, ed., *Lincoln as They Saw Him* (New York: Rinehart, 1956), 234; "Gunpowder Plots," *Charleston Mercury*, March 8, 1861.

14. *Cleveland Plain Dealer*, February 26, 1861.

15. Elihu B. Washburne, "Abraham Lincoln in Illinois," *North American Review* 141 (1885): 456–57; *New York Times*, February 25, 1861, quoted in Edward Steers, Jr., *Blood on the Moon: The Assassination of Abraham Lincoln* (Frankfort: University Press of Kentucky, 2001), 21.

16. "The Flight of Abraham. (As Reported by a Modern Daily Paper)," *Harper's Weekly*, March 9, 1861.

17. *Vanity Fair*, March 9, 1861; *Harper's Weekly*, March 9, 1861. Long the standard reference, Rufus Rockwell Wilson, *Lincoln in Caricature* (New York: Horizon Press, 1953), esp. 102–9, was recently supplanted by the excellent Gary L. Bunker, *From Rail-Splitter to Icon: Lincoln's Image in Illustrated Periodicals, 1860–1865* (Kent, Ohio: Kent State University Press, 2001), 86–95. *Frank Leslie's Illustrated Newspaper* was inexplicably behind the curve of this phenomenon. Its March 9 issue featured woodcuts of Lincoln's Springfield parlor, the flag-raising ceremony at Philadelphia, and an outdated gatefold engraving of a beardless Lincoln, surrounded by scenes from his youth, including one panel incorrectly claiming the president-elect's father had been killed by Indians. To add injury to insult, however, *Leslie's* front page was filled with the portrait of another new president—Jefferson Davis.

18. Ironically, Jefferson Davis would also be mocked for wearing an unusual overcoat—his wife's raglan—as he fled, rather than entered, his capital

more than four years later. Cartoonists exaggerated the Confederate president's disguise into a woman's hoopskirts, subjecting Lincoln's counterpart to the same kind of derisive hilarity with which they had greeted the Union leader upon his arrival in Washington. See Mark E. Neely, Jr., Harold Holzer, and Gabor S. Boritt, *The Confederate Image: Prints of the Lost Cause* (Chapel Hill: University of North Carolina Press, 1987), 79–96.

19. Volck's *Passage Through Baltimore* is printed in George McCullough Anderson, *The Work of Adalbert Johann Volck, 1828–1912* (Baltimore: privately printed, 1970), 85.

20. Wilson and Davis, eds., *Herndon's Informants*, 323.

21. Washburne, "Abraham Lincoln in Illinois," 456.

22. *New York World*, February 27, 1861, reprinted in Michael Burlingame, ed., *Lincoln's Journalist: John Hay's Anonymous Writings for the Press, 1860–1864* (Carbondale: Southern Illinois University Press, 1998), 43–44.

23. Mark E. Neely, Jr., discovered one hitherto unnoticed example, Maryland artist Adalbert Volck's etching, *Worship of the North*, in *The Last Best Hope of Earth: Abraham Lincoln and the Promise of America* (Cambridge: Harvard University Press, 1993), opp. 118. Stefan Lorant published another, a panel from the 1864 anti-Lincoln pamphlet, *Only Authentic Life of Abraham Lincoln, Alias "Old Abe,"* in *Lincoln: A Picture Story of His Life*, orig. pub. 1952, rev. ed. (New York: W. W. Norton, 1969), 230–31.

24. To Chicago congressman Isaac N. Arnold, Lincoln said much the same thing: "I did not then, nor do I now, believe I should have been assassinated had I gone through Baltimore as first contemplated, but I thought it wise to run no risk where no risk was necessary." See Arnold, *The History of Abraham Lincoln and the Overthrow of Slavery* (Chicago: Clarke & Co., 1866), 171; Henry Clay Whitney, *Lincoln the Citizen* (New York: Current Literature Publishing Co., 1907), 306.

25. A. K. McClure, *Abraham Lincoln and Men of War-Times: Some Personal Recollections of War and Politics During the Lincoln Administration* (Philadelphia: Times Publishing, 1892), 55.

26. For more on alleged ringleader Cipriano Ferrandini, see Steers, *Blood on the Moon*, 17.

27. William L. Schley to Lincoln, February 23, 1861, ALPLC.

28. Charles Gibbon, in "Proceedings of The Union League of Philadelphia Regarding the Assassination of Abraham Lincoln," *Magazine of History*, Extra No. 19 (New York: William Abbatt, 1912): 509; Henry J. Raymond, *Life and Public Services of Abraham Lincoln* (New York: Derby & Miller, 1865), 158. See also the view that by outsmarting the plotters, Lincoln "exasperated" the "traitors and their sympathizers," in *Illustrated Life, Services, Martyrdom, and Funeral of Abraham Lincoln . . .* (Philadelphia: T. B. Peterson & Bros., 1865), 85.

29. *New York Times*, October 31, 1867.

30. [Allan Pinkerton], *History and Evidence of the Passage of Abraham Lincoln from Harrisburg, Pa., to Washington, D.C. on the 22d and 23d of February, 1861* (New York: privately printed, 1868).

31. Mark E. Neely, Jr., *The Abraham Lincoln Encyclopedia* (New York: McGraw-Hill, 1982), 178; Ward Hill Lamon, *The Life of Abraham Lincoln from His Birth to His Inauguration* (Boston: James R. Osgood, 1872), 512–13. Lamon's "memoir" was ghosted by Chauncey Black, whose father, Lamon's law partner, Jeremiah S. Black, had been secretary of state in Buchanan's cabinet.

32. John Nicolay and John Hay, *Abraham Lincoln: A History*, 10 vols. (New York: The Century Co., 1890), 3:313.

33. Ward Hill Lamon, *Recollections of Abraham Lincoln, 1847–1865*, ed. Dorothy Lamon (Chicago: A. C. McClurg, 1895), 46–47.

34. Ibid. More recent and thorough scholarship, particularly by Lincoln assassination expert Edward Steers, Jr., has demonstrated that a specific and very dangerous plot had indeed been organized in Baltimore by a group called the National Volunteers, a paramilitary arm of the anti-Lincoln group known as the Knights of the Golden Circle. See Steers, *Blood on the Moon*, 17–20.

35. Judd to Pinkerton, in [Pinkerton], *History and Evidence of the Passage of Abraham Lincoln*, 23.

36. L[ucius]. E. Chittenden, *Recollections of President Lincoln and His Administration* (New York: Harper & Brothers, 1891), 66.

37. Carlos Mertyn, *William E. Dodge: The Christian Merchant* (New York: Funk & Wagnalls, 1890), 187–88. Dodge remembered Lincoln as a "master of the art of putting things."

38. *Illinois Daily State Journal*, December 18, 1860; John Sullivan to Henry Carey, March 1, 1861, Edward Carey Gardner Collection, Historical Society of Pennsylvania; Ezra Cornell to Mary Ann Cornell, March 3, 1861, Cornell University *Alumni News*, February 27, 1938, reprinted in Harry E. Pratt, *Concerning Mr. Lincoln . . .* (Springfield, Ill.: Abraham Lincoln Association, 1944), 67–68.

39. Nathaniel Hawthorne, "Chiefly About War-Matters," *Atlantic Monthly* 10 (July 1862): 59–60.

40. *Washington Evening Star*, February 23, 1861.

41. Ibid.; Mark Washburne, *Elihu Benjamin Washburne: Congressman, Secretary of State, Envoy Extraordinary*, 2 vols. (Xlibris: 2000), 1:466; Frederick A. Seward, *Seward at Washington, as Senator and Secretary of State: A Memoir of His Life with Selections From His Letters, 1846–1861* (New York: Derby & Miller, 1891), 505.

42. Walt Whitman, *Specimen Days in America*, orig. pub. 1883, rev. ed. (Lincoln: Walter Scott, 1887), 49–50.

43. Albert Gallatin Riddle, *Recollections of War Times: Reminiscences of Men and Events in Washington* (New York: G. P. Putnam's Sons, 1895), 17.

44. *Philadelphia Inquirer*, February 25, 1861.

45. *Washington Evening Star*, February 23, 1861; [Washington] *Daily National Intelligencer*, February 26, 1861.

46. *Washington Evening Star*, February 26, 1861.

47. Quoted in "How Lincoln Was Warned of the Baltimore Assassination Plot," 65; Seward, *Seward at Washington*, 511.

48. *New York Times*, February 27, 1861.

49. M. Garnett McCoy, ed., *Inauguration Day March 4, 1861: A Young Detroit Girl's Witness to the Stirring Events in the City of Washington on the Day of Abraham Lincoln's First Inauguration as Revealed in a Letter to Her Sisters* (Detroit: Friends of the Detroit Public Library, 1960), 4–5.

50. A. D. White, *Autobiography*, 2 vols. (New York: The Century Co., 1905), 1:78. The description was well used in Mary Panzer, *Mathew Brady and the Image of History* (Washington, D.C.: Smithsonian Institution Press, 1997), 93.

51. Henry Adams, *The Education of Henry Adams*, orig. pub. 1905 (Boston: Houghton Mifflin, 1973), 100.

52. Leonard Swett to "Dear Shell," February 25, 1861, Swett Papers, Library of Congress.

53. Jerome B. Wass to Lincoln, February 25, 1861, ALPLC. Wass was the proprietor of a bill-collecting firm on Pacific Street in Brooklyn.

54. *Philadelphia Inquirer*, February 27, 1861. Robert was accompanied on his visit by his Springfield pal George Latham.

55. Dispatch of February 26, 1861, printed in the *New York World*, March 4, 1861, reprinted in Burlingame, ed., *Lincoln's Journalist*, 45–49.

56. *Washington Evening Star*, February 24, 1861.

57. Riddle, *Recollections of War Times*, 10–11.

58. Francis Fisher Browne, *The Every-Day Life of Abraham Lincoln . . .* (Chicago: Browne & Howell, 1913), 282.

59. *Washington Evening Star*, February 25, 1861.

60. Winfield Scott to Lincoln, March 3, 1861, ALBLC.

61. Diary of Charles Francis Adams, February 23, 1861, Adams Papers, Massachusetts Historical Society.

62. *New York World*, February 27, 1861.

63. *Charleston Mercury*, March 8, 1861.

64. *Philadelphia Inquirer*, February 25, 1861; *Washington Daily Intelligencer*, February 26, 1861.

65. *New York Times*, February 25, 1861.

66. *New York Times*, February 24, 1861; James D. Horan, *The Pinkertons: The Detective Dynasty That Made History* (New York: Bonanza, 1967), 58. Sup-

posedly, a "horde" of "ruffians" menaced Hannibal Hamlin when his own train arrived in Baltimore, parted the curtains of his compartment to glare, but after failing to recognize him, stormed away, "leaving an atmosphere of profanity and whiskey behind them." See Charles Eugene Hamlin, *The Life and Times of Hannibal Hamlin*, 2 vols. (Cambridge, Mass.: Riverside Press, 1899), 2:390.

67. John G. Nicolay to Therena Bates, February 24, 1861, NPLC. According to the Willard's cash book, which survives, Robert Lincoln shared a room with his cousin Lockwood Todd; Nicolay and Hay shared room 127; and David Davis bunked with Ward Hill Lamon. Willard Family Papers, Library of Congress.

68. Margaret D. Williams, "A Brief Reminiscence of the First Inauguration of Abraham Lincoln as President," typescript in Robert Todd Lincoln Papers, January 4, 1921, ALPLM.

69. Harriet Lane to Sophie Pitt, February 24, 1861, quoted in William Seale, *The President's House: A History*, 2 vols. (Washington, D.C.: White House Historical Association, 1986), 1:86, 2:1101n3.

70. *Chicago Daily Press & Tribune*, March 4, 1861. Historian David Herbert Donald paints a vivid picture of the Lincolns' utter lack of preparation for running so vast a mansion in *Lincoln at Home: Two Glimpses of Abraham Lincoln's Family Life* (New York: Simon & Schuster, 1999), esp. 19–23.

71. *Washington Evening Star*, February 24, 1861; newspaper report quoted in Robert W. Johannsen, *Stephen A. Douglas* (New York: Oxford University Press, 1973), 841. Mrs. Douglas later paid a courtesy call on Mary.

72. George B. Loring, quoted in Whipple, *The Every-Day Life of Lincoln*, 282.

73. *Philadelphia Inquirer*, February 25, 1861.

74. Lucius E. Chittenden, and subsequent conversations, quoted in Charles M. Segal, ed., *Conversations with Lincoln* (New York: G.P. Putnam's Sons, 1961), 81–84; Chittenden, *Personal Reminiscences, 1840–1890, Including Some Not Hitherto Published of Lincoln and the War* (New York: Richmond, Croscup & Co., 1893), 391–92. It should be noted that Chittenden published his recollections more than thirty years after the events he described.

75. Francis B. Carpenter, *Six Months at the White House with President Lincoln: The Story of a Picture* (New York: Hurd & Houghton, 1866), 229–30.

76. Segal, *Conversations with Lincoln*, 82–83; Robert Gray Gunderson, *Old Gentlemen's Convention: The Washington Peace Conference of 1861* (Westport, Conn.: Greenwood Press, 1961), 84.

77. Segal, *Conversations with Lincoln*, 82–83.

78. Ibid., 84; Chittenden, *Recollections of President Lincoln*, 68.

79. Ibid., 78.

80. Riddle, *Recollections of War Times*, 10.

81. Diary of Charles Francis Adams, February 24, 1861, Adams Papers, Massachusetts Historical Society.

82. *Washington Evening Star*, February 25, 1861. Seward's pew and pastor are described in Wayne C. Temple, *Abraham Lincoln: From Skeptic to Prophet* (Mahomet, Ill.: Mayhaven Publishing, 1995), 133.

83. *Washington Evening Star*, February 25, 1861.

84. Frederick W. Seward, *Reminiscences of a War-Time Statesman and Diplomat* (New York: G. P. Putnam's Sons, 1916), 147.

85. "Diary of a Public Man, Part II," 266–67.

86. Diary of Charles Francis Adams, February 24, 1861. Adams Papers, Massachusetts Historical Society. Adams also provided the testimony that Corwin, Wade, and Sumner had preceded him in conference with Lincoln.

87. *Harper's Weekly*, April 27, 1861. Unfortunately for Lincoln, the engraved adaptation did not appear in print for two more months.

88. D. Mark Katz, *Witness to an Era: The Life and Photographs of Alexander Gardner . . .* (New York: Viking, 1991), 109. The note is something of a mystery; why Brady would assume Gardner would *not* have his equipment ready is difficult to explain—unless the famous photographer was simply acting the impresario. See also Lloyd Ostendorf, "President Lincoln," in Brooks Johnson, *An Enduring Interest: The Photographs of Alexander Gardner* (Norfolk: Chrysler Museum, 1991), 61.

89. George H. Story testimony, 1916, quoted in Rufus Rockwell Wilson, *Lincoln in Portraiture* (New York: Press of the Pioneers, 1935), 167; Katz, *Alexander Gardner*, 106.

90. "The card photograph has swept everything before it, and is the style to endure," wrote the *American Journal of Photography* in 1862. See William C. Darrah, *Cartes de Visite in Nineteenth Century Photography* (Gettysburg: William C. Darrah, 1981), 4.

91. Because war had broken out, the portrait was relegated to the inside of the April 27 issue of *Harper's*, but published near a two-page woodcut of the bombardment of Fort Sumter, neatly implying that Lincoln was a worthy commander-in-chief. The weekly accompanied the engraving with a flattering biographical sketch. George Henry Story took even longer than *Harper's Weekly* or the publishers of separate-sheet prints to create his adaptation. His Lincoln painting was not completed until 1916. See Wilson, *Lincoln in Portraiture*, 168.

92. *The* [New York] *Independent*, February 28, 1861.

93. Henry L. Dawes, "Washington the Winter Before the War," *Atlantic Monthly* 72 (August 1893): 167.

94. See David Herbert Donald, *"We Are Lincoln Men": Abraham Lincoln and His Friends* (New York: Simon & Schuster, 2003), 101.

95. *Philadelphia Inquirer*, February 26, 1861. King went on to serve as a Lincoln

elector in 1864, but seven months after the president's assassination, took his own life by leaping off a New York ferryboat.

96. *Washington Evening Star*, February 25, 1861.

97. Some sources suggest that these meetings occurred on separate days, but the best evidence indicates that Lincoln made at least the first of his courtesy calls on the Senate, House, and Supreme Court on a single visit. For a contrary view, see *Lincoln Day by Day*, 3:22–23.

98. *Washington Evening Star*, February 26, 1861; *Washington Daily National Intelligencer*, February 26, 1861; *New York Times*, February 27, 1861.

99. Nicolay and Hay, *Abraham Lincoln*, 3:317; David M. Silver, *Lincoln's Supreme* Court, orig. pub. 1956 (Urbana: University of Illinois Press, 1998), 5. For the letter laying out the schedule for the court visit, see William H. Seward to Lincoln, February 25, 1861, ALPLC. Lincoln was invited to attend the justices either in their Capitol reception room at 3 P.M., or at their 4-½ Street consultation room at 3:30. For Lincoln's history as an attorney before Taney's Court, see Brian McGinty, *Lincoln and the Court* (Cambridge: Harvard University Press, 2008), 18.

100. *Washington Evening Star*, February 26, 1861.

101. Ibid.

102. Ibid. That same day, the pro-Union paper predicted that Cameron would be named treasury secretary, and Caleb Smith secretary of war—both wrong. Two days later, the *Star* thought Lincoln might add Andrew Johnson of Tennessee.

103. "Diary of a Public Man," Part II, 267.

104. *CW*, 4:246. The surviving draft is in John Nicolay's hand.

105. *Lincoln Day by Day*, 3:22–23; *CW*, 4:246–47.

106. John G. Nicolay, "Lincoln's Speeches on the Journey to Washington . . ." typescript of pencil notes written for, but not used in, the Nicolay book, *Outbreak of the Rebellion*, NPLC.

107. *Lincoln Day by Day*. 3:23. Wool was even older than Winfield Scott: although technically seventy-six, he was born on February 29, 1784, and without a leap year in 1861 could be called seventy-seven by the 28th.

108. *Lincoln Day by Day*, 3:23.

109. *CW*, 4:247.

110. See Rudolph Schleiden invitation, February 23, 1861, ALPLC; *Philadelphia Inquirer*, March 4, 1861.

111. The gift, from Brewster & Co. of Broome Street in Manhattan, was reported in the *Washington Evening Star*, February 26, 1861. See *Philadelphia Inquirer*, March 4, 1861.

112. The phrase "flourishing about" is used with apologies to Lincoln: beginning his career in Springfield, he had pointedly complained that there was much "flourishing about in carriages" there—despite which he was still "quite as

lonesome here as I ever was anywhere in my life." Lincoln to Mary Owens, May 7, 1837, *CW*, 1:78.

113. *New-York Semi-Weekly Tribune*, March 1, 1861, reprinted in Gunderson, *Old Gentlemen's Convention*, 83.

114. *Lincoln Day by Day*, 3:22–23; Gunderson, *Old Gentlemen's Convention*, 88; *Cleveland Plain Dealer*, March 1, 1861; *Boston Daily Courier*, March 1, 1861.

115. "Diary of a Public Man, Part II," 268; Robert W. Johanssen, *Stephen A. Douglas* (New York: Oxford University Press, 1973), 843.

116. Esther Cowles Cushman, "Douglas the Loyal: A Hitherto Unpublished Manuscript by James Pollock . . . ," *Journal of the Illinois State Historical Society* 23 (April 1930): 168–69.

117. Wilson and Davis, eds., *Herndon's Informants*, 41.

118. Speech of Charles S. Moorehead, published in the *Liverpool Mercury*, October 13, 1862, reproduced in Charles Segal, *Conversations with Lincoln* (New York: G. P. Putnam's Sons, 1961), 85–90.

119. Thomas Turner to Lincoln, February 28, 1861, ALPLC.

120. Gunderson, *Old Gentlemen's Convention*, 95.

121. Nicolay and Hay, eds., *Abraham Lincoln*, 3:323.

122. Gunderson, *Old Gentlemen's Convention*, 105–7.

123. John J. Crittenden and Mrs. Chapman Coleman, *The Life of John J. Crittenden, with Selections from His Correspondence and Speeches*, 2 vols. (Philadelphia: J. B. Lippincott, 1871), 2:282.

124. Allan Nevins and Milton Halsey Thomas, eds., *The Diary of George Templeton Strong*, 4 vols. (New York: Macmillan, 1952), 3:105.

125. *Congressional Globe*, 36th Congress, 2d Session (1861), 1285, 1403.

126. See, for example, Lincoln to "His Excellency the Governor of the State of North Carolina," March 16, 1861, copy in the Abraham Lincoln Papers Project, Springfield, Illinois; John A. Lupton, "Abraham Lincoln and the Corwin Amendment," *Illinois* Heritage 9 (September–October 2006): 34; "Abolition's Evil Twin," *Charlotte Observer*, reprinted in *Washington Post*, October 26, 2006. A Web campaign began in 2006 calling for the official rescinding of the Shadow Amendment as a gesture of apology for American slavery.

127. Modern Constitutional amendments must now achieve ratification within a prescribed time.

13. The Ultimate Justice of the People

1. *Washington Evening Star*, March 1, 1861.

2. Richard S. West, Jr., *Gideon Welles: Lincoln's Navy Department* (Indianapolis.: Bobbs-Merrill, 1943), 93–94. As late as March 2, 1861, the *New York Times* confidently reported that Welles would be postmaster general.

3. *Lincoln Day by Day*, 3:22–23. One Ohioan wrote to Lincoln to warn that he would "commit political suicide" by appointing Chase. See Alexander Waddle to Lincoln, February 17, 1861, ALPLC.

4. Loring, quoted in Francis Fisher Browne, *The Every-Day Life of Abraham Lincoln* (Chicago: Browne Howell, 1913), 283.

5. Diary of Charles Francis Adams, March 1, 1861, Adams Papers, Massachusetts Historical Society.

6. CW, 4:248.

7. According to one source, Lincoln met with Pennsylvania's Republican leadership during his visit to Philadelphia on February 21, and there learned that opposition to Cameron had been formally withdrawn. See *Lincoln Day by Day*, 3:20.

8. *New York Tribune*, March 2, 1861; William Baringer, *A House Dividing: Lincoln as President Elect* (Springfield, Ill.: Abraham Lincoln Association, 1945), 321.

9. *New York Times*, February 22, 1861; John Hay, writing in the *New York World*, in Michael Burlingame, ed., *Lincoln's Journalist: John Hay's Anonymous Writings for the Press, 1860–1864* (Carbondale: Southern Illinois University Press, 1998), 46.

10. William H. Seward to Lincoln, March 2, 1861, ALPLC.

11. Allan Nevins, *The Emergence of Lincoln*, 2 vols. (New York: Charles Scribner's Sons, 1950), 2:455.

12. John G. Nicolay and John Hay, *Abraham Lincoln: A History*, 10 vols. (New York: The Century Co., 1890), 3:371. Lincoln made the remark on Inauguration Day.

13. Howard K. Beale, *The Diary of Edward Bates, 1859–1866* (Washington, D.C.: U.S. Government Printing Office, 1933), 175; *National Intelligencer*, March 2, 1861; Diary of Charles Francis Adams, February 28, 1861, Adams Papers, Massachusetts Historical Society.

14. *National Intelligencer*, March 4, 1861; Albert G. Riddle, *Recollections of War Times: Reminiscences of Men and Events in Washington, 1860–1865* (New York: G. P. Putnam's Sons, 1895), 12.

15. Lincoln to William H. Seward, March 4, 1861, CW, 4:273.

16. Frederic J. Blue, *Salmon P. Chase: A Life in Politics* (Kent, Ohio: Kent State University Press, 1987), 132; "The Diary of a Public Man, Part III: Unpublished Passages of the Secret History of the American Civil War," *North American Review* 124 (October 1879): 375.

17. R. Gerald McMurtry, "From Our Archives: Lincoln's Proposed Cabinet," *Lincoln Lore* 1553 (July 1967), 2.

18. Joseph H. Medill, editor of the *Chicago Press & Tribune*, quoted in H. I. Cleveland, "Booming the First Republican President: A Talk with Abraham Lincoln's Friend, the Late Joseph Medill," *Saturday Evening Post* 172

(August 5, 1899): 85; Doris Kearns Goodwin, *Team of Rivals: The Political Genius of Abraham Lincoln* (New York: Simon & Schuster, 2005), 319.

19. One Sarah A. Robinson, for example, believed she deserved employment as a governess. Offering to pray for his "prosperity and happiness," opera singer Amalia Majocchi Valtellina audaciously demanded financial help. And at least having the decency to summarize fourteen petitions in support of his quest, rather than forwarding the bulky documents themselves, Samuel H. Parker wrote to request the office of postmaster of San Francisco. See Robinson to Lincoln, February 25, 1861; Valtellina to Lincoln, February 27, 1861; Samuel H. Parker to Lincoln, March 1, 1861, ALPLC.

20. See, for example, Henry S. Lane to Lincoln, February 25, 1861 (recommending Henry Winter Davis); Francis S. Corkran to Lincoln, February 26, 1861 (opposing Davis and favoring Montgomery Blair); Alexander K. McClure to Lincoln, February 24, 1861 (opposing Cameron); Edward D. Baker to Lincoln, February 24, 1861 (favoring Cameron), all ALPLC.

21. Salmon P. Chase to Lincoln, January 28, 1861, ALPLC. The Chase wing's fear of Seward dominance is recalled in Adam I. P. Smith, *No Party Now: Politics in the Civil War North* (New York: Oxford University Press, 2006), 31.

22. "Gulliver Abe in the White House . . . ," *Frank Leslie's Budget of Fun*, March 15, 1861, reprinted in Gary L. Bunker, *From Rail-Splitter to Icon: Lincoln's Image in Illustrated Periodicals, 1860–1865* (Kent, Ohio: Kent State University Press, 2001), 78.

23. *Washington Evening Star*, February 27, 1861.

24. Burlingame, ed, *Lincoln's Journalist*, 46, 51.

25. Henry Villard, *Memoirs of Henry Villard, Journalist and Financier, 1835–1900*, 2 vols. (Boston: Houghton Mifflin, 1904), 1:156; The "Diary of a Public Man, Part II," *North American Review* 129 (September 1879): 266; William E. Baringer, *A House Dividing: Lincoln as President Elect* (Springfield, Ill.: Abraham Lincoln Association, 1945), 303–4.

26. Francis S. Corkran to Lincoln, February 26, 1861, ALPLC.

27. The guidebook, published in New York, is illustrated in Thomas F. Schwartz, *Mary Todd Lincoln: First Lady of Controversy* (Springfield, Ill.: Abraham Lincoln Presidential Library and Museum, 2007), 35.

28. Villard, *Memoirs*, 1:156–57.

29. *Washington Evening Star*, March 2, 1861.

30. Lecture on discoveries and inventions, February 11, 1859, CW, 3:360.

31. Allan Nevins and Milton Halsey Thomas, eds., *Diary of George Templeton Strong*, 4 vols. (New York: Macmillan, 1952), 3:104–5.

32. Nicolay and Hay, *Abraham Lincoln*, 3:319.

33. Stephen Trigg Logan to Lincoln, January 13, 1862, with Lincoln's March 26, 1861 endorsement: "The writer of this is almost a father to me." Un-

earthed by the Papers of Abraham Lincoln Project at the National Archives, the text was reported in Daniel W. Stowell, "Almost a Father to Me," *Lincoln Legal Briefs* 84 (October–December 2007), 1.

34. First draft of the inaugural address, *CW*, 4:254.

35. From Logan's remarks after Lincoln's death, quoted by Charles S. Zane in a 1912 article for *Sunset*, "Lincoln as I Knew Him," quoted in Don E. Fehrenbacher and Virginia Fehrenbacher, *Recollected Words of Lincoln* (Stanford: Stanford University Press, 1996), 304.

36. Final inaugural address, *CW*, 4:266.

37. William H. Bailhache to his wife, March 1, 1861, Bailhache–Brayman Papers, ALPLM; and March 3, 1861, Lincoln Collection, Indiana University, first published in Douglas L. Wilson, *Lincoln's Sword: The Presidency and the Power of Words* (New York: Alfred A. Knopf, 2006), 62.

38. "Diary of a Public Man, Part III," 380, 384

39. *New York Herald*, March 4, 1861.

40. *Diary of George Templeton Strong*, 3:104–5.

41. Nicolay and Hay, *Abraham Lincoln*, 3:320.

42. Second draft of the inaugural address with Lincoln's handwritten emendations, ALPLC.

43. Wilson, *Lincoln's Sword*, 55.

44. William H. Seward to Lincoln, February 24, 1861, in Nicolay and Hay, *Abraham Lincoln*, 3:319–20.

45. Ronald C. White, Jr., *The Eloquent President: A Portrait of Lincoln Through His Words* (New York: Random House, 2005), 69.

46. William H. Seward to Lincoln, February 24, 1861, in Nicolay and Hay, *Abraham Lincoln*, 3:320.

47. Seward to Lincoln, February or March 1861, ALPLC.

48. *Proceedings of the Massachusetts Historical Society* 41 (1909): 147–48.

49. Nicolay and Hay, *Abraham Lincoln*, 3:321.

50. Ibid., 321–22.

51. "Suggestions for a closing paragraph," William H. Seward to Lincoln, late February 1861, ALPLC.

52. Douglas Wilson dismisses such speculation as "Occam's razor," pointing out that the sentence "does not seem to have anything much to do with Browning's advice, which was narrowly cast." But he adds: "It is, of course, possible that things happened as you hypothesize." And Ronald White agreed that "Seward started from scratch, and from his own sense of superiority to Lincoln, with his task of revision." E-mail correspondence, December 11, 2007. I am grateful to both scholars of Lincoln's words for sharing their views.

53. Seward draft in ALPLC; reproduced in Wilson, *Lincoln's Sword*, 65.

54. Don E. Fehrenbacher, "The Words of Lincoln," *Lincoln in Text and Context*

(Stanford: Stanford University Press, 1987), 285. Fehrenbacher argues that "Lincoln's literary skill is most readily observable in those instances when he took someone else's prose and molded it to his own use," including the inaugural peroration Fehrenbacher judges "the first oratorical summit of his presidency."

55. *CW*, 4:271.

56. *Washington Evening Star*, March 4, 1861.

57. *Philadelphia Inquirer*, March 4, 1861.

58. *Washington Evening Star*, March 4, 1861; William Burger to Eben H. Burger, March 8, 1861, "Lincoln Young and Handsome at 1st Inaugural," undated clipping from the *New York Herald Tribune*, in the Lincoln Museum, Fort Wayne, Indiana.

59. Diary of Charles Francis Adams, March 4, 1861, Adams Papers, Massachusetts Historical Society.

60. *New York Times*, March 5, 1861.

61. *Frank Leslie's Illustrated Newspaper*, March 4, 1861; *Boston Post*, March 3, 1861.

62. Elizabeth Todd Grimsley, "Six Months in the White House," *Journal of the Illinois State Historical Society* 19 (October 1926–January 1927), 44–45.

63. "Diary of a Public Man, Part III," 382.

64. *Boston Post*, March 4, 1861.

65. Ibid.

66. Browne, *The Every-Day Life of Abraham Lincoln*, 284.

67. Solomon Foot (chairman of Committee of Arrangements) to Mary Lincoln, March 3, 1861, ALPLC.

68. *Baltimore Sun*, March 4, 1861; *New York Times*, March 5, 1861.

69. Browne, *The Every-Day Life of Abraham Lincoln*, 285.

70. Willard family papers, Manuscript Division, Library of Congress. The bill included hefty liquor charges, presumably to lubricate hard-drinking guests in the hospitality suites. See also Lincoln to "Messrs. Willards," April 19, 1861, in Roy P. Basler, ed., *The Collected Works of Abraham Lincoln: Supplement, 1832–1865* (Westport, Conn.: Greenwood Press, 1974), 68.

71. *Baltimore Sun*, March 5, 1861; *National Intelligencer*, March 5, 1861.

72. Report by Stephen Fiske, correspondent for the *New York Herald*, in the *Ladies' Home Journal*, March 1897, reprinted in Rufus Rockwell Wilson, ed., *Lincoln Among His Friends: A Sheaf of Intimate Memories* (Caldwell, Idaho: Caxton Printers, 1942), 308. The kissing episode was reported in a clipping preserved by Gideon Welles in his news scrapbook, now in the Library of Congress, and noted in West, *Gideon Welles*, 94.

73. Charles P. Stone, "Washington on the Eve of the War," *Century Illustrated Magazine* 26 (July 1883): 466.

74. Wilson, *Lincoln Among His Friends*, 308.

75. *Charleston Mercury*, March 7, 1861.
76. *Douglass' Monthly*, April 1861, in Philip S. Fouer and Yuvall Taylor, eds., *Frederic Douglass: Selected Speeches and Writings* (Chicago: Lawrence Hill, 1975), 432.
77. *Baltimore Sun*, March 5, 1861.
78. Benjamin Brown French, *Witness to the Young Republic: A Yankee's Journal, 1828–1870*, ed. Donald B. Cole and John J. McDonough (Hanover, N.H.: University Press of New England, 1989), 348.
79. *National Intelligencer*, March 5, 1861.
80. Philip S. Klein, *President James Buchanan: A Biography* (Newtown, Conn.: American Political Biography Press, 1962), 402.
81. *Boston Post*, March 5, 1861; *National Intelligencer*, March 5, 1861; Wilson, *Lincoln Among His Friends*, 309; Diary of Charles Frances Adams, March 4, 1861.
82. *New York Times*, March 5, 1861.
83. *Arrangements for the Inauguration of the President of the United States on the Fourth of March, 1861*, Manuscript Division, Library of Congress.
84. Julia Buel, in *Inauguration Day March 4, 1861 . . . 3–4.*
85. *New York Times*, March 5, 1861; *National Intelligencer*, March 5, 1861.
86. "Diary of a Public Man, Part III," 383.
87. William Burger to Eben H. Burger, March 8, 1861.
88. *New York Times*, March 5, 1861.
89. Ibid.; Chittenden, *Recollections of President Lincoln*, 87.
90. Chittenden, *Recollections of President Lincoln*, 87.
91. Grimsley, "Six Months in the White House," 46. See also *Cincinnati Daily Commercial*, March 11, 1861. Eyewitnesses Ben: Perley Poore and Carl Schurz both corroborate this often disputed story. See Allan Nevins, "He Did Hold Lincoln's Hat," *American Heritage* 10 (February 1959): 98–99.
92. "Diary of a Public Man, Part III," 383.
93. Charles Aldrich recollections, first published in the *Annals of* Iowa in 1907, reprinted in Rufus Rockwell Wilson, *Intimate Memories of Lincoln* (Elmira, N.Y.: Primavera Press, 1945), 366; Wilson, *Lincoln Among His Friends*, 309.
94. Stone, "Washington on the Eve of the War," 466.
95. *New York Tribune*, March 5, 1861; Mercier quoted in Ernest B. Furgurson, *Freedom Rising: Washington in the Civil War* (New York: Alfred A. Knopf, 2004), 60. Furguson cites "Henri Mercier in Washington" an unpublished Ph.D. dissertation by Daniel Carroll, University of Pennsylvania, 1968.
96. Wilson, *Intimate Memories of Lincoln*, 366.
97. Diary of Charles Francis Adams, March 4, 1861, Adams Papers, Massachusetts Historical Society.

98. *Washington Daily Intelligencer*, March, 5, 1861.

99. Wilson, *Intimate Memories of Lincoln*, 366; W. A. Janny to Will Thomson, April 6, 1861, W. D. Thomson Papers, Emory University; *New York Times*, March 5, 1861.

100. *New York Times*, March 5, 1861; CW, 4:262–71.

101. Wilson, *Intimate Memories of Lincoln*, 366; *New York Times*, March 5, 1861; Wilson, *Lincoln Among His Friends*, 309.

102. Browne, *The Every Day Life of Abraham Lincoln*, 325; *Frank Leslie's Illustrated Newspaper*, February 23, 1861; Wilson, *Lincoln Among His Friends*, 310.

103. As historian James F. Simon put it, Lincoln had made certain that "the Taney Court would not have the final word on the issue of slavery." See Simon, *Lincoln and Chief Justice Taney* (New York: Simon & Schuster, 2007), 175.

104. Wilson, *Intimate Memories of Lincoln*, 366; Crimsley, "Six months in the White House," 46.

105. Grimsley, "Six Months in the White House," 45.

106. Nicolay and Hay, *Abraham Lincoln*, 3:344.

Epilogue. Mystic Chords of Memory

1. Allan Nevins and Milton Halsey Thomas, eds., *The Diary of George Templeton Strong*, 4 vols. (New York: Macmillan, 1952), 3:106. "I like the way this document opens," Strong enthused.

2. Both papers, from March 5, 1861, quoted in Lois J. Einhorn, *Lincoln the Orator: Penetrating the Lincoln Legend* (Westport, Conn.: Greenwood Press, 1992), 55.

3. *The* [New York] *Independent*, March 7, 1861; *Charleston Mercury*, March 9, 1861.

4. *Chicago Daily Times*, March 6, 1861; *Chicago Press Tribune*, March 5, 1861. These and other contrasting press accounts are superbly analyzed in Ronald C. White, Jr., *The Eloquent President: A Portrait of Lincoln Through His Words* (New York: Random House, 2005), 93–95.

5. William Burger to Eben H. Burger, March 8, 1861, "Lincoln 'Young and Handsome at 1st Inaugural," undated clipping from the *New York Herald Tribune*, Lincoln Library and Museum, Fort Wayne, Indiana.

6. "The Diary of a Public Man, Part III," *North American Review* 124 (October 1879): 382.

7. *New York Herald*, March 6, 1865. Second quote cited in White, *The Eloquent President*, 94.

8. Benjamin Brown French, *Witness to a Young Republic: A Yankee's Journal,*

1828–1870, ed. David B. Cole and John J. McDonough (Hanover, N.H.: University Press of New England, 1989), 348.

9. *Diary of George Templeton Strong*, 3:106.

10. Henry Watterson, quoted in Rufus Rockwell Wilson, *Lincoln Among His Friends: A Sheaf of Intimate Memories* (Caldwell, Idaho: Caxton Printers, 1942), 287.

11. William Kauffmann Scarborough, ed., *The Diary of Edmund Ruffin*. 2 vols. (Baton Rouge: Louisiana State University Press, 1972), 1:560.

12. *Douglass' Monthly*, April 1861, in Philip S. Foner and Yuvall Taylor, *Frederick Douglass: Selected Speeches and Writings* (Chicago: Lawrence Hill, 1975), 434–35.; see also James Oakes, *The Radical and the Republican: Frederick Douglass, Abraham Lincoln, and the Triumph of Antislavery Politics* (New York: W. W. Norton, 2007), 142.

13. Albert G. Riddle, *Recollections of War Times: Reminiscences of Men and Events in Washington, 1860–1865* (New York: G. P. Putnam's Sons, 1895), 14–15.

14. Rufus Rockwell Wilson, ed., *Intimate Memories of Abraham Lincoln* (Elmira, N.Y.: Press of the Pioneers, 1945), 369.

15. Edward Everett to Abraham Lincoln, November 20, 1863, ALPLC.

16. Seward proposed, without success, the following: "While so great a diversity of opinion exists on the question of what amendments if indeed any would be effective in restoring peace and safety it would only tend to aggravate the dispute if I were to attempt to give direction to the public mind in that respect." Lincoln generally avoided using the pronoun "I."

⊰ INDEX ⊱

Page numbers in italic refer to illustrations.

abolition, abolitionists, 107, 120, 132, 178, 216, 428
  H. Adams's views on, 192–93
  Lincoln alleged as, 12, 134, 211, 245
  Lincoln as viewed by, 27, 50, 51, 55, 125
Adams, Charles Francis, 24, 120, 131, 192, 417–18, 433, 477
  cabinet selection and, 107, 167, 180, 209, 532n, 535n
  compromise efforts and, 155, 193, 214
  on inaugural, 446, 450–51, 453
  inaugural trip and, 339, 340
Adams, Henry, 1, 192–93, 243, 410, 532n, 539n
Adams, John, 2, 41, 69
Adams, John Quincy, 102, 200, 495n
advertising, 107, 237, 335, 366, 575n
Aesop's Fables, 426–27
Alabama, 48–49, 175, 344
  in election of 1860, 25, 38
  secession and, 12, 47, 111, 127, 162, 211–12, 222, 244, 275
Albany, N.Y., 277–78, 284, 348–50, 383, 405
Albany Evening Journal, 171, 237, 460
Aldrich, Charles, 455

Alexandria, Va., 280, 478–79
Allberger, F. A., 569n
Allen, Cyrus M., 65
Alley, John B., 288
"almost chosen people," Americans as, 374, 576n
Alschuler, Samuel G., 8, 109–10, 519n
American Bank Note Company, 335
American Revolution, 51, 259, 371–74
Anderson, Robert, 163, 221–22
Andrew, John A., 51, 143
Andrews, Rufus D., 554n
Anticipations of the Future (Ruffin), 23–24
anti-slavery movement, 75, 81, 98–99, 107, 129, 344
  see also abolition, abolitionists
Arkansas, secession and, 327
Arnold, Isaac N., 4, 109, 582n
Ashmun, George, 106
Aspinwall, William Henry, 361–62
Atwood, Jesse, 88

Bailhache, Ada, 93
Bailhache, William H., 237, 270, 438
Baker, Edward Dickinson, 34, 173–74, 431, 447, 452

Baker, Edward L., 237, 302
Baker, Jean, 524n
Balance, Charles, 123
Baldwin, J. D., 209
Baldwin, Roger, 321–22
Ballard, Frank W., 233
Ballo in Maschera, Un (Verdi), 365–66
Baltimore, Md., 27, 405, 412, 585n
    Lincoln in, 273, 284, 394–95, 399
Baltimore Plot, 377–83, 385, 387,
        388, 390–405, 411, 418, 458
    genuineness of danger in, 403–5,
        412, 418, 582n, 583n
    pictorial rebuttal and, 418–19,
        586n
    and reactions to Lincoln's
        clandestine passage, 397–403,
        402, 434
    secrecy of plan to escape from, 388,
        579n
Banks, Nathaniel P., 107, 143, 180,
        209–10, 430, 535n
Baptist State Convention, Alabama,
        111
Barbee, David Rankin, 278
Barney, Hiram, 204, 235–36, 361,
        532n, 541n
Barnum, P. T., 358, 364, 366,
        575n
Barrett, Joseph, 237
Bartlett, D. W., 322–23
Bateman, Newton, 39, 117–18, 297,
        501n
    on Lincoln's confiding, 138, 526n
    as Lincoln's office neighbor, 20, 83,
        115, 153
Bates, Edward, 184, 232, 261, 530n
    cabinet selection and, 59, 105, 107,
        144, 149–52, 169–70, 180,
        181–82, 201, 203, 208, 209, 430,
        433, 528n, 529n
    inaugural trip and, 286–87
Bayard, James A., 51–52

Beason, Father John, 337
Bedell, Grace, 87, 333–34, 570n
Bell, John, 71, 281, 314, 477
    cabinet selection and, 144, 148–49,
        180, 534n
    in election of 1860, 13, 42, 46, 77,
        339, 340, 423, 427, 495n, 496n,
        500n
Benjamin, Judah, 244
Benjamin, Park, 510n
Bennett, James Gordon, 543n, 549n
Beresford-Hope, Alexander J., 283
Beringer, Richard E., 558n
Berlin, 118, 548n
Berret, James G., 423
Bible, 69, 132, 153, 178, 187, 225,
        374, 457
Bissell, William H., 498n
blacks, 225, 280–81, 283, 409
    citizenship denied to, 127
    in Illinois, 118, 280–81, 290, 296,
        521n, 560n
    voting of, 27
    see also slavery, slaves
Bladensburg, Ill., 46
Blair, Francis P., Sr., 169, 411, 437,
        440
Blair, Francis Preston, Jr., 104, 121,
        149, 207, 528n, 547n
Blair, Montgomery, 383, 411, 578n
    cabinet selection and, 59, 104, 107,
        169, 170, 180, 207, 430
Blair House, 383, 578n
Bloomington, Ill., 19, 97, 497n, 512n
Bonham, Jeriah, 210
Boone, J.H.A., 298
Booth, John Wilkes, 179, 349, 405,
        572n
Booth, Junius Brutus, 323
Border Ruffians, 71, 511n
border states, 151, 155, 217, 314, 322,
        434, 558n
    see also specific states

Boritt, Gabor, 77, 359

Boston, Mass., 51, 125, 200, 284, 365, 415, 499n, 524n

Botts, John Minor, 106, 167

Bowen, F. W., 247, 297

Bowen, Henry C., 381–82, 388

Bradley, William C., 396

Brady, Mathew, 335, 418–19, 479, 586n

Brainerd, Cephas, 359

Brayman, Mason, 70

Breckinridge, John C., 239, 314, 323, 417, 477
   in election of 1860, 14, 15, 24, 42, 50, 136, 146, 284, 495n, 500n
   as president of Senate, 136

Briggs, James A., 338

Brockett, L. P., 3–4

Broderick, David, 49, 507n

Bronson, J. A., 104

Brooks, Noah, 3, 19

Brown, Albert Gallatin, 244, 245

Brown, John, 178, 380, 415

Brown, John Howe, 204, 520n

Browne, Charles Farrar (Artemus Ward), 123–24, 368, 523n

Browne, Robert H., 304

Browning, Orville Hickman, 19, 291–92, 413, 477
   inaugural address and, 312, 345–46, 439, 440, 444, 591n
   inaugural trip and, 286, 297, 308, 312, 565n

Bryan, Thomas B., 110

Bryan Hall, 110

Bryant, William Cullen, 15, 53–54, 113, 135, 237, 238, 359
   cabinet selection and, 142, 180, 205

Buchanan, James, 3, 14, 38, 69, 70, 126–33, 171, 174–76, 261, 437, 524n, 547n, 558n
   cabinet of, 104, 132, 163, 211, 416, 421

congressional message of, 112, 126, 127, 129–33, 212, 255

Corwin Amendment and, 429

in elections, 35, 42, 146

Fort Sumter relief and, 221–22

inaugural address of, 128, 523n

inaugural journey of, 272–73, 384

Lincoln's inaugural and, 447, 449, 450–51, 453

Lincoln's visits with, 408, 413, 421

Scott's correspondence with, 77–78

secession and, see secession, Buchanan and

slavery and, 127–28, 172, 523n

Southerners in administration of, 47–48, 132, 211

Wheatland estate of, 388, 450

Buel, Julia Maria, 409

Buffalo, N.Y., 41, 199, 275, 284, 336–38, 347, 569n

Burgess, James M., 279, 297

Butler, Preston, 525n

Butler, William, 297, 501n

cabinet selection, 5, 59, 64, 83, 118, 121, 140–52, 154, 174, 179–83, 195, 200–210, 227, 233, 234, 262, 423, 430–34, 534n–35n
   Chicago discussions of, 101–9
   on Election Night, 59–60, 141, 209, 431
   hesitancy in, 1, 6, 140, 141
   inaugural trip and, 330, 342
   Lincoln-Weed summit and, 166–70, 532n
   Mary Lincoln and, 199, 279
   rumors about, 101–2, 106, 141, 144, 149, 199, 208, 370, 430, 432, 587n
   Senate approval of, 176, 244
   Southern representation and, 60, 106–9, 144–45, 149–52, 167–70, 180, 520n, 527n, 528n

Caldwell, Alfred, 545n–46n

California, 49, 173, 207, 368

Cameron, Simon, 36, 37, 323, 424
  alleged corruption of, 146, 181, 182,
    201–2, 260, 431, 432, 535n
  cabinet selection and, 107, 134,
    146–47, 148, 170, 174, 180–83,
    201–8, 221, 227, 240, 260, 262,
    280, 330, 431–34, 528n, 535n,
    542n, 587n, 589n
  Lincoln's withdrawing of offer to,
    202, 205–6, 221, 540n

Campbell, A. W., 545n–46n

Canada, 275, 279

Canisius, Theodore, 149

Capitol, Illinois State, 18–22, 43, 73,
    93, 265, 286
  Lincoln's headquarters in, 19–22,
    30–33, 35, 40, 41, 60–63, 73, 81,
    90, 115–18, 123, 134, 174, 177,
    185, 186, 226, 255, 256,
    533n–34n
  Lincoln's move from, 177, 185, 197,
    256, 534n
  overcrowding in, 533n–34n
  Representative Hall in, 32, 33
  Senate Chamber of, 88, 135–36
  visitors at, 80–84, 90–91, 116–20,
    123, 150, 172–76, 185, 226

Capitol, U.S., 322, 409, 410, 421, 422,
    587n
  Lincoln's inauguration at, 450–58

Carman, Harry J., 522n

Carter, R. C., 71

cartoons, 400–403, 402, 582n

Carwardine, Richard, 4, 507n, 511n

Case, Henry, 501n

Cass, Lewis, 104, 163, 421

Castle Pinckney, 162, 163

Chandler, Zachariah, 143, 431, 433

Chapman, Augustus H., 249–51

Chapman, Harriet Ann, 250, 551n

Charles II, King of England, 231, 398

Charleston, Ill., 246, 248, 250–51,
    550n

Charleston, S.C., 24, 72, 77, 506n
  reaction to Lincoln's election in,
    48, 49
  secession and, 111, 160–61, 165,
    550n

Charleston Mercury, 12, 47, 161, 399,
    412, 460

Chase, Salmon P., 107, 154, 194–95,
    424, 430–35, 481
  cabinet selection and, 59, 64,
    102, 142, 148, 154, 166–67,
    180, 183, 184, 185, 202–5, 208,
    210, 262, 284, 430–34, 542n,
    590n
  Cooper Union engagement
    declined by, 233, 547n
  election of 1860 and, 361, 541n
  Peace Convention and, 259, 413

Chenery, James N., 560n

Chesnut, Mary Boykin, 55

Chicago, Ill., 46, 86, 88, 95–113, 292,
    519n, 545n, 547n
  Election Day in, 25, 35
  Lincoln-Hamlin meeting in, 66, 72,
    95–96, 98–99, 101, 103–5, 109,
    110, 516n
  Lincoln-Speed meeting in, 68, 72,
    95, 107–9
  Lincoln's reception in, 99–101
  post office in, 235, 237
  Republican convention in, 99, 102,
    103, 106, 134, 142, 146, 203,
    261, 266, 367, 497n
  Tremont House in, 98–101, 108,
    109

Chicago Tribune, 50, 91, 100, 137, 198,
    298
  cabinet selection and, 206, 210

Chittenden, Lucius, 406, 414,
    415–16

Churchman, James, 187

Cincinnati, Ohio, 154, 284, 316–18, 338, 377
    Burnet House, 317–18, 566n
civil religion, 374
civil war:
    avoiding of, 130
    predictions of, 158, 216, 530n
Civil War, U.S., 6, 245, 280n, 401, 452, 477–82, 502n, 563n
Clay, Cassius M., 144
Clay, Clement C., Jr., 244, 245
Clay, Henry, 66, 102–3, 174, 185, 188, 414, 556n
    inaugural address and, 256, 257, 264
Clay, James B., 414
Cleveland, Ohio, 187, 328–29, 565n
Cleveland Plain Dealer, 310, 329, 343, 400
Cobb, Howell, 56, 132
Coles County, Ill., 247–52, 295
Colfax, Schuyler, 106, 107, 144, 149, 180, 330, 430, 557n
Columbus, Ohio, 284, 318–21, 324, 325, 328–29
Confederacy, 262, 280, 321, 365, 440, 477, 478, 479, 481
    birth of, 258–59, 276, 553n
    Davis made president of, 283
Congress, U.S., 6, 38, 147, 175, 206, 241, 322, 421
    Buchanan's message to, 112, 126, 127, 129–33, 212, 255
    gag rule and, 53
    inaugural address and, 466, 469
    Lincoln's courtesy calls on, 421–22, 587n
    Lincoln's relations with, 50, 56, 156, 180, 193
    secession and, 132, 155–60, 162, 163–64, 165, 175, 176–77, 211–16, 223

    slavery and, 26, 53, 56, 127, 128, 155–60, 163, 164–65, 168, 213, 469, 532n
    Thirteenth Amendment proposals and, 428–29
    see also House of Representatives, U.S.; Senate, U.S.
Conkling, James Cook, 31, 43, 134–36, 286, 302
Conkling, Mercy, 61, 134, 286
Constitution, U.S., 13, 38, 57, 72, 133, 264, 292, 314, 371, 373, 376, 415, 428–29
    Buchanan's views on, 130
    inaugural address and, 266, 267, 443, 453, 455, 465–67, 469, 471–72
    Lincoln's views on amendments to, 175, 176, 429
    secession and, 94, 130, 223, 224–25, 256, 257, 259, 326
    slavery and, 26, 56, 66, 128, 164–65, 168, 224, 225, 469, 471–72, 545n
Constitutional Union party, 13, 71
Cook, Isaac, 235
Cooper, Peter, 504n
Cooper Union, Lincoln at, 20, 53, 66, 113, 136, 204, 233, 255, 261, 267, 294, 351, 361, 373, 382, 418, 497n, 498n, 532n, 541n
Cornell, Ezra, 407
Corwin, Thomas, 104, 417, 429, 586n
Corwin Amendment (Shadow Amendment), 429
cotton, 73, 75, 129
Couch, E. R., 104
Cover, Daniel, 235
Covode, John, 206, 527n
Cowan, Edgar, 205
Crittenden, John J., 104, 144, 155, 163, 211, 214, 244, 417, 424, 427–28, 433, 478, 543n

Crittenden Compromise, 163–64,
165, 175, 176–77, 213, 240, 252,
274, 428
Crofts, Daniel W., 545n
Cromwell, Oliver, 398
Cullom, Shelby M., 501n
Cummings, Alexander, 181, 207–8
Curtenius, P. W., 529n
Curtin, Andrew, 259, 388, 392, 393,
404
Cuthbert, Norma B., 577n

daguerreotypes, 290, 291
Danville, Ill., 306
Daily Illinois State Register
(Springfield), 50, 148, 152, 211,
305, 340, 345
Davis, David, 97, 120, 165, 199, 227,
292, 440, 478, 517n
cabinet selection and, 106, 107,
151, 169, 199, 534n, 535n
as campaign manager, 12–13, 61,
102, 497n
inaugural trip and, 282, 297,
354–55, 391
office-seeking of, 228
Seward's senatorial replacement
and, 260
in Washington, 420, 433, 585n
Davis, Henry Winter, 102, 106, 107,
167, 169, 228, 433, 517n
Davis, Jefferson, 3, 38, 47, 412, 477,
479, 534n, 558n
Buchanan's relations with, 129, 132
as Confederate president, 283
inaugural trip of, 321, 343–44
inauguration of, 344–45, 372
Lincoln compared with, 283, 321,
343–45, 399, 581n–82n
resignation of, 244, 245
secession and, 212, 243–44
on Senate resignations, 243–44
Davis, Varina, 244

Dawes, Henry L., 420
Day, Benjamin, 156
Dayton, William L., 59, 369–70, 431
Decatur, Ill., 246, 247, 305–6, 331
Declaration of Independence, 224–25,
376, 385
Defrees, John, 139, 144, 147, 150, 159
Deiffendorf, John, 227
Delahay, Mark, 121
Democrats, Democratic party, 42, 49,
56–57, 65, 71, 75–76, 80, 119,
174, 241, 246, 421, 422, 478,
479, 482, 495n, 556n
antiwar (Copperheads), 401, 483
cabinet selection and, 59, 107, 167,
209–10, 535n
federal bureaucracy and, 121,
234–36, 547n
inaugural trip and, 297, 310, 326,
329, 332, 340, 341, 343, 345,
347, 348, 368, 375
Lincoln's clandestine arrival and,
397, 400
in Lincoln's coalition, 120, 434
Northern vs. Southern factions of,
13, 14
pro-South, 212, 362–63
Senate resignations of, 243–45
Southern, 13, 14, 69, 84, 323
Springfield ministers as, 138, 526n
see also specific people and elections
Dennison, William, 319, 324
Dewey, Joshua, 362
Dickens, Charles, 186, 520n
Dixon, James, 431, 447
Dodge, William, 406, 415, 433
Donald, David Herbert, 585n
Doolittle, James R., 213, 421, 431
Douglas, Stephen A., 89, 128, 281,
314, 326, 397, 502n
cabinet selection and, 143–44,
176
death of, 477, 478

in election of 1860, 12, 14, 25, 27,
    35, 37, 38, 44, 96, 114, 138, 274,
    284, 427, 495n–96n, 500n, 504n,
    543n
Electoral College and, 567n
inaugural address and, 438–39,
    455–56
Kansas issue and, 128, 157
Lincoln's 1860 win and, 56–57
Lincoln's debates with, 66, 75, 110,
    172, 248, 456, 497n, 498n, 563n
at Lincoln's inauguration, 452,
    455–56
Lincoln's reunion with, 413, 421
popular sovereignty and, 128,
    157
in Senate races, 12, 15, 66, 155,
    261, 499n
slavery compromises and, 155, 164,
    425, 543n
Douglass, Frederick, 216, 243, 499n
    election of 1860 and, 13, 26–27
    on inauguration, 450, 461–62
    on slavery, 15, 55–56, 125
Drake, J. R., 298
Draper, Simeon, 37, 432
Dred Scott v. Sanford, 107, 127–28,
    129, 422, 523n
Dryden, John, 76
Dubois, Jesse K., 33, 237–38, 501n
    inaugural trip and, 297, 308, 313
Dutton, O. H., 298

Eckert, George Nicholas, 133–34
economy, 73, 217, 424
    Buchanan and, 128–29
    election of 1860 and, 23, 55
    financial panics and, 75, 128–29,
        144, 164
    New York City and, 52, 76–77, 199,
        212, 361–62, 424, 437, 461,
        574n
Edwards, Elizabeth, 371

Edwards, Ninian W., 290, 547n
Election Day and Night, 18–45, 58, 77
    cabinet selection on, 59–60, 141,
        209, 431
    record-breaking voting on, 16,
        496n
    rumors on, 37–38
    in Springfield, 11–12, 18–22,
        27–41, 29, 43–45, 59–60, 63,
        494n
    telegrams on, 32–41, 36, 297
    weather on, 18–19, 24
election of 1860, 11–67, 77, 113, 129,
    149, 173, 175, 284, 339, 340,
    344, 370, 400, 427, 477, 541n,
    573n
    amalgam of Lincoln supporters in,
        107
    four candidates in, 13, 495n
    Hanks's role in, 246
    historic significance of, 14, 23
    House and, 13–14, 26, 36, 42–43,
        127, 136, 196
    ice cream parlor celebration in,
        38–40, 504n
    Illinois electors and, 31, 134–36
    Lincoln's lack of campaigning in, 6,
        14–18
    party tickets in, 27–28, 29, 30,
        500n, 501n
    popular vote in, 5, 42, 68–69, 97,
        126, 277, 362, 504n
    racism and, 54–55
    Republican convention in, 99, 102,
        103, 106, 134, 142, 146, 203,
        261, 367, 497n
    slavery and, 11, 14–17, 26, 55–56,
        155, 156, 156, 157, 213
    Southern reactions to, 46–57, 66,
        67, 111, 138–39, 211
    victory celebrations in, 43, 45, 46,
        71, 79, 90–95
    see also Electoral College

elections, 2, 41, 77, 102–3, 264, 479
  of 1800, 41, 437
  of 1824, 102, 495n
  of 1856, 35, 42, 143, 155, 275
  of 1858, 248, 261, 499n
  of 1864, 58, 263, 403–4, 482, 533n,
    554n
  Lincoln's knowledge of figures in,
    35, 502n
Electoral College, 5, 14, 69, 73, 126,
  152, 196, 277, 322–24, 423, 495n
Ellsworth, Ephraim Elmer, 30, 420–21,
  478–79, 500n
  Baltimore Plot and, 388, 391
  inaugural trip and, 280, 281–82,
    296, 297, 318, 375, 377, 388,
    391, 557n–58n
Emerson, Ralph Waldo, 51
England, 201, 230
Epstein, Daniel Mark, 573n
equal rights, Lincoln's views on, 55,
  154–55, 374, 529n, 550n
Etheridge, Emerson, 107
Evans, T. C., 298
Evarts, William M., 260, 554n, 574n
Everett, Edward, 71, 339–40,
  495n–96n
Ewing, Thomas, 143, 184, 527n
Ex parte Milligan, 478

Farewell Address (Lincoln), 298–304,
  301, 319, 338, 374, 563n
Farewell Address (Washington), 264
Farmington, Ill., Lincoln's trip to,
  246–51
Farwell, James V., 109
Fawcett, Henry, 123
federal jobs, 233–38, 547n
  see also cabinet selection
Fehrenbacher, Don E., 444, 526n,
  577n, 592n
Felton, Samuel M., 377, 382
Fenton, Reuben E., 97

Fessenden, William Pitt, 431
Fido (Lincoln's dog), 291, 560n–61n
Fillmore, Millard, 35, 104, 336, 337
  Lincoln's transition and, 274, 275
Fitzpatrick, Benjamin, 244
Flanders, A. W., 285
Florida, 175
  secession and, 12, 159, 162, 211,
    222, 244
Florville, William, 85
Floyd, John B., 163
Fogg, George G., 64, 118, 180, 207,
  210, 521n
Forbes, Burnett, 281, 297
Ford's Theatre, 405, 480, 575n
foreign service, 234, 547n
Fort Gaines, 212
Fort Morgan, 212
Fort Moultrie, 162, 163
Fort Pike, 245
Fort Pulaski, 211
Fort Sumter, 162, 163, 221–22, 427,
  439, 478, 481, 482, 586n
Foster, Lafayette, 431
Fralick, Elias, 302
France, 230, 398
Francis, Simeon, 237
Franciscus, G. C., 393
Frank Leslie's Illustrated Newspaper,
  88–89, 115–16, 136, 298, 356,
  515n, 525n, 581n
Franklin House, 93
Freehling, William W., 495n, 506n
Free Soilers, 107, 120, 157
Frémont, John C., 35, 143, 200
French, Benjamin Brown, 450, 461
Fugitive Slave Laws, 75, 160, 164–65,
  252, 275, 415, 428, 532n
  inaugural address and, 266, 442,
    461

Gage, George W., 98
Galloway, Samuel, 496n

Gardner, Alexander, *218*, 418–19, 479, 586n
Garnett, Muscoe, 323
Georgia, 55, 76, 175, 228, 545n, 574n
  militia of, 48, 211
  secession and, 12, 138–39, 162, 211, 222, 244, 283, 362, 506n, 543n
German, Christopher S., 190–91, 291, 538n
German-Americans, 42, 80, 101, 149, 238, 316, 435
Germany, 80, 118
Gettysburg, Pa., 340, 480, 558n
Giddings, Joshua, 118
Gillespie, Joseph, 171, 239
Gilmer, John A., 161, 213–14
  cabinet selection and, 107, 145, 167–68, 170, 180, 195
God, 138, 153, 337, 342, 345, 349, 374, 416
  Farewell Address and, 299, 303, 304, 338
Goodell, Lavinia, 356
Goodwin, Doris Kearns, 5, 60, 202
Gould, Charles, 382
Gourley, Harry, 331
Graham, William A., 127, 201, 540n
Grand Union Meeting, 179
Grant, Ulysses S., 25, 479, 480, 499n
Gray, J. W., 329
"Great Secession Winter, The" (H. Adams), 192–93
Great Western Railroad, 247–48, 289, 296–300, 302, 304–7
Greeley, Horace, 14, 53, 54, 227, 260–62, 423, 479
  inaugural trip and, 329–30, 382
  senatorial ambitions of, 260–61, 554n
  Springfield visit of, 230, 261–62
Green, Duff, 174–76, 533n
Grimshaw, Joseph Jackson, 297

Grimsley, Elizabeth Todd, 447
Grinnell, Moses H., 200, 213, 361
Griswold, A. W., 298
Gustav III, King of Sweden, 365
Guthrie, James, 108, 427

Hale, James T., 222–23
Hale, John Parker, 131, 447
Hall, Perry, 565n
Hamlin, Hannibal, 2, 25–26, 55, 71, 135, 166, 211, 479, 518n, 585n
  assassination threats and, 152, 194
  cabinet selection and, 101, 103, 109, 140–41, 143, 180, 210, 517n, 535n
  inaugural trip and, 364–65, 371
  Lincoln's Chicago meeting with, 66, 72, 95–96, 98–99, 101, 103–5, 109, 110, 516n
  at Seward's home, 417, 440
  speeches of, 98–99, 366
  swearing-in of, 450–51
Hanaford, Phoebe, 3
Hanks, Dennis, 249–50, 306, 426, 551n
Hanks, John, 246–49, 331
Hanks, Sarah Elizabeth Johnston, 551n
Hanscom, Simon P., 95, 516n
Harper's Weekly, 295, 401, 418, 419, 526n, 586n
Harris, George Washington, 392
Harris, Ira, 261, 433, 554n
Harris, William C., 510n–11n
Harrisburg, Pa., 259, 284, 379, 387–88, 390–93, 412, 420, 565n
  Lincoln's departure from, 392–93, 398–401, 411
Harrison, William Henry, 70–71, 103, 174, 556n
  inaugural journey of, 272
Hartford Life, 288–89
Harvard University, 18, 51, 72, 557n

Harvey, James E., 263
Haskell, Helen, 65
Hatch, Ozias M., 81, 120, 237, 297
    election of 1860 and, 30, 32, 33,
        501*n*
Hattaway, Herman, 558*n*
Hawthorne, Nathaniel, 407
Hay, John M., 30, 35, 116, 226, 230,
        232, 298, 443, 479–80, 481
    Baltimore Plot and, 392, 401,
        404–5
    cabinet selection and, 59–60
    inaugural trip and, 279, 282, 297,
        298, 302, 305, 306, 313, 315,
        317, 318, 330, 347, 348, 370,
        371, 374, 392, 563*n*
    on Lincoln, 87–88, 251–52, 287
    in Washington, 410, 420–21, 422,
        435, 452, 585*n*
Hay, Milton, 116
Haycraft, Thomas, 67
Hayne, Robert, 256–57
Hazzard, George W., 280, 281, 282,
        375, 391
Healy, G.P.A., 86, 88, 110
Hendee, John J., 123
Henderson, Isaac, 238
Henry, Alexander, 376
Herndon, William H., 30, 72, 122,
        163, 330, 480, 511*n*, 521*n*, 556*n*
    Baltimore Plot and, 404
    library of, 256, 553*n*
    on Lincoln, 20, 210, 215, 238, 240,
        256, 298
    Lincoln's pre-departure visit with,
        293–94, 561*n*–62*n*
    on Lincoln's voting, 28, 500*n*, 501*n*
    on Lincoln's writing, 255, 256, 263,
        265
Hesler, Alexander, 519*n*
Hicks, Thomas, 425
Hill, James L., 288–89, 559*n*
Hitt, Robert Roberts, 563*n*

Hoffmann, Francis A., 501*n*
Holmes, Oliver Wendell, 215
Hopper, John, 501*n*
House of Representatives, U.S., 50,
        163, 173, 428, 429, 478
    Committee of Thirty-three in, 155,
        158, 214, 240
    Committee on Elections of, 213
    constitutional amendment and, 176
    election of 1860 and, 13–14, 26, 36,
        42–43, 127, 136, 196
    Lincoln as member of, 26, 99, 143,
        173
    Lincoln's courtesy call to, 422, 587*n*
    presidents selected by, 13–14, 36,
        42–43, 495*n*–96*n*, 510*n*
Houston, Sam, 144
Howard, Joseph, Jr., 299, 332–33, 348,
        400, 408–9, 412, 558*n*
Hudson, E. B., 210
Hunter, David, 153, 162
    inaugural trip and, 280, 281, 282,
        318, 336, 375
Hunter, Robert, 244
Hutchison, Thomas, 527*n*
Hyer, Tom, 360

Illinois:
    blacks in, 118, 280–81, 290, 296,
        521*n*, 560*n*
    cabinet selection and, 106, 118, 180
    congressional delegation from, 413
    Corwin Amendment and, 429
    1860 election returns in, 35, 44,
        344, 505*n*
    electors in, 31, 134–36
    federal jobs in, 236
    founding of Republican party in,
        134
    inaugural journey in, 295–306, 331,
        344, 389
    neglect of Lincoln's friends from,
        237–38

Peace Convention and, 259, 427, 438

Republican state convention in, 246

Illinois & Mississippi Telegraph Company, 33–41, 36, 44, 45

Illinois Daily State Journal, 80, 88, 133, 148, 237, 289, 514n

Dec. 12 editorial in, 145, 528n

inaugural trip and, 298, 302

Lincoln at, 229, 270

Illinois Senate, 555n

Illinois State Capitol, *see* Capitol, Illinois State

Illinois State Library, 255

Illinois Supreme Court, 20, 534n

Inauguration Day, 438–39, 446–58, 449

Hamlin's swearing-in on, 450–51

inaugural address on, 452–57, 454

Lincoln's oath-taking on, 452, 457

military presence on, 446–47, 449

parade on, 447–50, 449

Indiana, 227, 306–14, 561n

cabinet selection and, 106, 180, 207

in election of 1860, 12, 26, 35–36, 39, 344

Lincoln's stops in, 276, 281, 284, 297, 307–14, 344, 565n

Indiana Asbury University, 65

Indianapolis, Ind., 281, 284, 286, 307–14, 317, 319, 320, 338, 565n

Bates House in, 308–13

Ingmire, F. W., 560n–61n

Interior Department, U.S., 132, 235, 522n, 548n

Lincoln's appointment to, 106, 143–44, 200, 201, 430, 529n, 540n

interregnum, 2–3, 69

inventions, 137, 410, 525n–26n

Irwin, Joseph I., 71

Irwin, Robert, 289–90, 297

Jackson, Andrew, 58, 81, 90, 104, 174, 383, 461

in election of 1824, 495n

inaugural journey of, 273, 297–98

Lincoln compared with, 59, 297–98

Nullification Crisis and, 78, 131, 256, 257

Jayne, William, 501n

Jefferson, Thomas, 2, 41, 69, 75, 274, 461, 510n

Lincoln compared with, 274, 316, 437, 441

Jeffords, H., 66

Jenkins, Jameson, 296

Jerome, William, 522n

Johns, Henry F., 123

Johnson, Andrew, 245, 421, 587n

Johnson, R. V., 540n

Johnson, Waldo Porter, 406

Johnson, William H., 280–81, 348, 558n

Johnston, Adam, 91

Jonas, Abraham, 194

Jones, Thomas D., 184–86, 188–92, 229, 264, 536n

patronage ambitions of, 191–92, 538n

Jones, William, 186–87

Juárez, Benito, 229

Judd, Norman, 121, 227, 290, 420

Baltimore Plot and, 377–79, 382, 384, 388, 390–93, 404, 405

cabinet selection and, 59, 105–6, 118, 148, 180, 199, 203, 279

inaugural trip and, 279, 282, 298, 332, 361, 377–79, 382, 384, 388, 390–93

Kansas, 128, 155, 177, 307, 386, 511n

Kansas-Nebraska Act (1854), 157

Kasson, William M., 335–36

Keene, Laura, 575n

Kellogg, William Pitt, 31, 101, 135–36
 in anti-secession efforts, 155, 158
 in Springfield, 240–41, 252
Kennedy, John A., 380, 381, 404,
 577n–78n
Kennedy, Robert Lenox, 439
Kentucky, 102, 119, 149, 174
 in election of 1860, 15, 27, 42, 67
 inaugural trip and, 285, 313–16,
 338
 secession and, 102, 161, 239, 244,
 314, 327, 344, 478
Ketch, Jack, 231
King, John Pendleton, 144
King, Preston, 140, 421, 433,
 586n–87n
King, R. P., 146
Know-Nothing party, 149, 273, 495n,
 537n
Koerner, Gustave, 118, 180–81, 203
Kohn, Abraham, 187
Kreismann, Hermann, 238, 548n
Kunhardt, Dorothy Meserve,
 560n–61n

Lady of the Lake (Scott), 189
Lafayette, Ind., 307
Lamon, Ward Hill, 12–13, 30, 45, 58,
 59, 82, 120, 421, 480, 585n
 Baltimore Plot and, 388, 391–95,
 400, 404, 405, 580n
 inaugural trip and, 279, 282, 287,
 296, 297, 305, 311, 313, 320,
 325, 377, 379, 384, 388
Lane, Harriet, 413
Lane, Joseph, 422
Latham, George C., 279, 297, 308,
 557n
Lecompton Constitution, 128, 523n
Lee, Robert E., 380
Lee, Samuel P., 534n
Lewis, Joseph J., 171, 236
Lexington, Ky., 103, 235

Libby, L. P., 237
Life of Washington (Weems), 271, 373
Lincoln, Abraham:
 as abolitionist, 12, 134, 211, 245
 affability of, 21, 61, 229, 327, 343
 anxiety of, 33, 57–58, 62, 125–26,
 221, 294, 296, 323, 387, 446
 assassination of, 3, 58, 290, 403,
 405, 538n, 557n, 560n, 575n,
 587n
 birthday of, 276, 312
 burned in effigy, 48, 71
 cabinet of, 533n; see also cabinet
 selection
 campaign biographies of, 235, 496n
 compromise efforts and, 155–60,
 164–65, 174–76, 179, 211,
 213–17, 221, 222–23, 240–42,
 252–53, 263, 268, 290, 292, 411,
 413–16, 424–28
 confidence of, 105, 231–32, 263,
 291, 328, 342, 421, 434
 cowardice allegations and, 15,
 378, 391, 397–403, 402, 419–20,
 434
 diet and eating habits of, 18, 39, 62,
 101, 114–15, 136, 310, 358, 365,
 497n
 dreams, signs, and omens of, 58–59,
 142, 294, 387
 exercise of, 117, 520n
 finances of, 72, 288–90
 firmness of, 90, 154, 159, 162, 293,
 343
 gifts received by, 20–21, 115, 136,
 161, 187–89, 232, 264, 285,
 497n
 greatness of, 1, 2, 6
 as "Honest Abe," 181, 215, 291,
 409
 humor and wit of, 1, 4, 22, 38,
 82–83, 99, 117–18, 352, 368,
 416, 426

inauguration of, 5, 104–5, 144, 153, 155, 163, 171, 194–97, 217, 240, 245, 267, 368, 421, 434, 436; see also Inauguration Day
insomnia of, 59, 231, 446
as inventor, 137, 410, 525n–26n
legal career of, 20, 72, 250, 293–94, 426, 511n–12n, 561n
loneliness of, 199
melancholy of, 44–45, 61–62, 148, 230–31, 287, 294, 296, 306, 412
moderation and conservatism of, 53, 55, 558n
poetry reading of, 76
preinaugural silence of, 1–7, 53, 57, 69–70, 72–75, 92, 125, 126, 133, 155, 157, 162–63, 193, 233, 239, 242, 254, 266, 283, 302, 424, 428, 432, 458, 498n, 524n–25n
religious views and practices of, 53, 109, 114, 138, 153, 204, 299, 303, 304, 337, 416–17, 445
resignation recommended for, 71, 152
in Senate races, 12, 15, 20, 37, 66, 155
smallpox of, 558n
theater going of, 186, 365–66, 480
as "Uncle Abe," 184, 536n
voting of, 28–31, 29, 500n, 501n
warnings and threats received by, 62, 70–71, 89, 115, 152, 194–96, 231–32, 251, 273, 278, 327, 410; see also Baltimore Plot
weariness of, 81, 84, 89, 111, 155, 230–31, 332–33, 354, 408–9
as Westerner, 305–6, 342
Lincoln, Abraham, appearance of, 1, 22, 53, 150, 153, 221, 313, 408
beard, 8, 85–89, 110, 184, 291, 333–35, 354, 375–76, 416, 445–46, 514n

in cartoons, 156, 400–403, 402, 435
C. F. Adams's views on, 417–18
clothes, 18, 101, 136, 188, 247, 285, 292, 364, 365, 393, 394, 399, 400–401, 416, 421, 447, 452, 517n
height, 100, 364, 365, 371, 393, 394, 414, 417, 421
in paintings and prints, 86–89, 110, 115–16, 49?n, 515n
in photographs, 8, 89, 109–10, 218, 283, 290, 291, 335–36, 386, 418–19, 479, 538n
in portrait busts, 184–86, 188–92, 536n
Lincoln, Abraham, inaugural address of, 5, 242–43, 254–59, 262–71, 337, 459–75, 592n
advice for, 263–64
baggage mishap and, 310–11, 565n
Blair Sr.'s review of, 411, 437, 440
Browning's views on, 312, 345–46, 439, 440, 444, 591n
delivery of, 452–57, 454
final text of, 463–75
"husband and wife may be divorced" section in, 268, 309, 472
Kentucky and, 314–15
polishing of, 437–46
reactions to, 455–56, 459–62, 594n
research for, 255–57
Schurz's discussion of, 292–93
secrecy of, 265–66, 270–71, 292–93
Seward and, see Seward, William H., inaugural address and
speech fragment and, 225, 545n
Lincoln, Abraham, inaugural trip of, 38, 189, 196–97, 259, 273, 276–87, 295–321, 324–96, 420, 458, 546n, 557n, 573n, 575n
disguises and, 89, 391

Lincoln, Abraham, inaugural trip of (*cont.*)
  guest list for, 279–81, 297–98
  journalists in, 298, 299–300, 302, 318, 332–33, 348
  office-seekers and, 330–32, 359, 569*n*
  oversight in, 282–83
  predecessors' inaugural journeys and, 271–74, 384
  preparations for, 265, 276–83, 288–95, 560*n*–61*n*
  Regular Army and, 280, 281
  rules and regulations for, 281–82
  security concerns in, 377–84
  stops in, 276–77; *see also specific places*
  Washington, arrival in, 6, 395–96
  Wood's role in, 277–82, 297, 298, 308, 347, 354, 375, 384
  see also Baltimore Plot
Lincoln, Abraham, inaugural trip speeches of, 1, 4, 6, 314–21, 324–29, 336–48, 368, 376, 385–90, 398
  Farewell Address, 298–304, *301*, 319, 338
  Indiana, 307–10, 312, 314, 319, 320, 321, 338, 389
  for Kentucky, 314–15
  New York, 347–48, 350, 352–54, 358–59, 389
  Ohio, 316–21, 324, 338, 389
  Pennsylvania, 326–28, 376, 385–90, 398
  Trenton, 371–74
Lincoln, Abraham, speeches of, 12*n*, 53, 75, 76, 83, 250, 314–21, 325–29, 336–48, 368
  during Chicago trip, 96–98
  "equal rights," 529*n*
  fragment of, 224–25, 545*n*
  in House, 99

"House Divided," 20, 53, 66, 139–40, 265
  impromptu, 96–97, 516*n*
  "jollification" day, 91–92, 93
  see also Cooper Union, Lincoln at
Lincoln, Edward Baker, 173, 303
Lincoln, Ill., 97
Lincoln, Mary Todd, 83, 91, 114, 134, 136, 204, 247, 317, 344, 436–37, 477–78, 561*n*, 562*n*
  alleged insanity of, 480
  anxiety of, 197
  appearance of, 198, 286, 575*n*
  Baltimore Plot and, 388, 391
  Chicago trip and, 68, 95–96, 98, 99, 101, 108, 111, 518*n*
  election of 1860 and, 18, 39, 45, 505*n*, 510*n*
  engraving of, 136, 525*n*
  exhaustion of, 61, 111
  at farewell soiree, 285, 286
  gifts and, 188, 189, 238
  husband's premonition and, 58
  inaugural and, 447, 452
  inaugural trip and, 189, 265, 273, 279, 281, 282, 290, 296, 297, 315, 319, 329, 332, 334, 337, 348, 350, 353, 354, 364, 376, 384, 387, 388, 391, 394
  in New York, 197–200, 238, 286, 364, 557*n*, 575*n*
  political role of, 198–99, 238, 279, 331, 332, 422, 436
  press views on, 53
  volatile outbursts of, 238, 548*n*
  Washington arrival of, 412
  in White House, 188, 197, 413
  Wood's relationship with, 483, 557*n*
Lincoln, Robert T., 161, 186, 286, 480
  baggage mishap and, 310–11, 565*n*
  celebrity treatment of, 198, 200, 311
  education of, 18, 51, 64, 72, 525*n*

on father's writing, 255
inaugural and, 446, 451
inaugural trip and, 279, 282, 296,
    297, 308, 310–11, 319, 325–26,
    332, 353, 379, 563n, 575n
in New York, 198, 199, 575n
office-seekers and, 331, 569n
parents' exhaustion and, 111
in Washington, 410, 422–23,
    585n
Lincoln, Sarah Bush Johnston,
    246–47, 249–51, 551n
Lincoln, Thomas "Tad," 18, 91, 189,
    197, 247, 412, 560n–61n
engraving of, 136, 525n
inaugural trip and, 265, 279, 281,
    291, 297, 315, 319, 332, 353,
    364, 388, 575n
Lincoln, Thomas, 249, 515n, 581n
Lincoln, William Wallace "Willie,"
    18, 91, 189, 197, 247, 412,
    560n–61n
death of, 478
engraving of, 136, 525n
inaugural trip and, 265, 279, 281,
    291, 297, 315, 319, 332, 364,
    388, 575n
Lincoln and the Patronage (Carman and
    Luthin), 522n
Livermore, Mary, 367, 575n
Logan, Stephen Trigg, 259, 438,
    590n–91n
Loring, George B., 430–31
Lossing, Benson J., 577n
Louisiana, 175
    secession and, 49, 127, 162, 244,
    245, 331, 362
Louis Philippe, King of France, 398
Lovejoy, Owen, 215
Lovie, Henri, 115–16, 298, 356
Lowell, Charles Russell, 215, 314
Luthin, Reinhard H., 522n
Lyons, Lord, 424

McClintock, John, 230
McClure, Alexander K., 181, 201–2,
    403, 405, 540n
McCormick, Richard, 233, 359
McIntire, C. F., 502n
McLean, John, 105, 144
McPherson, James M., 4, 524n
Madison, James, 316, 461
Magrath, Andrew Gordon, 506n
Maine, 12, 26, 323, 330
Mallory, Stephen R., 244
Manierre, Benjamin F., 233
Marshall, Thomas A., 247–48, 295,
    562n
Maryland, 37, 54, 164, 169, 180, 429
    inaugural trip in, 273, 284, 344
    secession and, 239, 441, 481
Masloski, Richard, 572n
Massachusetts, 37, 51, 135, 227
Mather, Thomas, 196
Medill, Joseph, 91, 149, 195, 434,
    528n
Melvin, Samuel, 153, 289, 529n
Memminger, Christopher, 162
Memphis, Tenn., 54, 321
Mercier, Henri, 453
Mexican War, 174, 230, 384, 448
Mexico, 229–30
Militia Acts (1794 and 1807), 131
Minturn, Robert Browne, 574n
Minutemen, 48–49
Mississippi, 38, 172, 175, 344
    secession and, 12, 47, 111, 159,
    162, 222, 244
Mississippi River, 77, 216
Missouri, 42, 57, 504n
    secession and, 161, 327
Missouri Compromise, 157–60, 163,
    166, 222, 253, 428
Missouri Democrat, 38, 151–52,
    215–16, 298
Missouri Republican, 75–76
Mobile, Ala., 25, 127, 282–83

Monroe, James, 144
Montgomery, Ala., 259, 321, 344–45, 372
Moody, Dwight L., 109
Moore, Clifton H., 66
Moorhead, James K., 181, 207–8
Morehead, Charles S., 425–27
Morey, George, 524n–25n
Morgan, Edwin D., 259, 349, 383
Morrill Tariff Act, 328
Morrison, William, 297
Morton, Oliver P., 297, 307, 312, 322, 561n, 565n
Moulton, J. S., 100
Murdoch, James, 186, 536n
music, 117, 365–66, 395, 399, 412, 424

Napoleon III, emperor of France, 285
Nast, Thomas, *414*
Navy Department, U.S., 235
    Lincoln's appointment to, 106, 195, 430, 433, 540n
Neely, Mark E., Jr., 4
Nevins, Allan, 4
Newark, N.J., 50, 370
New England, 50–51, 107, 275
    cabinet selection and, 106, 143, 167, 180, 207, 209–10, 535n
New Hampshire, 64, 169, 541n
New Jersey, 41, 50, 369–75, 504n
    federal jobs in, 236
    Lincoln's stops in, 271, 276, 284, 344
New Mexico, 177, 252
New Orleans, La., 49, 56, 127, 152
newspapermen, federal jobs for, 237
New York (state), 41, 135, 227, 233, 259, 262, 333–38, 347–67
    corruption scheme in, 142
    in election of 1860, 14, 21, 22–23, 36, 37, 38, 40, 41, 44, 65–66, 127, 344

Lincoln's stops in, 276, 284, 333–34, 336–38, 344, 347–50, 354–67
    secession and, 275
    suffrage referendum in, 27, 499n, 500n
New York, N.Y., 51–54, 145, 272, 351, 573n–74n
    Academy of Music in, 365–66
    Astor House in, 355–59, 362, 366, 573n, 575n
    business and financial community in, 52, 76–77, 199, 212, 361–62, 424, 437, 461, 574n
    City Hall reception in, 362–64, 482
    in election of 1860, 22–23, 37, 38, 51–52, 356, 573n
    Lincoln in, 284, 354–67, 482, 573n, 575n, 577n; *see also* Cooper Union, Lincoln at
    Mary Lincoln in, 197–200, 238, 286, 364, 557n, 575n
    port of, 235–36, 532n, 554n
    reaction to Lincoln's win in, 52–54
    secession and, 212, 354, 363, 482
New York Evening Post, 15, 92, 113, 142, 237, 255–56, 398, 482, 574n, 577n
New York Herald, 94, 101, 111, 136, 157, 216, 343, 398, 439, 461, 482, 499n, 516n, 540n
    cabinet predictions of, 105–6, 200–201
    on compromise efforts, 212, 214, 543n
    inaugural address and, 461
    inaugural trip and, 310, 319–20, 338–39, 345, 356
    on office-seekers, 81–84, 104, 119, 228–29, 436
    see also Villard, Henry
New York *Independent*, 368, 381, 382, 420, 460

New York Sun, 341, 363
New York Times, 22, 93, 132, 133, 154,
    198, 214, 237, 278, 321, 404,
    408–9, 457, 588n
    inaugural trip and, 298, 299, 310,
        332–33, 341
    secession and, 111–12
New York Tribune, 14, 37–38, 72–75,
    79–80, 227, 298, 339, 399, 453,
    479, 482
    Election Day coverage of, 30–31,
        37–38, 44
New York World, 23, 52–53, 127, 298,
    369, 512n
Niagara Falls, 572n
Nicolay, John George, 17, 20, 80, 145,
    150, 163, 212, 226, 278, 434,
    481, 536n
    Baltimore Plot and, 388, 404–5
    on Buchanan's cabinet, 47–48
    cabinet selection and, 59–60,
        542n
    on Election Day and Night, 30–35,
        43, 44–45
    on electors, 135, 136
    inaugural address and, 254–55,
        265–66, 270, 292, 443, 463
    inaugural trip and, 279, 282, 285,
        296, 297, *301*, 305, 308, 311,
        312, 320–21, 326, 327, 328, 332,
        355, 372, 388, 390, 565n
    on Lincoln, 44–45, 90, 140
    Lincoln's correspondence and, 16,
        62, 64, 70–71, 80, 87, 116, 232,
        233
    Lincoln's hiring of, 16, 496n
    in office relocation, 177, 534n
    victory celebration and, 79, 93
    in Washington, 412, 420–23, 452,
        585n
    as White House secretary, 237,
        548n
    in woodcuts, 115–16

North, Northerners, 6, 32, 42, 125,
    415, 428, 434, 441, 448
    anti-slavery movement in, 75, 129
    Buchanan's alienating of, 132, 133
    cabinet selection and, 109, 200
    economic problems in, 129
    inaugural address and, 460
    reactions to Lincoln's win in,
        50–54
North Carolina, 55, 327
North Market Mission Sabbath
    School, 109
nullification, 112
Nullification Crisis (1832), 78, 131,
    256, 257

Oakes, James, 499n
office-seekers, 1, 104, 334, 570n
    "Artemus Ward" parody of, 123–24
    inaugural trip and, 330–32, 359,
        569n
    Lincoln as, 272, 556n
    by mail, 232–33, 330
    in Springfield, 61, 79–84, 90, 96,
        117–24, 148, 153–54, 186,
        191–92, 226–29, 292, 295, 436,
        545n–46n, 560n, 561n, 562n
    in Washington, 273, 419, 430,
        434–37, 590n
Offutt, Denton, 331–32
Ogden, William B., 106
Oglesby, Richard, 331
Ohio, 66, 128, 313, 315–21, 389,
    429
    cabinet selection and, 106, 180,
        542n
    election of 1860 and, 12, 344
    Lincoln's stops in, 276, 284,
        316–21, 324, 325–26, 328–29,
        332, 333, 344
    Peace Convention and, 259
Ohio River, 314, 316, 326
Opdyke, George, 200, 542n

Page, S. D., 298

Painter, Uriah Hunt, 298

Palmer, John M., 31, 134–36

Paludan, Phillip Shaw, 4–5

Panic of 1857, 128–29, 144, 164

Parker, Samuel H., 590n

Paschall, Nathaniel P., 75–76

Patent Office, U.S., 410

patronage, 56, 64, 84, 104, 170, 191, 262, 278, 279, 280, 522n
  see also office-seekers

Paul, Ron, 6

Peace Convention, 259, 275–76, 321–22, 384, 406, 424–28, 438, 482, 561n
  Lincoln's meetings with members of, 413–16, 414, 425–27
  Lincoln's views on, 291–92
  Thirteenth Amendment proposed by, 428

Pearce, James, 447

Pease, Edward D., 139

Peck, Ebenezer, 105, 313

Peekskill, N.Y., 353–54, 572n

Pennsylvania, 41, 60, 131, 174, 227
  cabinet selection and, 106, 134, 146–47, 180–81, 203, 205–8, 260, 330
  in election of 1860, 12, 14, 26, 36, 37, 39, 127, 344
  Lincoln's stops in, 276–77, 284, 326–28, 344, 375–87

Pennsylvania State Assembly, 389

Petit, John, 247

Pettis, Solomon N., 553n

Peyton, Balie, 167

Philadelphia, Pa., 36, 39, 51–52
  Baltimore Plot and, 388, 393–94
  Continental House in, 375–81, 384
  flag-raising ceremony in, 386–87, 581n
  Grand Union Meeting in, 179, 405
  Independence Hall in, 384–85
  Lincoln in, 174, 259, 276–77, 284, 375–87, 398, 575n, 589n
  Lincoln memorial service in, 403

Philadelphia Inquirer, 298, 446

Phillips, Wendell, 50

photography, 8, 89, 109–10, 218, 290–91, 519n
  cartes-de-visite, 283, 291, 419, 586n
  of Fido, 291, 560n–61n
  by German, 190–91, 291, 538n
  inaugural trip and, 335–36, 347, 386
  in Washington, 418–19, 479, 586n

Piatt, Donn, 84, 95, 101, 104–5, 106

Piatt, Louise, 95

Pickwick Papers (Dickens), 186

Pierce, Edward L., 209

Pierce, Franklin, 104, 108, 121, 128, 274, 275, 276, 355, 507n
  inaugural journey of, 272
  postelection fears of, 50, 507n

Pinkerton, Allan, 384, 388, 391–97, 400, 401, 404
  arrival in Washington and, 395–96, 580n
  Lincoln's meeting with, 377–82, 579n

Pittsburgh, Pa., 36, 37, 259, 326–28, 386, 389

Pollock, James, 425

Poore, Ben Perley, 270

Pope, John, 280, 281, 375, 481

popular sovereignty, 128, 157–60

Porter, Charles Leland, 179–80

Post Office Department, U.S., 237
  jobs in, 235, 237, 238, 522n
  Lincoln's appointment to, 106, 143, 201, 430, 433

Potter, David M., 4

Prentice, William H., 137–38

Prince, William P., 142

public opinion, 63–71, 179, 509n

"public-opinion baths," 80
Pyne, Smith, 416

Quincy, Mass., 19, 24

racism, race, 27, 81, 117, 155
    Lincoln's views on, 54–55, 117,
        154–55, 521n, 550n
railroads, 144, 174, 199, 272–73, 482
    Chicago trip and, 96–98, 110
    Coles County trip and, 247–48
    inaugural trip and, 277–79, 281,
        289, 296–300, 302, 304–7, 313,
        318–19, 325–26, 328, 332, 336,
        347, 351, 354, 370–71, 378,
        387–88, 389, 393–95, 562n,
        567n–68n
    Southern, 48, 321
Randall, Alex, 279
Randall, James G., 4
Rankin, Henry B., 286, 293, 559n,
    561n
Ray, Charles H., 206
Ray, D. E., 172–73
Raymond, Henry J., 112, 154–55, 237,
    403–4
Rayner, Kenneth, 107, 180
Read, John M., 495n
Reagan, Ronald, 537n
Reeder, Andrew, 118, 203
Reich, C. Gustave, 100
Republicans, Republican party, 5, 310,
    421, 495n, 502n
    Chicago convention of, see
        Chicago, Ill., Republican
        convention in
    federal jobs for, 234–38
    Illinois, founding of, 134
    inaugural trip and, 332, 340–41,
        343, 358–59, 375, 383
    Lincoln's clandestine arrival and,
        397–99, 403
    Lincoln's coalition in, 107, 120

Lincoln's critics in, 112
platform of, 26, 156, 175, 223, 241,
    253, 266, 342, 441, 499n
in state elections, 12–13, 26
unity of, 4, 5, 6
see also specific people and elections
Rice, Allen Thorndike, 183
Richards, F. DeBourg, 386
Riddle, Albert Gallatin, 330, 411, 416
Ridgely, Anna, 63, 89, 93
Rives, William C., 413, 427
Robinson, A. R., 569n
"Robinson, Mother," 228
Robinson, Sarah A., 590n
Robison, William L., 235
Rochester, N.Y., 27, 347, 571n
Rodgers, John, 250
Roll, Frank, 291
Roll, John, 291
Romero, Matias, 229–30
Roosevelt, Franklin D., 2
Roosevelt, James W., 236
Ruffin, Edmund, 23–24, 32, 47, 111,
    161, 461, 481, 530n
Russell, Henry M., 520n
Russell, Lord John, 230

St. Louis, Alton & Chicago railroad,
    96–98
Sanderson, John P., 181, 205
Sanford, Henry S., 73, 74
Sangamon County Court House,
    27–28, 30–31
Sartain, Samuel, 88
Scammon, Jonathan, 110
Schaepper, Adam, 236
Schenk, Robert C., 102, 104, 106
Schleiden, Rudolph, 424
Schurz, Carl, 64, 101, 215, 241–42,
    259, 292–93, 481
Scotch cap story, 400, 412, 418
Scott, Dred, 107
Scott, Robert E., 150, 540n

Scott, Walter, 189
Scott, Winfield, 93, 131, 144, 162,
    212, 424, 433, 512n, 587n
  inaugural trip and, 281, 379–81, 411
  Jones's bust of, 185, 191
  Lincoln's visit to, 410–11
  secession and, 77–78, 196
  Washington military presence and,
    196, 245, 322, 323
Scripps, John L., 235, 237
Secchi, G. F., 236
secession, 1–7, 21–24, 75, 83, 104–5,
    111–13, 129–33, 145, 155–65,
    172–73, 184, 211–17, 221–25,
    256–59, 377, 416, 458, 554n
  Baltimore Plot and, 378, 391
  Buchanan and, 78, 111–12, 126,
    127, 129–33, 158, 161–63, 211,
    212, 274
  cabinet selection and, 149
  coercion vs. invasion and, 308–9
  congressional efforts at prevention
    of, 155–60, 163–64, 165, 175,
    176–77, 211, 213–16
  Douglass's views on, 125, 216
  election of 1860 and, 23–24, 32, 47,
    49, 52, 68
  federal jobs and, 236, 440
  former presidents and, 274–76
  Grand Union Meeting and, 179
  H. Adams's views on, 192–93
  inaugural address and, 460, 461
  inaugural trip and, 326–29, 342
  Jackson's views on, 257, 265
  Lincoln's military options and, 411
  Lincoln's views on, 21–22, 69, 76,
    84, 104, 109, 112–13, 126, 133,
    160–61, 222–23, 239, 256–57,
    267, 308–9, 511n, 549n
  Montgomery conference on, 259,
    275
  Peace Convention and, see Peace
    Convention

popular support for, 531n
  Ruffin's views on, 23–24, 32, 111,
    161
  Scott's views on, 77–78, 196
  Senate resignations and, 243–45
  Seward blamed for, 142
  Stephens's views on, 138–39, 140,
    526n
  Trumbull's speech and, 94, 95, 112
  writers' support for, 179–80
  see also specific states
Seddon, James A., 406, 414, 415
Senate, Illinois, 555n
Senate, U.S., 50, 51, 163, 174, 196,
    428, 429, 542n
  Baker in, 173
  battle for Seward's seat in, 260–61,
    433
  Breckinridge as president of, 136
  Committee of Thirteen in, 155,
    160, 164, 176–77, 211
  constitutional amendment and, 176
  Douglas's races for, 12, 15, 66, 155,
    261, 499n
  Hamlin in, 26, 98–99, 140, 479
  Hamlin's swearing-in in, 450–51
  Lincoln races for, 12, 15, 20, 37, 66,
    155
  Lincoln's appointments and, 183,
    205, 236, 244, 557n
  Lincoln's visit to, 421–22, 587n
  Murdoch's readings at, 536n
  secession-induced resignations in,
    243–45
  Seward's speech to, 214–15
  Trumbull in, 37, 96, 232, 482
Seward, Frederick, 379–81, 384,
    442–43
Seward, William H., 122, 192–96,
    323, 416–17, 420, 424, 430–35,
    482
  Baltimore Plot and, 379–81, 384,
    394

battle for Senate seat of, 260–61, 433, 554n

cabinet post rejected by, 432–33, 434

cabinet selection and, 59, 102–3, 140–43, 145, 147, 148, 150–51, 159, 166, 167, 180, 181–82, 201, 203–5, 208, 209, 213, 262, 430–34, 517n, 590n

compromise efforts and, 155, 156, 159–60, 164, 166, 192–94, 213–15, 252–53, 362, 432, 531n, 532n

election of 1860 and, 13, 24, 81, 102, 103, 106, 107, 146, 165, 213, 261, 340, 497n, 541n

inaugural address and, 269, 346, 346n, 417, 433, 439–46, 457, 459, 463, 465, 468, 469, 471, 595n

Lincoln compared with, 539n

Lincoln's Senate visit and, 421–22

Lincoln's Washington arrival and, 407–8, 410, 412, 413

secession and, 131, 155, 252

Senate speech of, 214–15

Wood's appointment and, 278, 556n

Seymour, Horatio, 554n

Shepherd, Nicholas H., 290

Sherman, John, 433

Shoaff, James, 65

Shoaff, Nancy Hanks, 65

signs and omens, Lincoln's belief in, 58–59, 142, 294, 387

Simon, James F., 594n

Sixth Massachusetts Infantry, 405

slavery, slaves, 1, 53, 54, 66, 94, 127–31, 211, 428

admission of states and, 128, 177

Clay's views on, 257

Constitution and, see Constitution, U.S., slavery and

containment of, 6, 15, 16–17, 26, 77, 127, 156–59, 172–73, 253, 257, 266, 268, 416, 425, 554n

in District of Columbia, 164, 168, 252, 409, 428

Dred Scott decision and, 107, 127–28, 129, 422, 523n

election of 1860 and, 11, 14–17, 26, 55–56, 155, 156, 156, 157, 213

fugitive, 75, 160, 164–65, 168, 252, 266, 268, 397, 415, 428, 442, 469, 471–72, 532n

inaugural address and, 461–62, 469, 471–72

Kansas-Nebraska Act and, 157

Lincoln's views on, 15, 16–17, 26, 47, 112, 117, 128, 138, 139–40, 154–60, 156, 172–73, 178, 193, 213, 252–53, 265–68, 342, 422, 425, 456, 458, 461–62, 469, 545n

Missouri Compromise and, 157–60, 163, 166

railroad built by, 48

revolts of, 55, 95, 125, 193

Thirteenth Amendment and, 429, 482

trade in, 164, 168, 252, 428

Webster's views on, 256–57

in Western territories, see Western territories, slavery in

Wilmot Proviso and, 173–74

Slidell, John, 47

Smedes, William C., 154

Smith, Ann, 265

Smith, Caleb Blood, 107, 149, 180, 208, 227, 430, 534n, 587n

Smith, Clark M., 265, 555n

Smith, G. Rush, 147

Smith, Henry M., 298

Smith, John W., 501n

Smith, Truman, 73–74, 76

Smith, William F., 65
Snethen, Worthington, 383
South, Southerners, 1, 75, 175–80,
    194, 414, 428, 441
  blockade of, 411, 439
  in Buchanan administration, 47–48,
    132, 211
  Buchanan's alienating of, 132, 133,
    211
  considered for cabinet, 60, 106–9,
    144–45, 149–52, 167–70, 180,
    520n, 527n, 528n
  Crittenden Compromise and,
    163–64, 175, 176–77
  Democrats in, 13, 14, 69, 84,
    323
  in election of 1860, 5, 13–14,
    16–18, 23–24, 25, 37, 42, 66,
    106, 495n, 504n
  Green-Lincoln talks and, 175–76
  inaugural address and, 262, 266–68,
    270, 440, 441, 442, 460, 464
  Lincoln's attempted reassurance of,
    4, 16–18, 53, 89, 133–34, 178
  Lincoln's clandestine arrival and,
    397, 399
  Lincoln's conciliatory message to,
    92, 94–95
  Lincoln's inauguration and, 153,
    368, 448–50, 455
  Lincoln's name kept off ballots in,
    25, 42, 106, 344
  Lincoln's threats from, 115, 152,
    189, 194, 231–32
  Lincoln voters in, 42
  NYC's links with, 212, 361, 362,
    363
  Peace Convention and, 275–76,
    414–16
  railroads in, 48, 321
  reaction to Lincoln's win in, 46–57,
    66, 67, 69, 111, 138–39, 211,
    510n–11n

Scott's views on, 77–78
  secession in, see secession
South Carolina, 55, 76, 144, 228,
    368
  coercion vs. invasion of, 309
  election of 1860 and, 11–12, 24, 32,
    47
  federal garrisons in, 162, 163, 175
  firing on Star of the War in, 221–22
  nullification and, 131, 256, 257
  reaction to Lincoln's election in,
    48, 49
  secession and, 12, 23–24, 32, 56,
    68, 94, 104, 111, 127, 131, 153,
    159–65, 257, 265, 362, 506n
Spaulding, Elbridge, 433
Speed, Fanny, 68, 95, 107–8, 518n
Speed, Joshua Fry, 67–68, 72, 95,
    107–9, 263
  Lincoln's cohabitation with, 108,
    518n
Speer, William S., 534n
spoils system, 81, 262
Sprague, William, 574n
Springfield, Ill., 57–64, 71–97,
    110–26, 132–55, 165–77,
    181–92, 194–97, 238–43,
    251–71, 559n
  blacks in, 118, 290, 296, 521n,
    560n
  Capitol in, see Capitol, Illinois
    State
  Capitol Square in, 22, 33, 35, 37,
    38, 40, 44, 152, 293
  departure preparations in, 288–95
  descriptions of, 19, 116, 148
  Election Day and Night in, 11–12,
    18–22, 27–41, 29, 43–45, 59–60,
    63, 494n
  electors' gathering in, 134–36
  farewell soiree in, 285–86
  First Presbyterian Church in, 114,
    153, 204, 520n

German-language newspaper in, 149

hotels in, 79, 90, 93, 134, 150, 174, 177, 181, 185–87, 191, 202, 290, 295–96, 536n, 560n

inauguration considered for, 195

insurance in, 288–89, 559n–60n

Johnson Building in, 177, 226

Lincoln's departure from, 276, 286–87, 295–305, 338, 374, 437, 548n, 563n

Lincoln's home in, 18, 32, 45, 84, 85, 91, 114–15, 165, 171, 177, 190, 197, 210, 226, 230–31, 238, 265, 285–86, 289, 290, 291, 581n

Lincoln's law office in, 293–94

Lincoln's sale in, 289

Lincoln's visitors in, 78–84, 90–91, 116–20, 149, 150, 153–54, 165–76, 181–87, 201–8, 226–32, 238–42, 259–62, 277, 290, 292–93, 528n, 545n–46n

ministers in, 137–38, 526n

office-seekers in, see office-seekers, in Springfield

Republican-Democratic split in, 63

Sangamon County Court House in, 27–28, 30–31

telegraph office in, 33–41, 36, 44, 45, 297, 300

turkey shortage in, 114–15

victory celebrations in, 43, 45, 71, 79, 90–95

William W. Watson & Son in, 38–40

Woods & Henckle in, 136

Yates & Smith in, 265–66, 555n

Springfield Marine and Fire Insurance Company, 288

Stager, Theodore, 298

"Stand by the Right" (Porter), 179–80

Star of the War, 221–22

State Department, U.S., 163, 237

Lincoln's appointment to, 102–3, 105, 107, 140–43, 147, 148, 150–51, 166, 180, 181–82, 200–201, 205, 213, 433, 434

states, slave vs. free, 128, 177

Statesman's Manual (Williams), 255–56, 552n

states' rights, 1, 309, 464

Steers, Edward, Jr., 583n

Stephens, Alexander H., 106, 140, 177–78, 222, 225, 267, 456, 534n

cabinet selection and, 144, 150, 527n

as Confederate vice president, 283

state legislature addressed by, 138–39, 178, 526n

Stevens, Walter B., 511n–12n

Stoddard, William O., 3, 60, 122–23, 237, 522n, 548n

Stone, Charles P., 380

Story, George Henry, 418–19, 586n

Stowe, Harriet Beecher, 132

Strong, George Templeton, 23, 52, 76–77, 324, 481

dinner guest diatribe and, 217, 544n

inaugural and, 437, 439, 461, 594n

inaugural trip and, 356

Stuart, John T., 562n

Stuyvesant Institute, 53–54

Summers, George W., 414

Sumner, Charles, 51, 53, 71, 208, 239, 417, 497n

Sumner, Edwin Vose "Bull Head," 280, 281, 282, 297, 318, 354–55

Baltimore Plot and, 391, 392

Sumner, George, 239–40

Supreme Court, Illinois, 20, 534n

Supreme Court, U.S., 49, 56, 228,
    346, 478, 481, 594n
  Dred Scott v. Sanford and, 107,
    127–28, 129, 422, 523n
  inaugural address and, 440, 442,
    470, 471
  Lincoln's courtesy call on, 421, 422,
    587n
Sutton, Frederic W., 505n
Sutton, Goyn, 34, 505n
Swett, Leonard, 120, 181, 205, 410,
    525n, 535n
  as Illinois elector, 31, 134–36
  Lincoln's relationship with, 227–28,
    237, 546n
  Weed-Lincoln summit and, 165,
    166

tailors, 101, 136, 289
Taney, Roger B., 127, 346, 422, 481,
    594n
  at Lincoln's inauguration, 451, 453,
    457, 458
tariffs, 131, 208
  high, 77, 107, 120, 431
  Pittsburgh speech and, 327–28, 386
taxes, 131, 361
Taylor, Zachary, 70–71, 185
  inaugural journey of, 272
telegraphy, telegraphs, 297, 300, 502n
  Baltimore Plot and, 388, 393, 412
  in election of 1860, 32–41, 36, 297
Temple, Wayne C., 526n, 563n, 572n
Tennessee, 54, 344
  secession and, 283, 321, 327
Terrell, W. G., 298
Terry, David S., 49, 507n
Texas, 162, 175, 239
Thackeray, William M., 298
Thanksgiving, 114–15, 116, 127,
    520n
Thayer, James S., 14
theater, 186, 349, 536n, 575n

Thirteenth Amendment, 429, 482
Thirteenth Amendment, proposed,
    428–29
Thompson, Jacob, 132
ticket-peddlers, 27–28, 30, 500n
Tilton, Lucian, 289
Titsworth, A. D., 101
Todd, L. B., 235
Todd, Lockwood, 279, 585n
Toombs, Robert, 139, 155, 244, 245,
    361, 574n
trade, 212, 217, 338–39, 361
  free, 77, 203
  slave, 164, 168, 252, 428
Treasury Department, U.S., 132, 235,
    570n
  Lincoln's appointment to, 106, 146,
    166–67, 181, 182, 183, 200–205,
    208, 260, 431, 432, 433, 532n
Trenton, N.J., 271, 284, 371–75
"True Republicans," 87
Trumbull, Julia Jayne, 95–96
Trumbull, Lyman, 36–37, 40, 41,
    93–96, 163, 175–76, 423, 482
  cabinet selection and, 101, 140,
    142–43, 169, 204–5, 431
  in Chicago trip, 95–96, 98, 101,
    105
  compromise efforts and, 155, 158,
    159, 166
  Herndon's correspondence with,
    240
  Lincoln's advice from, 120–21
  speeches of, 91, 93–95, 98, 112
  Stoddard's office-seeking and,
    122
Tuck, Amos, 321
  cabinet selection and, 119, 203,
    208, 321, 535n, 541n
Tuckerman, Henry, 538n
Turner, Thomas J., 427
Tyler, John, 272, 274, 275–76, 414,
    482

Ullmann, Daniel, 187–88, 537n
Underwood, William H., 297
Union, 6, 42, 315, 320, 365, 371, 409,
    434, 478
  admission of states to, 128, 177,
    511n
  inaugural address and, 466–70
  preservation of, 43, 47, 54, 69, 130,
    149, 152, 165, 192, 223, 245,
    251, 257, 267, 292, 307–8, 322,
    329, 342, 373, 374, 438, 440,
    460
  in speech fragment, 224
Utica, N.Y., 347, 348, 571n

Valtellina, Amalia Majocchi, 590n
Van Buren, Martin, 272, 274–75
Vance, Mariah, 290, 560n
Vanity Fair, 242, 368, 401
Vanity Fair (Thackeray), 298
Verdi, Giuseppe, 365–66
Villard, Henry, 80–86, 110–11, 117,
    124–25, 162, 216, 239, 482,
    543n
  on Baker, 173
  on Chicago trip, 96, 113
  doubts about Lincoln, 81, 89–90,
    115
  Farewell Address and, 299–300,
    302, 563n
  on farewell soiree, 285–86
  on Fogg, 521n
  on Greeley, 262
  inaugural trip and, 196–97, 298,
    299–300, 302, 308, 317, 324,
    328, 333, 348, 350, 353, 367,
    571n
  on Lincoln as housekeeper, 197
  on Lincoln's appearance, 86, 89,
    111, 153, 221
  on Lincoln's correspondence, 115,
    116, 232
  on Lincoln's departure, 294–95

  on Lincoln's melancholy, 231,
    287
  on Lincoln's speeches, 254, 257–58,
    271, 324, 328
  on Mary Lincoln, 200, 286, 436
  on office-seekers and visitors,
    81–85, 119, 153–54, 226–29,
    436
  on Robert Lincoln, 200
  on victory celebration, 93
  on Wood, 277, 278
Virginia, 125, 164, 272, 339
  Brown's raid in, 178
  in election of 1860, 37, 38, 42
  Peace Convention and, 275–76,
    406, 427
  reaction to Lincoln's win in, 46, 49,
    54, 111
  secession and, 111, 161, 196, 244,
    326, 327, 427, 441
Vliet, G. L., 528n
Volck, Adalbert, 401, 402, 582n
Volk, Leonard Wells, 185, 536n
voting, 22, 135
  of Lincoln, 28–31, 29, 500n, 501n
  New York referendum on, 27, 499n,
    500n
  popular, 2, 5, 42, 68–69, 97, 126,
    275, 277, 362, 504n

Wade, Benjamin, 155, 417, 586n
Wales, Prince of, 51, 278, 349, 355,
    356, 499n
Walker, William, 504n
Wallace, William S., 279
Ward, Artemus, (Charles Farrar
    Browne), 123–24, 368, 523n
War Department, U.S., 163, 235,
    478
  Lincoln's appointments to, 106,
    143, 144, 182, 183, 195, 200,
    201, 205, 280, 431, 434
Warne, Kate, 377, 394

Washburne, Elihu B., 134, 142, 162, 208, 413, 423, 433
  Lincoln's Washington arrival and, 396, 400, 407, 580n
  on secession, 158–59, 243, 245
  Washington hotel selected by, 273, 383–84
Washington, D.C., 77–78, 105, 198, 395–458
  Brady gallery in, 418–19, 586n
  description of, 409–10
  inaugurations in, 2, 105, 153, 271, 272
  Lincoln in, 218, 383–84, 395–458
  Lincoln's arrival in, 395–416, 580n
  military presence in, 196, 245, 322, 323
  National Hotel in, 273, 384, 433
  office-seekers in, 273, 419, 430, 434–37, 590n
  Peace Convention in, see Peace Convention
  slavery in, 164, 168, 252, 409, 428
  Southern invasion predictions for, 153, 195
  Stephens's attempted visit to, 534n
  Willard's Hotel in, 276, 384, 396, 406–8, 411–19, 414, 421–27, 430–36, 445–48, 585n
Washington, George, 2, 131, 362, 461, 558n
  birthday of, 277, 322
  Farewell Address of, 264
  inaugural journey of, 271, 371, 555n–56n
  Lincoln compared with, 59, 157, 299, 300, 303–4, 305, 316, 371–74, 427, 444
  Lincoln's Farewell Address and, 299, 300, 303–4, 374
  portraits and statues of, 313, 363, 458
  in Trenton, 271, 371, 372, 373

Washington Constitution, 43, 44, 243, 536n
Washington Monument, 409
Watterson, Henry, 461
Webb, James Watson, 361
Weber, George R., 501n
Webster, Daniel, 53, 103, 104, 170, 185, 265
  reply to Hayne of, 256–57, 553n
Weed, Samuel R., 22, 61–62
  Election Day and, 32–33, 35, 37, 38–39, 498n
Weed, Thurlow, 75, 103, 141, 151, 160, 208, 233, 349, 429, 433, 482, 497n
  in corruption scheme, 142
  inaugural trip and, 361, 383
  Seward's senatorial replacement and, 260–61, 554n
  in Springfield, 165–71, 532n
  Wood's relationship with, 277–78
Weems, Mason Locke, 271, 373
Weik, Jesse, 562n
Weldon, Lawrence, 134–36
Welles, Gideon, 45, 211, 323, 592n
  cabinet selection and, 59, 101–2, 103, 141, 143, 144–45, 167, 180, 201, 209–10, 430, 431, 433, 532n, 535n, 542n, 588n
  Lincoln countermyth and, 59
  Lincoln defended by, 193, 539n
Wellsville, Ohio, 326, 330
West, Westerners, 42, 59, 75, 107, 129
  Lincoln as, 305–6, 342
Western territories, slavery in, 15, 127–28, 129, 156, 158, 159, 163, 168, 174, 222, 469, 543n
Westfield, N.Y., 333–34
Whigs, 70, 77, 102–3, 173, 174, 178, 460, 502n, 556n
  cabinet selection and, 59, 102, 167, 170, 180
  Conscience, 107

in election of 1824, 102, 495n
in Lincoln's coalition, 107, 120, 434
White, A. D., 409
White, Horace, 110, 152
White, Hugh, 118
White, Ronald C., Jr., 441, 571n,
    576n, 591n
White House, 131, 192, 290, 406,
    478, 479, 480, 522n, 557n, 570n,
    585n
  Davis at, 129
  employment at, 234
  Lincoln's visit to, 408, 410
  M. Lincoln in, 188, 197, 413
  "public-opinion baths" at, 80
Whitehurst, Stephen S., 501n
Whitman, Walt, 357–58, 408, 573n
Whitney, Henry Clay, 109, 118, 228,
    230–31, 237, 403
  Lincoln's travel with, 247–48
Whittier, John Greenleaf, 135–36,
    186, 212, 524n
Wide-Awakes, 93, 98, 152, 153, 448
  in New England, 50, 51
  in New York, 22–23, 358–59, 366,
    534n
  in Springfield, 91, 92
Wigfall, Louis, 421
Wigwam, Chicago, 99
Willard, Henry A., 396, 407
Williams, Edwin, 255
Williams, Frank J., 486, 491
Williams, John S., 323

Williams, Margaret, 412
William W. Watson & Son, 38–40
Wilmot, David, 174, 200, 203
Wilmot Proviso, 173–74
Wilson, Douglas L., 270, 440, 554n,
    571n, 591n
Wilson, John J. S., 34, 297, 502n
Wood, Fernando, 212, 362–63,
    482–83, 574n, 578n
Wood, John, 20, 104, 114, 135, 498n
Wood, William P., 557n
Wood, William S., 277–82, 297, 298,
    308, 347, 354, 375, 430, 483
  appointment of, 277–78, 556n
  Baltimore Plot and, 384, 388
  confusion about, 557n
Woodruff, Jesse, 235
Woods, Harry, 206
Wool, John, 424, 587n
"Word for the Hour, A" (Whittier),
    212
Worship of the North (Volck), 582n
Wright, John Vine, 283
Wright, Presco, 569n

Yancey, William Lowndes, 344
Yankee Doodle, new version of, 399
Yates, Richard, 28, 135, 177, 196, 297,
    501n, 562n
Young Men's Christian Union, 337
Young Men's Republican Union, 53,
    65–66, 359
Yulee, David, 244

⊰ ABOUT THE AUTHOR ⊱

HAROLD HOLZER has authored, co-authored, and edited thirty books on Abraham Lincoln and the Civil War, including *The Lincoln Image*, *Lincoln Seen and Heard*, *Dear Mr. Lincoln: Letters to the President*, *Lincoln as I Knew Him*, *Lincoln on Democracy*, and *Lincoln at Cooper Union*, which won a Lincoln Prize in 2005. He has won a number of awards, including the Lincoln Diploma of Honor from Lincoln Memorial University, and the Civil War Round Table's Nevins-Freeman Award, and sits on historical advisory boards for a number of the nation's Civil War museums. Holzer, who is senior vice president for external affairs and marketing for The Metropolitan Museum of Art, serves also as co-chairman of the U.S. Abraham Lincoln Bicentennial Commission, and as founding vice chairman of the Lincoln Forum. He lives in Rye, New York.